Thomas Beecham
An Obsession with Music

JOHN LUCAS

Thomas Beecham
An Obsession with Music

THE BOYDELL PRESS

First published 2008
The Boydell Press, Woodbridge

ISBN 978 1 84383 402 1

The Boydell Press is an imprint of Boydell & Brewer Ltd
PO Box 9, Woodbridge, Suffolk IP12 3DF, UK
and of Boydell & Brewer Inc.
668 Mt Hope Avenue, Rochester, NY 14620, USA
website: www.boydellandbrewer.com

A catalogue record of this publication is available
from the British Library

This publication is printed on acid-free paper

Designed and typeset in Garamond Premier Pro
by David Roberts, Pershore, Worcestershire

Printed in Great Britain by
CPI Antony Rowe, Chippenham, Wiltshire

Contents

List of Illustrations

Title page Beecham sketched by Marc Kosloff, who played in the orchestra for his recording of *Carmen*, Paris, 1958–9

Plates between pp. 116 and 117

Preface

I first saw Beecham conduct in the late 1940s. I had witnessed Malcolm Sargent in action, and Boult and Barbirolli, and I even retain a vestigial memory of Henry Wood, but I was very young at the time and far more interested in the music that was being played than who was conducting it. The Beecham concert was at the Royal Albert Hall, promoted by the impresario Victor Hochhauser, who in an advertisement had announced that the great man would be giving an introductory talk about the items to be performed. Beecham walked on to the platform purposefully, stepped on to the rostrum, eyed us up and down with an air of hauteur, and paused. 'Ladies and gentleman', he said in a voice pitched a bit higher than I was expecting, with the words articulated very precisely, even primly. 'Mr Hochhauser has said that I shall be talking about tonight's programme. I shall be doing no such thing.' And he turned and plunged straight into the most vigorous performance of the National Anthem I had ever heard. (I had no idea that his conducting of it was famous.)

This was pure theatre, pure Beecham. He had caught the audience's attention and he held it until the end of the concert. I can still recall the magical, diaphanous effect in that first programme of Liszt's symphonic poem *Orpheus*, with the perfect balance in the orchestra (it was the year-old Royal Philharmonic) and the subtle grading of the dynamics. Suddenly, for the first time, I was made aware that conducting was not just a matter of beating time but, at its best, an inspired act of recreation.

Beecham is arguably the finest executant musician this country has produced. He was certainly the most influential. He raised orchestral standards in Britain to an unprecedented height. He proved by example that opera was for everyone, and not just for the society-led coterie which, for social as much as musical reasons, attended the short summer seasons at Covent Garden. And, however incredible it might now seem, he was responsible for the works of Mozart and Haydn becoming staples of the concert repertory in Britain and, in Mozart's case, the operatic repertory as well.

What he was unable to do, despite his tireless advocacy, and his incomparable performances and recordings of the music, was to persuade audiences that Delius was indeed, as he claimed, the 'last great apostle in our time of romance, emotion and beauty in music'.* I recall turning up for an all-Delius concert at the Festival Hall in 1958 to find that so few people had bought tickets for it that Beecham had had to change the second half of the programme to Sibelius's First Symphony in the hope of attracting more customers. I cannot pretend that it bothered me. Beecham was one of the best Sibelius conductors of his time, a verdict with which the composer himself concurred. (Anyone who has not heard the recording of Beecham's performance of the Second Symphony, captured live at the Festival Hall four years earlier, should hasten to get hold of it.)†

* Beecham, *Delius*, p. 221
† BBC Legends, BBCL 41547; also includes a live performance of Dvořák's Symphony no. 4.

It is now almost fifty years since Beecham died. This book is an attempt to place him, musically, politically and socially, in the troubled times in which he lived. Cutting through the myths that surround his life has not always been easy. His enjoyable book of memoirs, *A Mingled Chime: Leaves from An Autobiography*, written in a uniquely orotund and oratorical style, is often casual in its treatment of facts, while Neville Cardus's brief memoir, *Sir Thomas Beecham*, published in the year of the conductor's death, is more misleading still, though at least its author admits to inventing stories about Beecham.

Even Beecham's music-making is subject to myths, the most common being that when it came to Beethoven's symphonies he was an even-numbered man; that the *Sturm und Drang* of the odd-numbered ones did not appeal to him. Statistics show that the symphonies he conducted the most were the Seventh, Second and Third, in that order. The Eighth, alleged to be one of his favourites, comes well down the list. Beecham's huffings and puffings about Beethoven – he once called him 'the Mr Gladstone of Music' – can be safely ignored. His incandescent performance of the *Missa solemnis*, recorded at the 1937 Leeds Festival, reveals him as a Beethoven conductor to be reckoned with.*

With the help of family papers and a mass of new material that has come to light in libraries and archives, not only in Britain, but also in Germany, France, Holland and Italy, North and South America, and Australia, I have been able to lay many of the myths to rest. Some may miss their favourite Beecham stories, but a number of them have proved to be apocryphal; I have included only those I believe to be authentic (or as near as dammit.) If there is a tendency now to regard Beecham as a joke-book figure, rather than as a serious and hard-working musician, then he had only himself to blame. In his old age he took to playing the role of the Old Entertainer and revelled in it, indulging audiences with speeches marked more by waggishness than wit.

Beecham belonged to a group of autocratic international conductors – Toscanini, Furtwängler, Koussevitzky and Stokowski among them – who bestrode the musical world. With the passing of time, however, his reputation, in Britain at any rate, has faltered in comparison with that of the others. In an age devoted to specialisation and authenticity, suspicions have sprung up about a conductor who was master of so many styles, whose diverse enthusiasms ranged from Grétry and Méhul, through Mozart and Schubert, Berlioz, Massenet, Balakirev and Rimsky-Korsakov, and on to Richard Strauss, Sibelius and, of course, Delius.

His Handel arrangements may now be outdated, yet in their time they helped propagate a taste for the composer's music that went way beyond *Messiah* and *Judas Maccabaeus*, and it is interesting to find an authority like William Christie of Les Arts Florissants defending Beecham's approach to the composer: one can mock his extravagances, he has said, but 'Beecham had perhaps something that is lacking in our baroque scholars of today, a rhetoric that is naturally related to the Grand Siècle. There is something in common between the grandiloquence of Handel's language and Beecham's flamboyant

---

* Somm-Beecham CD 11.

side.'* If this book succeeds in reigniting interest in this great musician, then all well and good.

In my quest for Beecham I have spoken to literally hundreds of people, and I must apologise in advance if some have got left out of the list of acknowledgments that follows. Above all I must thank four members of Beecham's family, who have been unswerving in their enthusiasm and support:

> Sir Thomas's son, Paul Strang, who has not only helped me build up a picture of his mother, the soprano Dora Labbette; but also guided me unerringly through what seemed at first sight to be the near impenetrable thickets of the Chancery Court.

> His granddaughter, Jane Brabyn – daughter of Beecham's eldest son and heir to his baronetcy, the late Sir Adrian Beecham – who produced for me a cornucopia of family papers and photographs.

> His stepson, Sir Jeremy Thomas, whose memories of his mother Betty Humby, Beecham's second wife, and of the war years in America have been invaluable.

> His niece, Anne Wintle, who (using the *nom de plume* Anne Francis) wrote *A Guinea a Box*, a fascinating biography of Sir Thomas's grandfather, the inventor of Beecham's Pills. Sadly she died before the book was finished, but her son Christopher Wintle has kindly allowed me to use some of the earliest-known family photographs.

I also owe a debt of gratitude to Beecham's third wife, Shirley, Lady Beecham, who has given me permission to quote from Sir Thomas's published writing and private correspondence.

One of my greatest bits of good fortune was to meet and interview the last four surviving players (none of them, alas, still with us) from the London Philharmonic Orchestra's inaugural concert in October 1932: Gwydion Brooke, Richard 'Bob' Walton, Leo Birnbaum and George Roth. Many other players have shared their graphic memories of the Royal Philharmonic Orchestra in its Beecham heyday, among them the late Leonard Salzedo, the late Harry Legge, Denis Vaughan, Raymond Ovens and the late Reginald Giddy. Denham Ford, orchestral manager of the RPO and later Beecham's secretary, has proved a wonderful source of information about the late 1940s and early 1950s.

Ford was chairman of the old Beecham Society of London that did so much to help keep the Beecham flag flying until its untimely demise in 1988, and I owe special thanks to three other of its members: Tony Benson, who over the years has kept me supplied with a constant stream of information about Beecham's conducting engagements, Norman Morrison, expert on Beecham recordings, and Lyndon Jenkins, author of a recent book about Beecham and Delius, who has helped me sort out many knotty problems with the text. Others who have been generous with their time have been the

---

* Jean-François Labie, *William Christie: sonate baroque* (Aix-en-Provence, 1989).

composer Richard Arnell, Alan Jefferson, a previous Beecham biographer, Dr Erik Dervos, who gave advice on medical matters, the late Felix Aprahamian, Celia Baylis, Mike Ashman, and the discographer Michael H. Gray. Originally it was intended to include a Beecham discography, but in recent years there has been such a flood of issues and reissues that it would need a separate book to list them all.

British archivists and librarians who have been specially helpful include Lionel Carley of the Delius Trust; Vivien Hainsworth of the St Helens Local History and Archives Library; Lawrence Aspden, curator of Special Collections at the University of Sheffield, and Tom McCanna, the university's music librarian (both departments have important Beecham collections); Clifford Davies (Wadham College, Oxford), Ros Edwards (Henry Watson Music Library, Manchester), Maureen Hopkins (Glyndebourne archives); Eleanor Roberts (Hallé Orchestra); Libby Rice (London Symphony Orchestra); Edmund Pirouet (London Philharmonic Orchestra); and Michael Goold, who has built up an impressive private collection of information about the LPO. Laurie Watt of Charles Russell, solicitor and horn player, cast an eagle eye over the manuscript for me.

Among American helpers, I must single out Robert Tuggle and John Pennino of the Metropolitan Opera, supreme operatic archivists; Professor Paul Jackson, authority on Met recordings; Paul Ganson, bassoon player and historian of the Detroit Symphony Orchestra; Michele Smith of the New York Philharmonic Orchestra archives; David Peter Coppen of the Sibley Music Library, Eastman School of Music, Rochester; the singers Patrice Munsel and Regina Resnik, and the late Belle Schulhof, widow and business partner of Beecham's American manager, Andrew Schulhof. The Australian chapter could not have been written without the help of Guy Tranter of the Australian Broadcasting Corporation Document Archives in Sydney; Sir Charles Mackerras provided additional background information.

Some research expeditions turned out to be not only useful, but sheer fun, notably the successful treasure hunt for Luigi Illica's libretto for Beecham's projected opera, *Christopher Marlowe*, led by Massimo Baucia, conservator of the Fondo Antico at the Biblioteca Comunale Passerini-Landi at Piacenza. (My thanks, too, to my son Mark and Nell Rose for translating the voluminous correspondence between Illica, Beecham and the composer-conductor Emilio Pizzi that also emerged). Italy was an unexpectedly rich source of Beechamiana: the enormous package of material that arrived from Annalisa Bini of the Accademia di Santa Cecilia in Rome was another cause for celebration. Some of the other archives consulted are listed in the Source Notes.

Lastly I must thank David Lloyd-Jones, not just for his shrewd comments on the manuscript, but also for putting me in touch with Bruce Phillips of Boydell & Brewer, the publishers. My thanks to the Boydell staff for the enthusiasm they have shown towards the book. David Roberts has been a peerless editor. I had no idea that such meticulous and imaginative practitioners of his art still existed.

JOHN LUCAS
London, June 2008

To the countless musicians who helped
Beecham make us a more musical nation.

CHAPTER I

The Birth of the Pill

ALTHOUGH Sir Thomas Beecham was born and brought up in industrial south Lancashire – and proud of it – his family roots lay in a quite different part of the country, in the agricultural plain of south-west Oxfordshire, where for generations his forebears worked on the land. Family legend has it that the Beechams were of French origin, and were once called Beauchamp, but this has never been proved. The earliest known fact about them is that in the second half of the eighteenth century they were living and labouring in the village of Curbridge, fourteen miles to the west of Oxford.

The conductor's grandfather, also called Thomas Beecham, was born there in 1820, the son of a shepherd. Although it was unusual for children of farm workers to receive any formal education at that time, grandfather Thomas had a year's schooling at Witney when he was seven, though he left a year later to work in the fields for one shilling and sixpence for a seven-day week (the equivalent of £3.90 in 2008). As he himself put it many years later, his 'brief holiday with childhood' was over,[1] but at least, with extra help from his mother, he could read and write. Before long he, too, was tending sheep, sometimes spending all night with them in the open. He learned how to cure their ailments with herbs he found in the fields. He also used the herbs to treat himself.

After leaving home at the age of ten or eleven, Thomas found work on a large farm at Cropredy, near Banbury, where his skills as a veterinary herbalist so impressed his employer that eventually he was given the task of treating all the farm's livestock. In his spare time he began to make hand-rolled herbal pills for human consumption. Basically purgatives, they were held to cure all manner of ailments. When he was twenty, Thomas decided to sell his preparations to the public. After peddling them round Oxfordshire without much success, he went north, and in early 1847 reached Liverpool, which at the time was crowded with refugees from the Irish potato famine. Few of them could afford bread, let alone herbal pills, and to make ends meet Thomas was forced to take up casual labouring. In Liverpool he met and soon married Jane Evans, a Welshwoman eight years his senior and originally from Bangor, who was maid to a chemist. She was reputed to have a good singing voice. Anne Wintle, Thomas's great-granddaughter, has described the couple as being singularly ill suited: 'Unable to write, possibly wholly illiterate, Jane had a dour personality and was subject to fits of neurosis. Thomas, who had a bad temper and could be impatient with illness, was hardly the calm companion she needed.'[2]

In the summer of 1847 the Beechams moved to Wigan, where Thomas, who described himself variously as 'Quack Doctor', 'Worm Doctor' and 'Medicine Vendor', sold his products in the market-place. They included the herbal laxative pill that before long would make his name famous, another called 'Female's Friend', a 'Royal Toothpowder', a 'Golden Tooth Tincture' and 'a never-failing remedy for Deafness, providing the Drum of the Ear is not broken'. He augmented his earnings by casting horoscopes. By 1857 he had made enough money to set himself up as a 'Chemist, Druggist & Tea Dealer' at a shop in the centre of Wigan. With typical impudence he incorporated the royal coat of arms into his trademark and, to the irritation of the town's genuine medical practitioners, styled himself 'Dr Beecham'.

By now Thomas and Jane had four children – two boys and two girls. The future looked promising, but in August 1858 an incident occurred that was to have far-reaching consequences for the family. A young Wigan girl, Elizabeth Smith, had called at the shop for some laudanum for her father, who was 'ill with the flux'. Jane Beecham, who was serving, put it in a bottle bearing an old label for a harmless medicine, which she failed to replace with one marked 'laudanum', a tincture of opium that could prove fatal when administered to children. When Elizabeth arrived home, her father refused to take the laudanum and she put it in a cupboard. Three days later her small brother felt unwell and her mother, mistaking the mislabelled laudanum for the boy's regular medicine, gave him a spoonful of it. The boy died of convulsions. The coroner, recording a verdict of accidental death, said that it was the duty of all druggists to label all dangerous substances correctly.

Though in law Jane had been exonerated – it seems the coroner did not question her state of literacy – the affair had a disastrous effect on Thomas's business. The Pharmaceutical Society of London, which at the time was lobbying Parliament to introduce tighter regulations for the sale of potentially poisonous substances, published a report on the case in its journal.[3] Two months later Thomas felt obliged to put the shop up for auction, along with all its contents. In December he and his wife suffered a further blow when their five-year-old daughter Jane died of scarlet fever. The family left Wigan and moved to the nearby town of St Helens, whose collieries, glass factories and copper-smelting and alkali works placed it in the forefront of the Industrial Revolution. It boasted England's first canal, the Sankey, opened in 1757, which enabled coal to be transported directly from St Helens to the Mersey, and which in turn led to a huge expansion of the local coalfield. So great was the industrial pollution in St Helens that it stripped trees of their leaves and ruined farmers' crops within a four-mile radius. The rotten-egg stench of hydrogen sulphide could be detected at an even greater distance from the town.

That St Helens lacked any kind of visual attraction cannot have bothered Thomas, for by all accounts he was almost entirely lacking in aesthetic sensibility. Cocky, arrogant, opinionated, full of charm and a notorious philanderer, he revelled in the town's rumbustious mix of local and Irish coal miners, French and Scottish glassmakers, and Welshmen who had crossed the Mersey in search of employment. Drunkenness, prize-fighting, prostitution and general unruliness were endemic, but in St Helens Thomas found just the place to restore his battered fortunes.

He now concentrated on two products – the familiar Beecham's Herbal Pill (though it no longer contained any herbs) and Beecham's Magic Cough Pill – which he sold at St Helens market on Mondays and Saturdays, and at Wigan on Tuesdays and Fridays. An obituarist and friend of this 'ever genial modern Aesculapius' noted that his success arose from his 'having to deal mainly with the bulk of the labouring population in most matters concerning their physical well-being. Whatever may have been the merits of his various nostrums, he believed in them himself, and they were always popular with the people, and faith in a specific goes a long way in bringing about its ultimate efficacy'. Thomas's sales pitch, delivered in an Oxfordshire brogue, was peppered with biblical allusions that came some way after the Book of Exodus. 'What', he once asked a St Helens audience, 'did the Lord say to Moses when he appeared in the burning bush on Mount Sinai? He said, "If I have sent you plagues, if I have sent you pestilence, have I not sent you a remedy also? Go into the woods and fields and gather those flowers, roots and leaves the Almighty has sent you!"' [4]

In August 1859 Thomas placed his first, extravagantly worded, advertisement in the *St Helens Intelligencer*. Headed 'Worth a Guinea a Box', a slogan he had almost certainly coined himself, it claimed that Beecham's Pills were not simply a laxative, but 'the best in the world for bilious and nervous disorders, wind and pain of the stomach, headache, giddiness, fullness and swelling after meals, drowsiness, cold chills, loss of appetite, shortness of breath, etc., etc.' [5] By the early 1860s the demand for Thomas's products had grown so great that he gave up his stall and turned to full-time manufacturing. He no longer rolled pills by hand, but instead made them with a machine of his own devising in a shed behind his cottage in Westfield Street, where, said his advertisements, 'a box of the Finest Medicine in the World can now be had for 9d (£1.73).

Thomas sold pills by post and appointed wholesale agents to distribute his products throughout the country. Far from following the Almighty's alleged injunction to go into the woods and fields to gather ingredients, he now bought them by the hundredweight from wholesalers. His formulae were a closely guarded secret, but it was noted that large amounts of aloes and ginger, both common purgatives, were being delivered to his door. Such was the faith of Thomas's clients in the pill's curative powers that some took to standing outside his cottage in order that they might inhale the fumes wafting from the shed. Analysis carried out later for the British Medical Association revealed that the proportions of each pill were approximately 40 per cent aloes, 45 per cent powdered ginger and 15 per cent powdered soap, which bound the mixture together.[6] With cheap ingredients and low overheads, the business was very profitable.

But not everything was going well for Thomas. Jane Beecham, in poor health, began to suffer from hallucinations. In her misery she turned to drink for consolation. Thomas, who paid more attention to his business than he did to his family, was unsympathetic. In 1861 he was bound over to keep the peace for throwing Jane into the street following an argument and then brawling with an ostler who had intervened in the dispute. In the following year Jane's misery was compounded when Thomas fathered an illegitimate daughter. This incident broke up the marriage.

At the age of fifteen the Beechams' eldest child, the shy and introverted Joseph, began work as his father's full-time assistant. He had recently left the Moorflat elementary school for the sons of respectable tradesmen, where he had been taught 'Euclid, Algebra, Mechanics, Book-keeping by double entry, Mensuration, Drawing, Painting, Chemistry and Music (use of harmonium).'[7] Joseph, who had a remarkable head for figures, helped the business begin to grow at an even faster rate. An annual sales figure of £2,500 in 1865 (£120,300) leapt to £13,000 (£562,000) in 1872, when Thomas boasted to a friend that his sales extended to every town in Britain and to some parts of Australia, as well as to Africa.[8] Yet despite its success, the pill operation was small beer by St Helens standards. To the town's industrial grandees – the Pilkingtons (glass manufacturers), the Greenalls (brewers and coal owners) and the Gambles (chemical manufacturers) – Thomas was an upstart, and, with his flowing beard and capacious trousers hitched up to his chest, an uncouth and eccentric-looking upstart at that. To Thomas's embarrassment, a Pilkington had been on the bench when he was bound over to keep the peace.

Jane Beecham died in August 1872 at the age of fifty-nine. The circumstances of her death, reported at length in the local press, can have done little to improve her estranged husband's standing in the town. Her alcoholism had become so advanced that on the day before she died Joseph, believing she had become insane, had gone to the police office to ask how he should proceed to have her put in an asylum.[9] A coroner's jury returned a verdict that she had died of 'excessive intemperance'. Thomas quickly put the matter behind him, however, and five months later married Sarah Pemberton, a milliner from Lambeth, twenty-three years his junior. The local press ignored the event, as it did the marriage in April 1873 of Joseph, now twenty-five years old. His bride was a striking, raven-haired dressmaker, Josephine Burnett, daughter of a St Helens silk-dealer who doubled as a barber. Slight in build, with a regal bearing she never lost, Josephine claimed she had Spanish blood in her veins. Emily, the first of their ten children, was born the following year. A son, Harold, followed in 1875, though he lived for only a short time. A second daughter, Laura, was born two years later.*

Business was now growing so fast that Thomas found it necessary to build a small, single-story factory in Westfield Street to meet the demand for pills. During the previous three years the Beechams' only helpers had been a teenage packer and a general dogsbody who had joined the business at the age of eleven. Now extra staff had to be taken on. Next door to the factory Thomas built a decent-sized house for Joseph and Josephine and their daughters, with stables attached and room for a housemaid and children's nurse. There, on 29 April 1879, a second son was born. He was named Thomas after his grandfather, though to the family he would always be known as Tom. Grandfather Thomas was jubilant, for it seemed inevitable that, despite the death of Harold four years earlier, the business would pass eventually to a third generation of Beechams after all. It did, but not in the way that he – or anyone else – could have expected.

---

* No birth or death certificates have been found for Harold. His name and year of birth appear in Josephine Beecham's petition to the President of the Probate, Divorce and Admiralty Division of the High Court, 14 December 1900 (NA, J77/708). Laura died on Christmas Day 1881, two weeks before her fifth birthday.

CHAPTER 2

The Mecca of Globules

ACCORDING TO Beecham's own account, written when he was in his sixties, his first musical memory was of being taken at the age of five to a piano recital that included several pieces by Grieg. That night, he says, he could not sleep, for the music revolved distractingly in his head. Eventually he went downstairs and asked his surprised parents if he could be taught to play the piano.[1] The following morning a local church organist was asked to give him his first lesson.

The organist was James Unsworth of Holy Cross Roman Catholic church in Corporation Street. Joseph, who had been taught to play the organ by Unsworth, might have been a committed Congregationalist, but he harboured no sectarian prejudices: the large Roman Catholic community in St Helens and its schools in particular would benefit greatly from his munificence. It was Unsworth who gave Beecham his first taste of Mozart. He had introduced several of Mozart's liturgical works into the services at Holy Cross (a particular favourite being the spurious 'Twelfth Mass' ĸa232), and he recounted the stories of the Mozart operas to his young pupil, illustrating them with musical examples on the piano. Unsworth recalled telling Joseph, 'This boy has music in him, and it will come out.'[2]

A year later, in 1885, Joseph took a lease on a sizeable, cream-painted villa called Ewanville, set in eight and half acres of land in the village of Huyton, six miles from St Helens. The family's old home in Westfield Street, together with the original factory, was demolished to make way for a new three-storied factory, planned and completed by Joseph at a cost of more than £30,000 (the equivalent of £1,826,000 in 2008). Joseph was now virtually in sole charge of the business. Old Thomas had been unwell and had been advised by doctors that the industrial pollution in St Helens was damaging his lungs. His second wife had died and he had married yet again, this time Mary Sawell, a merry widow thirty-two years younger than himself, whom he had met by chance on Banbury railway station. Mary disliked the smell and dirt of St Helens and, in the hope of both pleasing her and restoring his health, old Thomas bought 300 acres in the Buckinghamshire village of Mursley, on which he built a large, rather forbidding-looking house, which he called Mursley Hall. He even took up farming on a small scale. Though a long way from Lanca-shire, he was now reasonably close to his Oxfordshire relations, with whom he had always kept in touch. In 1889 he gave Joseph a half-share in the pill-business.

Under Joseph's guidance, sales rose ten-fold. The new factory, designed jointly by H. V. Krolow and Harry May of Liverpool and built of red brick with local sandstone dressings, was described at the time of its opening as being 'in the Queen Anne style of architecture',[3] though that particular monarch might not have recognised it as such. Nonetheless, it remains one of St Helens's most distinctive buildings. At first-floor level a terracotta frieze portrays various members of Joseph's family in relief, including, on the south side, the infant Tom, who with flowing locks and a lace collar is shown peering out of a window. A bust of Joseph himself, sculpted in stone, sits above the main door with, on either side of him, the female figures of Health and Beauty bearing scrolls emblazoned with the words, 'Worth a guinea a box' and 'Largest sale in the world'. With its grand Tudorbethan entrance-hall and 150 ft clocktower (both still intact), as well as its nickel-plated Otto engines that provided lighting and power for the pill-making machinery, the factory was truly – as one of Joseph's advertising pamphlets put it – a 'Mecca of globules'. In a ten-hour day it could turn out enough pills 'to give the whole population of Ireland and London a mild aperient every night'.[4]

Meanwhile the Beecham family was growing apace: in all there would be six daughters and two sons, the younger one, Harry, being born in 1888. To provide room for them, Joseph added an extra wing to Ewanville, as well as large conservatories in which he grew tropical ferns and orchids, palms and pineapple trees. A keen, though not particularly proficient, musician, he installed in his music-room a two-manual Hill organ, an American harmonium and a Broadwood grand piano (as well as a full-size billiard-table). The house was one of the first in Lancashire to have a central-heating system, as well as its own electricity generator. Joseph, an enthusiast for gadgetry, attached to the organ an electric pump, which tended to fuse all the lights when switched on.

When Tom was nine or ten, Joseph bought an electrically driven orchestrion, or mechanical organ, which could reproduce with reasonable accuracy the sound of a large wind band, backed by drums, cymbals and triangle. Built by G. Baker & Co. of Geneva and encased in a massive glass-fronted cabinet of Cuban mahogany, it stood thirteen feet high and seven and a half feet wide, and seemed to the boy as big as the side of a cottage. By inserting into it specially perforated music-rolls – Joseph owned 131 of them – the listener could enjoy a wide selection of 'Overtures, Operatic Selections, Sacred Music, Dance Music, etc'.[5] Beecham particularly liked the operatic items, and later his parents took him to the Carl Rosa Opera Company's seasons in Liverpool, travelling there and back in the family brougham.

Not only had the Beechams grown rich, they were also making their mark socially. When the daughters were old enough, they went to Cheltenham Ladies' College. Joseph was now a Justice of the Peace and a Tory member of the St Helens council, active in improving the town's electricity supply and sewerage system. As an employer, he had a reputation for treating his staff with respect. But, if to an outsider, life at Ewanville seemed idyllic, things were far from tranquil beneath the surface. Relations between Joseph and his wife were on the verge of collapse. Since the birth of their ninth child, Elsie Olive, Josephine had been suffering from depression, a state not helped by her habit of steadying her nerves with a glass of brandy. She began to spend long spells recuperating in Eastbourne.

Beecham writes in his 1944 autobiography, *A Mingled Chime*, that her absences hardly made Ewanville the cheeriest place for children. Joseph seemed to them a severe and remote figure who found it hard to communicate with his young family. A libertine like his father, he took full advantage of his wife's absences. The youngest children could not help but notice the embraces he exchanged with one of the nursemaids, and even speculated that she might be the mother of a new and unexpected baby who had suddenly appeared in the nursery.[6] On at least one occasion Josephine bombarded her husband with crockery. In later life Elsie Olive remembered her father as being 'very reserved and secretive. He was very shy and might have opened up if I had known how [to get] him to do it. But he terrified me. I am sure he lacked confidence in himself and that made him very aggressive on occasion.'[7]

Tom began his education at a local school, but in the autumn of 1892, when he was thirteen, he was sent as a boarder to Rossall, the North Country public school set on a bleak and isolated stretch of the Lancashire coast between Blackpool and Fleetwood. The new boy's arrival caused something of a stir, for news spread quickly that he was sporting a moustache. 'Sure enough', one of his contemporaries recalled, 'there was to be seen a short, stout boy with a definite dark-brown moustache and a lively eye, destined in the end to be one of the world's great men.'"[8] Tom's housemaster ordered the immediate removal of the facial hair. At first Tom found life at Rossall a dislocating experience, but his musical talent was soon recognised by the school's music master, Edward Thomas Sweeting, who was taken aback by his pupil's ability to sight-read his way through a volume of Beethoven's piano sonatas that he had won as a prize.*

During the summer holiday that followed his first year at Rossall, Tom accompanied his father to New York, where Joseph rented a factory in Brooklyn for

---

* Sweeting left Rossall in 1897 to become organist at St John's College, Cambridge. In 1901 he was appointed master of music at Winchester College, a post he held for twenty-three years.

making his pills. On the way over on the Cunarder *Campania*, the boy played at the ship's concert for a group of British singers who were to perform at the Chicago World's Columbian Exposition of 1893. Tom, too, visited the Exposition, as well as the Niagara Falls, and ended up in Boston, where his father, delayed by business meetings, sent him back to Britain on his own. Tom again took part in the ship's concert, this time playing for the Swedish baritone Carl-Frederik Lundquist, who made a strong impression on him with his singing of the 'Evening Star' aria from *Tannhäuser*.*

During Beecham's second year at Rossall the school marked the fiftieth anniversary of its foundation with a 'Grand Jubilee Concert', which featured an orchestra of some forty players, most of them drawn from the Hallé Orchestra in Manchester. Lacking a percussion-player, Sweeting, who conducted, asked the fifteen-year-old Beecham to play the cymbals and the bass drum, an instrument with which the boy was familiar, since, dressed in a uniform of scarlet tunic, blue trousers and helmet, he played it regularly as a member of the Rossall cadet-corps band.† A year later, in 1895, Tom's playing of one of Schumann's *Novelletten* at the annual school concert earned him a perceptive note in the *Fleetwood Chronicle*: 'Mr T. Beecham's pianoforte solo was exquisitely played, his style being generally admired, and it is safe to prophesy that he has before him a brilliant musical career. An immediate recall was accorded, and acknowledged with an exceedingly delightful *morceau*.' [9] ‡ In 1896 Tom conducted his house choir in the school's annual singing competition. *The Rossallian* found the choir 'distinctly the best, Beecham's spirited conducting being quite one of the features of the evening's entertainment'. His singing in the vocal quartet contest met with less appreciation, his bass voice being considered 'very incorrect'. In the following year he won second prize in the solo voice competition with an aria from Victor Nessler's recently composed *Der Trompeter von Säkkingen*, an opera still be heard occasionally in smaller houses in Germany and Austria. His rendering, said *The Rossallian*, was expressive, though some of his notes were 'rather strange'. [10]

In *A Mingled Chime* Beecham suggests that he took part in school sports infrequently, for fear that if he showed too much zeal he would be kept away from his books and music. In fact he was an enthusiastic and valued sportsman,

---

* Beecham claims in *A Mingled Chime* (p. 29) that Lundquist had by then grown so fat as a result of a growth disorder that he had been forced him to give up his stage career, though in fact he was to continue singing at the Stockholm Opera for another eleven years.

† The programme included Schubert's *Rosamunde* Overture, Mendelssohn's *Capriccio brillant* and a rousing *Festal March* that Sweeting had composed for the occasion.

‡ Many years later Beecham told the American critic Irving Kolodin that Schumann was 'not the greatest of composers, perhaps, but one who expressed a certain intimacy of emotion better than anyone else' (*Saturday Review* [New York], 25 March 1961).

playing football, cricket and Rossall's own version of hockey for his house, as well as football (at centre-half) and cricket for the school. A group photograph of the Rossall cricket XI in 1897 shows him leaning nonchalantly against a pillar and wearing not the conventional cap worn by his team-mates, but a hat that looks like a Stetson. 'T. Beecham', noted *The Rossallian*, 'bats in good style though is too inclined to play forward, having several times lost his wicket this way on a slow pitch. A good field at cover-point.' [11] Now in his last term, Beecham was head of his house, a member of the sixth form and the first pupil at Rossall to be allowed a piano in his study. At his final school concert he played Chopin's *Fantaisie-Impromptu*. His performance, wrote the Fleetwood paper, was 'to the uninitiated a storm of notes, to the initiated a beautiful design with an ornate and elaborate setting. Needless to say he was encored.' [12]

After leaving Rossall in the summer of 1897, Beecham took his friend Charles Stocks, who had been captain of school, on a cruise to Norway. 'I used to land, and climb the high mountains alone', Stocks remembered, 'while he stayed on the ship all the time, playing the piano non-stop to admiring audiences of ladies.' [13] Stocks was due to go up to Wadham College, Oxford, at the end of the holiday, but Beecham appeared to have no plans at all. Back at Ewanville he told his father that he thought he might study abroad, but Joseph thought it an inappropriate step for his eldest son, who, he assumed, would join him at the factory. After consulting his local Congregational minister, Joseph, curiously indecisive when it came to family matters, eventually agreed that Tom could go to either Oxford or Cambridge, whichever he preferred. No sooner had Stocks settled in to start his first term at Wadham than he was startled to hear from the hall porter that a Mr Beecham had arrived at the college and was inquiring for him – 'He's *up*, sir.' It was true. Beecham had taken private rooms in Walton Street, where he could have his own piano. He was planning to read history and classics.

During his first term at Oxford Beecham took an active part in college life, attending lectures, playing football for Wadham and joining its musical society, which, the college magazine noted, 'began the term with a very good Smoker, for which we have chiefly to thank the freshmen, who in music are distinctly above the average, particularly Beecham (piano) and H. M. Tennent (song)'. [14] * There is no record of Beecham's participation in any more of the society's events, nor is there any evidence to support a claim he made two years later that he had 'a little to do with an orchestra at Oxford'. [15] He found university dull. Music was barely acknowledged outside the college chapels and musical societies. There was no faculty of music. Though there had been a professor of music at Oxford

---

* Tennent was to become one of London's leading theatrical managers.

since the seventeenth century (in Beecham's time it was the church musician Sir John Stainer), he was not obliged to reside in the city; his duties were confined more or less to overseeing the music at ceremonial occasions and examining candidates for music degrees, for which residency was not a requirement – in 1866 the future composer Hubert Parry had gained an Oxford degree in music while still a schoolboy at Eton.

During his second term Beecham gave up attending lectures and restricted his college activities to playing football for the Wadham team, which, noted the *Gazette*, had enjoyed 'the most successful season they have had for some years past'. The forwards, of whom Beecham was one, were judged 'a good scoring lot'. For much of the time he shut himself away in his rooms, playing the piano, devouring books on theory and composition, including Berlioz's *Traité de l'instrumentation et d'orchestration modernes*, and composing songs and other small-scale works. These he took to a down-to-earth Yorkshireman, Dr John Varley Roberts, composer of church music, conductor of the University Glee and Madrigal Society, and organist at Magdalen College, whose choir was in Beecham's opinion the best in Oxford. Beecham appreciated his mentor's solid musicianship, though, as the *Musical Times* reported a decade later, Varley's lessons in harmony and composition only served to convince him 'that he was not made the right way to appreciate the usual English methods of approaching these subjects'. [16]

By his third term, which turned out be his last, Beecham seems to have virtually abandoned Wadham. The Bursar's Book for 1898 shows that he ate in the dining hall only once, on 22 April, when he paid four pence (£1 in 2008) for food and four pence for beer. He also made a single appearance with the college cricket team. In *A Mingled Chime* he leaves the manner of his parting vague. When the composer Ethel Smyth later asked him if he had been sent down from the university, he told her that, on the contrary, the Warden had seemed sorry to see him go, despite his parting observation that 'Your untimely departure has perhaps spared us the necessity of asking you to go.' [17] Smyth's question was more pertinent than Beecham was prepared to admit, for in 1961 Charles Stocks confirmed in an obituary of his friend that Beecham had indeed been dismissed by Wadham, which had failed to realise 'that he was the only one of us undergraduates destined to win them real fame'. [18] *

During Beecham's last term at Oxford, Joseph had invited a young American girl, Utica Celestia Welles, to stay with the family at Ewanville. Utica was the

---

* After a spell of schoolmastering at Eton, Stocks (1878–1975) joined the Civil Service, where his posts included Secretary of the Royal Commission on Oxford and Cambridge, and Commissioner of Crown Lands. He and Beecham remained friends for some years after leaving Oxford.

daughter of Dr Charles Stuart Welles, former superintendent of New York's Polyclinic Hospital, with whom Joseph had become friendly after being treated by him during one of his trips to the United States. Recently Welles had brought his family to Britain, following his appointment as physician to the American Embassy in London. Emily, the eldest Beecham daughter, had stayed with the Welleses in New York and now the hospitality was being reciprocated. Joseph asked Utica to prolong her stay at Ewanville, so that she might meet his son when he returned from university.[19] Tom was greatly struck by the sixteen-year-old Utica's vivacity and good looks, and in due course was invited to stay at the Welleses' house at 9 Roland Gardens, South Kensington.

Welles had a colourful background. Though he adopted the dress and mutton-chop whiskers of a Confederate gentleman, he was a direct descendant of a New Englander, Thomas Welles, who had emigrated from Warwickshire in the 1630s and later became Connecticut's second governor. His uncle, Gideon Welles, had been Secretary of the Navy in President Lincoln's cabinet. Not only was Welles a medical practitioner and diplomat, but he also dabbled in poetry, painting and hypnotism, and earlier in his career had been a canal-builder. His wife Ellie was the niece of Tennessee Cook, American wife of the hugely rich City merchant, draper and baronet, Sir Francis Cook.

After leaving Oxford, Beecham was given a job in the pill company's advertising department, though there is no record of what he did there, apart from playing the piano that Joseph had installed in the factory for his own rare moments of relaxation. We can discount the old story that Tom was responsible for a promotional hymnal that included the verse, 'Hark! The herald-angels sing / Beecham's pills are just the thing / For easing pain and mothers mild, / Two for adults, one for a child.' By now Beecham knew that music was to be the dominant force in his life, and he took lessons in harmony and composition from a young teacher at the Liverpool College of Music, Frederic Austin. To familiarise himself with the orchestral repertoire, he haunted the concerts of the Liverpool Philharmonic Society and the Hallé in Manchester, as well as the concerts of contemporary British music that Granville Bantock initiated at New Brighton, on the Cheshire side of the Mersey estuary. Elgar, Parry, Stanford, Edward German, Alexander Mackenzie and Bantock all conducted programmes of their works there.

Since there was no chance of an existing orchestra offering him an opportunity to conduct, the twenty-year-old Beecham decided to form one of his own, and at a meeting at St Helens in May 1899 he called on local musicians to join him in an enterprise that would provide the town with concerts of 'high-class music'.[20] The response was enthusiastic, and Beecham announced the formation of the St Helens Orchestral Society, which would give its first concert in the autumn. With that settled, he departed for Bayreuth, where he heard his first *Ring* cycle, produced by Wagner's widow, Cosima, and conducted by the composer's son, Siegfried. He had looked forward to the experience with some excitement, but found the standard of playing, singing and staging lower than he had expected.[21] He was not alone in thinking that what Cosima claimed to be a faithful copy of the Master's own production of twenty-three years earlier was disappointingly time-worn.

Back in St Helens, Beecham set to work with his new, mostly amateur, orchestra. Rehearsals took place at the Congregational School in Brook Street, where players soon discovered that he knew a good deal more about the scores he was conducting than they imagined. Finding a cello passage hard to play, Andrew Kay, a chemist from the Kurtz chemical works at St Helens, substituted the much easier double-bass line in the belief that the conductor would not notice. 'Kay', shouted Beecham in his first recorded rebuke to a player, 'what the devil do you think you're doing?'[22]

The first concert, which marked Beecham's debut as an orchestral conductor, took place at St Helens Town Hall on 8 November 1899. With a stiffening of professionals from Liverpool and Manchester, the orchestra numbered sixty-two players. The programme, a typical rag-bag of its time, opened with Mendelssohn's *Ruy Blas* Overture and closed with Rossini's Overture to *William Tell*. In between came Grieg's first *Peer Gynt* suite, Elgar's *Spanish Serenade* for chorus and orchestra, arias and ballads sung by a local baritone, Samuel Coleridge-Taylor's *Four Characteristic Waltzes*, and a group of piano solos played by Osborne Edmundson, director of Liverpool's German School of Music, who was also the soloist in Mendelssohn's Piano Concerto no. 1. The *St Helens Reporter* judged the event a 'musical treat', though it 'was not so largely attended as it ought to have been ... Mr T. Beecham, jun., conducted the orchestra from beginning to end in a manner which indicated considerable knowledge of the requirements of orchestration.'[23]

On the following day Joseph Beecham took a further step up the St Helens social ladder when he was unanimously elected mayor of St Helens in succession to a member of the Pilkington family. To mark his year of office, he asked the Hallé Orchestra to give an invitation concert at the Town Hall under its recently appointed chief conductor, the illustrious Hans Richter.* Joseph might have been shy and retiring, but paradoxically he liked making flamboyant gestures,

---

* At the time of the St Helens concert, the Hallé Orchestra, founded in 1858 by the German emigré musician Charles Hallé, was the country's only fully fledged professional symphony orchestra outside London. A third of Hallé's members also played in the orchestra of the Liverpool Philharmonic Society, a tradition that continued until 1943, when it was re-established as the full-time Liverpool Philharmonic Orchestra.

particularly if the results showed him off to advantage. A date for the concert was agreed – 6 December, which was only a month away – but because of an administrative muddle, the orchestra failed to tell Joseph that Richter could not appear, as he was leaving England at the end of November for long-standing engagements in Vienna. The Hallé suggested that its leader, Carlo Risegari, should conduct the concert instead, but Joseph demanded a conductor with a name. When it became clear that no such conductor was free on the day, Tom suggested to his father that he might take Richter's place. Joseph vacillated, but then told the Hallé that he wanted his son for the concert. Risegari said he would rather withdraw than play under a novice. Incensed, Joseph threatened to go to London for an orchestra, at which point the Hallé capitulated.

Since there was only one rehearsal, on the afternoon of the concert, Beecham agreed that the programme should consist of works that the Hallé had recently performed under Richter: the prelude and the introduction to Act 3 of *Die Meistersinger*, the *Tannhäuser* Overture, Beethoven's Fifth Symphony, the third movement from Tchaikovsky's 'Pathétique' Symphony, the prelude to Act 3 of *Lohengrin* and Berlioz's Hungarian March. In addition, the American soprano Lillian Blaufelt, who had recently scored a success at the Royal Albert Hall in London, was to sing some familiar operatic arias by Gounod, Delibes and Verdi. During preparations for the concert, Utica Welles paid another visit to Ewanville. She and Beecham walked across the fields, while he sang the Beethoven symphony at the top of voice and gave cues to imaginary players. 'That', she recalled sixty years later, 'was why I fell in love with him – because of his genius.'[24]

The *St Helens Newspaper & Advertiser* described the audience as 'one of the most brilliant which has been witnessed in the municipal buildings for some considerable time'. The Town Hall square was lit by specially erected arc lamps and the building's interior was decorated with exotic plants from Ewanville's conservatories. A large, specially commissioned, drawing in the London-based *Illustrated Sporting and Dramatic News* shows Joseph, his chain of office round his neck, receiving his guests, the men in white tie and tails, the women in décolleté and tightly cinched long dresses. If it had been the artist's aim to flatter the new mayor by evoking the aura of a Paris salon, rather than that of a northern town hall, he achieved it successfully.

The local press was particularly taken by the fact that Beecham appeared to conduct the Beethoven symphony and some of the other pieces from memory. Even the Hallé players (minus Risegari, who boycotted the event) seemed impressed – at least, they gave him a round of applause. If any doubts about working for the unknown Beecham still lingered, they were soon dispelled by the supper and Havana cigars that Joseph laid on for them after the concert. It was generally agreed that the feast had been equalled only by the one provided by Earl Fitzwilliam a fortnight earlier, when Richter and the Hallé had given a private concert at his Yorkshire seat, Wentworth Woodhouse.

The *St Helens Newspaper and Advertiser* consulted the St Helens Choral Society's conductor, J. T. Elliott, for 'an expert's opinion' on Beecham's performance. At first, said Elliott, the brass had been too loud in relation to the rest of the orchestra, though later the balance had improved; also, Beecham had a tendency to exaggerate sforzandos, 'perhaps due to over-enthusiasm'. But on the whole 'his work was very clever indeed. It was more than a merely correct interpretation of the music; he put energy and life into his conducting.'[25] According to Beecham himself, Lillian Blaufelt declared herself well satisfied with the orchestral accompaniment to her arias, even though there had been no time to rehearse them.[26]

A week later the same paper published an interview with the twenty-year-old Beecham that showed him by turn confident and unsure of himself, boastful and modest, and not above inventing things that made him sound more experienced than he actually was – for example that he played 'the clarionette and tympani in orchestras'. He also claimed that he had been going to take a musical degree at Oxford, but 'was not so well at the time'. The rest of the interview was less contentious:

> N & A. *People have commented, Mr Beecham, on the fact that you seemed so thoroughly at home on the conductor's pedestal. You seemed to like it.*
>
> T.B. Yes, I have drifted into conducting because I am fond of it. It is by far the most enjoyable branch of music to me. I detest solo-playing. In fact, I am more or less nervous when solo-playing, but not the slightest when I am conducting. That is a little strange, too, because there is far more responsibility about conducting an orchestra.
>
> *Now you have found how well you like conducting, do you intend to stick to it?*
>
> I think I may. I hardly know yet.
>
> *Is Hallé's band the best in this country?*
>
> It is certainly the best in the North of England, but Mr [Henry] Wood's orchestra in London is one I like very much, and is one of the best in the world.

The Hallé and Queen's Hall orchestras, said Beecham, could stand comparison with any Continental orchestras, adding that he had 'heard all the best of the latter', which was improbable. At this point the interview ended, though the reporter added a postscript: 'There is no doubt about Mr Beecham's enthusiasm for music, and no doubt also that in a young man of twenty his talents are of a quality that may some day make his name as well known as a musician as it is already in another capacity.'[27]

Beecham's second – and, as it turned out, last – concert with the St Helens Orchestral Society, a joint affair with the choral society, came on 18 December 1899. The centre-piece of the programme was Beethoven's First Symphony. Beethoven, he told the *Newspaper & Advertiser*, was 'hardly, perhaps' his favourite composer, though all his symphonies were 'interesting'. One of his favourite symphonic writers was Brahms, and Schubert was another. The young Beecham was nothing if not opinionated.[28]

CHAPTER 3

Banishment

FOR BEECHAM a deep shadow lay over the success of the Hallé concert. His mother had not attended it and his eighteen-year-old second sister, Josie, had acted as lady mayoress in her place. Ten months earlier Joseph had successfully petitioned to have Josephine certified by doctors and two magistrates as being a person of unsound mind, on the grounds that she was 'sullen of demeanour, with a certain amount of violence, talked loudly and refused to answer questions, suffered from epileptic hysteria, and suffered from delusions'. Shortly afterwards, in March 1899, Josephine had been taken on her husband's instructions to St Andrew's Hospital, a privately run lunatic asylum near Northampton, where she was still being detained.[1] Beecham and his eldest sister Emily protested that an asylum was not the proper place for their mother, but Joseph, who twenty-seven years earlier had contemplated putting his own mother in an asylum, took no notice of their objections.

Re-examined in the light of twentieth-first-century medicine, the original diagnosis would seem to be incorrect. If Josephine, at the time aged fifty, had indeed been suffering from a form of epilepsy, she would not have survived for long, because there was then no effective treatment for the condition, yet she was to live on for another thirty-three years. Josephine's initial fits were more likely to have been brought on by eclampsia, a common complication in middle-aged women who have experienced multiple pregnancies. The precisely worded grounds given for her certification also indicate chronic post-natal depression. In the absence of modern drugs, depression was treated with bromide, which had a calming effect on bouts of agitation, but made depressive states worse. Josephine's subsequent 'seizures' were almost certainly fainting fits caused by hyperventilation syndrome or over-breathing. If this re-diagnosis is correct, Josephine's two eldest children were right in their instinctive belief that what she needed most was sympathetic care in a private environment.

At the time of Josephine's certification, Emily, a small, energetic figure afraid of no one, had left Ewanville and was lodging with the Welles family in South Kensington. Beecham, upset by the turn of events, had wanted to join her there, but Dr Welles persuaded him that, in order to prevent a total family breakdown, it would be wiser if for the time being he were to remain in Lancashire with his father.[2] In the months that followed the Hallé concert it became clear to both Beecham and Emily during visits to their mother that she was being held at the asylum against her will, and that her condition was not as serious as Joseph made out. They vowed to secure her release, but found they could achieve nothing without their father's agreement, which he withheld.

Emily and Beecham received strong support from Mrs Welles's uncle, Sir Francis Cook, who called in solicitors to advise Josephine. They recommended that the best way to break the impasse was for her to seek a judicial separation from her husband, to which she readily agreed, for Cook had discovered that Joseph kept a mistress, a Mrs Bennett, at 3 Craven Park, a Victorian villa with Gothic detailing in the then prosperous north-west London suburb of Harlesden. Joseph was known there as 'Mr Bennett'. 'Mrs Bennett' was also an alias. Her real name was Helen McKey Taylor, who had been a governess at St Helens. Sixteen years younger than Joseph, she had been 'on terms of intimacy' with him (her own phrase) for at least twelve years.[3]

On hearing that Tom supported his mother's wish for a separation, the enraged Joseph threw him out of Ewanville. They would not see each other again for nine years. Dr Welles agreed that Tom could stay at Roland Gardens, where at least he had the compensation of seeing Utica every day. Before long he proposed to her and was accepted, though her father insisted that in view of the couple's ages, twenty and eighteen, their engagement should be regarded as unofficial. During the summer of 1900 Tom and Utica were invited by the Cooks to spend a few weeks at their magnificent Portuguese estate, the Quinta de Monserrate at Sintra, which had once belonged to William Beckford, author of *Vathek*. It was there that Byron had written the stanzas in *Childe Harold* lauding the wild beauty of Sintra's countryside. On the site of Beckford's now ruined neo-Gothic castle Francis Cook had built, to J. T. Knowles's designs, a fantastical *palácio* that welded together Gothic, Islamic and Renaissance influences to magical and romantic effect. In its library Beecham read for the first time the plays of Shakespeare's contemporaries, beginning with Christopher Marlowe and running on to Beaumont and Fletcher. He never lost his enthusiasm for them.

With the St Helens link severed, money became a problem for Beecham, though he made ends meet by playing the piano at private functions; he also played on occasion in the sixteen-strong De La Warr Orchestra, formed by the eighth Earl De La Warr at Bexhill-on-Sea in Sussex to provide concerts of light music for the enjoyment of holidaymakers and residents. Beecham harboured ambitions to become a composer, and approached Charles Stanford, Dublin-born professor of composition at the Royal College of Music, in the hope that he might give him lessons. Stanford did not take private pupils, however, and passed Beecham on to a fellow Irish composer, Charles Wood, now best remembered for his church music. Beecham submitted several works to Wood, including a grand opera based on Walter Scott's *Marmion*, for which he had written his own libretto. None of them appears to have survived. Charles Reid, Beecham's first biographer, writes that 'a professional friend to whom he played some of the *Marmion* music testifies that it was tuneful, well-shaped, and professional in quality'.[4]

Some months passed before Josephine could file her petition for a decree of separation. When her solicitor's managing clerk, accompanied by a commissioner for oaths, took the petition to Northampton for her to sign, the superintendent of the asylum refused to let them see her, citing an order of the Commissioners in Lunacy that no person of unsound mind could sign any document other than a will or codicil affecting his or her property or income. The Commissioners upheld the superintendent's action, but backed down in December 1900, when the president of the Probate, Divorce and Admiralty Division of the High Court ordered them to allow Josephine to sign the petition. 'It is quite clear', said the judge, 'that the lady must be allowed to take all steps that are necessary for her to bring her case before this court.'[5] Several days before the ruling was handed down Joseph threatened both Tom and Emily with irrevocable disinheritance should they continue to support their mother, but they held their ground.[6]

When the case finally came to court on 8 February 1901, Josephine's counsel revealed that when Emily had visited the asylum two days earlier with a solicitor, she had been told by its superintendent's son that her mother was no longer there. Joseph had taken her away that morning. The judge called Joseph's action a 'very grave' contempt of court, in that he had molested the petitioner in the suit now pending against him, and ordered that Josephine's whereabouts should be discovered as soon as possible. When the hearing resumed three days later, her counsel told the court that she was in Lancashire, where she was 'a close prisoner in her husband's house, which is guarded by commissionaires'. Joseph's counsel claimed that 'the whole trouble had arisen through the children's intermeddling between husband and wife', to which the judge replied that 'If the husband has been guilty of the acts alleged against him I think the children were justified.' He ordered that Josephine should come to London in the care of a medical expert nominated by the court, so that he could decide for himself on the state of her health.[7]

Joseph protested that he was innocent of the adultery alleged by his wife, but the judge did not believe him. No doubt recognising that the court's sympathies lay with Josephine, and that his case looked bleak, Joseph decided not to defend the suit. Josephine was placed in Dr Welles's care and on 25 June 1901 was finally granted her decree on the grounds of her husband's adultery. Her alimony was set at £2,500 (£154,300) a year. In order that she should have no difficulty in seeing her children, the judge ordered Joseph to provide a house in London for the governess Mrs Davidson and the younger Beecham daughters. It was to be 'within a drive' from where Josephine lived. Henry, now twelve and known to the family as Harry, was to remain in Lancashire, so that he could continue to attend Liverpool College, but he was to come to London during the holidays.[8]

Joseph, used to getting his own way, was hugely resentful of the outcome, though to comply with the judge's order he bought West Brow, a large Victorian house at 9 Arkwright Road, Hampstead. He accused Welles of influencing Tom against him, a charge Welles vigorously denied, citing letters he had written to Joseph urging a reconciliation with his children. Perhaps embarrassed by the disclosure of his secret life in Harlesden, Joseph sold the house there for £950 (£58,600) and bought Helen McKey Taylor another, more expensive, home, 14 Holland Park Villas in Kensington. At the same time he increased the allowance he gave her to £1,000 (£61,700) a year. She was to remain Joseph's friend and confidante for the rest of his life.

Tom's and Emily's persistent support for their mother proved in the end to be justified. Once free of the asylum and of her husband, Josephine began to improve physically, though her mind could still become confused, and she would never get over her depression entirely. Beecham left no clues as to what he felt about this extraordinary episode – in *A Mingled Chime* he merely refers to a serious difference of opinion with his father – but it can only have been deeply disturbing for someone who was still only nineteen when it started. It says much for his strength of purpose that he remained determined to pursue his musical ambitions.

In early 1902 Beecham acted as accompanist for the singing lessons given in Chelsea by a German baritone, Josef Claus, who was about to start a tour of London's inner suburbs with the grandly named but decidedly ramshackle Imperial Grand Opera Company. Claus gave Beecham an introduction to Kelson Trueman, the enterprise's founder, manager and leading tenor, who was looking for an assistant conductor. When Beecham turned up at the Old Vic theatre, where rehearsals for the tour took place, Trueman asked him if he knew the operas to be performed. Beecham said that he did and proved it by playing selections from all of them on the piano from memory. He was signed up on the spot.*

Beecham was allotted *Carmen*, *Pagliacci* and the three old chestnuts known satirically as 'the English Ring', Michael Balfe's *Bohemian Girl*, Vincent Wallace's *Maritana* and Julius Benedict's *Lily of Killarney*. *Il trovatore*, *Faust* and *Cavalleria rusticana* were in the hands of the company's chief conductor, Emilio

---

* This version of the meeting with Trueman, based on interviews Beecham gave much nearer the time, is less colourful, but seemingly more accurate, than the one he gives in *A Mingled Chime* (pp. 46–7).

Pizzi, an Italian then living in London.* Orchestra, chorus, sets and costumes left much to be desired, but there were some good principal singers, among them the Irish tenor Joseph O'Mara, who sang the role of Don Caesar in *Maritana* for Beecham, Blanche Marchesi, the Santuzza in *Cavalleria rusticana*, and Marie Duma, whose Leonora in *Il trovatore* was recalled by Beecham forty years later as being unmatched in his experience for its tone quality, phrasing and understanding of the character.[9]

The tour opened on 31 March, Easter bank-holiday Monday, with a matinée performance of *The Bohemian Girl* at the Shakespeare Theatre in Lavender Hill, Battersea. Of the national newspapers, only the *Daily Telegraph* noticed the event, though it cannot have been the operatic debut of the twenty-two-year-old conductor that prompted its representative to attend, for at that point nobody in London had heard of Beecham:

> Though often assailed by ridicule, the old work – which, by the way, will attain its Diamond Jubilee in November, 1903 – still retains its popularity, and the large audience that assembled yesterday welcomed the time-honoured melodies, at once tuneful and unpretentious, with plenty of applause, a repetition in most cases being sought and obtained. Miss Marie Titiens, the Arline of the occasion, won her way easily to favour by her graceful singing of 'I dreamt that I dwelt' and 'Come with the Gipsy Bride.' Her acting, too, had vivacity to recommend it. Mr Henry Beaumont was only moderately satisfactory as Thaddeus, his intonation at times being faulty, though he sang the music allotted to the Polish rebel in spirited fashion ... Chorus and band discharged their respective tasks fairly well, and Mr. Thomas Beecham conducted.[10]

Two days later Beecham conducted his first-ever *Carmen*, which earned him a mention in the theatrical weekly, *The Era*: 'Overlooking a slight tendency to drag, the performance went exceedingly well, due no doubt in a measure to the assistance of Mr Harry Brooklyn (stage-manager) and Mr Thomas Beecham, the latter of whom very ably conducted and presided over an augmented and hard-working orchestra.' The writer expressed surprise at the size of the 'exceptionally large' audience and forecast a successful tour for the company, which could 'hold its own with any other on the road'.[11] †

The five theatres visited by Beecham and the Imperial Grand Opera had all been built in 1896–7 in response to a theatrical boom that before long would be seriously dented by the cinema. All were designed by one or other of the two

---

* Emilio Pizzi (b. Verona 1861; d. Milan 1940), a pupil of Ponchielli, was eighteen years older than Beecham, but was to prove a good friend to his much younger colleague. He wrote several operas, a setting of the Requiem Mass, instrumental works and songs.

† The Imperial Grand Opera was one of four touring companies performing opera in English in London and its suburbs that week. The others were the Neilson Grand English Opera Company at Alexandra Palace; the Carl Rosa at the Grand Theatre, Islington High Street; and J. W. Turner's company at the Standard Theatre, Bishopsgate.

most prolific theatre architects of the day, Frank Matcham and the Australian-born W. G. R. Sprague. They boasted electric light, heating systems, a greatly reduced fire-risk because of steel and concrete construction, and, thanks to cantilevered balconies that did away with the need for weight-supporting pillars, better sightlines. Box-offices were equipped with telephones.

From Sprague's Shakespeare Theatre, Battersea, the tour progressed to the Brixton Theatre (Matcham), the Grand Theatre, Fulham (Sprague), the Borough Theatre, Stratford (Matcham) and the Broadway Theatre, New Cross (Sprague), where Beecham's Carmen was the popular mezzo-soprano Zélie de Lussan, an American of French parentage who had been singing the role regularly at Covent Garden since 1888. With tickets ranging from 4 shillings (£12.64) in the dress circle to sixpence (£1.58) in the gallery, the operas drew large and enthusiastic houses, except at Stratford, where most of the more expensive seats remained empty. After a return visit to Battersea at the end of May, the company disbanded. 'Mr Beecham's recollections of this tour', the *Musical Times* reported a few years later, 'are pleasant, inasmuch as he gained so much valuable experience. But there were difficulties fairly often, some of which were owing to the inconvenient thirst of many members of the orchestra. They were in the habit of taking a bar's rest before the performance began.' [12] *

There was talk of a further tour by Kelson Trueman's company, but nothing came of it. Nonetheless, Beecham kept in touch with Emilio Pizzi, and later in the year attended the British premiere of his one-act opera, *Rosalba*, which the Moody-Manners company gave at Covent Garden. *The Times* thought Pizzi's score abounded 'in reminiscences of Puccini tempered by occasional Wagner'. The words for it were by one of the leading librettists of the day, Luigi Illica, co-author with Giuseppe Giacosa of the texts for Puccini's *La bohème* and *Tosca*, and now collaborating on the composer's latest work, *Madama Butterfly*.† Beecham wondered if Illica might not provide a libretto for him, too, and Pizzi, who looked after the librettist's affairs in London, said he would sound him out on the possibility. Illica was a colourful figure, irascible, unpredictable and a fierce Republican who had lost half of his left ear in a sabre duel with a conservative newspaper editor. He was frequently in financial difficulties, which may explain why, when writing to him in October, Pizzi painted an over-rosy picture of the young Beecham's prospects. Beecham, he assured

---

* Of the five theatres, only the Borough in High Street, Stratford, or rather parts of it including its façade, has survived. The Shakespeare and the Brixton were both bombed during the Second World War, while the Fulham and New Cross theatres were demolished in post-war property developments.

† Illica had written librettos for several other leading Italian composers, among them Catalani (*La Wally*), Franchetti (*Cristoforo Colombo*), Giordano (*Andrea Chénier*) and Mascagni (*Iris* and *Le maschere*).

Illica, was 'a good musician (and, what's more, extremely rich)' who intended to have the resulting opera performed by the Carl Rosa company, 'of which he is a shareholder'.[13]

Illica took the bait. Pizzi's reference to Carl Rosa must have helped. If Beecham really did have a connection with that company, it can only have been a very tenuous one, but five years earlier it had given the British premiere of *La bohème*, in Manchester, which Puccini had supervised.* Before long Illica produced a contract for Beecham's signature: the libretto, it said, was to 'consist of a single act or an act of two scenes depending on the development of the synopsis and by common agreement; and will have the title *Christopher Marlowe*'. (In its final form the libretto consisted of a single act of four scenes.) Why Beecham should claim in *A Mingled Chime* that by good fortune Illica already had on the stocks a libretto based on the life of the Elizabethan playwright is a puzzle. Not only was it Beecham's, rather than Illica's, idea that the opera's protagonist should be Marlowe, but he also supplied the librettist with background material about him.[14] Under the terms of the contract Illica was to receive £40 sterling (£2,500) on signing and a further £60 (£3,800) on delivery of the complete libretto, which was to be finished by May 1903. In addition he was to receive 25 per cent of all earnings from the opera.[15]

In December 1902 Illica produced a synopsis, with which Beecham was delighted. Writing to Illica in French (their regular form of communication), he complimented the librettist on the story's fresh charm, adding that it was 'tout à fait "Elizabethan"'.[16] The relationship between the two was to prove rocky, however. To Illica's irritation, Beecham often took weeks, sometimes months, to answer his letters. Worse, he failed to make an initial payment on receipt of the synopsis, as the contract stipulated. He also kept asking Illica for changes to the libretto, which only added to the size of the final bill. When Beecham did get round to sending a cheque, it bounced, and the long-suffering Pizzi had to save the situation by giving Illica a cheque for £100 drawn on his own account. 'This one will <u>not</u> be returned', Pizzi assured the librettist, adding that Beecham was 'un vero tipo' (roughly, 'a real handful').[17] In further letters to Illica, Pizzi described his protégé as 'un vero enigma' and 'quel matto Beecham' ('that madman Beecham'). He urged Illica not to send Beecham too much of the libretto until he had paid for it.

Following the Trueman opera tour Beecham had no other musical engagements in London until 14 July 1903, when he appeared as 'conductor' at 'Herr Josef Claus's Grand Morning Concert', which took place 'at 3.15 o'clock sharp' in

---

* Ricordi, the publisher, offered *La bohème* to the Carl Rosa, which sang it in English, after Covent Garden had turned it down. It finally reached the Royal Opera House two years later.

the afternoon at the Steinway Hall in Lower Seymour Street.* Though Beecham conducted the sextet from Donizetti's *Lucia di Lammermoor*, his main task was to act as piano accompanist for a series of arias, ballads and instrumental solos performed by Claus himself and his pupils and colleagues, some of whom had been on the Trueman tour. The *Daily Telegraph* noted that the hall was not full, but described the occasion as being 'one of considerable vivacity and enjoyment'. It did not comment on Beecham's contribution.[18]

Utica Welles, who attended the concert, kept two copies of the programme among her private papers to her dying day. Thirteen days later, on 27 July, she and Beecham married at St Peter's Church, Cranley Gardens, in South Kensington. The bridegroom was twenty-four, the bride twenty-one. Emily Beecham, who was Utica's bridesmaid, signed the register, as did Josephine and Dr Welles. The vicar told Utica that she was the most beautiful bride he had seen.[19] The honeymoon was spent touring some of Britain's cathedral towns. Joseph Beecham did not attend the wedding – indeed, he may not even have known about it. He had always opposed the couple's engagement, claiming that the Welleses had long ago sized up Tom as a good catch for their daughter, which may have been true once, but could hardly be the case now. Five days before the ceremony, in the hope of better days to come, Tom covenanted to give Utica £50,000 (£3,109,000), by way of a marriage settlement. There was to be an initial payment of £805 (£50,000), with the rest to follow when Tom came into his inheritance.[20] All Utica ever received was the £805.

Josephine Beecham's financial prospects, on the other hand, had taken a turn for the better. On learning that Joseph's income was a vast £80,000 (£5 million),† she appealed against the £2,500 she had been awarded as alimony on the grounds that she deserved to have more. The appeal court accepted her plea, and the alimony was raised to £4,500 (£280,000), though Joseph managed to secure a concession from the judges. In return for the money, Josephine had to agree that she would not contract to pay any part of it to Tom, his wife Utica or their issue. A list of any casual payments she might make to Tom was to be sent to Joseph annually. Dr Welles was to submit a similar list of payments for Josephine's board and lodging.[21]

In the early summer of 1904 Beecham went to Paris, where he took private

---

* The use of 'morning' to denote an event that took place at any time during the day, as opposed to the evening, was already giving way to the more snobbish 'matinée'. Lower Seymour Street was the name of what is now the western section of Wigmore Street. The 400-seat hall, which adjoined the premises of the American piano-manufacturers Steinway, was renamed Grotrian Hall in 1925 and remained open until 1938. It was demolished following bomb-damage in the Second World War.

† Joseph's income came not only from the St Helens operation, but also from the American factory and other large-scale investments.

lessons in orchestration from the German composer, Moritz Moszkowski, and searched the Bibliothèque Nationale for scores by forgotten eighteenth- and early nineteenth-century composers, among them Grétry and Méhul, which he arranged to have copied. In July he joined Utica and her parents for a holiday in Lucerne. Utica was by now seven months pregnant. Convinced that the clear air of the Swiss lakes would be better for the baby's health than the smoke and fog of London, she decided that she would remain in Switzerland for the birth. Dr Welles supported the idea, and Beecham found that he had little alternative but to go along with it. The Beechams' first child, Adrian, was born at two minutes past midnight on 4 September at the Pension Dreilinden, Lucerne, with a local doctor and Utica's father in attendance. Utica kept a journal of Adrian's first year of life, an effusion of cloying sentimentality, in which her husband barely features and the baby is revealed as the all-consuming passion of her life. To pass the time, Beecham began work on *Christopher Marlowe*.

A month after Adrian's birth the party left Lucerne and went first to Lugano and then, in early November, Milan, where Beecham and Utica scoured the antique shops; they bought an inlaid chest of drawers, which was shipped back to London. In Milan they met Illica, who was busy revising *Madama Butterfly* with Puccini, following the opera's disastrous premiere at La Scala the previous February. The librettist described 'Signor Tom Beecham' as a little Englishman with a nervous facial twitch and a chronic sniff. He introduced Tom and his wife to Puccini, who, though he showed little interest in Beecham, was greatly charmed by Utica and her fractured Italian.[22] When Utica went off to Venice with her parents, Beecham stayed at Piacenza, near to Illica's home at Castell'Arquato, so that he might discuss *Christopher Marlowe* at length with the librettist. In *A Mingled Chime* he says he found their meetings absorbing, but Illica was less happy about them, complaining to Pizzi that his visitor never once brought up the subject of payment. Sympathising with Illica, Pizzi said that he had hoped that marriage would have made Beecham 'more grown-up, but he seems to be just the same to me'.[23]

By now Beecham was impatient to return to London, but Utica, more influenced by her parents than by her husband, was not yet ready to go home, and once again Beecham fell in with her wishes. The Welleses went next to Florence, where they rented the top floor of the Hotel Minerva. Beecham, who joined them there after seeing Illica, struggled on with his opera. Finally, in January 1905, he set off for Britain alone, breaking his journey at Piacenza, where he again saw Illica. Utica noted in her journal that, with her husband gone, she had even more leisure to be with 'the little sweetheart', now four months old. The situation did not bode well for the future of the marriage.

Although a typescript of the libretto for *Marlowe*, written in Italian, survives in the Illica archive at Piacenza, there is no sign of any music for it. Indeed, there is no evidence that Beecham ever resumed serious work on it after his initial efforts in 1904. Perhaps he concluded that he lacked the inspirational fire for composition; perhaps he was simply too preoccupied with other projects to bother with it. Or perhaps he had come to dislike the libretto, for which he can hardly be blamed, for it is pure hokum. Set in an Elizabethan England that has a curiously Italian flavour, it tells of two feuding recusant families who are reconciled through the forced marriage of the daughter of one to a son of the other. Unfortunately the daughter, Helena, is smitten with love for one Christopher Marlowe, who leads a theatrical troupe that is performing his play *Doctor Faustus* in the local town. Marlowe, distraught, turns up at the wedding. ('Gloriana will descend triumphant and destroy the Papists.') To cut an unlikely story short, a lot of duelling ensues, which results in the death of both Helena (accidentally) and Marlowe.

Realising that there was little hope of Beecham's ever completing the opera, Illica discussed with the publisher Ricordi the possibility of Puccini taking over the libretto, though nothing came of it.[24] Illica decided to recycle the libretto as a three-act play, which he called *Kit Marlowe*, but was unable to get it published, because legally Beecham held the rights to the story, which for an unfathomable reason he was unwilling to give up. In 1912 Illica engaged a London solicitor to recover the manuscript of the libretto from Beecham, as well as the sum of £150 (£9,370) that Beecham still owed him.[25] He received the money, but not the libretto. A compromise was reached, formalised in a new contract between the two men. In return for agreeing that the play could go ahead, Beecham would receive a share of the royalties on it; he would also benefit from the sale of any cinematographic rights. He promised Illica that he would get the play put on in London at a theatre owned by his father (presumably the Aldwych), but war intervened and Illica gave up all hope of a production until hostilities ended. He died in 1919, and his Marlowe play, like his Marlowe libretto, still remains unpublished and unperformed. Emilio Pizzi, who spent most of the Great War working in a munitions factory in Shepherd's Bush, eventually returned to Italy, where he died in Milan in 1940.

On returning from Italy, Beecham began to look for a house for his family in the countryside on the outskirts of London, although he had no idea when they might be back. A brief but telling vignette of him at this time by the English composer Cyril Scott describes him as a 'shy, groundward-glancing little figure in a frock coat, brown boots, pork-pie hat, and dark woollen gloves (with a pattern)', who was full of 'musical schemes upon which he would soliloquise as, with body bent and arms on knees, he stared at the carpet'.[26] Unfortunately the schemes demanded money, which Beecham did not have, though unexpectedly he received a windfall from his grandfather, to whom he had remained close. Old Thomas's third marriage had collapsed, and he was now living at Southport on the Lancashire coast. Because he was seeing less and less of Mursley Hall, he let it and then gave it in trust to his grandson as a belated wedding present. The rent from Mursley provided Tom with a modest allowance. It was not enough to underwrite a concert he was planning to give at the Bechstein Hall* on 5 June 1905 with a small orchestra, but it was a start.

In the forlorn hope of achieving a reconciliation with his father, he commissioned a South Kensington solicitor, Edgar Todd-Jones, to visit Henry Oppenheim, his father's solicitor and close friend at St Helens. Todd-Jones told Oppenheim that his client's desire for a reconciliation was so great that he was even 'prepared to reside near St Helens and to take part in his father's business', no matter what his wife Utica might have to say on the matter. Whether or not Beecham really intended to take such an extreme step is not known, but it seems unlikely.

Oppenheim said that Joseph might consider a reconciliation, but on two conditions. First, Josephine had to remove herself 'from the household and influence of Dr Welles' and move into a home of her own, and secondly, Tom had to sever all relations with Utica's family. If Tom had views on these conditions, Oppenheim continued, he should put them in writing to his father. If he wanted a meeting with his father, he should approach him 'in one character only, viz: as a contrite son willing to acknowledge his disobedient conduct and asking for his father's forgiveness and to be re-instated in his favour.' Oppenheim went on to assure Todd-Jones that Joseph was quite happy about 'the music business' and that 'so long as Tom earned a living honestly he did not mind in what way he did it.' Todd-Jones asked Oppenheim if, as a trustee of the Mursley estate, he would sanction an application by Tom to borrow around £500 (£31,575) to enable him to make headway with his musical plans. Oppenheim turned the proposition down flat[27] and as a result no interview between father and son took place.

In the end the money for the concert was almost certainly put up by Josephine. Publicity for it announced that, 'owing to the great attention given of late to modern composers, the works of the earlier masters have been very much neglected. We believe that an effort to bring again before the attention of the public rarely heard works, and to produce many which are totally unfamiliar – in short, to attempt something of the nature of a classical revival – should meet with approval and support.'[28] The programme included three rarities that

---

* The 550-seat Bechstein Hall, situated at the opposite end of Wigmore Street to the Steinway Hall, was opened in 1901 by the German piano-manufacturers Bechstein, who ran it until the outbreak of the First World War. In 1917 it was given the more patriotic-sounding name, Wigmore Hall.

Beecham had brought back from the Continent – the overtures to Méhul's *Stratonice*, Paisiello's *Nina, o sia La pazza per amore* and Cherubini's *Faniska* – as well as Haydn's 'Drum Roll' Symphony and two works by Mozart, the aria 'Rivolgete a lui lo sguardo', K584,* sung by Beecham's composition teacher from Liverpool, Frederic Austin, and the C minor piano concerto K491 with Fanny Davies, a pupil of Clara Schumann, as soloist. Utica did not return to London for the concert, but, knowing her husband's liking for lucky signs, she sent him a four-leaf clover she had found in a field at St Moritz, where the Welleses were now staying.

Mozart's music featured rarely in London's programmes in 1905. The *Daily Telegraph*'s comprehensive concert-listings for that week included only one other event that included a work by the composer, an unidentified minuet to be played by a solo cellist at a Sunday afternoon concert at the Royal Albert Hall. When it came to Haydn, Beecham had the field to himself that week. The players for his concert were drawn from the Queen's Hall Orchestra, London's only symphony orchestra that played regularly throughout the season. Robert Newman, the hall's lessee and manager, had created it in 1895 for a series of promenade concerts with, as conductor, a then unknown twenty-six-year-old, Henry J. Wood. Now, ten years later, Wood had established himself as Britain's first full-time conductor, in charge not only of the promenade concerts, but also of the Queen's Hall's regular concert-series.†

Beecham's concert was not widely reviewed, but the critics who did turn up were complimentary. The *Sunday Times* thought Beecham's enterprise 'very commendable, for the programmes of our concerts run very much in ruts'. The *Times* reviewer, J. A. Fuller-Maitland, called Beecham 'a conductor of remarkable ability, with a firm and expressive beat and decided views of his own', though he thought that neither in the Paisiello overture nor elsewhere 'were the players any too attentive to the conductor's wishes.' Later Fuller-Maitland accused the orchestra of sabotaging Beecham's efforts 'by deliberately opposing his directions, playing loud when he was trying to soften things, and so forth'. It was not, he said, the first time he had witnessed a new conductor being subjected to such behaviour.[29] Although Beecham does not mention the players' boorishness in

---

* Originally written for Guglielmo in *Così fan tutte*, though Mozart replaced it with 'Non siate ritrosi'.

† Hitherto, Britain's best-known conductors had been primarily composers, among them Elgar, Stanford and Alexander Mackenzie. Henry Wood (1869–1944), son of an Oxford Street jeweller and pawnbroker, was ten years older than Beecham. Queen's Hall, then London's main concert hall, opened in 1893. With 2,492 seats and excellent acoustics, it stood just to the south of All Souls' church, Langham Place, on a site now occupied by the St George's Hotel. To the dismay of both performers and audiences, it was destroyed by a German incendiary bomb on the night of 11 May 1941.

A Mingled Chime, he says that the concert produced in him a definite feeling of disappointment with himself: the sound of the music in performance was strangely different from the conception of it he had in his head.

It was announced before the concert that if public support for it turned out to be 'adequate', a series of similar concerts would be given during the winter, but the audience was not as big as had been hoped and Beecham's only other appearance on a public platform in 1905 came a month later, on 4 July, when he sang as lead bass at the inaugural concert of Charles Kennedy Scott's pioneering Oriana Madrigal Society at the Portman Rooms, Baker Street. Madrigals were not a new experience for Beecham. He had sung them regularly at Rossall with a small group of enthusiasts who included his housemaster, while later he made a special study of them with Charles Wood. The Oriana Society had grown out of informal evenings at Roland Gardens, where Beecham, Kennedy Scott and other friends gathered round a table to sing the works of the Tudor masters. Beecham did not sing with the Oriana choir again, though he wrote the pro-gramme notes for its second and third concerts, and remained a close friend of Kennedy Scott's.* As the Rossall magazine discretely suggested more than once, singing was not one of Beecham's more obvious talents.

Another of Beecham's friends at this time was George Morley, a harp-maker with premises in Old Brompton Road who lived above his work. The congenial Morley invited Beecham to musical evenings at his home, played billiards with him until well into the night, exchanged books with him, taught him to play chess, a game that became one of Beecham's lifelong enthusiasms, and took him to meetings of the Fabian Society, which Beecham joined, though it seems that his interest in socialism was short lived.[30]

Meanwhile Joseph remained obsessed with Dr Welles's influence on Jose-phine. The two solicitors, Oppenheim and Todd-Jones, went so far as to take counsel's advice on how her alimony might be suspended until what they called 'proper arrangements' could be made for its distribution. The fact that both solicitors were involved in this legal move indicates that Beecham, too, was worried about the situation. A joint memorandum they drew up claimed that Welles would not allow Josephine to have any visitors except those who met with his approval; that she was not allowed to receive any letters until he had read them first; that he had wasted her money on expensive and useless litiga-tion (which was certainly true); that behind Tom's back he had procured her power of attorney, which allowed him to 'administer' her finances; and that he would not allow her to visit her three youngest daughters at Arkwright Road,

---

* It is a mark of the catholicity of Beecham's musical taste that occasionally he conducted madrigals in his later years, for example Hilton's 'Fair Oriana, Beauty's Queen' at a concert at Bolton in 1918, and Morley's 'Now is the Month of Maying' in Detroit in 1946.

on the grounds that 'she might be at any moment seized by the emissaries of her husband and confined once more to an Asylum.'[31] By now Welles was no longer in the embassy's employ, and it seemed to Joseph that he was almost entirely dependent on the rent that Josephine paid for her and Emily's accommodation at Roland Gardens. In the following year it would amount to the huge sum of £1,400 (£86,000) – almost a third of her annual alimony.*

In early October 1905, just when it seemed that an ugly round of legal wrangling was about to erupt, the Welles ménage arrived back in London, which had the effect of calming what could have become an explosive situation. Utica agreed that in the following spring she would leave Roland Gardens to set up home with her husband and their small son Adrian at Highfield, a recently built house at Borehamwood, which today is a busy commuter town in south Hertfordshire, but was then a rural hamlet in the parish of Elstree. The house, one of six, each standing in a third of an acre of land, looked out over fields and satisfied Utica's wish that Adrian should live in a healthy environment.† It was also reasonably close to London. Elstree station was a brisk, ten-minute walk away, and from there Beecham could catch a train that took only half an hour to St Pancras. For the time being peace reigned.

---

* The figure comes from the account submitted to Joseph Beecham by Welles (StH). When Welles died in 1927, the gross value of his estate was put at only £1,830 (the equivalent of £63,500 in 2008).

† Highfield was situated on a country road, now called Theobald Street, leading north to Radlett. A post-Second World War block of flats now straddles the site.

CHAPTER 4

Orchestral Fireworks

BEECHAM concluded that the main reason for his dissatisfaction with not just his own performances, but also those of other conductors, was the lack of a properly balanced sound, the result of imperfect co-ordination between the various sections that was endemic in British orchestras. In the early twentieth century London's players were (and still are) widely admired for their sight-reading skills – a prerequisite for survival, given the general shortage of rehearsals – but by most accounts the performances they gave were not noted for their subtlety. Exhilarating evidence of just what could be achieved was provided in June 1906, when the Vienna Philharmonic Orchestra visited London for three concerts under Franz Schalk. 'The sonority of the band as a whole and the splendid precision with which everything went were more striking than the playing of any individual instrument or group of instruments', wrote the *Times* critic, 'but, if anything is to be singled out for special praise, it would perhaps be the brass, which ... was splendidly full and powerful without ever becoming raucous, and the tympani, which were always admirable, especially in the soft and resonant pianos.'[1]

Beecham was anxious to conduct further concerts, but finding an orchestra for them was not easy. Given its dismal behaviour at his Bechstein Hall debut, the Queen's Hall Orchestra was not an option, and there were few alternatives. All players in London, including those of the Queen's Hall Orchestra, were poorly paid freelancers, hired for individual engagements or series of concerts. During Henry Wood's 1904 Promenade Concert season, most of them received only £2 10s (£151.20) for a week of six concerts and the inadequate three or four rehearsals allotted for them. Even the best players combined their orchestral work with a job in a West End theatre-pit, for which they might earn a further £2 10s for an eighteen-hour week.[2] They also played in cafés, hotels, restaurants and dance halls, or performed at the ubiquitous concerts given in private houses. Members of the Queen's Hall Orchestra did not think twice about sending deputies to rehearsals or concerts if they found better-paid dates elsewhere. Wood was so exasperated by the deputy system that in 1904 he banned it in his orchestra. In protest, some forty players walked out to found the capital's second large-scale orchestra, the London Symphony, as a players' co-operative.

For the 1905–6 season the LSO hired some of the leading international conductors of the day: Hans Richter, Fritz Steinbach from Cologne, Ernst von

Schuch from Dresden, the Russian Vasily Safonov and Arthur Nikisch, the magnetic Hungarian, on whose pointed beard Beecham modelled his own. (Henry Wood went one step further, modelling not only his beard, but also his wild and woolly moustache, on Nikisch's.) To ensure good houses, the LSO chose programmes that were conservative in the extreme. When Beecham approached the LSO to see if it might play for him he was met with scepticism and condescension. Covent Garden did not have a permanent orchestra, while the hand-picked players of the orchestra of London's most august musical institution, the Philharmonic Society, met for only seven concerts a year.*

By the spring of 1906 Beecham and Utica had settled down to family life at Borehamwood. Very little is known about their domestic life, except that Josephine paid frequent visits to see her first grandchild and that Beecham had a dog, which eventually he got rid of, because it bit the neighbours.³ In late May he and Utica went to Lancashire to see Henry Oppenheim, in the hope that Joseph had had a change of heart. But Oppenheim brought cold comfort. As far Joseph was concerned, he said, there could be no progress towards a reconciliation until there was 'a complete and final' break with Dr Welles, which, for the sake of his wife, Beecham refused to countenance.⁴

In the following month, Beecham had a visit from one of the country's leading instrumentalists, Charles Draper, principal clarinet of the Philharmonic Society's orchestra. Draper was also a founder-member of the New Symphony Orchestra, made up of forty-six good freelance players, who the previous winter had given a handful of Sunday concerts at the Imperial Theatre, Notting Hill Gate, under the pianist-conductor Evlyn Howard Jones. The New Symphony was about to give its first concert at Queen's Hall, with one of its cellists, Edward Mason, as conductor. Draper had learned from the musical grapevine that Beecham was on the look-out for an orchestra, and invited him to attend a rehearsal.

Beecham liked what he heard, and hired thirty-five of the players for four concerts at the Bechstein Hall, for which Josephine provided a limited guarantee.† The programmes consisted mainly of works by 'the earlier masters' that he had unearthed in Paris, a prospect that worried his concert manager Leslie Hibberd, who thought that something more popular was called for. Beecham had no such qualms, and his confidence only increased when, walking with Hibberd in the fields at Borehamwood, he came across, not one, but three 'lucky'

---

* The Philharmonic Society, founded in 1813, was not granted its 'Royal' prefix until the end of its centenary season in 1912.

† Early photographs taken at the hall show that an extension was added to the front of the platform to accommodate large ensembles (Wigmore Hall archives).

horseshoes. Beecham's optimism was justified. The concerts were enthusiastically received.

The first, on 2 November 1906, included overtures and arias by Méhul, Cimarosa, Paisiello, Grétry and Dalayrac, plus Mozart's 'Prague' Symphony. The *Times* review makes it clear that on this occasion Beecham encountered no problems with his orchestra, which performed with 'a fine energy and that deference to the wishes of the conductor which was conspicuously absent from the performance of some well-known players a year ago ... He got many effects that can only be got by a fine musician with his forces absolutely at his command; and, while the details of phrasing were often admirable, they were presented as part of one organic whole.' It was noted that, like Safonov, Beecham dispensed with both baton and score.[5] Further concerts followed on 21 November and 12 December, when Beecham ended the evening with a piece that was to features in his programmes for another forty-eight years, Méhul's exuberant overture to *La chasse du jeune Henri*. The three concerts attracted good-sized audiences, but the fourth, advertised for 23 January 1907, failed to materialise. The limit of Josephine's guarantee may have been reached.

Impressed by Beecham's youthful enthusiasm and obvious talent, Draper and his colleagues asked him to become their regular conductor, an offer he accepted, though he warned them that he was not in a position to speculate on concerts of his own, and that he and the players would have to go out and tout for work. Advertisements began to appear in the press announcing that the New Symphony was available for public concerts and charity events, as well as for garden parties and concerts in private houses involving small groups of players, 'with or without Mr Beecham'. His first appearance under the new arrangement with the orchestra – or, rather, a contingent drawn from it – came on 25 March 1907 when, at a charity matinée organised by the Duchess of Somerset at the Playhouse in Northumberland Avenue, he conducted the first professional performance of *The Dryad*, a dance-play by the English composer Dora Bright, with Adeline Genée, *prima ballerina* at the Empire music-hall, Leicester Square, in the title-role. 'La Genée', wrote one critic, 'was seen at her terpsichorean best.'[6]*

There were not enough dates to provide Beecham with a living, however, and to help support his family he played the piano for singing lessons given by the illustrious French bass-baritone, Victor Maurel, who had recently opened an

---

* Adeline Genée (1878–1970), Danish-born but British by adoption, had an important influence on the growth of British ballet; she was made a Dame of the British Empire in 1950. Dora Bright (1863–1951) was the first woman to win the Royal Academy of Music's composition prize and the first to be commissioned to write a work for the Philharmonic Society.

opera academy in London. Though Maurel had created two of Verdi's greatest male roles, Iago and Falstaff, Beecham found him disappointing as a teacher, for he seemed incapable of communicating his ideas to his students. Maurel was still only fifty-eight, but the top of his voice was losing focus and he had begun to sing flat in that register, though so compelling was his artistry that he could still draw large audiences for the recitals he gave in Paris, London and New York.

Thanks to Maurel, Beecham made his Queen's Hall debut on 12 April 1907, conducting the NSO at 'Victor Maurel's Grand Operatic Orchestral Concert'. Maurel sang a number of solos, including Falstaff's 'Quand'ero paggio', and joined some of his pupils in excerpts from *Otello* and *Ernani*. The *Musical Standard* thought the singer was in 'capital voice', but found Beecham's conducting style disconcerting: 'He has a good rhythmic beat but has a jerky awkward manner of exhibiting it and an exceedingly irritating habit of putting his left hand on his hip as if he didn't know what to do with it.'[7] Beecham appeared again with Maurel on 24 June, when he conducted a small band of players for what was 'probably the first London staging of Grétry's one-act opera *Le tableau parlant*, yet another work he had found at the Bibliothèque Nationale. It was given as a late-night entertainment at 22 Hyde Park Square, Bayswater, home of the wealthy chemical engineer Emile Mond, whose wife, a pupil of Maurel's, played the comic role of the servant Colombine. Maurel took the role of the old guardian Cassandre.

Beecham and the orchestra soon concluded that if the NSO were to compete on equal terms with the Queen's Hall and London Symphony orchestras, it would have to expand from around forty-five members to full symphonic strength. By the start of the 1907–8 season the orchestra could offer an ensemble of any size, from thirty players at a cost of £48 (£2,770) a concert, to 100 at £138 18s (£8,000).* Beecham's fee was extra. On occasion the orchestra was hired by agents as a showcase for the performers they represented. Child prodigies, in particular, were much in vogue, and Beecham's first concert of the season, at Queen's Hall on 14 October 1907, featured the fifteen-year-old Hubay pupil Joseph Szigeti (then billed as Jóska Szigeti), who played the Tchaikovsky and the Bach E major violin concertos. Szigeti, who was to enjoy a long and successful career, recalled that Beecham, who 'radiated authority far beyond his years', told him at rehearsal that 'the tempi of allegros in Bach's time were much brisker than I was inclined to take them'. Szigeti thought it good advice: 'It is probable that my allegro tempo *was* on the stodgy side – "Victorian organist's Bach."'[8]

Not all the young soloists found Beecham helpful, notably the seventeen-

---

* In 2008 the cost of hiring equivalent-sized orchestras might be £6,000 and £20,000 respectively.

year-old pianist Myra Hess, a recent gold-medal winner at the Royal Academy of Music. When her teacher, Tobias Matthay, heard that Beecham and the orchestra had been hired for her debut concert at Queen's Hall on 14 November, he sent her a postcard: 'Who is this fellow Beecham? If he doesn't accompany you properly, I shall come and do it myself.'[9] Matthay's worries were not unjustified. Hess, who won good reviews for her playing of the fourth concertos of both Beethoven and Saint-Saëns, found Beecham unnerving. With an insouciance bordering on arrogance, he spent most of the available rehearsal time on the purely orchestral items: Mozart's Symphony no. 34, a new set of *Variations on an Irish Air* by his former teacher, Charles Wood, and a piece by the French composer Vincent d'Indy, the symphonic overture *Max et Thécla*.* Hess found herself still rehearsing the Saint-Saëns concerto as the audience started to arrive, which was particularly unjust, bearing in mind that the cost of hiring the orchestra was to be deducted from any receipts she might receive from the box-office.

The Szigeti concert had unexpected consequences for Beecham. A newspaper advertisement for it caught the eye of the German conductor Fritz Cassirer, who had booked Queen's Hall for a concert on 22 November that was to include two pieces not previously heard in Britain, the *Appalachia* variations of the Bradford-born composer Frederick Delius and the 'Dance of the Seven Veils' from Richard Strauss's opera *Salome*, which had been premiered eleven months earlier in Dresden. Though very little of Delius's music had been heard in London, it had met with some success in Germany, where Cassirer had conducted the premieres of two of his operas, *Koanga* at Elberfeld in 1904 and *A Village Romeo and Juliet* at the Komische Oper, Berlin, in February 1907.

The London Symphony Orchestra had agreed in principle to play for Cassirer's concert, but had offered him only one rehearsal; if he wanted extra, he would have to pay for them. 'Just imagine', Cassirer wrote to Delius from Germany, 'the London Symphony Orchestra asks 1000M. per rehearsal! ... Horrendous!' He asked the composer, who was visiting London at the time, to make inquiries about the NSO.[10] Delius did more than that. He turned up at the Szigeti concert, and at the end of it went backstage to see Beecham, who was surprised by his visitor's air of asceticism and shrewdness that suggested he might be a bishop rather than a composer.

Despite having lived in France since 1888 and being of German parentage, the forty-five-year-old Delius had retained his Yorkshire accent, though his

---

* Beecham was introduced to Vincent d'Indy (1851–1931) in London in 1905 by Charles Kennedy Scott, who shared the Frenchman's interest in plainchant and polyphony. Over the next nine years Beecham conducted a number of d'Indy's works, but then virtually dropped them until 1946, when he returned to them.

vocabulary was liberally peppered with foreign words. He was impressed by Beecham's orchestra, and Cassirer took his advice that he should employ it, rather than the LSO. Delius's meeting with Beecham marked the beginning of a uniquely close musical partnership that was to last until the composer's death twenty-seven years later. Beecham was, in his own words, 'startled and electrified' when he heard *Appalachia*,[11] finding in it a melodic inspiration, as well as an originality of form and orchestration, that seemed to him quite new. He started to conduct Delius's music himself, beginning with the orchestral nocturne *Paris*, whose British premiere he gave in Liverpool with the NSO on 11 January 1908. After the concert, Delius wrote to his wife Jelka that the work's success had been only 'mediocre. I don't think anybody but a few musicians understood it.'[12]

Beecham became a magnet for other British composers, who soon realised that if they could persuade him to conduct their compositions, they would be assured of properly rehearsed performances. In the course of the 1907–8 season Beecham gave Ralph Vaughan Williams's *Norfolk Rhapsody* and a string of pieces by other British composers whose names are now rarely seen on concert programmes, among them Granville Bantock, W. H. Bell, Joseph Holbrooke, Balfour Gardiner and Cyril Scott (then widely hailed, more in hope than with conviction, as the English Debussy). Beecham worked hard on their behalf, though his efforts were not always appreciated. When he took the NSO to Birmingham for a concert with the City Choral Society, of which he was briefly conductor, he gave a further performance of Charles Wood's *Irish Variations*, which the *Birmingham Daily Post*'s young music critic, Ernest Newman, laid into with gusto: 'Mr Wood's thirty-one variations might just as well number a hundred and thirty-one so far as any logical approach to continuity is concerned.'[13]* In his three concerts with the choir, Beecham included Handel's coronation anthem, *The King shall rejoice*, Cherubini's Requiem Mass in C minor, Brahms's *Ave Maria*, Franck's Psalm 150, scenes from Elgar's *King Olaf*, 'Spring' from Haydn's *Seasons*, a madrigal by Marenzio and Joseph Holbrooke's symphonic poem with chorus *Byron* (which the composer conducted). The society's committee disliked Beecham's adventurous programming and did not ask him back for the following season.

No work given at the NSO's London concerts received more publicity than Holbrooke's ninety-minute 'illuminated symphony', *Apollo and the Seaman*, which Beecham premiered at the Queen's Hall on 20 January 1908. It had been commissioned by the Irish poet Herbert Trench to accompany a narrative poem

---

* Ernest Newman (1868–1959), later the distinguished music critic of the *Sunday Times* (1920–58) and an authority on Richard Wagner, was one of Beecham's earliest supporters. They remained good friends.

he had written on the subject of immortality, which was projected by magic-lantern, stanza by stanza, on to a huge white sheet stretched across the platform. Behind it were hidden, or rather half-hidden, the chorus and vast Straussian orchestra, which Beecham conducted in his shirt-sleeves, with a box of biscuits and siphons of soda-water at his side to sustain him.[14]

The *Morning Leader*'s review, published on its front page, complained that 'the great evening which was to have inaugurated a new Art Form [was a] dire disappointment to all who expected something really worth serious considera-tion ... The whole scheme was nearly wrecked by a singularly ill-advised piece of theatricality at the outset. There was a long held organ note, then a terrific bang on a tam-tam, and then on the screen we saw the head of Apollo, larger than life-size. Some of the audience tittered.'[15] (The head had disappeared when the work was repeated a week later with the composer conducting.) To many ears there was little relation between music and words, which Ernest Newman thought was not surprising, for some of the score had been recycled from an unpublished work *The Masque of the Red Death*, which the prolific and cantan-kerous Holbrooke had played to him on the piano some years earlier. Trench's poem, wrote Newman, was 'quiet and philosophical', Holbrooke's music 'noisy and lurid'. The orchestra had 'got through the difficult score well, apart from some bad horn-playing'.[16]*

Beecham, who includes a famously comical account of the preparations for the performance in *A Mingled Chime*, was unperturbed by the general press reaction to *Apollo*, and went on to give a number of Holbrooke's other pieces, despite his belief that the composer was incapable of self-criticism and lacked aesthetic judgement.[17] Holbrooke's enormous output, influenced in turn by Liszt, Wagner, Strauss, Rachmaninov and several other composers, may have been wildly uneven in quality, but in the best of it Beecham detected a willing-ness to take risks that appealed to him.

After introducing Delius's *Paris* and *Brigg Fair* to London, Beecham tackled *Appalachia* for the first time on 14 June 1908. He wrote to Delius that the per-formance at Queen's Hall had gone well and that he had enjoyed the experience greatly. He had doubled, not only the harps in places, but also the brass, which, he said, had produced a splendid effect, particularly in the crescendo to *fff* in the funeral march (Variation XII), though he admitted that in the finale the doublings had probably not helped the choir, which had not sounded strong enough.[18] Presumably it had been drowned out. What Delius made of this is

---

* There seems to have been a dearth of good horn players in London at the time. On 21 March 1908 Beecham wrote to Delius, asking for the names of the best horn players in Paris in the hope that one or two of them might be free to accept an engagement for the whole of the following season in London.

not known, but he cannot have been too put out, because he invited Beecham to join him on a month-long walking tour in Norway in late July.

Delius, seventeen years older than his companion, turned out to be an experienced walker and climber, and Beecham was relieved that he had kept himself reasonably fit by playing tennis and taking long walks in the countryside at Borehamwood, though it had hardly prepared him for what was to come. With a guide they traversed the Jostedalsbreen glacier, an undertaking that Delius described in a letter to Jelka: 'It was a frightfully tough walk up to the glacier. 5 hours almost as steep as a house – Beecham seemed quite done up & faint & I thought we should have to turn back – he pulled together however very pluckily – I carried his knapsack & the guide carried mine – The walk over the glacier was grandiose & nothing but snow in sight & snow covered peaks – after we crossed the glacier we descended gradually to Mysahytta Saeter which was a frightful distance – We were 14 hours walking – with only a couple of sandwiches each – B could scarcely walk any more – we had to wade a stream which took me almost up to the waist. The man carried B across.' [19] By the next morning Beecham had recovered and he and Delius continued on their way. Three days later they hiked to the top of Galdhøppigen, at 2,469 meters Scandinavia's highest peak. Delius went fishing and got Beecham to wield the landing net. 'Beecham is an excellent travelling companion', Delius told Jelka. 'I like him more and more – he does nothing that I do not like.' [20]

Back in London Beecham began to make plans for a special series of six concerts at Queen's Hall with the NSO, starting in January 1909. He complained to Delius that he was having difficulty in finding good new British works for them. 'I have a pile of stuff here by V. Williams, [Norman] O'Neill, Scott, Holbrooke & C° but it is all very weak', he wrote. 'These fellows do not seem to advance at all.' [21] Beecham was also dissatisfied with the NSO. Annoyed that players had been sending deputies to rehearsals and concerts, he warned that unless the practice stopped he would sever his connection with the orchestra and form a new one. The NSO thought he was bluffing, for it was no secret that Beecham was short of funds. Where, it wondered, would he find the players and the money? Beecham bided his time. Meanwhile the *Daily Telegraph*'s music critic wrote that he looked forward with enthusiasm to the concerts with their promise of interesting programmes, because so far the 1908–9 season had been nothing but 'a tedious round of recitals of all kinds, of all qualities … varied by an occasional orchestral concert the scheme of which rarely includes that fillip so necessary to the jaded palate – a new or rarely heard work'. [22]

In early December 1908 Beecham and the NSO went to Hanley for a concert organised by the North Staffordshire District Choral Society, one of the most versatile amateur choirs in the country. There was a long programme, not all of it conducted by Beecham, who found he had not been left enough rehearsal time to do justice to a new, lavishly orchestrated work, *Hero and Leander*, by the local-born composer Havergal Brian. Beecham's first instinct was to drop it, but then, unwisely, changed his mind. The performance went badly. 'The tone-poem still awaits a fitting baptism', wrote the local critic, echoing the feelings of the discontented composer.[23] It never got one. Beecham, who presumably had promised the unfortunate Brian a repeat performance in more auspicious circumstances, managed to lose both the full score and the orchestral parts. Next on the programme was Delius's *Sea Drift*, which Beecham had rehearsed thoroughly. When the piece had received its British premiere two months before at the Sheffield Festival, Delius thought that the conductor, Henry Wood, had not always taken 'the right Tempi – Sometimes too slow & and then too fast.' At Hanley he found Beecham's performance, conducted from memory, 'wonderful'.[24]

On the following day, 4 December, Beecham took his forces to the Free Trade Hall, Manchester, for a repeat performance of *Sea Drift*. It shared an enterprising but financially risky programme of music by living composers that included three other pieces new to the city – d'Indy's *La forêt enchantée*, the first movement from Max Reger's *Serenade* and the finale from Holbrooke's *Apollo and the Seaman* – as well as Debussy's *Prélude à l'après-midi d'un faune** and Richard Strauss's song with orchestra, *Pilgers Morgenlied*, with Frederic Austin as soloist. The concert, Beecham's first in Manchester, was a box-office disaster, with only 432 paying customers in a hall seating 3,910.[25] Among them was the future theatre critic and diarist James Agate, whose brother Edward was one of the viola players. He remembered the audience being 'dotted about like islands in a sea of nothingness'.[26]

The local music critics had a field-day, praising Beecham for his enterprise and castigating the city for its conservatism. The *Musical Standard*'s Manchester correspondent wrote that Beecham had performed almost as many new orchestral works in one programme as had been heard in the city in the whole of the past three years. The audience, he continued, might have been scanty, but its enthusiasm 'was more real and intense than that given twenty-four hours previously in the same Hall to Elgar's [first] Symphony'. This was fighting talk, for the critic was referring to the symphony's premiere by Richter and the Hallé. So pointed was the general enthusiasm in the press for the NSO's playing – the 'delicacy of nuance, purity of tone and an absolute precision in intonation were remarkable', wrote one critic – that it is impossible to miss the barely concealed message that such qualities were not to be found in Richter's orchestra.[27]

---

* It is likely that Beecham heard Debussy himself conduct the *Prélude* in London with the Queen's Hall Orchestra on 1 February 1908.

Impressed by the North Staffordshire choir, Beecham decided he would use it for his concerts in London, but he felt let down by the NSO. Some of his leading players had declined to play in either Hanley or Manchester, and he repeated his ultimatum that if the orchestra would not abandon the deputy system, he would leave it. The players still assumed Beecham was bluffing, but this time he went, and within a month had formed a new orchestra. At first he thought of calling it the Metropolitan Orchestra, but then settled for the Thomas Beecham Orchestra. Before long it was renamed the Beecham Symphony Orchestra. The NSO was thunderstruck by Beecham's hitherto unsuspected ruthlessness. It had lost not only its conductor, but also the concerts that Beecham had planned for it at Queen's Hall. The orchestra put out a statement saying that *it* had severed its connection with its conductor, rather than the other way round, a claim that was effectively scotched by Beecham in a letter to *Musical News*. He had never had any contract or written agreement with NSO, he wrote, and it was his decision alone not to conduct it any more.[28]* To help finance his new orchestra, Beecham invited prominent members of the public to join a syndicate of ten subscribers who would each contribute £250 (£14,000). The response was disappointing, but enough money was raised to get the series under way.

Some of the new orchestra's principals came from the NSO, others from the London Symphony and, to Wood's chagrin, the Queen's Hall Orchestra. The fine string-player Lionel Tertis, who had given up orchestral work five years earlier to pursue a solo career, could not resist the call to lead the viola section. Beecham's 'fixer', Verdi Fawcett, himself a violinist in both the NSO and the new orchestra, scoured the profession for talented young instrumentalists who were prepared to give Beecham their undivided loyalty.† Their average age was reckoned to be around twenty-five. Many were straight out of music college; others had received no formal training, for example the twenty-three-year-old Albert Sammons, who had been taught to play the violin by his father, a London shoemaker, and had begun his career at the age of twelve in the Earl's Court Exhibition band. Since then he had gained most of his experience in theatre pits.

At Fawcett's suggestion, Beecham went to hear Sammons at the Waldorf Hotel in London, where he was playing in the restaurant band. Beecham's account of the occasion in *A Mingled Chime* is well known: after Sammons had

---

* Under Landon Ronald's direction, the New Symphony Orchestra became house-orchestra at the Royal Albert Hall, where it gave regular series of concerts. Eventually it was renamed the Royal Albert Hall Orchestra. Ronald (1873–1938), a versatile, if conservatively minded, musician, had a successful career as conductor, composer, music critic and educator. He was knighted in 1922.

† Verdi Fawcett was a member of a large family of musicians. Three of his brothers, Handel, Mendelssohn and Weber, played the trombone, clarinet and oboe respectively.

dashed off the finale of the Mendelssohn Violin Concerto, Beecham sent up a note, suggesting he should repeat it, but at a different tempo, which later in the evening he did, to Beecham's satisfaction. It makes a good story, but Sammons was not as inexperienced as Beecham would have his readers believe, for on Sunday evenings he led the 100-strong British Symphony Orchestra in concerts of popular classics at the London Coliseum.*

Sammons joined the Beecham Orchestra as a rank-and-file member of the first violins, though by the second concert he had been promoted to sub-leader. Within eight months he was leader, and in time came to be recognised as the outstanding British violinist of his generation. Ironically, Sammons almost threw away his chance of joining Beecham. When he received the conductor's note at the Waldorf, his first reaction was to send back a rude reply – he reckoned he knew the concerto as well, if not better, than any conductor – but his elder brother, Tom, a violinist in the New Symphony Orchestra who was also playing in the band that night, persuaded him to be co-operative.[29]

The Beecham Orchestra made its debut on 25 January 1909 at Queen's Hall, though a number of promised players were unable to extricate themselves from other commitments in time to take part in it. Because of this, Beecham and his new manager, the impresario and agent Thomas Quinlan, decided to play for safety with an undemanding programme that included Paganini's Violin Concerto no. 1, with a young Canadian player, Kathleen Parlow as soloist, and a number of operatic arias sung by Signor Tamini, a tenor with a loud if not very subtle voice from the Vienna Volksoper, who was beginning to make a name for himself in London.† *The Times* declared the next morning that 'the orchestral playing was admirable. The strings are particularly good both in the richness of tone which comes from a well balanced force with a solid bass, and in the vividness of their phrasing.'

Beecham, still only twenty-nine years old, assured Delius that by the next concert on 22 February, he would have an ensemble that would 'wipe the floor' with all London's other orchestras combined.[30] With an ambitious programme that included the premiere of Vaughan Williams's *In the Fen Country*, the first London performance of Delius's *Sea Drift* and the first in London for twenty-two years of Berlioz's *Te Deum*, the concert was an undoubted artistic success, even though the orchestra and the North Staffordshire choir had been unable

---

* The British Symphony Orchestra had been formed in 1908 by the Amalgamated Musicians' Union to provide work for its members on Sundays. Beecham conducted two of its concerts in 1910.

† Born Otto Haselbaum in 1880, Tamini was the son of a German father and an Italian mother, whose maiden name he adopted when he gave up his job as a bank manager in Mannheim to become a singer. Despite Beecham's heavy-handed suggestions to the contrary in *A Mingled Chime* (p. 84), Tamini never made any secret of his German background.

to rehearse together before the concert began, because 'the Suffragettes were in possession of the Queen's Hall, and would not be dispossessed until long past the time fixed for the band and the choir to meet.'[31] It failed to attract much of an audience, however. Quinlan reported a big loss. Utica helped to pay the players' wages by donating the money she had received from an insurance company for some stolen jewellery.[32] Quinlan told Delius that Beecham was 'at his wit's end' about finding the money for the four remaining four concerts: 'What we want is a strong subscription list, & until this comes, his Concerts will never pay', said Quinlan. 'The blasted public won't come.'[33] Beecham, in a new hunt for subscribers, managed to secure enough support to enable the series to continue, albeit in a hand-to-mouth fashion.

Quinlan found Beecham a difficult and capricious client. He had a prodigious musical talent, but lacked the social graces that could help both his own and the orchestra's prospects. At the first concert Quinlan was infuriated by Beecham's gauche reaction to the audience's applause – he could hardly bring himself to acknowledge it. 'I got hold of him one night in my office, and simply went for him', Quinlan told Delius, '[though] he is really a good fellow & we understand each other.' A month later the loyal but exasperated Quinlan complained to the composer that although Beecham had the best orchestra in London, he was 'the most unpunctual devil imaginable'. In addition he incurred extra expenses without bothering to mention them. 'If only he could see himself through a mirror', Quinlan continued, 'he would be the first to recognise how foolish he sometimes is. I speak to you as no-one else, and what I really want is to get you and Beecham in my little Study for a few hours, because I feel you would back me up and drive home my argument. ... I have induced fifty people to attend his Concerts, and without a single exception he has rubbed everybody up the wrong way. If you do not come, I shall tackle him myself, and if he does not see what I mean ... it will take him years to reach the goal that he ought rightly to take immediately.'[34]

One of Beecham's earliest champions, the music critic Edwin Evans, who understood the contradictions in his character better than most, ascribed his odd behaviour to a lack of self-confidence when in the presence of strangers. 'He used to seek refuge in a superficially aggressive self-assertion which earned him a reputation for arrogance', wrote Evans, 'whereas, however improbable it might seem, a close observer would have been tempted to diagnose a curious indefinable shyness concealing itself behind a mask.'[35] The soprano Maggie Teyte said that before joining a room full of people Beecham could be 'so unsure of himself that he had to create an attitude ... to put himself into the part before we went in.'[36] The writer Gerald Cumberland recalled a curious encounter in a restaurant. Beecham 'brought a tin of tobacco, placed it on the table, and proceeded to fill his pipe. He was not communicative. He simply sat back in his chair, smoking quietly, and behaving precisely as though he were alone, though, as a matter of fact, there were four or five people in his company. He was not shy: he was simply indifferent to us. If you spoke to him, he merely said "no" or "yes" and looked bored. He *was* bored. And so he sat for ten minutes; then, with a little sigh, he rose and departed from among us, without a word, without a look. He just melted away and never returned.'[37]

Quinlan had one more complaint about Beecham, that all too often it was hard to discover his whereabouts. This was not surprising, for Beecham had begun to spend many of his spare moments with an American artist, Maud Christian Foster, who was painting his father-in-law's portrait. On Beecham's own testimony they had met for the first time at Dr Welles's home on 21 March 1909.[38] Mrs Foster was of the same age as Utica, twenty-seven, but a good deal more worldly wise than her compatriot. She lived at 34 Redcliffe Square, Kensington, with her English husband George, whom she had married in 1906, though by now their relationship had grown tenuous. They were sleeping in separate rooms and there was talk of a separation. George Foster was also a portrait-painter, but made his living from buying and selling property. At this stage there was no suggestion of any impropriety in Beecham's liaison with the elegant Maud, though eventually it would erupt in a spectacular *cause célèbre*.

Two days after meeting Mrs Foster, Beecham happened to conduct a concert at Queen's Hall for one of her close friends, the American pianist Katherine Ruth Heyman,* who had hired the Beecham Orchestra for the occasion. She played Mozart's D minor concerto k466 and Anton Arensky's concerto in F minor, as well as the prominent piano part in César Franck's symphonic poem *Les djinns*. The *Daily Telegraph*'s critic wrote that none of the works 'was really familiar', a revealing comment on Mozart's place in London's concert life. For *The Times*, the Mozart concerto 'brought out the best qualities of Miss Heyman's playing, a smooth, lean touch, musical phrasing, and refined feeling for beauty of outline ... Mr Beecham's reading of the orchestral part of the work was full of warmth and colour, yet never violent or crude in the contrasts of tone he used.'[39]

Heyman rented rooms in the Fosters' house as a base for her European tours. Like Maud Foster, she moved in a Bohemian milieu that Beecham, who at heart was still a provincial unsophisticate, found enticing. Her friends included Ezra Pound, who dedicated several of his poems to her, while she in turn set

* Strongly interested in contemporary music, the California-born Heyman (1877–1944) championed Scriabin's piano works and wrote about his theosophic ideas. In 1928, in Paris, she founded the Group Estival pour la Musique Moderne. She composed a number of songs and piano pieces.

some of his verses to music. Before long Heyman was acting as intermediary for Beecham, who sent her letters and telegrams which she then passed on to Mrs Foster. Little is known about Maud Foster's background, but it seems that before marrying she had travelled extensively in Europe and had once had aspirations to be a singer. Beecham told Delius that she admired his music 'most fanatically' and sang all his songs.[40] Quick to recognise Beecham's talent, Maud offered to use her contacts to help him arrange a tour of the United States with the Beecham Orchestra that was planned for 1910. At first she appears to have found Beecham's manners disconcerting, for on 30 March he wrote to her soothingly from Borehamwood: 'It is evident my fascinating, off-hand manner, which is the despair of all my friends, has been perturbing your simple soul. Pray have no such fear, I am really only too delighted to find someone who is intelligent enough to be interested in my doings. ... Anything you care to do will be immensely appreciated by me. There are really few people who care twopence for the sort of thing I do.'[41]

On hearing that Joseph Beecham had been sitting in the Queen's Hall gallery incognito at some of his son's concerts, Quinlan decided that some financial help from that quarter would not come amiss. By chance his solicitor, Sir Henry Paget-Cooke, was also Joseph's London solicitor, and he got him to agree to test the atmosphere. Sir Henry 'doesn't know a note of music', Quinlan told Delius, 'but for all that a finer fellow never walked.'[42] In time Paget-Cooke engineered a meeting between Thomas and Joseph, whose new-found pride in his son's achievements was beginning to outweigh any hostility he felt towards him.

A letter Beecham wrote to Maud Foster on 25 May suggests that she, too, was involved in softening up Joseph: 'You will be interested to know that I am to have an interview with him to-morrow, the first for almost ten years, but whatever happens, please understand I have no intention of allowing you to relax your efforts on my behalf. On the contrary, as it is most necessary to prove to the "old boy" that my musical ventures are sound finance as well as "high falutin" art. This you can do better than anyone I know, so please don't slack off, there's a dear. Come to some of my rehearsals, and let us lunch together afterwards and talk. – Au revoir.'[43] It seems that Joseph made no promises at the meeting with his son, however. Meanwhile Beecham's relationship with Maud Foster was becoming closer. She was proving invaluable in securing new subscribers to the orchestra.[44] By the end of June she had brought in more than fifty.

The rehearsals to which Beecham referred were for his biggest undertaking to date, the first complete performance of Delius's *A Mass of Life*, which he gave at Queen's Hall on 7 June 1909. Written to a German text from Nietszche's *Also sprach Zarathustra*, it had been performed in a truncated version in Munich the previous year. For London, Beecham commissioned an English translation from the Scottish composer William Wallace, which Delius found 'ripping'. It 'reads like an English poem', he told the conductor.[45] The work divided the critics – Ernest Newman found it 'mostly great', the *Musical Standard* 'laboured' and 'wearisome'[46] – but there was general agreement that it had provided a fitting close to a notable series of concerts. *The Times* described the audience as being 'fairly large', which suggests that Quinlan suffered a further loss.

One of the keenest attenders at the Beecham Orchestra's concerts was the composer Ethel Smyth, who later declared that 'to some of us they were a revelation. Never in England, indeed only in Vienna under Mahler, had I heard music rehearsed to such a peak of perfection.'[47] After the second concert she asked Beecham if he would conduct her opera *The Wreckers*, which was due to be given four matinée performances at His Majesty's Theatre in June 1909. Set in a seventeenth-century Cornish village where ships are lured on to the rocky shore-line and then plundered, it had been premiered in Leipzig two years earlier, but had not yet been staged in Britain. Beecham had been sniffy about the piece when he heard Nikisch and the LSO give its first two acts in concert at Queen's Hall in 1908,[48] but he accepted Smyth's invitation, because it gave him a longed-for opportunity to conduct opera in central London. Better still, Smyth offered the Beecham Orchestra £1,000 (£59,350) to play in the pit, a sum put up by her patron, the reclusive American millionairess Mary Dodge, who lived at Warwick House, St James's. In return Beecham agreed to conduct without fee, and in addition promised to perform excerpts from the opera at one of his Queen's Hall concerts.*

Although at forty the redoubtable Smyth was older than most of the other British composers whose music Beecham performed at this time, he found her 'a tremendous ally', who was worth ten times all the male English composers put together.[49] As a girl of nineteen, she had browbeaten her father, a general who had helped to put down the Indian Mutiny, into allowing her to study composition in Leipzig, where she learned to write well-crafted pieces in the style of, first, Brahms (whom she came to know, but did not care for much) and then Schumann.

Musically, *The Wreckers*, completed in 1904, is an uneasy, though not ineffective, mix of Wagnerian romanticism and English heartiness. For Smyth it held a place of particular importance among her compositions, for its libretto was

---

* Beecham was as good as his word. On 19 April 1909 he included two excerpts from the opera in a concert at Queen's Hall that also included the first performance of the twenty-five-year-old Arnold Bax's tone poem *Into the Twilight*. Beecham found Bax's music much better than that of 'Holbrooke and C° ... Real imagination for once' (Letter to Delius, 11 April 1909).

by her late lover, the Anglo-American writer and philosopher Henry Brewster, who had died of liver cancer a year earlier. (Henceforth Smyth was to confine her romantic attachments to women.) The composer was cock-a-hoop about securing Beecham's services. 'I have at last found the ideal conductor for my opera', she told a reporter, 'and I cannot speak with too great enthusiasm on the subject.' [50] Smyth, who smoked cigars and insisted on wearing country tweeds, even at society dinner parties, was just the sort of outsize character to whom Beecham responded, and though he blew hot and cold about her music for the rest of his career, he appreciated its spirit and what he called 'guts'.

Not everything went smoothly at rehearsals, however. Unlike Delius, who trusted Beecham implicitly when it came to matters of tempo ('Take it just as you think best, my dear fellow'),[51] Smyth expected conductors to pay close attention to her metronome marks. 'I could not feel there was much affinity between my music and its conductor', she wrote later, for he 'seemed to me less bent on carrying out my ideas than on seeing what could be made of them by Thomas Beecham.' [52] Eric Coates, sub-leader to Tertis in the viola section and later a successful composer of light music, recalled a rehearsal with 'Smyth sitting on the floor of the stage beating one tempo and Beecham in the orchestra pit beating another.' [53] Though exasperated by such interventions, Beecham kept up a genial front.

Smyth had other criticisms to make of Beecham. For one thing he was never less than half an hour late for rehearsals; for another it was 'an effort to him to allow for the limitations of the human voice, to give the singers time to enunciate and drive home their words'. [54] As a rehearsal of the final act neared its conclusion, the tenor John Coates, who as the doomed hero Mark was about to meet his watery death, asked Beecham if he was supposed to be drowned by the waves or the orchestra.[55] Yet in spite of the complaints, it was Beecham who came out best in the reviews that followed the first performance on 22 June. Smyth's music was well enough received, but generally it was felt that she had been let down by a weak and poorly constructed libretto.

Aware that a royal visit to *The Wreckers* would bring both excellent publicity for her opera and increased sales at the box office, Smyth asked a friend of hers at Buckingham Palace, Frederick ('Fritz') Ponsonby, equerry to Edward VII, to persuade the King and Queen Alexandra to attend a special evening performance of the opera at the end of the run.* Edward agreed to the proposal. Before the news was made public, it was leaked deliberately to Joseph Beecham. At a rehearsal, Beecham whispered to Smyth that 'the left-hand man of the two men

---

* The royal pair were often seen at the opera. The *Musical Standard* (24 July 1909) reported that 'up to and including July 12 the Queen had been present this season at Covent Garden opera house no fewer than twenty times'.

hiding behind the pillars at the back of the stalls *is my father.*' Joseph did not attend the opening performance, but secretly bought a seat in the stalls for the royal performance, which took place on 8 July.[56] After the curtain came down the King sent for Beecham and complimented him on the work he had done.

Two days later, at 11.30 at night, Beecham wrote an ecstatic letter to Maud Foster from the Langham Hotel about a visit he had just made to Joseph's house in Hampstead: 'I have been with my father all day from 10.30 a.m. till the present moment. We have lunched and dined together, and played duets on organ and piano, and are once again as brothers. I think you will admit that your boy is developing diplomatic capacities ... All my heart is with you tonight and always, my love, my darling. – T.'* Maud Foster hid the letter in a white stocking, which inadvertently she put out to be washed. Mrs Nash, the housekeeper, found it, read it and handed it to George Foster. Unbeknown to Beecham and Maud, he called in a private detective called Roche to spy on them. Beecham's private life was becoming more complicated by the hour, for on 19 June, three days before the opening of *The Wreckers*, Utica had given birth at Highfield to their second son, who, like his great-grandfather and father, was named Thomas.

Despite his lack of funds Beecham had begun to stay quite often at the Langham Hotel. Commuting had begun to prove irksome, particularly on Sundays, when the last train to Elstree left London at just after 8 p.m. It was not unknown for him to catch the last train to Edgware, which left nearly three hours later. From there he had an hour's walk up Watling Street to Borehamwood, with a steep climb at Brockley Hill. 'It seems that our Tommy owes a great deal of money', the composer Norman O'Neill grumbled to Delius, '[but] that won't prevent him living in state at the Langham!'[57] Balfour Gardiner complained that Beecham had given him a cheque that was subsequently dishonoured: 'It is abominable treatment & I have had enough of Beecham to last me the rest of my life.'[58] † The Langham was convenient for a number of reasons. It stood opposite Queen's Hall and was close to Quinlan's office at the top of Regent Street. It was also a good place to meet Maud Foster, as Roche the detective was soon to discover.[59]

---

* Though Beecham was now reconciled with his father, his sister Emily remained unforgiven. After leaving home she had trained as a dancer and at Christmas 1909 performed in the pantomime, *Goody Two Shoes*, at the Shakespeare Theatre, Lavender Hill, where Thomas had made his operatic debut seven years earlier. She was billed as 'Premiere Danseuse Madamoiselle Dolli, who has had the honour of appearing recently before HER MAJESTY THE QUEEN'. *The Era* (25 December 1909) reported that she was 'conspicuous in several dances, which were executed with skill and grace'. 'Dolli' was Emily's family nickname.

† Gardiner's ire seems to have been short lived; a month later he was playing in the Beecham Symphony Orchestra's percussion section.

Meanwhile Beecham was being drawn into London society, thanks mainly to Ethel Smyth's wide circle of friends and relations, notably her sister, the hostess Mrs Charles Hunter. His Lancashire accent was beginning to disappear under a languid drawl, with vowels that would always remain a fraction too refined to be mistaken for those of an Edwardian upper-class gentleman. (His father, on other hand, made no attempt to lose his accent.) In August Beecham wrote to Delius that before long he would be moving with his family nearer to London, for he had come to the conclusion that, if he were to get anywhere, he would have to play the 'social game', for that was where the people were who had money to spend on music.[60]

In the event most of the money came, not from the ranks of society, but from Joseph Beecham, who told his son that he was ready to fund a season of opera in London. Stories abounded in the press that he was even prepared to put up the sum of £300,000 (£17.8 million) for the endowment of a National English Opera House,[61] though the *Morning Post* argued that, before any building was erected, it was necessary to create a public for opera, with prices 'within reach of all'. The music schools, too, would have to play their part by widening their scope 'so as to include the regular and exclusive study of opera in all its branches, beginning with the important matter of voice use'.[62]

That Joseph was in a position to make a significant financial contribution to opera in Britain was beyond doubt. He was now richer than ever, thanks to his widespread business activities. In 1908 his profit from the St Helens pill business alone had reached £98,200 (£5.9 million) and an even larger one was forecast for 1909. In addition he had inherited around £40,000 (£2.4 million) from his father, old Thomas, who had died in 1907 at the age of eighty-six. Joseph was now spending more time at his house in Hampstead and had built on to it a picture gallery (which also housed a pipe organ) for his growing collection of predominantly British art that included paintings by Constable and watercolours by Turner. There were also works by Bonington, Cox, Crome, Morland, de Wint, Dadd and others. In the evenings Joseph, who had become a familiar figure in London's salerooms, was known to sit for hours, examining the pictures in solitary wonder.

Beecham meanwhile was completing plans for a long tour of the British Isles that he was about to undertake with his orchestra. Because he was so busy, Utica left Highfield on 1 September 1909 for an extended holiday in Bournemouth with Adrian and the baby. A week after they had gone, Beecham lent the house for a month to a Russian couple, Prince and Princess Bariatinsky, who were friends of his. The prince, who was a playwright, and his wife, an actress, apparently wanted to spend time in the English countryside. But it was not just the Bariatinskys who stayed at Borehamwood. Katherine Ruth Heyman and

Maud Foster went with them, and from time to time Beecham turned up too. The servants took a more than casual interest in the comings and goings, as did Roche the detective.

One evening in mid-September Beecham was waiting at Elstree station for a train when Roche came up and introduced himself. As they travelled to London together, Roche explained that he was employed to watch Beecham's movements and warned him that George Foster might bring a petition against Mrs Foster and cite him as co-respondent. Roche suggested that if he were to leave George Foster's service and work for Beecham instead, he could then spy on Foster in the hope that he might discover something disreputable about him, which in turn would enable Mrs Foster to launch a counter-petition. Naively, Beecham agreed to the proposal and, after consulting Maud, signed up Roche.[63] It was to prove an unwise move.

The Beecham Orchestra's tour started in Cardiff on 6 October with the first of twenty-three concerts in the space of twenty-five days.* Though the pace was hectic, a strong sense of camaraderie developed between players and conductor, both on and off stage, and as a mark of his faith in their musicianship Beecham gave six of his principals the chance to play concertos during the tour.† In several of the towns visited the orchestra's football team took on local sides: key players included Albert Sammons (left winger) and Horace Fellowes, leader of the second violins (centre forward). While on their way to one match they bumped into Beecham, who was out for a stroll. On hearing that the team was short of a full-back that day, he offered his services, even though he had no proper boots. 'We were amazed at his defensive play', wrote Fellowes, 'and it was obvious he knew something of the game.'[64] After the match, which resulted in a draw, Beecham invited the players to refreshments at his hotel.

Beecham was also involved in some of the players' more boisterous escapades. Tertis recalled a night at the Adelphi Hotel in Liverpool,‡ where Beecham and leading members of the orchestra were staying after a particularly successful concert (presumably the one at nearby St Helens, his first in the town for nine years): 'We were in the best of spirits at the supper afterwards and it was well beyond

---

* The tour continued to Exeter, Torquay, Bournemouth, Southampton, Reading, Bedford, Cheltenham, Great Malvern, Burton-on-Trent, St Helens, Chester, Wigan, Lancaster, Bolton, Kendal, Barnsley, Harrogate, Belfast, Dublin, Preston and Hanley and ended at Cambridge on 30 October.

† The players were Sammons (Saint-Saëns's Violin Concerto no. 3), Fellowes (Vieuxtemp's Violin Concerto in E), Tertis (York Bowen's Viola Concerto), Warwick Evans (Boëllmann's *Variations symphoniques* for cello and orchestra), George Ackroyd (Chaminade's Flute Concertino) and Emile Gilmer (Mozart's Clarinet Concerto).

‡ This was the original Adelphi Hotel, opened in 1826 and demolished in 1912 to make way for its much larger successor of the same name that still stands in Ranalegh Place.

midnight when Beecham, Sammons, Warwick Evans, the principal cello, and I retired to our rooms. We did not deign to take the lift but tripped up the five or six floors of the staircase in jovial mood.' At each landing Beecham removed light-bulbs from their sockets and, when he and his companions reached the top floor, dropped the lot down the stairwell. As the bulbs hit the ground there was 'a tremendous explosion', which caused pandemonium in the hotel. The next morning, after Beecham had paid compensation for both the bulbs and the general disruption, the management agreed to forget about the incident.[65]

There were more explosions as players threw fireworks from the windows of their train. Preston station was a favourite target following an incident there in which an enormous 'cannon' firework with a time-fuse, deposited under a luggage-trolley, had exploded just as the orchestra's train was pulling out. The train stopped, and the station-master threatened to have everyone arrested, Beecham included. For Eric Coates, the general exuberance was reflected in the orchestra's playing. 'Never before or since', he wrote in 1953, 'have I heard an orchestra play with greater brilliance than the Beecham Orchestra of forty odd years ago. Beecham had an amazing way of getting the best out of his players by making some irrelevant remark in a high-pitched voice, just as he was about to raise his stick for the opening piece. "Now then, gentlemen, do your *worst!*" seemed to bring out the 'devil' in the orchestra, and the performance which followed after this misleading exhortation was never anything but terrific. I have seen audiences raised to a pitch of enthusiasm after a performance such as this which makes the plaudits of a Promenade gathering on a Saturday night appear lukewarm.'[66]

The tenor Tamini sang at thirteen of the concerts, but did not please Beecham with his habit of holding on to the climactic A flat at the end of 'Lohengrin's Farewell'. Coates claims that on one occasion Beecham took his watch out and timed the offending note. But if Tamini's top notes grew ever longer as the tour progressed, the main item in most of the programmes, Elgar's First Symphony, grew shorter. At the early concerts of the tour, the symphony, which was performed on seventeen occasions, seems to have been given complete. It certainly was at the ninth concert, given on 14 October at Great Malvern in the heart of the Elgar country, where the critic of the *Malvern News* noted that Beecham's reading lasted five or six minutes longer than Richter's. The *Malvern Gazette* considered the performance to be in 'the true Elgar spirit' and 'quite equal to that given at the recent Hereford Festival, and directed by the composer'. Yet at Preston a fortnight later the *Manchester Guardian's* correspondent wrote that 'to the amazement of those who followed the score the symphony was curtailed in a most unjustifiable manner; almost half of the first movement was sacrificed, principally in the development section, two minutes was chopped off the scherzo, even the serenely beautiful adagio, which only occupies eleven minutes in performance, was abbreviated, only the concluding movement escaped with its life.' At Hanley on the following night, 28 October, the last movement, too, suffered a cut, and a work that normally lasts more than fifty minutes came in at thirty-eight.

Havergal Brian, writing about the Hanley concert for the *Staffordshire Sentinel*, was so incensed by the butchery that he refused to discuss the performance of the symphony in his review, though he was even-handed enough to praise Beecham's 'extraordinary exposition' of Berlioz's *Te Deum*, which shared the programme. Brian wrote a letter to the *Musical Times* complaining that the performance of the symphony 'was an insult to the composer ... This is surely not the use to which so exceedingly fine an orchestra should be put, to say nothing of the misuse of the genius with which nature has endowed Mr Thomas Beecham.' At the final concert, at Cambridge, Beecham, perhaps stung by Brian's review, restored all the cuts. He got no thanks from the reviewer of the *Cambridge Daily News*, who said he agreed with an unidentified, but 'competent', critic who thought that 'the work would gain considerably if a quarter of an hour were chopped out somewhere'. [67]

Later Beecham would characterise the work as 'neo-Gothic, the equivalent of the towers of St Pancras Station'. [68] Whether he was bored by the symphony, or whether he thought listeners were bored by it, is impossible to say – a Torquay reviewer admitted he found it 'a trifle long', while at Cheltenham the local press reported that many members of an already sparse audience left the hall during the course of it, 'much to the annoyance of the performers and those who were anxious to hear every note of the work'. [69] The writer Reginald Nettel quotes Beecham as saying that, although the British public had placed Elgar on a pedestal higher than that of any composer since Purcell, he did not find this valuation shared by either our own or foreign musicians.[70] Presumably one of the musicians Beecham had in mind was Delius, who wrote that the 'only thing to be said in [the symphony's] favour is that it is better manufactured than the rest of the English composers' compositions – But it is a work dead born.' [71] Nettel, a friend and supporter of Brian's, revealed that there was an ironic sequel to the affair. After Brian's letter was published Elgar, his hero, cooled noticeably towards him. Brian realised, too late, that what Elgar craved was performances of his work – even cut ones.[72]

If Beecham's professional life was flourishing, his private life was in a state of confusion. His marriage was faltering. Whether or not Utica was aware of the affair with Maud Foster is not known, but according to legal testimony Beecham gave later in America she 'ceased cohabitation' with him against his express wishes after the birth of their second son, and 'never resumed such relationship'.[73] In November he took a flat in West Heath Road, Hampstead. It seems that Utica declined to go with him, and chose instead to remain at Borehamwood; she also spent long periods at her parents' house in Kensington. Her obsession with her children had grown in intensity, to the detriment of her husband.

CHAPTER 5

Elektra and the Baptist

JOSEPH kept his promise that he would fund an opera season in London, and booked the Royal Opera House, Covent Garden, for a period of three and a half weeks beginning on 19 February 1910. Rehearsals were to start on New Year's Day. Thomas was determined that the season should open with Richard Strauss's third opera, *Salome*, for which he had acquired the British performance rights. For a thirty-year-old conductor with very limited operatic experience it was a bold, some thought reckless, act.

Unlike his symphonic poems, none of Strauss's four operas to date – *Guntram, Feuersnot, Salome* and *Elektra* – had been performed in Britain. At its premiere in Dresden in December 1905, *Salome* had been an instant success with the public, and in the following year productions were mounted in Prague, Graz, Berlin and Turin. In 1907 it was seen at the Paris Opéra and at the Metropolitan Opera, New York, where, at the public dress rehearsal, the Swedish-American soprano Olive Fremstad as Salome startled the house with her fondling of St John the Baptist's severed head – 'she rolled around on the stage with it', wrote one observer, 'and slobbered over it and talked baby talk to it till some delicate creatures felt just a little queer in the midst'. [1] So scandalised were some of the theatre's richer and more influential patrons, notably Mrs Herbert Satterlee, daughter of the financier J. P. Morgan (it was Sunday morning and some of the audience had come straight to the theatre from church), that the opera was withdrawn after only one performance, on the grounds that it was 'objectionable and detrimental to the best interests of the Metropolitan Opera House'. [2]

In choosing *Salome*, Beecham risked falling foul of the Lord Chamberlain's office, which since 1737 had been responsible for stage censorship in Britain. Covent Garden had shied away from the work, not entirely without good reason, for Strauss had based his libretto on a German translation of Oscar Wilde's play of the same name (written in French), which had been refused a performing licence by the Lord Chamberlain in 1892 on the grounds that it portrayed on stage the New Testament figure of the Baptist. In 1909 the ban on the play was still in force, and Beecham was warned informally that Strauss's opera was likely to meet the same fate. The problem was not simply a matter of the story's New Testament origins. As would become clear, the necrophilism of the final scene was found extremely distasteful by the current Lord Chamberlain, Viscount

Althorp.* American newspaper reports of the Met débâcle had been widely reproduced in Britain, and their lurid headlines – 'Many Disgusted by the Dance and the Kissing of the Dead Head' (*New York Times*); 'Salome disgusts its Hearers' (*New-York Tribune*) – had not been forgotten. Few remembered, or even knew, that New York's critics had heaped praise on Strauss's score, the Met's production, the virtuoso playing of its orchestra under Alfred Hertz and the singers, led by Fremstad who for the first night had toned down her portrayal of Salome considerably. For the *New York Times*, she 'presented a figure of wonderful exotic beauty, of lithe and snaky grace, with the languor and the fire of the Orient, the passion of a perverted nature'.[3]

On 6 December 1909 the ever-hopeful Beecham submitted a copy of the libretto to the Lord Chamberlain's office. On the following day Ethel Smyth wrote a personal letter of support to Viscount Althorp, saying that 'Beecham is a friend of mine, & his one wish is to keep the acting of the last scene such as shall <u>not</u> make the sort of sensation Fremstad's performance did in America.' She added that, since Beecham was already in Berlin making tentative arrangements to cast the opera, she would 'be most grateful if the thing could be decided with the greatest possible expedition'. Althorp replied that although he would give the work every consideration, he was 'doubtful as to its prospects, for the same story [i.e Wilde's play] has already been discussed and decided upon.'

Confirmation that the opera would be refused a licence came in a letter sent to Beecham on 10 December by G. A. Redford, Althorp's examiner of plays. As was customary, the letter offered no explanation for the decision.[4] If Beecham wanted to know the precise reasons for the ban, he would have to appeal against the ruling. The ban was particularly absurd because, just over a year earlier, the Canadian-born dancer Maud Allan, heading the bill at the Palace Theatre of Varieties in Cambridge Circus, had enthralled London with more than 250 performances of a twenty-minute solo called *The Vision of Salome*. Danced to a score by the Belgian composer and critic Marcel Rémy, it had been inspired by a performance of Wilde's play that Allan had seen in Vienna. Like her slightly younger contemporary, Isadora Duncan, Allan eschewed the principles of classical ballet in favour of a freer style of dancing. *The Times* praised 'the dramatic force and finished beauty' of her performance which, it said, embraced 'allurement, exultation, rage, fear, despair, even exhaustion'. At its climax the scantily clad and bare-footed Allan not only fondled the Baptist's head, but kissed its lips – yet she escaped prosecution because acts performed in music-halls,

---

* Charles Robert Spencer, Viscount Althorp and later the 6th Earl Spencer (1857–1922), was the great-grandfather of Diana, Princess of Wales. He was a Liberal MP for twenty years before Edward VII appointed him Lord Chamberlain (1905–12), a post in which he was known for his illiberality when it came to play censorship. He was a noted dandy.

unlike stage plays, were not subject to the scrutiny of the Lord Chamberlain's office.*Among the thousands captivated by Allan's performance were the Prime Minister, Herbert Asquith, and his wife Margot, who introduced the dancer into society. Edward VII and Queen Alexandra saw *The Vision* at a private performance given at the home of the Earl of Dudley.†

With the start of the season only ten weeks away, Beecham had no time to appeal against the censor's decision, and decided to open instead with Strauss's fourth and most recent opera, *Elektra*, for which he also held the British rights. Premiered in Dresden eleven months earlier, with Ernst von Schuch conducting, it had one great advantage over *Salome*: it presented no censorship problems. The season was also to feature the British premiere of Delius's *A Village Romeo and Juliet*, a staging of Debussy's early cantata *L'enfant prodigue*, Humperdinck's *Hänsel und Gretel* and Bizet's *Carmen*, both sung in English, *Tristan und Isolde*, and new productions of *The Wreckers* and Sullivan's *Ivanhoe*, which had not been seen in London for almost twenty years. (Several critics thought it should have stayed that way.) On Ethel Smyth's recommendation, Beecham brought in for *Tristan* and one of *The Wreckers* performances a young conductor from the Vienna Court Opera, Bruno Walter, who was making his British operatic debut.[5]

Clearly Joseph Beecham's interest in endowing a national opera house on Continental lines was still alive, for a brochure for the season explained that one of its main purposes was to discover whether or not there was an audience that was large enough to justify the provision of a theatre where opera could be performed throughout the year in properly staged productions, with the conductor and orchestra playing as important a role as the singers. For London this was a revolutionary concept. Covent Garden, run by the Grand Opera Syndicate, a wealthy group of patrons who appointed a manager, did not have a permanent company. Each year, from April to July, it put on some twenty starrily cast operas in the course of a fourteen-week 'grand season' that occupied an important place in the London social calendar. During the rest of the year the theatre either played host to the occasional visiting company or

---

* The anomaly arose because the Theatres Act of 1843 had not taken into account variety acts, which at the time were still confined to public houses. As a result, the regulation of music-hall acts (as opposed to plays) became the responsibility of local authorities, which in the case of the London County Council tended to turn a blind eye to what was presented on stage. Manchester was Britain's only local authority to ban Allan's *Salome*, and, to its embarrassment, was widely mocked in the press for doing so.

† In 1910 Allan (1873–1956), anxious to follow up The *Vision of Salome* with something equally striking, commissioned Debussy to compose the music for a solo dance set in ancient Egypt called *Khamma*. Although the score was completed and paid for (Debussy got Charles Koechlin to orchestrate part of it), Allan never used it.

mounted brief autumn or winter seasons of its own. For much of the time it was dark.

It would be 'idle to pretend that Covent Garden is primarily concerned with opera as an art', wrote the critic Francis Toye in 1910. 'The audience demands first-rate singers, and cares very little what they sing; the Syndicate expects a profit and cares as little how it is earned. ... To a person of artistic ambitions, such a programme leaves something to be desired, and it is just this "something" that many of us would like to see cultivated in England.' [6] Thomas was hoping to provide that 'something', though, as he would soon discover, the difficulties involved were immense.

Because the Beechams' season was so short, it was not at first clear how they could hope to gather from it sufficient statistical evidence to draw any useful conclusions about the viability of a national opera house. It soon emerged, however, that the season was only the first instalment of a much bigger plan. Starting in May, there were to be eleven weeks of *opéra comique* at His Majesty's (which, cheekily, would run concurrently with the Grand Opera Syndicate's season), to be followed in the autumn by a further season at Covent Garden, which this time would last, not three and a half weeks, but three months. In all, the Beechams would be giving London an unprecedented twenty-eight weeks of opera in one year, with the Beecham Symphony Orchestra in the pit. Because of the sheer scale of the operation, the plan to take the orchestra on a tour of America was dropped.

Casting *Elektra* at short notice proved an expensive undertaking, for several of Europe's leading opera houses demanded considerable sums in compensation to release singers from existing contracts. Nonetheless, Beecham secured an impressive line-up, including the Hamburg-based American soprano Edyth Walker as Elektra; Anna Bahr-Mildenburg, a celebrated Isolde from the Vienna Court Opera, as Klytämnestra; a second American, Frances Rose from the Berlin Court Opera, as Chrysothemis, and another member of the Vienna Opera, the German baritone Friedrich Weidemann, as Orest. Each of the opera's five scheduled performance was estimated to cost at least £1,500 (£94,750), while Joseph Beecham's outlay for the whole season was put at £20,000 (£1,263,000).[7] Far from keeping the figures to himself, Joseph made sure that they reached the ears of the press, which was only too happy to print them. When it was discovered that Strauss himself would be conducting two of the performances, excitement in the press boiled over, particularly after the Beecham publicity machine let slip that his fee would be £200 (£12,600) a night.

The stage director, Willy Werk, was brought over from Germany to rework the original Dresden production, while Beecham held an unprecedented number of orchestral rehearsals, both sectional and with the full complement of 115 players.

The popular illustrated tabloid, the *Daily Sketch*, watched him at work: 'He is a man of hidden nerves. He takes his seat as if he were sitting down for breakfast. He opens his score in a manner which suggests that he is badly bored with the whole business ... A quick word to the musicians, a short rap [and] the flood of music fills the opera house.' The *Daily Mirror*, a rival of the *Daily Sketch*, told its readers that the 'composer represents musically the lowing of cattle, baa-ing of sheep, cracking whips and the halting steps of animals dragged to sacrifice. Drums are beaten with birches to indicate the flogging of the cattle.'[8] There were rumours of singers 'taking certain forms of exercise and special food', and of doctors standing by in the wings, though in a newspaper interview Edyth Walker poured scorn on them. 'I do not approve of getting fame by pretending that I must make almost superhuman exertions', she said, 'when, with the knowledge of how to breathe and of the proper routine, the task is not very difficult.' On being reminded by her interviewer that Ernestine Schumann-Heink, the Klytämnestra at the Dresden premiere, had called the whole opera 'nerve-racking', Walker retorted in true diva fashion that 'perhaps, had her part been suited to her better, her opinions would have been different.'[9]

The general frenzy had a gratifying effect on the box office. The most expensive seat in the stalls for *Elektra* nights cost £1 15s (£110.55), the cheapest in the amphitheatre 1s 6d (£4.74).* So great was the demand for tickets that Beecham announced that the number of performances of *Elektra* would be increased from five to nine.† The opening night was judged a triumph in every respect. Edward VII and Queen Alexandra and their guests, the Prince and Princess of Prussia, were in the royal box and 'persons of note in the musical and other worlds were to be seen in every row'.[10] Only senior members of the Government and the Opposition were missing, for they were attending the banquets and receptions traditionally held on the Saturday night before the opening of Parliament. Among the standees in the gallery was the future conductor Eugene Goossens, then a sixteen-year-old music student, who had queued in Floral Street for more than six hours to secure a ticket. He had taken some sandwiches to eat before the performance started, 'but such was the crush of people standing that I was unable to retrieve them from the tail pocket of my frock-coat for sheer inability to move my arms backwards or forwards'.

The following morning's *Observer* reported that an 'extraordinary

---

* The same seats for performances of *Elektra* at Covent Garden in 2003 cost £110 and £12 respectively.

† Since not all the contracted singers were available for the extra performances, Beecham brought in reinforcements from Germany: Zdenka Fassbender (Munich) and Annie Krull (Dresden) for Elektra; Ottilie Metzger (Frankfurt) for Klytämnestra; Luise Perard-Petzl (Hamburg) for Chrysothemis; and Paul Bender (Munich) for Orest. Frederic Austin sang Orest at the two final performances.

demonstration occurred at the conclusion. The audience seemed breathless for a few moments, then a spontaneous and continual outburst of applause, never excelled on any occasion at Covent Garden, brought the artists before the curtain again and again. More than a dozen times altogether the curtain had to be raised. A worthy and especial tribute was accorded Mr Beecham, who was presented with an enormous laurel wreath'. [11] On the Monday the *Daily Mirror*, *Daily Sketch* and *Daily Graphic* all devoted their entire front pages to photographs of the production, the singers, Strauss, Beecham and even the heckelphone (a bass oboe), 'one of the many strange instruments invented for use in *Elektra*', which actually had made its first appearance in *Salome*. [12]

The critics were almost unanimous in averring that *Elektra* was a masterpiece. Ernest Newman was one of the few who expressed serious reservations, though he admitted that the piece had some 'marvellous moments', particularly in the Elektra–Orest recognition scene. 'Is, then, the opera worthless?', he asked in the *Birmingham Daily Post*. 'I make bold to say that quite half of it is, and that few will want to hear this half more than once or twice.' A few days later Newman returned to the attack in a review for *The Nation*, for which he was taken to task by George Bernard Shaw, who, in a correspondence with Newman that was to enliven the pages of the London weekly for the next six months, declared that the production of *Elektra* was a 'historic moment in the history of art in England, such as may not occur again within our lifetime'. [13] According to Joseph Beecham, his son's interpretation of the work was not based on anyone else's; he had never seen a production of the work previous to his own. [14] Shaw said of it that 'sometimes the music sounded like a concerto for six drums', though the *Morning Post*'s critic reported that it was 'to the everlasting credit of the artistic powers of Mr Thomas Beecham that his huge force, with its volume of sound, was never once allowed to overwhelm the voices'.*

Strauss conducted the sixth and seventh performances. On arriving at the theatre to rehearse the orchestra, he was surprised to find the stalls filled with music critics and others anxious to watch him at work. He had them thrown out, saying that he would prefer to return to Berlin at once, rather than have them there listening. He rehearsed for exactly two hours and twenty minutes (not three-quarters of an hour as Beecham has it in *A Mingled Chime*), interrupting the orchestra only nine times, mostly to make brief points such as 'louder' or

---

* In a lecture delivered shortly after the opera's Dresden premiere, the British music writer and friend of Strauss's, Alfred Kalisch, who had assisted in the preparations for it, said that the legend, already given credence, 'that at rehearsals Strauss exclaimed to Herr von Schuch, "Louder! Louder! I still hear some of the voices"' was a 'fiction' and 'profoundly untrue'. Curiously, Beecham, who relied on Kalisch's expertise during the Covent Garden rehearsals for the opera, repeats the discredited story with approval in *A Mingled Chime* (pp. 104–5), where he ascribes it to the original *Salome* rehearsals.

'softer'. At the end of the session he congratulated Beecham and the players.[15] Though offered a second rehearsal, Strauss felt there was no need for one, which, he said, had not happened to him before with *Elektra*.

Queen Alexandra (though not the King) returned to Covent Garden for the first of Strauss's two performances. In an instructive review, the *Morning Leader*'s pseudonymous critic 'Staccato' wrote that the 'extraordinary clearness and sharpness of the melodic outlines are the chief things which strike one about Strauss's conducting. He seems to hammer the themes into one's brain. He insists on the accents which Mr Beecham sometimes softened down, and in many places he "pulled out" the dance rhythm which is hidden away in some inner part. The music of the sacrificial procession, and that of the symphonic passage which marks Klytämnestra's exit were astonishingly lurid, and the final scene was taken at a whirlwind tempo which took one's breath away. The music of the Recognition was also hurried along breathlessly, whereas Mr Beecham made it more reposeful. Very striking, too, was the mysterious pianissimo secured at the point where Elektra relates to her brother how she had sacrificed her youth and beauty to the task of avenging her father.'*

At the curtain-calls, the *Leader* reported, Strauss 'dragged on the modest and reluctant Mr Beecham and shook him warmly by the hand and applauded him enthusiastically'. The Queen invited them, along with the principal singers, to her box, where all were asked to sign her autograph book. 'Still attired in their primitive Greek costumes and with made-up faces, the artistes complied with her Majesty's commands', noted the *St Helens Reporter*, which was on hand to bask in its local hero's success.[16] Strauss, the Beechams and most of the company then adjourned to a supper at the Savoy for 150 guests, which continued well into the early hours.[17]

Given that so much money, time and energy was spent on *Elektra*, it is not surprising that other operas in the repertory suffered as a result. Bruno Walter was allotted insufficient rehearsal-time for *Tristan und Isolde*, and it was not until the second performance that his reading came into its own. The *Musical Standard* found a performance of *Carmen* under the composer-conductor Hamish MacCunn 'obviously under-rehearsed', both musically and in its staging. Ethel Smyth, who had been promised a much better production of *The Wreckers* than the one seen at His Majesty's, was disappointed with the result: 'This was to have been the great model performance to which I had looked forward for years.

---

* The *Musical Standard*'s editor, J. H. G. Baughan (19 March 1910), found Strauss's reading 'wonderfully illuminative, masterful and finished', but thought that his hurrying of the music in the Recognition scene 'made a far less impressive effect than Mr Beecham achieved at the slower tempi'. Similarly, 'the closing vocal music of the opera was taken at so swift a pace that the singers failed to make as much of it as when Beecham conducts.'

But Beecham ... did not give as much thought or time to it as to Strauss's *Elektra* and Delius's *Romeo and Juliet*. Once more *The Wreckers* was wrecked!'[18]

In fact, Delius's opera fared little better than Smyth's. The composer Philip Heseltine (later known by his pseudonym, Peter Warlock), who as a fifteen-year-old Etonian attended one of the performances, recalled that the production 'could scarcely be called a production at all in a theatrical sense. The orchestral playing [under Beecham] was superb and the singing passable, but old stock scenery ... combined with old stock gestures of the traditional "operatrical" order rendered the conception and design of the work wholly unintelligible'.[19] Delius found the production 'old fashioned' and Beecham promised him an improved staging in the autumn.[20] *The Globe* said that there was an additional reason for the three British operas' failure to make an impact on either the critics or the public: they all contained 'much charming music, but they are poor operas because their composers, or their librettists, or both, display a painful lack of knowledge concerning what is effective upon the stage and what is not'.[21]

When on 19 March the season ended with a final performance of *Elektra*, the cheering at the fall of the curtain was as loud and persistent as it had been on the opening night. The cast, holding hands, with Beecham in the middle, stretched itself in a line across the stage for the singing of the national anthem, which was led by the Elektra of the night, Annie Krull, who had created the role in Dresden.* In a speech Beecham paid a graceful tribute to his father which, Quinlan told him, had left Joseph 'greatly moved'.[22] Summing up the season, *The Globe* wrote that Thomas Beecham was 'the man for whom we have been so long waiting, the man who is prepared to act as pioneer of what is the most neglected branch of music in this country ... He has reaped great honour, he has established himself very firmly in a high position, and we trust that in the future he will meet with the full reward of his labours.'[23]

For Beecham any feelings of euphoria must have been clouded by worries about his personal life, for on the previous day George Foster, with deadly timing, had filed a petition for divorce from his wife Maud on the grounds that she had 'frequently committed adultery with Thomas Beecham' during the previous year. Beecham answered through his solicitors that he was not guilty of adultery as alleged, and asked the High Court, without success, to dismiss Foster's petition.[24] Maud also denied the allegation and counter-petitioned for a divorce from her husband on the grounds that he had been cruel to her and had himself

---

* *The Standard* (21 March 1910) wrote of Krull's Elektra that, compared with Edith Walker's, it was not 'vocally or dramatically as strong. Indeed, there were times when she appeared to give up the combat with the orchestra as hopeless ... On the other hand it was, perhaps, a more subtle rendering. With her round, childish face, and large, staring eyes, she suggested the school girl, ordained by fate to be the instrument and sport of its inevitable decrees, rather than the mad, bad, frenzied creature Miss Walker showed us.'

committed misconduct. It looked as though the case, which was unlikely to reach court for at least a year, would be a messy one. Instead of driving Utica even further apart from her husband, Foster's action had a galvanising effect on her. Fearful that her own marriage might be about to collapse, she decided to leave Borehamwood for good and rejoin Beecham in London, where they took a house, 32 Upper Hamilton Terrace in St John's Wood, on a fifteen-year lease. An uneasy truce ensued.

At the end of the Covent Garden season Joseph Beecham visited America for the twenty-fourth time. His purpose was to buy the lease of a new and larger factory building in Brooklyn to cope with the increasing demands of his business there. Bounded by Classon Avenue and Taffe Street, and providing 100,000 square feet of floor space, it cost him $108,250 (£6,021,000). 'A big deal in Brooklyn', proclaimed the headline in the *New York Herald*.[25] Joseph took just twelve days to pull it off and was back in London in time for the Beecham *opéra comique* season at His Majesty's. It should have opened on 9 May 1910, but Edward VII had died three days earlier, so, out of respect, the start was delayed until 12 May, when Thomas conducted Offenbach's *The Tales of Hoffmann*. Though premiered in Paris twenty-nine years earlier, it was still considered something of a novelty in London. The piece was lavishly presented, for the Beechams, anxious to avoid the variable production standards that had marred the Covent Garden season, had hired a designer from Milan, Signor E. Comelli, to supervise the costumes for all twelve operas in the repertoire.

Hoffmann, like everything else in the season, was sung in English by singers who, with few exceptions, were British. This was a gamble on Beecham's part. He thought that British singers – unlike their Continental colleagues and the many American artists who had had the foresight to study in countries that 'lived and breathed opera' – suffered from an obsession with oratorio and song, and had no feeling for the theatre.[26] Nonetheless, conscious that there could never be a truly national opera company until there were enough capable British singers to staff it, he knew he had to give them the chance to learn their craft. *The Observer*, applauding his attitude, said that as 'the State had never shown any inclination to render assistance', it was the musical public's duty 'to be with him every step of the way'.[27]

The singers at His Majesty's ranged from those with no stage experience at all – the baritone Harry Dearth resigned his post as a lay vicar in the Westminster Abbey choir to join the company – to a few seasoned artists like John Coates, who had sung extensively in Germany, and the twenty-two-year-old Maggie Teyte, who, though British, had made her name at the Opéra-Comique in Paris, where Debussy had chosen her to sing Mélisande in succession to the role's creator, the Scottish-born Mary Garden. Somewhere in the middle came singers with limited stage experience, among them Agnes Nicholls, Walter Hyde and Robert Radford, who had been given their chance by Richter in his pioneering English-language *Ring* cycles at Covent Garden in 1908 and 1909. Finally, there was a valued group of singers, including Ruth Vincent, Frederick Ranalow and Caroline Hatchard (the Woodbird in Richter's *Siegfried*), who had started their careers in musical comedy and so knew just how to tread the boards. As the season progressed, there was a marked improvement in both singing and acting.

It is a sign of Joseph's shyness that although he financed the 1910 seasons, he put his son's rather than his own name to them, and seemed happy for the public to think that it was Thomas who was putting up the money. Beecham told a reporter that, what with renting His Majesty's, providing new scenery and costumes for ten operas and paying an orchestra of sixty-five players, the losses on the *opéra comique* season would be not be far short of £10,000 (£631,700), and 'might easily run to double that amount'. Nonetheless, he said, he remained committed to establishing a permanent opera house in London and, if necessary, to spend £500,000 (£31.5 million) in doing it: 'I am only waiting until I can find a good site in a good position at a fair valuation.'[28]

The brochure for the His Majesty's season explained that the term 'opéra comique' embraced anything operatic that 'could be heartily enjoyed without the concentrated mental effort demanded by the more serious productions'. *Hoffmann* was an instant success and was given thirty-four performances in all, eight of them conducted by Beecham. He then conducted two more French pieces, Edmond Missa's *Muguette*** and Jules Massenet's *Werther*. Though Beecham claimed that *Werther* was a particular favourite of his, it proved so unpopular at the box office that it was given only one performance. (It had suffered exactly the same fate at its British premiere at Covent Garden in 1894.) Things looked up, however, with his next three offerings, Mozart's *Il seraglio*, *The Marriage of Figaro* and *Così fan tutte* (the last translated as 'They all do it'), which opened in the space of eight days. Contrary to general expectation, they drew large crowds.

By 1910 performances of Mozart's operas, *Don Giovanni* apart, had been all but swept off London's stages by a tidal wave of Wagner and Verdi. *Figaro*, once heard regularly at Covent Garden, had received only six performances there in the past twelve years; *Il seraglio* had not been given in the capital for almost thirty years. As for *Così fan tutte*, it had last been performed professionally in London in 1873, when the visiting Italian Company had included it in a season

---

* The French composer Edmond Missa (1861–1910), a pupil of Massenet's, based *Muguette* on Ouida's novel *Two Little Wooden Shoes*. It was premiered at the Opéra-Comique, Paris, in 1903 and opened at His Majesty's on 25 May 1910, with Maggie Teyte (1888–1976) in the role of Melka. It was her British operatic debut.

at St George's Hall, Langham Place.* The *Sunday Times's* critic looked forward to hearing all three works at His Majesty's, because, he wrote, they would 'throw some light on the problem of whether there is a future for Mozart in the opera house.' After hearing *Seraglio* and *Figaro* (*Così* was still to come), he declared that there most certainly was a future; it had been a 'red-letter week in our musical history'.[29] Among the singers, Maggie Teyte as Blonde and Cherubino and Agnes Nicholls as the Countess stood out, while Beecham's conducting was admired for its refinement and rhythmic vitality, though Francis Toye thought he used far too large an orchestra.[30]

In Beecham's hands *Figaro* lost several of its arias, including Barbarina's in Act 4, but gained an unexpected orchestral addition, two movements from Mozart's Divertimento in D, K131, which were played as entr'actes. In addition, the *secco* recitatives were replaced by spoken dialogue, a common practice in Vienna until Mahler reintroduced them into the opera in 1906. Nobody seemed to mind; indeed, some of the London critics thought the dialogue quickened the action and clarified the plot. In *Così* the recitatives survived, but Beecham again cut several arias, as well as the Ferrando–Guglielmo duet 'Al fato dan legge'. The ensembles remained intact.

A month later Beecham introduced Mozart's one-act opera, *The Impresario* (*Der Schauspieldirektor*) into the repertory, which one of his assistants, Cuthbert Hawley, conducted. To have reawoken in Britain an interest in Mozart's stage-works, not to mention his orchestral works, remains one of Beecham's most important achievements, but an unanswered question remains. Why, having so successfully established the viability of *Così*, did he never conduct it again, even though in *A Mingled Chime* he describes its music as being 'equal in beauty to anything the composer ever wrote'? Beecham continued to perform *Figaro* and *Seraglio*, but returned *Così* to limbo, where as far as Britain was concerned, it was to remain for a further twenty-two years.†

The season at His Majesty's ended with Johann Strauss's *Die Fledermaus*, conducted by MacCunn, and the British premiere of Richard Strauss's second opera, *Feuersnot*, under Beecham. The latter received a good deal of press

---

* The only performance of *Così* that most London critics could recall was a matinée at the Savoy Theatre in July 1890 with the students and orchestra of the Royal College of Music conducted by Charles Stanford. The Rev. Marmaduke E. Browne's English translation, specially commissioned for the occasion, was also used by Beecham at His Majesty's, and was widely given, with revisions, until the 1970s.

† In 1932 *Così* was given productions at both Glyndebourne (conductor Fritz Busch, producer Carl Ebert) and Sadler's Wells (Aylmer Buesst, Clive Carey), but it was not until 1944 that it finally got a firm foothold in the British operatic repertory, thanks to the soprano Joan Cross, wartime director of the Sadler's Wells Opera, who introduced a new production of it with a cast that included herself as Fiordiligi and Peter Pears as Ferrando. Toured throughout the country, it notched up fifty performances in its first year.

coverage but, unlike *Fledermaus*, was not much of a crowd-puller. Written in one act and playing for under an hour and a half, *Feuersnot* makes for an even shorter evening than either of its two immediate successors, *Salome* and *Elektra*, and in an attempt to provide better value for the audience's money Beecham preceded its two final performances with the Venetian act from *The Tales of Hoffmann*.

Feuersnot's story is based on a bawdy Netherlandish legend, reset in Munich by the librettist, Ernst von Wolzogen. It tells of a young student of sorcery, who, in revenge for being made to look a fool by the burgomaster's daughter, invokes his magic powers to extinguish all the lights in the town, as well as the town's traditional midsummer bonfire. To save the situation, the girl draws him into her house, where the two consummate their new-found relationship in a blaze of orchestral passion that pre-dates by ten years the celebrated musical orgasm at the beginning of Strauss's *Der Rosenkavalier*. The town's candles and the bonfire burst into flame once more.

When *Feuersnot* was given in Berlin in 1902, a year after its Dresden premiere, the Kaiser, on hearing of its disreputable dénouement, ordered the opera's withdrawal after five performances. Beecham forestalled possible problems with the Lord Chamberlain by commissioning an English translation from William Wallace that skilfully skated over the libretto's riskier passages, though thanks to the aural tumescence emanating from the orchestra pit, few in the audience can have failed to guess what the lovers were up to. Beecham considered reviving *Feuersnot* at Covent Garden in the autumn, but decided that if it could not fill His Majesty's, it was unlikely that it would do any better in the much larger house. It has not been staged in Britain since, though in his later years Beecham conducted the final love-music in concert on more than twenty occasions and also recorded it.[31]

During the final week of the *opéra comique* season, Beecham made his first gramophone records, when he went to the Gramophone Company's studio to conduct excerpts from *Die Fledermaus* and *The Tales of Hoffmann* with five singers from His Majesty's, a few members of the chorus and a small section of the Beecham orchestra. In the 'Doll's Song' from *Hoffmann*, Caroline Hatchard, displaying an unusual warmth in a voice so highly placed, impresses with clean, accurate coloratura that is never merely mechanical, while Walter Hyde makes a strong Hoffmann. Beecham, whatever Ethel Smyth may have said about his treatment of singers, accompanies with care. As so often in early acoustic recordings, the wind instruments sound lacklustre and out of tune, but there is no mistaking the brilliant attack of the string playing in the *Fledermaus* overture.[32]

The season at His Majesty's ended on 30 July. After a month's break the Beechams extended their opera crusade by sending out *Hoffmann* and

Fledermaus on a fifteen-week tour of Britain under Thomas Quinlan's management. The *Musical Standard*, reporting crowded houses in Birmingham, thought the tour a most 'suitable method of laying hold of the man-in-the street'. Indeed, it proved so successful that it was extended for a further fourteen weeks after Christmas with *Hoffmann* only. Beecham had intended to conduct some of the early performances, but found himself so embroiled in arrangements for his second Covent Garden season that he left the tour in the hands of MacCunn and another composer-conductor, Howard Carr.

The autumn season at Covent Garden got off to a bad start. It should have opened on 1 October with the British premiere of Eugen d'Albert's *Tiefland* with Beecham conducting, but on the previous day Marguerite Lemon, an American from the Mainz Opera who was singing the leading female role of Marta, fell ill. Some said she was suffering from stage-fright, others that she had matrimonial problems. Despite Beecham's claim to the contrary in *A Mingled Chime*, there was no understudy, and it was decided to open the season instead with the next opera in the repertory, Ambroise Thomas's *Hamlet*. At this point disaster struck again. The Ophelia, Mignon Nevada, fell ill, genuinely. Worse, she did not have an understudy either and, only eight hours before curtain-up, the embarrassed company had to announce that it had no alternative but to postpone the opening of the season until the following Monday, 3 October, when *Hamlet* would be given under one of Beecham's co-conductors, Luigi Camilieri. Beecham's sole contribution to what turned out to be limp evening was to conduct the National Anthem.

The episode said little for the company's planning abilities. Matters were not helped by the reviews for *Hamlet*, several of which mocked its composer and librettists for mangling Shakespeare's original. It attracted such a small audience that Beecham decided not to repeat it. *Tiefland*, which finally reached the stage on the third night of the season, was another disappointment at the box office, as was *Le chemineau*, by the Massenet pupil Xavier Leroux, which was withdrawn after just two performances. Even *Carmen* did poor business. The only crowd-pullers during the first three weeks were *Tristan* and *Tannhäuser*, both strongly cast and finely conducted by Alfred Hertz from the Metropolitan Opera,* along with the first night of a revival of *Elektra*, with Edyth Walker, Petzl and Bahr-Mildenburg, which, in *The Observer*'s view, was 'probably the finest Mr Beecham has yet given us.' Unfortunately, the public failed to support

---

* Hertz conducted only the first night of *Tristan* (with the Danish tenor Ejnar Forchhammer and Anna Bahr-Mildenburg as the lovers). Beecham, who had not conducted the work before, took over the remaining five performances. Later in the season he conducted his first *Don Giovanni* (with Giuseppe de Luca as the Don) and *Der fliegende Holländer* (with Frederic Austin as the Dutchman).

its three subsequent performances. *Elektra* even received a royal snub. Lieutenant Albert Williams, bandmaster of the Grenadier Guards, arranged a suite of extracts from the score, which, after many rehearsals, his men performed during the Changing of the Guard ceremony at Buckingham Palace. The writer and former Grenadier, Osbert Sitwell, recalled that 'a scarlet-coated page came out from the Palace with a personal message for Williams from the new King, George V. The note was brief and ran, "His Majesty does not know what the Band has just played, but it is *never* to be played again".'[33]

With ten weeks of the Covent Garden season still to go, even the Beechams were forced to admit that a national opera house was nothing but a pipe-dream. 'Ah', Beecham told a reporter, 'we shall never have that.'[34] The plan to revive Delius's *A Village Romeo and Juliet* was quickly dropped for fear that it would turn out to be yet another failure at the box office. Various explanations were offered for the poor attendances: that the season had failed to attract 'men and women of social importance' (*Musical Standard*); that London had become satiated with opera in 1910; that Beecham was using too many British singers who either lacked star-quality or were unable to hold their own in so large a house.

Poor organisation and the frequent changes to the programme cannot have helped, for audiences, unsure of what was coming up next, had grown wary of booking ahead. Landon Ronald, brooding on the problem in a Sunday newspaper column, found it 'difficult to resist the conclusion that the English public is constitutionally unsympathetic to the music drama. It will go to hear great singers in opera when it cannot hear them otherwise, but it has no genuine interest in opera as an art form, and it is only drawn to hear new works by some element of sensation such as "Electra" provided. I suppose the explanation lies in the emotional reticence which is characteristic of the Anglo-Saxon. ... He cannot bring himself to believe that the life of the operatic stage has any relation to himself or indeed any vital existence.'[35]

Beecham, recognising that only a new 'sensation' could rescue the season, decided to revive his plan to produce *Salome*. If he could secure the Lord Chamberlain's approval, he could open it in the second week of December. Time was short, a mere seven weeks, but there was no problem about finding a cast, for the leading roles could be taken by singers booked for other operas at Covent Garden. Switching them to *Salome* would be a simple matter. (Such flexibility would be unthinkable today, when productions are planned and contracts signed sometimes years ahead of performances.) The singers Beecham had in mind included the Finnish soprano Aïno Ackté, who had sung the title-role in Frankfurt and Dresden and had studied it with Strauss, the American baritone Clarence Whitehill, whose noble-sounding voice would be ideal for the Baptist, and two Germans, Ernst Kraus (Herod) and Ottilie Metzger (Herodias).*

On 24 October Beecham's company manager, Albert Archdeacon, sent a request to have the ban lifted to Lord Althorp who, though still Lord Chamberlain, had recently become Earl Spencer following the death of his half-brother. The Beechams, said Archdeacon, had suffered huge losses on both the first Covent Garden season and the one at His Majesty's, which together had amounted to nothing less than £50,000 (£3,158,000). The current season at the Opera House was likely to add a further £30,000 (£1,900,000) to the deficit. Only *Salome* could save the situation and, by extension, the livelihood of a large number of British singers and musicians. In his final paragraphs, Archdeacon (or perhaps Beecham, who must have had a hand in drafting the letter) pulled out all the stops:

> By the number of letters, and personal questions at the box-office, there is shown in all classes and on all sides a widespread desire to hear this musical work, and it cannot be that musical England alone in the world should be deprived of the opportunity of hearing the finest opera of modern days.
>
> In the event of your not giving permission for the opera to be given, there is no doubt whatever that this will be Mr Beecham's last attempt to give opera in London, as no one, however rich he may be, can stand so huge a drain on his purse.
>
> Surely in the face of what would be nothing short of a national calamity to the progress of musical art in our Country, you, my Lord, will kindly reconsider your decision, and give permission for this work to be reproduced here.[36]

Pleading 'stress of business', Lord Spencer got his Comptroller, Colonel Sir Douglas Dawson, to answer the letter on his behalf.† The Lord Chamberlain, wrote Dawson, had learned of Beecham's losses 'with infinite regret', but remained adamant that the ban could not be lifted unless it was agreed, first, that the Baptist would not appear on stage, and second, that the 'indecent and objectionable' introduction of his severed head would be eliminated, along with all the 'offensive' portions of the libretto.

If Spencer imagined that Beecham would admit defeat when faced with the bizarre prospect of a *Salome* without a visible Baptist, he underestimated the

---

* Ackté had been signed up for Senta in *Der fliegende Holländer*, Whitehill for Kurwenal (*Tristan*), Rocco (*Fidelio*) and Valentine (*Faust*), Kraus for Tannhäuser and Tristan, and Metzger for a much admired Carmen. Tragically, Metzger, who was Jewish, was destined to die in Auschwitz in 1943 after a successful career in Germany that lasted thirty-seven years.

† Sir Douglas Dawson (1854–1933) had his horse shot from under him in the Egyptian campaign of 1882. He became military attaché in several European capitals before joining the Royal Household in 1903.

latter's cunning and determination. Thanks to a loophole in the law, the Lord Chamberlain's powers did not extend to theatre clubs. Though officially banned, Wilde's *Salome* had been given its British premiere 'privately' in 1905 by the New Stage Club at the Bijou Theatre, Bayswater; members' subscriptions to the club included 'free' entrance to the play. Beecham reasoned that, since the play had been performed without interference from the authorities, there was no reason why he should not give private performances of Strauss's opera at Covent Garden by turning it into a club for *Salome* nights.

Through his widening circle of social contacts, Beecham secured a meeting with the Prime Minister. Asquith had attended Beecham's Covent Garden season on at least one occasion and, thanks to Maud Allan, was clearly not shocked by the thought of Salome and the Baptist being portrayed on stage. He listened sympathetically to Beecham's idea of a theatre club and instructed his senior private secretary, Vaughan Nash, to convey his views to Lord Spencer. In a convoluted letter dated 7 November, in which he did his best to avoid disturbing the Lord Chamberlain's sensibilities, Nash told Spencer that 'so far as he – Mr Asquith – is aware there are no obstacles of any kind in the way of the proposed production.'

Spencer was out of London when Nash's letter arrived, but was advised of its contents. Somehow he managed to miss the point completely. 'It is all capital about Beecham and Salomé', he wrote to his Comptroller from the country. 'With St John the Baptist altogether out of the scenes, and the filthy allocution to the head also omitted, I think all will be well ... I am touched at the care not to interfere with me shown by the PM. – it was most nice of him.' Negotiations dragged on for another twelve days. Then, on 19 November, agreement was reached at last. The Baptist was to be allowed back into the opera, though he was to be called, not Jokanaan or John, but 'a Prophet', while in the final scene the executioner was to hand Salome a blood-stained sword, rather than the saint's head on a silver charger. Salome's hymn to the head was to be bowdlerised and all Biblical allusions in the text eliminated. The action was to be moved from Judea to Greece and the Five Jews were to become Five Learned Men. For the sake of getting *Salome* produced in London at last, Strauss accepted the changes.

The opera was licensed on 1 December, one week before the opening. Tickets for its opening night sold out within eighty-five minutes of the box-office opening, and before long touts were offering seats at more than double their face-value. During the final dress rehearsal on 7 December the lissom Ackté, a gift to London's illustrated papers, found that the 'blood' dripping from the sword was staining her fingers and, using 'some very drastic words in French', wiped it off on the cloak of the nearest supernumerary.[37] It was not a problem she had encountered in Germany, where she had held the charger bearing the head. Beecham stopped the rehearsal and in the hope of finding a solution ordered one of his staff to make an urgent telephone call to the Lord Chancellor's office. After a long wait the shirt-sleeved stage manager rushed to the front of the stage and knelt before Beecham, who was waiting in the orchestra pit. 'We can use a tray instead of a sword', he shouted, 'so long as there is no head on it.'[38] The news was greeted with cheers. Comedy had finally turned into farce.

Beecham was tireless. The dress rehearsal took place in the afternoon. In the morning he had taken a three-hour rehearsal for his first concert for the Philharmonic Society, which he conducted that same evening at Queen's Hall. The concert came at an awkward moment, but he had postponed it once already, and for the sake of future relations with the society he could hardly delay it again.* It was not the only concert he conducted during the final week of *Salome* rehearsals. Three nights earlier he had conducted a programme of Wagner excerpts with his orchestra at the Opera House; and on the evening before that had given a concert of eighteenth-century operatic music at the Aeolian Hall in Bond Street, at which Maggie Teyte sang arias by Méhul, Grétry, Paisiello, Isouard, Monsigny and Dalayrac. Teyte claimed to friends that she had an affair with Beecham, but, if true, it seems it was a brief one.†

Not surprisingly, given the enormous amount of pre-publicity it had received, the first night of *Salome* on 8 December was a *succès fou*, though several reviewers found the opera less musically satisfying than *Elektra*. (Ernest Newman took the opposite view.)[39] The Lord Chamberlain's office came in for a good deal of criticism. 'Truly the ways of the Censorship are past finding out', wrote the *Times* critic, who wondered how anybody in the audience could possibly have been expected to miss 'the very striking coincidences' between the fate of the Prophet and that of John the Baptist. 'Of what avail was it', asked the *Sunday Times*, 'that Salome had to say "Ich will dir folgen" ["I want to follow you"] instead of "Ich will deinen Mund küssen" ["I want to kiss your mouth"], when

---

* Beecham's programme, the most adventurous of the society's 1910–11 season, though the least successful financially, included Mozart's Symphony no. 34 (last heard at a Philharmonic concert almost forty years earlier), Delius's *Paris*, d'Indy's *Sinfonie montagnarde* (with Katherine Ruth Heyman playing the piano part) and W. H. Bell's Phantasy-Prelude, *The Shepherd*. Beecham, who waived his fee (as did Heyman), got Bell to conduct his own work because, he told the society by telegram, he was too overworked to do it justice (BL, RPS MS 335, fol. 24).

† Teyte's biographer, Garry O'Connor (*The Pursuit of Perfection*, p. 117n), suggests that the affair was in 1914, but, if it did happen, 1910 is the more likely date, for that year she sang no fewer than five roles with Beecham as conductor: Melka (*Muguette*), Blonde (*Seraglio*), Cherubino (*Figaro*), Nuri (*Tiefland*) and Marguérite (*Faust*). She never sang with him again. Teyte's suggestion that the affair was resumed briefly in the 1930s (O'Connor, p. 177) must be taken with a large pinch of salt. She was a good exaggerator.

she expressed by every fibre of her being the very abandon of amorous desire?' [40] In the heat of the performance some of the textual alterations were forgotten by the singers, though if these were noticed by the members of the Lord Chamberlain's staff who were present, none of them mentioned it. Either they did not speak German or they chose to adopt a diplomatic silence.

By all accounts Ackté's performance in the title-role was remarkable. She expressed emotion 'not only by glance and gesture, but by sensuous curve of bodily movement', said one critic, who added that although the music was 'rather exacting' for her (recordings suggest that the top of her voice was not her strongest point), she sang 'skilfully' and with 'rare expressiveness'. [41] It was noted with approval that, contrary to the practice in Germany, she performed the 'Dance of the Seven Veils' herself, rather than handing over the task to a double. Less appreciated was the silver tray, which, though it lacked a head, was filled with 'gore'. Ackté found it 'inartistic and rather revolting' and, after the sixth of the ten performances, asked if it could not be covered with a cloth, so that 'people may imagine what they want'. Archibald Archdeacon passed on Ackté's request to Sir Douglas Dawson, who replied that 'Lord Spencer says "yes", the tray can be covered with a cloth, only care must be taken not to build up a great heap in it which would look suggestive.' [42] So great was the ridicule poured on the Lord Chamberlain's office for its part in the *Salome* affair that many imagined it could not be long before it was relieved of its licensing duties, but another fifty-eight years and two world wars were to pass before stage censorship in Britain, along with the Lord Chamberlain's role in it, was finally abolished in 1968.

On 31 December Beecham brought what had been a gruelling season to a close with a final performance of *Salome*, prefacing it with Strauss's tone poem *Ein Heldenleben*, which he had not conducted before. Albert Sammons played the long violin solo representing the hero's companion and, along with Beecham, was 'loudly and deservedly applauded' by a house, which, *The Times* noted, was only 'fairly full'. It was not the first time that there had been empty seats during the opera's run. A reporter from *The Observer* asked Beecham if he was satisfied with the season. 'Profoundly dissatisfied', he replied emphatically. 'There is no audience at all for opera.' But what of the furore caused by *Elektra* and *Salome?* 'It is no credit for people merely to patronise these productions and stay away from everything else', said Beecham. What, then, did the future hold? 'The future requires a good deal of consideration.' In a letter to Delius he was even more blunt. The season, he wrote, had been a 'failure'. [43]

CHAPTER 6

Guilty – or Not Guilty?

B EECHAM may have been angry and disappointed about the lack of support for his operatic endeavours, but his father took a sanguine view of what had happened. 'Some men spend their money on horses', he told an American reporter, 'some on yachts. I go in for music.'[1] Thanks to Joseph's instinctive grasp of advertising and publicity – the annual advertising budget for Beecham's Pills was one of the biggest in the country – business was booming. In 1910 his profit from the British company alone had grown to £104,900 (£6.6 million), and in 1911 would rise further, to £111,600 (£7.1 million). Joseph had recently been elected mayor of St Helens for the second time and on 24 January 1911 he marked the occasion, just as he had his first term in 1899, with an invitation concert at the Town Hall. This time his son conducted the Beecham Symphony Orchestra in a programme of popular classics.

The Beechams had plans for a summer season at Drury Lane in 1911, to run concurrently with the Covent Garden grand season. It would feature not only opera, but also the first appearance in Britain of Sergey Diaghilev's company of dancers from the imperial theatres of St Petersburg and Moscow that had made its sensational debut in Paris in May 1909. On hearing that a draft contract had already been drawn up, the Opera House syndicate panicked. Rivalry with a summer season of *opéra comique* in English at His Majesty's had been one thing, but having to compete with a glittering array of dancers headed by Vaslav Nijinsky and Tamara Karsavina was quite another. A deal was struck. Covent Garden would take over the Diaghilev–Beecham contract. In return, Thomas would become a member of the syndicate and be offered some conducting at the Opera House; in addition the Beecham Symphony Orchestra would be invited to play for the ballets during the 1911 grand season. The Beechams also agreed to drop attempts to forge a link with the Metropolitan Opera, New York.

Joseph was quite happy about the deal. He had plenty of other theatrical interests. He owned the Royal Court Theatre, Warrington, and a half-share of the Golders Green Hippodrome. He was chairman of the St Helens Theatre Royal (and a major contributor to its rebuilding following a fire), and had recently become a director of London Theatres of Variety Ltd, in which he had invested £10,000 (£638,000). The company owned a number of music halls up and down the country, the newest of which, the Palladium in London, had opened its doors to the public on Boxing Day 1910.

Joseph, pragmatic by nature, had no difficulty in accepting the main lesson of the 1910 seasons: that as yet there were not enough people in London willing to pay for year-round opera. He now changed tack. Believing that if opera were made easily accessible to everyone, the British public could not fail to become enthusiastic about it, he arranged for the 'Thomas Beecham Opera Company' to appear at the Palladium for twelve weeks as part of the variety bill, starting on 30 January 1911. Extracts from seven operas would be given twice daily by British singers and a large chorus; scenery and costumes would be lavish. The Palladium agreed to pay the Beecham company £1,050 (£67,000) a week to appear there.

Thomas had no outright objection to performing at a music hall – earlier in the month he and the Beecham Symphony Orchestra had given a concert, the first of many, at the Palladium for the National Sunday League, an organisation dedicated to enlivening the nation's traditionally gloomy Sabbath – but he made it clear that he did not see eye-to-eye with his father about the opera scheme. Perhaps thinking that Joseph should be spending his money on more serious operatic enterprises, he told *The Observer* huffishly that although he had lent his name to the company, the season had nothing to do with him: 'If the Palladium chooses to encourage a few of my artists when they are not otherwise engaged, I can't prevent it, and I don't want to prevent it.' But, he added, he would not be conducting, nor would his orchestra be participating. 'I am not', he said, 'the proprietor of a music-hall.' [2]

The Palladium's management, under the impression that it was getting the full international company that had appeared at Covent Garden, was infuriated by Thomas's petulant outburst. Joseph did not seem too happy about it either. Six days before the engagement was due to begin, the *Daily Mail* published a letter from an apparently remorseful Thomas, sent from his father's home at Huyton, saying that the principals and chorus had been 'selected' from those who had taken part in his recent Covent Garden season, and that to show his entire sympathy with the scheme he would, in spite of uncertain health, conduct both the afternoon and evening performances on the opening day.

Thomas's climb-down, presumably made at Joseph's insistence, marked a change in their professional relationship. When discussing their joint enterprises in public, Thomas no longer spoke as though it were he, rather than his father, who was making all the decisions, even the financial ones, and increasingly Joseph began to assert himself as an impresario in his own right. In the coming years Thomas would receive enormous financial support from Joseph, though never again would he be given virtual *carte blanche* when planning opera seasons, as had happened in 1910. In *A Mingled Chime* Beecham writes that, despite an affinity between them, he thought his father was a little afraid of him, which is hardly borne out by Joseph's behaviour towards him either during their period of estrangement or the years of reconciliation that followed. Thomas may have provided the artistic inspiration for the opera seasons, but it was Joseph's money that made them possible.

The operatic extract chosen for the first week at the Palladium came from the second act of *Tannhäuser*, beginning with Elisabeth's Greeting and continuing to Tannhäuser's departure for Rome. The title-role was sung by the company's principal tenor, Philip Brozel, who, though he had met with some success as Herod at the final performance of *Salome* at Covent Garden, was an inadequate Tannhäuser, frequently singing out of tune. Edith Evans, a stalwart of the *opéra comique* season at His Majesty's, was an excellent Elisabeth. For the first day's performances only, the Palladium's house orchestra, augmented by members of the Beecham Symphony Orchestra, overflowed into the auditorium. The BSO players had to transpose their parts up a semitone to match their Palladium colleagues, since at the time the pitch adopted in music halls and military bands was higher than that used in the concert hall and opera house.

'What a wonderful influence the excerpt had on the audience!', wrote the editor of the *Musical Standard* of the opening performances under Beecham. 'Not a soul smoked, and great outbursts of enthusiasm were frequent.' Such interruptions might have seemed inappropriate in a Wagner opera, he continued, but they 'showed that Wagner's wonderful dramatic music hit home'. *The Stage*, which found Joseph's experiment 'as satisfying both musically and spectacularly as anything yet shown on the variety boards', had just one criticism, that at some forty minutes (the *Tannhäuser* overture had been thrown in for good measure) it all seemed a bit long for a bill that also included a contortionist, a 'phonetic comedian', the singer Gertie Gitana of 'Sweet Nellie Dean' fame, Sam Stern 'in his Clever Hebrew and Italian Character Studies', a troupe of jugglers and the Forum scene from Shakespeare's *Julius Caesar*, performed by the actor-manager Lewis Waller and his company.[3]

Having done his filial duty, Beecham handed over the rest of the season to his chorus master and assistant conductor, Emil Kreuz. During the second week the *Tannhäuser* extract was replaced by scenes from *Carmen*. Outwardly, all seemed well, but backstage the Palladium and the opera company were locked in strife. The theatre, perhaps still smarting from Thomas's outburst, complained about vocal standards and demanded Philip Brozel's removal. Brozel claimed in defence that he had been thrown by the higher pitch of the Palladium orchestra, but even when Kreuz lowered it for him matters did not improve. The Beecham company admitted that Brozel's singing was sub-standard, but deferred sacking him. In exasperation, the Palladium ordered the company to pack its bags and leave the building at the end of the second week, even though Joseph was one of the theatre group's directors.

Joseph, by now in the south of France, ordered his solicitors to bring an action against the Palladium for breach of contract, and sent word to the company that his contracts with it would be honoured. Brozel was given notice, however, and later Edith Evans was also dismissed, for no better reason, it seems, than that she had stood up for Brozel. The Alhambra Theatre, Leicester Square, one of the Palladium's main rivals, came to the beleaguered company's rescue by hiring it for two weeks of a shortened version of the Venetian scene from *The Tales of Hoffmann*.* Finally the company moved on to the Alhambra, Glasgow, for a week of extracts from *Carmen* and *Tannhäuser*. 'Wagner in a music-hall', enthused the *Glasgow Herald*. '*Tannhäuser* a "turn". The old order changeth.' †

Joseph dropped his action against the Palladium in return for a gift of shares, but then found himself being sued in the High Court by Brozel for wrongful dismissal and breach of contract. Thanks to some virtuoso, if questionable, advocacy on the singer's behalf by F. E. Smith (later Lord Birkenhead), who relied on the jury's inability to grasp the minutiae of vocal technique, Brozel won his case and was awarded £540 (£34,450) for loss of earnings. He never sang for the Beechams again. Edith Evans also sued for wrongful dismissal and was awarded her full claim and costs after Joseph's counsel admitted there was no case to answer.[4] It was put out that there had been a 'misunderstanding' between Evans and the Beechams, who later re-employed her.

After appearing at the Palladium, Thomas travelled to Sheffield to rally the Beecham Opéra Comique Company which, nearing the end of its long and exhausting tour of Britain, was performing *The Tales of Hoffmann* to abysmally small audiences at the Lyceum. 'In proportion to its size', said Thomas Quinlan, who managed the tour, 'Sheffield is the worst town we have visited since we set out last September.' Besides conducting a single performance of *Hoffmann*, Beecham attacked the city for its apathy and lack of musical taste. Not even Sheffield's choral singers were spared. Referring to what was clearly the Sheffield Festival Choir, which he had heard performing Delius's *Sea Drift* under Henry Wood, Beecham told a reporter that its members were incapable of singing quietly. 'When they got to the end they were singing louder than ever. It made you think of engine-driving and that sort of thing.' The Sheffield press was flooded with letters about the affair. Some readers supported Beecham's stand, others were quick to point out that London had not been too ready to support his operatic activities either.[5]

---

* The Alhambra Theatre, on the east side of Leicester Square, was demolished in 1936 to make way for the Odeon Cinema.

† In the following year, 1912, a more ambitious season of music-hall opera lasting six weeks was given at the Palladium by the 'Beecham Opera Company under the personal supervision of Sir Joseph Beecham'. A six-month tour followed.

The Sheffield *Hoffmann* was Beecham's last conducting engagement for three months. Concerts announced for the Beecham Symphony Orchestra at Queen's Hall were cancelled. He was said to be 'indisposed'. Other conductors took over concerts he should have given in Birmingham and in Swansea, where a local paper reported that he was 'prostrate after the exertions of the London season and in a very serious condition of ill-health'. [6] There is little doubt that the previous year's opera seasons had taken their toll: Beecham makes several references to his poor health in his correspondence with Delius at the time. He was suffering from colitis, undoubtedly brought on by stress. His public statements were consistently gloomy in tone: he would not be giving another season of opera in English, he said, because there was 'practically no demand for native talent in London'. [7] The spectre of the forthcoming Foster divorce case, set down for hearing in October, must also have contributed to his feeling of depression.

That he failed to turn up for a programme of Ethel Smyth's works with the London Symphony Orchestra at Queen's Hall on 1 April had nothing to do with his health, however. He was to have shared the conducting with the composer, but he was in France with a new companion, Maud Cunard, American wife of the baronet and shipping-line heir, Sir Bache Cunard, and had omitted to tell Smyth that he would not be back in time for the concert.* Though he took Lady Cunard to visit Delius at Grez, the main purpose of his trip was to discuss with André Messager, co-director of the Paris Opéra, the possibility of giving the French premiere of Strauss's *Elektra* there with the Beecham Symphony Orchestra and some of the principal singers who had taken part in the Covent Garden performances – a plan that came to nothing, because of opposition from local musicians. [8] †

Beecham and Maud Cunard had been lovers for about six months, though they had known each other rather longer, having met for the first time in the winter of 1909, around the time Beecham had ended his affair with Maud Foster. They had been introduced at a supper party given in London by Ethel Smyth's sister, Mrs Charles Hunter. Six years older than Beecham, Lady Cunard was small and golden-haired, enthusiastic, witty and exceptionally well read. She did not know much about music, but she was already Beecham's most unswerving

---

* 'It was a rousing welcome that Dr Smyth received when she appeared on the platform', reported the weekly *Votes for Women* (7 April 1911), 'and the applause was increased rather than lessened when she announced that, owing to the unexpected defection of Mr Thomas Beecham, she herself would conduct the entire programme, which she accordingly did, and in right masterly fashion.' By now Smyth had been a committed suffragist for seven months and the concert ended with a chorus she had written specially for the movement, *March of the Women*.

† *Elektra* was not heard in Paris until February 1932, when it was given in French at the Opéra.

admirer. Cyril Scott believed that it was largely due to her influence and energy that out of 'that shy, groundward-glancing little figure' of five years earlier there had 'emerged a figure of such force and magnetism that the whole of musical England was to feel its grandiose effects'. [9]

Maud compensated for her conventional life as châtelaine of Nevill Holt, a sprawling pile in the heart of Leicestershire's hunting country, by inviting to the house writers (among them Somerset Maugham and the Irish novelist, George Moore), musicians (Joseph Holbrooke was remembered for turning up on a motor-cycle), politicians (Herbert Asquith was a visitor before he became Prime Minister), and some of the more interesting members of the aristocracy, notably the artistic Duchess of Rutland, who became a close friend. George Moore's visits to Nevill Holt were so frequent that some assumed he was Maud's lover, though in 1957 Beecham said he had 'always understood that Moore was a case of didn't kiss but told', [10] a view supported by the novelist's biographer, Tony Gray, who thought it 'most likely that he died as he was born, a County Mayo virgin', and that all his extravagant romantic memoirs were pure fantasies'. [11] *

Sir Bache, who had married his wife in 1895, was twenty-one years older than her. Unlike many other American women who had married into British society, Maud Cunard, born Maud Alice Burke, was not a member of the East Coast aristocracy, but a Californian, which was considered less socially acceptable. Nonetheless, she had come to England with a substantial inheritance from a friend of her mother's, the Civil War general Horace Carpentier, who had made a fortune from property dealing. Sir Bache had two passions – hunting with his own pack of hounds and working in his smithy, where he fashioned love-tokens in silver and gold for his wife, which as often as not she received with subdued enthusiasm. Early in their marriage Maud, too, had hunted, but gave it up with relief when she became pregnant with their only child, the poet Nancy Cunard.

Bearing in mind the unsettled state of his marriage to Utica and the unfortunate consequences of his affair with Maud Foster, Beecham might have been expected to steer clear of a liaison with another married American, yet he seems to have entered into it with few qualms. He first visited Nevill Holt on 16 August 1910 and over the next twelve months stayed there on seven further occasions, the last one on 14 August 1911. [12] Local villagers had no illusions about what was going on at the big house. Men working one day on the stable block's clock-tower got a clear, if unexpected, view of the lovers in Lady Cunard's bedroom. [13]

---

* Moore (1852–1933) always remained jealous of Beeecham's relationship with Lady Cunard. 'It is impossible for me to allow my name to appear among those who favour Sir Thomas Beecham's operatic schemes', he wrote to her in 1927. 'You will know why.' (George Moore, *Letters to Lady Cunard, 1895–1933*, ed. Rupert Hart-Davis (London, 1957), p. 159.)

Beecham and Maud Cunard returned from their visit to France in time for the opening on 22 April of the Covent Garden grand season. The *Musical Standard* expressed disappointment that, although Beecham had joined the syndicate, he was not down to conduct. The decision may have been Beecham's, rather than Covent Garden's. He was never much of a team-player – unless he was the captain. He did make one conducting appearance in London at this time, however, when on 16 June he gave an all-Delius concert with the Beecham Symphony Orchestra at Queen's Hall, which the composer attended. Besides *Appalachia*, *Paris* and the first *Dance Rhapsody*, the programme included the first performance of the *Songs of Sunset*. The audience was one of the largest of the season, but another four months were to pass before he conducted again.

The *Musical Standard* had one further complaint about the grand season, that despite Beecham's appointment to the syndicate, there was virtually no improvement in its choice of operatic repertoire, which, apart from the British premiere of Puccini's latest opera, *La fanciulla del West*, was frustratingly predictable, with not one German opera included. Where, asked the *Musical Standard*, was Strauss's new opera, *Der Rosenkavalier*, recently premiered with great success in Dresden? 'The stir an opera makes abroad, to say nothing of its composer's great reputation, has but little influence with the conservative directors of the Royal Opera Syndicate ... We long for another Beecham opera season, with its wonderful enterprise.' [14] * Perhaps the musical press expected too much of Beecham. On joining the syndicate, he had expressed doubts to a reporter that he was in a position to exert any influence on his fellow board members, who included the Marquis of Ripon, Viscount Esher, the banker and composer Baron d'Erlanger and, as chairman, the well-connected solicitor Henry Higgins. 'I am a young man', said Beecham (he was thirty-one at the time), 'and some of them are older, and I may want to go further than they are disposed to go. I have a tendency that way, but, still, they are very nice people.' [15]

Predictably the Russian ballet caused a sensation when it made its London debut on 21 June 1911. Diaghilev, perhaps playing for safety in the face of British conservatism, decided not to perform either of the company's most remarkable creations to date, the two Stravinsky ballets, *The Firebird* of a year earlier and *Petrushka*, which had been premiered in Paris only eight days before the London visit. Nonetheless, Covent Garden's society-dominated audiences were dazzled, first by the sheer expressiveness of the dancers, secondly by the originality of Michel Fokine's choreography, which in *Carnaval*, *Les sylphides*, *Le spectre de la rose*, *Scheherazade* and *Polovtsian Dances* brought a new dimension to classical dancing; and thirdly by the exotic designs of Benois, Roerich and

---

* Puccini's opera had been premiered at the Metropolitan Opera, New York, on 10 December 1910, *Der Rosenkavalier* in Dresden on 26 January 1911.

Bakst, which were to make a considerable impact on British design and fashion. The season, wrote the music critic of the *Daily News*, proved that 'the ballet, as developed in Russia, is a serious form of art, and not merely a frivolous excuse for showing pretty girls and dresses behind the footlights'.[16]

Beecham's orchestra played for the ballet with distinction. Diaghilev's musical director for the season, the composer-conductor Nikolai Cherepnin, was reported as saying that he had toured throughout Europe with the company, but that nowhere else had he found such sympathetic orchestral playing as he had in London. The string players all 'sang' on their instruments and took more pleasure in their work than their counterparts in the Continental orchestras he had encountered. (By then the company had also performed in Paris, Berlin, Monte Carlo, Brussels and Rome.) Cherepnin singled out Albert Sammons's fine playing of the solo violin part in *Scheherazade* as proof that British players had temperament.[17]

In September 1911 Beecham accompanied his father on a business trip to New York, the first time he had been to the United States since 1891, when as a schoolboy he had visited the Chicago World's Exposition. They sailed on the *Lusitania*. Writing to Delius from his hotel opposite Grand Central Station, Beecham said that he was now feeling much better than he had when they had last met, though he still felt disillusioned about musical prospects in Britain.[18] He told the *New York Times* that he was thinking of mounting festivals of Mozart and Strauss operas in the city, but in a leading article the paper warned him that such projects were doomed to failure. No more was heard of the idea.[19]

Beecham returned to London for what looked like a busy autumn season. He had contracts to conduct the concerts of the Birmingham Philharmonic Society, as well as those of the Cardiff Orchestral Society, which had signed him up in the hope that he would 'raise the prestige of Cardiff as a musical centre'.[20] He gave his first concert with the Liverpool Philharmonic Society's orchestra and his first official one with the Hallé. In November he was due to conduct the British premiere of Humperdinck's latest opera, *Königskinder*, during a special autumn season of German opera and Russian dance organised by the syndicate, but he withdrew from it at an early stage, for fear, it seems, that rehearsals would coincide with the Foster divorce case.

By awkward coincidence, Beecham's first Birmingham concert and the start of the Foster hearing both took place on Wednesday, 18 October 1911. He began the day at the Law Courts, where he and Maud Foster sat on either side of their joint solicitor, and at the adjournment in the afternoon he took the train to Birmingham for the concert. The case, heard before Mr Justice Bargrave Deane and a special jury, took eight days, spread over two weeks. It was a matter of wide public interest.[21] The *Daily Telegraph* published a 3,000-word report on the first day's proceedings (it printed around 36,000 words in all) and both the *Daily Sketch* and *Daily Mirror* devoted the whole of their front pages to photographs of the Fosters, Beecham, the judge, leading counsel and one of the witnesses, Prince Bariatinsky.* Two days later the *Mirror's* front page had a picture of a trilby-hatted Beecham hurrying along the pavement outside the court during the lunch-break, and another of Maud Foster, described as 'a handsome young lady with a profusion of brown hair', taking tea and a lobster salad at the Law Courts' restaurant. The judge, suspicious that she was courting publicity, was not at all pleased to see it.

As expected, George Foster asked for the dissolution of his marriage on the grounds of his wife's alleged misconduct with the co-respondent, Thomas Beecham, described in court as 'a gentleman connected with the music profession, who has had a great deal to do with concerts and operas'. Both Beecham and Mrs Foster denied the allegations made against them, and she in turn counter-charged her husband with misconduct and cruelty, because of which she asked for a divorce. Since the pair had not been observed *in flagrante delicto*, everything depended on circumstantial evidence. Much was made of Beecham's letter of July 1909 that Maud had hidden in her stocking, where it was found by the housekeeper. Mr Foster's counsel, Montague Shearman, KC, thought that the letter's final words, 'All my heart is with you tonight and always, my love, my darling. – T', could be only one thing – a declaration of love. But Beecham maintained that the effusive language merely reflected his elation over the success of *The Wreckers* and the reconciliation with his father. At the time, he said, he was 'so exalted' that he was not responsible for anything he wrote or said.

Shearman then produced a letter, also in Beecham's hand, which George Foster had intercepted, steamed open, photographed and put back in its envelope before leaving it for his wife. It read in part, 'Please tell me where we meet tomorrow ... I have a terrific day, but I will try and steal an hour to see you. No old princess I can assure you, only you, you, you.' The second 'you' was underlined twice, the third one three times and both the first and last four times. Shearman suggested to the court that 'Mr Beecham must have been madly in love to write such a letter to another man's wife.' Beecham replied there was no significance whatever in the words 'you, you, you'; they came from a music-hall song.†

---

* In 1911 newspapers were at liberty to report freely on divorce hearings, provided they did not transgress the obscenity and indecency laws. Change came in 1927 with the Judicial Proceedings (Regulation of Reports) Act, which still restricts what can be reported in such hearings.

† The judge said he had never heard of it, but two days later Beecham's counsel produced a copy of a song by Frank Leo called 'You, You, You', which had been made popular by the music-hall artist, Wilkie Bard.

There was also a good deal of discussion about a secret code, apparently devised by Katherine Ruth Heyman for use in messages passing between Beecham and Maud Foster. Beecham was 'Fire', Mrs Foster 'Beastie', George Foster 'Philanthropist', and Heyman herself 'Brangaene', named, most suitably, after the lovers' go-between in Wagner's *Tristan und Isolde*. There was little proof that it had been used much.

Domestic servants employed by both the Fosters and Beechams were called by Montague Shearman to give evidence that was then disputed by either Maud Foster or Beecham. Mrs Annie Wightman, who lived in the basement at Redcliffe Square and acted as both caretaker and Mrs Foster's cook, said that in May and June 1909 Beecham had frequently called on Mrs Foster and had dined alone with her at the house on about ten occasions. One evening, said Mrs Wightman, she thought Mrs Foster was out, because there were no lights on in the house, but, when she went upstairs, she discovered to her surprise that she had been in the drawing-room all along, in the dark with Beecham.

Next to be heard was Mrs Ostler, wife of a Borehamwood cowman, who had been called in to help in the kitchen when, at Beecham's invitation, the Bariatinskys, Katherine Ruth Heyman and Maud Foster had arrived on 9 September 1909 for their extended visit to Borehamwood while Utica and the children were on holiday at Bournemouth.* Beecham, said Mrs Ostler, had stayed there the first night to make sure that the arrangements went smoothly. On passing the drawing-room door that evening she had noticed him sitting at the piano with Mrs Foster's arms round his neck. Later, Mrs Foster had come to the kitchen and given orders for Beecham's breakfast the next morning. She told Mrs Ostler that she had been a widow for four years. Beecham slept in the nursery and went back to London the next morning, though he returned to Borehamwood several times later in the month. In an attempt to minimise the closeness of Maud Foster's relationship with Beecham, her counsel, George Elliott, KC, sought to establish that there was a strong bond between Beecham and Utica. Were not Mr and Mrs Beecham on the most affectionate terms? he asked Mrs Ostler. 'Not on such terms as I am with my husband', she replied to laughter. On 'good terms' then? asked Elliott. 'Favourable terms', said Mrs Ostler, who was not prepared to go any further.

Mrs Ostler's sixteen-year-old daughter, Agnes, who was employed as a maid in the house, said that Beecham had reappeared at Borehamwood for the last time on 12 October, when he and Mrs Foster were the only two people to spend the night there, apart from herself and the cook. By then the rest of the guests had gone. Both Beecham and Mrs Foster left the next morning. Beecham described

---

* At some point Ezra Pound also joined the party.

the story as 'a complete fabrication'. At the time, he said, he had been on tour with his orchestra and on that particular night had conducted a concert at the Corn Exchange, Bedford. Mrs Foster, he admitted, had been in the audience. Bedford was only thirty miles from Borehamwood by rail. There was a late train from there that would have taken them to Elstree station just before midnight, but Beecham insisted that after the concert they had travelled instead to London, where he had slept the night at an hotel in Endsleigh Gardens, opposite Euston station. It was not said where Mrs Foster had slept.

Maud Foster turned out to be a reckless witness. In her petition she claimed that in July 1909 her husband had committed adultery at the Cock Inn at Whitchurch, Hampshire, with Annie Wightman, the Redcliffe Square caretaker, but in court she failed to produce any evidence to support the accusation. Her charge that George Foster had been guilty of cruelty fell equally flat (she had accused him of, among other things, infecting her with gonorrhoea in 1906)[22] and her counsel was left with the sole task of trying to prove that she had not committed misconduct herself.

Beecham, the *Daily Mirror* reported, 'strode with as much easy dignity and grace into the witness-box as if he were taking his place in front of his orchestra'. To the *News of the World* he looked 'like a smart French army officer, being tall and slim, with neatly trimmed, glistening black hair, a thick black moustache and chin-beard, and large, dark, expressive eyes', a good description of him at the time, apart from the fact he was short, not tall. His counsel, Henry Dickens, KC, sixth son of the novelist, led him through a series of questions about both his career and the allegations made against him.

Beecham appeared confident, even when Dickens brought up the subject of Mr Roche, the detective. Dickens asked if there was the slightest foundation for a suggestion that Beecham had been a party with Roche in trying to get a woman into Redcliffe Square for the purpose of entrapping Mr Foster and then charging him with misconduct. 'Absolutely none at all', replied Beecham. Montague Shearman then rose to cross-examine him. He produced evidence that Mrs Foster was certainly implicated in such a plot, and suggested that Beecham, as Roche's paymaster, must have been aware of it too, even if he had not entirely approved of it. Beecham agreed that he had paid Roche around £326 (£20,800) for services rendered. He may not have realised it, but Shearman was closing in for the kill:

> Shearman: Did you appreciate that the man was collecting evidence for someone else, and that if you retained him he obviously could not use what evidence he had collected against you? – No, I did not. I was ignorant of those matters then.

> Shearman: Did it not occur to you that to undertake to pay a person watching

you was bribing him not to disclose the evidence he had obtained? – I did not think so at the time.

With these two questions Shearman firmly planted in the court's mind the thought that Beecham had employed Roche to stop him revealing damaging information about Maud Foster and himself.

On the penultimate day, in what seemed like an act of desperation, Henry Dickens called Utica to the witness-box to testify on behalf of her husband. The *News of the World*'s reporter described her as 'a very pretty woman, dressed in a black tailor-made costume and a large hat trimmed with blue ostrich feathers'. With Shearman on the rampage the risks involved were great. Two days earlier Beecham had assured the court that he had always been on very affectionate terms with his wife, and Utica agreed that this was indeed the case. Dickens asked her if she knew that her husband had been meeting Mrs Foster. 'Yes', Utica replied, 'and I encouraged him in it.' 'Why?', asked Dickens. 'She seemed quite enthusiastic and knew a great deal about music, and knew d'Indy in Paris and a number of people I thought would be a help to him.' Did she know that Mrs Foster had been staying at Borehamwood when she had been in Bournemouth? 'Yes.' Did she know that her husband went there during that time? 'Yes.'

In cross-examination, Shearman asked Utica if she had the letters that her husband had written to her in Bournemouth during the summer of 1909. She replied that she did not have all of them. Could she produce one in which he mentioned Mrs Foster's name? Utica had to confess that she couldn't, because, she claimed, her desk had been broken into and her letters were missing. It was not a convincing answer. In the end she admitted to Shearman that she knew almost nothing about the case, apart from what she had read in the newspapers, which, inevitably, suggested to the court that her relationship with her husband was not perhaps as close as had been made out.

Utica was the last witness. After she had finished her evidence Beecham's counsel began his final address to the jury, during which Maud Foster sat weeping quietly until, eventually, she left the court. 'If it had not been for the "darling" and the "you, you, you" letters, claimed Dickens, the case would never have got as far as it had – it was the weakest case of misconduct ever brought into court.*

Beecham was not present on the final day of the hearing, but Mrs Foster was. She sat with head bowed as her counsel, George Elliott, employed, in the words of a reporter, 'all the arts known to the Bar to stir the jury to sympathy with

---

* On the following morning, 28 October, the *Daily Sketch* published a three-column photograph of Utica with her two children, Adrian, now seven, and the two-year-old Tommie. Adrian is shown in a dress, a form of attire that Utica insisted on him wearing until he was eight.

her'. Shearman, who followed, was by contrast 'short, sharp and unsentimental'. The jury had heard some wonderful oratory, he said, but what had it heard of the true facts of the case? Mr Elliott, he continued, had quoted a passage from Gray's 'Elegy' ending with the words, 'living lyre', which, he would like to suggest, aptly described Mr Elliott's chief witness – Mrs Foster. Summing up, the judge told the jury that in cases such as this, where there was no actual evidence of guilt, it had to decide 'whether the parties charged had the opportunity as well as the inclination to commit misconduct'. It had heard the witnesses and now it must steer a way through the many contradictions and see where the truth lay.

It took the jury just a quarter of an hour to come to a verdict. The final words of the hearing were brief and to the point:

> Mr Widdicombe, clerk of the court, to the foreman of the jury: Do you find that George Sherwood Foster has committed adultery? – No.
>
> Do you find that he committed cruelty? – No.
>
> Do you find that Maud Christian Foster committed adultery with Thomas Beecham? – Yes.
>
> Do you find that Thomas Beecham committed adultery with Maud Christian Foster? – Yes.
>
> Mr Shearman (for George Foster): I ask for a decree nisi, with costs against the co-respondent.
>
> His Lordship: Yes.

Three months later Beecham was ordered to lodge the sum of £694 11s 6d (£44,300) in court to cover George Foster's legal costs.[23] The amount of his own costs is not known, but it must have been considerable. Nor is it known if he paid Maud Foster's costs as well.

According to Beecham's first biographer, Charles Reid, a duchess telephoned Utica after the hearing, urging her to start divorce proceedings against her husband. 'I do not believe in divorce', said Utica.[24] Remarkably, the Beechams' marriage struggled on. *Mrs Bull*, sister-paper of the weekly *John Bull*, castigated Beecham in an open letter to him signed 'Mary Bull': 'There is nothing more shocking in our human relations than for a woman to hold her marriage ties as lightly as Mrs Foster did, or for a man to intrigue for her affections as you did, to the wrecking of another man's home.'[25] Bishop Welldon, dean of Manchester and one of the Hallé's guarantors, publicly attacked the orchestra for not withdrawing its invitation to Beecham to conduct one of its concerts. The ladies of the Hallé choir, he said, might 'reasonably object to association with a man whom they would not wish to meet and know in private life'. The dean was widely ridiculed in the press for his Grundyism.[26]

In a burst of hypocrisy (readers of the Cardiff-based *Western Mail* had enjoyed some of the longest and most detailed reports of the hearing in the country), the Cardiff Orchestral Society dropped Beecham as its conductor even before he had had a chance to give his first concert, and replaced him, without explanation, with 'the greatest conductor living', the recently knighted Sir Henry Wood.[27] Beecham withdrew from the Birmingham Philharmonic concert he was to have conducted eight days after the case ended (he handed it over to Percy Pitt), but was there for the next one on 22 November. There were many empty seats, and the applause that greeted his entrance was tepid. 'Let us pray', he said, as he turned to the orchestra to conduct the opening item, Beethoven's Eighth Symphony. Even fewer people turned up for the first Birmingham performance of Elgar's Second Symphony, which Beecham conducted on 6 December. The *Birmingham Gazette*'s reviewer did not care for the work, but noted that 'thanks to the rich scoring, every movement was applauded, those most loudly that ended with the greatest crash'. In the *Post*, Ernest Newman thought it best to draw a veil over the occasion: 'What the cause of the thorough badness of the performance may have been we can only conjecture; it may have been due to insufficient rehearsal, or to a lack of sympathy with the work on Mr Beecham's part, or to the two combined.' *

It may have been a difficult time for Thomas, but his father was flourishing. In September 1911 Joseph had bought a ninety-two-year lease on the Aldwych Theatre in London, which, after refurbishment, he reopened with a popular Christmas show, *The Golden Land of Fairy Tales*, a compilation of fairy tales by the Grimm brothers with copious incidental music by the Hungarian operetta composer Heinrich Berté.† A contingent of the Beecham Symphony Orchestra played in the pit under Emil Kreuz. Two weeks into the run Joseph received a knighthood in the 1912 New Year's Honours, an accolade applauded by the press, which found the rest of the list dull, unimaginative and too full of Herbert Asquith's Liberal party supporters. 'Arise, indeed, Sir Knight of the Pestle!', proclaimed the *Saturday Review*. Joseph had recently begun a third term as mayor of St Helens, at the unanimous request of the town council, and in February 1912, as a gesture of gratitude, he brought *The Golden Land of Fairy Tales*, complete with the London cast and the Beecham orchestra, to the St Helens Theatre

---

* Elgar himself had conducted the work's premiere seven months earlier at Queen's Hall. The sparseness of the audiences in Birmingham was likely to have been the result of the city's general apathy for concerts in general, rather than anything to do with Beecham's private life. In 1913 the orchestra was wound up for lack of support.

† Berté (1857–1924) was best known for his 1916 operetta *Das Dreimäderlhaus*, based, without too much care for historical fact, on the life of Schubert. In the early 1920s it enjoyed success in New York as *Blossom Time* and in London as *Lilac Time*.

Royal for a week, at a personal cost of £1,200 (£76,500). More than 12,000 schoolchildren saw the show at special matinées, to which they were brought by trams paid for by Joseph.

In the same month Thomas's marriage to Utica finally disintegrated, and he moved out of Hamilton Terrace. Shortly before this he had written to Delius, telling him that he was now feeling stronger and more tranquil and that he had been spending time with Lady Cunard.[28] By now she had left her husband, taking her fifteen-year-old daughter Nancy with her, and was renting Asquith's palatial London house, 20 Cavendish Square, which was being let while he was at 10 Downing Street. Utica stayed on at Hamilton Terrace with the children, but her parents, together with Beecham's mother, Josephine, left South Kensington and went to live at Mursley Hall, the house in Buckinghamshire that Thomas had been left by his grandfather. Josephine, now in her early sixties and frail, occasionally accepted invitations from Joseph to attend the opera. Despite his earlier behaviour towards her, she asked him more than once to take her back, but, perhaps wisely, he refused to do so. Josephine, realising that there was no chance of a reconciliation, grew fretful and disillusioned.[29]

It seems that Beecham did not move into 20 Cavendish Square with Lady Cunard, though they spent a good deal of time in each other's company.* They went to Holloway Prison in the hope of visiting Ethel Smyth, who in early March had been arrested during a suffragette demonstration for throwing a stone through a window of the Belgrave Square home of the Secretary of State for the Colonies, Lewis Harcourt, and in consequence had been given a two-month prison sentence by the Bow Street magistrate. Smyth was in the next cell to the movement's leader, Mrs Pankhurst, but Beecham and Cunard were not allowed to see her, because they had failed to obtain the necessary permit.[30] Beecham writes in *A Mingled Chime* that he caught a glimpse of her beating time with a toothbrush from the window of her cell as her fellow inmates marched round the prison courtyard singing a suffragette anthem.

Despite the upheavals in his private life, Beecham pressed on with conducting engagements in London, Birmingham and Manchester. On 20 March he gave another mayoral invitation concert for Joseph at St Helens Town Hall with the Beecham Symphony Orchestra. On the following night he and the orchestra were at the Victoria Hall, Hanley, for a concert promoted by the North Staffordshire District Choral Society. The main work was Elgar's *Dream of Gerontius*, conducted by the choir's director, Herbert Whittaker. Beecham opened the evening with the *Flying Dutchman* overture and, in an act of devilry that may have reflected his opinion of the oratorio, closed it with an unexpected encore,

---

* In a letter to Delius (12 December 1912), Beecham asked the composer always to write to him at the Devonshire Club. A year later he was staying at Carr's Hotel in Jermyn Street.

Johann Strauss's *Blue Danube* waltz, which he had conducted at St Helens the night before. The local paper was taken aback: 'One is hardly sure that the inclusion of this item in a programme which contained "The Dream of Gerontius" was the proper thing. Not a few present would feel strongly on the point in all likelihood, but it is notable that no one apparently left the concert room before this bewitching music was played; and the burst of cheering which broke out at its conclusion at any rate proved that the majority of those present were in no way offended at those responsible for the addition to the programmed items. Certain it is that never before has this music been interpreted locally with the swing, and feeling and poetry that were its special claims to recognition on this occasion.[31]

At the beginning of May, Covent Garden announced that Beecham would be one of conductors for the Diaghilev company, now named the Ballets Russes, when it returned to the Opera House in June to share the second half of the 1912 grand season. The press greeted the news with some incredulity, because, apart from the single performance of *The Dryad* with Adeline Genée five years earlier, Beecham had no experience as a ballet conductor. To Diaghilev, however, it made excellent sense. In order keep his company afloat financially, he needed the help and backing of theatrical entrepreneurs who had as much courage and artistic flair as himself. In Paris, after a bumpy start, he had come to rely on the French impresario Gabriel Astruc. Now, in London, he was forging links with the Beechams that would prove to be of great benefit to both parties. Since the Beecham orchestra had again been invited to play for his dancers, it was a logical and prudent step for Diaghilev to ask Beecham to conduct two of the ballets, a revival of *Scheherazade* and a piece new to London, *Thamar*, choreographed by Fokine to Balakirev's powerfully evocative symphonic poem *Tamara*.

Based on a poem by Lermontov, *Thamar* tells of a cruel queen in the Caucasus who lures a young prince into her castle and then, after dancing with him ecstatically, stabs him to death before turning her sights on the next unwitting passer-by. The ballet was premiered in Paris at the Théâtre du Châtelet only three weeks before it was seen in London. Beecham crossed the Channel in order, as one British newspaper put it, to study 'the intricacies of the elusive art'.[32] He attended the rehearsals and the initial performances under Monteux.

The piece left a strong impression on Cyril Beaumont, chronicler of Diaghilev's London visits, who saw the performance at Covent Garden on 18 June, the third of the eleven *Thamar*s that Beecham conducted that season with Karsavina dancing the title-role: 'The curtain rose slowly to reveal Bakst's setting – a great room with walls coloured mauve and purple, and slanting ceiling painted green. The lighting was subdued, save for the dull glow of a dying fire. The scene was dominated by a huge divan set against the far wall, and upon the divan reposed Karsavina in the role of Thamar, Queen of Georgia. Stretched at full length, she occasionally stirred uneasily in her sleep. A waiting-woman sat near her couch, other retainers stood in the shadows, their attitudes strained and watchful ... The curiosity aroused was intense. What was about to happen?'³³ * Not all the London critics shared Beaumont's enthusiasm. Some of them found *Thamar* gloomy, oppressive and altogether less enjoyable than the brilliantly coloured and, by comparison, superficial *Scheherazade*, which Beecham conducted seven times with a cast that included Nijinsky, Karsavina, Adolf Bolm and the veteran Enrico Cecchetti. It was generally agreed that he acquitted himself well.

After a holiday in Venice with Maud Cunard, Beecham returned to London, where he announced the formation of a new ensemble, the fifty-strong Beecham Wind Orchestra, with Emile Gilmer, principal clarinet of the Beecham Symphony Orchestra, as its principal conductor and trainer. The wind orchestra, which made its debut in mid-October, included a number of unusual instruments, including bass oboe, heckelphone, basset horns, sarrusophones and bass trumpet. In his prospectus, Beecham declared that his purpose was to raise the standards of brass and woodwind playing in London, which, he maintained, had declined steadily during the previous ten years.³⁴ Promising young players would be given the chance to play alongside experienced principals from the London orchestras. The idea was excellent, but after three months of concerts under Gilmer the project was abandoned for lack of support from the public. It might have helped if Beecham had had the time to conduct it more often. It seems he only appeared with it once, sharing the podium with Gilmer at a concert at St Helens Town Hall on 7 November 1912.

In December Beecham made his German debut, conducting two concerts in Berlin with the Beecham Symphony Orchestra, the first at the Hochschule für Musik on 16 December, the second at the Blüthnersaal five days later. The orchestra had already been in the city for some weeks, playing under Monteux for the Ballets Russes at the Kroll Opera House. Stravinsky was delighted by its performances of both *The Firebird*, with which it was familiar, and *Petrushka*, which it had not played before. (The work had still not been given in London.) 'I've never heard such marvellous sounds anywhere as this amazing orchestra revealed in my scores', the composer wrote to the Moscow concert promoter, Vladimir Derzhanovsky. 'Also their attitude to me and my works was highly

---

* A recording of Balakirev's *Tamara* that Beecham made with the Royal Philharmonic Orchestra in 1954 shows him to have had an almost uncanny affinity with the work's fusion of 'orientalism' and romanticism (Sony CD, SMK91171).

considerate and artistic. Oh, if only Russian audiences could hear my music played by them!' [35] *

Beecham's Berlin programmes included Mozart's 'Prague' Symphony and movements from his Divertimento K131, overtures by Paisiello (*Nina*), Méhul (*La chasse du jeune Henri*) and Berlioz (*Le carnaval romain*), and several British works by Delius, Vaughan Williams, Grainger, Holbrooke and Bantock. Despite their success at the Kroll, the players had anticipated the concerts with some trepidation. It seemed that no British orchestra had given a concert in the German capital before, and, as Beecham told *The Observer*'s Berlin correspondent, there was a widely held belief that the city's critics 'stood waiting for Anglo-Saxon artists at the frontier, tomahawk in hand, ready to massacre them on the mere notification or an intention to invade these artistic preserves'. [36] Such fears turned out to be groundless.

'The Beecham Orchestra is without doubt one of the best in the world', declared the *Vossische Zeitung*, a view shared by a number of other papers. 'Where on earth does England, and especially London, find all these excellent instrumentalists?', asked the musical weekly, *Signale*. 'Only young men have a place in Mr Beecham's organisation and every one of them seems to be a true artist. The violins have a rich and noble tone, the woodwind a fascinating lustre, and, if the brass perhaps does not quite match the dignity and amplitude of our best German brass, it displays an unusual sensitivity in its playing. It never blares.'

If some found Beecham's podium style idiosyncratic and distracting (*Germania* described it as an 'elegant agility scarcely known to us here'), they were happy to hail him as a 'geborene Dirigent', a born conductor. There was some disagreement about his abilities as a Mozart interpreter, but *Signale*'s critic averred that he had 'never heard a performance of Delius's *Brigg Fair* under any other conductor – Nikisch not excluded – that was so spontaneous, so wonderfully nuanced, so compelling.' † Delius's *Paris* was given at the second concert, which Strauss attended. Beecham told Delius that Strauss was 'immensely impressed' by the work, which he had not heard before. [37] Percy Grainger's jolly *Mock Morris* was such a hit with the audience at the first concert that it was repeated at the second, but, despite claims to the contrary made by Beecham on his return to London, the remaining British works in the programmes did not fare so well, at least not with the critics. Vaughan Williams's *In the Fen Country*

---

* In referring to the British musicians' positive attitude to him, Stravinsky was comparing them with the Parisian players who, when Monteux started to rehearse them for *Petrushka*'s premiere in June 1911, broke into incredulous laughter.

† High praise indeed. At the time Nikisch was conductor of the Berlin Philharmonic Orchestra.

was scarcely mentioned in the countless reviews; Joseph Holbrooke was taken to task for quite failing in his 'unenjoyable' symphonic poem *Ulalume* to match the unsettling atmosphere of Edgar Alan Poe's verses that had inspired it; and, while it was admitted that Bantock had talent, his *Fifine at the Fair* was criticised for lacking the inspiration that made the listener sit up in expectation of a revelation. For the *Vossische Zeitung*, the work left 'a flat aftertaste of disappointment on the tongue'. However, wrote the *Allgemeine Musik-Zeitung*, Beecham's 'mastery of these works was no less amazing than his capacity to make his orchestra receptive to the music.'[38]

After the concerts Beecham stayed on to hear Strauss conduct *Der Rosenkavalier* at the Hofoper on 23 December. His huge and very real success in the German capital established his international credentials and did much to strengthen Anglo-German musical relations. There was not even a hint that in just over a year and a half Britain and Germany would be at war.

CHAPTER 7

Towards the Abyss

TWO YEARS had now passed since the Beechams mounted a season of their own at Covent Garden. The reason for not returning there was a practical one. Before committing himself to another hugely expensive venture, Joseph Beecham had wanted to gauge the impact on the capital's operatic life of the new, luxurious London Opera House which was to open in November 1911. The theatre was being built by the free-spirited American impresario, Oscar Hammerstein* to a design by Bertie Crowe. Situated on the east side of Kingsway, between Sardinia and Portugal Streets, it would have 2,700 seats – 800 more than Covent Garden. A two-shilling (£6.32) unreserved seat in the gallery, said Hammerstein, would be as comfortable as an expensive one in the stalls. 'I trust to my ears and to my eyes', he said, 'and I have an unbounded confidence in my abilities.'¹ In 1909 the directors of the Metropolitan Opera in New York, anxious to eliminate the strong competition from Hammerstein's rival Manhattan Opera House, had handed him $1,200,000 (equivalent to £15.5 million sterling in 2008) in return for a written promise that he would not give any more opera in New York for ten years. To Hammerstein it seemed more than enough money to try his luck in London

Joseph told a New York journalist that although he felt no disrespect for Hammerstein, he had certain doubts about his plans. Selling the cheaper seats would not be difficult, he said, but to succeed, the American would need the support of Society subscribers, who might not want to enlist in his venture. The interviewer, accustomed to a more flamboyant kind of impresario, was impressed by Joseph's demeanour. 'In personal appearance', he wrote, 'he represents the quiet, pipe-smoking, tweed-clad type of Englishman. He has neither business nor artistic pose, and is modesty itself. He is of medium height and wears a closely cropped moustache. Asked for a picture of himself he said that he never had had one taken and did not intend to begin now.'²

Preceded by frenzied publicity, Hammerstein's theatre opened with the London premiere of *Quo Vadis?*, a spectacular, but worthless opera by the French

---

* Oscar Hammerstein I (1847–1919) was born in Germany (it is not clear where) and brought up in Berlin. At the age of fifteen he left home and emigrated to New York, where, after doing menial work in a tobacco factory, he invented and patented cigar-making machines. An enthusiasm for the theatre and opera in particular led him to build twelve theatres in all. His celebrated grandson, Oscar Hammerstein II, wrote the lyrics for some of Broadway's best-known musicals, stretching from *Show Boat* to *The Sound of Music*.

composer Jean Nouguès, set in Nero's Rome. The first-night audience included a pair of dukes (Marlborough and Rutland), Prince Nicholas of Greece, the American, Austro-Hungarian and Portuguese ambassadors, Lady Cunard (doubtless acting as a spy for the Beechams) and 'a host of fashionable and distinguished visitors', [3] but unfortunately for Hammerstein few of them returned for subsequent performances. The repertoire of French and Italian operas was not uninteresting – it included Rossini's *Guillaume Tell*, Bellini's *Norma* (with recycled scenery from *Quo Vadis?*) and the London premiere of Massenet's *Don Quichotte* – but Hammerstein soon discovered that, just as Joseph Beecham had warned, he had to sell the expensive seats as well as the cheap ones, and this he was failing to do. He lacked the star singers and the Diaghilev dancers who proved such a draw at Covent Garden's 1912 grand season.

In desperation, Hammerstein first lowered seat prices and then introduced operas in English. He even premiered an English opera, Holbrooke's *The Children of Don*,* with Nikisch conducting its first performance. The *Times* critic found it well staged and decently sung, but 'quite unintelligible to all who had not spent hours of preliminary study upon it'; in short, it was probably 'the most severe blow which the struggling cause of British opera has sustained for many years'. In August 1912, nine months after his theatre had opened, Hammerstein admitted defeat. He told the press that he had lost £45,000 (£2.8 million) on the venture, though the true figure was probably four times that much. The London Opera House was sold to Oswald Stoll, who renamed it the Stoll Theatre and used it for variety shows.† Hammerstein returned to New York, built one last theatre there, the Lexington Opera House, and died, virtually penniless, in 1919.

Joseph was now ready to return to the fray with a series of events of extraordinary artistic splendour. In June 1912, by which time it had become clear that Hammerstein was already on the ropes, he had bought the British performing rights to Strauss's *Der Rosenkavalier*. The press jumped to the conclusion that Thomas would conduct it for the Covent Garden syndicate,[4] but he and his father had other plans. It was to open a season of operas by Strauss and Wagner, together with performances by the Ballets Russes, which they were to mount at Covent Garden in January 1913. Joseph had already paid Diaghilev an advance of £950 (£58,000).[5] As well as the new *Rosenkavalier*, there were to be revivals of *Salome* (again with Aino Ackté), *Elektra*, *Tristan und Isolde* and an opera

* *The Children of Don* was the first of a trilogy of operas, based on the cycle of Welsh stories, the *Mabinogion*, with librettos by T. E. Ellis, pen-name of the composer's (and Beecham's) patron, Lord Howard de Walden.

† The Stoll was eventually demolished in 1958 and replaced by an office block. In its basement is the small Peacock Theatre.

Beecham had not conducted before, *Die Meistersinger* (his reading of it, said the *Telegraph*, had an unusual 'freshness and youthfulness.') To avoid a repeat of the huge losses incurred in the winter season of 1910, this one would last only six weeks, half the length of its predecessor. It would also be far more strictly organised than its predecessors.

In Germany, *Der Rosenkavalier* had suffered some minor amendments at the hands of the court censor, so it came as no surprise when in London the Lord Chamberlain asked for changes to both the German libretto and an English-language version prepared by Alfred Kalisch. By now Earl Spencer had retired from the post; and his place been taken by Lord Sandhurst, a former governor of Bombay and by all accounts a genial fellow.* The surviving correspondence between his department and the company over *Der Rosenkavalier* suggests that his regime was more helpful than his predecessor's, though Charles Brookfield, his examiner of plays (a Spencer appointment), initially found the opera 'a sala-cious piece. The idea – & still more, the spectacle – of a man [Baron Ochs] getting his passions aroused by the appearance & <u>minauderies</u> [simperings] of another man dressed up as a woman [Octavian masquerading as the maid-servant 'Mariandel'] is very revolting.' Brookfield added that since the role of Octavian was to be sung by a woman, the situation was not, perhaps, as bad as it might have been.[6]

Though Hugo von Hofmannsthal's text was left more or less intact, problems arose over the beds that feature in both the first and last acts. At the Dresden premiere two years earlier the Marschallin had been obliged to receive her young lover's attentions at the beginning of the opera, not, as the stage-direction speci-fies, lying in a canopied four-poster bed, but sitting on a sofa. The Lord Cham-berlain's office went one step further. It insisted not only that the Marschallin should be seated, but also that the action should be moved from her bedcham-ber to a room described in a rewritten stage-direction as her 'petit salon', fur-nished with 'a small table, chairs, etc'. Similarly, in the last act, the curtained-off bed in the alcove, on which Ochs hopes to seduce 'Mariandel', was to remain invisible to the audience – even when the curtain was pulled back – though, oddly, Octavian was still allowed to refer to it, albeit in a slightly altered form.†

---

* Sandhurst's first wife was Spencer's daughter, Lady Victoria Alexandrina Spencer, who died in 1906.

† In von Hofmannsthal's original, Octavian, on pulling back the curtain, exclaims: 'Jesus Maria, steht a Bett drin, a mordsmässig grosses. Ja mei, wer schlaf denn da?' ('Jesus Maria, there's a bed there, an incredibly big one. Goodness me, who sleeps there?') Ochs: 'Das wird Sie schon seh'n.' (You'll see pretty soon.') At the Lord Chamberlain's request, Octavian's second sentence and Ochs's reply became: 'Ja mei, es ist gar gross' (or, as the officially approved translation had it, 'Bless me! 'Tis very big'); Ochs: 'Sie haben ganz recht' ('I think you are right').

Beecham regarded this particular change as a 'near perfect' example of British compromise.[7]

The first night of *Der Rosenkavalier* was sold out within hours of the box-office's opening, and business was brisk for the rest of the season, thanks to Joseph's decision to keep the price of the most expensive seats down to £1 (£61.50) on *Rosenkavalier* nights and fifteen shillings (£46.13) at other times. Best of all from a financial point of view, Lady Cunard succeeded – where Hammerstein, and indeed the Beechams themselves in 1910, had failed – in filling the boxes by dragooning royalty, the aristocracy, the diplomatic corps, the rich and the famous, into buying subscriptions for winter opera. Even Lord Sandhurst, the Lord Chamberlain, subscribed. 'The democrat may regret that support from "Society" is necessary if opera is to pay', said a St Helens newspaper, 'but the cost of operatic production before the curtain goes up is so great that democratic prices will not make the venture profitable.'[8]

'Really I never remember seeing such a gathering at this time of year', marvelled *The Lady*'s social reporter, who attended the performance of *Der Rosenkavalier* on the opening night, 29 January 1913. 'It might have been the height of the Season, so brilliant and fashionable was the audience.'[9] The novelist Arnold Bennett noted in his journal that the first act was received quite coldly in the more expensive parts of the house, where the piece was 'certainly not understood', but that at the end there was 'an explosive sort of shout when Thomas Beecham came to bow'.[10] In all, the seemingly inexhaustible Beecham conducted seventeen of the season's twenty-one opera performances, leaving his assistant, Hans Schilling-Ziemssen from Frankfurt, in charge of three further *Rosenkavalier*s and a single *Salome*.

A number of German critics arrived for the first night of *Der Rosenkavalier*, drawn by a fine cast that included two singers from the original Dresden production, Margarethe Siems (the Marschallin) and Eva von der Osten (Octavian), together with Claire Dux (Sophie) and Paul Knüpfer (Ochs), who had both sung in the first Berlin performances. The producer was the baritone Hermann Gura, director of the Berlin Komische Oper.* *Musik*'s reviewer thought that although Beecham allowed the first act to lose impetus, and that subtleties in the score were missed, cast and orchestra reached a peak of perfection in the last act.[11] One or two British reviewers noted problems of co-ordination between stage and pit in the early part of the evening, which was not surprising,

---

* Gura, producer for all the season's operas, sang the role of Faninal at some of the later performances of *Der Rosenkavalier*, as well as Beckmesser in *Die Meistersinger*. His wife, Anna Gura-Hummel, was the Annina in *Der Rosenkavalier* and the soprano soloist in a performance of Delius's *A Mass of Life* that Beecham conducted at Covent Garden on 10 March.

for although the opera had been rehearsed thoroughly by the majority of the company for several weeks, the four principal singers had not turned up until the dress rehearsal. Reviews of later performances suggest that the difficulties were soon resolved.

The season's second red-letter night came on 4 February, when Diaghilev, no longer shackled by the Grand Opera Syndicate's conservatism, at last introduced *Petrushka* to London, with Nijinsky as the eponymous marionette and Monteux conducting. Again the house was sold out. Lady Cunard, a Russian diadem in her hair, arrived with a large sheaf of Madonna lilies and pink carnations, which, at curtain-fall, she asked one of her guests, the former Austrian Prime Minister, Baron Gautsch, to throw to Karsavina, who took the part of the Dancer.[12] By now Lady Cunard was firmly established as one of London's most influential hostesses. Beecham tended to keep his distance from the social milieu she created, but was not blind to the benefits it brought him.

If many in the audience were disconcerted by Stravinsky's complex rhythms and Nijinsky's jerky, dislocated movements, London's music critics (there were no separate ballet critics at the time) were quick to recognise *Petrushka* as a groundbreaking work. 'The Russian dancers', wrote Richard Capell, 'have brought with them a novelty so extraordinary that it is now impossible to guess what may be the limits of their art'.[13] The evening had opened with a revival of *Thamar* conducted by Beecham, his only appearance with the ballet that season. It was the occasion of a rare *bon mot* from the normally taciturn Nijinsky, who was watching from the wings: 'Comme l'orchestre dirige bien Monsieur Beecham ce soir' – 'How well the orchestra conducts Mr Beecham this evening.'[14]

Petrushka was not the only ballet new to London. On 17 February Diaghilev introduced Nijinsky's first essay in choreography, the erotically charged *L'Après-midi d'un faune*, danced to Debussy's score of the same name with the twenty-five-year-old Nijinsky himself as the faun. Capell described him as 'the peerless dancer, who as the faun does no dancing ... half-boy, half-brute, consummate and also uncanny'.[15] Between performances Nijinsky held the first rehearsals for his next choreographic work, *The Rite of Spring*, down the road at the Aldwych Theatre, which Joseph Beecham had put at Diaghilev's disposal. It was to be premiered in Paris in May.

Stravinsky, who took a curtain-call at the end of *Petrushka*, again praised the Beecham Symphony Orchestra. His admiration for it, he said, had been further enhanced as a result of a recent incident – at the Court Opera in Vienna, though he did not identify it – when in *Petrushka* the orchestra (the Vienna Philharmonic), 'very widely regarded as the finest in Europe, gave endless trouble. Oboists and trumpeters declared their parts to be unplayable and, indeed, performed them as if they really were.' Diaghilev announced that in 1914 he would be taking the Beecham orchestra to Russia for the company's first tour there.[16] The tour never took place, however.

The season made a loss, though not a huge one, and Joseph pressed on immediately with his next enterprise, the British premiere of Strauss's *Ariadne auf Naxos*, which was given eight performances in May and June at His Majesty's Theatre in collaboration with its proprietor, Sir Herbert Beerbohm Tree. This was the original version of the work, now rarely seen, in which the opera is incorporated into von Hofmannsthal's shortened version of Molière's play *Le bourgeois gentilhomme*. Tree was to play the part of Monsieur Jourdain.

With a combined cast of thirteen singers, all of them German or Austrian, sixteen actors, a dancer and an orchestra of thirty-seven players led by Albert Sammons, another financial loss was inevitable, for the theatre had only 1,200 seats. Not that the prospect bothered either Joseph or Tree, for both were anxious to recreate the intimate atmosphere of the Kleines Haus of Stuttgart's highly subsidised Königliches Hoftheater, where Thomas and Tree had attended the work's premiere only seven months earlier and had secured the British rights to it on the spot. The Stuttgart producer, Emil Gerhäuser, was brought to London to direct the opera, which was to be sung in German, while Tree directed the play, which was given in an English version by Somerset Maugham. At the time it was much criticised in the press for being too colloquial, slangish and vulgar, but now, more than ninety years later, it strikes the reader as being not only funny and fluent, but faithful to the spirit of Molière.*

Tree's share of the deficit on *Ariadne* was £1,500 (£92,250) and it can be assumed that the Beechams' was the same.[17] † The loss would have been even greater had Tree not raised the normal price of a front stall at his theatre from ten shillings and sixpence (£32.29) to thirty shillings (£89.40). When a reporter asked him if the hike was not a bit steep for the West End, he countered that Stuttgart had charged the equivalent of fifty shillings (£153.75).[18] The *Daily Sketch* published a photograph of Beecham and Tree in the latter's office during rehearsals. Balloons come out of their mouths: 'What would they pay to hear you sing, Sir Herbert?', asks Beecham. 'I should say about thirty bob', replies the

---

* Maugham had adapted a translation of the complete play that Tree had commissioned from him a year earlier, but not used. Entitled *The Perfect Gentleman*, Maugham's 'Ariadne' version was never published, but at least two typed copies of it have survived, one in the Lord Chamberlain's collection at the British Library (MS LCP 1913/18, The Perfect Gentleman), the other, the annotated prompt-copy used for the performances at His Majesty's, in the University of Bristol Theatre Collection (BTC HBT/000229).

† Tree's loss was more than covered by the £13,554 (almost £807,800) profit he had made not long before on a production of Louis N. Parker's patriotic costume drama *Drake*.

lugubrious-looking Tree, who at the time was trying to master the little ditty that Strauss had composed for Jourdain. When a week later Beecham was asked how Tree was getting on as a singer, he replied tongue-in-cheek, 'For every three or four bars M. Jourdain has to wander out of the key, and Sir Herbert, I may tell you, does this quite admirably – as well, indeed, as many quite experienced singers'.[19]

Strauss, no doubt aware of the financial burden of putting on the work in an unsubsidised theatre, wrote a letter of gratitude to Beecham that was printed in the brochure for the performances. It bears signs of being translated, rather awkwardly, from Strauss's original German:

> My dear Mr Beecham,
>
> It is a necessity to me to express to you how much I am delighted that, through your constantly proved enterprise, in so short a time after the German *premiere*, "Ariadne" will be presented in England, and, from all anticipations, will have the same great representations which all my earlier works have received under your perfect guidance. What you, dear Mr Beecham, have done for my works in England cannot be sufficiently appreciated, but your kindness ensures you at all times my warmest gratitude. I am sure that under these conditions "Ariadne" will have as great a success as you have secured for my former works in London, at any rate I wish you the same much deserved artistic reward for all your trouble and whole-heartedness.
>
> It is much to be hoped that we Germans will have again next winter the great joy to greet you at the head of your wonderfully perfect orchestra here in Berlin, where your concerts had such a beautiful artistic success.
>
> I regret exceedingly not to be able to be present at your performances of "Ariadne", but I am strongly overwhelmed with work and also officially engaged with the festivities of the beginning of June in Berlin.
>
> Accept, my honoured colleague, the expression of my greatest esteem, and with the kindliest greetings
>
> Your devoted admirer,
> Richard Strauss[20]

As in the case of *Der Rosenkavalier*, critics from Berlin turned up for the first night on 27 May. 'The performance of the opera was brilliant and deserves the highest praise', wrote the *Berliner Zeitung*, though the *Berliner Tageblatt* thought that 'in passages of sheer Straussian rapture [*Straussbegeisterung*], Beecham and his masterly orchestra sometimes bolted ahead to the discomfort of the female singers, who were unable to keep pace.' The *Pall Mall Gazette*'s critic noted 'uncertainty' in some of the ensembles.[21] Eva von der Osten, enjoying as great a success as Ariadne as she had as Octavian in the Covent Garden *Rosenkavalier*, sprang to Beecham's defence. He 'conducts with wonderful sympathy and understanding', she told a reporter. 'He lives, one might say, in the music, knowing always exactly the right thing to do.' She regretted that Strauss was unable to see the production: 'He is missing much through not being here.'[22]*

Joseph appeared not to turn a hair over his loss on *Ariadne*. Three weeks after its final performance he opened yet another hugely expensive season, this time at Drury Lane. Lasting five weeks, it was billed as 'Sir Joseph Beecham's Grand Season of Russian Opera and Ballet (Organised by M. Serge de Diaghilew)'. Like *Ariadne*, it ran concurrently with Covent Garden's 1913 grand season, though Joseph denied that he was acting in a spirit of rivalry: 'Neither Paris, nor Berlin, nor Vienna, depends wholly on one opera house, and London surely has room for special seasons.'[23] That Thomas's name was not associated with the Drury Lane season was no accident, for he was still a member of the Covent Garden syndicate, in spite of his claim in *A Mingled Chime* that by now he had resigned from it.

The ballets at Drury Lane included the London premieres of, not one, but two new works created by Nijinsky: *The Rite of Spring*, the evocation of pagan Russia to a score by Stravinsky that had caused a near-riot at its historic premiere in Paris a month earlier, and the mysterious *Jeux*, loosely based on a game of tennis and danced to a specially commissioned score by Debussy. Cyril Beaumont observed of *The Rite*, which was given three performances, that 'everything possible seemed to have been done to make the poses as awkward, as uncouth, and as primitive as could be'.[24]† The work was greeted with bafflement and distaste by at least half the Drury Lane audience, though, unlike in Paris, nobody came to blows. The critics were respectful, but unsure of its merit. Beecham found the score 'striking and interesting', though for him *Petrushka* remained the composer's masterpiece.[25] Debussy's music for *Jeux*, which, like Stravinsky's for *The Rite of Spring*, would later come to be regarded as one of the defining orchestral scores of the early twentieth century, was barely understood or appreciated.

Three Russian operas were given during the season, all of them new to Britain: Musorgsky's *Boris Godunov* and *Khovanshchina*, and Rimsky-Korsakov's *The Maid of Pskov*, or *Ivan le Terrible*, as it was called in London and Paris, which were performed by singers from the imperial opera houses of St Petersburg and Moscow, led by the bass Feodor Chaliapin. At least Joseph had not had the expense of bringing the productions all the way from Russia. The two Musorgsky operas had just been given as part of Diaghilev's season at the new Théâtre des Champs-Élysées, built by Gabriel Astruc in the Avenue Montaigne. Astruc

---

* The cast also included Otto Marek as Bacchus and Hermine Bosetti from the Munich court opera, who dazzled with her F sharps *in alt* in the original, extended version of Zerbinetta's coloratura aria, 'Grossmächtige Prinzessin'.

† Monteux conducted both works. Nijinsky danced in *Jeux*, but not *The Rite of Spring*.

had not only paid for the sets and costumes, which had been specially made in Russia, but also the cost of transporting them to France.*

The name of Chaliapin, who was making his British debut, meant little to London, which was in thrall to Caruso, who for the first time in six years was back at Covent Garden singing, by all accounts superbly, the roles of Canio, Radames, Cavaradossi and Rodolfo, for which he was paid an astonishing £500 (£30,750) a night. The English writer on music, Alec Robertson, then a student at the Royal Academy of Music, was surprised to discover that, 'so incurious at first was the ordinary public about Russian opera', one could walk into Drury Lane half an a hour before curtain-up on all three first nights and secure an excellent seat in the cheaper parts of the house.

'We had nothing in our experience with which to compare this profoundly original music', wrote Robertson of the opening performance of *Boris Godunov*, which, like the other two operas in the season, was conducted by Emil Cooper, a Russian, despite his name. 'We had, also, never encountered a singer with such outstanding dramatic genius, allied to a glorious voice, as Chaliapin, and that bare statement conveys little of his unforgettable performance as Boris that night which had the effect of a great performance of King Lear, leaving one "purged with pity and terror". He could not only fill the house with a magnificence of sound, as when at the great moment just before Boris dies he drew himself up to his full height, and cried out "I still am Czar" ... but he could make the softest mezza-voce carry to the back of the gallery.'[26] Chaliapin had equal success as Dosifei in *Khovanshchina* and Tsar Ivan in *Ivan le Terrible*. Joseph was said to be paying him more than £300 (almost £18,450) a night. The second star of the performances was the chorus, which came from Maryinsky Theatre in St Petersburg, and sang with a power and acted with a conviction quite new to British opera audiences.

Following eulogistic reviews, the demand for tickets for the few opera nights that remained was so great that an extra performance of *Boris Godunov* was given on 21 July, which was attended by George V and Queen Mary. At the end of it Joseph came on stage, flanked by Chaliapin and the Shuisky, Nikolai Andreyev. Chaliapin addressed the audience, thanking it for its applause. Flowers rained down on the stage and were in turn thrown by the chorus to Emil Cooper and the Beecham orchestra, which had played throughout the season. The royal pair shook hands with the Beechams as they left the theatre, and said how much they had enjoyed the evening. It was not the first time that Queen Mary had met Joseph that month. On 4 July he had been present when she had opened the Bedford College for Women in Regent's Park, to

---

* The production of *Ivan le Terrible* was adapted from a staging that Diaghilev had mounted in Paris in 1909.

whose building fund he had made an unannounced donation of £30,000 (£1,845,000).

The royal pair were unaware that the performance of *Boris* had almost been brought to a premature end by the men of the chorus, a fractious lot, who at an earlier performance had refused to appear in the coronation scene because of an alleged slight by Diaghilev. This time the issue was one of money. The chorus's contract did not cover the extra performance, and it demanded to be paid before the curtain went up. Drury Lane's stage manager, Ernest D'Auban, described what happened next: 'Chaliapin went among them and argued hotly with them. Then he tried persuasion, and ended up by rating them soundly in his big powerful voice. But they stood firm, and it was only when they had been paid that the performance could begin.'[27]

It was not the end of the matter. Before the start of the third and last act, while the stage was being set for the Kromy forest scene,* the chorus-men were still in a volatile mood. Chaliapin, who during the second interval had been called to the royal box, reappeared backstage and began to reproach them for their earlier behaviour, at which point a chorister hit him with the branch of a tree. The rest of the men joined in the mêlée, with the tall, burly Chaliapin fending off their blows. Part of the stage had been elevated by hydraulic lifts, leaving big gaps in the floor, towards which Chaliapin was being driven. D'Auban brought down the safety-curtain to keep the sound of battle from the audience and stage-hands ran forward to extricate the bass, who retired to the safety of his dressing-room. Meanwhile interpreters were summoned to calm the chorus, apparently successfully. Chaliapin then returned to the stage and, amid expressions of goodwill and fraternity, the performance proceeded.†

Four nights later the Ballets Russes brought the season to a close with a quintuple bill of *Scheherazade*, *Prélude à l'après-midi d'un faune*, *Thamar*, *Les sylphides* and *Le spectre de la rose*. It was the company's 100th appearance in London. So great and prolonged was the applause that Karsavina and Nijinsky had to repeat the last item, and when they returned once more to the stage they brought with them Joseph, a small and rather nervous-looking figure. After yet

* The opera was given in Rimsky-Korsakov's second revision of 1906–8, but without the Polish act. *Khovanshchina* was shorn of its second act.

† Several versions of the incident have survived, none of them agreeing on what actually happened. Ernest D'Auban's account is by far the most convincing. The most picturesque – and improbable – is Beecham's (*A Mingled Chime*, p. 120), in which he claims that the police were called in to help restore order, and that, when Chaliapin finally reappeared, he was carrying a loaded revolver in each pocket. Beecham also says that the coronation-scene boycott and the brawl occurred on the same night, though Chaliapin's version, which does not mention revolvers, suggests the opposite (*Chaliapin: An Autobiography as Told to Maxim Gorky* (London, 1967), p. 183).

more applause he made a brief speech: 'Your Excellencies, my Lords, Ladies and Gentlemen. I thank you extremely much for the support you have given my season here. I hope at some future time to offer you something at least as good as, if not better than, you have had this season.'

When Joseph was asked how the season had fared financially, he was reticent. 'It won't have paid', he said, 'but I won't have lost much.'[28] A few days later he sailed to New York on the *Mauretania* for the start of a 16,000-mile tour of Canada and the United States 'in the interests of the world-famous Beecham's Pills'. It lasted three months. While he was away, a story was leaked to the British press, perhaps by Thomas, which appeared to confirm that plans were afoot for a new 4,000-seat opera theatre for London, with Joseph as one of its backers. It would be the largest house of entertainment in London, with the exception of the Royal Albert Hall, and would cost around £250,000 (£15.4 million). Seat prices would range from sixpence (£1.53) to five shillings (£15.38).[29] Some papers accepted the story at face value, others were sceptical. The *Evening Standard* said that, although 'conversations' were undoubtedly taking place, Thomas was refusing 'to confirm or deny the report, knowing, as he does, that nothing fires public imagination so much as a mystery, and that the more public interest in opera is excited the nearer becomes the solution of the operatic problem'.[30] Meanwhile Beecham resigned at last from the Covent Garden board. His place on it had become untenable, for he and his father were planning an even longer season of opera and ballet for Drury Lane during the summer of 1914, in which he intended to participate.

The Beechams' confidence in the future was well founded. Not only had the 1913 seasons lost a good deal less money than those of 1910, but they had also been far better organised, thanks to the management skills of a young man, recently turned thirty-one, called Donald Baylis, whose origins remain obscure. No birth certificate has turned up, but his death certificate gives his real name as Donald Herbert Goas. The 1891 census lists him as plain Herbert Goas, nine-year-old adopted son of Edward, a schools attendance officer, and his wife Deborah of Corporation Street, St Helens. By the 1901 census Herbert is described as Donald H. Baylis, the now widowed Mrs Baylis's 'son'; his birthplace is given as Manchester. As a lad he had been taken on at the Beecham factory as a commercial clerk. Such was his efficiency that by 1909 he had become secretary to its manager, Charles Rowed. There was speculation in St Helens (shared to this day by members of the Baylis family) that Donald was an illegitimate son of Joseph's. Many of his acquaintances noticed that, like both Joseph and Thomas, he was small of stature, had the same magnetic eyes and displayed formidable energy. Baylis, who had a good tenor voice, took singing lessons in Liverpool, which were paid for by Joseph, who in January 1910 brought him to

London, not only to sing in the chorus for the first Beecham season at Covent Garden, but also to work as a member of the opera company's management. In 1911 Baylis became deputy manager at the Aldwych Theatre, and two years later was put in charge of all the Beechams' theatrical operations. The press called him Joseph's 'right-hand man'.*

Thomas was now appearing infrequently in the concert hall, though on 2 June, in the middle of the *Ariadne* performances, he conducted his orchestra at a seventy-fifth anniversary concert for Camille Saint-Saëns at Queen's Hall, given under the auspices of Paul Cambon, the French ambassador in London. It turned out that the event marked, not the veteran composer's birthday (he was, in fact, seventy-seven years old), but the seventy-fifth anniversary of his first piano lesson. Saint-Saëns himself was the soloist in his *Africa* fantasia, movements from his second and fifth piano concertos, and Mozart's B flat concerto K450. Eric Coates recalled a moment when Beecham and Saint-Saëns, a noted pianist, had different ideas about how a particular passage should be played: 'The diminutive Frenchman cursed our conductor in voluble French.' At supper after the concert Saint-Saëns told Beecham that as far he was concerned there were only two kinds of conductor: the first took the music too fast, the second too slow; there was no third kind.[31]

On 22 June 1913 Beecham at last made his Paris debut, not, as he had always hoped, at the head of his own orchestra or opera company, but at a concert of contemporary music at the Théâtre du Châtelet, at which he shared the conducting of a large *ad hoc* orchestra† with the German conductor Oskar Fried and the Italian composer Alfredo Casella. In a long programme that seems to have suffered from insufficient rehearsal, Beecham gave the first performances in Paris of Vaughan Williams's *Norfolk Rhapsody* and Delius's *Appalachia*. Casella conducted his Second Symphony (described in the programme as *Prologue pour une tragédie*), while Fried was responsible for a batch of pieces that reflected some of the most vital trends in current European music: Debussy's *Ibéria*, 'The Song of the Wood-dove' from Schoenberg's *Gurrelieder*,‡ the introduction to

---

* Baylis's future wife, the soprano Gwen Trevitt, was also in the chorus for the Beecham's seasons and was occasionally given small parts, including the 'grosses Mädchen' in *Feuersnot*, the Milliner in *Der Rosenkavalier* and the Train-bearer in *Elektra*.

† Previews in the London press said that the orchestra was to be the Orchestre Colonne, but it was not identified as such in either the printed programme or the many reviews in the Paris press. The concert was given under the auspices of the Grandes Auditions Musicales de France, whose patron was the Comtesse de Greffulhe, supporter of the arts, society beauty, acquaintance of Lady Cunard, and Marcel Proust's inspiration for the Duchesse de Guermantes in *À la recherche du temps perdu*.

‡ The singer was the Polish-born soprano Marya Freund, who four months earlier had sung the Wood-dove at the first performance of *Gurrelieder*, given under Franz Schreker in Vienna.

the second tableau of Stravinsky's *Rite of Spring* and the 'Danse générale' from Ravel's *Daphnis et Chloé*.

Neither of the British works fared very well at the hands of the Paris critics, who were almost unanimous in their belief that, as far as the future of music was concerned, Beecham was barking up the wrong musical tree in espousing Delius's cause. M. D. Calvocoressi, an influential propagandist for new music, at least wrote favourably of the Vaughan Williams rhapsody, but was at one with his colleagues in pouring scorn on *Appalachia*. 'I found nothing to praise in it', he wrote, 'nothing at all. Neither the conception, which seemed puerile, nor the developments, which were conventional and meagre, nor the orchestration which often sounded harsh and hollow.'[32] Delius, who was present, complained to Philip Heseltine that the 'Orchestra was 2nd rate & the Chorus awful & Beecham seemed to be entirely out of his water [*sic*] & made nothing of the Orchestra or Chorus.'[33] Beecham admitted to an English journalist in Paris that he was disappointed with the reception given to the British works, and put the blame on the audience, an assertion that failed to impress his interviewer.[34] Perhaps it is not surprising that Beecham should have omitted to mention the concert in his memoirs.

With Joseph away in America and no plans for an autumn opera season in London, Thomas accepted an invitation to act as chief conductor for a tour of opera in English that was being organised by the Edinburgh-based impresario Ernst Denhof. For Beecham, its main attraction was that it offered him the opportunity to conduct his first *Ring*. No other British conductor had tackled a complete cycle of Wagner's tetralogy before. The Swiss-born Denhof was a man of lofty ambitions. In 1910 he had mounted in Edinburgh the first complete *Ring* in Britain to be seen outside London, which was sung in English and conducted by Michael Balling, Bayreuth's *Ring* conductor at the time and Richter's successor at the Hallé. In 1911, again with Balling, Denhof toured *The Ring* to Leeds, Manchester and Glasgow, and in the following year was responsible for the first performances of *Elektra* in English. (It opened in Hull.)

The 1913 tour with Beecham was Denhof's biggest enterprise to date. Lasting fourteen weeks, from September to December, it was scheduled to visit Birmingham, Manchester, Sheffield, Leeds, Liverpool, Newcastle upon Tyne, Edinburgh, Aberdeen and Glasgow. Beecham was to conduct *Tristan und Isolde*, *The Mastersingers*, *The Magic Flute* and at least three cycles of *The Ring*,*

---

* *The Ring* was sung in Frederick Jameson's English translation, *The Magic Flute* in a translation prepared by Edward J. Dent, with shortened dialogue, for a production at Cambridge in 1911 that attempted to restore the opera to its original state. Though not entirely unknown in Britain, the *Flute* had suffered from years of inadequate touring productions that played fast and loose with the piece both musically and dramatically. It had not been seen at Covent Garden since 1888, when it received a single performance.

while Hans Schilling-Ziemssen, his assistant at Covent Garden earlier in the year, was to be responsible for the first performances outside London of both *Der Rosenkavalier* (given as *The Rose-Bearer* in Alfred Kalisch's translation) and Debussy's *Pelléas et Mélisande*, along with *The Flying Dutchman, Elektra* and Gluck's *Orpheus and Euridice*. The stage director was another of Beecham's colleagues from Covent Garden, Hermann Gura.

Money seemed to be no object. There was an orchestra of sixty-five players drawn from Scotland and London, a good-sized chorus augmented by local choral groups from each of the cities visited, and, for the *Orpheus* performances, a troupe of twenty-four dancers. Many of the principal singers, among them Agnes Nicholls, Cicely Gleeson-White, Caroline Hatchard, Frederic Austin, Walter Hyde and Frederick Blamey, had performed in Richter's English *Ring* cycles at Covent Garden and Beecham's 1910 *opéra comique* season. In contrast, the tenor Frank Mullings, who was to enjoy a remarkable success as *Tristan*, had had virtually no stage experience at all.

The tour began on 18 September with two weeks at the Prince of Wales Theatre, Birmingham. Ernest Newman wrote of the opening night's *Tristan* that Beecham and the orchestra had provided 'by far the best orchestral playing we have ever had in a Birmingham theatre ... the wonderful score was given with extraordinary brilliance and eloquence', while in *The Mastersingers*, 'what [Beecham's] performance lacked in breadth and solidity, it made up for in vivacity, sensitiveness, and lucidity'. The Birmingham reviewers noted an alarming number of empty seats, particularly in the more expensive parts of the theatre. At the second *Tristan* on 23 September there was 'a very poor house in every department'. Denhof, it soon became clear, had made a disastrous miscalculation. His earlier seasons had taken place in the spring. In September, many of Birmingham's citizens had not recovered from the expense of their summer holidays and were in no mood to spend money on the opera.[35]

At the next venue, the Theatre Royal, Manchester, the situation was not helped by the fact that the first week there coincided with the Jewish New Year, which, a letter from a reader in the *Manchester Guardian* pointed out, meant that on the Wednesday and Thursday, as well as on the Sabbath, many of the city's Jews, 'liberal patrons of the opera', felt compelled to attend the synagogue rather than the theatre.[36] This did not explain, however, why advance bookings for the second week (which was to feature the first *Ring* of the tour) were even worse than they were for the first. After only four days in the city Denhof announced that his losses, already estimated at £4,000 (£246,000), were so great that the Saturday-night performance of *The Flying Dutchman*, with Schilling-Ziemssen conducting, would be the last. He could not afford to continue, and was abandoning the tour. The 200-strong company, faced with the loss of eleven weeks' work, was shocked. The débâcle did nothing for Manchester's image. 'Well may she hang her head in shame!', wrote the *Musical Times*.

Beecham, in London on the day the news broke, sent a message to the company, asking it to stick together and not leave the city. He said he was returning to Manchester post-haste, and would make a statement after the final *Flying Dutchman*, which, ironically, had attracted the largest audience of the week. At the end of it, cast and conductor were given a long ovation and there were cries of 'Denhof! Denhof!' in the hope that the unfortunate impresario, for whom there was plenty of sympathy, might make a speech. But he was not to be found, so Charles Knowles, who had sung the part of the Dutchman, spoke in his place. 'We cannot condemn Mr Denhof alone for what has happened', he said. 'It is the British public that has not come forward to our support ... I hope, however, that this will not be the end of opera on a large scale in the provinces. I am a Yorkshireman [laughter], and we are all Britishers, and we are not all going under on account of what has happened [cries of 'Bravo!' and applause].'

With the curtain finally down, Beecham, with Donald Baylis at his side, told the assembled company that although it was now too late to rescue the second week in Manchester, he would do all he could to resurrect the tour. Much depended, he said, on talks he was holding on the Monday with United Theatres, which controlled the touring circuit. He asked everyone to leave their home addresses, so that they could be contacted as soon as a solution was found, and added that he hoped to meet them again in a week's time at the Lyceum Theatre, Sheffield. He was heartily cheered.

Questioned by the press, Beecham said that he had no great faith in large-scale opera outside London, either as an artistic or a financial undertaking – when it came to opera, the provinces were as bad as 'the cannibal islands' – but he was concerned for the artists, whose work was endangered, and anxious that the cause of opera in Britain should not 'be allowed to suffer a set-back'. He also took the opportunity to poke fun at Manchester for its lack of musical adventurousness. The managing director of United Theatres handed each member of the company a railway ticket and a portion of his or her salary, and the next morning most of them left, along with all the scenery and costumes, by special train for London, where they were met by a representative of the *Daily Dispatch*. 'Mr Beecham', a member of the orchestra told him, 'is a brick.'[37]

With Joseph still away in the United States, Beecham had to raise the money himself and, as subsequent events would make clear, he borrowed a lot of it. On the Tuesday Beecham confirmed that the tour would be resumed as promised, though the last two venues, Aberdeen and Glasgow, would have to be dropped. Sheffield, which Beecham had attacked two years earlier for ignoring his production of *The Tales of Hoffmann*, was subjected to a hurricane of publicity. 'MR THOMAS BEECHAM', ran an advertisement in the local press, 'APPEALS TO THE SPORTING INSTINCTS OF THE SHEFFIELD PUBLIC TO SUPPORT HIM IN HIS GREAT EFFORT'. In a further move, the price of seats in the cheaper parts of the house was reduced. The strategy worked. Though the cost of mounting the Sheffield week was not quite covered, takings at the box office were £400 (£24,600) more than Baylis had originally estimated. After the final performance, of *The Mastersingers*, Beecham spoke to the audience. The last time he had conducted in Sheffield, he said, 'nobody came to hear me [laughter and cries of 'Shame'] – and I grossly insulted you in the press the next day. Tonight I take it all back [loud cheers].'[38] Beecham, for once out of the shadow of his father, was enjoying himself immensely.

The following week's takings at the Grand Theatre, Leeds, where Beecham at last conducted his first *Ring*, showed a small profit, though the technical problems of putting on a complete cycle under touring conditions within the space of only five days defeated even Baylis. Because of the unusual circumstances of the tour, he and the stage staff had not had an opportunity to handle the *Ring* sets, which were 'more or less strange to them', until the day before the cycle opened.[39] 'It is perhaps as well to say at once that the mounting, the lighting, and the scenery of the work fell very far short indeed of the standard required by the composer', wrote *The Times* of the Leeds cycle, 'but their very imperfection served to throw the music itself into stronger relief.' The *Yorkshire Post*, reviewing *The Twilight of the Gods*, found it 'hard to pardon the absolute fiasco at the close, when the curtain descended twice before its proper time, or the terrible muddle when the funeral procession was delayed till the bearers had to rush away under a descending cloth which, for some unaccountable reason, represented colossal Egyptian statues!'[40] In *A Mingled Chime*, Beecham makes a joke of the premature curtain-falls, but he must have found them extremely galling at the time.

At the next venue, the Shakespeare Theatre, Liverpool, advance bookings were so disappointing that Beecham cancelled the second week there and instead, to everyone's surprise, returned to Manchester, where he conducted his second *Ring* cycle.* Samuel Langford, reviewing it for the *Guardian*, found the conducting in *Rhinegold* 'clever, effective and alert rather than imaginative', but thought that as the week progressed Beecham's conception of the work grew in stature. By *The Twilight of the Gods* it had become 'broad and sweeping, and one felt as secure of the onward course of the music as if we were listening to it fresh from the well of the composer's imagination.' When it came to the singers,

---

* Beecham, 'apparently a victim of the strain of the last few weeks', did not appear in Liverpool, where the financial loss was 'considerable' (*Liverpool Courier*, 3 November).

Langford had particular praise for Cicely Gleeson-White, the Brünnhilde in *The Valkyrie* and *The Twilight of the Gods*. 'If only our singers generally could cast their coldness off as Madame Gleeson-White has ventured to do', he wrote, 'a new era would arise in English singing.'*

Beecham's feat of mastering all four *Ring* operas at once was widely noted. In 1913 getting to grips with the complete *Ring* was a vastly more arduous undertaking for a conductor than it is almost a century later, when recordings, broadcasts and DVDs of the operas are widely available to aid familiarisation. Beecham, who had first heard the *Ring* fifteen years earlier at Bayreuth, would doubtless have attended cycles at Covent Garden, and studied the works at the piano, but his achievement was particularly remarkable, because, unlike many of his contemporaries in Germany and Austria, he had not had the opportunity to absorb the epic work bit by bit, year by year, as a *Kapellmeister* on the staff of an opera house.

Although audiences in Manchester were much larger than they had been the first time round, the return visit still made a loss. Beecham was resolute. He felt that if opera was going to flourish anywhere in the provinces, it would be in Manchester. The city was awash with rich citizens and it had the best orchestra outside London. He told the *Guardian* that he would guarantee £5,000 (£307,500) for a month of opera a year in Manchester, provided an equal sum could 'be found within the city itself.' He hoped that Michael Balling and the Hallé might be involved: 'Only by some such pooling of interests can great opera in Manchester be made quickly a vital and popular thing. The representative moneyed men of Manchester have need to do their part. A Socialistic subsidy of opera is not to be looked for.' Beecham was firmly of the opinion that court and municipal support for opera only led to official meddling in artistic matters, a belief that, for better or worse, he held on to for the rest of his life.

He also gave an interview to the Manchester *Dispatch*. 'So far from being a really musical city, you have not begun seriously to think about music', he railed. 'The class that is chiefly to blame for this is, of course, the wealthy upper class, as they take hardly any interest at all in music. The only things they seem to be concerned with are hospitals or lunatic asylums ... It seems that the only way to make opera pay in the provinces is to run a third-rate company, and produce the works in a tenth-rate fashion. The public don't know

---

* The two Siegfrieds, Frederick Blamey in *Siegfried* and Walter Hyde in *The Twilight of the Gods*, were also picked out by Langford for special mention, as were Charles Knowles (the *Rhinegold* Wotan), Lewis James (Alberich) and Frederick Ranalow (Gunther), who were all 'advancing confidently to heights that their concert singing has never led us to expect them to reach'.

the difference.' The outburst had one immediate and positive effect: a group of citizens met at the Midland Hotel to discuss his proposal for opera in the city. Meanwhile Beecham and Balling inspected Manchester's New Theatre* to see if it might not be more suitable for opera than the much smaller Theatre Royal.[41]

After a disappointing week at the Theatre Royal, Newcastle upon Tyne, the tour reached its final destination, the King's Theatre, Edinburgh, on 17 November. There, in the course of a fortnight, Beecham conducted *Tristan*, *The Ring* and, on the final night, with Joseph, now returned from America, watching from a box, *The Mastersingers*. At its close, soloists and chorus massed on stage to sing the National Anthem under Beecham's baton. When he came up from the orchestra pit to join them, he was greeted with repeated calls for a speech. He declined to make one, even though Edinburgh, like Leeds, was one of the only two places where the box-office takings had cleared the expenses. Perhaps Joseph thought that his son had said quite enough about the tour already. The *St Helens Newspaper* reported that, despite a final loss on the tour running to 'several thousand pounds', there were good reasons for hoping that Thomas would be returning to the provinces with grand opera on a similar scale in the future,[42] but as far as Joseph was concerned such a tour was out of the question, for he was becoming increasingly alarmed by his elder son's profligacy with money.

Since the reconciliation of 1909 Joseph had been generous to Thomas, lending him a total of £39,000 (£2.4 million) in addition to paying for the opera seasons. Joseph was in no hurry to get his money back, but discovered that Thomas had numerous debts, some of them arising from the Denhof tour. He owed £5,000 (£307,500) to one of his patrons, Lord Howard de Walden, and £6,000 (£369,000) to one of his father's business associates, the flamboyant speculator James White. Even Donald Baylis was a creditor. Thomas had also made an unwise investment in an Australian gold mine, which turned out to be valueless.[43] Debt-collectors and professional money-lenders were hovering, and at least one bankruptcy notice had been issued against him.

Moving quickly to avoid public embarrassment, his father asked James White to help sort matters out, and by March 1914 a breathtaking £100,219 (£6,163,460) had been repaid, no doubt out of Joseph's pocket. In order to provide Beecham with a proper home, rather than a series of expensive hotel rooms, White arranged for him to acquire The Cottage, at 8a Hobart Place, Belgravia, which Thomas described to Delius as being 'a pretty house with a garden'.†

---

* The New Theatre in Quay Street, built in 1912, was renamed the New Queen's Theatre five years later. In the 1930s it became the Opera House, the name it still retains.

† The house stood on part of what is now the site of the Italian Embassy.

The money for the purchase of its lease, £12,000 (£738,000), plus £1,200 for furniture, came from a Beecham trust. Thomas, Delius reported to Jelka, 'seems to be rolling in money again'.[44]

By way of compensation for all the money that had gone to Thomas, Joseph made an outright gift of the American pills business to his younger son Harry. Unlike Thomas, Harry had remained in Lancashire, working diligently, though without Joseph's flair, for the Beecham company at a salary of £1,000 (£61,500) a year. His passion was for fast motor-cars, which had already led to frequent court appearances. In 1910, while driving his two-seater Siddeley through Prescot, near Huyton, the twenty-one-year-old Harry had knocked down a retired mill-engine driver, who later died of his injuries. A witness told the coroner's court that the car had been going 'like a ball from a cannon', though Harry claimed he was doing only about 12 mph.

The evidence was inconclusive, and the jury delivered a verdict of accidental death, though its foreman said that he and his colleagues did not 'altogether exonerate Mr Beecham from blame'. The coroner said that Harry had 'not impressed him as a straightforward witness.' The official speed limit at the time was 20 mph, though local authorities were empowered to vary it in built-up areas; fines for infringement were heavy. At East Retford in Nottinghamshire the magistrates not only fined Harry £10, plus £4 3s costs (the equivalent of £883 in all), for driving dangerously in the town, but also suspended his driver's licence for a month, because 'fining a man in a position of great wealth was not likely to bring home the seriousness of his offence'. There was an even larger fine – £20 with £15 costs (£2,150) – at Warrington, where another offence of dangerous driving was compounded by Harry's initial refusal to say whether the figure at the wheel, wearing goggles and skull-cap (the attire, the court was told, of a 'motor-racer'), was himself or his chauffeur. In time, Harry would suffer calamitous consequences as a result of his penchant for speed.

Having sorted out most of Thomas's money problems, Joseph announced details of a second Drury Lane season. Billed as 'Sir Joseph Beecham's Grand Season of Russian Opera, German Opera, and Russian Ballet', it was as glittering – and at almost ten weeks twice as long – as its predecessor. It opened on 20 May 1914 with a revival of *Der Rosenkavalier*, which Thomas conducted from memory; he did not even have the score in front of him in case of accidents.* On the following night he unveiled a new production of *Die Zauberflöte*, held

---

* At the two final performances of the opera the twenty-eight-year-old Lotte Lehmann made an inauspicious London debut as the Sophie. In the printed programme for the press night, 4 June, Lehmann's name was transposed with that of Johanna Lippe, the Oktavian. Few of those present noticed the mistake. *The Times* thought Lippe – in reality Lehmann – sang Sophie's music 'charmingly when it does not rise so high as to be trying to her voice'.

to be the most complete version of Mozart's opera yet heard in London. It was performed in German, though eccentrically the spoken dialogue was replaced by sung recitative, which Beecham had commissioned from Emil Kreuz. Several critics used the word 'enchanting' to describe Claire Dux's Pamina. Beecham, wrote *The Times*, 'handled the orchestra as if he loved every note of the score. There was no attempt to force effects, no haste; he just let the characterization of the music make its own effect'.*

Because Joseph was unsure how a London audience might react to *Die Zauberflöte*, only three performances were scheduled, but it proved so popular that a fourth was added. The press noted that although an immense number of people were being attracted to Drury Lane, Covent Garden was enjoying an equally good season. That both houses could be filled simultaneously suggested that the audience in London for opera and ballet was at last beginning to grow, just as Joseph and Thomas had always hoped it would, though as yet it was too early to say just who the new patrons were.

The Russian part of the season followed in June. This time there were no fewer than four operas new to London – Borodin's *Prince Igor* and Rimsky-Korsakov's *May Night*, both produced specially for Drury Lane, Rimsky's *Golden Cockerel*, performed in a version more balletic than operatic, and Stravinsky's *The Nightingale*, which had been premiered at the Paris Opéra by the Diaghilev company only three weeks earlier. Chaliapin was back, doubling the roles of Galitzky and Konchak in the new *Prince Igor* and repeating his previous successes in revivals of *Boris Godunov*, *Khovanshchina* and *Ivan le Terrible*.

This time the Maryinsky chorus was replaced by the equally magnificent, but more pacific, chorus from the Bolshoy Theatre in Moscow. The combined contribution of the chorus and the Ballet Russes in the Polovtsian dances in *Prince Igor*'s second act, choreographed by Fokine, electrified audiences, whose enthusiasm at the first performance 'was not abated until everyone concerned, including M. Steinberg [the conductor], had appeared before the curtain several times'.[45]† So grateful was Tsar Nicholas II for Joseph's support for Russian art that before the season opened he conferred on him the Order of St Stanislaus.

---

* Beecham gave many of the smaller roles to singers who had taken part in the Denhof performances of the opera.

† Leon Steinberg conducted *Prince Igor* (shorn of the Prince Vladimir–Konchakovna scene in Act 2 and the whole of Act 3) and *May Night*, while Emil Cooper was responsible for the other operas. *The Golden Cockerel*, which Monteux took over after the first night, had the uniformly dressed singers placed on tiered benches on either side of the stage. The eminent Russian violinist Efrem Zimbalist complained in a letter to the *Daily Telegraph* (27 June 1913) that the balletic treatment of the piece, not to mention the cuts imposed on its score, was a 'libel to Rimsky-Korsakov's fame'.

Chaliapin was now being paid £400 (£24,600) a performance,[46] but as far as Joseph was concerned it was worth every penny, for on Chaliapin nights – there were seventeen in all – the theatre was packed from top to bottom. Bumping into the singing teacher and critic Herman Klein at Drury Lane one evening, Joseph admitted that his opera seasons also had their commercial uses; they helped to keep the Beecham name before the public.[47]

By now Diaghilev had become more dependent on Joseph than ever before. His main Paris backer, Gabriel Astruc, was facing bankruptcy following a financially disastrous opening season at the Théâtre des Champs-Élysées, and as a result Diaghilev was heavily in debt. Taking advantage of the situation, at a cost of a mere 40,000 francs, Joseph bought from the beleaguered Astruc the sets, costumes and props for both *Boris Godnov* and *Khovanshchina*. (They had cost Astruc 700,000 francs.)[48] Now, by footing the bill not only for the new *Prince Igor* and *May Night*, but also for *The Golden Cockerel* and *The Nightingale*, Joseph became owner of those four productions as well. Hearing that Diaghilev owed Karsavina a large amount of back-pay, he went to her dressing-room one night and handed her £2,000 (£123,000) in notes; later Diaghilev touched her for a £400 loan.[49] Joseph put Diaghilev even further in his debt by advancing him 100,000 francs to pay Richard Strauss for the sole performing the rights to *The Legend of Joseph*, which, following its premiere in Paris on 14 May, was to receive six performances in London. In return Diaghilev lent Joseph the scenery for *Ivan le Terrible* free of charge and undertook to repay the advance in instalments after each performance of the Strauss ballet.[50] When Diaghilev failed to maintain the payments, Joseph kept the *Ivan* sets in lieu.

Hugo von Hoffmannsthal and his collaborator, Count Harry Kessler, based their scenario for *The Legend of Joseph* on the story in the Book of Genesis of the lust of Potiphar's wife for the young Ishmaelite slave Joseph. The keenly anticipated London premiere, with Strauss himself conducting, took place on 23 June, almost exactly the half-way point of the season. It very nearly did not happen. On 4 June José-María Sert's scenery and trunks full of Bakst's costumes were seized at the Paris Opéra by some of Diaghilev's creditors before they could be shipped to London. The dance historian Lynn Garafola surmises convincingly that it was Joseph Beecham who eventually secured their release by bailing out Diaghilev.[51]

Although Diaghilev had intended that Nijinsky should not only dance the role of Joseph, but also act as choreographer, the plan did not work out. In the autumn of 1913, during a visit to Buenos Aires, Nijinsky married a young Hungarian dancer, Romola de Pulszky, without informing the impresario, who expelled his one-time lover from the company for what he regarded as unforgivable disloyalty. As a result, the role of Joseph was danced instead by Diaghilev's latest discovery, the handsome, but inexperienced, Leonid Myasin, later to achieve fame as Leonide Massine. Fokine replaced Nijinsky as choreographer.* The artist Charles Ricketts reported that 'all little London' – the alliance of society leaders and aesthetes who formed the backbone of the subscription audience – attended the ballet's dress-rehearsal, at which Lady Diana Manners, the madcap, but ethereally beautiful daughter of the Duchess of Rutland, 'clambered over the balcony from one box to another before an enraptured house'.[52] Like her mother, the twenty-one-year-old Diana was a Drury Lane regular. On the first night of *Joseph* she was a guest in Lady Cunard's box, along with the Prime Minister and Margot Asquith, Delius, Chaliapin and the Russian ambassador.

Contrary to expectation, *The Legend of Joseph* was an artistic flop. The Veronese-inspired sets and costumes seemed overblown, while the *Morning Post*'s critic spoke for many in describing Strauss's score as 'a triumph of workmanship, but not of inspiration', a verdict that has hardly changed over the years. On the day of the opening performance, Diaghilev received a telegram from Kessler, who, besides sending regrets that he could not be present, expressed concern that the company's visit to Germany, scheduled for the autumn, might not now take place. Diaghilev, failing to recognise that Kessler, who had court connections in Berlin, was warning of dangers ahead, told his *régisseur* Sergey Grigoriev and others that the count must be ill.[53]† Although the war was by now only six weeks away, few Britons outside the govenment seriously believed that it could happen, despite the worrying signals from abroad: the build-up of the German army and navy, Russia's huge increase in the size of its army in response, the Serbian threat to Austrian hegemony in the Balkans, and territorial claims by all and sundry. With only a small standing army, it seemed unlikely that Britain could even contemplate taking on the vast conscript forces of the central European powers.

Joseph must have been as unconcerned about the international situation as Diaghilev, for it is hard to deduce why otherwise he would have chosen this moment to embark on the largest business deal of his life, the purchase of eighteen and a half acres of Covent Garden from the Duke

---

* Nijinsky danced in London for the last time in March 1914, when he led a small company of his own for a brief, unhappy season at the Palace Theatre. Eventually forgiven by Diaghilev, he rejoined the Ballets Russes in New York in 1916. In the following year he showed the first signs of the mental disorder from which he never recovered, and danced for the last time in public on 26 September 1917, in Buenos Aires.

† Strauss conducted the first three performances of the ballet. Although it was announced that Beecham and Monteux would share the last four, it seems that Monteux conducted all of them.

of Bedford at a cost of £2 million (£123 million). The *Daily Express* broke the news on its front page on the day before Diaghilev received Kessler's telegram.* It was announced on the same page that Joseph had been created a baronet in the King's birthday honours list, in recognition, it was widely assumed, of his contribution to the arts and philanthropy. More than one paper commented approvingly that in this instance the Liberal party could hardly be accused of rewarding a rich man for putting money in its coffers, for Joseph had always been a staunch Tory.

Delius, reporting on the baronetcy to his wife, observed that 'Lady C[unard] – who has brought it of course all about, is exultant.'[54] Maud Cunard's involvement is confirmed by an entry in Duff Cooper's diary, in which he reveals a 'profoundest secret', told to him by his future wife, Diana Manners, that Joseph had paid out a total of £10,000 (£615,000) in connection with the baronetcy – £4,000 of it to Lady Cunard, £5,500 to Edward Horner, brother of the Prime Minister's daughter-in-law Katharine Asquith, and £500 to Diana. Presumably all three had used their friendship with the Asquith family to put in a good word on Joseph's behalf.[55] Later in the year Maud Cunard decided that Delius, too, should have an honour and went to work on the Prime Minister. 'She is a wonderfully active woman', Asquith wrote to his close friend Venetia Stanley, 'only yesterday she sent me 2 boxes of cigars (which made me a little suspicious), and I now find she has been even more generous to Bongie,† with a hint that one Delius (who composes) should have a Knighthood.' Although Asquith thought Maud 'quite undefeatable' – 'I hear her nasal accents at this moment in the next room, exhorting or threatening or wheedling poor Bongie' – he stood firm in the case of Delius, who did not receive his honour. Asquith remained fond of Maud, however: 'She certainly adds to the gaiety of life & and is one of the persons we should miss.'[56]

Included in the Covent Garden deal were the freeholds of buildings as diverse as the Drury Lane and Strand Theatres, the Royal Opera House, Bow Street police court and police station, Covent Garden Market, the Waldorf Hotel, the Roman Catholic church of Corpus Christi in Maiden Lane, and the National Sporting Club, as well as the Aldwych Theatre, of which Joseph was already the lessee. Interviewed at his home in Hampstead, Joseph

---

* Herbrand, eleventh Duke of Bedford, had decided to sell the Covent Garden estate in 1910, after the Liberal government introduced new land duties on urban estates. Joseph Beecham, who was advised on the deal by James White, was not the first person to make an offer for it. In November 1913, the duke agreed to sell the estate to the Tory MP for Harrow and land-speculator, Harry Mallaby-Deeley. When in June 1914 Joseph Beecham offered Mallaby-Deeley £250,000 (£15 million) for his option to buy the estate, the MP was happy to accept the money and leave the scene.

† Maurice Bonham Carter, Asquith's private secretary and future son-in-law.

admitted the story was true, though he added that negotiations could 'drop through even now'.[57] He made it clear that he had no plans for the Royal Opera House, since the syndicate's lease on it ran for another thirty-three years.

What Joseph did not say was that he intended to raise the money through a flotation arranged in conjunction with a Manchester stockbroker, Alexander Lawson Ormrod. Furthermore, the two had agreed that once the sale was complete, Joseph would sell on the estate to Ormrod and make a quick profit of £50,000 (£3 million) in the process.[58] On 28 June, four days after news of the scheme leaked out, the young Bosnian Serb anarchist Gavrilo Princip shot dead Archduke Franz Ferdinand, heir to Emperor Franz Josef of Austria-Hungary, and his wife in Sarajevo and in doing so lit the fuse that led to war. Regardless, the cool-headed Joseph signed a contract with the Duke of Bedford on 6 July to buy the estate and paid an initial deposit of £200,000 (£12.3 million).

Meanwhile the Drury Lane season proceeded in what in retrospect seems its rather surreal way. The Asquiths continued to attend, as did the German ambassador, the popular anglophile Prince Lichnowsky, who in June had received an honorary doctorate of civil law at Oxford, where he told his hosts that Britain and Germany were in agreement in their policies 'to secure for their peoples the blessings of undisturbed intellectual and economic development'.[59] Lichnowsky had recently invited Beecham and the orchestra to give a concert at the German embassy, while as late as 25 July it was reported that both conductor and orchestra would be making a three-week tour of Germany in the autumn.[60]

Beecham's last scheduled appearance during the Drury Lane season came at the beginning of July with the premiere of Joseph Holbrooke's *Dylan*. This was the second instalment of the composer's trilogy of operas, with a libretto by Lord Howard de Walden based on the Welsh *Mabinogion* stories. Howard de Walden's wife found the rehearsals for it 'enthralling and entertaining', with 'arguments about lighting, battles over advantageous cuts, [and] Beecham, baton in right hand and stroking his tiny pointed beard upwards with the back of his small left-hand, loudly drawling "give it hell boys!" '[61] But not even Beecham's committed conducting of the vast orchestra, which included four saxophones, four saxhorns, tubaphones, a bass flute, an oboe d'amore and an organ, could disguise the inconsistencies of Holbrooke's score and the undramatic quality of the libretto. 'It is really impossible to get up much interest of any sort in the doings of these prehistoric invertebrate Welshmen', grumbled the *Evening News*.[62] After the last of the three performances (the only ones *Dylan* ever received) the costumes went to Seaford House, the Howard de Waldens'

London home in Belgrave Square, where later they came in handy for fancy-dress balls.*

On the night of 2–3 July, a tragedy occurred that shocked the members of Beecham's orchestra and caused consternation among the denizens of Mayfair and Belgravia. After the performance of *The Golden Cockerel* that night some of the younger members of the audience left Drury Lane for Westminster pier, where they met up with other friends before boarding a large pleasure-launch, the *King*, for a midnight supper-party as they steamed up-river to Kew. A small group of Beecham's players had been hired to provide music for the trip, among them a young musician from Islington, William Mitchell, who was the orchestra's librarian and platform manager. The revellers, fifteen-strong, included Diana Manners and Duff Cooper, who in the previous year had joined the Foreign Office; the Prime Minister's eldest son Raymond Asquith; Herbert Beerbohm Tree's daughter Iris; the Russian ambassador's son Count Constantin Benckendorff; Nancy Cunard, at eighteen probably the youngest member of the group; and Sir Denis Anson, a young baronet with a reputation for being a prankster, who had inherited his title only a month earlier.

At around 3 a.m., as they neared Battersea Bridge on the return journey, the party was sitting in groups on deck under the light of Chinese lanterns. Anson, who, egged on by some of the women in the party, had been climbing on top of the deck-cabin, suddenly took off his watch and jacket and dived into the Thames, apparently as the result of a wager. He struck out for the Battersea shore, but was carried away by the strong tide and was heard calling out, 'Quickly! Quickly!' Though his fellow musicians tried to deter him, William Mitchell, a good swimmer, but in poor health at the time, immediately jumped into the water to rescue Anson. Count Benckendorff followed suit, but because of the current was unable to reach either man and was eventually picked up by the launch. Despite a search by the river police and local boatmen, neither the twenty-five-year-old Anson nor Mitchell, two years younger, was found. On disembarking at Westminster, the shaken party went to Anson's lodgings in Half Moon Street, Piccadilly, in the hope that he might have reached the shore and gone home, but there was no sign of him. Two days later Mitchell's body was discovered on the foreshore at Fulham, and on the following day Anson's turned up by Lambeth Bridge.[63] The Lambeth coroner paid tribute to Mitchell's bravery after the jury had returned a verdict that both men had been accidentally drowned.

---

* *Dylan*'s cast included Frederic Austin, Frank Mullings and Doris Woodall. The first opera of the trilogy, *The Children of Don*, had been given in 1912 at Oscar Hammerstein's London Opera House. The third, *Bronwen*, was performed by the Carl Rosa company at Huddersfield in 1929; Claud Powell conducted. It met with as little success as its predecessors.

Delius was in London at the time and on the fateful night had, like Diana Manners, been a guest in Maud Cunard's box for *The Golden Cockerel*. He wrote to his wife Jelka: 'Luckily I & Beecham & Lady Cunard did not go [on the boat trip] but came home & had a nice supper & chat – The young men must have been shewing off & playing the fool & and perhaps drinking too much ... I hear Lady Diana looked quietly on & said – What does it matter – 2 human lives are nothing at all – perfectly unmoved – Nancy got home at 6. a m & had to be put to bed quite hysterical – Nice goings on eh! They go it strong here in this lot – I can tell you'. [64] * (At an earlier encounter with Diana Manners, Delius had found her 'very nice – & spirituelle'.) [65]

Joseph Beecham acted quickly to assuage disquiet among William Mitchell's colleagues in the orchestra by letting it be known that he was 'interesting himself in the welfare of the widow and child'. [66] The Anson family made a similar pledge. The Beechams also saw to it that the musician was given an impressive funeral at the Islington cemetery at East Finchley. After a short service in the chapel, the coffin was carried outside and placed on a bier at the spot where the Beecham Symphony Orchestra and the principals and chorus from *Dylan*, 150 performers in all, were assembled. Beecham conducted an arrangement of Chopin's Funeral March and then, after an address by the officiating priest (a cousin of Anson's), chorus and orchestra, with Emil Kreuz conducting, performed Mozart's motet *Ave verum corpus*. Finally, at the graveside, the chorus sang 'Fight the Good Fight', 'Abide with Me' and, accompanied by a small group of instrumentalists, Joseph Barnby's 'Sleep thy Last Sleep'. Among the dozens of floral tributes was one from Beecham, who wrote on its card, 'In remembrance of my faithful hero'. [67]

Beecham's final appearance at Drury Lane was unscheduled. On 17 July, a Friday, Monteux went to Paris, where his wife was about to give birth, and on the next day sent word to the company that he would not be back in London in time for the performance of *Petrushka* he was due to conduct on the Monday. Neither Beecham, nor Emil Cooper, the only other conductor available, had performed the piece. Rather than change the programme, Beecham decided he would sit down and learn it. Having done so, he rounded up what few players could be found for a scratch orchestral rehearsal. At the actual performance, the orchestra was alarmed to discover that Beecham intended to conduct the most difficult piece in its repertory, apart from *The Rite of Spring*, not from the

---

* On 8 July Delius attended an afternoon concert of his works that Beecham gave with his orchestra at the Royal Academy of Music before a disappointingly small audience. The programme included *Brigg Fair*, the final scene of *A Village Romeo and Juliet* and the first *Dance Rhapsody*. Delius wrote to Jelka: 'I never heard Beecham play my things so wonderfully ... he feels my music like no one else'.

score, but from memory, a typical act of bravado that might have been considered unfair to both players and dancers. Wynn Reeves, who was now leading the orchestra, recalled that 'Tommy started off with great gusto. He hadn't got far before mistakes began to creep in, and it soon became evident that he was going to bluff his way through. Those who know the score well will realise what this meant: a terrific effort of nerve and speed of uptake on his part. We observed that he kept his eyes glued on our desk, so we began indicating the various changes of tempo. He got through without a breakdown. A prodigious exploit!'[68]* Mistakes or no mistakes, the *Daily Telegraph*'s critic, Robin Legge, thought Beecham's performance was one 'of real splendour'.[69] With Nijinsky no longer available, the title-role was taken by Fokine, with Karsavina in the role of the Ballerina.

The season ended five days later on 25 July with a triple-bill of ballet conducted by Monteux – *Papillons*, *The Legend of Joseph* and *Petrushka*. Headlines in the evening papers were full of gloom: 'IN THE BALANCE – GOVERNMENT IN GRAVE DILEMMA', ran the *Standard*'s. Two days earlier the Austrians had delivered an ultimatum to Serbia, demanding among other things that it should punish anyone circulating anti-Austrian propaganda, and that it should condemn Serbian military involvement in the archduke's assassination. Most of those arriving for the performance were probably unaware that a few hours earlier Serbia had rejected the demands and was mobilising its army. At the end of the evening there were the usual scenes of enthusiasm, but Joseph, who in that day's *Evening Standard* was reported as saying that Chaliapin had already been retained for the following year, was cautious in his end-of-season speech. He told the audience that he would be giving another season of Russian opera and ballet, but he did not put a date to it.[70]

On 28 July Europe took a further step towards the abyss. Austria declared war on Serbia. On the same day Joseph paid the Duke of Bedford a second instalment on the Covent Garden estate of £50,000 (£3 million), with the remaining £1.75 million (£107.6 million) to be paid in full on 11 November. On 3 August, Germany invaded Belgium, whose neutrality Britain had guaranteed by treaty in 1839, and on the following day, somewhat unwillingly, the British government declared war on Germany. Before long the Treasury stopped all further issues of capital for anything unconnected with the war. As a result Ormrod found himself unable to honour his agreement to purchase the estate. Joseph had a problem.

---

* Earlier in the season, on 9 and 23 June, Beecham had conducted two performances of *Thamar* for the ballet.

1 'The ever genial modern Aesculapius': grandfather Thomas, inventor of the pill

2 Beecham's parents, Joseph and Josephine, at the time of their engagement, c. 1872

3 'Worth a guinea a box': the Beecham's factory at St Helens, c. 1907

4 The infant Beecham, c. 1882

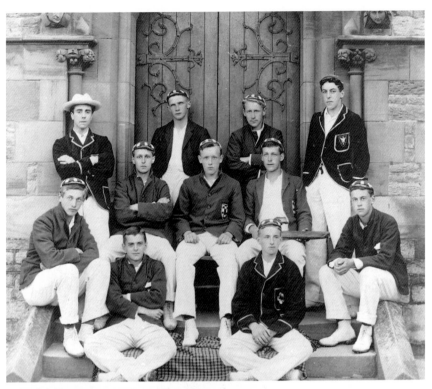

5 Beecham in Stetson-type hat with the Rossall cricket team, 1897

6 The undergraduate Beecham with his future father-in-law, Dr Charles Stuart Welles, c. 1898

7 Engagement idyll: Thomas and Utica at the Quinta de Monserrate at Sintra during the summer of 1900

8 The fireworks tour, October 1909: Beecham at Reading station

The Daily Mirror

THE MORNING JOURNAL WITH THE SECOND LARGEST NET SALE

No. 2,493.   Registered at the G.P.O. as a Newspaper.   SATURDAY, OCTOBER 21, 1911   One Halfpenny.

MRS. FOSTER, THE RESPONDENT IN THE "SECRET CODE" DIVORCE SUIT, LUNCHING AT THE LAW COURTS YESTERDAY.

During the interval yesterday Mrs. Foster did not leave the Law Courts, but lunched within the precincts of the building with Prince and Princess Bariatinsky and Miss Hayman. All the three last-named have been mentioned during the hearing of the divorce suit in which Mrs. Foster is the respondent and Mr. Thomas Beecham, the well-known conductor and producer of grand opera, the co-respondent. (1) Mr. G. Sherwood Foster, the petitioner. He is an artist. (2) Mr. Beecham leaving the Law Courts at the luncheon interval yesterday. (3) Mrs. Foster at lunch.—(Daily Mirror and Langfier.)

9 Divorce sensation, October 1911: the plaintiff George Foster (top left); the defendant Maud Foster lunching on lobster at the Law Courts restaurant; and Beecham, her trilby-hatted co-defendant, taking a break during the hearing

10 Enthusiastic, witty and exceptionally well read: Lady Cunard in 1919

11 *The Musical Mirror* celebrates Beecham's return to the concert platform after a three-year gap, May 1923

12 Initial subscriptions pour in: Beecham at his desk at the Imperial League of Opera offices, November 1927

13 Utica with her sons Adrian (left) and Tommy, 1927

14 Beecham with the principal dancers in *The Gods go a'Begging* at the Opera House, Manchester, during Diaghilev's British tour in November 1929. Rear: Alexandra Danilova and Léon Woizikovsky. Foreground: Lubov Tchernicheva and Felia Dubrovska.

15 Delius Festival, October 1929: a porter from the Langham Hotel pushes Delius to the Queen's Hall with, from left, Philip Heseltine, the composer's wife Jelka and his male nurse

16 Beecham orates at Delius's graveside, Limpsfield, May 1935. Eric Fenby, with bow tie, is second from left in the front row.

CHAPTER 8

Battle for Music

B EECHAM was confident of Allied victories that would bring an end to the war within a matter of months. On learning that Delius and his wife, fearful that the conflict might soon reach their home at Grez, had briefly sought refuge in Orléans, he wrote to the composer on 1 October 1914, assuring him that he was unlikely to be troubled again, since there was no doubt that 'the neck of the German attack' had now been broken.[1]

Presumably Beecham was buoyed up by the recent Anglo-French success in driving back the Germans at the battle of the Marne, thus preventing the occupation of Paris. But his optimism was premature. Shortly afterwards the first battle of Ypres began in southern Belgium. The British army managed to halt the German push towards Calais and Boulogne, but the cost was great. Both sides dug in and the stalemate of trench-warfare began. Belgian refugees started to appear in St Helens, drawn by offers of help made jointly by the town's Roman Catholic community and the municipality, which set up a committee, with Joseph Beecham as one of its members, to oversee their welfare. Among the first to arrive were the nuns of the order of Notre Dame, who with their mother superior had fled from their convent near Antwerp after the city had been besieged and then overrun by German forces.

One of the committee's first acts was to organise a fund-raising 'Grand Patriotic Concert' of orchestral music and popular songs at the flag-bedecked Theatre Royal, St Helens, on 17 October. After the local conductor had led the amateur players of the St Helens Orchestral Society* through the national anthems of Britain, France, Belgium and Russia, Beecham took over for one of Elgar's *Pomp and Circumstance* marches, the overtures to Gounod's *Mireille* and Nicolai's *Merry Wives of Windsor*, and Saint-Saëns's Violin Concerto no. 3, with Albert Sammons as soloist. A reviewer noted tactfully that if the musicians at Beecham's disposal were not of 'the very best', at least they had produced the best that was in them.[2] The plight of the refugees may have helped to bring home to Beecham the true nature of the situation, for on 25 October he wrote again to Delius, urging them to come to England with Jelka before it was too late. He leased for them Grove Mill House in a rural part of Watford, where they stayed until July 1915, when they left for Norway and Denmark

---

* This was not the orchestra that Beecham had founded and conducted at St Helens in 1899, but a later body bearing the same name.

before returning in November to Grez, which had not been overrun by the Germans after all. Delius wrote the Double Concerto for violin and cello at Watford, and completed his Violin Sonata no. 1 and the *North Country Sketches* there.[3]

One of the most immediate effects of the war on Britain's musical life was the exodus, or in some cases internment, of hundreds of German and Austro-Hungarian musicians who traditionally had made a living playing in every kind of ensemble from symphony orchestra to restaurant trio. The most prominent German musician working in the country, the Hallé's conductor Michael Balling, was at least spared the embarrassment of being publicly shown the door: when war broke out he was conducting *The Ring* at Bayreuth. Several British musicians thought it prudent to change their German-sounding names to something less suspicious, among them the Torquay Municipal Orchestra's conductor, Basil Hindenberg. Born in Reading, the son of a Berlin-born piano-tuner domiciled in Britain and a British mother, he decided to adopt the surname of his maternal grandmother and call himself Basil Cameron. He recalled bumping into Beecham at the Savage Club. 'Hello, Basil', said Beecham, 'what alias are you trading under these days?'[4]*

When Henry Wood's 1914 promenade concerts opened at Queen's Hall on 15 August, only eleven days after Britain entered the war, the hall's lessee, the music publishers Chappell, insisted on German works being removed from the programmes. As a result, Tchaikovsky's *Capriccio Italien* was substituted for Strauss's *Don Juan* on the first night, while at the second concert, originally an all-Wagner event, works by French, Russian and British composers were played instead. Wood and Robert Newman, manager of the concerts, disputed the ban, and as a result music by dead German and Austro-Hungarian composers was allowed back into the programmes, where they were to remain for the rest of the war. The compromise came to be widely regarded as an acceptable rule-of-thumb.

The prospects for opera in wartime London looked bleak. In September 1914 both the Carl Rosa and O'Mara companies (the latter announcing itself patriotically as 'an all-British concern') managed to open their autumn tours in Notting Hill and Wimbledon respectively, though for the time being it was the closest they got to the West End. Joseph Beecham had suspended his operatic activities, while the Royal Opera House was being used as 'the leading station for swearing in special constables',[5] and in time would be taken over as a store for furniture removed from buildings that had been requisitioned for wartime purposes.

* Basil Cameron (1884–1975), a dedicated, dependable musician, was to become one of the pillars of Britain's musical life during the Second World War.

Covent Garden opened briefly on 5 November 1914 for a matinée in aid of members of the artistic professions who had suddenly found themselves in strait-ened circumstances as a result of the war. The event marked the final appearance of the Beecham Symphony Orchestra, which was then disbanded, since there was insufficient work to justify its continued existence. In a mixed bill, Beecham conducted the ballet *Carnaval* and the first performance of *Phoebus and Pan*, a comic-opera version he had devised himself of Bach's secular cantata, *Der Streit zwischen Phoebus und Pan*. Its score, wrote the critic of *The Times*, 'had been provided with some modern orchestration, but otherwise the music was practi-cally as Bach wrote it'. The claim in the programme that *Carnaval* was being performed by the 'Russian Ballet under the direction of M. Serge de Diaghilev', was misleading, for although the performance featured Fokine's choreography, Bakst's original designs and several of Diaghilev's dancers, the Ballets Russes company had broken up after the last Drury Lane season and would not be reformed until 1915, in Switzerland.*

Concert-giving bodies, the Royal Philharmonic Society among them, lost a significant number of subscribers who failed to return for the first wartime season. The society had another problem: Willem Mengelberg, the charismatic conductor of the Amsterdam Concertgebouw Orchestra who was to conduct most of its 1914–15 season's concerts, found himself stuck in neutral Holland because of travel restrictions. He telegraphed the society urging it to engage British conductors for at least the first four dates. Shrewdly it offered three of them to Beecham, and then, when Mengelberg pulled out altogether, gave him two more. Beecham declined to accept a fee for his appearances, and in addition paid for the Hallé Choir to come to London for Berlioz's *Te Deum*. Better still, he subsidised the society's orchestra, which allowed the players, who had agreed on a 50 per cent pay-cut should it prove necessary, to be paid in full. In all Beecham handed over £400 (£21,900) during the season.[6] Though British soloists replaced more famous foreign ones and programmes included more contemporary works than ever before, audiences held up surprisingly well.[7]

Beecham's benevolence, fuelled by loans and hand-outs from his father, also extended to the Hallé Orchestra. Rather than appoint a new chief conductor to replace Balling, it had decided to rely on guests, including Elgar, Beecham, the Irish conductor and composer Hamilton Harty, the Belgian Henri Verbrugghen

---

* *Carnaval* was danced to Schumann's piano pieces of the same name in orchestrations that Diaghilev had commissioned from Rimsky-Korsakov, Liadov, Cherepnin and Glazunov. Beecham conducted the score several times in concert during the Great War. *Phoebus and Pan* was sung in English with a cast that included John Coates, Frank Mullings and Edna Thornton.

and the Russian Vasily Safonov. Beecham conducted ten of the season's concerts, seven in Manchester and one each in Bradford, Liverpool and Sheffield. Again he conducted without a fee, as did some of the other conductors. The only person unhappy about Beecham's involvement with the Hallé was the dean of Manchester, Bishop Welldon, who repeated his complaint of five years earlier that the orchestra had no business hiring an adulterer who was guilty of 'a flagrant offence against morals'.[8] * The Hallé's board held its ground, saying that while it would never employ a conductor convicted of a grave crime, it would not make judgements on grounds of 'public morals'.

It could hardly have said anything else. In its last pre-war season the orchestra had made a loss of £1,648 (£101,350). Now, largely thanks to Beecham, it had ended its first wartime one with a profit of £404 (£22,115), a sum that was handed to the players who, like their Philharmonic Society colleagues, had volunteered to take a 50 per cent drop in pay. Beecham brought the orchestra a further benefit. His skills as an orchestral trainer, and the challenges presented by the new repertoire he introduced, led to a striking improvement in the Hallé's playing-standards. After a concert in 1915 that included Stravinsky's *Firebird* suite, Mozart's Freemasons' Cantata and the Polovtsian dances from *Prince Igor*, the Manchester critic of the *Musical Standard* wrote: 'Under no other baton has the Hallé Orchestra ever played so consistently, so superbly, so thoroughly nobly. For the first time (it is scarcely too much to declare) has Manchester seen what her orchestra can do. That they could scale the Promethean heights one fondly dreamed, or blindly hoped: but the proof was wanting. Now we have it. And Mr Thomas Beecham has the credit of having vouchsafed it.'[9] It was agreed that he should return for the 1915–16 season, not only as conductor, but also as musical adviser, with overall responsibility for programming. As if conducting the Philharmonic Society and Hallé orchestras were not enough, Beecham also accepted an invitation from the London Symphony Orchestra to become its principal conductor for the 1915–16 season. The flood of engagements came at an opportune moment, first because Beecham no longer had an orchestra of his own to conduct, and secondly because he needed to revitalise his concert career, which as a result of his multifarious operatic activities had stagnated.

Uniquely among the leading conductors of his generation, Beecham had at the time a concert repertoire that was not grounded in the music of Bach, Beethoven and Brahms. It was highly individual, and in 1914 included curious gaps. He had still to conduct Beethoven's Fourth, Seventh and Ninth Symphonies, and had given only the Second Symphony and the Violin Concerto of

---

* In justice to the dean, although he resigned in protest as one the orchestra's guarantors, he then reversed his decision and continued to give his support.

Brahms. Not that this posed a problem in wartime Britain, where for reasons of patriotism and Beecham's own preferences his programmes were dominated by the music of French, Russian and British composers, though paradoxically one of the composers featured most often at his concerts was Wagner, whose music was particularly popular in Manchester and the North. There was plenty of contemporary music. Beecham not only gave frequent performances of Stravinsky's *Firebird* suite and the complete *Petrushka*, but in January 1915 he conducted the first British performance of the composer's *Three Japanese Lyrics* at an enterprising concert of Anglo-Russian music* at the Grafton Galleries in Bond Street and then repeated them with the Hallé. Two months later he introduced Ravel's *Trois poèmes de Stéphane Mallarmé* to London at a concert at the Aeolian Hall.

Stravinsky benefited not just from the performances Beecham gave of his works, but also from the conductor's personal munificence. 'He sent 2,500 Swiss francs to me at the beginning of the 1914 war, in the event I might be cut off from my income in Russia', the composer recalled. 'The money came like manna, too, on the very day I had to pay my mother's passage back to Russia.' [10] Stravinsky was not the only composer to receive financial help. In 1915, in order to support Delius while he was living in England, Beecham agreed to pay him £900 (£42,900) for several new pieces – the Violin Sonata, a revised version for violin and piano of *Légende*, the *North Country Sketches* and three songs – and then, once they had been published, to hand back the copyright to him. The money was to be paid in three annual instalments. [11]

Though tireless in promoting British music, Beecham found it an uphill struggle. In May 1915 he and the Polish conductor Emil Młynarski collaborated on three concerts of British works at Queen's Hall with the LSO, but they were poorly attended. After he had conducted the premiere of Cyril Scott's Piano Concerto at the final concert, Beecham was heard to remark wryly as put on his coat, 'Well, I think we have successfully paved the way this afternoon for another quarter of a century of German music.' [12] † Even Scott, who had played the piano part himself, was of the opinion that the series 'was not a success, nor even approaching one'. [13] Nonetheless, there was more British music a month

---

* The concert, on 25 June, also included the first performance of Delius's *Légende* for violin and orchestra with Sammons as soloist, Bax's *Fantasia* for harp and strings, three songs for baritone and orchestra by Ethel Smyth, and a suite from Glinka's incidental music for *Prince Kholmsky*. The soloist in the Stravinsky *Three Japanese Lyrics* was Carrie Tubb.

† Besides Scott, the festival's featured composers were Delius, Elgar, Vaughan Williams, Bax, Norman O'Neill, Stanford, Bantock, Holbrooke, Smyth, Grainger, Stanford, William Wallace, Harty, Graham Peel, Austin, Pitt and J. B. McEwen. Of the twenty-seven works performed, only Elgar's Violin Concerto and his *Introduction and Allegro* for strings can truly be said to have survived into the twenty-first century repertoire.

later, when Beecham and Landon Ronald shared a month-long series of promenade concerts at the Royal Albert Hall with the New Symphony Orchestra.

The two conductors had cooked up the scheme during a chance meeting at Pagani's restaurant in Great Portland Street, close by Queen's Hall, believing that in the absence of the usual opera season at Covent Garden, the music-loving public would welcome the concerts as a worthwhile substitute. It didn't, partly because Beecham and Ronald, who were sharing the expense of the enterprise, took a patriotic step too far in deciding that works by dead German and Austrian composers, as well as by living ones, should be excluded from the programmes. Even Haydn and Mozart were out, though illogically the Hungarian Liszt was allowed in.

An even greater obstacle to success arrived on the night of 31 May. At around 11 p.m., not long after the second concert had ended, a German Zeppelin dropped ninety incendiaries and thirty small explosive bombs between Stoke Newington and Leytonstone, killing nine people and injuring thirty-two others. It was London's first air-raid. Ronald relates in his memoirs that at lunch the next day the ever-optimistic Beecham tried to persuade him that the raid 'would drive the people into the Albert Hall for the purpose of taking shelter as well as to listen to music'. It had exactly the opposite effect. People considered the hall 'a large and convenient target for the Germans to hit and preferred to keep to their own homes. We continued bravely for a fortnight, when I found I had lost all the capital I had promised to contribute, so I suggested closing down. Beecham wouldn't listen to it and insisted on continuing. But he equally insisted ... that I should not contribute one penny more towards the expenses and begged me to continue doing my share as conductor. To this eventually I agreed though I thought it very foolhardy of him.' [14] *

It says a lot for Landon Ronald's equable temperament that he agreed to co-operate on the promenade concerts at all, for only six months earlier Beecham had, by implication, impugned his ability as principal of the Guildhall School of Music, a post Ronald had held since 1910. In a knockabout and deliberately provocative address to the Royal Manchester College of Music that caused a good deal of offence, Beecham not only insulted the Mancunian institution, but also claimed that he never troubled to listen to any singers who came from London's 'useless' music colleges – 'especially that great bazaar, the Guildhall School' – because he knew they would be bad. 'When I think of that vast number of innocent, harmless people', he said, 'diverted from their useful spheres of labour, and passing through those portals over which it is written, "Abandon hope, all ye

---

* Zeppelins did not return to London during the Albert Hall season, though there were raids on Kent (Gravesend), Essex, the East Riding of Yorkshire (Hull), Lincolnshire (Grimsby), Northumberland and Durham.

that enter here", I assure you that my eyes shine with more than crocodile tears ... Out of all the singers in England today I should have the greatest difficulty in getting together a second-rate opera-company.' [15]

It was an odd assertion, coming as it did from someone who in 1910 at His Majesty's Theatre, and during the Denhof tour three years later, had proved conclusively that it was possible to put on opera of commendable quality using British singers. Archie Camden, first bassoon with the Hallé, and a professor at the Royal Manchester College, asked Beecham mischievously if it were true that he was about to become the college's principal. 'That damn place', Camden reported him as saying. 'They needed stirring up and I thought I was the one to do it. I hope you admired my restraint. It doesn't do to upset people.' Camden noted that 'he was enjoying the uproar he had created and sailed through the storm with exaggerated calm'. [16]

To help him keep track of his myriad concert engagements and mark up his scores, Beecham now had the assistance of Eugene Goossens, who as a student five years earlier had stood immobile in the crush of the Covent Garden gallery at the British premiere of *Elektra*. Now twenty-two years old, Goossens was a violinist in the Queen's Hall Orchestra and had aspirations to conduct. Beecham discovered him at a concert of British music at Queen's Hall conducted by Wood. Half-way through the programme Goossens had stepped from his place in the orchestra to conduct his own *Symphonic Prelude*, a new and noisy work inspired by lines from Ossian, which called for an orchestra that included an organ, bells and thunder-machine. Impressed by the young man's ability to master the large forces involved, Beecham asked him to call on him. Goossens asked if he should he bring his violin. 'Heaven forbid', said Beecham, who the next morning engaged him as his general secretary. To Goossens's surprise, his new employer greeted him in mauve silk dressing-gown and pink pyjamas, a style of dress that Beecham continued to favour for informal morning meetings.*

Because so much of Beecham's time was now taken up with the Hallé, he had let Hobart Place and was staying at Lady Cunard's home, 20 Cavendish Square, whenever he was in London. In Lancashire he stayed with his father at Huyton. The St Helens pill business was doing better than ever. The war, far from damaging pill sales, had actually increased them. More people, particularly women, were in employment and had more money to spend, while the Government bought huge quantities of the pills for the purpose of relieving the effect on troops of a diet much richer in protein than they had been used to. [17]

---

* In his somewhat wayward autobiography *Overture and Beginners*, written in Australia thirty-five years after the event, Goossens gets the date of the Queen's Hall concert wrong – it was on 29 April 1915, not, as he has it, in mid-November. He also confuses his first meeting with Beecham with another that took place eight months later.

In contrast, the problems thrown up by the Covent Garden deal were as acute as ever. Completion day, 11 November 1914, had long passed, and all attempts to raise the money for the final payment on the estate had failed. Under the terms of his contract with the duke, Joseph faced the possibility of losing the £250,000 he had paid already in instalments, while the duke was free to rescind the agreement and offer the property to someone else, in which case Joseph would find himself responsible for the expenses of such a transaction. Joseph tried to sell his interest in the estate, but nobody wanted to buy it.

He asked for a new completion date, to which the duke agreed in principle, and after months of bargaining a supplemental agreement was signed in September 1915, which postponed completion to 24 June 1917. Its terms were far from favourable to Joseph. The duke remained in possession of the property until the new completion day, and retained all rents and market tolls. In addition, until completion, Joseph had to pay the duke interest on the outstanding sum at the rate of 5 per cent, an annual sum of £87,500 (£4.1 million).[18] Although he still had plenty of money, Joseph was depressed by the situation. His mistress Helen McKey Taylor reported that he was also 'much worried' by the depreciation in the value of his securities since the beginning of the war.[19]

To add to his woes, Joseph had lost the affection of his second youngest child, Elsie Olive, twenty-five years old and thought to be his favourite daughter. Lady mayoress during her father's second and third terms of office, and his social hostess during the Drury Lane seasons, Elsie Olive had wanted to marry William Ellis, a St Helens accountant who looked after some of her father's business accounts. Joseph, assuming wrongly that Ellis was only after the Beecham money, forbade her to do so. There were ferocious verbal exchanges. Elsie Olive, fully aware of Joseph's philandering, accused him of gross hypocrisy in trying to control his daughters' private lives. When Joseph refused to back down, she defied him and married Ellis at Kensington register office.[20]

Joseph showed a good deal more understanding towards his daughter-in-law, Utica, and his two grandsons, who spent their summers with his estranged wife, Josephine, at Mursley Hall and their winters at Upper Hamilton Terrace. 'Dear Grandpa', one of Adrian's letters to Joseph begins, 'I am writing to thank you for the nice pen. The Encyclopedias arrived too.'[21] Adrian and Tommy had seen little of their father since he left the family home in 1912, an event that the shy and retiring Adrian in particular found hard to accept. He had shown an aptitude for music from an early age and by the start of the war (when he was nine) had begun to compose modest pieces. The boy's letters to his father have a poignant tone. In August 1914 he complains that he had seen him only twice in six months: 'I have been very busy writing a ballet and I want to talk to you about it and a lot of other things.'[22] Another (undated) letter is headed, 'The Men of

England', the title of a song Adrian had written: 'Dear Father, Can I send a copy of the above to the King and cheer the soldiers in the war. Please reply by return or come and see me, which would be better.' But Adrian's pleas had little effect on the frequency of his father's visits.

The boys' schooling would remain a constant source of friction between their parents. Utica held the view that most of her husband's faults could be attributed to his boarding-school education, and saw to it that both her sons were taught at home by private tutors. This was particularly problematic for the younger boy, Tommy, who, when he reached the age for his education to begin, was not allowed to start with simple lessons of his own, but had to join his brother's, even though Adrian was almost five years older, and by then grappling with subjects such as trigonometry. More than once Beecham resorted to the courts to secure a more conventional education for Tommy, but Utica would have none of it. It says much for the younger boy's tenacity that in spite of the difficulties he would later succeed in qualifying as a structural engineer. Music remained Adrian's main interest.

Though the Beechams had nothing to do with it, opera returned to the West End rather earlier than expected, when in February 1915 the lessee of the Shaftesbury Theatre,* the actor-manager Robert Courtneidge, in partnership with the opera manager H. B. Phillips, mounted a season of popular pieces sung in English, among them *Hoffmann*, *Butterfly*, *Bohème* and *Rigoletto*. Hubert Bath and Hamish MacCunn shared the conducting, while Courtneidge himself directed the well-rehearsed productions. With 1,196 seats and a tiny orchestra-pit (the players spilled into the first three rows of the stalls), the theatre was small for opera, but such was the season's success – there were 104 performances during the fourteen-week run, with seats at normal West End prices – that Courtneidge decided to repeat the experiment in the autumn. He invited Beecham to join him as his partner.

Beecham launched the new Shaftesbury season on 2 October 1915 by conducting Gounod's *Romeo and Juliet*, but otherwise confined himself to providing scenery and costumes from his own large stock and advising on singers, conductors (Percy Pitt,† Landon Ronald, Hamish MacCunn and Julius Harrison) and orchestral players, a number of whom had been in the Beecham

---

* This Shaftesbury Theatre is not to be confused with the present establishment of the same name at the Holborn end of Shaftesbury Avenue. Courtneidge's Shaftesbury, which opened in 1888 and was destroyed by bombing in 1941, stood on the site now occupied by the Shaftesbury Avenue fire-station.

† Pitt (1870–1932), a cosmopolitan, innovative musician, was not an inspired opera conductor, but he was an experienced one, having been 'musical director' (more exactly head of music staff) at Covent Garden since 1907. He was also a prolific composer, though his music has long been forgotten.

Symphony Orchestra. Many members of the cast were familiar names to him, but the much-liked Juliet was a twenty-three-year-old newcomer, the Cheshire-born Miriam Licette. Beecham, wrote the *Daily Telegraph*'s critic, 'conducted throughout without a score, though how he came to know by heart every tiny detail of an opera that one would have thought to have but small attraction for him is unknown to us'.²³ After a second performance Beecham vanished northwards, but not before he had taken a contingent of the orchestra into the Columbia Graphophone Company's studio to record a deftly played perform-ance of the *Magic Flute* overture and a truncated, dim-sounding version of the Polovtsian dances from *Prince Igor*. The labels on the original discs say 'Beecham Symphony Orchestra', which was accurate up to a point.*

The second season proved as popular as its predecessor, and Courtneidge decided to extend it into 1916 with fresh repertory. Beecham, with Donald Baylis's help, organised productions of two new operas, Charles Stanford's *The Critic* and Ethel Smyth's *The Boatswain's Mate*, as well as a staging of Elgar's *Une voix dans le désert* for reciter, soprano and orchestra, a brooding, atmospheric, but now forgotten piece set on the banks of the war-ravaged River Yser, with words by the Belgian poet Émile Cammaerts.† On 21 November 1915 Beecham visited Elgar at his Hampstead home, Severn House, to discuss the production of *Une voix*, which the composer himself was to conduct. (It was sandwiched incongruously between *Cavalleria rusticana* and *Pagliacci*.) Perhaps not surpris-ingly, given his ill-concealed views on some of her husband's music, Alice Elgar was suspicious and disapproving of Beecham. She noted in her diary that after a long talk with the composer in the library he 'came into tea & ate cakes & drank cold water'. The following March, after the Elgars had lunched at Lady Cunard's, with Beecham as a fellow-guest, Alice described him enigmatically as being 'very phantasmagoria [*sic*], & not appealing to us at all'.²⁴

Beecham had intended to conduct both the Stanford and Smyth operas him-self, but in mid-December 1915 found that he could not do so, because he had been invited to conduct in Rome. He asked Eugene Goossens if he would take them over. Goossens seized the chance to further his conducting career, not realising that the first piano-rehearsal for Stanford's opera was scheduled for the

---

* Beecham continued to make records for Columbia with the so-called Beecham Symphony Orchestra until 1918. Of particular interest is a seven-and-a-half-minute suite from *The Firebird* (Dance of the Firebird, Scherzo and Infernal Dance), recorded in 1916 and played with considerable panache. It is one of the earliest recordings, if not the very first, of music by Stravinsky.

† Lasting only twelve minutes, *Une voix* seems to this listener to be greatly superior to its musically banal but at the time more popular predecessor, *Carillon*, also with reciter. Beecham conducted *Carillon* twice in 1915, first with the LSO at Queen's Hall and then with the Hallé.

following morning. Blessed with an ability to assimilate new works quickly, he stayed up most of the night to master the score, though to his chagrin, when it came to the performances, Smyth butted in and insisted on conducting the first night of *The Boatswain's Mate* herself. As reward for his efforts, Goossens was asked to join the company as one of its regular conductors.

The invitation to visit Rome came from Count San Martino, president of the Accademia di Santa Cecilia, whose symphony orchestra was then the only one in Italy that did not play in the opera house, but instead devoted itself entirely to concert work. Lady Rodd, wife of the British ambassador in Rome, was instrumental in persuading Beecham to accept the offer, while the British Foreign Office quickly recognised that the visit was a heaven-sent opportunity for a much-needed display of Anglo-Italian solidarity. It was agreed that in addition to two concerts at Rome's main concert hall, the Teatro Augusteo, there would be a third at the British embassy.*

Italy's position in December 1915 was complicated. Since 1882 she had been linked to Austria-Hungary and Germany in a Triple Alliance, but on the outbreak of war her liberal government had refused to support either of its partners, on the grounds that they were acting aggressively rather than defensively. At first neutral, Italy waited until 24 May 1915 to declare war on Austria-Hungary, largely in the hope – actively encouraged by London – of capturing both Trieste and the Italian-speaking region of Trentino in the Tyrol. During its first seven months of fighting, much of it in treacherous conditions high in the Dolomites, Italy had achieved only small territorial gains but had paid a heavy price in casualties. Some voices questioned the wisdom of continuing the war. Britain and her allies were anxious that Italy should not lose her nerve, for the Italian campaign tied up vast numbers of Austro-Hungarian troops who otherwise would have been fighting the hard-pressed Russians on the eastern front.

Beecham travelled to Italy by train via Paris. He arrived in Rome, four days later than expected, on the morning of Christmas Eve 1915, much to the relief of Count San Martino, whose telegrams and letters to him about travel arrangements, contracts and programmes had been largely ignored.† Beecham insisted that rehearsals should be held, not at the times specified by the Accademia, which he found inconvenient, but outside normal working hours, which suited

---

* The Augusteo, a large circular hall seating 3,500 people, was built on the site of the tomb of the Emperor Augustus. Closed by Mussolini in 1936, it was subsequently demolished to make way for the tomb's restoration, an action that left Rome without a decent hall for symphony concerts for many years.

† Provided one could obtain the right visas it was possible to travel by train to Italy via Paris, since the route lay to the south of the Western Front. The Channel crossing from Southampton to Le Havre, though under threat from German mines and submarines, remained open throughout the war.

him better. If this raised a few eyebrows with the management, it made him highly popular with the players, who as a result received, not only their usual rehearsal fee from the Accademia, but also a large overtime payment from Beecham. It was not just the musicians who enjoyed his extravagance. Each time the orchestral attendant placed Beecham's scores on the conductor's lectern, he was tipped handsomely. The attendant, an old Accademia retainer who had observed all the leading musicians of the day, assured his colleagues that Beecham was 'truly a great maestro. People make me laugh with their talk of their Toscaninis, their Mottls and the rest. There's just no comparison.' Some tips were unexpected, as the director of the Accademia discovered. Coming out of a rehearsal into a torrential downpour, he accompanied Beecham to his waiting cab and opened its door for him. He then put out his hand, expecting a farewell handshake. Beecham put a gold sovereign in it.[25]

The embassy concert was a grand ceremonial affair attended by the French and Russian ambassadors, the Serbian and Belgian ministers, the Italian secretary for war and leading Italian musicians. There was a speech of welcome from the ambassador, Sir Rennell Rodd, much playing of national anthems and a programme of music by Allied composers. Beecham's efforts to introduce British music to Roman audiences proved no more successful than they had in Berlin and Paris. Summing up the first Augusteo concert, which took place on 26 December, *L'Idea Nazionale*'s reviewer criticised 'the unhappy composition of the programme', which was 'too heavy with anodyne, mechanical and insignificant English music', a view shared by many of his colleagues. It had included Smyth's overture to *The Wreckers* ('well-made, but trifling'), Grainger's *Mock Morris* ('fairly picturesque') and Delius's *Paris*, which the critic of *La Tribuna*, kinder to the work than most, noted was 'received coldly with little applause and, in contrast to normal good manners, some whistling'. In his memoirs Beecham claims that the whistling had started while *Paris* was still in progress, and that he had had to bring the performance to a premature end because of it, but there is nothing in either the reviews seen or the Accademia's archives to suggest that he took such drastic action.* For the critics there was ample compensation, however, in two Beecham specialities – the Polovtsian Dances and, to end the concert, an electrifying performance of Berlioz's overture *Le carnaval romain*, which, said *La Tribuna*, provoked an outburst of applause that was 'long, unusually frenzied and absolutely joyful'.[26]

A day or two after the concert Beecham heard from his solicitor in London, Sir

---

* Beecham's account of the visit in *A Mingled Chime* includes other curious assertions, e.g. that Rome's opera house, the Teatro Costanzi (now known as the Teatro dell'Opera), was closed at the time. In fact the first performances in Rome of *Boris Godunov*, as well as revivals of several other operas, took place at the Costanzi while he was in the city.

Henry Paget-Cooke, that a letter had arrived from the Prime Minister, Herbert Asquith, offering him a knighthood in the 1916 New Year's Honours. Beecham was still only thirty-six years old. No reason was given for the honour, but it was generally accepted that it had been awarded in recognition of his extraordinary achievements since his first Bechstein Hall concert a mere ten years earlier. Paget-Cooke wrote to Downing Street accepting the knighthood on his client's behalf.[27] It is likely that the honour came about partly through Lady Cunard's machinations. Ten months earlier Asquith had written to Venetia Stanley: 'Just as I was beginning to write this, there was a sudden incursion into the Cabinet room (like an Atlantic tornado) of Maud Cunard & Diana Manners ... Maud had her usual lot of small & big axes to grind: A. J. B[alfour] for the Garter, a certain Ld Oranmore of Ireland for anything that is going, Thomas Beecham for God knows what, and the raising of a fund to give me £15,000 or £20,000 a year when the War is over!'[28]

The second Augusteo concert, on 2 January 1916, was predominantly of Russian music – *Thamar*, the *Firebird* suite and *Scheherazade* – and the feeling of relief in the reviews was palpable. Critics fell over each in their enthusiasm for the colours and exoticism of the music, while Beecham's conducting of it was lauded for its 'perfect Russian "accent"'.[29] Beecham cheerfully admitted to Samuel Langford of the *Manchester Guardian* that he could understand why Italian audiences were 'far more apt' to appreciate the beauties of the Russian works than those of the British ones; indeed, he himself, 'when living under the influence of the blue Italian sky', had found 'something a little discordant between the austerity of English musical style and the brightness of Italian surroundings.'[30]

Despite general distaste for the British pieces, and mild surprise over Beecham's idiosyncratic conducting style (one critic wrote of his 'Dionysian poses'), the warmth of his reception in Rome was such that after the first concert Rodd sent a ciphered telegram to the Foreign Office in London asking permission to extend the validity of Beecham's passport, so that he might remain in the city longer.[31] It was Rodd's belief that Rome's privileged classes felt a natural affinity with the autocratic Austro-Hungarians, rather than the more democratically minded British and French, and Beecham was asked to keep an ear open for any subversive views that might be expressed in that quarter, though he failed to discover any strong prejudices one way or the other.[32] Indeed, Rome's aristocracy took Beecham to its bosom, if not literally, then certainly metaphorically, and it turned up in force for two specially arranged charity concerts with the Santa Cecilia orchestra in which he took part.

At the first, given at the Augusteo on 14 January in aid of the war-wounded, Beecham shared the rostrum with the orchestra's regular conductor and artistic director, Bernardino Molinari. Half the audience consisted of Italian soldiers in uniform, along with representatives of the British, French, Russian and Serbian armies, while the other half was 'made up of the best names in Rome, of the most elegant of our ladies'.[33] *La Tribuna* complained bitterly about the inadequate heating in the hall ('When is someone going to mend that accursed broken skylight?'), but reported that Beecham received 'copious and affectionate applause' for Grieg's *Peer Gynt* suite and, once more, the Polovtsian Dances.[34] The soloists included the soprano Gemma Bellincioni, a particular favourite of Rome audiences who twenty-five years earlier had created the role of Santuzza in *Cavalleria rusticana* at the Teatro Costanzi.

Bellincioni also sang at the second charity concert, which took place three days later at Rome's Grand Hôtel for the benefit of conscripts' families. Given under the patronage of three princesses, two duchesses, a marchioness, three baronesses and numerous other women of rank, it marked Beecham's farewell to the city. This time he had the programme to himself.* In *A Mingled Chime* he chose to mock the visit to Rome and his role in it, no doubt because in June 1940, at the time he was writing, Italy had entered the Second World War on the side of Germany. But twenty-four years earlier the Roman adventure was seen in a positive light by those who witnessed it. Writing to Beecham, Count San Martino thanked him for his 'warmth and unselfishness' and expressed the hope that soon he would return to Rome and the Accademia, where he had 'aroused a truly universal feeling of affection.' The concerts, said the count, 'had been an ever-intensifying demonstration of the close ties between our two countries.'[35]

For all its success, the gesture of solidarity could not hide the fact that the war was going badly for the Allies. Austria and Germany had defeated Serbia, the Gallipoli campaign had ended in humiliating failure, and on the Eastern Front the Russians had failed to break the Austrian line in Galicia. Britain's all-volunteer army was fighting heroically, but the number of new recruits was drying up, and on 5 January 1916 Asquith brought in a Military Service Bill which introduced compulsory conscription for all men between the ages of eighteen and forty inclusive. Inevitably the bill, given overwhelming support in both Houses of Parliament, affected the musical profession. Beecham himself was a potential conscript.

After a brief stop-over in Florence, Beecham finally reached London on 25 January 1916. No sooner had he done so than he received an SOS from the London Symphony Orchestra. The state of the its finances had grown so parlous that

---

* It included Italian arias sung by Bellincioni, Bizet's *L'Arlésienne* suite, Debussy's *Fêtes*, Tchaikovsky's *Francesca da Rimini*, Delius's *On Hearing the First Cuckoo in Spring*, Stravinsky's *Firebird* and, yet again, the *Polovtsian Dances*, for which Rome seemed to have an insatiable appetite.

its directors had called an extraordinary general meeting to discuss a proposal that its current season should be suspended forthwith. Beecham saved the situation by accepting financial responsibility for the season's remaining concerts and giving the orchestra a cheque on account for £100 (£4,000).[36] The players asked him to stay on for the 1916–17 season, and at first he went along with the idea, telling the Royal Philharmonic Society that because of his commitment to the LSO he would no longer have time to conduct its concerts.

In despair the society decided that it had no alternative but to suspend operations for a year – at which point Beecham suddenly changed his mind, telling the society's directors that he was prepared to continue their concerts after all, but on terms that he would present to them in due course.[37] The LSO, waiting anxiously for news, eventually received a letter (from Donald Baylis) saying that Beecham would be unable to conduct its concerts 'as his plans were very unsettled'. Beecham, a natural dissembler, had been trying to keep more balls in the air than he could manage, and the LSO suffered as a result. Audiences for its concerts grew so thin that it decided to stop promoting its own concerts until the war was over.[38]

The Shaftesbury season ended on 26 February 1916. With a break at Christmas, it had lasted twenty-one weeks, which made it London's longest opera season on record. As far as audiences were concerned, it could have gone on indefinitely, but it had to make way for a long-scheduled musical comedy, *My Lady Frayle*, which Courtneidge was directing. After conducting *The Tales of Hoffmann* on the last night Beecham ceded to calls for a speech, but if his supporters hoped to hear that another opera season was in the offing they were to be disappointed. A week later, however, *The Queen* magazine's well-informed music critic reported whisperings that 'a well-known knight of harmony' was planning a new season of opera in English, to take place at a West End theatre in the near future.[39] Not unexpectedly, the knight turned out to be Beecham, who now took over the Shaftesbury company lock, stock and barrel, and based it at the Aldwych Theatre, of which his father was still the lessee.

The move marked the birth of one of Beecham's most important contributions to Britain's musical life, the Beecham Opera Company. Unlike any of the Beechams' other operatic enterprises, this one aspired to permanence, a true ensemble of singers, with able conductors, répétiteurs and imaginative designers that would provide virtually year-round seasons of opera of a musical and dramatic standard that none of the other touring companies could hope to achieve.* Though the Beecham company lacked international singers, it made its own stars and was to become the closest thing to a national opera company,

---

* Beecham's assistant conductors were Goossens, Pitt and Harrison.

albeit one that did not receive a penny of public subsidy, that Britain had yet known. The subsidy was provided by Joseph.

After an initial three-week run in April 1916 at the Aldwych, the new company moved to the New Queen's Theatre, Manchester, with the Hallé in the pit. At the Aldwych the repertory had been more or less identical to that at the Shaftesbury, but in Manchester Beecham expanded it dramatically with three key operas that he conducted himself: Musorgsky's *Boris Godunov*, given in the magnificent sets and costumes that had been used at Drury Lane; Verdi's *Otello*, still something of a rarity in Britain, with beautiful designs that Beecham had commissioned from the Russian scene-painter Vladimir Polunin;* and Wagner's *Tristan*, for which the painter Adrian Allinson produced striking new scenery influenced by the Vienna *Sezession*, though for *The Times* its 'daring contrasted quaintly with conventional dresses (especially those of Isolde) and old-fashioned stage properties such as the time-honoured sofas on which Wagnerian characters have reclined at Bayreuth since 1876'.[40]

Neither *Tristan* nor *Otello* could have been mounted successfully had it not been for Frank Mullings, who uniquely in the company had the strength and stamina for the two title-roles. His recordings reveal a flawed technique with an unstable top to the voice, but by all accounts he was a most affecting performer. *Tristan*, in which Mullings was partnered by the New Zealand soprano Rosina Buckman as Isolde, was sung in English, but, to the puzzlement of many reviewers, *Otello*, whose cast also included the Belgian bass-baritone Auguste Bouilliez as Iago, and Mignon Nevada as Desdemona, was given in its original language, which went against the company's declared policy. Even more confusingly, *Boris Godunov* was sung in French because, it was said, Bouilliez, the only Boris available, did not know the role in any other language and was too busy (or perhaps disinclined) to learn it in English.†

On the last night of the Manchester season Beecham told the audience that 'many people have remarked about the all-round excellence of enunciation in my singers, declaring that in some of the operas every single word can be heard with ease in any part of the house. I may say that this is a point to which I attach the greatest importance, as, of course, without such results the whole propaganda

---

* On hearing that Polunin was unfamiliar with Verdi's opera, Beecham, with assistance from Goossens, performed the entire opera for him on the piano, to which he added a running commentary on the action. When Lady Cunard put her head in to ask what was going on, Beecham told her that he 'was playing the scenery' (Vladimir Polunin, *The Continental Method of Scene Painting*, ed. Cyril W. Beaumont (London, 1980), p. 34).

† In subsequent seasons both *Boris Godunov*, with Robert Radford in the title-role, and *Otello* were sung in English. The Nottingham-born Radford had been Beecham's original choice for Boris when the production was new, but he had been unwell and was unable to learn it in time.

of opera in English falls to the ground.' [41] In London, thanks to Lady Cunard's tireless advocacy, even the most die-hard supporters of the old Covent Garden grand seasons came to accept that opera in English could be not only artistically satisfying, but also socially acceptable.

When the company returned to the Aldwych in mid-June, a critic wrote of *Otello* that although its three principal singers could not hope to erase memories of Tamagno, Maurel and Melba at Covent Garden, the performance was nonetheless remarkable for the 'general excellence of ensemble, fine chorus singing and brilliant orchestral playing'. The burly Mullings looked the part of Otello 'to the life, and if at times the voice did not prove quite equal to Verdi's difficult demands, his reading of the character was sound and convincing.' [42] In London (though not in Manchester) *Tristan* provoked angry criticism from some who thought its inclusion in the repertory unpatriotic, but it played to full houses nonetheless. A reviewer pointed out that 'a very large proportion of the audience on each occasion consisted of British officers. Furthermore, many worthy fellows on active service specially requested that *Tristan* be given on a Saturday, so that they might have an opportunity of enjoying its strains whilst on weekend leave ... [Those] who stay at home and complain may draw their own conclusions.' [43]

Because of conscription, the company found it increasingly difficult to plan ahead, since 'at any moment a leading soloist or an important member of the orchestra may have to forsake the musical for the military life.' [44] Frank Mullings was called up and even started training, but was then released and allowed to return to singing.[45] The spectre of war constantly hovered over the performances. The opening night of Mozart's *Il seraglio*, conducted by Beecham on 24 July, was given for the benefit of the six orphaned children of the Spanish composer Enrique Granados, who with his wife had died when the passenger ferry *Sussex* was sunk in the English Channel by a German torpedo. To ensure that the children received the largest amount possible, Joseph personally defrayed the total costs of the performance.

The company began its summer break on 5 August 1916. Beecham's industry during the sixteen weeks of opera had been prodigious. In addition to masterminding all the productions, he had conducted thirty-eight of the performances himself: four of *The Magic Flute*, two of *Hoffmann*, five of *La bohème*, three of *Boris Godunov*, two of *Lucia di Lammermoor*, seven of *Tristan*, eight of *Otello*, one of Gounod's *Romeo and Juliet*, four of *Il seraglio* and two of *Faust*. During one of the *Magic Flutes* he had noticed that the celesta player, due to produce the sound of Papageno's bells, was missing. Jumping down from the rostrum, he whispered to Wynn Reeves, who was leading, to conduct while he played the instrument himself. Reeves found to his consternation that the score on the conductor's desk was closed. Beecham had been conducting from memory and Reeves, with no time to find the right page, had to manage as best he could.[46]

In September 1916 Beecham at last revealed his proposals for the future of the Royal Philharmonic Society. They were Draconian. First, he was to be a elected a director; secondly he was to be chairman of any board meeting he attended; thirdly he was to be given complete control of the society's orchestra, programming and concert arrangements; lastly, Donald Baylis was to be elected honorary secretary, a post that happened to be vacant. For his part, Beecham would conduct a season of six concerts, for which he and Baylis would be entirely responsible financially. Knowing that they had no alternative if the society were to survive, the directors voted unanimously to accept the demands. Furthermore, in return for a pledge that Beecham would raise a special guarantee fund of £10,000 (£400,500), they agreed to appoint him the society's conductor for the next five years, with the option of a further five years after that.[47]

Beecham had one more iron in the fire. He had been approached by Neville Chamberlain, Lord Mayor of Birmingham and future Prime Minister, to advise on the creation of a first-class symphony orchestra for the city. Chamberlain, a genuine and knowledgeable music-lover, believed that the money should come from an endowment fund with, a revolutionary idea for a British politician, additional funding from the rates, though he believed it unlikely that anything could be achieved until the war was over.[48] Beecham thought otherwise, and started to lay plans for such an orchestra.[49]

By now Beecham was the most powerful figure in British music, eclipsing his nearest rival, Henry Wood. Wood's promenade concerts remained immensely popular and he still conducted the regular concerts of the New Queen's Hall Orchestra, but his wartime programmes lacked the pioneering spirit that had once brought forth the British premieres of Schoenberg's *Five Orchestral Pieces*, op. 16, and Mahler's First, Fourth and Seventh Symphonies, as well as *Das Lied von der Erde*.* Wood found Beecham's success galling, and it is no accident that in his autobiography, *My Life of Music*, published in 1938, he does not mention his rival's name once. Five years later Beecham reciprocated by not mentioning Wood in *A Mingled Chime*.

On 19 October 1916, a Thursday, Beecham opened the Hallé's new season with an all-Wagner programme at the Free Trade Hall. The Canadian bass

---

* The orchestra had acquired the prefix 'New' following a reorganisation in 1915. For a non-Central European conductor of his generation, Wood was unusual in performing a number of Mahler's works (later he would introduce the Eighth Symphony to London). For Beecham, Mahler's music held little appeal. He conducted only the Fourth Symphony, which he gave with the New Symphony Orchestra at Queen's Hall in 1907 with Blanche Marchesi as the solo singer in the last movement, and *Kindertotenlieder*, which he conducted twice in 1934, on both occasions with the Russian bass Alexander Kipnis.

Edmund Burke, billed as Captain Edmund Burke, sang Wotan's Farewell from *Die Walküre* and Hagen's Watch from *Götterdämmerung*. If any of the critics thought it rather odd, even comic, that an Allied army officer should have elected to sing these very German pieces, none of them mentioned it. Unfortunately the captain was not in good voice and Beecham had to tell the audience that he was suffering 'from hoarseness as the result of exposure to the rigorous weather in carrying out his military duties'. [50]

Joseph Beecham was in the audience. At the end of the concert Thomas saw his father on to the local train back to Huyton and then took the sleeper to London. The new opera season had just opened at the Aldwych, where on the following night he conducted a performance of *La bohème*. The Mimi was the soprano Bessie Tyas, 'a high soprano of considerable variety and charm', [51] who had first sung for him eight months earlier, when she had taken the role of Olympia in *The Tales of Hoffmann* at the Shaftesbury. She and Beecham were now engaged in a passionate affair, though it seems that Maud Cunard knew nothing of her rival. In August she wrote to Jelka Delius saying that Beecham was 'delightful, but so nervous that he must go alone to the country to have a fortnight's rest cure'. [52] *

On the Saturday morning after the Hallé's Wagner concert Joseph worked in his office at St Helens for a few hours before catching the train to London, where he spent the weekend at Arkwright Road. Durant, his butler, found him 'quite happy and cheerful'. [53] Joseph had business meetings planned for the Monday, after which he intended to spend the evening with his brother William at the National Sporting Club. When at eight o'clock on Monday morning Durant knocked on his master's bedroom door to wake him, he got no response. On opening the door he found Joseph in bed, as if asleep. Durant thought he looked ill. He put out his hand to arouse him, only to find that Joseph was dead.

---

* At the time Beecham had a country retreat at Markyate in Hertfordshire.

CHAPTER 9

A Mountain of Debts

JOSEPH'S DEATH at the age of sixty-eight was unexpected, and an inquest was held. Thomas, who identified the body, told the coroner that at times during the past three months his father had been feverish and had suffered from fatigue, but that there was nothing in his condition that had led him to believe that he might die suddenly. When he had last seen Joseph, on the night of the Hallé concert, he had seemed 'unusually well'. Others who gave evidence included the pathologist Bernard Spilsbury, who conducted the post-mortem. Himself something of a celebrity – six years earlier his findings had helped to secure the conviction of the wife-murderer Dr Crippen – Spilsbury said that Joseph had died of disease of the arteries; his heart was enlarged and its cavities dilated. The jury returned a verdict of death from natural causes.[1]

Joseph was given a funeral befitting one of St Helens's most generous bene-factors. His coffin, topped with a heart-shaped wreath from his estranged widow Josephine, was escorted by mounted police on its six-mile journey from Ewanville to St Helens parish church, where the mourners, several hundred strong, were led by Josephine and her eight children – Thomas, who as the elder son had inherited the baronetcy; Harry, now serving in France as a lieutenant in the Army Service Corps; and her six daughters, including the eldest, Emily, whom Joseph had never forgiven. Edna Thornton, the Beecham opera compa-ny's Delilah and Amneris, came from London to sing 'O rest in the Lord' from Mendelssohn's *Elijah*. At the end of the service many shops closed in tribute as the cortège passed on its way to St Helens cemetery, where Joseph's remains were placed in a new family vault.

Joseph had made a fresh will only a month before his death, which suggests that he may have had an intimation of his imminent demise. In it he directed that the pill business should become a private limited company. The major shareholders were to be his two sons, who were each to receive 460 out of every 1,000 shares issued, a hefty and valuable holding. But if Thomas imag-ined that this would give him access to the capital, he was to be disappointed. Joseph, knowing his elder son's cavalier attitude to money, and anxious to protect the interests of Utica and the children, made sure that he could not touch it. His shares were to be placed in a trust administered by the execu-tors of the will, who were to be responsible for distributing the dividends. On Thomas's death the shares were to pass to his eldest son. No such restrictions applied to Harry's shares. It is a further sign of Joseph's lack of confidence in Thomas's financial sense that he did not appoint him one of his four executors, but instead chose Harry, Charles Rowed, his manager at the pill factory, and two of his sons-in-law, one a Manchester doctor, the other a Liverpool leather-importer.

For Thomas, his father's death could not have occurred at a worse moment. His debts had once again grown alarmingly, to around £50,000 (£2 million). He claimed that the sum had been incurred in connection with his operatic activities and that Joseph had planned to reimburse him. 'Had he lived three weeks more I should have owed nothing at all', he said later.[2] Joseph's executors were helpful, but only up to a point. They accepted responsibility for all liabilities known to have been sanctioned by Joseph, but refused to pay the majority of Thomas's debts because, they argued, there was no evidence that they had arisen from his musical activities.

The holdings of Thomas and Harry represented 92 per cent of the company shares. The remaining 8 per cent was split – a typical Victorian touch – between four of Joseph's daughters. The two left out were his eldest daughter, Emily, and his second youngest, Elsie Olive, who had married against his wishes. Just as he had threatened sixteen years earlier, Emily had been left out of his will altogether, while Elsie Olive received no shares, but was bequeathed an annuity, modest in the circumstances, of £250 (£10,000). Joseph's mistress, Helen McKey Taylor, who had been in Australia visiting friends when he died, was also left nothing. She appealed to the executors for support, and in 1918 they eventually agreed to pay her a lump sum of £6,000 (£172,560) and to invest £9,000 (£258,600) in trust funds, the income from which would be paid to her during her lifetime. (She died two years later.)[3]

Several other former paramours of Joseph appealed for financial help, but only one of them, a Mrs L. Hill, was thought to have a case. She had borne Joseph a son, described by Thomas as a lusty specimen of juvenile masculinity.[4] Elsie Olive remembered her as having 'piles of yellow hair' and paying visits to the nursery at Ewanville, where on one occasion she gave her a children's story, *What Katy Did Next*. Elsie had no idea who she was and, because of the book, thought kindly of her, until she discovered her true identity.[5] The executors came to the conclusion that they had no legal responsibility for either Mrs Hill or her son, and it was left to Thomas and Harry to provide them with a modest £250 (£8,000) a year out of their own pockets. The brothers also promised to make provision for their eldest sister, Emily.

The executors were all but overwhelmed by the complications of the Covent Garden estate, made harder still by family in-fighting over the terms of the will. Because of this, it was decided that, despite the huge costs involved, the more intractable problems should be placed before the Chancery division of the High Court for adjudication. Louis Nicholas, a leading Liverpool accountant, was called in as financial adviser. At first it seemed doubtful if Harry could play much part in administering the will, but in December 1916 he was seconded from the army to help run the munitions industry in Britain, which allowed him to attend more executors' meetings than would have been possible had he remained in France.

Completion day for the Covent Garden purchase, 27 June 1917, was approaching fast, but the executors had no chance of meeting it. Their immediate priority was to find £190,000 (more than £6.3 million) to pay an initial instalment on Joseph's death duties – the final figure was £295,669 (£9.8 million)[6] – together with £79,600 (£2.6 million) due to the Inland Revenue for underpayment of income tax by Joseph over the previous seven years. But even this was as nothing compared to the vast sum still owed to the Duke of Bedford – £1.75 million (£58 million).* Fortunately the duke was prepared to delay completion by yet another year, which gave the executors time to raise the money by disposing of some of Joseph's assets, beginning with his cherished picture collection, the Royal Court Theatre at Warrington, seventeen houses and shops at St Helens, property in Liverpool, three farms bought for investment in Warwickshire, and his Hampstead house in Arkwright Road. Ewanville was closed up and the servants' employment terminated.

With property prices depressed by the war, it was not a good time to be selling. Arkwright Road went for only £5,700 (£188,700). The pictures, to which Joseph had been adding almost up to his death – they included thirteen Constables and twelve watercolours by Turner, plus one of his paintings of Walton Bridges – raised far more, a total of £97,068 (more than £3.2 million), when they were auctioned at Christie's in May 1917. The highest prices paid were for two of the Constables, *On the Stour*, bought by Joseph from the artist's family, and *Salisbury Cathedral from the Bishop's Grounds*, which fetched £6,300 and £6,510 respectively. Turner's view of *Constance*, once owned by Ruskin, sold for £4,252 (£140,800), the largest sum yet paid at auction for one of the artist's watercolours.† When Ewanville's contents were auctioned a year later, the

---

* In *A Mingled Chime* (pp. 157–8) Beecham writes that when Joseph died he was close to signing an agreement with the duke that would delay completion until the war was over. However, there is no evidence in the Bedford Estate archive, the Chancery papers or the minutes of the executors' meetings to suggest that such an arrangement was ever discussed.

† By way of comparison, fourteen Turner watercolours sold at Sotheby's in July 2007 fetched an average £768,570 each. Among Joseph Beecham's pictures, Turner's *Constance* is now at York Art Gallery, the view of Salisbury Cathedral (Constable painted at least four of them) belongs to the Metropolitan Museum of Art, New York, and *On the Stour* is part of

mighty orchestrion that had made such an impact on the infant Beecham was bought for £1,650 (£47,400) for use in a Preston cinema.

Not unreasonably Thomas assumed that, even if he could not touch the capital he had been left, he could at least expect to enjoy the dividends it generated, which he estimated at around £75,000 (more than £2.48 million) a year. But the executors decided, and the Chancery court concurred, that their first duty was to meet Joseph's liabilities, and that practically all dividends from the business should be diverted to that end. As a result Thomas received around £8,000 (£264,800) a year, a large sum by most standards, but insufficient to make an impression on his debts.

Joseph's death had very little effect on Thomas's musical activities, however. Four days after the funeral he returned to the Aldwych for a period of work almost manic in its intensity. On two consecutive Saturdays he conducted both the matinée and evening performances – *Tristan* and *La bohème* on the first Saturday, *The Tales of Hoffmann* and *Faust* on the second – and during the intervening days conducted *Il seraglio* and a second *Bohème*.

Conscription continued to pose problems for the company. In November 1916 Beecham was himself the subject of a question in the House of Commons. Pointing out that at thirty-seven Beecham was eligible for military service, the Tory member for Ludlow, Major Rowland Hunt, asked the government which tribunal had granted him exemption. Amid derisive laughter directed at Hunt, Henry Forster, financial secretary to the War Office, replied that inquiries were being made. Four days later the *New Statesman* rebuked Hunt for his intervention:

> Ever since the day of his maiden speech some years ago, the name, which *Punch* then gave him, of "Boadicea" Hunt has been a convenient synonym for the more extreme degrees of asininity. Such qualities are not changed even by the greatest of wars, so there is no need to press the question of why a "Major" is making inquiries of this sort at Westminster instead of being with his regiment. If the military authorities have granted him leave of absence, we dare say they are acting in the best interests of all concerned* ... The combination of taste, wealth and public spirit represented in the person of Sir Thomas Beecham is one of the most fortunate accidents that could befall a country. On his life depends in an extraordinary degree the future of English music. It ought not to be so, but it is so; and if Sir Thomas were a whole regiment instead of one man, the question of his right to exemption ought not to be in doubt for a second.[7]

the Phillips Collection, Washington DC. Since 1921 the Arkwright Road house has been the headquarters of the railway union ASLEF. Ewanville was demolished after the Second World War to make way for a housing estate.

* An entertaining jest, though by now Hunt, who had once served with Lovat's Scouts in South Africa, was fifty-eight and no longer eligible for military service.

The government must have shared the *New Statesman*'s view, for the matter was dropped.

A month later Beecham was pleading with the House of Commons appeals tribunal to rescind the call-up of Horace Halstead, his principal oboe player. Halstead got a two-month deferment, but that was all.[8] Donald Baylis was luckier. Called up in July 1917 and commissioned as a second-lieutenant in the Royal Flying Corps, he was posted to its stores department at Regent's Park, where he managed to combine his duties as an equipment officer with work for the opera company. (Correspondence in Baylis's service file suggests collusion between Beecham and the Military Aeronautics Directorate.)[9] The conductor Julius Harrison was equally fortunate. As a lieutenant in the technical branch of the Royal Flying Corps, he served at a camp within easy reach of London and continued to conduct for Beecham, often in uniform, whenever his duties allowed it. He recalled an occasion when, in the course of being examined by the medical officer, an orderly interrupted to say that he was wanted on the telephone. Stark naked, he walked over to take the call and found the opera company on the other end, asking if he could manage *Tosca* the following night.[10]

Some of the problems thrown up by the war were unsolvable. A well-advanced plan to stage Glinka's *A Life for the Tsar* at the Aldwych had to be abandoned on grounds of political prudence after Tsar Nicholas II was forced to abdicate during the first Russian revolution of March 1917. Purcell Jones, who had designed the sets, sued Beecham in the High Court for unpaid fees, and was awarded £100 (£3,310) and costs, money that Beecham could ill afford.[11] The British government, alarmed by the possibility that, with the Tsar gone, Russia might now pull out of the war, mounted a propaganda campaign in favour of the new provisional government led by Prince Lvov. Beecham was made an adviser to a hastily arranged Russian Exhibition at the Grafton Galleries devoted to the country's art, literature, theatre, music, customs and even cookery.* In the exhibition brochure the novelist John Galsworthy unctuously declared that 'only one who has loved Russian literature, art, and music, will understand the numb horror of the long yesterday – the relief of the wonderful to-day.'[12] After Field-Marshal Lord French had opened the exhibition on 30 April 1917, Beecham conducted an orchestra of forty in music by Glinka, Tchaikovsky, Stravinsky and Musorgsky. The dreams of a 'wonderful today' were short-lived, shattered by the events

---

* Lloyd George, who had succeeded Asquith as Prime Minister in December 1916, was president of the exhibition's organising committee. Its senior patron was, somewhat cynically, George V, who had persuaded the government to withdraw its offer of asylum to the Tsar (his first cousin) for fear that the British public might be tempted to agitate against his own position.

of November 1917, when the Bolsheviks overthrew Russia's provisional government, and Lenin and Trotsky came to power.

At the time of the Russian exhibition the opera company was paying its second visit to Manchester, where on 4 May Beecham conducted the British premiere of Bizet's *Fair Maid of Perth*. The company then moved on to Birmingham and Edinburgh, and ended the 1916–17 season with a further eight weeks in London, this time at Drury Lane which, with almost 2,300 seats, was more than twice the size of the Aldwych and, as the Beechams' pre-war seasons had already proved, an admirable venue for opera. Additions to the repertoire included a new production by the innovative actor-director Nigel Playfair of *The Marriage of Figaro*, Beecham's version of Bach's *Phoebus and Pan* and a staging of Puccini's *The Girl of the Golden West* by the company's resident producer George King, which caused *The Era*'s critic to enthuse that 'nothing could have been better managed even on the film, than the row over the cards in the bar-scene'.

Figaro was the company's biggest success of the war years. Conducted by Beecham, it was set, not in Spain, but in the France of Louis XVI, with elaborate costumes to match. Spoken dialogue, some of it from Beaumarchais's original play, replaced the *secco* recitative. No fewer than six stage-rehearsals in costume were held to enable the women in the cast to grow accustomed to their towering wigs and hugely wide farthingale skirts.* Some thought Hugo Rumbold's designs absurdly overdone, while George Bernard Shaw took Beecham to task for taking several musical liberties, which included introducing Act 3 with the Fandango from the wedding scene, only to repeat it later in its proper place.[13] Yet Shaw found the evening 'ravishing', as did audiences and most of his fellow reviewers. Summing up the Drury Lane season, 'Saxonus' of the *Musical Standard* wrote that it had provided most welcome 'relief from the strain of war'. At a *Figaro* performance he had found 'the house aflame with cabinet ministers and political celebrity'.[14]

Meanwhile Beecham, perhaps intoxicated by the general acclaim, let his mind run wild with schemes that even he must have known had little of hope of being realised. He told the Manchester *Evening Chronicle* that if the city were to provide a suitable site, he would build an opera house on it. Was the proposal to be taken seriously? asked his incredulous interviewer. 'Absolutely', said Beecham. 'I don't ask for money.' Manchester was agog over its apparent good fortune. Within days the *Guardian* was discussing suitable sites, while Beecham told *The Observer* that he would run the opera house for ten years: 'At the end

---

* The cast included Frederick Ranalow (Figaro), Frederic Austin (Count Almaviva), Miriam Licette (Countess), Desirée Ellinger (Susanna), Bessie Tyas (Cherubino) and Gwen Trevitt (Barbarina).

of that time I will present the house to the town on the proviso that during my lifetime I shall remain in control and also that I shall draw up a constitution for its future government.' The Lord Mayor read out to the city council a letter from Beecham which promised that in size and importance the opera house would be the equal of any in Europe, 'with the exception of Paris and Petrograd', and that it would be built as soon as labour conditions and the price of materials made it possible.[15] The scheme came to nothing.

Beecham maintained his furious pace throughout the 1917–18 season, which began on 17 September with three weeks of promenade concerts with the Hallé in Manchester. After conducting the first three concerts, he handed over the task to assistants and returned to Drury Lane, where the opera company opened on 22 September with Rimsky-Korsakov's *Ivan le Terrible*, given with the sets that Joseph Beecham had acquired from Diaghilev in 1914 and conducted by Eugène Goossens senior, father of Beecham's assistant. On the second night Beecham conducted a revival of *Figaro* that unluckily coincided with the first of six night-raids on London and southern England by German Gotha bombers taking advantage of the bright harvest-moon. Margot Asquith was in a box that evening with her fourteen-year-old son 'Puffin' (the future film director Anthony Asquith) and her twenty-year-old daughter Elizabeth. Her husband, no longer Prime Minister but still leader of the Liberal Party, joined them shortly after curtain-up. In her diary she described the extraordinary sang-froid displayed not only by Beecham and the company, but also by the audience:

> On Mon. 24th we went to *Figaro* <u>divinely</u> given & conducted by Thomas Beecham ... In the middle of the delicate music we heard <u>thunder-claps</u> of guns & all in an instant knew it was a gigantic German raid. I felt the tension and danger of the situation, and watched it dawn slowly on the Huge house. The police cleared the top gallery & about 7 people got up and left but otherwise <u>no one turned a hair</u>. I whispered to H. who had joined us after the overture – Had he known the raid was coming? He said before he left Cav[endish] Sq only anti aircraft and flash lights were going.*
>
> Puff hardly looked up from the score. He was following every bar & [illegible word] lent against me in an ecstasy. Eliz looked very pretty [...] On and on the guns <u>boomed</u> and the fiddles played – it was a curious sensation and I wondered who were being killed.[16]

One German bomb landed only 800 yards from the theatre, killing thirteen people and injuring twenty-two others who were sheltering in the foyer of the Bedford Hotel in Southampton Row.[17] Much of the racket heard by the

---

* Following his resignation as Prime Minister, Asquith had returned with his family to their house in Cavendish Square. Lady Cunard, who had been living there, moved to Carlton House Terrace, while Beecham went to The Albany, the fashionable chambers situated between Piccadilly and Vigo Street.

audience came from London's new anti-aircraft barrage, which was being used for the first time. Thousands sheltered in tube stations as shrapnel from the guns' exploding shells crashed down on streets and roof-tops. In all, twenty-one people were killed and seventy injured that night. Only one of the seventeen bombers was brought down. Gunfire was heard again on the following night, when Beecham conducted *Aida*, though the raiders only got as far as South London, while on the Saturday night – *Cav* and *Pag* under Percy Pitt and Wynn Reeves, now one the company's conductors – there were bombs in Seven Sisters Road and Waterloo Road.

The last and heaviest of the raids came on the following Monday, 1 October, when bombs fell on Victoria Station, the Grosvenor railway bridge (the gas-main it carried across the Thames was set alight to brilliant effect), Pimlico and Hyde Park, though miraculously only eleven people were killed. At Drury Lane it was a *Tristan* night, with Lieutenant Julius Harrison conducting. Act 1 had to be halted, so that performers and audience could take shelter in the corridor running round the stalls, which was said to be as 'safe as houses'.[18] 'Really the Germans have no sense of the fitness of things', wrote *The Queen*'s reviewer. 'Had it been a French or Italian work that the Beecham company were playing they might have claimed that the interruption was of high military value; but "Tristan" forsooth!' After a lengthy break Isolde and Brangäne (Rosina Buckman and Edna Thornton) 'resumed magnificently, and with the other members of the cast showed a worthy determination to see the opera through at all costs'.[19]

Lady Diana Manners, as fancy-free as ever, spent that evening at Wimborne House (just behind the Ritz Hotel in Arlington Street and not far from the main action), where she dined in the safety of the basement with its owner, the famously lecherous Lord Wimborne, Lord-Lieutenant of Ireland and one of her many unrequited admirers. She reported to Duff Cooper, now in the army: 'Later arrived Jenny Churchill and Maud Cunard, both a little tipsy, dancing and talking wildly. They had been walking and had got scared and had stopped for a drink. Maud had a set purpose to get to the opera, because it being raid-night the public required example. She really, I expect, wanted to die with Thomas Beecham if Covent Garden was to be hit.[20]* So we let her out at ten. I hope she was all right.' In fact Beecham was not in London that night, but in Manchester, where he had returned for further promenade concerts. Presumably Maud was anxious to reach Drury Lane to fly the flag on his behalf.

---

* She was referring to the area in general rather than the Opera House, which in any case was closed. Jenny Churchill (properly Mrs Cornwallis-West – she had remarried following the death of her first husband, Lord Randolph Churchill) was the mother of Winston Churchill.

The programme for the final Hallé prom on 6 October included a concert performance of *Cavalleria rusticana*, though, as often happened in wartime Britain, the orchestral parts failed to arrive. Undaunted, Beecham accompanied extensive excerpts from the opera on the piano. He appeared quite frequently as pianist at this time, mostly accompanying singers, though he also joined the Hallé's leader, Arthur Catterall, for performances of Delius's *Légende* in its version with piano and, on another occasion, sonatas for violin and piano by Mozart and Grieg. In October 1918 Beecham and Hamilton Harty brought the house down at a Hallé prom when they were the soloists in Bach's double concerto BWV 1061. The last movement had to be repeated.

Reviewing the sonatas, Samuel Langford noted that in Mozart's B flat sonata Beecham's eloquent playing was 'far from the placid equanimity which so often does duty for the Mozart lyric style. Sir Thomas emulated rather the full ebb and flow of the vocal style, which is the foundation of all musical expression'. True, there were technical slips. The 'hazardous' opening of the last movement of Grieg's C minor sonata 'involved here and there a real hazard in Sir Thomas's execution, but the spirit of the music was there, and the long continued applause at the close of the recital showed that the expectation of a reading above the common had not been disappointed'.[21] On more than one occasion Beecham said that he might have become a concert pianist had it not been for a wrist injury caused by a cricket ball (Utica attributed the problem to lifting heavy luggage), but it is more likely that his imperfect technique was the result of small hands that could not stretch to the demands he made on them. If Beecham's piano-playing was often notable more for its enthusiasm than its accuracy, it remained extremely effective in conveying his view of the music.

From Manchester Beecham went to Birmingham, where he had fulfilled his promise to create a new orchestra for the city. It was called, simply, the Birmingham Orchestra. Its birth had not been easy. Beecham had no time to train the orchestra himself and instead got the ever-faithful Goossens to do the job. Goossens did his best, but conscription had caused a shortage of first-class players in the Birmingham area and some of the positions in the orchestra were still unfilled. For the season's opening subscription concert, which Beecham conducted on 10 October 1917, he had to import a number of players from London. In his review of the event Ernest Newman was enthusiastic about the orchestra's potential, but reported 'a regrettably large number of empty seats'. When Henry Wood conducted the second concert two weeks later, Newman thought that 'altogether the playing had not the electric quality of that of a fortnight ago'. If Beecham had appeared with the orchestra more frequently he might have built up a loyal audience, but in all he conducted only three of the nine subscription concerts (his last one was 'crowded to overflowing'), leaving the remainder to Wood and Landon Ronald, who both lacked Beecham's drawing-power. Although the orchestra had dates with several other local musical organisations, its future already looked precarious.[22]

In London the Drury Lane season should have continued until mid-December 1917, but on 24 November it was brought to a sudden and premature conclusion. The decision puzzled and disappointed both press and public, because houses had been particularly good during the previous two weeks; indeed, London theatre generally was enjoying a boom and 'even moderately good entertainments' were doing excellent business.[23] Nonetheless, the chairman of the company that ran Drury Lane announced that the season had been losing £1,000 (£33,100) a week. Various explanations were offered for the losses: that the air-raids had had a disastrous effect on the box-office; that a new entertainment tax was driving people from the higher- to the lower-priced seats; that operas such as *Ivan le Terrible* and the revival of *Khovanshchina* that followed it were 'too lugubrious, too charged with unrelieved gloom, to appeal here at the present time'.[24] Beecham himself laid the blame on the general apathy of the London public, claiming tetchily that 'in London grand opera in English is supported by the rich and the poor. The middle classes know nothing about it. They have a meat tea, and then go to the pictures or the music-hall.'[25]

Beecham might have been forgiven if he had chosen to throw in the operatic towel at this point, but with heroic if reckless obstinacy he decided to carry on, even though he had to resort to a number of money-lenders, who assumed, wrongly, that they would be repaid from the profits of the pill business. Beecham's debts grew even greater, but the company managed to visit Manchester and then in March 1918 opened another season at Drury Lane, where this time houses were gratifyingly large. Beecham, joked one critic, 'must now be in the unhappy position of King Gama [in Gilbert and Sullivan's *Princess Ida*], who found life intolerable when he had no cause to grumble.'[26]

Audiences even held up in early June, when most other theatres suffered a slump as the German army made an alarming series of advances on the Western Front. So great was the demand for tickets for the first night of Wagner's *The Valkyrie*, which Beecham introduced into the repertory on 14 June, that extra rows of seats had to be placed in the stalls; 'scores of people stood and many more were turned away'.[27] It was the first time a *Ring* opera had been heard in London for four years. With its ancient sets borrowed from Covent Garden and capricious lighting, the production was far from perfect, but for George Bernard Shaw it was, 'at its best moments, a superb fulfilment of the composer's intentions', with Beecham 'the star of the evening'.[28] Wagner-lovers in the audience, noted the *Daily Telegraph*, 'made no concealment of their joy'.[29] The sixth and last performance of the opera closed the season on 27 July.* In a curtain-speech Beecham drew groans from the gallery with his announcement that the company would not be back at Drury Lane until February 1919. When he promised new additions to the repertoire, supporters called out for *Lohengrin* and *Parsifal*, but were told that Wagner was to be given a rest and that they should learn to appreciate other (and presumably cheaper) things.[30]

Three days later, on 30 July 1918, the purchase of the Covent Garden estate was at last completed. Joseph's executors handed to the Duke of Bedford £500,000 (£400,000 of which had been loaned to them by Parr's Bank) and in return the duke granted them a mortgage of £1,250,000 (£36 million) to cover the outstanding balance of the purchase price, repayable over five years. Beecham, his brother and some of his sisters now found themselves joint-freeholders of the Royal Opera House, Drury Lane Theatre and much else besides, but it was no time for rejoicing. They were still faced with gigantic repayments on both bank loan and mortgage, which between them amounted to £1,650,000 (£47.4 million), plus interest. Rents and tolls were now coming in from the Covent Garden market, but were well below their pre-war level owing to restrictions on the import of foreign fruit and the shortage of transport for distribution.

Since no one wanted to buy the entire estate, the executors' only hope was to sell it off piecemeal – not an easy task, for much of the property was in a run-down condition and needed a good deal of money spending on it. To facilitate sales, the Covent Garden Estate Company was formed, with Thomas as chairman (his operatic activities left him no time to play a significant role in its affairs) and Harry and Charles Rowed as directors. Louis Nicholas, who by now had assumed the status of *éminence grise*, was appointed company secretary. For Beecham the most useful thing about being chairman was the £2,500 (£71,850) salary that went with the post. An even better bonus came in July 1918 when a judge in Chancery decreed that Thomas's annual income from the pill business should be increased to £15,000 (£431,000). Most of it went to his creditors.

To his embarrassment, Beecham found himself unable to fulfil his obligation to pay the deficit of £811 (£23,000) on the Royal Philharmonic Society's 1917–18 season. The society, already displeased that he had failed to create the special guarantee fund of £10,000 he had promised a year earlier, was growing restless and in September 1918 a group of its directors asked Beecham to 'suspend operations'. Recognising that his position was untenable, he produced a cheque for £500 'on account' and along with Baylis handed in his resignation,

---

* Beecham conducted four of the *Valkyrie* performances, Pitt two. The first-night cast included Walter Hyde (Siegmund), Miriam Licette (Sieglinde), Robert Parker (Wotan) and Agnes Nicholls (Brünnhilde).

still owing £300 (£8,600) for players' unpaid fees.[31] It was an unhappy end to his relationship with the society though, as one of the directors had the grace to acknowledge, he had indisputably ensured its survival during four difficult years.*

There was no hope of the Birmingham Orchestra surviving without further help from Beecham, and it collapsed after only one season (not two, as he claims in *A Mingled Chime*). The city council was unwilling to rescue the situation, and Neville Chamberlain was proved right in his belief that the formation of the orchestra should have waited until the end of hostilities. Delius also suffered from Beecham's insolvency: he failed to receive the final instalment of the money he had been promised in return for new works. When in September 1918 the composer and his wife came to London for a visit that was to last almost a year, Beecham was in no position to offer them lodgings, so at first they rented Henry Wood's house in St John's Wood before moving to a furnished flat at 44 Belsize Park Gardens.

By now the prospect of an Allied victory was beginning to look more promising by the day. London was full of American servicemen on their way to the Western Front and on 22 September 1918, under the aegis of the Ministry of Information, the full Beecham company, dancers included, gave 'a grand operatic concert' for some of them at a packed Palace Theatre. Beecham shared the podium with Pitt. It was the first time he had conducted in London for two months. On the day the armistice was signed, 11 November 1918, the company was in Edinburgh, where a meeting of the War Loan campaign in the Waverley Market turned into an impromptu peace celebration, with the assembled crowd singing 'O, God, our help in ages past'. Bands of jubilant young women, freed from their munitions work, roamed the streets, singing and displaying red, white and blue colours, and at noon 'a covey of aeroplanes performed spectacular evolutions and dropped smoke balls, while three of them at one point flew along Princes Street low down over the heads of the crowd.' In the afternoon the company gave a concert for wounded soldiers at Craigleath Hospital and in the evening performed *Figaro* under Pitt at the King's Theatre. Before the overture was played the entire ensemble, 'some in the costumes of the opera, others in walking dress', came on stage to sing 'Land of Hope and Glory'.[32]

Beecham had been advertised to conduct the performance of *Tannhäuser* that closed the Edinburgh visit five days later, but Pitt took his place.[33] His absence

---

* The composer Balfour Gardiner agreed to guarantee the society's concerts until the end of the war, but thought it would be impossible to replace Beecham with a 'really good' conductor, who was an 'attraction for the public' and 'reliable without being dull' (BL, RPS MS 370, fols. 44–6). The 1918–19 concerts were conducted by Landon Ronald, the twenty-nine-year-old Adrian Boult and Geoffrey Toye.

was not unexpected. His liabilities, now estimated at £80,000 (£2.3 million), had become a matter of public speculation, with the official receiver showing an unwelcome interest in the matter. The opera company continued on its travels, but apart from a single *Aida* in Birmingham, Beecham did not conduct it again until March 1919, when it returned to Drury Lane for its first post-war London season.

The Deliuses seem to have had little sympathy for Beecham at this difficult time, perhaps because of his failure to complete his payments to the composer, perhaps because in the three months since their arrival in England he had failed to conduct any of Delius's music, apart from a couple of performances in the North of *The Walk to the Paradise Garden*. The Deliuses found it hard to track Beecham down. A letter Jelka wrote to a friend in December 1918 has more than a touch of sour grapes about it. After saying that Beecham was nearly bankrupt and had sold all his furniture at Christie's, she continued: 'We have not seen him. [Maud Cunard] says he does not "wish to see Musicians just now" ... She is helping to run his Opera scheme "on a proper financial basis". They play mediocre operas and give them mediocre performances. The seats are awfully expensive – absurd.'[34] *

By now Beecham's concert appearances had dwindled to almost nothing. During the 1918–19 season he turned up for only two of the five concerts he had agreed to conduct for the Birmingham Festival Choral Society and handed over a number of his Hallé dates to other conductors, most often Hamilton Harty, a habit that infuriated the orchestra's management, not least because often he failed to carry out his promise to pay the substitute's fee. On such occasions Beecham was said to be 'ill', on one occasion 'extremely ill'. In the 1919–20 season he gave just one concert for the Hallé. It included Delius's *Brigg Fair*, but important premieres of new works by the composer were now left to other conductors, among them Wood (*Eventyr* and the Double Concerto), Boult (the Violin Concerto, with Albert Sammons, the work's dedicatee, as soloist) and Albert Coates (*A Song of the High Hills* and the Requiem).

Meanwhile, and not before time, the Beecham opera company was indeed being put 'on a proper financial basis'. Even when Joseph was alive the accounts it kept were rudimentary. He had a special overdraft at the bank for the opera, from which he could tell at a glance just how much money he was losing at any moment. At the end of each season he simply paid off the overdraft, which on average amounted to £30,000 (£1.2 million) a year.[35] Now the opera's 'furniture, scenery, costumes, scores of music and all other property and effects' were to be

---

* In fact, tickets for the opera were not unreasonably priced. At Leeds, where the company was then playing, they ranged from 12 shillings (£17.24) for a seat in the circle to 1s 5d (£2.04) in the gallery. The furniture Beecham sold came from his country home at Markyate.

transferred to a new limited company, the Sir Thomas Beecham Opera Co. Ltd, which had a properly constituted board of directors. Thanks largely to Maud Cunard's cajolery, some of the grandest names in London paid a total of £71,302 (£1.93 million) for shares in it, with Maud herself, the Aga Khan and Lord Howard de Walden topping the list at £5,000 (£135,000) each; the Columbia company, for which Beecham recorded, invested £3,000 (£81,000).[36] Beecham strengthened the artistic side of the company by appointing as its principal conductor Albert Coates, three years his junior and a gifted pupil of Nikisch. After many difficulties Coates, the son of an English father and a Russian mother, had recently reached London from Petrograd, where he had conducted at the Maryinsky Theatre. America was wooing Coates with several lucrative offers but, he said, it was his 'happy lot to help in the great work of English national opera'.[37]

The company was incorporated on 1 April 1919 and four weeks later, on 29 April, Beecham celebrated his fortieth birthday by conducting it in a performance of *Il seraglio* at Drury Lane. A fortnight after that, on 12 May, he conducted the first night of Covent Garden's first post-war Grand Season. The reopening of the Opera House had been announced the previous January. The syndicate had reconvened, and its chairman, Henry Higgins, had asked Beecham, not only to return as a member of the board, but also to act as artistic director.* The repertory for the thirteen-week season was to consist predominantly of French and Italian operas, with no works by German or Austrian composers. The highlight was to be the British premiere of *Il trittico*, Puccini's triptych of one-act operas, *Il tabarro*, *Suor Angelica* and *Gianni Schicchi*, which had been given for the first time only a month earlier, at the Metropolitan Opera, New York.

Stories appeared in the press that *Il trittico* was to be conducted by Toscanini, making his British operatic debut. It was a surprising choice, for earlier he had enraged Puccini by telling him that he considered the libretto of *Il tabarro* the worst kind of Grand Guignol, and unworthy of the composer.[38] When in March news of Covent Garden's interest in the Italian conductor reached Puccini's ears, the composer told his close English friend Sybil Seligman that he did not want 'that <u>pig</u> of a Toscanini' ('il <u>pig</u> di Toscanini'), and asked her to intercede with Higgins on his behalf. He wanted Beecham to conduct, but claimed that Higgins was against the idea. (It is possible that Beecham had no wish to conduct *Il trittico*.)[39] The dispute fizzled out, however, because it proved impossible to organise the production in the time available, so it was postponed until the following year. (Toscanini, like Beecham, never did conduct *Il trittico*, nor did he ever conduct opera in London.) The most important, and successful, novelty

---

* Beecham's fellow conductors during the season were the Italian Leopoldo Mugnone, Coates and Pitt.

of the season turned out to be the British premiere of Ravel's *L'heure espagnole*, which Pitt conducted. Two other operas new to London, Massenet's *Thérèse* and Mascagni's *Iris*, sank almost without trace.

The season might have had a makeshift air about it, but it was a miracle that it took place at all. Removing all the stored furniture from the Opera House took longer than anticipated, and the opening had to be delayed by a week. Money was short, as were labour and materials for building new scenery. There were also considerable difficulties when it came to assembling casts. A few familiar stars from earlier grand seasons were there, including Nellie Melba, who had spent most of the war in Australia, Emmy Destinn, now calling herself Ema Destinnová following the freeing of her native Bohemia from the Austro-Hungarian yoke, the young Italian tenor Giovanni Martinelli and the French-Canadian soprano Louise Edvina. But many other leading foreign singers who had been invited either could not obtain passports or were defeated by insu-perable transport problems. When it was discovered that key members of the *Madama Butterfly* cast had been delayed in Italy, the Beecham company's cast was brought down from Manchester by overnight train for the revival's first night. Sung in English, with Rosina Buckman in the title-role and Pitt conduct-ing, it came as 'a revelation to the regular subscribers; for once the occupants of the stalls and boxes did not chatter'. [40] The company also contributed two performances of Isidore de Lara's *Naïl* under Beecham, and a single *Prince Igor* with Coates conducting.

Melba was the Mimi in the performance of *La bohème* that opened the sea-son, with George V and Queen Mary in the royal box. (The King told Beecham that *Bohème* was his favourite opera, because it was the shortest one he knew.) [41] The *Telegraph*'s critic detected in the house 'a suspicion at least of tristeness aris-ing from the absence of old familiar faces', but found the occasion 'joyous' none-theless. Melba's tone, he wrote, was 'as full, as easy as ever.' [42] The imperious diva was just a week short of her fifty-eighth birthday, though no one was ungallant enough to suggest that she might have been a trifle old for the role of a young Parisian seamstress. Post-war London came as a shock to Melba, who had not seen the city for five years. Tiaras and white ties were on view in many of the boxes, but for her it was not enough. 'Can you imagine in the old days', she wrote in her memoirs, 'men walking into Covent Garden on a Melba Night, or on any other night, in shabby tweed coats?' [43]

Beecham claimed that after initial differences with Melba – she had objected to the green colour in which her dressing-room had been newly painted – they became 'excellent friends', though he felt that as a singer she was 'wanting in genuine spiritual refinement, which deprived the music she was singing of some virtue essential to our pleasure'. [44] Melba, for her part, told friends that she liked neither Beecham nor his work.[45] For her, opera was solely about singing. She was not interested in stage-craft, nor did she care for the new concept of conductor-led opera espoused by Beecham, and it comes as no surprise to read in the *Morning Post*'s review of *La bohème* that Beecham's reading of the score had 'a point of view which did not always coincide with that taken by those on the stage'.

Even more acerbic were Beecham's relations with Destinnová, a favourite with London audiences since 1904. Although she was still only forty-one, her once magnificent voice was beginning to fade and she had grown stout. It seems Beecham thought she was doing less than she might to bring the role of Amelia to life in Verdi's *Un ballo in maschera*, which he was conducting. He made an unflattering comparison with the professionalism of the Beecham company and threw in some critical remarks about the behaviour of foreign singers in general. Destinnová, who had been put under house-arrest by the Austrians during the war for her support of the Czech national movement, was not afraid of Beecham. She slapped his face and stalked out of the Opera House and the rest of the season. She never sang at Covent Garden again.[46]

The season was not only an artistic disappointment, but a financial one too. For all Lady Cunard's efforts, seats in the more expensive parts of the house had proved hard to sell, and many of the pre-war subscribers had failed to take boxes for the whole period. It seemed unlikely that the syndicate could afford to underwrite another season the following year. But if the syndicate's financial position was rocky, Beecham's looked even worse. A fortnight into the season, a clerk from a firm of Mayfair money-lenders had gone to The Albany to serve him with a petition for bankruptcy, but was told by the caretaker that he was no longer using his flat there. (In an attempt to keep his creditors at bay, Beecham was using at least four addresses.) The clerk then went to the Opera House, where Beecham, who was between performances of *Manon* with Edvina in the title-role, refused to see him. Eventually the petition, which claimed that Beecham had defaulted on two promissory notes each worth £450 (£12,150), was sent to him by registered post, care of his solicitors.[47]

With the season over, Beecham might have been expected to pause and take stock of his situation, but typically, heedless of the consequences, he leapt once more into the operatic breach, persuading the Covent Garden syndicate to grant the Beecham Opera Company an eight-month sub-lease on the Opera House for a season of opera in English to begin on 3 November 1919. Better still from the syndicate's point of view, he said that he and his company would be entirely responsible for the management of the 1920 grand season. The winter season, which opened on schedule, ran for twenty-three weeks – fifteen of them at Covent Garden and, at the midway point, eight in Manchester, but the *frisson* that had marked so many Beecham seasons in the past seemed to be missing. There were a few successes, however, notably the company's first attempts at *Parsifal* (Coates)* and *The Mastersingers* (Beecham), both done in Covent Garden's ageing sets. There was also a new production of Delius's *A Village Romeo and Juliet* with atmospheric designs by Adrian Allinson and a cast led by Miriam Licette and Walter Hyde as the young (though in Hyde's case not so young) lovers. For the composer, the opera 'went off as well as could be expected & much better than 10 years ago – Beecham and his orchestra were perfectly splendid'.[48] †

Some commentators, notably 'Schaunard' of *Musical Opinion*, felt that Covent Garden was simply too big for the company. A small group of its principals, among them Frank Mullings, Rosina Buckman and Sylvia Nelis, could project their voices into the large auditorium, but many of their colleagues sounded 'strangely shrunken'. It was like listening, 'as it were, through the wrong end of a telescope'.[49] For another reviewer, Edward J. Dent, it was 'not a sign of good management' that the company's performances of stock classics had been 'allowed to become slack and indifferent. Sir Thomas has not been seen very often at the conductor's desk, and this is the more to be regretted, since he has a most remarkable genius for pulling through a performance which in other hands would be always trembling on the verge of disintegration.'[50] But it was not just Beecham's presence that was missed. The company had lost the steadying hand of Donald Baylis, who was suffering from laryngeal tuberculosis.

The lack of attention to detail was all too obvious in the first revival of Stravinsky's *The Nightingale* since its 1914 premiere, sung in a translation by Edward Agate and conducted by Goossens. For Dent, Sylvia Nelis in the title-role was 'the only singer who was certain of the notes to be sung, and almost the only singer who was taking the opera seriously ... A modern opera of such intricate difficulty ought to be staged properly and conscientiously or not at all.' Stage-lighting was often disastrously haphazard. The composer R. O. Morris, reviewing a performance of *The Golden Cockerel*, noted that instead of the instant black-out that should have followed the killing of King Dodon by the eponymous bird, the lights 'were reduced in a series of leisurely gradations, until we began to wonder if this really was King Dodon's palace after all, and not one

---

* It is likely that *Parsifal*'s religiosity held little appeal for Beecham, for he never conducted the work in the theatre. However he often gave excerpts from it in concert during the earlier part of his career. In 1953 he made a refulgent recording of the 'Good Friday Music' with the Royal Philharmonic Orchestra (Sony CD SMK89889).

† In *Overture and Beginners* ((London, 1951), p. 151), Goossens says that he, rather than Beecham, conducted the last of the *Village Romeo*'s three performance, but no evidence has been found to support this claim.

of the stately homes of England, with the old family butler tottering round and turning off the switches one by one before going to bed.'[51] The incident could have been taken as a metaphor for the company's decline.

If audiences thought they would be offered greater vocal allure during Covent Garden's second post-war grand season, which opened on 10 May 1920, they were soon to be disillusioned. Publicity described it as an 'international' season, yet many of the singers were members of the Beecham company, and most of the foreign artists who did appear were of the second rank. There was no tenor to match the previous year's Martinelli. Melba did not return either. She had told a friend, 'I dislike Beecham and his methods. I'll sing only if the King commands me.'[52] The King did not oblige her. Lady Cunard found it harder than ever to dragoon society into buying subscriptions. Britain was suffering from a post-war slump, and unemployment was high. The repertoire, made up entirely of French and Italian works (German opera was still out), was even more unbalanced than in 1920. There were five operas by Puccini, but to the press's irritation only one, *La traviata*, by Verdi. Eccentrically Bizet's *Les pêcheurs de perles*, which Beecham conducted, was sung, not in French, but in Italian. Beecham later hailed the Spanish coloratura soprano Graziella Pareto, who sang the role of Leila, as one of the 'most accomplished' singers of the age,[53] but not all reviewers agreed with him. The forthright critic of *The Times* found her 'a disappointment. A light voice, easily obscured by the orchestra except on the highest notes, with only a very moderate command of technical agility.'[54]

The second week of the season was marked by the death of Donald Baylis at the age of only thirty-seven. The chorus and a contingent of the orchestra from the Opera House performed at his funeral at Hampstead parish church, with Beecham and Pitt conducting. Agnes Nicholls sang 'From thy love as a Father' from Gounod's *La rédemption* and the 'Requiem aeternam' from Verdi's Requiem. In a graveside oration Beecham said that no one but he himself could know how untiring had been Baylis's devotion to his work, to which it was literally true that he had sacrificed his life.[55]

The British premiere of Puccini's *Il trittico*, postponed from the previous year, took place at last on 18 June, with the Italian Gaetano Bavagnoli conducting. The composer came to London to supervise rehearsals. Beecham took advantage of his presence to go through the score of *La bohème* with him 'in very close detail'.[56]* *Il trittico* should have been the high point of the season, but for the most part it was disappointingly cast and audiences found it intolerably long. After the second performance, Beecham and Higgins took the decision to drop

---

* Beecham told the American critic Irving Kolodin that his celebrated recording of the work, made in New York the previous year with Victoria de los Angeles and Jussi Björling, 'reflects Puccini's desires about this score as of 1920'.

the least-liked of the three operas, *Suor Angelica*, and for the next two evenings presented *Il tabarro* and the genuinely popular *Gianni Schicchi* as a double-bill. When that failed to attract the public, first *Schicchi* and then *Il tabarro* shared the bill with the Diaghilev company, which was collaborating with Beecham for the first time since 1914. Puccini, furious with Beecham for ditching *Suor Angelica*, took to calling him 'the Purge'. To Sybil Seligman he expressed a desire to 'tie up all three in a sack together: the Purge, the Ship [Lady Cunard] and Higgins!' [57] More than thirty years later Beecham said of Puccini, 'I never liked him too well, but we managed.' [58]

The Ballets Russes, which had spent most of the war in the Americas and Spain, and since September 1918 had been reduced to dancing in London's variety theatres, brought a much needed touch of glamour and excitement to the lacklustre season. It presented a large repertoire that included three works new to Britain, the Stravinsky–Matisse *Chant du rossignol*, the Stravinsky–Picasso *Pulcinella* and a reworking as an opera-ballet of Cimarosa's *Le astuzie femminili*, all of them choreographed by Massine. Karsavina and Massine were among the principal dancers; Ernest Ansermet conducted.

Diaghilev's reunion with Beecham, which had begun amicably enough, went from bad to worse. Because the grand season was losing so much money, Beecham fell behind with payments to the impresario. Diaghilev, who ironically had so often been saved from financial ruin by Joseph Beecham, consulted a firm of London solicitors, which advised him to cut his losses and withdraw from Covent Garden before the end of the season. He took the advice, and cancelled the last ballet performance, scheduled for the penultimate night. It was replaced by a hastily arranged *Tosca* conducted by Bavagnoli, who on the following night, 31 July, brought the season to a close with *La bohème*. There was nothing to celebrate, and for once Beecham failed to make a last-night speech from the stage.

Largely as a result of its ill-advised involvement in the grand season, the Beecham company faced liabilities estimated at £20,000 (£466,800). Diaghilev put in a claim for £3,000 (£70,000), though in the end he had to settle for a third of the sum. [59] In a last-ditch bid to save a six-month opera tour of the provinces due to start in the autumn, Beecham tried to raise money for it by mortgaging the company's sets, costumes and scores, but it was too late. [60] On 31 August a shareholders' meeting confirmed a resolution that the company should be voluntarily wound up. Liquidators were appointed. [61]

That seemed to be that, but still Beecham refused to give up. In response to pleas from members of the company who were in imminent risk of being thrown out of work, he set about rescuing the tour. Prudently staying in the background, he got Arthur Lomas, a Manchester businessman and talented amateur musician, to act as front-man.* The plan was for Lomas to set up a new organisation, whose board of directors would include representatives from the cities to be visited. With the support of Henry Higgins of Covent Garden (which was owed more money by the Beecham company than anyone else),[62] Lomas approached the liquidators, who agreed to rent him all the company's effects ranging from scenery to musical scores. He then travelled to the first five stops on the planned tour – Birmingham, Edinburgh, Glasgow, Leeds and Manchester – to sell the scheme and raise enough money to allow it to take place. In Scotland he told a meeting of potential backers that Beecham would be conducting without fee 'when he turned up', an enigmatic assertion that was greeted with laughter.[63]

Birmingham failed to produce a penny of support, but thanks to one or two of Beecham's friends who came up with last-minute donations, the tour opened there as promised on 27 September with a month-long season at the Prince of Wales Theatre. It soon became apparent, however, that the visit was making a loss. The liquidators, on discovering that Beecham had failed to secure a guarantee to cover the cost of renting the scenery and costumes, threatened immediate closure. The tenor Webster Millar, a company veteran, saved the situation with a deposit of £1,000 (£23,340) for the scenery and a pledge to pay £200 a week in rent for it. Beecham gave Millar a promissory note for £2,000.† The Birmingham season was allowed to continue, but still it lost money. Beecham summoned the tour manager to London, where he told him that he had just sent a telegram to the company terminating his agreement with it, and ordering its immediate return to London. The manager, together with the singers and music staff, fought back. They pointed out that Lomas had raised sufficient guarantees to justify carrying on to Edinburgh and declared that they would run the company themselves as a 'commonwealth', to which Beecham agreed.[64]

In Edinburgh the company called itself the 'Sir Thomas Beecham Grand Opera', though when it moved to Glasgow in early November, the word 'Grand' was dropped, perhaps because it was felt that the performances hardly justified the word. Both orchestra and chorus were noticeably smaller than in past years. Albert Coates was no longer on the conducting staff and, despite Lomas's hopes, Beecham did not appear anywhere. To make matters worse, a number of the company's best singers had abandoned ship. As a result, wrote the *Musical Herald*, there was 'wholesale recasting, much of it not for the better.[65]

---

* Lomas had founded and trained the Manchester Beecham Operatic Choir, which acted as an unpaid extra chorus for the Beecham company's visits to the city. He also conducted the performance at the Hallé proms of the Bach double concerto that featured Beecham and Harty as soloists.

† Beecham repaid the money three years later, but Millar was unable to enjoy it for long. In June 1924 he died aged fifty-one from blood-poisoning after accidentally cutting himself with a chisel.

The Glasgow season ended on 4 December 1920. Though houses in Scotland had been respectable, the company had still made a loss. After failing to obtain the guarantees needed to continue to Leeds and Manchester, Lomas admitted defeat and the company was closed down. Manchester's lack of support came as a particular disappointment, for Beecham had so often used the city's apparent enthusiasm for opera as a handy stick with which to beat London's apathy. The company's demise brought an end to Beecham's dream of a national opera for Britain. It also marked a watershed in his career. He would not conduct again for almost three years.

CHAPTER 10

The Bull of Bashan

IT IS AT THIS POINT in *A Mingled Chime* that Beecham's account of his life veers into outright fiction. He gives the impression that during the next three years he sat at his desk daily, solving the problems of the Covent Garden estate almost single-handedly. In reality he played little part in the task. True, he kept an office in the Central Market Building, but he was rarely there and spent a lot of time abroad in the company of Lady Cunard. Because of both the failure of the Beecham Opera Company and the petition for bankruptcy he had received during the 1919 Covent Garden season, his financial competence was in serious doubt, and there was no possibility that he could be seen to be involved in property transactions worth thousands, even millions, of pounds. The petition was not, as he claims in *A Mingled Chime*, 'harmlessly dormant', but a constant and very public reminder that he could be declared bankrupt. Were that to happen, the court could sequester dividends due to him from the pill company, with disastrous consequences, not only for Beecham himself, but also for Utica and the boys.

His examination in the Bankruptcy Court was set for 24 November 1920, but had to be adjourned until February 1921, first because the statement of affairs he submitted was 'very imperfect', and secondly because new claims were being made against him all the time.[1] Beecham's solicitor promised more accurate information within the week. A month before the new date a Belgravia doctor wrote to the court saying that Beecham was suffering from colitis and in a very run-down condition, and that unless he went to the South of France for two or three weeks he faced 'a very serious risk of a complete breakdown'. There is little doubt that the condition, from which he had suffered before, had been brought on by worry over his financial difficulties. In a written statement Beecham added melodramatically that if he failed to take the doctor's advice, there was 'a considerable danger' that he would have to enter a nursing home, where he would be 'unable to see anyone except my medical attendants'.[2] The court, which assumed he would be back in London in time for the hearing, agreed to his going abroad.

On the appointed day there was no sign of either Beecham or the promised documents. His solicitor explained that his client had been unable to complete the accounts because of his illness, and that he was now in Paris under the care of a specialist. Another adjournment was granted – and then, as a result of further

procrastination by Beecham, three more. The examination finally took place on
12 October 1921 and took two days. It was an uneasy encounter for both parties. For much of the time Beecham seemed to lack a firm grasp of his financial
affairs (he confessed that, compared with his father, he possessed 'no financial
ability whatsoever'), while the receiver, whose task it was to find a solution fair
to both debtor and creditors, had to grapple with inaccuracies and inconsistencies in the set of accounts that had been filed only that day.[3] There was a further
adjournment to allow both sides time to consider their positions.

There is no reason to doubt that Beecham consulted a specialist in Paris, for
he spent much of the early part of 1921 there with Lady Cunard. Jelka Delius
reported that he was now 'disgusted' with England's 'indifference and ungrate-
fulness' over his musical activities,[4] yet he still harboured hopes of resurrecting
the opera company, even hiring a Mr George Robinson as general manager of
his musical enterprises at a promised salary of £1,200 (£30,850) a year. Robinson
was to look into the possibility of buying the company's sets and costumes from
the liquidators for a future tour, but nothing came of it and he went unremuner-
ated. When he sued for payment in the High Court, Beecham at first denied
that he had engaged him, but then backed down in the face of evidence to the
contrary. Robinson received his money and costs, a further financial blow for
Beecham.[5] In the end a group of artists from the company itself bought most
of the effects* and set themselves up as the British National Opera Company
(the BNOC), with Percy Pitt as musical director. It opened its first season, in
Bradford, in February 1922.

Meanwhile the Beecham family was struck by turmoil of a different kind. In
1917 Harry had bought Lympne Castle on the Kent coast near Hythe from Francis Tennant, brother of Margot Asquith. He and his family could not live there
immediately, for during the war it had been commandeered by the Royal Flying
Corps. While waiting for the military to move out, Harry rented Knebworth
House, Hertfordshire, seat of the Earl of Lytton, who at the time was living in
Switzerland. On 2 January 1921 Harry, who had not lost his love of speed, took
three of his Knebworth house-guests for a Sunday afternoon spin in his high-
powered Vauxhall Special. As they were driving along the Baldock–Royston
road, the car skidded at a sharp bend. Harry lost control and hit three children
who were walking along a bank by the roadside, an eight-year-old girl and her
two brothers aged six and three. Though injured, the girl and the younger boy
survived, but the other brother, Charles Collis, died of a fractured skull.

Harry was quick to pay the family compensation, but local feeling ran high
against him. The children had lost their father in the war and their mother was

* The sets and costumes for *Boris Godunov*, designed for Diaghilev's 1913 seasons in Paris and
at Drury Lane, were acquired by the Paris Opéra.

now married to an unemployed farm-hand. Harry was charged with manslaughter and committed for trial at the Hertford assizes. The two-day trial began five months later, on 23 June, when he was accused of causing Charles Collis's death by driving at excessive speed. Although his passengers testified in court that he had been travelling at only a moderate pace, villagers who witnessed the accident painted a different picture. One described the car's speed as 'terrific'; another put it at 65 mph, the speed the Great Eastern express trains reached as they passed nearby. It was noted that the Vauxhall's gear-lever had been found in the 'top-speed' position.

Giving evidence in his own defence, Harry said he had been going at only 20–25 mph. Sir Richard Muir, leading for the prosecution, asked if he had bought the car 'because it was capable of a very high speed'. No, said Harry; he had bought it because it had appealed to him, adding unwisely, 'I don't care for going at a high rate of speed myself.' 'Is that true?', Muir asked. 'It is true', said Harry, apparently unaware that he was walking into a trap. Muir pressed on: 'Is it not the case that you have been repeatedly convicted of driving to the public danger?' Harry asked the judge whether he was compelled to answer the question. 'You have brought it on yourself', said Mr Justice Rowlatt. Harry admitted that Muir was correct. After the jury brought in a verdict of guilty, the judge said that the case demonstrated 'wicked and selfish negligence' on Harry's part; it was not the first time that someone had died as a result of his dangerous driving. Harry was sentenced to twelve months' imprisonment. A month later an attempt by his counsel to have the conviction overturned was quashed by the Court of Criminal Appeal.[6]

With Harry out of circulation, the task of Louis Nicholas and the executors grew yet more burdensome. Beecham sniped from the sidelines, at one point accusing them of incompetence in their efforts to sell off the Covent Garden estate.[7] In fact, large sales of property had been achieved since 1920 and, to the unconfined relief of everyone concerned, the mortgage with the Duke of Bedford was at last paid off on 7 September 1922, eight years after Joseph had embarked on his unwise speculation. The Beechams even found themselves still in possession of several Covent Garden properties that no one had wanted to buy, including the Royal Opera House and the Market.

The Opera House had become something of a white elephant. The syndicate had not recovered financially from the débâcle of the 1920 grand season, and for the time being was not prepared to risk further international seasons. What little opera there was at Covent Garden in 1922 – just thirteen weeks in all – was given in English by either the Carl Rosa or the BNOC. The latter enjoyed the public's goodwill, but while some reviewers bent over backwards to be kind to it, others found it a shadow of the old Beecham company, with low orchestral standards and unpredictable casting. The spark and imagination, not to mention the money, that Beecham had brought to the original enterprise was missing.

By mid-1922 Beecham was aching to return to music. He wrote to the Hallé, offering to conduct two of its concerts during the forthcoming season.[8] It was a gamble. Thanks largely to his energy and generosity, the orchestra had survived the war, but he still owed it £733 (£23,300) in respect of fees for substitute conductors and other expenses for which he had accepted responsibility during the 1917–19 seasons. The Hallé needed the money and was one of the many petitioners anxiously awaiting the outcome of Beecham's bankruptcy proceedings. The orchestra's executive committee was in two minds about inviting Beecham back, but Hamilton Harty, who with Beecham's approval had been appointed the Hallé's chief conductor in 1920, had no such qualms. He felt that Beecham could help him restore the reputation of the war-wearied orchestra. Harty's wishes prevailed, and Beecham was promised a pair of concerts at the end of the season.

The autumn of 1922 was a nerve-racking time for Beecham. The final hearing at the Bankruptcy Court was scheduled for 2 November. Should he fail to satisfy the court that he was in a position to pay all his debts, he would be declared bankrupt. In desperation he asked the executors, who had been rejoined by Harry following his discharge from prison, if they would raise a bank-loan sufficiently large to pay off all his creditors.[9] They were sympathetic to the idea. With the Covent Garden affair settled, they now had much greater financial freedom. Also, they were anxious that Thomas's bankruptcy, which looked to them inevitable, should not compound the public embarrassment already caused to both family and pill business by Harry's conviction

Louis Nicholas estimated that for Thomas to discharge his debts and pay his legal costs he needed at least £118, 825 (£3.8 million). If his unpaid supertax and a sum of £15,000 he owed to Harry were also taken into account, the total could rise to £150,000 (£4.7 million).[10] The executors decided to go ahead with the loan, which was sanctioned by Chancery, and the Bankuptcy Court agreed to adjourn the hearing until 28 March 1923. As a result of the delay the final stages of the drama became unexpectedly entwined with Beecham's Hallé dates.

The first of the concerts was scheduled for 15 March at the Free Trade Hall. Gustav Behrens, the Hallé Society's chairman, had to be prodded by Harty into writing courteously to Beecham to ask about his date of arrival ('I expect he wd like his old suite in the Midland', wrote Harty) and to invite him to supper with the executive committee after the concert.[11] But if the chairman's welcome was half-hearted, the audience's was quite the opposite. Beecham, it was noted, was 'genuinely moved' by the demonstration of affection and gratitude that followed a programme of music by some of his favoured composers – Weber, Delius, Berlioz, Mozart (the 'Linz' Symphony, described as 'little known' by the *Musical Times*'s reviewer), Méhul and Bizet – plus, as a gesture of friendship, Hamilton Harty's Piano Concerto with Harty himself as soloist.[12] The Manchester critics urged readers not to miss Beecham's second appearance, on 30 March, when he would be sharing the conducting with Harty at a special Good Friday concert.

Two days before it took place, the bankruptcy order against Beecham was lifted at last. His relief, and that of the executors, was manifest. 'I have an appointment with the official receiver', Beecham quipped to friends. 'For what he is about to receive may the Lord make him truly thankful.' No doubt the receiver was truly thankful to see the back of him, and vice versa, though not everyone was satisfied by the outcome, Gustav Behrens for one. On reading in the following morning's *Times* that Beecham's debts were to be paid in full, he telephoned the Hallé's solicitors to ask when the orchestra might get its money, but soon discovered that, instead of the expected £733, it would receive only £200, which, after the deduction of lawyers' fees, would shrink to £142, a shortfall of £591 (£18,800).[13] The news did nothing to improve his feelings about Beecham, who a few days earlier had pulled out of the Good Friday concert.

Notice of Beecham's withdrawal reached the Hallé in a none too convincing letter from his secretary saying that he had 'a bad attack of influenza', as a result of which his doctor had 'sent him to the South Coast, where he is to remain for two weeks at least'.[14] A more likely reason for his absence, and one that must have occurred to the Hallé, is that Beecham knew that some of the unsecured creditors would not be paid in full and could not face a confrontation with Behrens. Beecham also pulled out of a concert arranged for the following November, at which he was to have conducted the first British performance of Strauss's *Alpine Symphony*, a task that fell instead to Harty, who by the end of the decade had succeeded in turning the Hallé into what was widely acknowledged to be the best orchestra in Britain.

If musically minded Mancunians imagined that on the afternoon of Sunday 8 April 1923 Beecham was somewhere on the South Coast still recuperating from influenza, they were being naive. He was at the Royal Albert Hall in London, apparently fighting fit, for a mammoth concert that had been organised by the artists' manager and concert promoter Lionel Powell. The *Daily Telegraph* was overjoyed to see Beecham back in business: 'True, several of his former lieutenants have obtained promotion in the last few years, but it would be foolish to say that any of them has as yet succeeded in displacing the commander-in-chief, or even remotely suggested a comparison with him as orchestral conductor.'[15] The *Musical Mirror* celebrated the event with a drawing on its front-cover of Beecham, in tails and baton in hand, springing up through a hole in the floor like a Jack-in-the-box with a balloon from his mouth proclaiming, 'Here we are again!'[16] But Beecham himself seemed unsure about his future. In a pessimistic article for the *Sunday Times*, which appeared on the morning of the concert, he wrote that he had certain vague projects in mind, but knew that he had to adapt to altered circumstances. Those who had most liberally supported opera before the war had been hit hard by post-war taxation, and few of them could continue to support it now; nor was there any chance of their contribution being replaced by state subsidy, for unlike other countries that were striving to maintain their artistic institutions, Britain had other priorities.

In an attempt to overcome the hall's famously indistinct acoustics, the London Symphony and Royal Albert Hall orchestras were combined for the concert to provide an ensemble of 170 players. Further ballast was provided by the soloist, the statuesque contralto Dame Clara Butt, of whom Beecham once said that, with the wind in the right direction, she could be heard on the other side of the English Channel. She proved troublesome. Down to sing two items with orchestra in the programme, Beethoven's 'Die Ehre Gottes' (in English) and 'Divinités du Styx' from Gluck's *Alceste*, she responded to demands for encores from a band of her fans by giving them six in all to piano accompaniment – mostly trifles, said one critic, that did 'neither artist nor audience credit.'[17]

Beecham's supporters grew restless. As Butt prepared to start her fifth encore, there was a shout from the gallery, 'We want to hear the orchestra', but she ploughed on regardless. Reviewers castigated her for her behaviour – she was not after all the occasion's *raison d'être* – though for the *Musical Times* 'the time we spent with her was perhaps not wasted, as it enabled us to see Beecham's conducting more clearly for the finely wrought, fine-edged thing it is.'* Conducting from memory, he gave the audience Weber, Berlioz (the 'Royal Hunt and Storm' from *Les troyens*), Mozart, Delius and Wagner, and ended with a performance of Strauss's *Ein Heldenleben* which, even with such a vast orchestra, was so transparently clear 'that it was difficult to recognise it as the same muddy and noisy work which most conductors make it.'[18] The applause for him was tumultuous.

The success of the Albert Hall concert encouraged Lionel Powell to take Queen's Hall for four dates with the LSO under the banner 'Sir Thomas Beecham Symphony Concerts', starting in the autumn of 1923. There were well-known soloists – Fritz Kreisler, Wilhelm Backhaus and Eugen d'Albert among them – and programmes less hackneyed than most heard in London at the time. The critics found Beecham's conducting inspirational, but there were grumbles

---

* Butt was not an entirely inappropriate choice as soloist, since she had also participated in Beecham's last appearance before he went into musical exile – a performance at Covent Garden on 13 July 1920 of Gluck's *Orfée*, in which her dignified Euridice (her only operatic role) stood out in what was otherwise considered a most unmemorable production.

about the quality of the playing. For the *Musical News*, 'the nadir of our system of doing with a minimum of orchestral rehearsal' was reached at the third concert on 3 December, when the coloratura soprano Selma Kurz and the orchestra drifted so far apart in 'Sweet bird' from Handel's *Il penseroso* that Beecham had to call a halt and start the aria again.[19]

The concerts coincided with important discussions about the future of the pill business. Following his conviction for dangerous driving, Harry had lost all interest in it and he and his fellow executors were casting around for a possible buyer. In preparation for such an eventuality Harry sold the American pill business to Joseph's estate for a nominal £32,500 (£835,400).[20] It seems, however, that it was Thomas who came up with the eventual purchaser, the financier Philip Hill, who, with a group of colleagues, formed in May 1924 a new company, Beecham Estates and Pills Ltd (with Louis Nicholas as managing director), which took over not only the patent-medicine operations in both St Helens and New York, but also what still remained in the Beechams' hands of the Covent Garden estate. Besides the Market and the Opera House, this included the Tavistock Hotel, a large office block, Bedford Chambers, and numerous shops and small business premises in Russell Street, James Street and Floral Street. In all, Hill and his colleagues paid out £2,800,000 (£89 million). It is a further indication of Harry's withdrawal from public life that, on the Beecham side, negotiations for the sale were formally conducted in Thomas's name, rather than that of his more qualified brother. Thomas was invited to join the hybrid company's board, but after attending two meetings tendered his resignation.

The deal did not bring the Beechams limitless riches. Far from it. A large chunk of the money received from Hill was used to pay off the loans that had enabled the executors to complete the original purchase from the Duke of Bedford. In compliance with the terms of Joseph's will, Thomas's share of what was left was invested by the executors, and placed in trust, to provide him with an annual income equal to what he would have received from the pill business before it was sold. In 1921 this income had been fixed by a judge in Chancery at around £20,000 (£514,200) gross, to be paid for the rest of Beecham's life, provided he was not declared bankrupt. After income and supertax had been deducted, and fixed payments made to Utica and the children, as well as to his eldest sister Emily and his father-in-law, Beecham was still left with a large sum of money, but one that remained inadequate for someone who had to pay off the loan that the executors had raised to stave off his bankruptcy. In addition, he was facing yet more costly court-hearings relating to claims that had not been covered, or not been paid, under the terms of the 1923 bankruptcy agreement. He was also involved in an embarrassing dispute with his wife.

Utica, still living in Upper Hamilton Terrace, had become secretary of the

Marriage Defence Council, an organisation with offices in Victoria Street that had been set up to fight 'any Legislation which aims at making Separation a Ground for Divorce, whether by mutual consent, accidental circumstances, or legal separation order. As Christian citizens we believe that legislation on these lines would weaken the life-long bond of marriage, endanger the happiness of home life, and seriously injure the welfare of the children of the nation.'[21] The message for Beecham could hardly have been clearer.

When in early 1925 the lease on Hamilton Terrace came to an end, Beecham agreed to help Utica find a house in central London. What he had not bargained for was that, without his knowledge – he was abroad at the time – she would take a six-year lease on a grand but unfurnished eighteenth-century mansion in Mayfair, 19 Grosvenor Square. The choice of house, on the north side of the square, was not accidental. As her son Adrian later acknowledged,[22] it provided a good vantage-point for Utica to spy on the comings and goings at 7 Grosvenor Square on the east side (at the corner with Brook Street). No. 7 had recently been acquired by Lady Cunard who, said Utica, had for a long time been exercising 'an undue and pernicious influence' over her husband.[23] That his wife should be residing in such close proximity to his mistress was a matter of intense irritation to Beecham, who throughout the 1920s chose to live, not at Lady Cunard's house, but in a succession of London hotels, among them the Hyde Park and Grosvenor House.

In anticipation of moving to Grosvenor Square, Utica spent huge sums on furniture and pictures that she bought both at Christie's and from leading London dealers and carpet suppliers. Beecham was sent the bills, which amounted to around £15,975 (£527,000).[24] Utica's excesses were not restricted to furnishings. She also ordered close on £20,000-worth of jewellery from Cartier of New Bond Street, most of which was delivered to the house. When the firm asked for settlement of the bill, she said that it should look to her husband for payment. Disquieted by the news, Mr Cartier himself went round to Grosvenor Square, where after a lengthy discussion he secured the return of the jewellery. But even this failed to put a stop to Utica's machinations. She inveigled the women's page editor of the *Evening Standard* into publishing a story about the new house; this appeared in the paper on 28 May. Beecham was astonished to read that, 'At the moment Sir Thomas and Lady Beecham are busy settling down in their new home, some of the furniture for which, by the way, was bought at the Carnavon sale [at Christie's] last week. It is, I learn, the aim of the new tenants to make 19, Grosvenor Square a meeting place for distinguished people in art and literature. In short, Lady Beecham hopes to revive the Salon.'

The next day, Beecham secured a meeting with the paper's editor, which resulted in an immediate correction: 'Sir Thomas Beecham desires us to state that he has not taken No. 19, Grosvenor Square, and has no intention of residing there. Any statements to the contrary are entirely unfounded.' He also instructed his solicitors to place advertisements in the personal columns of several newspapers asserting that he was not responsible for any debts contracted by his wife, and that she had no authority to pledge his credit in any way.[25] Utica responded by seeking an injunction in the Chancery Court to prevent Beecham repeating his claim either publicly or privately. The judge, Mr Justice Eve, found her evidence 'inadequate' and declined to make an order in her favour.[26]

Beecham believed that what he called Utica's 'financial eccentricity' was designed to ruin him, but what upset him most was that their two sons Adrian and Tommy, now aged twenty and sixteen respectively, had signed a joint affidavit, produced in court, that was very critical of him. In his own affidavit, Beecham claimed that the boys were entirely under Utica's influence and would do anything she asked them to do. He complained that the money she received from him via the trustees for maintenance and the boys' education was being used instead for, among other things, 'costly and ruinous operatic enterprises'.[27]

This was a reference to a lavish production that Utica had financed in 1922 of an operatic treatment of Shakespeare's *The Merchant of Venice* by the seventeen-year-old Adrian. With Sir Frank Benson of the Stratford Shakespeare festival directing, a professional cast that included singers from the old Beecham company, a thirty-five piece orchestra conducted by Howard Carr and a large chorus, the Sullivan-inspired piece went down well at previews in Brighton and Bristol, but landed with a bump when it was subjected to the London critics at the Duke of York's Theatre. *The Times* hoped that the experience might enable the young composer to recognise his shortcomings: 'the lack of skill to develop ideas, to make climaxes, to decide whether a melody is quite good enough for the situation (as so many are obviously not), and the need of a far greater control over the orchestra.'[28] The production was taken off during its fourth week for want of an audience, and lost Utica a lot of money.

The squabble between Beecham and Utica ended in a compromise that was reached outside court. Utica was to return a proportion of the furniture to the sellers, and she and her husband would share the cost of what remained. For Beecham this still meant bills amounting to many thousands of pounds. In addition he had to find the money he owed his counsel. Once more he resorted to money-lenders, one of whom took him to court in October 1925 demanding repayment of £10,000 (£330,000) plus interest. Worse, as would emerge during the hearing, bankruptcy notices had been issued against him by various other creditors, though for the time being he managed to side-step them. 'Don't you take the slightest interest in the amounts you borrow from money-lenders, up to £50,000 or so?', he was asked rhetorically by the plaintiff's counsel, Sir Patrick Hastings.[29]

Professionally, the mid-1920s were a period of acute frustration for Beecham, who was now enduring the lowest point in his entire career. International opera had returned to Covent Garden in May 1924, but without his participation. The German performances, the first to be heard at the house in their original language since 1914, were not perfect, with uneven casting and orchestral playing that was sometimes rough and ready, but they were remarkable for the singing of a nucleus of artists, all of them making their Covent Garden debuts, who would continue to bring glory to the house for some years: Frida Leider, Lotte Lehmann, Maria Olszewska, Elisabeth Schumann, Lauritz Melchior, Richard Mayr and Friedrich Schorr. Much of the conducting was in the hands of the admired Bruno Walter, who ironically had first appeared at the Opera House in 1910 at Beecham's invitation. He would remain Covent Garden's *de facto* musical director for the next seven years. Beecham had not conducted an opera since the Covent Garden fiasco of 1920, though shortly after Walter's first season ended, he was at His Majesty's Theatre to conduct a single performance in English of *The Mastersingers* for the BNOC, for which there had been inadequate rehearsal with the less than first-rate orchestra.* It must have seemed small beer to those who had relished the recent Wagner performances in Bow Street.

Even Beecham's concert engagements in London dwindled. Most of his appearances were on tour with the LSO for the 'International Celebrity Concerts' that his agent, Lionel Powell, promoted throughout Britain. The first tour, in February–March 1924, stretched from Dundee to Cardiff. In the course of it Beecham conducted twenty concerts in twenty-two days, with a basic programme that included Mozart's 'Prague' Symphony, the overture and Venusberg music from *Tannhäuser*, and the Polovtsian dances from *Prince Igor*. The soloist throughout was the Spanish soprano Elvira de Hidalgo, who sang 'Ombre légère' from Meyerbeer's *Dinorah* with orchestra in the first half of each concert, and a group of Spanish songs to piano accompaniment in the second. Later she would secure a footnote in musical history as Maria Callas's teacher in Athens.

The self-governing LSO and Beecham made strange bedfellows. Though the orchestra included many of the best players in London, its work-practices embodied much that he had fought against before the First World War, in particular the deputy system, which as always had a lamentable effect on playing standards. Returning from a visit to America, Ernest Newman was to write sarcastically, 'I was afraid that after the splendid American orchestras our own

* The cast included Andrew Shanks as Sachs, Miriam Licette as Eva, and Walter Widdop, who later would achieve some success as a Wagner singer, as Walther.

would sound very poor, but I was agreeably disappointed. The L.S.O., I suppose, ranks as our premier orchestra; and I am glad to be able to record that at its concert last Monday [conducted by Felix Weingartner] it compared not unfavourably with the orchestras in some of the New York picture houses.' Newman went on to note that 'the strings often sounded thin, scratchy and disorganised, the wood-wind sour, and the brass blatant.'[30]

As Beecham's 1924 tour with the LSO progressed, and orchestra and conductor got used to each other, the quality of the playing improved noticeably, though Beecham must have been severely tried by the indiscipline and even drunkenness of some of the players. Two of them were each fined ten shillings and sixpence (£17.45) by the directors for arriving late for the second half of the Dundee concert, while a third was threatened with 'severe measures' should there be a repetition of his (unspecified) behaviour on the platform on several occasions.[31] The LSO's directors, all of them players, acknowledged the orchestra's deficiencies, but could do little about them. The deputy system was enshrined in the orchestra's tradition, and even modest changes in personnel were all but impossible. Wynn Reeves, who after the war had returned to the orchestra as sub-leader, remembered a long rehearsal at which Beecham displayed unusual calm as the four members of the horn section were replaced, one by one, by four quite different players. 'Gentlemen of the horn department', he said at last. 'Perhaps you will be so kind as to acquaint me as to whom I am to expect at the concert. At the present rate we shall have heard all the horn-players known in London.' He was reminded, he continued, of a limerick inspired by Einstein's theory of relativity:

> There was a young lady named Bright,
> Whose movements were quicker than light.
> She went out one day
> In a relative way
> And came back the previous night.[32]

Beecham could not afford to lose the LSO's goodwill, however, for he needed the work and the fees, though he did conduct one engagement at this time without payment, the Hallé's annual pension-fund concert in March 1926, which traditionally was organised by the players themselves. Gustav Behrens, now retired as chairman though still on the orchestra's executive committee, made no attempt to interfere with their choice of conductor. On the night before the concert Archie Camden, the Hallé's pension-fund secretary as well as its first bassoon, met Beecham off the last train from London. On hearing that the concert was not sold out, Beecham decided that more publicity was needed. Arriving at the Midland Hotel after midnight, he called for the manager – who appeared in his overcoat – and persuaded him to lay on a supper of 'hors-d'œuvre, cold meat, salad and of course champagne. Plenty of it and at once.' He also arranged for the city's newspapers to send round their night-reporters.

Camden described what happened next: 'Tommy was at his most genial. He loved to create a splendid scene, and urged his guests to eat and drink. He was a charming and attentive host, and told them how important they were; that they had the power to influence people's minds and actions; that they could ensure the success of any venture with their pens. The waiters, meanwhile, were refilling the glasses, and I heard Tommy say to one rather down-at-heel man: "Tell me, is this the vintage you like, or would you prefer a rather earlier one?" ... He painted a picture of poor, ill and ageing musicians unable to play any longer and thrown on the scrap-heap, penniless. "You, gentlemen," he said, "have it in your power to alter this. ... I rely on your help. You will not fail me! We will now toast the great Hallé Orchestra." With great drama he lifted his glass, making sure all other glasses were filled. Having rendered these representatives of the press almost speechless and full of emotion (as well as champagne) he added, "Now to finish our supper and afterwards to work". Sir Thomas gave his services, paid all his own expenses and even those of some players he had brought from London (who would arrive next morning) because he had put *Heldenleben* in the programme and this needed five trumpets and eight horns. The Free Trade Hall was packed and we made a lot of money.' [33]

Beecham spent most of the summer of 1926 on the Continent with Maud Cunard. In Venice he had an altercation with the American master of musical comedy, Cole Porter. Hoping for peace and quiet, he found his nights shattered by the noise emanating from a black jazz band that Porter had imported from Paris to play on a barge moored outside the Salute. (Diaghilev, also in Venice, was another complainant.) Beecham, using the pseudonym Didymus Belcampus, wrote a poem that he arranged to have printed called *The Tragical History of Young King Cole*, who was finally swept out to sea and drowned.[34]

From Venice he and Lady Cunard moved on to Switzerland, where, from the Beau Rivage Palace at Ouchy, the latter wrote a letter to her old admirer George Moore which she signed 'Maud Emerald (a new name)'. On receiving it, the distraught Moore telegraphed her: 'WHO IS EMERALD ARE YOU MARRIED? G.M.' He consulted the London telephone book and trade directories, but could find only one Mr Emerald, a paint manufacturer. Eventually, to his relief, he discovered that she had not become Mrs Emerald. It was simply that at the age of fifty-three, and not long widowed, she had decided to adopt a name more sparkling than Maud.[35] * (Emeralds were her favourite jewels, and she wore

* Her estranged husband, Sir Bache, had died in November 1925, aged seventy-four, leaving most of his estate to their only child, the poet Nancy Cunard.

them with style.) To many of her friends (though not to Moore or Beecham) she remained Emerald for the rest of her life.

Beecham's first engagement of the 1926–7 season, a Sunday afternoon concert with the LSO at the Albert Hall on 31 October, attracted a pathetically small audience. He called a press conference. 'Concerts have no future', he ranted, 'I have no future, nobody has any future in this country. There is only one thing left for the musician who cares for his art ... and that is to get out of the country as quickly as possible and go to America.' He had, he said, been invited to conduct the Philadelphia Orchestra in a year's time: 'When I go I shall take with me as many good musicians as possible, and my advice to every young musician in England is, get ready to go. It is the end; it is the twilight of the gods. ... Do you suppose any decent person is going to remain here to play in cinemas or for the gramophone companies or in front of the [wireless] microphones?'

A reporter managed to squeeze in a question: 'Would you appear before the microphone if the terms were good enough?' 'I would not be seen anywhere near it', Beecham retorted. 'The microphone has ruined all art. You have got this elaborate machinery of music, the beautiful human voice, or the marvellous fabric of an orchestra, and what does it sound like on the wireless? It sounds like the most horrible gibbering and chattering of goblins and devils, and they have the impudence to tell me that it is Beethoven and Wagner. It has got as much relation to music as the roarings of the Bull of Bashan.'[36]

Typically, Beecham omitted to mention that not only had he been making records since 1910, he had also by now made his wireless debut. The British Broadcasting Company, only four years old and working hard to improve the sound quality of its music programmes, had relayed the Hallé pension-fund concert via transmitters in Manchester and London, and even included an appeal he made to the audience for money. The musical periodical *The Sackbut* thought it 'better that people should hear Beethoven even as a shrieking of goblins than they should not hear him at all. ... The B.B.C. becomes at a bound the most important patron of musicians in the country, and it gives many of us a positive thrill to think of public money being spent to provide any sort of semi-musical entertainment to the mass of the people.'[37]

That Beecham should also have mentioned the gramophone companies in his attack is a typical example of his habit of biting the hand that fed him. In 1926 he made several successful recordings with the LSO (his first using the new electrical system), including one of Beethoven's Second Symphony that in sheer vitality is unmatched by either of his two later versions of the work. If the LSO plays far better on these records than one might have been led to expect by the critical drubbings it so often received for its concerts, the reason is not hard to find: to the orchestra's irritation, the Columbia company insisted on the right to vet the players used for its recording sessions, even importing musicians from outside the LSO's ranks when it was thought necessary.[38]

Few seriously believed that Beecham was preparing to leave the country, though he repeated the claim, as well as his strictures on broadcast music, during a provincial tour with the LSO that followed the London concert. Faced with empty seats in Nottingham, he told a local journalist that he would not be returning to the city. 'I could get a better audience in the middle of Africa, among primitive people', he said. 'They would love it.'[39]

There were more unsold seats a month later when, on 15 December 1926 at Queen's Hall, he conducted a pioneering and revelatory performance of *Messiah*, for which, instead of the unwieldy, elephantine choir traditionally thought suitable for the work in London, he used the smallish Philharmonic Choir, trained by Charles Kennedy Scott and full of fresh, talented and enthusiastic young voices. The LSO's playing was unusually surefooted, which the *New Statesman's* critic, W. J. Turner, attributed to the fact that the orchestra had been playing on tour under Beecham for some weeks, and as a result 'had got thoroughly into form and accustomed to his style'.[40] Tempi were fleet, textures light. Some reviewers expressed regrets about the lack of a harpsichord for the recitatives, and there were doubts about Beecham's decision to move the Hallelujah Chorus to the end of the work at the expense of the Amen Chorus, which was dropped. But most concurred with the *Guardian's* reviewer, who wrote that the performance was 'a welcome substitute for the ballasted, coarsened, and square-cut versions that are too often so confidently given out as the real Handel, but may, for all we know, err as far on the wrong side as Sir Thomas errs on the right.' Turner deemed it 'one of the greatest musical achievements of a generation of concert giving in London'.

The soprano soloist was a dark-haired, down-to-earth beauty with a racy sense of humour called Dora Labbette, who maintained that Beecham chose her for the event after seeing a photograph of her during a visit to her agents, Ibbs & Tillett. Born Dorothy Bella Labbett at Woodside, near Croydon, the daughter of a railway porter, she had shown a talent for singing from an early age and during the First World War had won a scholarship to the Guildhall School of Music, where in 1917 she crowned a series of awards by winning the Gold Medal. In the following year, seven months before the Armistice, Labbette married a captain in the Royal Engineers, David Strang, son of the artist William Strang. Her husband wanted her to give up her career, but she resisted, and nineteen months later walked out of the marital home for good, pulling behind her a hand-cart piled with her belongings.

Labbette's voice was once perceptively described as being 'of a timbre which is peculiarly individual in its charm – the clear purity of a boy soprano touched with womanly warmth and sweetness'.[41] Beecham fell in love with the sound. He also fell in love with the twenty-eight-year-old Labbette, and in due course began an affair with her that would last thirteen years. At the time of the *Messiah* Beecham was forty-seven. Whether Lady Cunard was aware of the liaison at this point remains a matter of conjecture, for she made no public comment on it and even the sharpest diarists in her circle failed to note a change in her own relationship with Beecham.

Some idea of the *Messiah* performance can be gained from the recording of the work that Beecham made six months later for Columbia with different soloists (apart from Labbette), an unnamed orchestra and the BBC Choir, whose women in particular, a contemporary review suggests, were no match for Kennedy Scott's singers.[42]* Nonetheless, if at Queen's Hall the chorus 'Let us break their bonds asunder' was unleashed with the same punch as it is in the recording, the audience must have jumped out of its collective skin.

The knock-about speechifying, the triumph of the *Messiah* and the arrival in his life of Labbette marked Beecham's emergence from the doldrums. He began 1927 with a series of engagements in central Europe, starting on 23 January with a concert with the Czech Philharmonic in Prague. One reviewer found him in many ways 'the most striking of the galaxy of great conductors' who had been guests of the orchestra; 'he conducted without a note of music before him and so was in the most perfect and intimate sympathy with his players.'[43] † There was no score either in Vienna, when he conducted a gala performance of Gounod's *Faust* on 1 February at the Theater an der Wien, an odd, polyglot affair, attended by the Austrian president, in which the roles of Faust (Jan Kiepura), Méphistophélès (the Latvian-born Georges Baklanoff) and Marguérite (Vera Schwarz) were sung in Polish, French and German respectively. The rest of the cast and the chorus, who all sang in German, came from the Vienna Volksoper, along with the orchestra and scenery. The *Neues Wiener Tagblatt* found Beecham 'a conductor full of temperament, with music in his every gesture'. There was also a concert with the Vienna Symphony Orchestra, though favourable reactions to it were somewhat blunted by Beecham's unannounced decision to switch the order of Delius's *Paris* and Lord Berners's Fugue in C minor, to the bemusement of those following the detailed analytical notes in the printed programme.

Between the two Vienna dates came a performance of *Tristan und Isolde* on

---

* Records were expensive at the time. Beecham's *Messiah*, consisting of forty-three of the Prout score's fifty-three numbers, was issued on eighteen double-sided 78 rpm discs, which came in two albums with printed text for a hefty £5 17s (£205). Individual discs cost 6s 6d (£11.40) each. An extra number, the 'Pastoral Symphony', was issued separately.

† The programme, given at an overflowing Smetana Hall on 23 January, included Mozart's 'Prague' Symphony, Delius's *Walk to the Paradise Garden* and Strauss's *Ein Heldenleben*.

11 February in Budapest, given in Hungarian, though with the Tristan (Hubert Leuer from Vienna) singing in German. The choice of Beecham as conductor caused some surprise, both inside and outside the opera house. A number of eminent Austrian and German conductors had made guest appearances there since the collapse of the Habsburg empire, among them Erich Kleiber, Richard Strauss and Clemens Krauss, but one from England was a novelty. The future conductor Antal Dorati, then a twenty-year-old répétiteur at the opera, recalled watching Beecham in the pit, rehearsing 'efficiently, with broad gestures, obviously savouring the music and the occasion to the hilt. He had a little black goatee and sparkling eyes. He talked a lot of English, which nobody in the house understood. That did not seem to bother him at all and things went swimmingly.' Dorati noticed two stagehands, leaning against the scenery and chewing bacon and bread as they looked down at Beecham. 'What does he want here?', asked one suspiciously. 'They won the war', came the reply, which seemed to settle the matter.[44]

CHAPTER 11

The Twopenny Opera

BACK IN LONDON and buoyed up by his successes on the Continent, Beecham announced in a news-agency interview that he had up his sleeve a new scheme for rejuvenating Britain's musical life which would be 'the largest and the most ambitious that I have yet put my hand to. People will be astonished when they find how simple it is – and it is terribly cheap.' It would, he said, be mainly concerned with opera. Would it include broadcasting? 'Certainly not', he replied. He hoped to release more information shortly: 'For the last twenty years I have been starting one musical enterprise after another in this country. One after another they have foundered. However I am going to have another try. If that fails, it will be my last.'[1]

The interview, which appeared on 12 March 1927, was not given wide coverage, and many of those who did read it were understandably sceptical. Only four months earlier Beecham had said he was leaving for America. Now he was clearly intending to stay in Britain, but where would he find the money for his scheme, however 'cheap' it might be? And was this a propitious moment to be launching a major new enterprise? Music in London was in a state of turmoil. Chappell & Co., lessees of Queen's Hall, had just announced that it could no longer afford to maintain either Henry Wood's Promenade Concerts or the New Queen's Hall Orchestra's concert series, which Wood had conducted since 1896. He and the orchestra were to give their last concert on 17 March. There were even stories, unfounded as it turned out, that Queen's Hall was to be sold; in the previous year there had been rumours that it was to become a cinema.

William Boosey, chairman of Chappell's, approached Beecham in the hope that he might help to save the Proms,[2] but Beecham must have turned him down, because nothing happened until May, when the BBC announced that it would be responsible for the 1927 season.* Reduced from ten to six weeks, it would feature 'Sir Henry Wood and his Symphony Orchestra', consisting mostly of players from the Queen's Hall Orchestra. That the BBC should have been responsible for the rescue was a supreme irony, for Boosey, in the belief

---

* By the beginning of 1927 the British Broadcasting Company Ltd, basically a commercial operation subsidised by a proportion of the licence fees for receiving sets levied by the General Post Office, had been transformed into the public-service British Broadcasting Corporation.

that the broadcasting of music could only have a devastating effect on concert-attendance – a view shared by Beecham and a number of concert organisations, agents and impresarios, including Lionel Powell – had kept the BBC's microphones out of the Queen's Hall. Now, for the sake of the hall's future, he had no alternative but to let them in.

Because of Boosey's intransigence, the BBC had until now been forced to hire the Central Hall, Westminster, the Royal Albert Hall or Covent Garden for its public concerts, which provoked accusations of unfair competition and, given the modest subsidy it received from licence fees, 'socialistic' competition at that. The standard of playing of the *ad hoc* orchestra that had been cobbled together for the concerts – sometimes called the Wireless Orchestra, sometimes the National Orchestra – was poor, but the BBC's imaginative programming did much to enliven London's musical diet. During the BBC's 1926–7 season Strauss gave a concert of his own works, including the *Alpine Symphony* (*The Times* complained of 'audible wrong notes and out-of-tune playing on the wind'); Honegger conducted the first British performance of his dramatic psalm *Le roi David*, Hermann Scherchen gave Schoenberg's *Verklärte Nacht*, and Hamilton Harty Berlioz's *Grande messe des morts*, not heard in London for a quarter of a century.*

The significance of broadcasting might have eluded Beecham, but other British conductors were quick to grasp its potential for cultivating a new audience for serious music, among them Percy Pitt, the BBC's first full-time director of music, and Landon Ronald, who acted as a musical adviser to the corporation's director-general, Sir John Reith. In a speech to the Incorporated Society of Musicians conference, the composer and organist Sir Walford Davies, a conservative figure who later succeeded Elgar as Master of the King's Music, called Beecham's anti-wireless tirade 'as foolish as it was useless', adding that he sounded 'like an annoyed Canute, watching the tide surround him'.[3]

Beecham spent much of 1927 working on his new opera scheme. Details were promised for June, but it was not until 13 November that a manifesto was at last issued to an enthusiastic press. The *Daily Telegraph*'s headline, 'SIR T. BEECHAM AND DEMOCRATIC OPERA', was typical of many in the next day's papers. As Beecham had promised, the basic idea was indeed simple. He calculated that in London, Manchester, Liverpool, Birmingham, Leeds, Glasgow and Edinburgh there existed a pool of at least 150,000 people who were interested in opera. If, for a minimum five years, each one of them subscribed ten

---

* Much of the credit for the repertoire goes to one of Pitt's programme-planners, Edward Clark, a one-time pupil of Schoenberg. In the following BBC season Schoenberg conducted the first British performance of his *Gurrelieder*.

shillings (£17) a year – or, as Beecham put it, less than the cost of a bun, a slice of Yorkshire pudding or a half-pint of beer a week – there would be an annual sum exceeding £60,000 (£2 million), enough to mount five or six months of opera in English in London and shorter seasons in the other cities. There would be a new orchestra, which would not only play for the opera, but also give concerts. Subscribers would be offered cut-price tickets. Beecham, who would not receive a salary, would be artistic director with responsibility for casting and productions, which would be of the highest standard.

The scheme was to be run by a new organisation, the Imperial League of Opera, with three floors of offices at 161 New Bond Street. To head off criticism that the League would suffer from the same financial and administrative muddles that had troubled the old Beecham company, all funds received from subscribers would be held and administered by a board of trustees of proven probity: Lord Islington, a former governor-general of New Zealand and organiser of the National Savings movement, Sir Vincent Caillard, a director of the Vickers engineering company, and the banker Sir Eric Hambro. The League's business affairs were in the hands of Lionel Powell (manager and general secretary), Harry Beecham and the BNOC's legal adviser, Paget Bowman.

Beecham hoped that an initial season could be mounted in the autumn of 1928. He had two or three London theatres in mind for it, he said, though he would not be going to the Royal Opera House, since 'sooner or later' it was going to be pulled down, a prospect he appeared to view with equanimity. It was no secret that he considered Covent Garden inadequate as a national opera house, because, though large as a building, it held only 1,900 people, which was uneconomic in a country where theatres received no state support. Eventually, said Beecham, if the League turned out to be a success, he would examine the possibility of building a new, more suitable, opera house in London.*

The likelihood of the demolition of the Opera House was no jest on Beecham's part. A fortnight earlier it had been reported, accurately, that the freeholders, Covent Garden Properties, were negotiating with the syndicate for the surrender of its lease, due to run until 1947, so that the building might be replaced by a much-needed extension to the fruit and vegetable market. The property company's chairman, Sir Arthur Wheeler, reckoned that the 1928 and 1929 international seasons would be the last,[4] a prediction that seemed a

---

* Earlier in the year a Unionist MP, Sir Arthur Holbrook, had asked in the Commons if the government might establish a committee to look into the possibility of building a national opera house in Britain, 'the only country in Europe' without one. The Prime Minister, Stanley Baldwin, replied – to cheers – that 'in the present state of the country's finances no such proposal as is suggested by my honourable and gallant friend could be entertained' (*The Times*. 31 March 1927).

certainty when on 15 November 1928 it was announced that the freeholders had signed a provisional contract to acquire the lease.*

Shoals of postal applications for League membership arrived at the London offices and Beecham had to telephone for extra clerical staff. The pianist Wilhelm Backhaus, in town for a series of recitals, turned up in person to hand him a cheque for a five-year subscription.[5] The Prince of Wales, not noted for his interest in opera, sent a modest £1 (to cover two years), no doubt at Lady Cunard's prompting.[6] But if London was responding with alacrity, the other cities were disappointingly slow on the uptake. Invoking the spirit of his grandfather's barnstorming oratory in the market-places of Wigan and St Helens, Beecham set off to harangue potential subscribers in Liverpool, Manchester and Birmingham, where, perhaps exaggerating for effect, he claimed that in the first ten days of his campaign not one of its citizens had signed up.[7] He spoke at the Eastbourne music festival and at a special lunch in Bradford, and in London addressed a rally at the Royal Albert Hall and a group of MPs at the House of Commons.

He would have made even more speeches had he not tripped on the pavement in Parliament Square after his Commons meeting and hurt his back, which forced him to cancel several engagements, including an LSO concert at Queen's Hall on 12 December, at which he was to have conducted Haydn's C major Cello Concerto, with Pablo Casals as soloist, and Elgar's Second Symphony. He was replaced by the twenty-eight-year-old John Barbirolli, who had little more than two days to learn the symphony. As a teenager he had played the cello for the Beecham Opera Company at the Aldwych Theatre and was now on the conducting staff of the BNOC. The concert was Barbirolli's lucky break. As he came off the platform at the end he was grabbed by a small man wearing a hat, who said, 'Don't sign any contracts. I'll see you tomorrow at ten. I'm Gaisberg, HMV.'[8] Before long he was accompanying some of the finest artists of the age in the recording studios. Frederick Gaisberg was HMV's artistic director. In spite of his accident Beecham still managed to conduct a performance of *Messiah* at the Royal Albert Hall and record Delius's *On Hearing the First Cuckoo in Spring* and *The Walk to the Paradise Garden* for Columbia, as well as some Grieg songs and French arias with Dora Labbette.

On 28 December Beecham left Southampton on the Cunarder *Aquitania* for his transatlantic debut. He was to conduct not only Stokowski's Philadelphia Orchestra, but also the two other great East Coast orchestras, the New York Philharmonic, so closely identified with Toscanini, and Koussevitzky's Boston Symphony. In a characteristic parting shot Beecham expressed the hope

---

* In January 1928 Beecham Estates and Pills Ltd had been split into Covent Garden Properties Company Ltd, which owned the freehold of the Opera House, and Beechams Pills Ltd.

that during his seven-week absence the funds needed for the League would be secured. 'I want money and not guarantees', he said, 'and I want the money quickly.'[9]

News of Beecham's musical prowess, as well as his ready tongue, had preceded him, and a bevy of reporters was on hand when his ship docked in New York on 4 January 1928. Press conferences were held both on board and at his suite at the Hotel Plaza. Beecham did not let his questioners down. He apologised for being unable (because of Prohibition) to offer them 'illegal beverages', but provided them with plenty of quotable copy, e.g. 'English music today is in that extraordinary state of perpetual promise. It is perhaps the nearest approach to perpetual motion we have, for it goes on promising and promising and has done so for three-hundred years. In fact, it might be said to be one gigantic promissory note.' As for the English people, 'We are the laziest nation in the world. People are having their music brought to them [by wireless]. I feel sure that in another fifty years they will never even get out of bed in the morning if this present tendency goes on.'[10]

The *Musical Courier*'s verdict on Beecham was that he 'was a cynical humorist of the Bernard Shaw type, but a brilliant, virile and enterprising man'.[11] Back in Britain, however, the president of the Incorporated Society of Musicians called his reported remarks 'unpardonable' (though they contained little that Beecham had not said already at home),[12] while the *Scottish Musical Magazine* complained that one of the jokes he had told – that thanks to its echo the Albert Hall was the only hall in the world where the same composition could be heard twice at one time – 'had long ago served its purpose, and had become stale about the time that Sir Thomas Beecham had been born'.[13]

New York was bowled over by Beecham's four concerts. 'Gone from the Carnegie Hall podium is the benign paternalism of Herr Mengelberg', wrote the *Evening Post*'s reviewer, in full rhapsodic flight after the first, on 12 January. 'Gone the exquisite synthesis of poetic motion and sensitive gesture that is Stokowski. Gone the stern beating of Fritz Busch and the courtly and polished virility of Koussevitzky. Instead, we gaze upon a conductor who seems to speak a new language to the Philharmonic, who shakes his fist, who fondles the strings into the most gentle of pianissimos, who sweeps his rhythms with large scoopings of his arms, who seems to hew music with the manual strength of a sculptor.' Olin Downes of the *New York Times* hailed Beecham as 'a musician of unusual enthusiasm, magnetism and purpose' who was quite unlike the 'conductors who play war-horses season in and season out in this city, and profess it difficult to find unfamiliar music that is worthwhile'.[14]

Beecham's programmes featured pieces by Handel, Grétry and Paisiello, Berlioz and Delius, as well as two of Mozart's C major symphonies – no. 34

and the 'Linz' – both of which had the word 'unfamiliar' attached to them by one critic or another.* The only true 'war-horse' was Tchaikovsky's B flat minor Piano Concerto, whose inclusion in the opening concert was nonetheless fully justified, for it featured as soloist the twenty-three-year-old Vladimir Horowitz who, too, was making his American debut. The occasion was an undoubted triumph for Horowitz – he had, wrote Downes, 'amazing technic, amazing strength, irresistible youth and temperament' – though the performance was disappointingly untidy, thanks partly, Downes thought, to insufficient rehearsal, which had led to 'a scarcity of understanding' between the two protagonists. In the first movement, the *Musical Courier* complained, Beecham, conducting as usual without a score, 'took the pace too slowly. Later Horowitz pushed ahead too rapidly. There seemed little excuse for lack of cooperation.' The concerto was repeated at Beecham's second concert and again at his fourth and last, when the *Herald Tribune*'s critic noted that Horowitz 'played with more discretion than he exhibited at his first appearance last week'. The pianist enjoyed telling the story of his tussle with Beecham to the end of his days, on each occasion embellishing it further at the conductor's expense.

Beecham's programmes with the Boston and Philadelphia orchestras were similar to those in New York, though with the Tchaikovsky concerto replaced by his familiar visiting-card, Strauss's *Ein Heldenleben*. After the first concert in Boston, Koussevitzky wrote to Ernest Newman in London: 'I hasten to tell you what a brilliant performance it was. Händel and Strauss (Heldenleben), – impressed me especially. The success was enormous, the orchestra played beautifully, and I was very enthusiastic about it. I was really very glad to see before me such a great artist.' [15]

The tour put the seal on an international reputation that no other British conductor had come close to matching. It had been full of unexpected incident. At the first concert in New York Beecham's braces had snapped towards the end of Mozart's Symphony no. 34 and, though he was using both hands to conduct, he just managed to stop his trousers falling to his ankles before the final note. In Philadelphia he had an attack of gout, which was to plague him for the rest of his life, and had to be pushed on to the platform in a wheel-chair by his valet, Smith. (It was put out that he had sprained an ankle while avoiding speeding traffic.)[16] Such episodes only enhanced Beecham's popularity. Arthur Judson, the New York Philharmonic's manager, whose idea it had been to bring him to America in the first place, had no difficulty in persuading the orchestra's board to give Beecham four further dates in January 1929 at a fee of $750 dollars a

---

* The three Handel pieces Beecham conducted in America were the Overture to *Teseo*, Musette (*Il pastor fido*) and Bourée (*Rodrigo*). Programme notes described them as being 'edited' by him.

concert (the equivalent of £5,400 in 2008).[17] Judson's support was an invaluable asset for any conductor. Regarded as the tsar of musical America, he not only had his own concert-management firm, but also managed both the New York Philharmonic and Philadelphia Orchestras.

Back in London, Beecham was disappointed to find that the League's membership had not increased significantly and that there was no chance of there being sufficient funds for an initial season in the autumn. Scotland and some of the English cities, he said, had barely begun to organise themselves.[18] Almost immediately he set out on a mammoth 'Operatic Party Tour' of twenty-three towns, set up by Lionel Powell to publicise the League. There was a quartet of foreign singers, now mostly forgotten, and an orchestra of forty players from the LSO, hailed in the publicity with a pre-Trades-Descriptions-Act flourish as 'The World's Greatest Orchestra'.* Beecham was to speak about the League at each one. The tour failed to inflame the country with operatic fervour, however, partly because Beecham had miscalculated when it came to choosing the basic programme. A veritable hotchpotch, it contained too many of his favourite eighteenth-century morceaux for orchestra, and too few rip-roaring arias from the popular repertoire that might have inspired the citizens of towns off the normal operatic track like Middlesbrough and Stirling to hand over their cash. For the *Guardian*'s new music critic, Neville Cardus, who attended the Manchester concert on 25 February, the evening lacked 'glamour and style', two attributes he had always thought inseparable from Beecham.

Throughout the tour, Beecham was frantically trying to complete a new performing edition of Handel's *Solomon*, which the Royal Philharmonic Society had commissioned the previous year and which he was to conduct at Queen's Hall in the presence of George V and Queen Mary on 22 March, just five days after the tour ended. 'Those who attended the final rehearsal', reported an onlooker, 'will not easily forget the odd spectacle of an army of copyists bringing sheets of manuscript on to the platform at frequent intervals.'[19] There had been several attempts at a reconciliation between Beecham and the society in the ten years since he had been forced to resign as a director, but all had fizzled out, even though the money he had once owed it was no longer an issue. (It had been paid off long ago by Balfour Gardiner.)[20] The new *modus vivendi* came as a relief to the society, which, as usual, was in financial trouble and badly in need of the réclame that Beecham could bring to its concerts. At a supper given after *Solomon* he was presented with the society's gold medal.

Critical reaction to the performance was favourable, though one of the music monthlies struck an interestingly prophetic note: 'The tempos were generally on

---

* The singers were two Italians, the soprano Anna Maria Guglielmetti and the tenor Enrico di Mazzei, the Dutch mezzo Maartje Offers and the Russian bass Kapiton Zaporojetz.

the quick side, and everything was made out of the pomp and brilliance of the work. There were considerable cuts and rearrangements to bring it within modern notions of proper concert duration. More questionable was the re-scoring. This was cleverly and not glaringly done; but there is a growing feeling that a composer like Handel knew better what he was at than any modern improver. Another generation will probably look on us as barbarians for our arrangements of seventeenth and eighteenth century music.'[21]

Not even the League was enough to absorb all Beecham's ferocious energy. Fired first by the Berlin Philharmonic's sensational London debut under their conductor Wilhelm Furtwängler in December 1927,* and then by his experiences with the privately endowed American orchestras, he was now determined to provide London with a 'super-orchestra' that would be their equal. The Royal Philharmonic Society seemed to him a useful partner in the enterprise, since he wanted, and was given, the society's permission to call the new ensemble the Royal Philharmonic Orchestra, which, he reckoned, would give it a suitable aura of importance and gravitas.

On 1 April 1928, ten days after the performance of *Solomon*, he met a delegation from the society at his suite at the Hyde Park Hotel, where both 'verbally and in writing' he laid out his rather over-optimistic proposals. The new orchestra, he said, would enjoy an annual guarantee of £10,000 (£348,000). In addition to playing for the Opera League's seasons, it would give an estimated 140 concerts a year, twenty of them under the sole control of the society, which would be represented on both the League's business and artistic committees. There would also be forty recording sessions a year for Columbia.[22] The society was impressed, though, no doubt remembering Beecham's failure to deliver his promised guarantee-fund ten years earlier, it wanted to know who his sponsors were. Beecham hedged on the subject and, despite repeated requests from the society for further information, was still hedging six months later.[23]

Coincidentally the BBC, stung by continuing criticism of its current orchestral arrangements, was also thinking of creating a permanent orchestra. The last straw had come in January 1928, when the *Musical Times* wrote that the Corporation, 'with all its assured and conspicuous wealth, has given and is giving us the worst orchestral performances ever heard in London. Last year their six trombones at the Albert Hall proclaimed an utter lack of artistic sense and judgement. This year at Queen's Hall they have assembled an orchestra which

---

* For the *Times* critic, writing about the Berliners' first concert at Queen's Hall on 2 December, 'it seemed impossible to imagine that the playing of individuals and their balance in *ensemble* could be bettered in any particular. Such a style in performance is the result of a concentration on the art of symphonic playing which the conditions of the great Continental orchestras make possible, and indeed imperative, and which the conditions of orchestral engagement in this country render unattainable.'

sounds as if it were composed in great part of "substitutes" '. The BBC knew that, to ensure success, it needed a strong chief conductor. Landon Ronald, who besides advising the BBC was chairman of the Opera League's advisory board, assured John Reith and his director of programmes, Roger Eckersley, that, unlikely though it might seem, Beecham, the arch-critic of broadcast music, was just the man for the job, since, quite apart from his abilities as a conductor, he was planning an orchestra of his own. The chances were that he would welcome co-operation with the BBC, for it had the one thing he needed most – money.

There were already signs that Beecham was beginning to accept that wireless might have its uses after all. One of his New York concerts had been broadcast, and during the interval he had taken over the announcer's microphone to address a few remarks to the listeners at home. The radio station, WOR, Newark, reported that comments it had received from the public 'clearly showed that reception of last night's concert was the best of any of the series so far radiated', which prompted Beecham to promise the *New York Times* that he would try and find time to hear some 'complicated compositions through up-to-date American apparatus'.[24] After lunching with Beecham in London two months later Landon Ronald was able to write to Eckersley at the BBC: 'I think I may go so far as to say that I have, at last, entirely broken Beecham's opposition to broadcasting.'[25] Negotiations for a joint Beecham–BBC orchestra began at once, a situation that the Philharmonic Society was content to accept, since it would receive extra revenue from having its concerts broadcast.

Meanwhile Diaghilev had asked Beecham to choose and arrange music by Handel for a new one-act ballet, to be choreographed by the twenty-four-year-old George Balanchine. The impresario's gesture was probably a response to Beecham's and Lady Cunard's help in securing support for his forthcoming London season at His Majesty's.* Drawing on the operas *Admeto*, *Alcina*, *Il pastor fido*, *Rodrigo* and *Teseo*, and the Concerto grosso in B flat, op. 6 no. 7, Beecham produced a suite of eleven numbers, for which Boris Kochno, Diaghilev's secretary and librettist, concocted a simple story-line. Based on an eighteenth-century pastoral allegory, it tells of a shepherd who comes upon a *fête champêtre*, where two noblewomen flirt with him. To their irritation he prefers a serving-maid, who responds enthusiastically to his attention. Derided by the company for their behaviour, the pair throw off their humble outer garments to reveal themselves as two glittering divinities who have descended to earth.

---

* The first public sign of a reconciliation between impresario and conductor had come a year earlier, when it was announced that Beecham would conduct at a Ballets Russes gala at the Palace Theatre, London, in honour of King Fuad I of Egypt. In the event he withdrew on grounds of indisposition.

The piece was given the title *Les dieux mendiants* or *The Gods Go a'Begging*. Diaghilev, who held no particular hopes for it, decided that it should be premiered at His Majesty's. To save time and avoid the cost of ordering new designs, he decreed that Bakst's backcloth for *Daphnis et Chloé* and Juan Gris's costumes for *Les tentations de la bergère* should be used for it. Beecham conducted the premiere on 16 July 1928 and the seven subsequent performances, all with the beautiful Alexandra Danilova as the serving-maid, and Léon Woizikovsky the shepherd. Nobody could guess how the new ballet would be greeted, for it was in stark contrast to the season's opening work, the classically austere Stravinsky–Balanchine collaboration *Apollon musagète*, which the composer himself conducted.*

There were a few critical voices – one commentator complained that the Handel ballet, 'considered in the sequence of the work of the Russians, was extremely dull and safe'[26] – but Diaghilev's *régisseur*, Sergey Grigoriev, reported that 'far from appearing half-baked, as might have been expected, *The Gods Go a'Begging* presented an extraordinarily satisfying combination of subject, choreography and *décor*; and its success was prodigious. ... During the all-too-short remainder of the company's career, it was never out of the programme.'[27] 'It became our bread and butter', said Danilova.[28] The score, both in the theatre and through the excerpts from it that Beecham recorded, proved unexpectedly educative, for it alerted many of its hearers to the delights of Handel's operas, then still a closed book to the British public.

The BBC's discussions about a new orchestra with Beecham were supposed to be secret, but on 27 July, the penultimate day of the ballet season, the *Daily Mail* published a report, supported by an interview with him, headed, 'WORLD'S BEST ORCHESTRA. B.B.C. IN SIR THOMAS BEECHAM'S BIG SCHEME'. The Corporation was furious, particularly because it was portrayed as the junior partner; indeed, Beecham scarcely mentioned it in his explication of the plan, which included confidential details of players' salaries. The orchestra's financial backing, he said, was to be shared between a (still unspecified) syndicate of his friends, who would provide an unspecified but 'substantial' guarantee, the BBC and a gramophone company. No deputies would be allowed, and, uniquely for a British orchestra, its members would be employed for twelve months a year, which would include a month's holiday in July. The orchestra would be entirely independent of the Imperial League of Opera.

Beecham was quite unabashed by the BBC's reaction, and in a letter dated 27/28 July airily assured Reith that he did not think there had been 'anything in today's article to embarrass you or your Corporation'. The *Mail*, he said, had

---

* On its first night, *The Gods* shared the bill with two Massine ballets, *Les matelots* (music by Georges Auric) and *Le tricorne* (Manuel de Falla), both conducted by Roger Desormière.

informed him that it was about to publish a story about the new orchestra that had been leaked to it by an 'influential but indiscreet' guarantor. He had thought it advisable to give the interview to keep the record straight. He had tried to reach Reith on the telephone twice, but without success.[29] As an explanation it was not very convincing, but the BBC decided to accept it, and put out a statement that negotiations over the orchestra would be resumed in November. The press, however, sensing that plans were not as far as advanced as Beecham had made out, would not let the story go.

The Era (22 August) put its finger on the problem: 'The BBC has strong views about business, and is fond of control. Not unnaturally, Sir Thomas will not tolerate dictation on matters concerning the artistic side of his work. In that respect he insists on unfettered liberty. The result is something like an impasse.' In an attempt to disguise his differences with the BBC, Beecham agreed to conduct the opening concert of its new season on 18 October. When broadcasting, the orchestra, still an *ad hoc* body, continued to be known variously as the National Orchestra or the Wireless Orchestra, but for its public concerts it was now called the BBC Symphony Orchestra. Reviewing the first concert, the *Times* critic thought that 'bad playing by the woodwind' had spoilt Delius's *Brigg Fair*, but the composer, who picked up the performance on his radio at Grez, was pleased with it. His amanuensis, the twenty-two-year-old Eric Fenby, reported that reception had been very clear: 'Only once did it show signs of fading. When the music had ceased, Delius called out, "Splendid, Thomas! That is how I want my music to be played."'[30]

Three weeks earlier Beecham had appeared for the first time at the Leeds Triennial Festival, sharing the conducting with its director, Sir Hugh Allen, an influential figure in British music who was both director of the Royal College of Music and Professor of Music at Oxford. It was the occasion of more than one authentic Beecham 'story'. Finding himself in conversation with an affable woman in her early thirties, whom he recognised but could not quite place, he remembered that she had a brother who was quite well known. How was he and what was he up to? asked Beecham, hoping that the answer might provide a clue to her identity. 'Oh, he's very well, thank you', came the reply, 'he's still King.' It was Princess Mary, Countess of Harewood, a patron of the festival and sister of George V.[31]

The schedule for the four-day festival was stupefying, with two concerts of inordinate length each day, the first starting at 11 a.m., with an hour's interval for lunch, and the second at 7.30 p.m. On the final day, 6 October 1928, Beecham conducted a barely credible number of works: Vaughan Williams's *A Pastoral Symphony*, Brahms's Four Part-songs for female voices, two horns and harp, Walton's first *Façade* suite, a *Gaelic Pipe March* by his musical assistant

Henry Gibson, Brahms's Double Concerto (with the Harrison sisters, May and Beatrice, as soloists), Berlioz's *Te Deum*, Wagner's *Flying Dutchman* overture, the Grail scene from Act 1 of *Parsifal*, and Tchaikovsky's Fourth Symphony. Though the choir had been rehearsed thoroughly before the festival began, there was much less time for the orchestra, the LSO, to go through everything properly, with the result that performing standards varied widely, not just from concert to concert, but also from work to work.

Mishaps caused by tiredness were inevitable. In the first movement of the Vaughan Williams symphony, Beecham, conducting without a score, had an all-too-obvious memory-lapse and was only saved from having to call a halt by quick thinking on the part of the leader, Willie Reed, who kept the orchestra on track. For the rest of the performance Beecham used a score. To some, the incident seemed, if not divine, then certainly musical, retribution, for at the final rehearsal, keen to score a point off a composer for whose music he did not care that much, Beecham had deliberately continued to beat time after the soprano soloist, Dora Labbette, had brought the work to its peaceful conclusion. 'Why aren't you playing?', asked Beecham, who had conducted the whole rehearsal from memory. 'Because it's finished', said Reed. 'Thank God', said Beecham. The orchestra enjoyed the joke. Vaughan Williams would always resent Beecham's lack of interest in his music. In the course of his career Beecham conducted the Vaughan Williams *Pastoral* on four occasions. At the end of the last one, a studio performance in 1951 with the BBC Symphony Orchestra, he is reputed to have leant down to the leader, Paul Beard, and commented, 'A city life for me!'

A month later Beecham conducted ten further performances of *The Gods Go a'Begging*, again with Danilova and Woizikovsky, during the Ballets Russes' winter tour of British cities, which opened in Manchester on 12 November 1928 and continued to Birmingham, Glasgow, Edinburgh and Liverpool. Beecham himself selected the fifty-five-strong orchestra – from 'Leading London Orchestras' [32] – and conducted without fee. (Roger Desormière was responsible for the rest of the repertoire.) After each of his own performances Beecham spoke to the audience about the League. The Liverpool week produced a feat of endurance and industry that was remarkable even for him. Having arrived there by train late on the Monday afternoon, and conducted *The Gods* and given his usual talk that evening, Beecham left for the station, still clad in his tails, to catch the night-train back to London, where the next morning he looked in on a preliminary rehearsal for a forthcoming performance of *Messiah*, recorded *Brigg Fair* at the Portman Rooms in Baker Street, and gave a lunchtime talk about the League before catching the 2.35 p.m. train back to Liverpool, where he arrived in time to conduct the ballet and speak once more about the League. [33]

A fortnight after the tour ended, Beecham conducted one more performance of *The Gods Go a'Begging* for the Diaghilev company, on 27 December at the Paris Opéra. The occasion had a poignant link with the early Diaghilev–Beecham seasons. Watching from a box, though few in the audience realised it, was Nijinsky, seated between Diaghilev and Alexandre Benois, designer of *Petrushka*, which was to conclude the evening. The Paris correspondent of the *Dancing Times* wrote touchingly: 'As everyone knows, Nijinsky's genius passed to madness and he is now the inmate of a private asylum in the neighbourhood of Paris. M. Diaghileff conceived the idea of bringing him to witness this performance of "Petrouchka," in the faint hope that it might awaken memories of the glorious past and clear the cloud from his mind. To enhance the effect he induced Mme. Karsavina, Nijinsky's former partner, to dance "Petrouchka" with Serge Lifar. But alas! not even she, whom Nijinsky used to call "the inner perfume of his life," was able to supply the magic touch. Though the whole vast audience rose to greet her, she danced for one man alone, but that man sat motionless with unseeing eyes and the terrible vacuous smile never changed.'[34]* The evening marked the last occasion on which Beecham conducted for Diaghilev, who died in Venice eight months later.

It had been a tumultuous year for Beecham, but 1929 was to bring him little respite so far as both his campaign for the League and his convoluted negotiations with the BBC were concerned. So involved was he with the League in particular that, pleading an invented illness, he cancelled the four concerts he should have given with the New York Philharmonic in January 1929. Instead, he continued to traverse Britain, speaking at dinners, rotary-club meetings, theatres and even, at Harrogate, a fancy-dress dance. He also conducted concerts in aid of the League, not all of them successful. So few people turned up for one he gave in Portsmouth, with Labbette in arias by Handel, Grétry and Mozart, and an orchestra made up mostly of Naval and Royal Marine musicians, that instead of making his customary speech from the platform, he came down into the hall for what the local paper called 'an intimate chat with the faithful few enthusiasts'. They were, he told them, the smallest audience that had ever listened to him.[35]

At least he did not lambast Portsmouth for its philistinism, a tactic that had proved fatal in Leeds where, addressing the city's Luncheon Club during rehearsals for the festival, he said that in Vienna, which spent £120,000 a year on opera, the idol of the State Opera was an English tenor from Lincolnshire (Alfred Piccaver). 'You have never heard him in Leeds', declared Beecham, warming to his theme, 'and from my experience up to date I venture to say you

---

* Karsavina was forty-three at the time and living in semi-retirement in London; Nijinsky was thirty-eight. *Petrushka*, like the Stravinsky–Matisse *Chant du rossignol* that opened the evening's triple-bill, was conducted by Desormière.

never will. ... What have you got here? You have that superannuated, obsolete, disgusting, noisy, horrid method of making music in super-abundance, known as the brass band.'[36] The remarks sent shock-waves throughout the band-loving North of England and beyond, losing Beecham more potential subscribers than he gained. It was not the last time that, out of frustration and impatience, he would bite the hand that might otherwise have fed his musical ambitions.

Meanwhile the operatic scene in Britain had begun to look gloomier than ever, with the BNOC in terminal financial difficulties. On 5 April 1929, in an attempt to restore the company's flagging morale, as well as its bank-balance, Beecham conducted a single performance of *The Mastersingers* for it at the 3,000-seat Golders Green Hippodrome, an event that also gave him an opportunity to deliver what was claimed to be his 145th oration on the subject of the League. His presence attracted a huge crowd, many of whom, notably the Marchioness of Londonderry and her two debutante daughters who occupied a box, can have had but a passing acquaintance with the place. The opera, heavily cut in Act 3, was all too clearly under-rehearsed, the cast 'seemed smitten by self-consciousness' and the woefully unresponsive orchestra was only half the size it should have been.[37]

The performance came in the middle of sessions for Beecham's first recording of a virtually complete opera, Gounod's *Faust*, sung in H. F. Chorley's already antiquated English translation and featuring a cast of BNOC principals, a feeble-sounding BBC Choir and a decent, though unidentified, orchestra. Unfortunately on this occasion not even Beecham's lively, idiomatic conducting can save the opera from sounding like a quaint period-piece. Only Miriam Licette as Marguérite, sole survivor in the cast from the Beecham Opera Company, has a real sense of operatic style. The elegant-voiced Heddle Nash in the title-role comes noticeably to life whenever he shares a scene with her, but most of his colleagues fail to break the bonds of the oratorio tradition from which they sprang, with Robert Easton a tremulous and wooden Méphistophélès, and Harold Williams, so impressive in Beecham's *Messiah* recording of two years earlier, a stuff-shirt Valentin who sounds more like Marguérite's butler than her brother. It is hard to escape the conclusion that if this was the best the BNOC could manage, it is not surprising that it should have collapsed three months later for want of support. Beecham claimed in more than one League speech that in the previous ten years the standard of British operatic singing had declined noticeably. He expressed the hope that his organisation might help to reverse the trend.

There seemed little chance of that happening. On 29 April 1929, his fiftieth birthday, Beecham announced that the League now had 40,000 subscribers, four times as many as there had been in 'any similar undertaking in any other country'.[38] It was an over-estimate. After seventeen months of punishing endeavour,

Beecham was not even close to securing sufficient funds to mount an initial sea-son. Yet even in the midst of adversity he could conjure up a memorable event – the London Delius Festival of October–November 1929, his personal tribute to a man who, stoically suffering from the effects of what was undoubtedly ter-tiary syphilis, was by now paralysed and completely blind. Beecham had been thinking of such a festival for some time, though his plans do not seem to have crystallised until the beginning of 1929, when Delius was created a Companion of Honour in the New Year's Honours list.* 'What good news!', the composer exclaimed to Beecham, on hearing that the festival would definitely take place. 'What would musical England do without you?' [39]

To help with organisation, Beecham called in the composer Philip Hesel-tine, who in April was dispatched to Grez in search of new works for the fes-tival. Two unfinished manuscripts of music for solo voice and orchestra were unearthed there, *A Late Lark* and *Cynara*, both of which Delius managed to complete with the help of his young amanuensis, Eric Fenby. In the first week of September Beecham himself went to Grez, where, on a sweltering day, he descended like a musical shaman, bringing life and magic to what Fenby called 'the most extraordinary household in Europe, where everything, on every day, was done according to plan, according to rule'. [40] As Fenby's kaleidoscopic rec-ollections of the visit make clear, routine was thrown out of the window that day. It began with Beecham, bearing 'a great armful of scores and puffing on an enormous cigar', arriving in a taxi from Fontainebleau, six miles away. The driver was asked to wait until he was needed again. After greetings and much embrac-ing, Beecham sat on a little chair next to Delius and, taking his hand, talked about programmes for the festival and asked him to attend it. 'Impossible, quite impossible', said Delius, who seemed more interested in the latest musical gossip from London

After a convivial lunch, Beecham looked on in astonishment as Delius's male nurse put his charge over his shoulder like a sack of potatoes and carried him off for a rest. Revived, the composer reappeared for tea, when Beecham said, quite casually, that 'one of our English nightingales happens to be in Paris and I have asked her to come down. Miss Labbette. She would like to sing some songs, so there will be one more for the evening meal.' Jelka went out to impart the news to the kitchen. Meanwhile Beecham's taxi remained outside the house, its meter ticking away. 'At half-past four', Fenby recalled, 'another taxi arrived and Dora stepped out, looking absolutely, amazingly, ravishing in a pink dress. Jelka picked two red roses and pinned one on Dora and the other on Thomas – and the party began.'

---

* Two years earlier Beecham had campaigned, without success, for Delius to be awarded the Order of Merit, which is in the gift of the monarch (*Evening Standard*, 14 June 1927).

After supper, when normally Delius would have gone to bed, the company, in high spirits, at last ascended to the upstairs music-room where, with vocal contributions from Labbette, Beecham played through the *Songs of Sunset* – 'very badly', Fenby recalled. Instead of co-ordinating his hands, Beecham put down one before the other, 'like a broken-down Sunday school teacher'. Next came *The Nightingale*, which Beecham described as 'our battle-horse'. * When, some time after midnight, he eventually left with Labbette, presumably in the same taxi that had brought him from Fontainebleau in the first place, he told Fenby to be sure to be there when he returned to Grez the next day for lunch.

This time, and for the next day or two, the atmosphere was intensely serious as Beecham, playing from piano scores, worked his way through a number of Delius's large-scale pieces, calling out the instrumental entries as he went, while Fenby followed the music from the full scores. Fenby 'marvelled at the accuracy with which he retained the orchestral detail in his head.' Suddenly he realised what Beecham was up to: since only a tiny handful of recordings of Delius's music existed for reference, he was preparing himself the hard way for the task of conducting the festival concerts from memory. Nothing was to be left to chance. Though Fenby was aware that Beecham was dubious about his efforts to extend Delius's composing life, he felt nonetheless that he and the conductor had established 'quite a harmonious relationship'. This was confirmed for Fenby when, at the end of the last session, Beecham handed him a number of letters addressed to various of his acquaintances, which were to be posted on given dates after his departure, so that the recipients might think he was still hard at work at Grez, rather than holidaying for a few days, no doubt with Dora.

The festival, which began on 12 October 1929, comprised six concerts spread over three weeks, four of major orchestral and choral works at Queen's Hall and two devoted to smaller orchestral pieces, unaccompanied choruses, songs and chamber music at the 500-seat Aeolian Hall in New Bond Street. Despite his earlier protestations that he was too frail to visit London, Delius came from Grez by motor-ambulance. He and Jelka stayed with Beecham's guests at the Langham Hotel in Portland Place. From there he was wheeled across the street in a Bath chair for rehearsals and concerts at Queen's Hall, where he made an unforgettably pale and wraith-like impression in the front row of the grand circle. *A Late Lark* and *Cynara* (sung by Heddle Nash and the baritone John Goss respectively) were not the festival's only novelties. Beecham also conducted the first public performance of *Air and Dance* for strings, which he had given at a private concert at Lady Cunard's home in 1915, the first London performance of *An Arabesk*, which, though written in 1911, Delius had not had a chance to hear

---

* No. 2 of Delius's *Nine Songs from the Norwegian* of 1888. In June 1929 Labbette had recorded *The Nightingale* for Columbia, with Beecham accompanying.

before,* and the first British performance of the two final scenes from the opera
Fennimore and Gerda.

The festival ended on 1 November with a performance of *A Mass of Life* in
which, by all accounts, Kennedy Scott's Philharmonic Choir excelled itself. At
its conclusion Beecham called for a round of cheers for the composer, who
responded in 'a surprisingly strong clear voice'. [41] After thanking the audience
for its appreciation, Delius expressed his gratitude to Beecham 'for the inspired
manner in which he has played my music. This festival has been the time of my
life.' [42] As his cross-Channel steamer left Folkestone for his return journey to
France, he asked for his chair to be positioned so that he was facing the English
shore.

Yet despite full houses – and despite the support of the Columbia record
company, the BBC and the Royal Philharmonic Society, which had all provided orchestras for the concerts – the festival lost money. Bumping into Fenby
in Bond Street a year or two later, Miriam Licette, the soprano soloist in *A Mass
of Life*, told him with amused resignation that she was still waiting for her fee. [43]
Beecham had wanted the LSO to give one of its subscription concerts as part
of the festival but, afraid that an all-Delius programme would only result in a
deficit it could not afford, it told him to look for another orchestra. Incensed,
Beecham sent the LSO an intemperate letter, which its directors found to be 'an
unwarranted & unmerited insult'. [44]

That the LSO, which had seen little of Beecham since he threw in his lot
with the BBC, felt confident enough to stand up to him was a reflection of a
major change in its constitution. In May 1929, alarmed that it might lose its best
players to Beecham and the BBC, it had decided to put its house in order by
reorganising itself into an orchestra of seventy-five contracted players, whose
services could be terminated at any time should they prove unsatisfactory. In
addition, the deputy system was to be abandoned at last. [45] With this achieved,
the LSO secured contracts with the Covent Garden syndicate, which agreed to
employ it for the 1930 international season and subsequent seasons, the Gramophone Company (HMV), and Lionel Powell, who undertook to hire it for at
least forty-one concerts a year.

During the summer of 1929 Beecham helped to audition players for the latest – but still not final – version of the BBC Symphony Orchestra, which he
was scheduled to conduct nine times during the 1929–30 season at Queen's
Hall. 'Women, whether married or single, are eligible and will receive the same
consideration as men', said a BBC official, signalling what looked like an important change of attitude towards women orchestral players. 'Selection will be

---

* Its first performance had been given at Newport on 28 May 1920, with Arthur E. Sims
  conducting the Welsh Musical Festival Chorus and the LSO.

based on merit and experience.'[46]* The auditions proved fruitful. Reviewing Beecham's second concert, Eric Blom wrote in the *Guardian* that although there were details in his conception of the music that might be questioned, he got 'such entrancing sounds from the players that one realised with a shudder how near one had come in London recently to forgetting what an orchestra ought to sound like. Debussy's enchanting *Iberia* seemed like a clear landscape which hitherto one had seen only through a fog.'[47] But if all was well on the platform, behind the scenes there was still serious disagreement between Beecham and the BBC hierarchy over both financial responsibility and artistic control.

Matters came to a head on the last day of 1929, when the BBC received a letter from Beecham's solicitors, which contained a list of objections to the scheme made by his guarantors, who remained unnamed. (Some wondered if they even existed.) Beecham might have been an awkward and even untrustworthy partner in the enterprise from the start, but the list's key reservation was incontrovertible: 'The Guarantors are of the opinion that the scheme has been modified and moulded by the Broadcasting Corporation less with an eye to the visible than to the invisible audience. ... They are reluctantly forced to the conclusion that their aims and those of the Corporation are not identical.' Beecham conducted just two of his six remaining concerts for the BBC (he complained that the music department had interfered with his programmes) and then withdrew, leaving the way open for the Corporation to draw up a new plan altogether.† It had come to realise that it needed a safer pair of hands than Beecham could provide and its choice fell on Adrian Boult, who as conductor of the City of Birmingham Orchestra had shown himself to be a musician of wide sympathies and a good administrator.

Bruised but undaunted, Beecham soldiered on with his opera campaign, announcing in January 1930 that the League would give a preliminary London season in May (later amended to June), to be followed in September by a longer season 'somewhere outside London'.[48] The enterprising repertory would be drawn from Rossini's *Italian Girl in Algiers* and *The Thieving Magpie*, Berlioz's *Damnation of Faust* (to be designed by Augustus John) and *The Trojans*, Smetana's *The Bartered Bride*, Offenbach's *The Tales of Hoffmann*, Borodin's *Prince Igor*, Tchaikovsky's *The Snow Maiden* and Delius's *A Village Romeo and*

---

* Five women appear in the list of players printed in the programme for Beecham's first concert on 13 November 1929 – two first violinists, two seconds and a cellist. The orchestra's principals, headed by Arthur Catterall, late of the Hallé, as leader, included some of London's best-known players, among them Bernard Shore (viola), Lauri Kennedy (cello), Robert Murchie (flute), Frederick Thurston (clarinet), Aubrey Brain (horn) and Ernest Hall (trumpet).

† The substitute conductors were Basil Cameron, Leslie Heward, Frank Bridge and Oskar Fried.

Juliet.[49] No venue was mentioned, but Beecham signed up Harald André of the Stockholm Opera as producer of all stage-works mounted by the League during the next five years, at an annual salary of £3,000 (£110,370) a year.[50]

Many wondered how Beecham could hope to get a season up and running in, at most, four months. The answer was that he couldn't. His hoped-for new subscribers failed to materialise. Like other European countries, Britain was entering a period of economic depression, heralded, though not caused, by the Wall Street crash of October 1929. Nervous for the future, Beecham's main source of subscribers, the British middle-classes, shied away from spending money on an opera scheme, though paradoxically they would emerge from the depression with barely a financial scratch. It was the families of the unemployed in the coal-fields, the shipyards and the cotton mills who would suffer poverty and hunger.

In January 1930, realising that the League's days were numbered, Beecham approached Lt-Colonel Eustace Blois, who was now running Covent Garden, to sound out the possibility of an amalgamation with the syndicate.* Blois showed interest, even though the future of the Opera House itself was as precarious as the League's. Its freehold was up for sale at a reported £250,000 (£9 million), though the syndicate had managed to secure a new lease that ran until February 1933. What would happen after that was anyone's guess. The threat of the theatre being demolished had been lifted temporarily, but Philip Hill, who had negotiated the deal to buy it from the Beecham family and was now chairman of Covent Garden Properties, told his shareholders that 'the importance of the development of the Market may be such as to demand [the Opera House's] inclusion in some scheme in the near future'.[51]

Blois was interested in Beecham's proposal because, for the first time in its history, the syndicate had taken up the cause of opera in English. In the previous autumn it had set up the Covent Garden Touring Company, which had taken over the BNOC's dates, as well as a number of its artists, and was now performing a repertory of popular pieces in the major cities and London's suburbs, with John Barbirolli as musical director. It was not much of an improvement on its defunct predecessor, though it was generally agreed that in one respect it was superior: it had a reasonably sized orchestra of fifty players. Blois recognised that Beecham's artistic acumen, coupled with the League's financial assets, amounting to almost £56,000 (£2 million),[52] could transform the company's standards. Beecham had one more carrot to offer Blois. He claimed that in the

---

* Following Henry Higgins's retirement as chairman of the Covent Garden syndicate in 1924, Blois, who had experience of both the business and music worlds, was appointed managing director of a new syndicate. As a young man he had studied singing in Leipzig and composed an opera, *Giuliana*, which in 1913 he conducted for the Moody-Manners company.

previous spring the Labour Prime Minister, Ramsey MacDonald, had promised him that, in the event of his being returned to power in the imminent general election, he would be prepared to give the League the first public opera subsidy that Britain had ever known, a sum of £30,000 (£1 million) a year. Beecham told Blois that, if the amalgamation went through, the money would be shared with the syndicate.[53]

In fact, the subsidy did not materialise. Labour had more pressing matters to deal with: it had won the election, but without an overall majority in the House of Commons. Nonetheless, negotiations between Beecham and Covent Garden reached a successful conclusion in October 1930. All that was now needed was for the League's members to approve the merger. Fully expecting an overwhelming vote in favour, Beecham got a shock. A significant number of the 35,300 paid-up supporters[54] (not 44,000, as he claimed at the time) wanted their money back; some wanted it spent on other operatic enterprises; others turned out to be untraceable or dead. The trustees, thoroughly perplexed as to how they should proceed, turned for guidance to the Court of Chancery. The League's agreement with the syndicate was effectively scuppered.

Almost immediately the BBC jumped into the operatic vacuum with an announcement that it had signed an agreement with Blois allowing it to broadcast at least sixty operas a year. Yet another syndicate was formed, chaired by Frederick Szarvasy, Hungarian-born financier and Covent Garden's main backer. Significantly, it included one of the BBC's governors, the formidable and attractive Ethel Snowden, suffragist, peace campaigner, friend of the rich and well connected, and wife of Philip Snowden, Ramsey MacDonald's Chancellor of the Exchequer.

To add insult to Beecham's injury, on 20 November 1930, only six days after the BBC–Covent Garden link had been made public, Philip Snowden told the Commons that the government was proposing to subsidise Covent Garden. It would receive £5,000 (£184,000) for the last quarter of 1930, plus £17,500 (£644,000) a year for the following five years. The annual sum was to come out of wireless licence fees and be passed on to Covent Garden via the BBC. Inevitably there were rumours, never substantiated, that the Government's change of mind on the subsidy had been prompted by Ethel Snowden, rather than by her husband, a stern Nonconformist Yorkshireman, whose known musical aspirations were confined to occasional renditions of 'The Red Flag' and 'On Ilkla Moor baht 'at'.[55]

News of the subsidy was greeted with joy by the musical press – 'a wonder of wonders', gasped one journal[56] – but elsewhere it provoked widespread protests. Lord Beaverbrook's *Daily Express* (21 November) called Snowden's intervention 'utterly frivolous and feminine. Marie Antoinette told the starving Parisians to eat cake. Two-million unemployed are clamouring today for a chance to live. Mr Snowden is going to give them grand opera.' Eight Conservative MPs tabled a motion that, 'In view of the present industrial situation and the growth of unemployment, this House declines to agree to the proposal for the expenditure of public money on Grand Opera.'[57] A Mr Ford of Albert Gate, Knightsbridge, went to the Court of Chancery in an unsuccessful attempt to secure an injunction restraining the Postmaster-General from paying out the subsidy.[58]

Beecham, ignoring the fact that if things had gone his way he would have been the recipient of the money, claimed that the amount on offer – just over half what MacDonald had promised him – was too small to be useful, and that it could only 'have the effect of discouraging private benefactors and of continuing the modern habit of making the public look to the State.'[59] There was, he said, not 'a millionth chance' that it would go through.[60] He was wrong. The subsidy received the Royal Assent in the following July. Typically, Beecham also managed to find a funny side to the situation, telling an audience in Eastbourne that he had been under the impression that *he* 'had saved opera in England, having collected a large sum of money. Then I found that the BBC had saved opera in England. Now I find that the government is saving it and very soon, no doubt, we shall hear that the Colonies are saving it. But joking apart, I am hopeful that out of all this welter something will happen to opera in England. I, at least, am an optimist.'[61]

Ironically, at the same time that Beecham's plans for transforming Britain's orchestral and operatic life were turning to dust, he was enjoying a series of successes in Germany, where conductors of genius did not have to exhaust themselves – and their pockets – trying to create organisations worthy of their talents. First, on 29 January 1930, came his debut with Furtwängler's Berlin Philharmonic. The concert, at the orchestra's home, the Philharmonie, had been arranged by a local impresario and was given under the patronage of the British ambassador, Sir Horace Rumbold. Not only did Beecham and the players achieve an immediate rapport – at rehearsal they gave him a standing ovation. They were amused too by his friendliness and informality: as he walked on to the platform at the start of the concert he noticed that his shoelace was undone and, instead of bowing to the audience, he turned his back on it and bent down to do it up again.[62] The critics showed little interest in the programme's two British works, Elgar's *Cockaigne* ('superficial entertainment', said the *Börsen-Courier*) and Delius's *Eventyr*, but were full of enthusiasm for Beecham's readings of Mozart's Symphony no. 34 and Strauss's *Ein Heldenleben*. For the *Lokal Anzeiger* the latter possessed 'a sweep and balance between its various elements such as is seldom heard here'. Furtwängler was sufficiently impressed to invite Beecham to return to Berlin the following November to conduct one of the orchestra's subscription concerts.* In doing so he inaugurated what would become a fruitful and affectionate relationship between the two conductors. Beecham took to greeting Furtwängler, his junior by seven years, as 'My boy'.

In October, Beecham went to Leipzig for a concert with the Gewandhaus Orchestra, given in conjunction with Mitteldeutscher Radio. The programme consisted of Mendelssohn's *Hebrides* Overture, Delius's *Brigg Fair* and, again, Mozart's Symphony no. 34 and Strauss's *Ein Heldenleben*. More than one reviewer compared him favourably with Nikisch, who had conducted the orchestra until his death eight years earlier. It was not the first time (nor would it be the last) that Beecham was compared to the great Austro-Hungarian. For the composer Arthur Bliss, for example, 'Nikisch had a special gift shared by few other conductors I have seen – the apparent ability to generate at will some electric current which galvanised both players and audience alike. Beecham had the same power. Each might be proceeding with no more than professional musicianship through a score, when suddenly a musical passage would excite them either by its beauty or its rhythmic vitality and the heat was on.' [63]

Between the Berlin and Leipzig concerts came several opera performances with local casts, including *Tannhäuser* and *Lohengrin* in Wiesbaden, and *Der Rosenkavalier* in Hamburg, where Beecham was judged to be a first-rate Strauss conductor. Not everything went smoothly. When he turned up to open Cologne's Easter opera festival with *Die Meistersinger*, he discovered that virtually no rehearsal time had been allocated to it. Expostulation with the management resulted in 'a rehearsal and a half', but it was not enough for Beecham to go through the whole opera, which was being given uncut. He had a Sachs for the rehearsal, Emil Treskow, a member of the company, but the Walther, the popular Fritz Krauss from Munich, was not expected to arrive until the performance itself. Nonetheless, wrote the British critic Richard Capell, who was present, 'the performance went from strength to strength, [though] the orchestra could not give him the sheer beauty of tone which he invited, for instance, in the prelude to the third act. And even in the last scene – which was by far the best, with truly heartening merry-making in the Pegnitz meadows and splendid choral singing – Sachs and Walther still thought it was up to them to set the pace. [But] the audience was won – was won hands down. The fifteen minutes' applause at the end was Beecham's; he had earned it.'

Capell admitted to coming away from the performance elated, but at the same time shamefaced 'at the thought that at home a proper sphere of action is still denied this rare spirit, who (can it be questioned?) is so far and away the

---

* For the subscription concert, on 13 November 1930, Beecham, perhaps wisely eschewing British music, conducted the 'Royal Hunt and Storm' from *Les troyens*, Haydn's Symphony no. 93, Tchaikovsky's *Francesca da Rimini* and Franck's D minor Symphony.

finest musician our race and generation have produced in the executive field.' [64]
Absurdly, Beecham's sole opera appearances in London in 1930 took place at
the Scala Theatre in Charlotte Street, where, as an act of goodwill, he stepped
in to save from ruin the ill-attended London Opera Festival, a brave but incompetent attempt by a group of Oxford and Cambridge graduates to present several rarely heard operas. With a small professional orchestra, a cast consisting
mostly of young professionals, and an amateur chorus whose lack of concentration at rehearsal drove him to distraction, he conducted five performances of
Der Freischütz, on five consecutive nights, for nothing.* It was hard to see how
Beecham's prospects, at least in Britain, could improve.

---

* Designed by Frank Verity and opened in 1905, the Scala was demolished in 1969 after a fire.
 The *Freischütz* performances took place on 14–18 January 1930. The cast included Thea
 Philips as Agathe, Tudor Davies as Max, and Arthur Fear as Caspar.

CHAPTER 12

'Just listen to this'

R ESTLESS AS EVER, Beecham refused to accept that the Opera League would not live to fight another day. In January 1931 he tried to turn it into a private limited company, but was rebuked by its trustees, who refused to hand over the funds in their custody, 'because there appeared to be no reasonable prospects of the objects of the League being accomplished.'[1] But the problems facing the League were small beer compared with Beecham's personal financial difficulties. His debts stood at £142,000 (£5.6 million), which included £60,000 (£2.4 million) due to the Inland Revenue for unpaid super-tax. On 16 January he appealed in the High Court against a receiving order that had been issued against him, but the Master of the Rolls ruled that it could not be rescinded. Beecham, he said, had made no attempt to live within his income and had signally failed to satisfy his numerous creditors. There were at least ten other petitions on file.[2] The judgment opened the way for bankruptcy proceedings to begin.

At his public examination on 1 July, Beecham admitted that he had not been solvent since 1919, a situation which, he said, had been exacerbated not just by the super-tax he owed, but also by his wife's extravagance, the large amounts of interest he had to pay on further borrowings from money-lenders, expenses incurred in the sale of the Covent Garden estate, and 'very heavy' legal charges. Finally, he claimed that he had paid out an estimated £15,000 (£591,000) of expenses on behalf of the Opera League, which he had been unable to reclaim or offset against tax because he had failed to keep a proper record of what he had spent.[3]

Beecham's creditors, including the Inland Revenue, had already agreed to accept an offer he made to pay them ten shillings in the pound, i.e. half the amount he owed them.[4] For Beecham it was a big concession, but to avoid being declared bankrupt he still had to find the remaining half amounting to £71,000 (£2.8 million). Because he could no longer call on his father's executors for help, there was only one solution. He would have to persuade the Court of Chancery to allow him access to the capital in the trust fund that had been set up by the executors to provide him with an income. Both his creditors and the Bankruptcy Court agreed to await the outcome of this drastic course of action.

With the BBC now closed to him, and the League inactive, Beecham had no alternative but to mend his fences with the LSO. As usual he got excellent results from it, both in London and on tour, but in general, despite its contracts with Covent Garden and HMV, the orchestra was in poor shape. In the previous year there had been widespread grumbles in the press about its playing at the Opera House. 'Orchestrally', wrote one critic bluntly, 'the performances were not adequate.'[5] Covent Garden complained that players left rehearsals without permission, and that one horn-player read newspapers at rehearsal 'instead of seriously attending to his work'. The LSO's board fined the offending players ten shillings and sixpence (£19.30) each. Blois wrote to say that he expected a considerable improvement in both playing and general conduct in future.[6]

To add to the LSO's embarrassment, it found itself compared unfavourably with the orchestra of sixty-nine players, at least a third of them regulars from the Royal Philharmonic Society's orchestra, which in May and June 1931 performed for a six-week season of Russian opera presented by Lionel Powell at the Lyceum Theatre. The company was the émigré Opéra Russe à Paris, based at the Théâtre des Champs-Élysées and co-directed by the former director of the People's Theatre in St Petersburg, Prince Alexis Zereteli, and the Cossack officer-turned-impresario Colonel Wassily de Basil. It boasted striking sets and costumes, a vigorous chorus,* a ballet troupe that had inherited some of Diaghilev's dancers and an all-Russian roster of singers of varying talent, led by Chaliapin, no less. The guest artistic director for the visit was Beecham, involved at last in a worthwhile operatic enterprise.

The season proved beyond doubt that even in times of economic depression there was still an audience for opera in Britain when it was performed by a committed, artistically homogeneous company. Here, wrote Herman Klein in the *Musical Mirror*, was 'the model that our native performers must bear in mind and strive to imitate when they have the chance.'[7] More than 100,000 people were drawn to the Lyceum (Opera League members were given priority booking), though the enterprise still made a loss, borne largely by Lady Cunard and other backers, who were reported to have put up £4,500 (£177,000) between them.[8]

If the Russians could not match the glamour of the Diaghilev–Beecham evenings at Drury Lane of 1913–14, they nonetheless provided serious competition for Covent Garden's international season which, Chaliapin aside, had better singers, but also productions that were as hand-to-mouth as ever. Beecham chose works from the company's repertoire that would 'give the public a

---

* It was augmented, at Beecham's invitation, by the chorus of the Carl Rosa company, which a month earlier had been forced to suspend operations temporarily following a financial crisis.

chronological idea of Russian opera', from Glinka's *Russlan and Ludmila* and Dargomïzhsky's *Rusalka*, through Musorgsky's *Boris Godunov* and Borodin's *Prince Igor*, to Rimsky-Korsakov's *Sadko* and *The Tsar's Bride*.* All except *Boris* and *Prince Igor* were receiving their first London performances. Beecham conducted *Prince Igor*, Eugene Goossens *Sadko* and Michel Steiman, the company's musical director, the rest of the repertory. There were also ballet evenings, which included the first British staging of Falla's *El amor brujo*, choreographed by the company's ballet master Boris Romanoff. Beecham conducted *The Gods Go a'Begging*, revived by Woizikovsky, who once again danced the role of the shepherd, this time with Edna Tresahar as the serving-maid.

The highlight of the season was unquestionably *Prince Igor*, for which Fokine recreated his spectacular version of the Polovtsian dances that had astounded London audiences seventeen years earlier. Chaliapin sang the role of Khan Konchak at four of the seven performances, and at two of them doubled it with Galitzky, just as he had at Drury Lane.[9] Though, wrote one observer, 'his voice has lost something of its early physical robustness, a greater nursing of his forces has brought to light exquisitely shaded tones that, completely charged with human feeling as they are, move one to the depths'.[10] Chaliapin expressed strong admiration for the orchestra; as for Beecham, he said, he was 'one of the few men who come near to understanding music.'[11] The reason for the singer's enthusiasm can be gauged from a review of *Prince Igor* by Ernest Newman: 'The orchestra, feeling thoroughly at home under Sir Thomas Beecham, gave us some brilliant playing. The accompaniments to the vocal parts were often miracles of elasticity and precision; one does not quite know, indeed, how the thing was done. Sir Thomas gave the singers complete liberty, and they took full advantage of their privilege.'[12]

In contrast, press criticism of the LSO's contribution to Covent Garden's international season was even fiercer than it had been the previous year. *The Observer*'s anonymous reviewer (10 May) wondered why Bruno Walter, in his eighth consecutive season at Covent Garden, turned a blind eye to 'strings that have no conscience, horns that out of a hundred references of Siegfried's call can only once or twice play it correctly, trumpets and trombones that keep hitting the wrong note or the right one flat, a drummer who hardly misses a chance of vulgarity, upsets the rhythm (funeral march) with an extra note added in high spirits, and doesn't always tune.' Walter may have thought the orchestra beyond redemption, though Newman was not alone in noticing a distinct improvement in the playing when Tullio Serafin, conductor at the Metropolitan Opera, New

---

* During the season Chaliapin also sang the roles of Boris, the Miller in *Rusalka* and, at a gala on 23 June with Beecham conducting, Don Quixote in the death-scene from Massenet's eponymous opera.

York, and now making his Covent Garden debut, arrived to take charge of the Italian part of the season. Nonetheless, there was a widely expressed feeling that an air of routine lay over the Opera House and that it might be time for a fresh hand on the house's musical tiller.[13]

Beecham spent much of the summer of 1931 on the Continent with Lady Cunard. On 30 August, at the Salzburg Festival, he gave his first concert with the Vienna Philharmonic Orchestra, which featured three symphonies, Haydn's no. 93, Mozart's no. 34 and Brahms's Second.* Perhaps because he declined the offer of an interpreter ('I have a little colloquial German, thank you'),[14] he did not achieve as immediate a rapport with the orchestra as he had with the Berlin Philharmonic. Although he had brought with him his own marked orchestral parts for the Mozart symphony, there were initial misunderstandings over points of phrasing, though by the second rehearsal the players had been won over. Neville Cardus, who attended the concert, produced a couple of reviews for the British press that amounted to little more than an unashamed display of Britannic flag-waving – Beecham's interpretation of the Brahms symphony, he enthused, 'clinched an experience of genius'.[15] Cardus's Salzburg counterparts were equally chauvinistic, displaying in their reviews a woolly mixture of dislike for Beecham's energetic conducting style – one complained it was 'old-fashioned'[16] – and a generalised feeling that his readings lacked the proper German *Innigkeit*. In the absence of aural evidence it is impossible to say which view was the more justified. Beecham did not conduct the orchestra again. He was invited back to conduct an all-Mozart programme at the 1934 festival, but withdrew when Austrian Nazis, involved in an abortive putsch, shot dead the country's Chancellor, Englebert Dolfuss, three days before the festival began.

According to Cardus, one of the Vienna orchestra's players threw up his hands in amazement when told that in Britain Beecham did not at present lead an orchestra of his own. It was not for want of trying. At the beginning of 1931 he had resurrected his plan for an orchestra that would combine playing for the Opera League's seasons with concerts and recording sessions, but had failed to get any support for it.[17] In the autumn he came up with a scheme for an orchestra that, first and foremost, would be a high-quality recording ensemble, though it would also give concerts. By now Beecham no longer attacked the gramophone as a medium for disseminating music, having at last come to realise the importance of recording contracts to an orchestra's finances, not to mention his own. With flattery and bluff (he mentioned 'guarantors', but once again they remained amorphous), he set about selling his latest idea to the new

* The Vienna Philharmonic's other Salzburg concerts that year were conducted by Bruno Walter and Clemens Krauss.

conglomerate, Electric and Musical Industries (EMI), set up to counter the effects of the Depression. It absorbed both HMV and Columbia, though the two companies were allowed to keep their original names and identities.

Beecham told Fred Gaisberg, HMV's artistic director, that he would not make any more records until he had his own recording orchestra, a project that only he and EMI could carry through. He said that his recent recording of Mozart's 'Jupiter' Symphony with an *ad hoc* orchestra provided by Columbia had been unsuccessful because, though the individual players had been good, there had been no chance to weld them into a proper ensemble. It was never issued. The orchestra he had in mind would be the equal of those of Philadelphia, Berlin and Vienna, and far better than the BBC Symphony Orchestra which, he averred, could never match them because of all the studio work it carried out and the type of music it had to play. If the two EMI companies would offer him a minimum forty sessions a year for a 'nucleus orchestra' of forty to forty-five players, he would guarantee that each one would be 'a first-class recording man'.[18]

Negotiations broke off briefly while Beecham went to Leeds for the 1931 Triennial Festival, for which he had been appointed artistic director in succession to Sir Hugh Allen. Once again the LSO was the resident orchestra. The festival was marked by the first performance of William Walton's high-voltage cantata *Belshazzar's Feast*. According to the composer's later testimony, it was Beecham who advised him to 'throw in a couple of brass bands', manifested in the form of two extra brass ensembles, each consisting of three trumpets, three trombones and a tuba.[19] Beecham handed over the work to his ambitious assistant, Malcolm Sargent, already a seasoned choral conductor. Sargent, said Beecham admiringly, could make choirs 'sing like blazes'. Beecham's advice about the bands was more than a simple jest. Plenty of extra brass players would be available in Leeds, because he was planning to conduct his first-ever performance of Berlioz's *Grande messe des morts* two days later. Also, as he had discovered to his cost at the previous festival, Beecham knew the local predilection for brass bands, and no doubt felt that the extra instruments would help make the piece more accessible to the Leeds audience. In any event, *Belshazzar*, and Sargent's performance of it, was a triumph.

If not in the top flight of conductors, Sargent was a highly competent, hard-working musician and Beecham quickly formed a good relationship with him. They shared the same birth-date, 29 April – Sargent was then thirty-six, Beecham fifty-three – and in future would unfailingly exchange greetings on the day. There was a snobbish side to Sargent that appealed to Beecham's sense of humour. The son of a Lincolnshire coal-merchant's clerk, he was greatly smitten by London society, particularly its women, several of whom reciprocated his admiration with amorous enthusiasm. Sargent was also a natty dresser, which gave rise to his nickname, 'Flash Harry'

Beecham was not above making jokes at Sargent's expense. When at the Garrick Club Sargent told a group of acquaintances including Beecham that he had been shot at by an Arab in Palestine, Beecham exclaimed, 'So they're musical!'[20] Their collaboration in Leeds was opportune, for Sargent's widespread musical connections would prove useful to Beecham. Sargent not only conducted the Royal Choral Society's concerts and the popular children's concerts founded by the German-born metal broker Robert Mayer, he was also music director of the innovative Courtauld–Sargent concerts, created and run by one of the most enlightened musical patrons of the inter-war years, Elizabeth Courtauld, wife of the textile magnate and art-collector Samuel Courtauld.* The LSO played for all three series.

Beecham returned from Leeds convinced that, rather than spending time finding entirely new players (the BBC Symphony Orchestra had recruited many of the best), it would be more practical to base his proposed orchestra on a rejuvenated and reconstructed LSO, a decision that seems to have satisfied Gaisberg and his opposite number at Columbia, Arthur Brooks, for they made Beecham an offer of fifty recording sessions.[21] But when Beecham wrote to the LSO inviting its co-operation, its directors declined to give him an immediate answer. They wanted details of both the contract to be offered and the changes in personnel he said might be necessary.[22] They never received the answers. On 23 December the LSO's future was thrown into turmoil by the death of Lionel Powell, who managed its concerts.

Almost immediately Powell's executors announced that they were not in a position to underwrite either the LSO's forthcoming concerts in London or its nine-day tour with Beecham that was due to start in Newcastle upon Tyne on 15 January 1932. Beecham urged the players to press on with the tour 'for the sake of the orchestra's good name', and together with his old patron, Lord Howard de Walden, produced an advance of £450 (£18,200) that allowed it to take place.[23] He also arranged a guarantee, this time with Robert Mayer, that allowed another Powell promotion, the Berlin Philharmonic's forthcoming visit

---

* Elizabeth Courtauld inaugurated her scheme in 1929, basing it on a similar one run by the Berlin Volksbühne. Its purpose was partly to give London a new concert-giving organisation with a coherent artistic policy that was not afraid to embrace new music (Stravinsky and Hindemith both performed their own works), and partly to open up concerts to people who might otherwise not attend them. Businesses, schools and other organisations were invited to make block-bookings of seats, which were then sold on to employees or students at greatly reduced prices. Such was the scheme's success that each concert was repeated. Mrs Courtauld hired Sargent on the recommendation of the pianist Arthur Schnabel, who found him an attentive accompanist.

to Britain with Furtwängler, to go ahead as planned, a gesture that cemented Beecham's relationship with both orchestra and conductor. The tour broke even, and the guarantee did not have to be called in.

By the end of January, Powell's executors had a better grip on the late impresario's disorganised estate, and agreed to honour existing contracts for the London concerts, but the LSO then suffered a further blow. Following a financially poor season at Covent Garden the previous summer (caused partly by the Russians' competition), and disastrous ones of opera in English both in London and on tour, Eustace Blois announced in mid-February that there would be no international season at the Opera House in 1932. For the orchestra it meant the loss of ten weeks' work. Beecham and EMI, anxious to keep the plan for the recording orchestra afloat, urged the LSO to accept 'a certain measure of reorganisation', which they, rather than the orchestra itself, would undertake. The LSO's directors admitted that changes were needed, but insisted that only they could make them. Stalemate ensued.[24]

At the end of February 1932 Beecham sailed to New York. Toscanini, suffering from neuritis in his right arm, had been forced to withdraw from his engagements with the New York Philharmonic-Symphony Orchestra for the rest of the season, and Arthur Judson had asked Beecham to take his place.* In all he conducted twenty-four concerts with it, plus a twenty-fifth, at the Metropolitan Opera House, with an orchestra consisting of 200 musicians who had all lost their jobs because of the depression. Once again Beecham was applauded by the press for programming works unfamiliar to New York audiences: Bax's *Garden of Fand*, Elgar's *Cockaigne* and Delius's *Brigg Fair*, Rimsky-Korsakov's *Antar*, Balakirev's *Tamara*, Dvořák's *Golden Spinning-wheel*. For the *New York Times*, Haydn's Symphony no. 93 was given 'one of the most eloquent readings of this great master's music we have had in seasons',[25] while American Columbia was so taken by Beecham's performances of Strauss's *Don Quixote* that it took the opportunity to record the work while he was still in New York. The solo instrumentalists were two of the Philharmonic-Symphony's principals, the cellist and future conductor Alfred Wallenstein and the viola-player René Pollain.

In seven weeks Beecham earned $27,420 (the equivalent of £316,250 sterling in 2008), which, even after federal and state taxes had been deducted, still left him with a hefty sum.[26] He needed it, because in the Chancery Court his otherwise shy and retiring elder son Adrian, firmly under Utica's thumb, was claiming with justification that, since the fracas over the house in Grosvenor Square seven years earlier, his father had not paid his family a penny of the allowances due to it under the terms of the trust.[27] He was also demanding the replacement

* The New York Philharmonic and the New York Symphony Orchestras had merged in June 1928 to form the New York Philharmonic-Symphony Orchestra.

of the trustees, on the grounds that they had been paying all the money to Beecham, despite a court order giving them the discretion to make payments to other members of the family as well. The judge, Mr Justice Bennett, was not sympathetic to Beecham, particularly when he heard that the Inland Revenue had accepted his offer of ten shillings in the pound for the tax he owed. 'Why', asked his lordship, 'should he get off with half the surtax, when other people have to pay, just because he refuses to do so?' It was, he said, 'disgraceful'. He was not at all mollified when Beecham's counsel, William Swords KC, told him that his client had spent a great deal of money on public service.

Mr Justice Bennett: 'What public service?'

Mr Swords: 'The cultivation of music in England.'

Mr Justice Bennett: 'There are things more important than that.'

By mid-June 1932 the Chancery Court had succeeded in brokering a deal that would at last bring an end to the acrimony. It was agreed that capital from the trust could be released to pay off Beecham's creditors – the sum involved had by now risen sharply to £84,000 (£3.4 million)[28] – and also to settle the huge legal bills he had incurred in the Chancery and Bankruptcy Courts, as well as sundry other debts. His solicitor, Philip Emanuel, alone was owed £500 (£20,200). In return, Beecham had to give an undertaking that he would not 'incur any further liability in connection with any operatic, musical or theatrical enterprise or undertaking'. Adrian, heir to the trust money under the terms of Joseph Beecham's will, was to receive a sum equal to that released to his father. It was to amount to £235,000 (£9.5 million), a proportion of which was to provide an annuity for Utica.[29] Later the court would make provision for her younger son as well.

The agreement was conditional on the Bankruptcy Court approving Beecham's settlement with his creditors of ten shillings in the pound, which it did, in mid-July. It also lifted the receiving order against him, though the official receiver said that he had 'brought on, or contributed to, his insolvency by unjustifiable extravagance and by culpable neglect of his business affairs'.[30] For the second time in his life Beecham had escaped the humiliation of bankruptcy. What little capital remained in the trust was left there for his own benefit, but never again would he enjoy the luxury of a sizeable private income, and he would have to rely entirely on others to fund his future projects. He became very good at spending their money.

Adrian used some of his new-found riches to buy Clopton House, an historic house on the edge of Stratford-upon-Avon, to which Utica and her sons moved on the expiry of the Grosvenor Square lease. Once there, the twenty-eight-year-old Adrian fulfilled a long-held wish to live the life of a country gentleman, buying up a large collection of farms in south Warwickshire that had lost their value as a result of the Depression. Later in the 1930s, when both he and his brother married, Adrian moved to Compton Scorpion Manor, near Shipston on Stour, while Tommy lived in another manor house at Tidmington. Their wives were sisters, Joyce and Mozelle, whose mother had remarried into the Tollemache family.

Adrian farmed and hunted, and became an expert on the county's weather, sending occasional reports to the Meteorological Office, which presented him with a barograph. In *Who's Who* he listed his recreations simply as 'country life', but his interests were more widespread. Like his father he had a retentive memory for poetry and the plays of Shakespeare and he continued to compose. His works included a ballet, a pair of Biblical cantatas, operettas, arrangements of Irish Gaelic songs and settings of W. S. Gilbert's *Bab Ballads*. None of them received wide circulation, though Victoria de los Angeles included his *Six Spanish Songs* in a London recital in 1952.* Adrian once confessed that his father disapproved of his admiration for Arthur Sullivan: 'I think he was afraid Sullivan's music would influence me unduly. And it did, of course.'[31]

As if in compensation for his financial set-backs, Beecham's musical prospects were improving considerably. In mid-March, while still in New York, he had received a cable from Eustace Blois asking if he would collaborate as conductor-in-chief on a four-week Wagner festival at Covent Garden, which Blois and the syndicate, startled by a public outcry over the cancelled international season, had decided to mount in its place. A number of leading Wagner singers agreed to come to London at reduced fees.† The festival, Blois informed Beecham, would start in early May – 'All this absolutely conditional on your conducting. Personally beg you to accept as if season not given matters may be brought to a final close.'[32] The suggested fee was £800 (£32,000) for around ten performances. Beecham cabled back his acceptance. Time was short. There was only a fortnight – five days of which would be taken up by a transatlantic crossing – between his last scheduled concert in New York and the opening night in London. With Judson's connivance Beecham sailed for England five days earlier than he had originally intended, leaving his last three scheduled concerts to the Philharmonic-Symphony's assistant conductor, Herbert Lange.

The only casualty of the Wagner festival was Bruno Walter, who in a letter

---

* Royal Festival Hall, 20 October 1952. The accompanist was Gerald Moore. The *Times* critic wrote: 'In the first three [Adrian Beecham] was too fond of Moorish arabesque in his piano writing, but in the last three he left arabesque to the voice and used a more varied rhythm in the accompaniment, much to the benefit of the total effect.'

† Gaps in casting were filled by an unusually large contingent of British singers, including Florence Easton, Walter Widdop and Norman Allin.

to Blois said he was 'deeply hurt' that it should have been from the press, and not from Blois himself, that he had learned that he been dropped by the Opera House.[33] There was no doubting that the audience was happy to see Beecham in the pit. When on 9 May he stepped up to the conductor's desk for the opening *Meistersinger*, with Friedrich Schorr as Sachs and Lotte Lehmann as Eva, he was greeted with warm applause. It was his first appearance at Covent Garden for twelve years. Two nights later he conducted *Tristan* with a magnificent cast: Frida Leider and Lauritz Melchior as the lovers, Maria Olszewska as Brangäne, and Herbert Janssen as Kurwenal. 'Perhaps the most remarkable thing about this performance', wrote the *Times* critic, 'was that even with a cast of Bayreuth singers Sir Thomas Beecham made the orchestra the most potent, expressive force; not that he ignored or slighted the singers' importance, but that the voices were incorporated into the instrumental texture.' The orchestra was the LSO, playing as though its very life depended on it, which in a way it did.

All twenty of the season's performances were sold out. Beecham conducted three performances of *Die Meistersinger*, three of *Tristan und Isolde* and two each of *Götterdämmerung* and the Dresden version of *Tannhäuser*. The rest of the *Ring* and *Der fliegende Holländer* were conducted by Robert Heger from the Vienna State Opera, who had assisted Bruno Walter at Covent Garden for the previous seven years. Not everything ran smoothly, particularly on stage, where there had been even less time than usual at the Opera House for proper rehearsal. Beverley Baxter, then editor-in-chief of the *Daily Express* and a friend of Beecham's, recalled that when on the closing night the curtain went up for Act 3 of *Götterdämmerung*, a bowler hat was clearly visible in the middle of the Rhine's 'waves' as its wearer crossed from one side of the set to the other. The audience laughed – and laughed again when 'the mechanism which controlled the waves got out of hand, and they began to move with the rapidity of an angry bird flapping its wings on a rock. Beecham's face was black with fury.' At curtain-call Beecham received an ovation that 'developed into a tumult', though he brushed it aside, claiming flippantly that it was merely 'the tribute of a sporting people to a fellow who had performed the splendid athletic feat of waving his arms from five-thirty to eleven'.[34]

Meanwhile Beecham had become involved in yet another scheme for a new orchestra. This time the initiative was not his, but had come some eight months earlier from Elizabeth Courtauld. Unhappy about the LSO's involvement in her concert series because it consistently brought in deputies despite a promise not to do so, she had begun to explore the possibility of putting together an orchestra of her own. Looking for collaborators, she sounded out first Covent Garden and then the Royal Philharmonic Society (both seemed interested),[35] but that was as far she got. Already stricken with cancer, she died on Christmas Day 1931 at the age of fifty-six. Samuel Courtauld decided not only that the Courtauld-Sargent concerts should continue in her memory, but also that the orchestra she envisaged should become a reality.*

Mindful of Sargent's contribution to the concerts' success, Courtauld asked him to form the orchestra with a preliminary budget of £30,000 (£1.2 million).[36] There would be a lot more to come. Most of the money came from Courtauld himself, but Robert Mayer also made a large contribution. Surprisingly for someone prone to conceit, Sargent felt he lacked the experience to undertake such a project, and instead Courtauld invited Beecham to become artistic director and chief conductor.[37] Sargent was to be his right-hand man. Beecham must hardly have believed his luck. His plan for the recording orchestra, which had not got far anyway, was dropped, though the idea of using the LSO as a basis for a new ensemble was retained. This, it was agreed, would at last be the great orchestra that London had been promised for so long.

The Royal Philharmonic Society and EMI's managing director, Louis Sterling, were drawn in, and in May 1932 a board of management was set up, consisting of Courtauld himself as chairman, Mayer, Lord Howard de Walden, and two experienced committee men, the banker Baron d'Erlanger and Lord Esher. Harold Holt, who had picked up the pieces left by his one-time partner Lionel Powell, was appointed business manager. Beecham had no executive power: he was not made a member of the board, nor did he have a say in finance. All that now remained was for the LSO to give its collective agreement to its players being offered individual contracts. But again it procrastinated – worried, not without reason, that only the younger players would be called to the Courtauld colours. Courtauld began to lose patience.

In June Beecham went to Paris with Labbette. They paid several visits to Delius at Grez, where Beecham played through *A Village Romeo and Juliet*, with Labbette singing most of the part of Vreli and 'he filling in Sali as best he could. Her singing ... was exquisite, and they stayed till almost midnight.'[38] † Evelin Gerhardi, who helped Jelka with secretarial and household work, reported that at dinner Beecham 'told us so many funny stories that I kept on laughing for three days afterwards'.[39] By now Labbette was at last divorced from her husband. Beecham often proposed marriage to her during the 1930s, offering to

---

* Following his wife's death, Courtauld also established and endowed the Courtauld Institute of Art in the University of London, giving it a substantial number of his French Impressionist and Post-Impressionist paintings.

† A month earlier, on 20 May, Labbette had sung the role in a BBC studio performance of the opera conducted by Beecham, with Jan van der Gucht as Sali. Barbirolli took over the performance of *Die Meistersinger* that Beecham should have conducted that night.

get a quick 'Reno'-style divorce from Utica in America. But Labbette thought it might not be regarded as valid in Britain, and urged him to seek a divorce in London, even though it would be hard to achieve, for Utica would undoubtedly oppose it.

Beecham returned from France to find that the LSO situation had still not been resolved. His own position was equivocal. When on 16 July the LSO's directors confronted him with a letter it had received from Holt informing them that Courtauld's board had decided not to negotiate any further, he confessed that he himself had dictated it, even though, he claimed, he still thought the LSO should be included in the plan. Preposterously, he even offered to draft a reply to Holt. The orchestra's minute-book records that 'divergent views were expressed by the board as to the reliability of Sir Thomas's statements'.

A few days later Holt sent the LSO a conciliatory letter inviting them to meet some of Courtauld's directors. But the orchestra said it would not attend such a meeting unless Courtauld's full board was present. For Samuel Courtauld it was the last straw. He would go ahead without the LSO. Beecham must have known about the decision and agreed to it, but he did not deliver the *coup de grâce* – he was in Germany at the time, conducting *Die Zauberflöte* and *Die Entführung aus dem Serail* at the Munich summer festival. The LSO was stunned by the turn of events. It excoriated both Beecham and Sargent for what was seen as their duplicity; indeed, it never forgave Beecham. Though by its indecision the LSO had all but brought about it own destruction, its anger was understandable. It had lost the concerts of the Royal Philharmonic and Royal Choral Societies, the Courtauld–Sargent concerts and the Mayer children's concerts, as well as the touring concerts now organised by Holt. The Oxford subscription concerts had also slipped from its grasp. There was further alarm when it was learned that Holt was to inaugurate a series of Sunday afternoon concerts at Queen's Hall for the new orchestra, to be called the 'Beecham Sunday Concerts'.

With the LSO out of the picture, London's wiseacres predicted that Beecham would never find the players he needed, but on 12 August he assured the Philharmonic Society that the opposite was the case, even though the debut concert, to be given at Queen's Hall on 7 October under the society's auspices, was only eight weeks away.[40] He already had up his sleeve twenty-odd regulars from the society's own orchestra, all of them excellent players, whom he had promised to take on in return for the society's agreement that in future all its concerts would be given by the new orchestra.

The group included three particularly fine wind-players: Reginald Kell, still only twenty-six, who had played first clarinet for the society's orchestra while a student at the Royal Academy of Music, the flautist Gerald Jackson and, perhaps best known of the trio, the oboe-player Leon Goossens, whose beautiful, refined tone was quite unlike the unyielding, vibrato-less sound produced by other oboists of the time. All three were appointed principals of the Courtauld–Beecham orchestra, which had at last acquired a name, the London Philharmonic Orchestra. Beecham had also found a leader for it, the thirty-one-year-old Paul Beard, who for the previous twelve years had held the same post with the City of Birmingham Orchestra. Beard was on Llandudno Pier, leading the local ensemble as a holiday job, when he received the telegram from Beecham offering him the job. 'Am packing my bags', he telegraphed back.[41]

The LSO called on its players not to defect, but in August one of its own board members, John Alexandra, resigned as first bassoon to join Beecham. His action, said his fellow directors, was 'of a most treacherous nature, and worthy of the strongest condemnation'.[42] Alexandra's defection opened the flood-gates. Before long the LSO had lost sixteen more of its members, including George Stratton, who was to lead the London Philharmonic's second violins. His three colleagues in the Stratton String Quartet were also roped in. To help in the hunt for more players, Beecham engaged Frederick Laurence as his orchestral manager. Fred Laurence had been responsible for picking the musicians for the Philharmonic Society's orchestra and had an encyclopaedic knowledge of London's orchestral world. He was married to Marie Goossens (sister of Leon, Eugene and Sidonie), who got the job of second harp and before long would become principal.

Having exhausted the pool of good available players with experience, Laurence turned to the music colleges, urging professors to send their best students to the auditions that Beecham was holding at EMI's Abbey Road studios. A fair number of young players were taken on, among them a twenty-year-old bassoonist, Gwydion Holbrooke, son of the composer Joseph Holbrooke and Laurence's nephew. He had left the Academy only that summer. When Beecham put the music for the bassoon cadenza from Rimsky-Korsakov's *Scheherazade* in front of him, Holbrooke remarked nonchalantly, 'I'll have a stab at it.' Beecham guffawed. 'Just like his father!', he said.[43] Holbrooke, who later would shorten his surname to Brooke, was made second bassoon to Alexandra.

Youngest of all was the trumpet-player Richard ('Bob') Walton, just nineteen and still at the Royal College, where he was to remain for another two years. Before his audition his teacher Ernest Hall, the BBC orchestra's principal trumpet, had advised him to take a look at *Ein Heldenleben* because, he said, it was a Beecham favourite. On arrival at Abbey Road, Walton found Beecham sitting at a grand piano. Beecham's first request was for the trumpet-calls from *Fidelio*, which Walton played from memory. Then, sure enough, came *Heldenleben*. As Beecham played from the full score, Walton peered over his shoulder to read the trumpet line as best he could. He was given third trumpet. 'Three years later',

Walton recalled, 'I was pitchforked by Tommy into first trumpet in the middle of a ballet season. It frightened the life out of me.' [44]

The orchestra's members were not salaried, but instead were guaranteed a specific number of engagements a year. Goossens was reputed to receive the highest fee; rank-and-file string players were paid twenty-nine shillings (£58.67) a concert. To avoid the indiscipline endemic in the LSO, strict rules were written into the players' agreements: 'Upon your attending any concert, rehearsal or gramophone session, you will be in your place with your instrument five minutes before the time advertised for commencing same, and will not leave the Orchestra or be absent from any part of the concert, rehearsal or gramophone session without the consent of the Conductor.' Players could accept outside engagements provided they were not needed by the orchestra, but no deputies would be allowed, 'except in the case of illness, in which case you must forward a doctor's certificate to the Manager who will then provide a deputy for you'.

An all-important recording contract with EMI was drafted on 19 September (though not signed until two months later) and, on that day and the next, forty of the players got a preliminary chance to work together when they went to Kingsway Hall to make the London Philharmonic's first gramophone records, choruses from *Messiah* and Haydn's *The Creation* for HMV, with Sargent and the Royal Choral Society. But even at this late stage the orchestra was not complete. It was not until 22 September, when by chance Beecham went to Folkestone to conduct its municipal orchestra, that he found the right cor anglais player, Horace 'Jimmy' Green, who had started his career as a boy in the Plymouth Royal Artillery Band and later moved to Folkestone because he liked the fishing and golf it offered. Green not only produced the magically wistful tone that Beecham sought, but also phrased beautifully. There were still gaps in the string sections. When the twenty-one-year-old viola student Leo Birnbaum called at the LPO's offices with a recommendation from Ernest Yonge, his professor at the Guildhall, Fred Laurence gave him a job on the spot. Such was Yonge's reputation as a teacher that his word was good enough for Laurence. [45] The average age of the orchestra was dropping by the hour. At thirty-five, Leon Goossens seemed like a grand old man.

On 30 September Beecham began intensive rehearsals for the opening concert, by now only a week away. There were sectional rehearsals each morning and afternoon at the Royal Institute for the Blind's Armitage Hall at 224 Great Portland Street, with extra ones for principals and other key players at his recently acquired flat in Park Road, close by Regent's Park. Rehearsals for the full orchestra – there were three of them, not six, or even seven, as has sometimes been claimed – took place at Queen's Hall. Beecham pushed his young forces hard, but ensured that they had energy in reserve for the night itself.

The strategy worked. The LPO burst upon London with an explosive force that few seem to have anticipated – to Beecham's outrage, the hall was by no means full. After the first item, Berlioz's *Carnaval romain* overture, the applause was tremendous, with the audience drumming its feet on the floor. There was more noisy enthusiasm for the rest of the typically Beechamesque programme: Mozart's 'Prague' Symphony, *Brigg Fair* and *Ein Heldenleben*. The Berlioz, wrote Ernest Newman, 'had an air about it of "You Londoners want to know what an orchestra ought to be like? Well, just listen to this"; nothing so electrifying has been heard in a London concert room for years.' [46] For Richard Capell, 'the brilliance, the clarity and the ensemble of the performances were marvellous; no one who did not know Beecham could have believed this to be a newly formed orchestra.' [47]

Only two things bothered the critics. The first was Beecham's introduction into the orchestra of the large-bore German horn, more mellow in tone and less capricious than the French horn then still used by other London orchestras. The second was that in the 'Prague' Symphony he had been unable to resist the temptation to show off the skills of individual players, particularly in the woodwind section, which had made for a rather mannered effect. The composer and conductor Constant Lambert picked up on both points in his column for the *Sunday Referee* (9 October). Though otherwise full of praise, Lambert said he missed the French horn's 'intense and beautiful timbre', and that the second movement of the 'Prague' had suffered from 'unimaginable longueurs (each bloom was laboriously held up for inspection, but we were never allowed to look round the garden) ... as for the gear change between the first and second subjects [from *andante* to an unmarked *adagio*, noted *The Times*] it would have made a French taxi driver turn in his grave.'

Beecham might have been infuriated by the poor attendance, and irritated by critical quibbles, but with the LPO's debut he came into his musical kingdom. The concerts he gave with the orchestra would be vast in number and remarkably consistent in quality. The first international soloist to appear with it was Vladimir Horowitz, who on 10 November played Tchaikovsky's B flat minor Piano Concerto. It was the first time he and Beecham had worked together since their notorious collaboration on the same piece in New York almost five years before. When Horowitz arrived to rehearse, Beecham broke the ice by shouting out, 'Librarian! Score!' Both laughed and got on with the job. 'Never', wrote the *Musical Times*, 'was a battle-horse so beautifully groomed.' [48]

The LPO was characterised by a virtuosity that Boult's BBC Symphony Orchestra, good though it was, could not quite match. A tantalising glimpse of the LPO at this time is caught in an item filmed at Queen's Hall in December 1932 for a British Movietone news-reel. It features the last pages of Tchaikovsky's

'Polish' Symphony (no. 3), played with blistering energy by Paul Beard and his colleagues under Beecham's piercing, hypnotic gaze. In a brief introduction Beecham, leaning on the podium-rail, extols the two-month-old orchestra as 'much the best that has ever been under my baton'. It did not just play well for Beecham. It was soon responding with enthusiasm to visiting conductors like Bruno Walter, the young Georg Szell and, in the recording studio for Beethoven's Fifth Symphony, Felix Weingartner.

Before the year was out Eustace Blois invited Beecham to act as musical director for the 1933 international season at Covent Garden. The London Philharmonic would play in the pit, yet another set-back for the LSO.* It seemed likely that the season would be the last ever to take place at the house, for the syndicate's lease was about to expire without any chance of further extension. The building no longer complied with London County Council safety regulations, and Philip Hill, as chairman of the freeholders, faced a large bill for putting the matter right. He hoped to recoup the cost by raising the annual rent to at least £15,000 (£617,000) a year, a figure beyond the means of the current syndicate, which had been paying one-third of that figure for the extension to its current lease.[49] To cover the possibility that no tenant might be found, Covent Garden Properties submitted plans to Westminster City Council for the theatre's demolition and the redevelopment of its site. The council indicated that it would approve the scheme, subject to certain conditions.[50]

The decision to use the London Philharmonic for the season was taken without the knowledge of Ethel Snowden, who had written to the LSO specifically denying such a possibility. On hearing what Blois had been up to, she resigned from the syndicate, saying that she found it 'less insulting to be insulted than ignored!'[51] Her departure was not a problem for Beecham, who considered her meddlesome. Nor was he bothered that the opera subsidy instituted by her husband was to be terminated prematurely, following lobbying by Tory MPs who considered it unacceptable at a time of economic hardship. With so few performances being given at the Opera House the subsidy was hard to justify anyway.

In March 1933 Beecham took the LPO on a fifteen-concert tour of England, Ireland and Scotland. It was the fiftieth anniversary of Wagner's death, and his music featured prominently in the programmes. Saturday 25 March, when the orchestra gave an afternoon concert at Edinburgh's Usher Hall, had special

---

* The LSO began to recover under the guidance of Hamilton Harty who, no longer with the Hallé, became its chief conductor for the 1933–4 season. It also acquired a new, rich sponsor, F. J. Nettlefold, by coincidence a director of Courtaulds. Lord Howard de Walden and Baron d'Erlanger, who had both disapproved of Samuel Courtauld's treatment of the LSO, were two of the season's guarantors.

significance for Beecham, for that day, at a nursing home in Welbeck Street, St Marylebone, Dora Labbette gave birth to his third son, Paul Beecham. Sunday was a rest-day for the orchestra, which gave Beecham the opportunity to rush down to London to see the new infant and return north in time to resume the tour at Newcastle on the Monday.

CHAPTER 13

The Shadows Lengthen

T HE COVENT GARDEN SEASON, which opened on 1 May and, like its predecessor, lasted only six weeks, was the first to be given there since Hitler became Chancellor of Germany on 30 January 1933. The harsh consequences for Germany's musical life were brought home to London music-lovers when, on the eve of the season, Beecham presided at a dinner given by the Music Club in honour of Bruno Walter. Though Berlin-born, Walter had become one of the first conductors (Otto Klemperer was another) to be barred from working in Germany because of their Jewish descent.

Coincidentally, in the second week of the season, Alfred Rosenberg, editor-in-chief of the rabid Nazi daily, the *Völkischer Beobachter*, arrived in London at the Führer's behest to discuss the deadlock at the Disarmament Conference and to gauge British opinion on the Nazi regime. His presence was marked by street protests and a snub by the Prime Minister, Stanley Baldwin, who declined to meet him. Hitler's waxwork at Madame Tussaud's was daubed with red paint. But the greatest fury came when, on Hitler's behalf, Rosenberg placed a wreath at the Cenotaph 'in honour of the fallen British'. It was decorated with a swastika. That night the wreath was thrown into the Thames. The *Daily Telegraph* reported that at Covent Garden a female singer, whom it did not name, had burst out laughing on hearing of the wreath's fate, a reaction that infuriated the Nazi sympathisers among her colleagues. One can only speculate on the singer's identity. Lotte Lehmann? Frida Leider? Both these German singers had Jewish husbands.[1]

Lehmann was the Marschallin in the opening opera, *Der Rosenkavalier*, which Beecham conducted. The Ochs was the fine bass Alexander Kipnis, a Jewish Ukrainian still singing at the Berlin State Opera, though not for much longer; in the following year he would emigrate to America. For Richard Capell, the singers and orchestra in this and other operas in the German part of the season were unbeatable. Not even at Bayreuth, he wrote, were such casts to be heard, night after night, but 'what Bayreuth gets and Covent Garden does not is thorough rehearsing. If only the singers had all come to London a fortnight before the season began, and the orchestra, during that fortnight, had had nothing to do but rehearse, the splendour of the performances would have been without blemish.'[2]

Capell's reviews and articles in the *Daily Telegraph* provide a graphic commentary on the season's ups and downs.³ Ten days after *Der Rosenkavalier* there were problems of a different kind, when Beecham conducted the first of two *Tristans*. Frida Leider, the Isolde, was unwell, and withdrew on the morning of the performance. There was no cover and Henny Trundt, a Bayreuth Sieglinde and Kundry, flew from Cologne in a specially chartered aeroplane to save the day. It was the first known instance of a performance at Covent Garden being rescued in this fashion. The gallant Trundt, deafened by the noise of the plane's engines, arrived at Croydon three hours before curtain-up. For Capell she 'proved to be worth a Covent Garden hearing', but the linchpin of the evening was the LPO under Beecham, which 'played with the utmost fineness and clarity, as well as quivering nervous life'.

Capell was not alone in finding the second half of the 1933 season, devoted to Italian opera with a French addition, disappointing. 'Is Italian singing in a bad way in these days', he asked, 'or was the selection of the company at fault?' The sopranos Rosetta Pampanini (Mimi in *La bohème* conducted by Barbirolli) and Gina Cigna (Elisabetta in *Don Carlo* conducted by Beecham) had both 'wobbled like jellies'. Beecham would claim that the performances of *Aida* he conducted, with the British soprano Eva Turner striking in the title-role, had the poorest cast of singers (presumably he was excluding Turner) that had ever sung this opera under my direction'. He would not, he said, put up with the 'vocal deficiencies' and 'musical slovenliness' of all too many Continental singers.⁴ Many a wayward artist would feel the lash of his tongue.

There was no chance of the performances being rescued by inspired stage-direction. Verdi's *Don Carlo*, not seen at Covent Garden for sixty-six years, was 'not so much produced as pitched upon the stage', while the scenery 'might have come from a factory[,] failing as it did, in its dull, conventional way, to recognise in any detail the character of the lurid tragedy.' The same went for Berlioz's *La damnation de Faust*, whose true home, Beecham believed, was in the theatre: as a fourteen-year-old schoolboy he had attended its only previous staging in Britain, in Liverpool in 1894 by the Carl Rosa company, with Sir Charles Hallé conducting. Capell shared Beecham's enthusiasm for the piece, but thought that the production, with its ancient, recycled sets from the scenery store, was 'deplorably and surprisingly bad, with staging suggesting an impecunious touring company of fifty years ago, and much execrable singing'. Beecham should have been 'not only conductor, but also producer'. The principal singers were a Spaniard, Giovanni Voyer, in the title-role, and two Italians – Gina Cigna (Marguérite) and Cesare Formichi (Méphistophélès). The language they sang in was described as 'French-Italian'.

Eustace Blois had been mainly responsible for the Italian singers, but no one had the heart to blame him publicly. He had fallen seriously ill before the season started, and his duties had been taken over temporarily by a Scot, Charles Moor, whose job for the past nine years as the house's stage director had been to get the operas on to the stage at minimum cost and in the shortest time possible. On 16 May, half-way through the season, Blois died following an operation, which threw the future of the opera house into further doubt. A memorial service was held for him at All Souls Church, Langham Place, with the LPO and the Covent Garden chorus packed into the south gallery. At various points Beecham conducted the slow movement of Beethoven's 'Eroica' Symphony, the Easter Hymn from Berlioz's *Faust*, the second movement from Schubert's 'Unfinished' Symphony and the Funeral March from *Götterdämmerung*. As the last item 'rose to its tremendous conclusion of emotion, many of the congregation wept unrestrainedly'.[5] With so thunderous a sound in so limited a space the rector must have feared that his roof might fall in.

On the closing night Beecham told the audience that he had no idea what was going to happen to the Opera House, though there would definitely be a season in 1934 – if not at Covent Garden, then elsewhere. In the next few days the news of the house's likely demise drew forth 'howls of joy and moans of indignant regret in about equal number'.[6] Ernest Newman was all for pulling the place down.[7] Prominent in the opposite camp was Margot Asquith (by now Countess of Oxford), who wrote to *The Times* deploring the demolition of fine buildings in London in the name of commercial gain – 'we shall be lucky if we do not live to see the statue of Charles the First removed by private enterprise to make room for public lavatories.'[8] Beecham kept his opinions to himself, but the chances are he was still in favour of a new, larger and more economically viable theatre.

In August Beecham again went to Munich for its summer festival, this time to conduct *Tristan* and *Die Meistersinger* at the Prinzregenten-Theater, and *Figaro* (with Elisabeth Schumann as the guest Susanna) at the Residenz-Theater. He also conducted the opera orchestra's annual pension-fund concert. When he asked if he could include Strauss's *Don Quixote* in his programme, he received a reply (written in English) from Baron Clemens von Franckenstein, the Austrian composer and General-Intendant of the Bavarian State Opera, that illustrated all too clearly the pressures to which Germany's cultural institutions were being subjected: 'The orchestra will gladly play "Don Quixote" under your direction', wrote Franckenstein, 'but they would like our first cellist Professor [Josef] Disclez to play the solo. There is a special reason for this. Professor Disclez is a Belgian and has been attacked a good deal lately by certain jingos. If he is left out on this occasion his enemies will double their crowing and say that he is not good enough, although he is an excellent musician and a very clever cellist. I feel certain that he will give you full satisfaction.'[9] Disclez played and the performance received a standing ovation. Within the year Franckenstein himself fell victim to the 'jingos' and was forced out of office.* In a gesture of moral support Beecham conducted his *Serenade* at an LPO concert at Queen's Hall.

Meanwhile the prospects for Covent Garden's survival were looking brighter. At the annual general meeting of Covent Garden Properties, Philip Hill told shareholders that 'an arrangement with parties prominently connected with opera' was on the cards.[10] Despite his fierce public statements threatening demolition and redevelopment, Hill appreciated the historic status of the Opera House. He had musical friends and was about to marry the sister-in-law of the composer and conductor Geoffrey Toye, who in 1931 had become co-director with Lilian Baylis of the Vic-Wells opera company, now spreading its wings at the rebuilt Sadler's Wells Theatre. Following discussions with Toye over dinner, Hill was instrumental in setting up a new syndicate, the Royal Opera House Company Ltd. Chaired by the Northumberland landowner Viscount Allendale, its board included Toye as managing director, Hill himself, a couple more peers of the realm, chosen more for their wealth than their operatic acumen, and Lady Cunard, still unrivalled at rounding up subscribers. Beecham, though not a board member, was appointed principal conductor and artistic director.[11]

A three-year lease on the theatre was granted for an undisclosed sum, in return for which Covent Garden Properties spent £60,000 (£2.5 million) on improving the front-of-house – the gallery at last got a bar – and modernising the decrepit back-stage facilities.[12] The orchestra pit was enlarged at Beecham's insistence to accommodate the complete *Ring* orchestra, and a new wing built at the back of the building to provide badly needed dressing-rooms and rehearsal-space, while the stage benefited from both a new lighting-plant, 'capable of producing any effect that may be required', and a huge cyclorama, on to which scenic effects and moving pictures could be projected.[13] Thus Hill became in effect the Opera House's first commercial sponsor, though the continuing generosity of both himself and the property company, of which he was the major shareholder, was never publicised, probably for fear of antagonising unmusical investors. Without Hill's intervention the Opera House would not have lasted out the 1930s, let alone survived into the twenty-first century.

There were just three months left to plan the 1934 opera season, which was to last eight weeks. Because of Beecham's heavy concert schedule, much of the early work was left to Toye. In the short time he had been at Sadler's Wells, Toye had been responsible for an improvement in production and design standards that *The Times* found 'astonishing' and 'of enormous value'.[14] He prophesied,

---

* Franckenstein's younger brother Georg was Austria's ambassador to Britain. Recalled to Vienna in 1938 following the *Anschluss*, Georg von Franckenstein chose instead to become a British citizen. He was knighted the same year.

correctly, that what was happening at Sadler's Wells was 'the first step towards the creation of a national school of operatic singing and a National Opera',[15] which ironically was just what Beecham had dreamed of achieving with the Beecham Opera Company and later the Imperial League.

Further proof of what could be achieved by properly rehearsed ensemble opera was provided in 1934 by the first Glyndebourne festival, which opened in the middle of the Covent Garden season. Lasting two weeks, it featured productions of *Le nozze di Figaro* and *Così fan tutte*, sung in Italian by polyglot casts (there was only one native Italian), and produced and conducted by two political exiles from Germany, Carl Ebert and Fritz Busch respectively. Summing up the fortnight, Capell said it was 'rare in England for the producer's part in an opera performance to be carried out so thoroughly'.[16] Originally, John Christie, Glyndebourne's begetter, had asked Beecham to conduct, but Beecham had not bothered to answer his letters.[17] It was just as well, for as time would prove, it was impossible for two such opinionated personalities to co-operate on an opera season.

Toye and Beecham did not always see eye-to-eye, but they agreed on the need to inject at least a small measure of dramatic credibility into Covent Garden's productions, though not a lot could be achieved in a theatre whose season lasted two months at most and which had no permanent roster of principals, but instead relied on singers who as often as not turned up two or three days before they were due to perform. The German operas tended to work much better than the Italian ones, because the singers belonged to a relatively small coterie who in the Wagner operas at least had learned the productions at Bayreuth and reproduced them wherever they went.

Toye brought in Otto Erhardt, one of Germany's most experienced opera directors, to do his best with a repertory of no fewer than twelve operas. It included *Fidelio* and the complete *Ring*, both conducted by Beecham; Rossini's *La Cenerentola*, which marked the Covent Garden debut of the Spanish mezzo Conchita Supervia; and the first British performances of both Jaromír Weinberger's comic opera *Schwanda the Bagpiper* and Richard Strauss's *Arabella*. The last two were conducted by Clemens Krauss, director of the Vienna State Opera, whose mistress and future wife, the Romanian soprano Viorica Ursuleac, sang the role of Arabella. Both she and Krauss had participated in the premiere of Strauss's opera in Dresden only ten months earlier. *Schwanda*'s sets and costumes were bought at a bargain-price from the Berlin State Opera, which had dropped the work from its repertory, because its Czech composer, who attended the London performances, was Jewish.

In an attempt to raise the standard of design *Fidelio* was given to the fashionable British painter Rex Whistler, the *Ring* to the Russian scenic-artist Gabriel

Volkoff, whose Appia-influenced sets did not please everybody – one critic grumbled that he had never seen glaciers on the banks of the Rhine before. *Arabella* went to Benno von Arent, who two years later would be appointed by Hitler *Reichsbühnenbildner* (Reich Stage Designer). The German casts were as good as ever, the Italian singers again disappointing. Attempts to lure Beniamino Gigli and Giacomo Lauri-Volpi to Covent Garden had failed miserably, because both tenors thought the fees offered – £300 (£12,350) and £150 respectively – were derisory. Singers for the German operas came cheaper.

Fidelio opened the season on 30 April, with Lotte Lehmann singing her first Leonore at Covent Garden. No sooner had Beecham started the overture than a group of chattering late-comers sought their seats at the front of the stalls, 'guided by the electric torches of the attendants, flashed to and fro as in a cinema'.[18] It was a common enough occurrence at the Opera House, but Beecham had had enough of it. Turning to face the offenders, he barked, 'Stop talking!' He was heard clearly, not only in the house itself, but also by listeners tuned to the BBC, which was relaying the first act only. There was more trouble in Act 2. At the end of the Florestan–Leonore duet, the curtain began to descend and Beecham went without pause into the third *Leonora* overture, played as an interlude before the final scene. Its introduction was all but drowned out by loud applause for the singers. Beecham shouted at the offenders to keep quiet.

The following morning's papers disagreed about the wording of Beecham's second rebuke. Some said it was 'Shut up, you!' Some, 'Shut up, you barbarians!' Some, believing that the actual phrase was too indelicate for the public prints, left it at 'Shut up, you --------.' Society gossip had it that the missing word was 'bastards'; the orchestra thought it sounded more like 'buggers'. Beecham was unrepentant. The *Evening Standard* asked him to identify the word. 'It had better be left in oblivion', he replied, adding that having people talking within six feet of him was 'savagery – they think they are in a cinema, but they are going to be damned well shown that they are not.' The Opera House had not enjoyed so much press coverage in years. In the following year late-comers on German nights would be barred from the auditorium until the first interval.

The interruptions were not the performance's only problem. Shortly before curtain-up Erhardt had found Lehmann in her dressing-room in a state of 'nervous depression', apparently the result of a dispute with Hermann Göring, who as Prime Minister of Prussia had been given responsibility for the State Opera in Berlin. The thought of getting through Leonore's notoriously tricky Act 1 aria, 'Abscheulicher', without mishap was weighing on Lehmann's mind. Beecham called her to the conductor's room where, he said, he would give her a 'sedative' that would calm her. When she arrived she found to her amazement that he had assembled a small group of horn and woodwind players who, with Beecham conducting and a répétiteur at the piano, went through the aria with her.[19] The gesture appeared to have a positive effect on Lehmann, but when it came to the performance she suddenly accelerated in the aria to a tempo that, Beecham claimed later, 'made two bars almost into one'. He decided not to go with her, because it would only cause chaos among the horns, who were about to come in. To Beecham's chagrin the *Times* critic blamed him, rather than Lehmann, for the fact that singer and orchestra were not together.[20]

The opera season was immediately followed on 19 June by eight weeks of Colonel de Basil's Ballets Russes company, which was to be become a regular visitor to the Opera House. The conductors were Antal Dorati and Efrem Kurtz, with the LPO in the pit. Beecham put in an appearance on the first night to conduct a one-act version of *Swan Lake*, with Danilova dazzling as the Swan Queen. The *Daily Express* claimed that his approach was so 'tempestuous' that the dancers in the *pas de quatre* 'nearly tripped over themselves'. This may have been the occasion, recalled by several members of the orchestra, when Beecham remarked, 'That made the buggers hop.'

As an overture to the evening Beecham conducted a suite from Bizet's *The Fair Maid of Perth*, which he then recorded with the LPO at Abbey Road. It was among the first of the many recordings he made with the orchestra that would remain a corner-stone of the Columbia catalogue for years to come. It followed a recording of Delius's *Paris* that he had made just before the opera season opened. The composer was eager to hear it, and on 21 May Walter Legge, Beecham's producer at EMI, dispatched a set of discs to Grez,[21] but they were held up in Paris by French customs while inquiries were made about their dutiable value. As a result, Delius never heard them.[22] He died on 10 June 1934, at the age of seventy-two. The records arrived two weeks later.

When Beecham received a telegram from Fenby informing him of Delius's death, he was deeply involved in the last week of the opera season. He asked Labbette to go immediately to Grez to help Jelka, who was still weak from a recent operation for a cancerous tumour. It was as well she went, for she found the household in some disarray. She set about bringing order to it. Fenby seemed so upset that he was incapable of organising anything.[23] Because it was impossible to carry out immediately the composer's wish to be buried in a country churchyard in the south of England, Labbette made the arrangements for his body to be given a temporary resting-place in Grez churchyard.

Five months later Beecham's mother died at the age of eighty-three. She had continued to live at Mursley Hall in Buckinghamshire, though she had been bed-ridden for some years. On 8 November her coffin was placed with Joseph's in the family vault he had had built at the St Helens cemetery. The inscription placed under that of her husband reads, 'Lady Josephine, his beloved wife', which, wrote one of her granddaughters, 'chills those who know her story'.[24] Utica was Josephine's executor and sole beneficiary of her estate, whose net probate value was put at £171 16s 6d (£7,000). Beecham chose not to attend the funeral. That night, at Queen's Hall, he conducted the Royal Philharmonic Society's memorial concert for Delius: a suite from *Hassan, Eventyr, Sea Drift, Paris, Cynara* and the closing scene from *Koanga*. Possibly he had not wanted to come face to face with Utica at the funeral. Possibly he regarded the concert as a suitable memorial to his mother as well as to Delius.

Jelka Delius was at the concert, and while in London took the opportunity to finalise with Beecham plans for setting up the Delius Trust, which would not only finance recordings and performances of her husband's music, but also publish a complete edition of his works to be edited by Beecham, who with Frederic Austin would act as artistic adviser. It was also agreed that he would write Delius's biography (which was eventually published in 1959). The sole trustees were to be Beecham's lawyer, Philip Emanuel, and Barclays Bank. Emanuel had been a key figure in Beecham's affairs since the 1920s and would remain one for at least another two decades. There is little doubt that Beecham would not have had as many lives financially as he did had it not been for this diminutive and resourceful man. Emanuel had one office in Kilburn, where he spent much of his time representing the villains of north-west London in court, and another at 74 Great Russell Street, by Bloomsbury Square, where he concentrated on keeping his distinguished musical client out of other kinds of trouble.

One of the highlights of the 1935 Covent Garden season, the second to be run by Toye and Beecham, should have been the first British staging of Alban Berg's *Wozzeck*. Boult had conducted a successful concert performance of the opera at Queen's Hall on 14 March 1934, and the BBC had offered Covent Garden the cast, chorus and orchestra free of charge. The Opera House's production budget for 1935 was already committed to new stagings of *Lohengrin* and *Prince Igor*, so Toye tried to buy in a production cheaply from Germany, but without success. Because the opera was now banned by the Nazis, theatres that had once had the work in their repertoire had already destroyed their sets. Vienna could not help, because its production was in use at the same time as it was needed in London. In consequence, *Wozzeck*, one of the key operas of the twentieth century, would not be given at Covent Garden for another seventeen years.

The 1935 season was not one of Covent Garden's best. Beecham's relationship with Toye had deteriorated. He chafed at not having overall control, and there were disagreements over casting and the ill-balanced repertory. Toye had chosen to put on no fewer than three Rossini operas, which did the box-office no favours, although two of them, *L'italiana in Algeri* and a revival of *La Cenerentola*, featured the highly popular and effervescent Supervia. She also took the title-role in *Carmen*, which Beecham conducted. (Vincenzo Bellezza was in charge of the Italian repertory.)

Contrary to Beecham's wishes, Supervia insisted on the original dialogue being used, rather than the spurious recitatives. Rattled by the dispute which, unusually for him, he failed to win, Beecham stalked out of the dress-rehearsal, complaining that the boys' chorus in Act 1 was incapable of singing at the right tempo. He would not, he said, conduct the first night. He did, though, change his mind. Supervia told her regular recital-accompanist, Ivor Newton, that in an act of reconciliation Beecham came to her dressing-room and, without saying a word, kissed her hand with tears in his eyes. Newton recounted the story to one of Beecham's woman friends. She believed it, she said, except in one detail: Beecham had 'never wept in his life. He's incapable of it.' [25] Later in the year Supervia was to have sung the *Cenerentola* 'Rondo' in concert with Beecham and the LPO, but she became pregnant and withdrew from the engagement. Six months later she died in childbirth. She was only thirty-six.

In Lady Cunard's eyes, Toye's biggest sin was to hire as the season's Mimi the glamorous American soprano Grace Moore, a good singer who combined appearances at the Metropolitan Opera, New York, with leading roles in popular movies that showed off her musical talent. Her best-known film, *One Night of Love*, had recently been released in Britain. Her fans were legion. They packed the Opera House, which more than made up for the large fee Toye was paying her. Moore got a fistful of favourable reviews, and police had to be brought in to control the crowds outside the stage-door. Cunard thought Covent Garden was not the place for Hollywood stars, and made no secret of her distaste for all the ballyhoo that the singer courted and so obviously enjoyed. Moore claimed in her memoirs that Cunard cut her dead and that Beecham ignored her. [26]

On 26 May, between conducting performances of *Siegfried* and *Götter-dämmerung*, Beecham went to Limpsfield in Surrey, where on the previous night Delius's coffin, brought over from France, had been placed in a grave and covered temporarily with boards in the churchyard. Jelka had chosen the village for her husband's reburial because it was near the home of May and Beatrice Harrison – Delius had dedicated works to them – and she knew they would look after the grave after she was gone. At a simple service in the church Beecham conducted a group of seventeen players from the LPO in *Summer Night on the River*, the Serenade from *Hassan* and *On Hearing the First Cuckoo in Spring*, while Paul Beard directed the *Elegy*, written for Beatrice Harrison, with Anthony Pini, the orchestra's principal cello, as soloist. Beecham then delivered a funeral oration at the graveside.

Despite her frailty Jelka had been determined to attend the ceremony, but on reaching Dover she was found to be suffering from pneumonia. She was taken by ambulance to a nursing-home in London, where she died two days after her husband's funeral. She was buried by his side. On the day before her death she signed a new will, in which she directed that the income from her estate, along with all future royalties from her husband's works, should go to the Delius Trust.

The Covent Garden season came to a bathetic close with an unhappy production of *Prince Igor*, which Beecham conducted. Only the chorus, imported from Paris, sang in Russian. To save the expense of importing Russian-speaking principals, the opera was cast mainly from singers who had been in London for the Wagner operas, among them Elisabeth Rethberg, Herbert Janssen, Alexander Kipnis and Paul Schöffler. They sang in German. The season might have been 'international', but this was ridiculous.*

Twelve days later Beecham took the LPO abroad for the first time, to Brussels for two concerts given with Government backing to mark British Week at the 1935 Exposition Universelle et Internationale. The programmes were to include a number of British works not heard in Brussels before. By accident the large baskets containing the orchestral parts were left behind at Ostend (the station-master had mistaken them for laundry-baskets) and the first concert started forty minutes late, with locally borrowed parts of the *Meistersinger* prelude and Mozart's Symphony no. 40. Announcements from the platform kept the audience abreast of what was being played. The orchestra's own parts turned up at the interval, but by now there was time only for two of the five British works that should have been played that evening, Vaughan Williams's *Wasps* Overture and Delius's *Paris*. The Brussels correspondent of *The Times* claimed that they 'aroused much enthusiasm', but the Belgian critics were not keen on either piece, though they were much taken by Beecham and the orchestra.

Beecham switched the three unplayed works – Berners's Fugue, Holst's *Beni Mora* and Smyth's overture to *The Wreckers* – to the second concert, at the expense of other pieces. This time there were no announcements about changes, nor were there correction-slips in the programmes. The resulting confusion was predictable. 'Cette suite de *Façade* de Walton', wrote the critic of *La Libre Belgique* of the opening item, 'eh bien! elle est médiocre', not realising that what he had actually heard was the Berners followed closely by the Holst. Similarly, Smyth's overture was mistaken by the reviewers for Bax's *Garden of Fand*. Two days later Paul Tinel, critic of *Le Soir* and ironically a supporter of British music, castigated Beecham and the LPO for misleading both audience and critics, for

---

* The 1935 international season was the first to be mounted under the banner of the London and Provincial Opera Society, the syndicate's 'twin-brother' (Beecham's description). Classified as a non-profit-making organisation, it was exempt from having to pay Entertainments Tax. It 'rented' the Opera House from the syndicate for £500 a week.

he had discovered that although the orchestra's 'régisseur de l'orchestre', presumably Fred Laurence, had wanted to announce the changes, Beecham had opposed the idea.[27] Given the streak of devilry in Beecham's character, it is not inconceivable he had wanted to get his own back on the critics for their unfavourable comments on *Paris*.

There was little rest for Beecham. Back in London he conducted *Thamar* for the Ballets Russes at Covent Garden, with Lubov Tchernicheva in Karsavina's old role, and Massine as the Prince, and led the LPO in Strauss waltzes, for dancing on the stage, at a late-night party for the company's supporters.[28] In late August he and the LPO went to Ealing film studios to record excerpts from *Figaro* and *Die Zauberflöte* with a group of British singers for the soundtrack of *Whom the Gods Love*, a winsome though inevitably shallow feature on the life of Mozart, directed by Basil Dean. And as if that were not enough to keep him occupied, in the first week of September he acted the part of Henry VIII's chief minister, Thomas Cromwell, in a chronicle-play, *The Holy Maid of Kent*, written by Ethel Beecham, wife of his brother Harry. An amateur-theatricals enthusiast, she also directed it and took the title-role. The seven performances, one of them brought to a premature conclusion by rain, took place in the courtyard of Henry's Kent home, Lympne Castle. Beecham, wrote the *Folkestone Herald*, gave 'a dignified performance'.

Without a break Beecham went into rehearsals for a somewhat ramshackle two-week season at Covent Garden consisting of six operas that were then toured to Birmingham, Liverpool, Manchester, Bradford and Leeds. The LPO played in London and Birmingham, but because the concert season had begun, they were replaced by an inferior pick-up band. However, there were some decent casts, predominantly British with a sprinkling of Italians, led by Eva Turner, Heddle Nash and Walter Widdop. The money came from the Imperial League of Opera, released at last by the Chancery Court, though judging by the poor quality of the stagings, the season could have done with a lot more funding. The *Liverpool Daily Post*'s erudite critic A. K. Holland reckoned that his city and others like it had been short-changed. He and Beecham fought a running battle over operatic standards in the columns of the *Post*. Beecham was given the last word, but it was Holland who emerged as the more convincing of the two antagonists.[29]

The season had begun at the Opera House on 23 September with the first British performance of Delius's *Koanga*, set on a Louisana plantation, which had been premiered in 1904 at Elberfeld in Germany. The Australian baritone John Brownlee sang the role of the slave Koanga. Beecham had long wanted to conduct the opera, and called in Fenby to help prepare the score. By all accounts the LPO's playing was spellbinding, but reviewers grumbled about Delius's lack of theatrical nous, and audiences found the story incomprehensible. The production, by Charles Moor, was all but non-existent – Otto Erhardt had by now been forced out of Germany and had accepted a post at the Teatro Colón in Buenos Aires. Contemporary photographs of the scenery and costumes suggest that they would not have looked out of place in an end-of-pier minstrel show.

The season is best remembered for a brilliant publicity stunt cooked up by Beecham and Harold Holt. It was announced that the Mimi in *La bohème* was to be an exciting new soprano called Lisa Perli. Nobody had heard of her, though it was not long before half musical London learned her true identity – Dora Labbette, who was about to make her operatic debut. 'Lisa' was Beecham's nickname for her, 'Perli' an Italianisation of Purley in Surrey, near to her birthplace. The popular papers, anxious to make the most of a good story, kept up the pretence until Perli's first night on 28 September. 'Mystery of Covent Garden's Phantom Singer', ran the *Daily Mail*'s headline the next morning. 'Who was Lisa Perli? Audience Say: Dora Labbette.' The reviewer from *The Times* chose to stick with Perli: 'her phrasing revealed an experienced singer behind the clear, almost girlish tones, and she had at her disposal a richer and more powerful quality when it was needed.' Labbette's Rodolfo was Heddle Nash, who 'revelled in the Italian *cantilena*'.[30] Clarence Raybould got few marks for his conducting. The last tour performance took place at Leeds on 23 November, still with Nash and Labbette, but this time with Beecham as conductor. A memento of the performance survives in a recording of Act 4 (with the LPO) that Columbia made at Abbey Road shortly afterwards.

News reached Mayfair's ears that the *Bohème* jape had sparked off a quarrel between Lady Cunard and Beecham. The former diplomat and secret-agent Robert Bruce Lockhart noted in his diary (missing several salient details in the process): 'Story goes back to last winter when Emerald discovered that Beecham had another girl round the corner. There was a row. Emerald threatened never to lift a finger for opera again unless Beecham gave up his fairy. Beecham agreed. Emerald discovered recently that he had not given her up. Hence these tears.'[31] Somehow a compromise was reached. To all outward appearances Beecham's relationship with Cunard continued normally. His career was about to enter a new phase and he needed her support. But he did not give up Labbette. She and Beecham remained very close. In Glasgow, during a second Covent Garden–ILO tour in the following spring, she sang both Mimi and Gounod's Juliette with Beecham conducting, though after that she opted for greater discretion, and did not appear with him for the time being, either in opera or concert, though she continued to sing for other conductors.

Because she was still working, Labbette did not ask for maintenance for either herself or their son Paul. But Beecham got Philip Emanuel to draw up a legal document that ensured financial support for her once her career had ended. Under the terms of a second document he agreed to provide Paul with an education such as 'befits the son of a baronet'. Labbette and Paul were living in Hampstead Garden Suburb, where Beecham called from time to time to listen to Paul's first steps in playing the piano.

When at the end of 1935 Beecham sailed to America for his third series of concerts with the New York Philharmonic-Symphony Orchestra, it was Labbette, not Cunard, who accompanied him. There were to be eleven concerts in all, spread over two and half weeks and starting on 2 January 1936. Arthur Judson had suggested to Beecham that, 'since we have Klemperer for the first half [of the season], who is a typical German Conductor, and Toscanini for the second half, who plays a classical repertoire, it might be interesting if we were to make your three weeks cover an exposition of English music.'[32] Beecham thought the programmes should be leavened with some Mozart symphonies.[33] Judson agreed. Works by ten British composers were chosen, ranging from Boyce's Symphony no. 1 (in an edition by Constant Lambert) to Vaughan Williams's *A London Symphony*.*

The reviewers were delighted to see Beecham back in New York. After the first concert Olin Downes wrote in the *New York Times* that he had 'won a sweeping triumph, and astonished and delighted the audience'. His reading of the Vaughan Williams symphony had been unequalled in its 'commanding eloquence and poetry', though Downes could not think why, 'wantonly and outrageously', Beecham had chosen to open his programme with Ethel Smyth's 'perfectly awful' overture to *The Wreckers*. For the *Musical Courier*'s critic the performance of Elgar's First Symphony at the fourth concert 'crowned the impression the English conductor had made during the week as a leader of the highest virtuosity and musicianship ... Conducting at fiery pace and with an energy that extracted every ounce of meaning from the work, Sir Thomas gave a glowing and memorable reading of the adagio and a powerful evocation of the exalted finale. There was a long ovation.'

Downes shied away from offering a final verdict on the series, but the *Musical Courier* thought that although contemporary British composers were 'serious in purpose and able craftsmen', none of them had 'either a great original voice or world-arresting manner of uttering it'.[34] That was debatable. What was undeniable was that the concerts had caused an alarming box-office deficit, which the

* The other British works Beecham conducted were Delius's *La Calinda*, *Hassan* Serenade, *Eventyr*, *Paris* and the closing scene from *Koanga*; Vaughan Williams's *Wasps* Overture and first *Norfolk Rhapsody*; Holst's *Beni Mora*; Elgar's *Cockaigne*, *Introduction and Allegro* and the *Serenade for Strings*; Walton's *Façade* suite, Bax's *Overture to a Picaresque Comedy* and Third Symphony; Butterworth's *A Shropshire Lad*; Bantock's *Fifine at the Fair*; and Berners's *Triumph of Neptune* suite.

orchestra could ill afford. The all-important non-subscribers had stayed away in droves. 'Unfortunately', Judson told the orchestra's board, 'the public not only did not want English music but most of them would not even come to find out whether it was any good.'[35] The outcome certainly damaged Beecham's reputation with the board. To his alarm he discovered that although, as Judson would remind them, the directors had agreed to the original plan, they were now blaming him for the débâcle, and even questioning his professional judgement.[36]

The Philharmonic-Symphony was not only facing financial difficulties. It was about to lose its crowd-pulling chief conductor, Toscanini, who on 14 February, a month after Beecham's final concert, confirmed his intention to leave the orchestra at the end of the season, following arguments over salary and other matters. An attempt by the board to appoint Wilhelm Furtwängler as his successor collapsed after a storm of protest from New York's Jewish community in particular. Judson then hit on an interim arrangement that would tide the orchestra over until a worthy successor to Toscanini could be found. To widespread astonishment, he invited John Barbirolli, virtually unknown in New York, to conduct the first ten weeks of the following season. Artur Rodzinski, Polish conductor of the Cleveland Orchestra and Toscanini's candidate to replace Furtwängler, was to take the last eight. In between, there would concerts with three composer-conductors – Igor Stravinsky, George Enesco and Carlos Chávez. Judson wrote to Beecham claiming that the situation was 'difficult and complicated'. He and a colleague at Columbia Artists had spared no effort in trying 'to arrange a satisfactory engagement for you. That we have not succeeded is entirely due to matters beyond our ability to solve.'[37]

No doubt Beecham was miffed by Judson's failure to secure him some guest concerts, coming as it did on top of Barbirolli's appointment, which had surprised him as much as anyone else. But there is no evidence in the Philharmonic's archives, either in the correspondence files or board minutes, to substantiate allegations made by Barbirolli that the older conductor bombarded the orchestra with letters of complaint about his engagement (though there is one from a furious Klemperer berating Judson for not appointing him in place of Furtwängler). Michael Kennedy makes it clear in his biography of Barbirolli that his subject had always been wary of Beecham, finding his arrogance 'distasteful'.[38] It is possible that Barbirolli's wariness had turned into an obsession. As will be seen, Beecham would later find an opportunity to make fun of it.

The reason for Judson's choice of Barbirolli remains obscure. Barbirolli himself thought the invitation might have been prompted by reports of his skill as an accompanist in both concert hall and recording studio from artists such as Jascha Heifetz, Artur Rubinstein and Pablo Casals.[39] As it turned out, Barbirolli was liked by both orchestra and audiences in New York (though not by Olin

Downes), and he was asked to return to conduct practically the whole of the Philharmonic-Symphony's 1937–8 season. By the end of the 1938–9 season he was musical director in all but name.

The overheated atmosphere surrounding Barbirolli's engagement has given rise to a number of myths about Beecham's 'behaviour'. The most wrong-headed is that Beecham had wanted the job for himself, for he was in no position to spend ten weeks in New York, let alone undertake a six-month season there. He was totally committed to both the LPO and Covent Garden, and had become chief guest-conductor of the Hallé, which had not appointed a successor to Harty. And it should be asked why, if Beecham really did have a low opinion of Barbirolli's abilities, he not only invited him to conduct both *Tosca* and the legendary *Turandot*s with Eva Turner and Giovanni Martinelli during the 1937 Coronation season at Covent Garden, but also agreed to his conducting concerts with the LPO in both Bristol and London. The gesture was not reciprocated by Barbirolli when Beecham was next in New York.

While Beecham was in America, Geoffrey Toye resigned as Covent Garden's managing director. It came as no surprise, for it had become obvious that there was no room for both Beecham and Toye at the Opera House. One of them had to go. In a statement to the press Toye admitted that there had been 'differences of opinion between the directors and myself with regard to questions of policy, management, and financial control'.[40] He was paid £5,000 (£204,000) in compensation, which indicates that he was pushed by the board. Though Beecham did not assume the title of managing director, he was now *de facto* in control of everything except the Opera House's finances.

Coincidentally, Beecham also found himself in complete charge of the LPO. Courtauld and Mayer had been aware for some time that Beecham resented their holding the purse-strings. The costs of the orchestra had risen, due largely to his uncontrollable habit of calling unauthorised extra rehearsals, and they felt that after four years of bankrolling the LPO it was time to withdraw, though the orchestra would continue to play for both the Courtauld–Sargent series and the Mayer children's concerts.[41] Beecham set up a new company to manage the orchestra, the Orchestral Concerts Society Ltd, whose directors included himself, Lady Cunard and Harold Holt.[42]

To help him run Covent Garden, Beecham brought in the former Beecham Opera Company baritone Percy Heming as assistant artistic director, but his key appointment was that of a German refugee, the formidably efficient Berta Geissmar, who had an unrivalled knowledge of the European musical scene. Now in her mid-forties, she had been Furtwängler's general secretary and organiser of the Berlin Philharmonic Orchestra's tours. When in December 1933 Beecham had conducted his first concert with the Berlin Philharmonic since Hitler became Chancellor (at that point the orchestra still retained its Jewish players), he told Geissmar that 'If ever you get into hot water here, you must come and work for me at Covent Garden.' Beecham was aware that her days with the Philharmonic were almost certainly numbered. Though she had been brought up a Protestant, her family was of Jewish origin.

Geissmar lost her job the next year in the wake of Furtwängler's defiant defence of Hindemith. She left Germany, ostensibly to research musical scores in New York. When Beecham arrived there to conduct his 'English season' in January 1936, she went to one of the concerts and secured an appointment with him at his hotel, the Savoy-Plaza, where she found him 'immaculate in his white silk pyjamas with his Turkish dressing-gown – the picture of elegance, comfort and detachment'. She asked if he might try her out during the forthcoming Covent Garden season. 'Why not?', said Beecham, thoughtfully stroking his beard. 'You are just the person I want.'[43] When she reached London, he appointed her his general secretary and organising manager of the LPO, paying her twice what she asked for. There was to be no probationary period; she was to come for good.

Covent Garden in 1936 remained an 'open house', where it was generally understood that political disputes between artists would not be tolerated, though inevitably the rule was sometimes broken. Jewish artists, among them Sabine Kalter (Brangäne) and Emanuel List (Hagen in the first *Ring* cycle), sang alongside dedicated Nazi supporters such as the bass-baritone Rudolf Bockelmann, who had succeeded the Hungarian-Jewish Friedrich Schorr as the Opera House's regular Wotan and Hans Sachs. Bockelmann liked to show off his gold and silver cigarette-case inscribed with a hand-written greeting: '30ten Januar, 1936. Dem grossen Künstler, Kammersänger Bockelmann, mit Dank für den schönen Abend. HERMANN GÖRING.'* The soprano Tiana Lemnitz, making her house debut as a much-admired Eva in *Die Meistersinger*, proudly informed a member of Beecham's staff that she had been appointed to the Berlin State Opera by Göring himself.[44]

Beecham was no admirer of Nazidom and despised its leaders, though some, like Otto Erhardt, were perplexed by his flippant habit of speaking of them as clowns, rather than purveyors of wickedness. During the regime's first three years in power Beecham had limited his German engagements to just two concerts with the Berlin Philharmonic, which he conducted as much out of friendship with Furtwängler and the orchestra as anything else. When, to Hitler's dismay, Toscanini withdrew from conducting *Parsifal* and *Die Meistersinger* at the 1933 Bayreuth Festival in protest against the treatment of Jewish musicians,

---

* '30 January 1936. For the great artist Kammersänger Bockelmann, with thanks for the splendid evening.'

Beecham was one of the conductors asked by the greatly embarrassed Winifred Wagner to take his place. It had been one of Beecham's ambitions to conduct at the holy of holies, but, given the circumstances, he turned her down.[45] He never would conduct at Bayreuth. In the end *Parsifal* went to Richard Strauss, while *Die Meistersinger* was shared between Karl Elmendorff and Winifred's artistic director, Heinz Tietjen.

Live recordings made by EMI during the German part of the 1936 Covent Garden season include extended excerpts from *Die Meistersinger* and *Götterdämmerung* with Beecham conducting. They reveal – and for once the cliché is justified – a golden age of Wagner singing, though the chorus is rough and ready by the standards of seventy years later. As might be expected, Beecham conducts with great rhythmic drive, but he also displays an unerring dramatic instinct in more introspective scenes, such as Brünnhilde's soliloquy in Act 2 of the *Ring* opera. Frida Leider, unequalled in her understanding of the role, is heart-breaking in her despair. In the *Meistersinger* 'Prize Song' the Swedish tenor Torsten Ralf is revealed as a wonderfully lyrical, ardent Walther. The season also saw the house-debut, as Isolde, of the Olympian soprano Kirsten Flagstad, with Fritz Reiner conducting. 'On a hundred occasions I felt tempted to stand up and thank Providence for Beecham', wrote Ernest Newman of the Wagner performances, 'and probably would have done so could I have been sure I was addressing my thanks for so demoniac a phenomenon to the proper quarter.'

Beecham prepared himself for the Wagner performances in the same way as he had for the Delius festival, by playing the scores on the piano. Douglas Steele, who became his music secretary, describes one such session at the Opera House:

> 'He called me in, and said, "Have a piece of birthday cake". This cake was made for him, so he told me, 'by a little old lady in St Helens." Then he said, "I want you to turn over for this terrible piece."
>
> He went to the upright piano and the "terrible piece" was *Götterdämmerung*. As fast as he roared, coughed, cursed, sang (and what singing!), I turned. When I missed a turn, he cursed, not me, but *The Ring*. "Damn awful thing, what – barbarian lot of Nazi thugs, aren't they?"
>
> If complications in turning brought us to a stop, he roared with laughter; stopped, told a marvellous short anecdote about some accident in performance, and the swearing and banging on the piano started all over again, along with the terrible, moaning sing-song. The following evening he gave an absolutely majestic performance of the work.[46]

Despite the coughing and cursing, Beecham had the greatest respect for Wagner's music – he conducted *Tristan* more times than any other opera in his repertoire.

In the middle of the 1936 opera season Joachim von Ribbentrop, grandly styled ambassador at large of the Third Reich and soon to be appointed Germany's ambassador in London, offered Beecham a cultural exchange. In return for the Dresden opera company coming to Covent Garden for a fortnight the following November, he would invite the LPO to make a tour of Germany at the same time. Beecham agreed to the plan with alacrity – the opportunity to compete with the Berlin Philharmonic on its home-ground was irresistible – though naively he failed to take into account the political implications of such an undertaking, particularly one financed with German money. The British government declined to give the tour its official support. The origins of Ribbentrop's invitation lay in the mistaken German belief that Beecham was a confidant of the new king, Edward VIII, whose reputed Nazi sympathies, Hitler hoped, would lead to an Anglo-German entente. Ribbentrop was persuaded that involving Beecham could only improve the chances of success. It was true that Beecham and Cunard on occasion dined with Edward and his paramour, Wallis Simpson, but Beecham (unlike Cunard) was not on close terms with the monarch and had no wish to be. For a start the feckless Edward was not remotely interested in music.*

No sooner was the 1936 season over than Beecham started to plan the following year's extended Coronation season. He decided to attend the opening week of the Bayreuth Festival in July in order to discuss casts for it with both Furtwängler and Tietjen, who, as well as being Bayreuth's artistic adviser, ran the Berlin State Opera. Beecham sent Geissmar ahead of him to make preliminary arrangements. She was aghast at the thought of returning to the country she had left as an exile only eight months earlier, but Beecham assured her she would be quite safe. He had personally extracted a promise from the obsequious Ribbentrop that there would be no trouble whatever.

Geissmar went first to Berlin. At her own suggestion the Philharmonic was helping Ribbentrop's office in the tour's organisation, and bizarrely she found herself in her old office discussing details with the Berlin orchestra's Nazi-appointed chairman. She arrived in Bayreuth to find that Winifred Wagner had arranged a lunch during the first *Ring* cycle, still three weeks away, at which the guests would include not only Beecham and Hitler, but also herself. The Führer had apparently decreed that she was to be treated as a member of the British

---

* In her autobiography, *The Heart has its Reasons* (London, 1956), Wallis Simpson, later Duchess of Windsor, remembers one of Lady Cunard's musical soirées at Grosvenor Square, at which Beecham played the piano for the entertainment of the guests. Emerald interrupted him. 'Won't you give us a little Handel?', she asked. 'But my good woman', Beecham replied, 'I've been playing Handel all evening.' 'Have you?', she said airily. 'We must have the piano tuned tomorrow.' (This sounds authentic. Another version of the story provides no context, and has Beecham conducting an orchestra, which is implausible.)

party. On the day before Beecham was due to arrive, Geissmar received a telegram from him saying that he would not be coming after all. Winifred, in Geissmar's words, was 'considerably displeased'. 'But this is impossible', she said, 'the Führer expects Sir Thomas and wants to sit with him in my box.' Geissmar set off for London, where she tracked Beecham down at the Euston Hotel, sitting in his dressing-gown having breakfast. He said that he would go to Bayreuth for the second *Ring* cycle, when it would be easier to work. Beecham's features, wrote Geissmar, 'were sphinxlike. Only his eyes twinkled mischievously.'

Arriving in Bayreuth after Hitler had departed, Beecham attended first *Parsifal* and then a spectacular new production of *Lohengrin*, which Furtwängler conducted. Its designer was Emil Preetorius, whom Beecham wanted for a new *Fliegende Holländer* at Covent Garden. Hitler had been so overwhelmed by the *Lohengrin* – in the bridal scene Elsa (sung by Maria Müller) was preceded by seventy pages carrying candles – that he decided to offer a replica of it to Covent Garden for the Coronation season, though the plan came to nothing, because the production would never have fitted London's much smaller stage, even in a cut-down version. King Edward was reputed to have said that he had no objection to the gift, as long he did not have to go to 'the damned opera' himself.[47] Beecham and Furtwängler completed the Covent Garden master-plan in the tranquil garden of the latter's lodgings. Tietjen promised to release the required singers, and Preetorius agreed to design not only the *Holländer* but also a new production of Gluck's *Orfeo*. Furtwängler was to conduct the season's two *Ring* cycles.

Rehearsals for the German tour were held in London at the beginning of November. Beecham decided there was no point in carrying coals to Newcastle by including Beethoven and Brahms in his programmes, and instead chose symphonies by Haydn (no. 93), Mozart (no. 39), Sibelius (no. 2), Dvořák (no. 8) and, provocatively, for his works were now banned in Germany, the Jewish-born Mendelssohn (the 'Scottish' Symphony). There would also be half a dozen British pieces, including Elgar's *Enigma Variations*. The decision to play the 'Scottish' Symphony caused consternation in Berlin, and ironically it was Geissmar who persuaded Beecham to drop it for the sake of peace and quiet. At rehearsal Beecham expressed the hope that the Jewish members of the orchestra would go to Germany, and all, after reflection, agreed to do so.[48] It was a handful of players who had fought in the Great War who expressed the strongest doubts about going; their mood was not improved when they discovered that they would be travelling to Germany on Armistice Day. By now the LPO had a new leader, David McCallum, who came from the Scottish Orchestra. Paul Beard had resigned before the opera season to join the BBC Symphony Orchestra, complaining that just one more Wagner day at Covent Garden, with a rehearsal starting at ten in the morning and the performance going on until almost until midnight, 'would be the death of me.'[49]

The tour opened on 13 November 1936 at the Philharmonie in Berlin. Beecham might have escaped Hitler in Bayreuth, but he could not avoid a private meeting him at the Chancellery an hour or two before the concert began. Little is known about what was said. 'Initiated circles' – Geissmar's phrase – reported the following exchange, though since the conversation was conducted through an interpreter, there is no guarantee of its accuracy:

> *Hitler*: 'I should have liked so much to come to London to participate in the Coronation festivities, but cannot risk putting the English to the inconvenience which my visit might entail.'
>
> *Beecham*: 'Not at all. There would be no inconvenience. In England we leave everybody to do exactly as he likes.'

According to Winifred Wagner's daughter Friedelind, Beecham said after the encounter, 'Now I know what is wrong with Germany.'[50] Later, during the war, Beecham informed reporters in both Australia and America that although, officially, *Die Meistersinger* was held to be Hitler's favourite opera, the Führer had told him at the Chancellery that he actually preferred Lehár's operetta, *The Merry Widow*.*

Hitler, wearing his Nazi party tunic with swastika armband and sporting his Iron Cross, sat in the Government box for the concert, flanked on his right by his similarly dressed propaganda minister, Dr Goebbels, and on his left by the war minister, Field-Marshal von Blomberg, in full army uniform. The interior and communications ministers were also in the box. Hitler's deputy, Rudolf Hess, sat in the front row of the stalls. There had been a longish pause before the Führer's entrance. Beecham, already on the platform with the orchestra, remarked none too quietly, 'The old bugger's late.'[51] After the first item, Dvořák's third *Slavonic Rhapsody*, which was greeted enthusiastically by the audience, Beecham spoke again: 'The old bloke seems to like it.' He had forgotten that the concert was being broadcast. His comments, picked up by the microphones, were greeted with particular mirth by a group of young diplomats at the German embassy in London who had been instructed to listen in by Ribbentrop, their pompous and unpopular boss, who had gone off to Germany for the tour.[52]

Goebbels, unconvinced of the tour's diplomatic importance, bristled with indignation, writing in his diary: 'Beecham conducts in a very vain and disagreeable way, and what's more is superficial. His orchestra's strings sound very thin, lacking precision and clarity. Putting Beecham in the same class as Furtwängler

---

* In the 1920s Hitler attacked *The Merry Widow* as kitsch, but then changed his mind about it. He came to revere Lehár, even though his wife, like his librettists, was Jewish.

is like comparing Kannenberg [Hitler's major-domo and chef, who sang popular songs to the accordion] with Gigli. Only Berlioz's "Roman Carnival" and a Dvorak Rhapsody made any impression; the Haydn symphony seemed downright boring. The evening dragged on. It was painful, as one had to clap out of politeness. Also the Führer was very discontented. How high Germany's musical culture stands in contrast, what with the Berlin Philharmonic and Furtwängler! I'm working on the press – no tearing to shreds!' [53]

On the following morning the *Berliner Zeitung* published a photograph of Beecham in the box with Hitler, Goebbels and the rest of the party, apparently taken in the interval. It had been faked. Beecham had remained in his dressing-room, where Furtwängler and the British ambassador, Sir Eric Phipps, went to see him. It is hard to tell whether or not the German critics were influenced by official edicts. The general tone of their reviews is overwhelmingly enthusiastic, though the *Deutsche Allgemeine Zeitung* ventures a comparison between the Berlin and London orchestras that seems to veer cautiously towards Goebbels's view of the visitors. The LPO's brass was 'slighter, more compact and at the same time lighter than ours'; the strings were 'soft as silk, slender and insinuating, fragrant and unweighty'; the 'expressive colouring of the oboe's vibrato' (presumably a reference to Goossens) called 'to mind a saxophone'.

The concert was followed by a riotous supper given by the Berlin Philharmonic for its British colleagues, at which wine, beer and schnapps flowed unceasingly. Before slipping away early, Beecham stood on a table to conduct his players in a chorus of 'The more we are together', as Furtwängler, leaning against a pillar, looked on in bemusement. There were a lot of sore heads when on the following morning the party travelled to Dresden for the second concert. Next came Leipzig, where Beecham received a number of clandestine letters from citizens mourning the loss of the statue of Mendelssohn that had stood outside the Gewandhaus concert hall until six nights earlier, when it had been pulled down and taken away on the orders of the Nazi deputy mayor. By the fourth concert, in Munich, Beecham had become greatly concerned about the enterprise. In Britain a tour of eight concerts in nine days was nothing unusual, but this one was being ruined by the exhausting round of social events laid on by Ribbentrop's office. The British consul in Munich reported to Sir Eric Phipps in Berlin that Beecham had told him he was

> very disgusted with the whole tour so far. He was a musician and he wished to be regarded and his orchestra to be regarded from a strictly musical point of view, instead of which it appeared that they were no more than objects of political propaganda and living instances of "Anglo-German cultural relations". All the emphasis in the press has been laid on this side of the tour and far too little on the musical side. He had wished, when in Munich, to see the town again

and meet some old friends in the musical world – this had been denied to him. He had seen Prime Ministers, Lord Mayors and Gauleiters and had had hardly time to rehearse. His orchestra was being ruined by festivities that lasted half the night.

Sir Thomas Beecham asked [me] during the dinner given by the Lord Mayor of Munich if he should reply to Herr Fischler; he was advised that he should make a short reply preferably about Munich. Sir Thomas remained silent for some ten minutes, apparently collecting his thoughts, then turned to [me] and said "I'm damned if I will".

He had expressed a desire while at Munich to see Pfitzner* and Hindemith. He had been unable to see the former and was told that the music of the latter was "politically unreliable".

The consul reported that the mayor's dinner had proved so congenial that 'very few of the orchestra got away much before 4 a.m. and some remained until 6 a.m., and thereby incurred Sir Thomas Beecham's wrath.'[54] Not surprisingly, the playing at the Munich concert, which took place on the following night, was the least good of the tour. After it, Rudolf Hess gave a party at his house for Beecham, Nazi party and government leaders, Winifred Wagner *et al*. Five members of the LPO were to have provided musical entertainment, but to Frau Hess's disappointment Beecham had ordered them to bed.

Stuttgart came next, followed by Ludwigshaven, where Beecham refused to go to the banquet that followed; the viola player Thomas Russell was roped in by Fred Laurence to make an impromptu speech, in German, in his place. The concert had been given at the concert hall of the local BASF works, which at the time was developing a new recording medium in the form of tough cellulose tape coated with iron-oxide. It was used to record the concert. Some years later parts of the programme were issued on cassette. The sound-quality is patchy, but there is no mistaking the quality of Beecham's and the orchestra's music-making in Delius's *First Cuckoo*, less introspective, faster flowing, than in his other versions, and two magical excerpts from *The Golden Cockerel*, launched by Richard Walton's piercingly brilliant trumpet fanfare.[55] This was one of the first, if not the very first, tape-recording of an orchestra ever made.

The tour ended with concerts in Frankfurt and then Cologne, where Beecham made a final speech in which he said diplomatically that British music had brought the two peoples nearer together. It had done nothing of the kind.[56] On 12 December 1936, just three weeks after the orchestra got home, Edward abdicated, to be succeeded by his shy and equally unmusical brother George

---

* Though he held strongly nationalistic views, the composer Hans Pfitzner was not a member of the Nazi party, and was much disliked by Hitler. Beecham conducted the British premiere of his Piano Concerto at Queen's Hall three months later, with Edwin Fischer as soloist.

VI. Hitler lost all interest in an entente, and the shadows over Europe began to lengthen. When the Berlin Philharmonic visited London the following year, the LPO organised a dinner for the two orchestras at the Savoy which, it was generally agreed, was dull in comparison with its Berlin predecessor. Beecham made a speech, whose impish wit was no doubt lost on his guests. 'While we were in Germany', he said, 'I made thirty-nine speeches, the same number as the articles of the English church, and every one of them was different. In reply to my orations a high German official of one designation or another made a similar number of speeches, each of which was identical, thus showing the superiority of the Teutonic mind.' [57]

Beecham's next concert abroad with the LPO, a concert at the Paris Opéra on 16 March 1937, would prove a far happier occasion than any in Germany. During the interval the Prime Minister, Léon Blum, invested him with the insignia of a *commandeur* of the Légion d'Honneur. Beecham included in his programme one French work, Berlioz's *Carnaval romain* overture, and one that was inspired by France, Delius's *Summer Night on the River*. 'It is astonishing', wrote *La Revue Musicale*, 'that a master who loved France so much, and felt so deeply the influence of Debussy, should still be unknown here.' [58]

Later in 1937 Beecham met briefly a young British pianist, Betty Humby, who in time, though neither of them could have guessed it, would play a prominent part in his life. With her co-organiser, William Glock, later the BBC's music controller, Humby was putting on a series of Mozart concerts at the Cambridge Theatre, London, on Sunday evenings. She and Glock went to Beecham's flat to ask him if he would provide a written introduction for the printed programmes. Without even pausing for thought Beecham, who had greeted the pair in his dressing-gown, scribbled down the following:

> The larger revelation of the transcendent gifts of Mozart is a crying need in our present condition of dubious culture and civilisation. His spirit, more than that of any other composer, is made of that stuff which can provide the most telling and efficacious antidote to the chaotic thought and action of a blatant age.
>
> If I were a dictator, I should make it compulsory for every member of the population between the ages of four and eighty to listen to Mozart for at least one-quarter of an hour daily for the coming five years.

Beecham promised his guests that he would conduct one of their concerts for nothing, which he did, on 10 April 1938, with a contingent from the LPO.*

To compensate for the loss of the Courtauld–Mayer money, the LPO had to work harder than ever. An increase in out-of-town dates, which included

---

* Glock had studied piano in Berlin with Schnabel. He first met Humby when she attended Schnabel's summer school at Tremezzo on Lake Como in 1933. (Sir William Glock, conversation with the author, 1992.)

the Sheffield, Norwich and Leeds festivals, helped to swell its income, but often the players were paid late, which led to a good deal of frustration. As an economy the Beecham Sunday Concert series was switched from Queen's Hall to the Opera House, whose acoustics were not ideal for concerts. An appeal for £20,000 (£750,000) to provide working capital and a reserve fund for the orchestra fell on deaf ears. Beecham relied heavily on his men's loyalty, but a number of them thought he asked too much of them and left. Yet the standard of playing remained as high as ever.

In London at least Beecham made few compromises in his programming, though he now left the knottier, post-*Elektra* works to others. He did, however, put a tentative toe into the world of the Second Viennese School, when in November 1935 at Queen's Hall, with Emanuel Feuermann as soloist, he gave the world premiere of Schoenberg's Cello Concerto, the composer's radical reworking of a keyboard concerto by the eighteenth-century Austrian composer Matthias Georg Monn. He preferred the works of more traditional composers, conducting the first British performances of Rachmaninov's Third Symphony and the *Rhapsody on a Theme of Paganini*, with Rachmaninov himself as soloist, and Bloch's Violin Concerto, with Szigeti. In November 1938 he organised a mammoth seven-concert Sibelius festival, during which he conducted a complete cycle of the symphonies. The festival would prove to be one of the last gasps of society-sponsored music-making in London. The list of subscribers and guarantors marshalled by Lady Cunard took up two pages of the printed programme.

Both the 1937 and 1938 Covent Garden seasons had their great moments, for example Furtwängler's *Ring* cycles, two in each year (though Newman thought his reading paled beside Beecham's more dramatic approach to the operas). In 1938 Gigli made a welcome return to the house* and Erich Kleiber conducted *Der Rosenkavalier*. No one could accuse Beecham of keeping star conductors out of the house for fear that they might outshine him. He opened the season with a finely sung *Die Zauberflöte*, whose sets, reproduced from Schinkel's beautiful designs of 1816, had been lent by the Deutsches Opernhaus in Berlin (now the Deutsche Oper). The celebrated Austrian tenor Richard Tauber was the Tamino, Lemnitz the Pamina. Three days later he conducted an overwhelmingly powerful *Elektra* with the Hungarian-born soprano Rose Pauly in the title-role. The Austrian writer Stefan Zweig, librettist of Strauss's opera *Die schweigsame Frau*, and now living in Britain, wrote to Beecham to tell him that he had 'heard many a performances of *Elektra*, from the very first one. I have heard those of Mahler and Richard Strauss himself (with the unforgettable Bahr Mildenburg)

---

* Labbette, again appearing as Lisa Perli, sang Mimi to his Rodolfo in *La bohème*, with Vittorio Gui conducting.

– but never in my life have I heard a more perfect than yesterday evening.'[59] It was a box-office failure. Indeed, the whole season made a significant loss.

In October 1938 the Covent Garden syndicate went into liquidation. It was not surprising. By now Hitler had annexed both Austria and the Czech Sudetenland. With the future so uncertain it had become increasingly hard to find money for opera. Jewish backers like the property magnate Moss Myers could no longer stomach supporting the German part of the season, particularly when it was sung by the likes of Bockelmann, Lemnitz, Erna Berger (Queen of the Night in *Die Zauberflöte*) and the Berlin-based Dane, Helge Roswaenge (Florestan in a revival of *Fidelio*). Such was the esteem in which the last two were held in Germany that Hitler had approved large cuts in the income tax they paid.[60] For Myers, employing Jewish artists like Rose Pauly and the half-Jewish Tauber did not compensate for the presence of Nazi supporters.

Even Beecham's resolve to keep musical avenues open had cracked. In June 1938, during the last weeks of the opera season, he told Geissmar that he would accept no further engagements in Germany. He had made his last pre-war appearance there three months earlier, when he conducted *Otello* and *Die Zauberflöte* at the Berlin State Opera, and took the opportunity to make the last few sides for his celebrated recording of the latter opera with the Berlin Philharmonic, which he had begun the previous year. Masterminded by Walter Legge, and featuring Roswaenge as Tamino and a number of the singers who not long afterwards would appear in the Covent Garden *Zauberflöte* production – Lemnitz, Berger, Gerhard Hüsch (Papageno) and Wilhelm Strienz (Sarastro) – it would become the model against which all later recordings of the opera would be judged until well into the post-war period.

Ideas about Mozartian style have changed, but Beecham's reading still casts a potent spell, even if some of the singers, Berger for one, have since been outclassed by their successors. Legge, who had now also become Beecham's assistant artistic director at Covent Garden, had wanted to use Tauber (Tamino), Alexander Kipnis (Sarastro) and Herbert Janssen (Der Sprecher), by now a political refugee, for the recording. But as Legge said later, 'none of them could be expected to expose themselves to the evident dangers' of recording in Berlin.[61]* Legge's future wife, Elisabeth Schwarzkopf, sang in the chorus, though they did not know each other at the time.

---

* Because Beecham returned to London just before the 1938 recording sessions had been completed, it was left to his assistant in Berlin, Bruno Seidler-Winkler, to conduct the Queen of the Night's first aria, 'O zitt're nicht', for which the Berlin State Opera's orchestra played. The American discographer Michael H. Gray has established that Seidler-Winkler also conducted the side used in the complete set of the Queen's second aria, 'Der Hölle Rache', made with the Berlin Philharmonic on 15 November 1937. That day Beecham was at Ipswich, conducting a concert with the LPO.

With the loss of the syndicate it seemed that an international season at Covent Garden in 1939 was an impossibility, but Beecham thought otherwise. He decided that the LPO would accept responsibility for it, and took a six-week lease on the Opera House beginning on 1 May. Financing the season would be a problem. For one last time Emerald Cunard rallied society to the cause, but the subscription list was much smaller than in previous seasons. To raise more money, she sold part of her jewellery collection, replacing it with paste substitutes. Philip Hill had burnt his fingers over the collapse of the syndicate, but provided extra income for the LPO by getting Beechams Pills Ltd, of which he was still chairman, to sponsor twenty-six half-hour radio programmes of popular classics featuring Beecham and the orchestra. Recorded in March and April at the Scala Theatre, they were broadcast each Sunday evening until late August by the commercial station, Radio Luxembourg. Beecham introduced the items.*

Beecham put what money he could into the opera season, but it did not amount to a lot. Dora Labbette witnessed an extraordinary moment at his new Bell Moor flat in East Heath Road on the edge of Hampstead Heath, when bailiffs arrived to seize goods in lieu of debts to unpaid creditors. They decided to take his large radiogram. 'Not that!', exclaimed his lawyer, Philip Emanuel, who was also present. 'He has promised it to me in payment of my fees.' The bailiffs took no notice and carted off the magnificent instrument.[62]

The season opened with *The Bartered Bride*. The cast included Tauber and several Germans, among them Hilde Konetzni, who may not have realised when they agreed to take part that Beecham had chosen to conduct the opera as a tribute to Czechoslovakia, which Hitler had invaded on 15 March. Tactlessly it was being sung in German. Rehearsals were tense, with endless disputes between Beecham and the singers. When one of them complained that Smetana was known to have taken a particular passage at a much slower tempo, he snapped back, 'Smetana, I regret to say is dead. I happen to be musical director here.' Tauber, singing the role of Jenik, advanced to the front of the stage and with great politeness addressed Beecham. 'You must be patient, Sir Thomas', he said. 'We have been singing it wrong for so many years that it will take us a few minutes to put it right.' 'Next number', said Beecham, amused but unrepentant.[63]

A recording of the first night shows Tauber to be the most polished of the singers; Konetzni is miscast. Ironically it is Beecham who provides the most idiomatic-sounding contribution. Beecham arranged for several of the season's operas to be recorded using the new Philips-Miller system. The sound was

* Seven of them are available in the Symposium CD-set 1096-1097.

captured, not on tape, but on film with a thick gelatine layer coated with mer-
curic sulphide. The film had to be played on a special machine. The few Philips-
Miller recordings that have survived, though in variable sound, give a good idea
of some of the season's highlights: the young Swedish tenor Jussi Björling making his house debut with a thrillingly sung Manrico in a *Trovatore* conducted by
Gui; and Gigli setting the Nile ablaze in Act 3 of *Aida*, with the equally impressive Maria Caniglia in the title-role and Beecham conducting with warmth and
intensity.[64] There is no recording of the last night of the season on 16 June, a
performance of *Tristan* conducted by Beecham, in which Lauritz Melchior
made his last appearance at Covent Garden. In the absence of both Leider and
Flagstad, his Isolde was the French soprano Germaine Lubin, whom most liked,
though Ernest Newman grew weary of her 'attitudinizing'.

Four days before the season ended, Beecham announced that he was taking
a year's rest from his musical activities, partly on account of medical advice he
had been given. He did not identify his condition, but later told the LPO that
he was suffering from throat and bronchial problems.[65] Nonetheless, ever the
optimist and despite the large loss incurred on the 1939 season, he issued a brief
prospectus for an international season at Covent Garden for the following year,
which listed Vittorio Gui and Felix Weingartner as conductors. Though the
season would be under his direction, Beecham told the press that he himself
would not be conducting because of his intended rest-period. The more likely
reason for his absence is that at the time he was in negotiation with the Australian Broadcasting Commission for a tour which, if it came to fruition, would
clash with the opera season. The ABC had been trying to get him to Australia
since 1935.

For the rest of June and all of July 1939 the LPO was fully engaged with the
Russian ballet at Covent Garden. Beecham conducted a few recording sessions
with the orchestra at Kingsway Hall, but otherwise stayed away. Now that his
sons Adrian and Tommy were both married and free from their mother's immediate influence, he had managed to effect a happy rapprochement with them.
He particularly enjoyed the company of Adrian's vivacious wife Joyce. At the
beginning of the year he had offered to provide her with her wedding trousseau,
and took her on a round of fashionable London *couturiers*, where he was magnanimous in ordering dresses for her. To her amusement she discovered later
that the shops had been instructed to send the bills to Adrian.

By late August it was obvious that war was inevitable. The evacuation of children from Britain's cities began. On 1 September Hitler invaded Poland. Two
days later Neville Chamberlain announced that the nation was at war. London's
theatres, cinemas, concert halls and art galleries closed. The LPO, which had
been on holiday throughout August, held its breath. On 4 September it should

have embarked on two further weeks of ballet at the Opera House and then given concerts in Harrogate and at the Norwich festival. Everything was cancelled. Covent Garden was to become a Mecca dance-hall for the duration of the war.

The orchestra's situation was desperate. Because it was unable to perform, the players were not being paid; many were still owed money for the opera season. Backers had faded away. A liquidator's meeting was held at the Holborn Restaurant on 18 September, at which Beecham managed to hold the commercial creditors at bay. As soon as they left, he spoke to the orchestra. Its members neither blamed him for the situation, nor demanded any money they were owed. Their main interest was to keep together as many players as possible, though a few, including Leon Goossens and Anthony Pini, had already left for the BBC. Beecham asked the orchestra for any ideas it might have about a possible rescue plan. Charles Gregory and Francis Bradley, the first and third horn, together with the principal trombone, Francis Stead, said they had already thought up a scheme. The players, they said, should run the LPO themselves. With Beecham's agreement a committee was formed with Thomas Russell as chairman, and a decision was taken to form a limited company. Beecham undertook to pay the costs involved.

By the end of September places of entertainment reopened. The LPO's new committee resurrected plans that had been made some time earlier for a tour in October with Felix Weingartner. He was now unable to get to England from his home in Switzerland, however, and Beecham agreed to take his place for a number of the dates. The first two were given in Cardiff on 1 October and in Swansea on the following day. 'War or Peace!', trumpeted the hastily produced newspaper advertisements for them. 'London Philharmonic Orchestra says: "We Carry On"'. There were no intervals, so that people could get home early in the blackout. Further concerts followed in Cheltenham with Beecham and in Southampton with Boult. Sidney Beer, racehorse owner, cotton broker, and an experienced amateur musician, conducted in Leicester and Wolverhampton, no doubt paying the costs of the concerts. He also provided money, channelled through Beecham, that enabled the orchestra to employ a professional manager and secretary.

Boult appeared again on 21 October for the orchestra's first wartime date in London, a Courtauld–Sargent concert at Queen's Hall. Beecham was there eight days later for the season's first Beecham Sunday Concert, given in association with Holt. A member of the audience asked Beecham what had persuaded him to reappear. 'My dear fellow', he said, 'we were given to understand that the country was in a state of emergency, and so I emerged.'[66] He resumed his concerts with the Hallé, which was now performing at the Paramount cinema, since the Free Trade Hall had been commandeered for war purposes. The printed programme for a Hallé concert Beecham conducted in Sheffield's City Hall in November asks listeners not to leave the hall in the event of an air-raid warning unless they could 'reach home or some other place of safety within a few minutes'. The best course, it continued, was to stay put. The building was of reinforced-concrete construction and afforded good protection. Despite the difficulties, music in Britain was definitely coming back to life. Audiences began to include large numbers of servicemen in uniform.

Negotiations over the Australian tour dragged on, largely because Beecham would not agree on a fee. The ABC's London representative wrote to tell his superiors in Sydney that Beecham 'often says one thing one day and quite another thing the next day'.[67] Agreement was finally reached at the end of November 1939, when the ABC accepted Beecham's demand that in addition to his fees he should be paid £750 sterling (£23,700) for a Philips-Miller recording of a Covent Garden *Don Giovanni* with Ezio Pinza. He stipulated that it could only be broadcast in Australia.* Dora Labbette was to go with him to Australia and sing at several of his concerts.

In the four months left before his departure, Beecham undertook an extensive recording programme that not only provided work for the LPO, but also gave Columbia a stockpile of discs that could be released at intervals over the next two years. He also accompanied on the piano the mezzo-soprano Nancy Evans (then married to Walter Legge) for a recording of three of his son Adrian's songs: a grave, atmospheric setting of Sir Henry Newbolt's 'Outward Bound' and two settings of words from Shakespeare's *Othello*, 'The Willow Song' and a delightful 'O Mistress Mine'.[68] By now Beecham was on the most affectionate terms with his sons, a situation which, he told Adrian, he could not have imagined possible a year earlier.[69]

In January 1940 Beecham launched an appeal on behalf of the LPO, which brought in more than £2,000 (£63,000). His last concert with the orchestra before he left for Australia took place at Queen's Hall on 4 April 1940. It was an all-Sibelius programme, given in aid of the Finland Fund – *Finlandia*, 'The Death of Melisande' from the *Pelleas and Melisande* suite, *Tapiola* (which, wrote *The Musical Times*, 'was played and conducted as if the whole world depended on it'), *Valse triste*, *The Swan of Tuonela*, *The Return of Lemminkäinen* and the First Symphony. In the interval a telegram from the Finnish government was read out: the Finns expressed their thanks to Beecham and the orchestra. At the end of the concert he asked the audience to continue to support the LPO in his absence, if only to ensure that upon his return it would be still in existence,

* The recording was duly dispatched to Australia by ship, but its eventual fate is not known.

'unimpaired by the ravages of war'.[70] He and the orchestra then adjourned to Pagani's restaurant for supper. In a farewell speech Charles Gregory expressed the orchestra's sense of loss at Beecham's departure.

Beecham had arranged to travel to Australia via America, where he would join up with Labbette in San Francisco for the final leg of the journey. He was to sail to America on the Italian liner *Rex*, leaving Genoa on 30 April. He left London early to allow himself a week in Rome. While there, news reached him that Joyce Beecham had given birth to his first grandchild, a boy. Writing to her, Beecham expressed his warmest love, and asked her and Adrian not to reveal his whereabouts. He did not say why, but the reason may lie in message sent by the ABC's man in London to his general manager in Sydney, saying that Beecham was travelling on a diplomatic passport and 'perhaps will be engaged en route on some war-work'.[71] That could mean anything, but it is possible he had been asked by the British government to use the links he had forged during earlier visits to Italy to discover what he could about the country's bellicose intentions. (Mussolini would not declare war on the Allies until two months later.)

Beecham arrived in New York on 9 May. Emerald Cunard, who had travelled with him, was mistaken by the press for his wife. The *New York Herald Tribune* reported that, on his own admission, he was on his way to Australia under the orders of the British Government as a 'lecturer-propagandist'. The paper tried to find out more, but Beecham was 'secretive concerning the British propaganda he would disseminate'. The war had reached a particularly dangerous point for Britain. Germany had overrun Norway and Denmark, and was poised to invade France and the Low Countries. Beecham told the *Tribune* that Chamberlain's government 'must go at once', because it was 'made up of complacent, acquiescent toy figures'. What was needed, he said, was a new cabinet under the leadership of Lloyd George, who was 'vigorous instead of weak' and had the all-important 'magnetic quality of attracting great leaders about him'.

Later that day news reached New York that Winston Churchill had been appointed Prime Minister.

CHAPTER 14

Adventures in Australia

FOLLOWING THE OUTBREAK OF WAR, the Australian Government ruled that visiting artists could not take their earnings out of the country. As a result, the violinist Nathan Milstein and the piano-duo Vitya Vronsky and Victor Babin cancelled their engagements for the 1940 season in Australia. There was speculation in the Australian press that Beecham might cancel too, so there was widespread relief when in April it was learned that he was on his way. He earned extra credit for agreeing to accept young Australians as his soloists, rather than more celebrated artists: Eunice Gardiner for the Schumann and Delius piano concertos and Liszt's Concerto no. 1 in E flat, and Lyndall Hendrickson for the Mendelssohn Violin Concerto.

Leaving Lady Cunard behind in New York, Beecham travelled by train to San Francisco, where on 21 May he and Labbette embarked for Sydney on an American liner, the Matson Navigation Company's *Mariposa*. During the three-week voyage he dictated chapters of *A Mingled Chime* to Labbette, who typed them up on a portable machine she had brought from England for the purpose. When she complained that he was sometimes being casual with the truth, Beecham told her to stop worrying – the embroidered version was much better than what had actually happened.[1]

There was a brief stopover at Honolulu and another on 7 June at Auckland, where they were met on the quayside by Andersen Tyrer, who had worked for Beecham as a pianist in Manchester during the First World War. By chance Tyrer was conducting a performance of Gounod's *Faust* at His Majesty's Theatre in Auckland that night, as part of the New Zealand Centennial Celebrations. He asked Beecham if he would like to conduct in his place. Beecham, who had not conducted anything for two months, jumped at the opportunity, but said that he would prefer to confine himself to Act 3, set in Marguérite's garden, since it would not involve the Auckland Operatic Society's chorus, which he would not have time to rehearse. Tyrer agreed to conduct the rest of the opera.

Delighted to find himself involved in such an improbable and unexpected arrangement, Beecham told the audience to much laughter that he had chosen the garden scene because it was 'the easiest to conduct'.[2] The principal singers posed no problems for him, for three of them were old colleagues – Heddle Nash, as Faust, Isobel Baillie, making a rare appearance in opera as Marguérite, and Gladys Ripley as Siebel.* The professional orchestra numbered thirty-six. The critic of the *Auckland Star* found the performance 'brilliant', though he admitted that he did not have much to compare it with, since *Faust* had not been given in Auckland since around the turn of the century. The next morning Beecham continued on his journey to Australia.

Press interest in his imminent arrival at Sydney was intense. *Picture-News* magazine hailed it 'as the most important news in the musical history of Australia' and devoted two pages to photographs of the great man at home in Hampstead, sitting at his chess-board, playing the piano, posing at his desk in a dressing-gown for a portrait painted by his son Tommy, sporting a bowler hat as he headed for a waiting taxi. There was a picture, too, of a bundle of batons being inspected by Smith, his pipe-smoking valet, who in the caption comments cryptically, 'It's this music that causes all the trouble.'[3]

When the *Mariposa* finally docked in Sydney Harbour on the afternoon of 11 June, Beecham was observed on the quayside 'waving a rolled newspaper like a baton as he directed the collection of his pieces of luggage'.[4] Reporters took particular note of his button-boots. After a late lunch ending at 5 p.m. – he had enjoyed the oysters, he said, but would reserve judgement on Australian hock – he gave a press conference. The assembled journalists expected lively copy, and Beecham, as attuned as ever to both their needs and his own, did his best to oblige them. Only when faced with a provocative question about the Australian accent did he refuse to rise to the bait.

What did he think of Germany's leaders? During his visits to Germany, he said, he had met several of them, including Hitler and Goebbels. They were 'an example of men of narrow mind, poorly educated but energetic, dominating a credulous and silly people'. Was he worried that on the previous day Italy had declared war on Britain and France? Not at all – a French general, asked by his government how many men he would need to fight the Italians, replied, 'I'd need 600,000 to fight against them, but 1,400,000 to fight with them.' Would he be giving a concert of Paganini's music, to mark the centenary of the virtuoso's death? 'I hope that that is a disaster that shall be spared Australia in my brief visit.'[5] The Australian Broadcasting Commission, elated by the wide coverage in the Sydney newspapers, asked Beecham if he would agree to meet a second group of journalists. He refused to do so. The ones he had met already, he said,

---

* Despite the outbreak of war, the New Zealand government had decided to continue with the Centennial Celebrations, though in modified form. Nash, Baillie and Ripley travelled out from England specially for them. In her memoirs, *Never Sing Louder than Lovely* (London, 1982), Baillie relates how, on the first leg of the journey across the Atlantic, a German U-boat shelled their ship, killing two members of the crew (p. 124). Before leaving for New Zealand, Baillie, who until then had only sung Marguérite in concert, went to Dora Labbette for advice on performing the role on stage.

had been 'the most brainless and incompetent' he had ever known and no useful purpose would be served by his giving any more interviews in the city.[6]

When interviewed for the radio by Neville Cardus, who was writing about the tour for the *Sydney Morning Herald* and other Australian papers, Beecham was uncharacteristically reticent. It seems he had never taken part in an unscripted broadcast before and found the experience unnerving. There was a lot of throat-clearing and nose-blowing, as well as long pauses between questions and answers. One pause was so long that Cardus had to repeat the question, a simple one about the future of music. 'Music?', said Beecham, suddenly coming to life. 'No future at all. None whatever.' Eventually he was coaxed into saying that he was keeping an entirely open mind about Australia. What he expected and looked forward to in the orchestras was a maximum of attention, industry and enthusiasm. From audiences he hoped for 'similar manifestations of these qualities'.[7] Listeners had been promised an hour of wit and scintillating chat, but it was generally agreed that what they actually got was something of a let-down.

During an initial six-day stay in Sydney, Beecham took stock of the Australian musical scene. He accompanied the Countess of Gowrie, wife of Australia's Governor-General, to a concert given by the Sydney Symphony Orchestra under the Finnish conductor Georg Schneevoigt, and on the following evening went with Labbette to a recital by the distinguished Polish pianist, Ignaz Friedman, who had recently decided to settle in Australia following a concert tour there. Despite the distressing news of the Nazis' entry into Paris on 14 June, Beecham kept up a calm and affable front. His only disappointment, he said, was that he had found it hard to find a suitable cigar in Sydney; the special ones he had ordered for the tour had been sent on to Melbourne, where he was to conduct his first concerts.[8]

On 16 June Beecham and Labbette left for Melbourne on the overnight train, a journey that in 1940 involved a change at the New South Wales–Victoria border, since the two states still used different rail-gauges. On arrival the next morning at Melbourne's Spencer Street station, the ABC reception committee missed Labbette altogether in the general kerfuffle; characteristically she had paused to help a mother laden down with children and luggage, and had alighted from the train carrying a baby. Meanwhile Beecham had buttonholed a reporter who was standing on the platform and subjected him to a harangue on the bankruptcy of contemporary composition – it was, wrote the journalist, 'a torrential requiem, performed in the first place for me, and secondarily for passing porters, fellow passengers and a group of officials from the Australian Broadcasting Commission'. Beecham thumped the young man on the chest to emphasise his points: 'My boy, creative music is dead. ... Not since a century before Bach have the wells sunk so low. ... I have an orchestra. I have an opera house. I can find nothing new that is worth listening to. It is over!'[9] The fact that Beecham no longer had either an orchestra or an opera house to call his own passed unnoticed. Antal Dorati, who was touring Australia at the time with de Basil's Ballets Russes, recalled in his memoirs another of Beecham's encounters with the Melbourne press. A gullible reporter who asked him what new works he would be introducing to Australia was told they would include a Tenth Symphony by Beethoven, which he had recently discovered in the British Museum; maybe an Eleventh and a Twelfth Symphony, too. 'The few of us who stood around listening to this remarkable interview', wrote Dorati, 'became concerned that it really might get printed and word was sent to the editor to take it easy.'[10]

At the start of his first rehearsal with the ABC's Melbourne Symphony Orchestra, Beecham complained that the double-basses were sitting in a 'preposterous' position and should be given seats higher up. Told by an official that this was impossible because of the design of the hall, Beecham said that it was not important; it was just that he had learned from experience that making a fuss at the outset usually put people on their toes.[11] The rehearsal went smoothly, though at one point Beecham almost fell off the rostrum and in trying to regain his balance stepped on, and broke, a cello bow. Admonishments were mildly expressed and sometimes given a quaint Australian slant: 'Let us hear the notes and not slide over them like a girl on a surf-board.'[12]

The Melbourne journalist Basil Burdett described Beecham at work on Tchaikovsky's 'Pathétique' Symphony: 'He sits during lyrical passages, eyes half-closed, beating with his hands in a half-dreaming way. Sometimes he ceases beating altogether ... Then suddenly the music changes ... Sir Thomas is on his feet, his baton sweeping in wide, strenuous curves ... He turns to the players like a man haunted, eyes distended as though with terror, making the urgent rhythms with a lunge of his whole body towards them ... Very, very good," he said at the end of the first movement. "Very attractive. Very little to be done to that."'[13] Joseph Post, the orchestra's regular conductor, who had rehearsed the work before Beecham arrived, was amazed by what he heard. 'It's hypnotism', he said, 'bloody hypnotism. I've been trying to get them to play like that for a week and they couldn't get near it.'[14] The players, expecting tantrums, were caught off their guard by what one music critic called the conductor's 'slightly mannered charm'.[15] Beecham had gauged his tactics accurately, and the orchestra responded with enthusiasm.

Extra chairs had to be crammed into Melbourne Town Hall for the opening concert on 22 June, the day of France's surrender. To the francophile Beecham it must have seemed a melancholy coincidence that the first three works in his programme should all have been associated in one way or another with France: music from the ballet *The Gods Go a'Begging* that he had arranged for Diaghilev and had conducted at the Paris Opéra; Delius's *Summer Night on the River* that always evoked for him Sisley's paintings of the Seine and the Loing,[16] and Mozart's 'Paris' Symphony, composed for, and first performed in, the French capital.

In their reviews of the concert, the music critics fell over each other in search of superlatives, while Cardus stoked the fires of adulation with phrases of deepest purple. Indeed, so extravagant was his enthusiasm for Beecham generally that stories began to circulate that he must be acting as the conductor's press agent, a claim that Cardus felt obliged to repudiate in print.[17] The only person who seemed to find the concert something of a disappointment was the social columnist of the Melbourne *Age*, who noted wistfully that 'the crowd had lost the lustre that marked pre-war days. Hair dressing styles were simpler, and the frocks, worn with comfortably warm fur coats, were not as elaborate as formerly.'[18]

The radio weekly, *Listener In*, remarked that the ABC had done much to foster musical culture in Australia in the past, but its 'supreme gift' was Beecham's visit.[19] The journal was not alone in prophesying that it would bring lasting benefits to the country's musical life, though Beecham expressed serious doubts about such a possibility on more than one occasion. As far he was concerned, there could be no improvement in orchestral standards until the Australian government and trade unions lifted the inflexible rules that banned the introduction of first-rate players from abroad who could also act as teachers. Such rules, he claimed, were unique in the musical countries of the world.[20]

Originally there were to have been four concerts in Melbourne, but so great was the demand for tickets that Beecham agreed to conduct two more, one of them a charity concert for the Red Cross, at which Dora Labbette made the first of seven appearances during the tour, singing arias from *Figaro* and *Don Giovanni*. She used her stage-name, Lisa Perli. If journalists noticed her closeness to Beecham, that she always travelled with him and acted as hostess when he entertained, none of them drew attention to it. Although the critics continued to marvel at Beecham's ability to stimulate the Melbourne orchestra, they had begun to notice that even he could do little to remedy its technical deficiencies. 'The C major symphony of Schubert was opened by accurate horn playing', wrote Cardus. 'I nearly fainted with relief.'[21] Beecham confided his impressions of the orchestra in a letter to his daughter-in-law, Joyce.[22] On the whole, he wrote, it was much better than he had expected, particularly in its general musicianship, though the players required more rehearsal than was necessary in Europe, partly because they were unfamiliar with much of the music they were being asked to play.

As for Australia itself, he told Joyce, he liked it. The people were amiable and well intentioned, though there was very little intellectual life and the newspapers were dull and full of sport. Live theatre was almost non-existent. What worried him most was that, although the war was now ten months old, Australia had been slow to face up to the issues at stake. Men were being trained to fight, but it would be some time before the country's factories and workshops could be organised for any substantial production of armaments. The next day Beecham told the music critic of the *Melbourne Argus* that if Australia was to make a serious war effort, as Britain was at last doing, it had to introduce conscription, both of manpower and of wealth and property. 'Once the plunge has been taken everyone will experience a great feeling of relief and united confidence. Then, and then only then, will there be a real unity among you, instead of an imperfect, or even fictitious, one.' Did he think that people might say he should stick to conducting and leave politics to politicians? 'Young man', said Beecham, 'I don't give a damn what they think. You have asked my opinion and I have given it.'[23] The British Government must have been delighted with his forthrightness.

Beecham's final concert in Melbourne took place on 11 July. Labbette joined the Australian baritone, Harold Williams, and the Melbourne Philharmonic Chorus in Brahms's *German Requiem*. The choir, wrote the critic of *The Australasian*, may have left much to be desired, but Beecham 'presented the work in all its grandeur'. The evening ended with an exhilarating performance of Borodin's Polovtsian Dances. After applauding the choir and orchestra, Beecham strolled among the players, shaking hands with many of them. 'It was a finale such as one is likely to see only at a Beecham concert', wrote the same critic. 'Melbourne will miss him.'[24]

Whether Beecham missed Melbourne is another matter, for his visit there had been marred by an incident which, though it seemed trivial enough at the time, was to have unpleasant repercussions for him. Not long after his arrival in the city he was told by the ABC that a reception in his honour had been arranged for 4 p.m. on 1 July at the Hotel Australia. Beecham pointed out that at that time he would be rehearsing for his third Melbourne concert. Nonetheless, he said, he would do his best to reach the reception by 4.45. In the event he got there just before five o'clock, only to be greeted with ill-concealed annoyance by his hostess, the president of the orchestra's committee. Her message was clear: no matter that Beecham's first duty had been to his players; he had kept 100 guests waiting, including Australia's Prime Minister, Robert Menzies, and his wife.

Although the couple, who chatted to Beecham at the reception, made no complaint about the incident, a group of reporters from the popular press decided that Beecham had insulted the Prime Minister and jumped on the story with

glee. One journal, ironically called *Truth*, even claimed that, far from rehearsing, he had been enjoying a motoring trip in the country.[25] Beecham made it
clear that he found it ridiculous that he should be expected to be at the call of
people who thought they were conferring a distinction on him by issuing an
invitation which he had no wish to accept and which, as in this case, was highly
inconvenient.[26] For the rest of his time in Australia he was to receive abusive
letters about the incident, most of them anonymous. The mail, he said, 'was so
various in invective that it might have been written by Elizabethan poets'.[27]

   The next stop was Brisbane, where Beecham gave two concert with the Brisbane Symphony Orchestra, one of them a performance of *Messiah* with the
Queensland State and Municipal Choir, augmented by members of practically
every other local chorus, ranging from the Brisbane Grammar School Old Girls
Association to the Brisbane Eisteddfod Choir. Eisteddfods were popular events
in Brisbane. It is possible that the Menzies affair weighed heavily on Beecham's
mind, for little seemed to please him in the city. As always, however, he showed
consideration and respect for the orchestra, even though it was regarded as one
of the ABC's weakest.* 'He gave the players confidence', wrote the Commission's controller of music, William James. 'He didn't try to get impossibilities
out of them. He told me that his method of conducting was to "give them their
heads" for the first rehearsal. Then he decided what standard of work he could
obtain from them, and worked for that. "If I can get higher," he said, "well and
good."'[28]

   At rehearsal in Brisbane's City Hall for the first concert, Beecham objected
to the orchestra having to sit huddled in a wooden, shed-like 'resonating chamber' that had been erected on the platform to improve the hall's acoustics. He
branded it 'a rabbit-hutch' and said that, far from improving the acoustics, it
made the music sound ugly and vulgar, with coarse woodwind tone and rowdy
brass. To make matters worse, since there was no room in the 'hutch' for either
the conductor's rostrum or the piano for the Liszt concerto, they had to be
placed on a special platform in the hall itself, with disastrous consequences for
the balance between soloist and orchestra.[29] Beecham demanded the chamber's
immediate removal.

   Civic uproar ensued, for it had been specially designed by George Sampson,
the city organist, who insisted that it was most successful 'in preventing musical
sounds wandering around the hall'. He claimed that Dorati and other visiting
conductors had made no objection to it; indeed, no less a person than Madame

---

* It has proved impossible to authenticate one of the most often repeated stories about the
Australian tour. According to Neville Cardus (*Sir Thomas Beecham: A Memoir* (London,
1961), p. 51), the ABC offered Beecham two extra rehearsals in Brisbane, which he turned
down on the grounds that the orchestra would 'only get worse.'

Lotte Lehmann had described it 'as an outstanding contribution to Australian music', when she had sung in Brisbane in 1937.[30] But it was Beecham who won the skirmish. By the time of the concert the 'outstanding contribution' had been dismantled. 'Never was the orchestra better heard', wrote the critic of the Brisbane *Telegraph*. 'And the change vastly enhanced the intimacy between orchestra and audience.'[31]

On the following day, Beecham and Labbette attended an informal bush picnic on the hill-top at Jolly's Look-out, organised by the Queensland Musical Association. He sat under a gum tree drinking sterilised milk, which, he said, was one of his favourite drinks, though actually he preferred the unsterilised kind, which appeared to be unobtainable in Australia. He assured his hosts that there were other drinks he liked too: claret, burgundy (which he was not allowed), brown Scotch ale, Rhine wines, whisky (in emergency) and brandy (in extremity). Replying to a speech of welcome, he resorted to below-par jokes about kangaroos, but at least he was friendly.[32]

As was his custom at the time, he made a number of cuts in *Messiah* and replaced the closing Amen Chorus with the Hallelujah Chorus. At the final rehearsal there were problems with the massed choirs. In the Hallelujah Chorus, Beecham accused them of sounding like a mothers' meeting: 'You drag, you drag', he shouted. 'It's dead and it's dull.' But he kept his strongest invective for the run-through that followed of Elgar's three-verse arrangement of the National Anthem that was to open the concert. The second strophe – 'O Lord our God arise, / Scatter his enemies, / And make them fall' – seemed to Beecham particularly apt for the times, but the choir's flaccid approach infuriated him. 'Don't get sentimental singing God save the King in wartime', he ranted, hurling his baton to the ground and burying his face in his hands. 'My God, what a desecration of a masterpiece. This is tragic, what with rabbit-hutches, sheds and now this.' The chorus was taken aback. One of its members ventured to say that Brisbane's choirs were not accustomed to singing the National Anthem right through. 'It is full of cuts', said Beecham, 'but I want it sung without cuts.'[33]

At the performance on the following day it was the audience's turn for a drubbing. Many latecomers missed the National Anthem altogether and were still taking their seats in the dress circle during the overture. Before starting the recitative, 'Comfort ye, my people', Beecham turned to face the auditorium. 'Would you mind closing the doors, please?', he barked. 'This is an oratorio, not a cabaret.'[34] The performance was broadcast live and the rebuke was heard over the air as far away as Perth on the other side of Australia. Asked afterwards by a reporter what he thought of the audience, Beecham made no attempt to be diplomatic. It was 'very, very cold, very chilly. There was no emotion at all. After a performance like that in England all would have got to their feet and shouted for ten minutes. Here, they sat and clapped politely for a few seconds.'[35]

The ecstatic reviews for *Messiah* may have mollified Beecham – 'a landmark in oratorio in Australia', wrote the critic of *The Telegraph* – because the next day he took a more conciliatory line with the press. Perhaps, he said, Australians 'like the music intensely, but do not demonstrate it'. He refused to be drawn on the capabilities of Brisbane's choirs and orchestra – 'Any advice that I can impart I can best do in private.' Asked if he considered Brisbane a musical city, he could not resist a parting salvo. How could it be described as musical, he said, when so few decent concerts were given there in the course of a year. But what about the eisteddfods? he was asked. Eisteddfods, he snorted, were 'competitions for grown-up children and not for serious people'.[36]

Beecham may have ruffled a lot of feathers in Brisbane, but he also had a lot of support there, notably from the city's leading daily paper, the *Courier-Mail*, which not only invited him to contribute a 1,200-word article on the 'rabbit-hutch' affair, but also published a leader saying that a conductor like him should be encouraged to spend longer periods in Australia, 'to develop the capacities of orchestras in a wider range of works, and enlarge the part of music in our cultural life.'[37] Australia's musicians and the ABC were quick to applaud the idea. The article on the 'hutch' was just one of several Beecham found time to write for the Australian newspapers on subjects ranging from Germany's war-aims to the future of music.

The month that followed in Sydney was relatively tranquil, though Beecham refused to give any interviews to the city's press. He banned reporters from his first rehearsal with the Sydney Symphony Orchestra, though following pleas from ABC officials he allowed three photographers to take pictures before it started. When they asked Beecham if he would read a score or hold his baton as if he were conducting, he replied that he never did anything requested by the press. They could, if they liked, photograph him winding his watch. The photographers stalked out of the hall in protest, and on the following day the ABC's public relations department complained about Beecham's 'unpleasant attitude' and 'high-handedness', which had led to the loss of photographs in three important newspapers.[38]

Rather than stay in an hotel, Beecham and Labbette chose to rent a flat with splendid views over the harbour. Among Beecham's first engagements was a speech at the University of Sydney, in which he urged all parts of the Empire to come together at a round-table conference to form a common scheme of national defence and foreign policy. 'Without this our Empire will go down', he said. 'We are of recent origin. The Roman Empire lasted in splendour for 700 years, but we have existed only a mere 200.'[39]

Sydney's concert-goers must have taken Beecham's strictures on Australian audiences to heart, because the performance of Berlioz's *Symphonie fantastique* that ended his first concert on 3 August provoked a storm of applause. 'If anybody comes here and says the Sydney Symphony Orchestra is no good, sock him on the conk', said the exhilarated conductor as he came off the platform; the players had given him 'every ounce they had'. [40] In all, there were six concerts in Sydney, two of them for war charities. Beecham waived his fee for both. The first, attended by the Governor of New South Wales, Lord Wakehurst, was in aid of the Naval War Auxiliary Fund and an Air Force hostel. In a Town Hall bedecked with patriotic flags, Labbette sang the old English song *The Nightingale*, in an orchestration by Beecham, who exhorted the audience to give generously. 'His musicianship was superb', noted one paper, 'his wit not quite on the same level. He gibed at the newspapers, rather like a young coquette who seeks notice by provocation. In short, he had a night out. But, heavens, how he made that orchestra play!' [41]

To swell the proceeds from the concert, Beecham also acted as auctioneer for a sale of amateur art at the Macquarie Galleries in Bligh Street. 'They say conductors never understand each other', he announced, holding up a grim-looking caricature of himself drawn by Antal Dorati. 'Here you see proof of this.' [42] The picture was knocked down for five guineas. Taken together, auction and concert raised a large sum of money. Lord Wakehurst showed his appreciation by also attending Beecham's second charity concert, held in the Sydney suburb of Marrickville in aid of the Lord Mayor's Patriotic War Fund. After Beecham's final concert in the city, a critic wrote that there was no longer any need to make allowances when judging the Sydney orchestra: 'Harty started it off, Schneevoigt trained it, Szell gave it precision, but Beecham inspired it.' [43]

Beecham reached Adelaide, the penultimate stop of his tour, on 27 August. By then the Battle of Britain was at its height. Twenty-one Australians pilots were flying with RAF fighter squadrons,* but Beecham warned a Rotary Club luncheon that the Australian people as a whole did not seem sufficiently stimulated by the grim intensity of the struggle in Europe. He wished that they would not look upon the war as a mere spectacle like a theatrical drama, but realise that their own interests were at stake. Australia, he claimed, was doing only a quarter of what a country of its importance could do.

Given the Australian press's tendency to reach for its gun whenever a prominent outsider criticised the country, the general reaction to Beecham's remarks was surprisingly cautious. In a long, reflective leader, Adelaide's morning paper, *The Advertiser*, admitted that it was 'almost impossible for us to realise the

---

* Thirteen of them were killed in the Battle of Britain.

nature of the ordeal to which our kith and kin are being subjected in Britain, or to understand the extent of our own good fortune, in a country to which no invader has ever come, and which has never yet been so much as threatened by a bombing aeroplane. For millions of Australians, war may indeed seem almost indistinguishable from peace ... but at least we can stimulate our perceptions by devoting our thoughts to these things; by giving full rein to our pride in, and gratitude for, the indomitable courage of the British people; by renewing, as often as may be, our own determination to be worthy of their sacrifice, and to support them to the utmost of our power.'

Beecham could be forgiven if he felt a mood of optimism as he travelled by rail from Adelaide to his final destination, Perth, 1,680 miles away, on Australia's western coast. Not only had his two concerts in Adelaide been warmly received, but his propaganda efforts on behalf of British interests seemed to be achieving some sort of acceptance. The journey to Perth, most of it on the Trans-Australian Railway across the vast, treeless Nullarbor Plain, took two days. Faced with the prospect of being badgered on arrival with yet more press questions about his alleged insults to Mr Menzies, choral singers, latecomers at concerts and others, Beecham decided to give no interviews. In Adelaide he had even been accused of insulting a member of the orchestra. At the start of the prelude to *Tristan* a clarinet player's reed had slipped and the resulting squawk had ruined the celebrated 'Tristan chord'. Beecham had quickly stopped the orchestra and restarted the piece, this time without mishap. The player did not feel insulted, but, in a rerun of the Menzies affair, reporters leapt to his 'defence', claiming that he had been publicly disgraced. The situation, said Beecham, was 'daily becoming more and more like Alice in Wonderland'.[44]

Any hopes that he might have had for a peaceful conclusion to the tour were soon dashed. On 13 September he was forced to abandon a lecture he was giving on education and culture at the University of Perth, because of noisy, unexplained demonstrations by students outside the lecture-hall. Then, on the following evening, he returned to his hotel suite after his first concert to find the furniture in his sitting-room overturned, his personal belongings scattered about, and what he called a 'highly scurrilous and defamatory document' pinned to the door. Exasperated, Beecham summoned the police, who caught the offenders, 'young men, in uniform, and in a fairly advanced state of intoxication', and paraded them before him. The youths claimed they had no personal grievance against Beecham, but had heard that three months earlier he had been disrespectful about their Prime Minister. After explaining the truth of the matter, Beecham asked the police not to take any further action.[45]

Beecham made no reference to the incidents in a letter he wrote to his son, Adrian, a few days later, but said that he had found the Australian public at large to be ignorant and narrow-minded to an extent unimaginable in Britain. Any kind of criticism was resented keenly, and even quite harmless comments by him had provoked offensive letters. With the musical community he had no quarrel, though even he, with all his years of experience, had been unable to cover up the technical deficiencies in certain sections of the orchestras, notably in the oboes, bassoons, horns and double-basses.[46]

Beecham's final engagement of the tour, on 18 September 1940, was a performance of *Messiah* at Perth's Capitol Theatre, with Labbette and Heddle Nash among the soloists. At the end of it 'there was a remarkable demonstration, with conductor and principals returning again and again'. The next day Beecham and Labbette set off on the four-day rail journey to Sydney, where there was a frustrating eleven-day wait before they could sail to Vancouver on the Canadian-Australasian liner *Aorangi*. The continuing Blitz on London filled Labbette with anxiety about the safety of their son Paul, now seven years old, and she longed to be on her way home. Beecham planned to follow her after he had completed his engagements in Canada and the United States. What he did not know at the time was that on the night of 25 September his Hampstead flat had been bombed and that many of his possessions destroyed, including the first and last manuscript pages of *Elektra* that the composer had given at the time of the 1938 Covent Garden revival with the inscription, 'To my highly honoured friend, Sir Thomas Beecham, the eminent musician and distinguished conductor of my works, in sincere gratitude. – Richard Strauss.' Berta Geissmar's flat in Holborn had suffered a similar fate on the previous night.

The ABC drew up a plan for him to return to Australia in 1941, but when it was put to him he turned it down. He said that he might like to conduct in Melbourne and Sydney again but, given the brief time available, it would be difficult for him to make any lasting impact on the orchestras in the smaller state capitals. Nonetheless, he was interested in the possibility of returning to Australia one day to establish some form of permanent opera company.[47]

On 3 October, the day before Beecham's departure, a reporter from the *Sydney Morning Herald* asked him for his final impressions of Australia. Beecham pulled on his cigar and smiled enigmatically: 'You can simply say, if you wish, that I have enjoyed my trip.'[48] But when his ship reached New Zealand on 6 October, he launched a ferocious attack on the country. Australia, he told the *Auckland Star*, was 'sublimely self-satisfied and complacent'. So far, its military contribution to the war had been 'smaller and less effective than that of any other purely British part of the Empire; incomparably less than that, for example, of Canada and New Zealand', while intellectually it was 'the most backward part of the British Empire and contributes nothing to the world's fund of creative literature, art, drama or music'.[49]

His opinion caused great offence. In a counter-attack, a leader in the *Sydney Sun* headed 'Epistle to the Australians' even threw in an untranslated quotation from Horace to underline its view: 'It may be that some Australians did write stupid letters to him, and came in late to his concerts, and misunderstood the intense seriousness which, we are told, lurks behind his witty sayings and his rather baroque platform, and public, manner. It may be that, indefensibly, some foolish youths, angered by his contemptuous references to us and our institutions, wrecked his flat in one of the minor capitals. But who threw the first stone? Sir Thomas's shrieks merely indicate that whatever his stature as a musician, his stature as a man-of-the-world and a philosopher is about equal to that of any bad-tempered old gentleman who cries "Odi profanum vulgus"* when inferior souls offend his vanity or disagree with his opinions.'[50]

There was one final incident. Details remain sketchy, but according to fellow passengers on the *Aorangi* some young Australians, on their way to Canada to train as aircrew under the Empire Air Scheme, took exception to Beecham's comments in Auckland and hatched a plan to cut off his beard. At 2 a.m. on the last night of the voyage, they went to his stateroom and at least one of them managed to get inside, but Beecham kicked up such a row that they left in a hurry. On the captain's orders a guard was placed outside the door until the ship docked on 26 October. Beecham was cautious when questioned about the episode by the press in Vancouver – 'my policy is to bury the hatchet', he said[51] – but it did not stop him making further remarks critical of Australia.

As hostilities spread across the Pacific, and Australia's commitment to the war effort became total, the wranglings that had bedevilled Beecham's tour faded into the background, so much so that when, only eight years later, Isabelle Moresby came to write her history of Australian music-making, she did not feel the need to mention them. 'His performances were thrilling', she wrote, 'and remain a glorious memory.'[52] The ABC made several more attempts to lure Beecham back to Australia, but in spite of his showing interest in the various offers, he never returned. In the post-war years the great migrations from Europe that helped to treble Australia's population were to have so wide ranging an influence on its cultural life that by the 1970s permanent symphony orchestras had been established in all the state capitals, and Sydney could boast an opera house that, as a piece of architecture, has come to be regarded as a symbol of national pride. It is doubtful if Beecham, even in his most optimistic moments, could have predicted so remarkable an outcome.

---

* 'Odi profanum vulgus et arceo' ('I hate and shun the uninitiated crowd'), Horace, *Odes*, iii, i, I.

CHAPTER 15

Enter Miss Humby

F ROM VANCOUVER, Labbette travelled with Beecham by train across Canada to Montreal, where at the beginning of November 1940 she took ship for Britain, an increasingly hazardous undertaking, for there was a high risk of being torpedoed by a U-boat. The circuitous voyage to Liverpool lasted a fortnight. Later, Labbette told her son Paul that when she and Beecham said goodbye on the dockside in Canada, she had a strong premonition that she would never see him again. It would prove to be the case, though clearly at the time Beecham had every intention of continuing their relationship. He and Labbette corresponded frequently during the months that followed their parting.

Once back in wartime Britain, Labbette picked up the threads of her career with a series of broadcasts for the BBC that included a programme of operatic arias with Boult and the BBC Orchestra, which had been evacuated to Bristol since the beginning of the war.* She also resumed work for the Motor Transport Corps, delivering medical supplies to hospitals; acted as a water sampler for the Metropolitan Water Board amid fears that the Germans might attempt to poison the reservoirs; and raised the money to buy and equip the London Philharmonic Mobile Canteen, which she drove to the scene of air-raids in order to provide refreshments for ambulance workers, firemen, demolition teams and the bombed-out people themselves. Sometimes, if the all-clear had sounded, she allowed Paul to go with her, an exciting and formative experience for an eight-year-old boy.

From Montreal, Beecham took the train down to New York, where he met up again with Lady Cunard. She had spent the summer with friends at Newport, Rhode Island, and in the autumn had taken a suite on the tenth floor of the old Ritz-Carlton Hotel in New York, in anticipation of Beecham's arrival from Australia. He moved in with her. At this point Emerald was sixty-eight, Beecham sixty-one. Their friendship had lasted for more than three decades, though according to Sir Thomas for the past ten years it had been 'only that'.[1]

At the end of November 1940 they went to Toronto, where, between rehearsals with the Toronto Symphony Orchestra, Beecham gave an address to the Canadian Club, in which he criticised Britain's pre-war politicians for failing

---

* Because Bristol docks became a target for German bombers, the city proved no safer than London, and at the end of July 1941 the orchestra moved again, to Bedford, where it remained until September 1945.

to spend money on the armed forces. Cunard hauled him off to Upper Canada College to visit one of its boarders, Duff and Lady Diana Cooper's eleven-year-old son, John Julius, who, much to the disapproval of both the *Daily Mirror* and Winston Churchill, had been dispatched across the Atlantic by his mother, who feared for his safety in Europe.[2] Churchill thought it inappropriate that the son of his Minister of Information should have been sent abroad.

The social writer of the Toronto *Evening Telegram* came across Cunard in the Royal York Hotel's palm court – 'blondish and fashionable in a Russian sable jacket [and] a black felt coachman's hat with four pale pink roses nestling on the side of the brim'. She was treating three British schoolboys, one of them John Julius, to large helpings of ice-cream.[3] Beecham's programme that evening included what was said to be the first performance in Toronto of Mozart's 'Paris' Symphony. The critics were full of enthusiasm, as were Montreal's reviewers a week later when he conducted the Montreal Symphony Orchestra in a programme that included Mozart's Symphony no. 40 and Sibelius's First. For *The Gazette*'s music critic, Thomas Archer, it was 'the greatest interpretative conducting heard here since Arturo Toscanini, then in his prime, came to Montreal in 1921. ... There are many accomplished conductors but very few masters. Sir Thomas last night demonstrated just what a great master of the orchestra can do with great music.'[4]

In mid-December, Beecham and Cunard embarked on an immense train journey that took them, first to Missouri for two concerts in St Louis, and then to Arizona, where they spent Christmas enjoying the winter sunshine at the El Conquistador Hotel in Tucson. From there they continued to Los Angeles, where Beecham discussed arrangements for concerts he was to give in February with the Los Angeles Philharmonic following the sudden departure of its musical director, Otto Klemperer, whose behaviour had become alarmingly erratic following an otherwise successful operation to remove a brain-tumour.

Since coming to America, Beecham's relationship with the press had been noticeably amicable and quite unmarked by the irascibility he had displayed in Australia. As wily and skilled a self-publicist as ever, he ensured wide press coverage of his arrival in a town by insulting some well-known local institution. Reporters enjoyed the game as much as he did. When he told the *Los Angeles Times* that Hollywood falsified all values and that the whole idea of musical pictures was artistically preposterous, the paper reported his views at length, though it noted with amusement that the closest he had got to Hollywood was his suite at the Biltmore Hotel, five miles away.[5] Before leaving Los Angeles, Cunard took Beecham to tea with the Woolworth heiress, Barbara Hutton, and insisted on staying on to meet Gary Cooper, who was due for dinner.[6]

At the next stop, San Francisco, Beecham, tongue in cheek, told a press conference that although he was giving some concerts in America, he was there mainly for a lecture-tour and a holiday. He would be returning to Britain by sea in the spring. When it was suggested to him that the bombing might have changed London's appearance since he last saw it, he replied cheerfully, 'Probably for the better. There are a number of buildings there – including Covent Garden and that huge object of terror, the Royal Albert Hall – that have long wanted destruction.' He did not mention the loss of his own flat. As to the future, he expressed 'complete confidence that Britain would eventually win the war'. [7]

John Barbirolli, who was due to conduct the San Francisco orchestra just after Beecham, took a poor view of the senior conductor's more flippant remarks. Barbirolli's wife, the oboist Evelyn Rothwell, wrote to her mother-in-law in Streatham that Beecham had been making 'an arrant fool' of himself with his 'idiotic and tactless' statements in the press and running down America and Americans in public wherever he went. He had, she said, gone down very badly in San Francisco. [8] In truth, he had gone down rather well. Alfred Frankenstein of the *Chronicle* thought that if the orchestra's 'energy outran its accuracy far more often than is usual in the concerts of the San Francisco Symphony, everything was alive and glowing and spirited; there was never an uninteresting moment; even the mistakes were interesting.' [9] Things went even better a month later in Detroit, where the review of a concert with the Detroit Symphony Orchestra was headed, 'Audience is overwhelmed by the Dynamic Sir Thomas'. [10] When Evelyn Barbirolli's letter arrived in England, it was opened by a Ministry of Information postal censor and passed on to the Foreign Office, which decided that the matter was not worth pursuing. An official in the American department deemed Beecham 'foolish, but quite harmless.' [11]

While he was in San Francisco, Beecham wrote to Walter Legge in London, saying that he would be returning to Britain for a six-week visit at the beginning of April 1941. He suggested that during that time he might record *A Village Romeo and Juliet*, with Labbette as Vreli, as an addition to EMI's Delius subscription series. Beecham claimed that there was 'a unanimous demand for this piece', though when Legge canvassed potential subscribers (including Ernest Newman) he found that most of them thought there were more important things on which to spend their money in wartime Britain. The project was dropped. Beecham told Legge that after his visit to Britain he would be returning to North America. [12] He seemed to think that it would as simple for him to travel back and forth across the Atlantic as it had been for him to cross the English Channel in the 1930s, though he would soon discover that this was far from being the case. With the United States still a neutral country, it was not impossible to secure a transatlantic passage to Britain, but there was no guarantee of being able to get back to America in time for specific engagements.

Beecham broke his return journey to New York at Provo, Utah, where on 13 January he gave a lecture on patronage and the arts to the Mormon students of Brigham Young University. It was just one of twenty-five lectures he delivered in early 1941, many of them in the Midwest and Northwest of America. Writing from Utah to his daughter-in-law Joyce in Warwickshire, he expatiated at length on Mormon history and customs, adding that he could not help thinking that his wife Utica in her more imaginative moods must often have associated him in her mind 'with this joyous band of connoisseurs in matrimony'. He also told Joyce that during his forthcoming visit to Britain he hoped to see as much as possible of her and Adrian, and that he looked forward to meeting his first grandchild, John, now nine months old. He made clear his gratitude for his daughter-in-law's achievement in bringing calm and stability to the family at Compton Scorpion.[13]

Beecham's second stop-over on the journey was at Cincinnati, Ohio, where he gave two concerts with the Cincinnati Symphony Orchestra. Eugene Goossens, the orchestra's principal conductor since 1931, asked his old chief if he would like to stay at his home, but Beecham wrote back saying that Lady Cunard (plus maid) would be travelling with him, and that in the circumstances it would wiser for him to go to a hotel, since she had no friends in the city and disliked solitude.[14] When Howard W. Hess, music critic of the *Cincinnati Times-Star*, visited Beecham at the city's Netherland Hotel on a cold January morning, he was surprised to find him sitting in his room with the windows wide open. Still wearing pyjamas and dressing-gown, he was studying manuscripts and scores, which were spread out on every available chair and table. He told Hess that he had an aversion to over-heated American hotels.[15] (He also had an aversion to air-conditioning. When, eight years later, he was told by a new hotel in Dallas that he could not open the window in his room because it was sealed, he took an umbrella and attacked the glass. After that, Beecham's American manager always made sure that he was installed in an older hotel with conventional windows.)[16]

By the time Beecham and Cunard got back to New York, they had travelled more than 10,000 miles in the space of a month. For Cunard it was more than enough; from then on she tended to visit only places that were within reasonable striking distance of Manhattan. When Lady Diana Cooper later passed through New York, she was disappointed to find that Emerald had gone off with Beecham to the New Jersey resort of Atlantic City. 'It's Blackpool', wrote Lady Diana in her journal, 'and she thinks it's Cannes.'[17]

By mid-February 1941 Beecham was back in Los Angeles for the concerts he had agreed to conduct in place of Klemperer. As he stepped off the train, waiting reporters asked him if it were true that, despite his earlier remarks about

Hollywood, he had accepted an invitation to visit the Walt Disney studios. Indeed he had, said Beecham; he was looking forward to it. He was surprised to discover that the Los Angeles Philharmonic Orchestra lived a hand-to-mouth existence and that, unlike many of its counterparts in the East, it had no large endowments to see it through difficult times. It seemed to him scandalous that in a city where so much talent and so many millions of dollars were lavished on the film industry, the orchestra should have to endure a constant struggle to survive. Beecham decided to speak out against Los Angeles's complacency when it came to music and art, but in choosing to do so at a lunch given in his honour by the women's committee of the Los Angeles Philharmonic he miscalculated, for had it not been for the heroic fund-raising efforts of these women, the city would not have had an orchestra at all.

After laying into Los Angeles, Beecham went on to attack what he believed to be the shortcomings of America's artistic life and to accuse the country of destroying through misuse its 'prime cultural asset', the English language. He turned on the nation's politicians, claiming that they were spending too much time in Congress debating the Lend-Lease Bill, which would enable the country to provide Britain with armaments without violating US neutrality. In the long run, he said, the Bill would not make a 'tuppence of difference'. To criticise this crucial support for Britain's war-effort was a strange act of political naïvety. Beecham was hissed by some of his listeners.*

The ensuing row provided the lead-story in the *Los Angeles Times*'s city section, with a seven-column banner headline: 'Beecham Blast at America Brings Storm of Protest Here'. The orchestra received telephone calls complaining that Beecham had not only been bad-mannered, but had harmed the British cause. A member of the women's committee sent a telegram to the Philharmonic: 'The insults to our nation publicly made at the Biltmore Hotel yesterday were un-British, un-American, uncalled for and should bar him from our auditoriums.' However, the orchestra's board of directors refused to cancel Beecham's concerts, saying that they would 'transcend anything politic or non-politic he may have said'.

The publicity did wonders for the orchestra. The public flocked to the Philharmonic Auditorium for the first concert and its repeat on the following day. (The programme included Mozart's 'Linz' Symphony and Sibelius's First.) The *Los Angeles Times* reported 'a record audience' and a long ovation for Beecham. Isabel Morse Jones, the paper's music critic, was even-handed in her reaction to Beecham's political *faux pas*: 'Undoubtedly, our visiting conductor had been

---

* The bill was finally approved by Congress a fortnight later, on 11 March 1941. On the following day President Roosevelt asked for an appropriation of $7,000,000,000 to finance the scheme, which Congress authorised in record time.

17 An immediate rapport: Beecham rehearses for his first concert with the Berlin Philharmonic Orchestra, January 1930

18 Beecham greets Willem Mengelberg and the Amsterdam Concertgebouw Orchestra on their arrival at Harwich for a British tour, May 1930

19 Transatlantic encounter, 1935: Beecham with the violinist Josef Szigeti

20 Planning Covent Garden's Coronation season with Furtwängler at Bayreuth in the summer of 1936

21 Fed up with the speeches and official receptions: Beecham with a Nazi official in Dresden, November 1936

22 Christmas dinner aboard ship, 1935: Dora Labbette and Beecham *en route* to America

23 Labbette, 1926: the photograph that caught Beecham's eye

24 Their son Paul in 1944

25 Great Wagnerians: Lauritz Melchior and Frida Leider with Beecham on the *Ring* set at Covent Garden during the 1930s

26 29 April 1938: Beecham celebrates his fifty-ninth birthday with members of the *Zauberflöte* cast at Covent Garden. Front row from left: Erna Berger (Queen of the Night), Irma Beilke (Papagena), Beecham, Tiana Lemnitz (Pamina), Heinrich Tessmer (Monastatos), Gerhard Hüsch (Papageno). Back row from left: Wilhelm Strienz (Sarastro), Ludwig Weber, who later in the season sang Rocco in *Fidelio* for Beecham, and Herbert Janssen (Der Sprecher)

27 'This tuppenny-ha'penny, mutton-headed pip-squeak': Beecham, in Seattle in 1941, brandishes a tax demand he has just received from an Inland Revenue solicitor in Llandudno

28 Beecham at the Met in New York in 1943 with Patrice Munsel, whom he rescued from near-disaster when she sang Philine in *Mignon*

29 7 October 1944: Beecham, back from America, rehearses at the Royal Albert Hall for his first London concert in four years

30 Historic reunion: Richard Strauss during a rehearsal for the festival of his works that Beecham organised in London in October 1947

31 Domestic happiness: Beecham with Betty Humby at Ringmer in the late 1940s

32 Rehearsing Mozart's 'Prague' Symphony with the City of Birmingham Symphony Orchestra, October 1954

33 A rare foray into Britten's music: Beecham with the composer and the soloist Bronislav Gimpel during a break in rehearsal for the revised version of the Violin Concerto, Royal Festival Hall, London, 12 December 1951

34 'I coo like the proverbial dove.' The eighty-year-old Beecham arrives with his new wife Shirley Hudson at Union Station, Seattle, 16 February 1960

waiting for the opportunity of telling a representative group what he thought of the USA ever since he landed. However, the women's committee of the Philharmonic really didn't deserve the blitzkrieg it took at Tuesday's Biltmore luncheon. It should have been heard by the men and women of prominence and ability who take no responsibilty in supporting orchestras, furthering the needed choral groups, building opera houses and orchestral halls. We should be creating something besides the cinema, money and the climate to be proud of.' [18] Jones was probably correct in her assumption that Beecham had been planning a public attack on American culture for some time. A month earlier, in the letter he sent from Utah to his daughter-in-law, Joyce, he wrote that America was suffering an intellectual decline and that the gods in its cultural firmament were no longer Homer, Dante, Shakespeare and Goethe, nor even Poe, Longfellow, Emerson and Whitman, but the Twentieth Century Fox film company and Warner Brothers.

Because the American press was, and virtually remains, locally based, the incident received little coverage outside Los Angeles. Even the *San Francisco Chronicle* ignored it; though the *New York Times* gave it three short paragraphs. [19] News of it did reach 10 Downing Street, however. On 4 March a Mrs Tibbals of Sierra Madre, California, wrote to Winston Churchill:

> Dear Sir:
>
> You will find enclosed several newspaper articles with regard to Sir Thomas Beecham, who has been visiting in our State.
>
> Possibly he speaks the English Language perfectly, but has he the manners of a gentleman? We are of the opinion he has not, even though he carries the title "Sir".
>
> It is difficult for the American people to understand why persons from foreign countries seek work in this country, often making large sums of money, then insult the American people. We are not honored by their presence.
>
> It is regrettable so many look upon the United States in a mercenary way, then biting [sic] the hand that feeds them.
>
> Respectfully yours,
> Elizabeth P. Tibbals

Downing Street passed Mrs Tibbals's complaint to the Foreign Office, which added it to the file containing Evelyn Barbirolli's letter. An official jotted a brief note on it: '[There] can be no doubt that Sir Thomas behaved badly. This is particularly unfortunate in so friendly a part of the U.S. as Los Angeles, and in such friendly company as that which he was addressing. Such remarks as those which are attributed to Sir Thomas are much more than foolish; in these times they are positively mischievous.' A second official added, 'It is fortunate that the supercilious musings aloud of this pampered maestro have not attracted wider notice.'

The prudish tone of the officials' complaints may read quaintly more than sixty-five years after the event, but the Foreign Office's disapproval of Beecham's speech is understandable. Isolationism was rife in the United States and it was feared that a speech such as Beecham's could only encourage its spread. Henceforth the Washington embassy tended to regard him as a loose cannon. The Secretary at the embassy, William Hayter,* replied to Mrs Tibbals on the Prime Minister's behalf. He told her that the ambassador, Viscount Halifax, entirely shared her opinions, but unfortunately the British authorities had no means of controlling the utterances of individual British subjects in the United States, however much they might deplore them.[20] Beecham was summoned to the embassy, where he was asked by an official, Gerald Campbell, to be more discreet in future. Beecham promised he would, but rather spoiled things when, descending to the exit in a lift crowded with Americans, he turned to Campbell and said loudly, 'You know, Campbell, these bloody Americans haven't big enough brains to get into this war!'[21]

If the embassy hoped that Beecham might stay for good in Britain once he got there, it was to be disappointed. He was still determined to return to the United States after spending six weeks at home. One reason was that he had agreed to become the Seattle Symphony Orchestra's principal conductor for the 1941–2 season. *Time* magazine expressed astonishment that 'this top-notcher' should have accepted 'a second-rank job', but put it down to Beecham's apparent liking for the climate of America's far Northwest, which, he said, reminded him of England's.[22] A more likely explanation is that Seattle was the only city in the United States where he had been offered a post with an orchestra on which he might put his personal stamp. Geographically, Seattle was remote from the main centres of American musical life in the East, but Beecham reasoned that if he could make a success of his time there, it might lead to something grander elsewhere

Beecham's concert diary for the first three months of 1941 had been, for him, unusually empty. In the hope of getting more work, he abandoned Arthur Judson and Columbia Artists, and joined a small concert agency that had been set up by the New York branch of Boosey & Hawkes, mainly to provide engagements for its most distinguished client, Béla Bartók, and his pianist wife, Ditta Pásztory, who had arrived in America during the winter of 1940 as near-penniless refugees. At Boosey's, Beecham's interests were looked after by the Hungarian-born Andrew Schulhof, who before the war had been Furtwängler's manager in Berlin.

Schulhof soon discovered that many American orchestras were wary of

* Later Sir William Hayter, British ambassador to the Soviet Union and warden of All Souls, Oxford.

Beecham, thinking him unreliable in his business dealings and irresponsible in what he might say next. Nonetheless, critical eyebrows were raised in the New York press when it was announced that Eugene Goossens, rather than Beecham, had been included in the list of guest conductors for the Philharmonic-Symphony's 1941–2 centennial season, alongside Stokowski, Walter, Rodziński, Dmitri Mitropoulos, Fritz Busch, Koussevitzky, Walter Damrosch and, for a grand finale, Toscanini. Beecham, however, knew only too well that the orchestra would always remain a closed book to him as long as Judson and Barbirolli were associated with it. As the British composer Richard Arnell, then living in New York, put it, 'You couldn't be arrogant in your dealings with Judson. It was like upsetting the Mafia.'[23]

An unexpected invitation to appear in New York came in a letter from the city's flamboyant mayor, Fiorello La Guardia, who asked Beecham if he would conduct two concerts at Carnegie Hall in early April 1941 for the city's WPA music project. The orchestra would be the New York City Symphony Orchestra, made up of unemployed musicians. The fee was a token $50 (£360) a concert, but it was an opportunity that Beecham could not afford to turn down. It was now five years since he had last conducted in New York, and he needed to make his mark there.

The WPA, or Works Project Administration, had come into existence in May 1935 as part of President Roosevelt's New Deal. Funded by Congress, its purpose was to provide work for the millions who had become unemployed as a result of the Depression. One of its programmes was the Federal Music Project, which organised all kinds of ensembles from dance bands to symphony orchestras (of which the New York City Symphony was one), set up music classes for those who could not otherwise afford them, and encouraged composers by arranging rehearsals and performances of new works. Tickets for the WPA's weekly Sunday evening concerts at Carnegie Hall ranged from 25 cents to just $1.10 (£1.80 to £8). Nathan Milstein and Emanuel Feuermann were just two of the leading instrumentalists who had agreed to appear during the 1940–1 season for $50. Klemperer had already conducted five of the concerts to some acclaim, but had walked out of rehearsals for a sixth in a rage after being ordered by the director of the New York project to use the full orchestra for Wagner's *Siegfried Idyll*, rather than the thirteen players the composer himself had conducted at the work's first performance on the staircase at Tribschen on the shore of Lake Lucerne.

The choice of Beecham to succeed Klemperer as a guest conductor who might pull in the crowds was shrewd. Interviewed about the forthcoming concerts by Ross Parmenter of the *New York Times*, he said that he liked 'conducting any orchestra that can play the notes. I like to get in touch with the human side of orchestras. ... There is no problem in conducting. You get the players to accomplish your purpose, or you don't. Up to the present I have never encountered an orchestra which failed to accomplish my purpose.'[24] The WPA musicians had a reputation for querulousness, but Beecham soon gained their confidence. Rehearsals were subsidised by the city, and there were plenty of them.*

The ensuing concerts were greeted with acclaim. The American composer Virgil Thomson, recently appointed music critic of the *New York Herald Tribune* in succession to Lawrence Gilman, hailed the first one, on 6 April 1941, as a 'triumphal success'. No orchestra, he wrote, 'has played better this season in New York City, by any imaginable standards, than Mayor La Guardia's WPA boys played for Sir Thomas. ... Nobody has to take seriously any longer the excuses of [Barbirolli's] Philharmonic for not playing any better than it currently does. Because if the WPA can play like that, the Philharmonic can too. The other certainty is that in sending us Sir Thomas Beecham as a musical ambassador Britain has certainly delivered the goods.'[25] Assuming that His Majesty's consul in New York kept his superiors posted about the activities of British citizens, Thomson's verdict must have caused a hiccup or two at the Washington embassy.

Olin Downes, still critic of the *New York Times*, thought that Beecham had 'conducted one of the best and the most exciting orchestral concerts that New York has heard this season. ... He appeared to be in top fettle last night, perhaps because he was pleased with the quality of the audience, one of enormous dimensions, consisting not of socialites or musical sophisticates, but of plain men and women from all over town, with a wholly exceptional number of young people in the assembly. These people had come, not for show, or with pharisaical lip service to art. They wanted to hear music, and what they asked was given them in memorable measure.'[26]

A few days later Downes analysed Beecham's qualities in an article that is of interest because it attempts to place the British conductor in the context of the extraordinary profusion of conducting talent to be found in America at the time. 'It is first and last the musical result and not the technical result that interests him', wrote Downes. 'He has never been the conductor for meticulous detail, or achieved the perfections that we have known at the hands of Koussevitzky and Toscanini ... Clearly Sir Thomas is not a virtuoso in the sense of a crack performer who achieves the surprising effect and the razor-edge efficiency with a crack orchestra. But he is too great a musician and he has born in him too many of the qualities of a man of genius to need to rest upon the qualities of an

---

* Programmes for the WPA concerts were: 6 April 1941, the Handel–Beecham *Faithful Shepherd* suite, Mozart's 'Paris' Symphony, Sibelius's Symphony no. 7, Tchaikovsky's *Francesca da Rimini*. 13 April, Haydn's Symphony no. 102, Mozart's 'Linz' Symphony, Delius's *Paris*, Dvořák's *Symphonic Variations*.

orchestra for the results he obtains ... Judged by the conventions of conducting, his technic, if such it can be called, and his style are precise examples, at least to the casual glance, of what a conductor should not do ... He may indicate a sforzando in the manner of a man hurtling a brick or a bomb at a foe, or beat the measure freely with one arm while holding the baton in a clenched fist, invisible to the orchestra, at his back. It remains that the orchestra understands him, and that singularly inspired music floods torrentially and with precision from him and the instrumentalists ... He is the living proof that we have been more concerned with the manner than the matter of orchestral music. This is not to disparage or to underestimate the wonderful performances of the leading orchestral conductors of this country and of the world, whom we have with us, and who, beyond all others, are responsible for the enormous popularity of orchestral music in the United States ... But the return of Sir Thomas has borne freshly and impressively upon us the distinction between vital interpretation and mere virtuosity as such.'[27]

Virgil Thomson echoed Downes's theme when he reviewed the second WPA concert a week later: 'Beecham alone of the great conductors, as Nikisch did before him, collaborates with an orchestra rather than conquers it. As a result his orchestra always sounds like an ensemble of skilled musicians rather than like a Panzer division on the march. This particular attitude toward music-making places him at once as the survivor of a vanished epoch and the hope of the next. He is the obvious rallying point for all those musicians, young and old, who have had enough of musical Caesarism.'[28] In the following year Beecham would achieve similar miracles with the fledgling Brooklyn Symphony Orchestra.

The fact that New York's two leading critics had both been unequivocal in their enthusiasm for the WPA concerts cannot have improved Barbirolli's feelings about Beecham. Barbirolli's star was by now waning in New York. He had successfully helped to bring the Philharmonic-Symphony through a difficult period, but he and the orchestra were living in the shadow of Toscanini's NBC Symphony Orchestra, and for the critics they were often found wanting. Virgil Thomson was as unsympathetic as Olin Downes to Barbirolli's continuing tenure. As the orchestra's historian put it, 'it is not unfair to say that for the two years from 1941 to 1943, as far as its over-all policy was concerned, the Philharmonic drifted'.[29] The glamorous line-up for the century season gave a clear indication that the directors were contemplating the need for a starrier figure to lead the orchestra.

That Toscanini, too, was unnerved by Beecham's presence in the city and jealous of him is more surprising. Later in the year the Italian maestro wrote a letter to Downes: 'I have just received the enclosed concerts-program with the love and greetings of all my english friends – all working with joy, faith, love and hope in their own fatherland – while that <u>nazi-sympathizer man</u> whom I do not even dare to call him by name lives here, in America protected, adulated and honoured by critics and american people ... Truly, it is a very <u>farcical</u> and <u>deploring thing</u>, but so is life!!!' [30] Had the letter been made public at the time, Toscanini might have found himself in court on a libel charge.

Downes paid no attention to Toscanini's rant and continued to give Beecham excellent notices, as did Virgil Thomson, who became friendly with both Beecham and Lady Cunard, and sometimes attended the latter's afternoon tea-parties at the Ritz-Carlton, where regular guests included Somerset Maugham, the American composer and pianist Courtlandt Palmer, the playwright Harley Granville-Barker, the English writer and tireless propagandist for British inter-ests Cecil Roberts, and the Irish writer and poet Oliver St John Gogarty, as well as assorted ambassadors, soldiers, society beauties and exiled politicians. Rob-erts wondered how Cunard managed to cast her net so wide; he also wondered 'how it was possible for one small head to hold so much', for although none of her New York admirers ever saw her with a book, 'her reading was wide and thorough ... She would quote Baudelaire, Paul Fort, Schiller and Maria Rilke. If the conversation veered to Euripides, Dante, Leopardi or Camoens, she kept up and was in at the kill.' [31] Another writer who left an evocative memoir of the salon, the American novelist Frederic Prokosch, remembered his hostess as having 'a small triangular face lined with wrinkles and a tiny red mouth and enormous blue eyes. She looked both painfully disillusioned and incessantly startled'. [32] Her guests sat in a circle and nibbled, not cakes or buttered toast, as Prokosch expected, but nuts and wafers.

Beecham was not keen on what he called 'the cultural chitchat' of these gath-erings, and rarely attended them, though occasionally he would put his head round the door to see who was there. He took refuge in his bedroom, where he had an upright piano. Sometimes, wrote Prokosch, 'he would oblige me with a minuet or rondo by Mozart. Once he played a little "Nocturne", which Samuel Barber had set to a poem of mine and he played it quite wonderfully, as though he had freshly discovered it.' * Beecham had his own visitors at the Ritz-Carlton, a steady stream of business managers, concert promoters, lawyers, music pub-lishers and composers.

One of the composers was Richard Arnell, at the time only twenty-four years old. At Virgil Thomson's prompting, Beecham had telephoned him, asking to see some of his music. Arnell said that he had several orchestral scores to hand. 'Bring a suitcaseful', commanded Beecham, adding that it should be left at the

---

* 'Nocturne' is the last of Barber's *Four Songs*, op. 13, which were given their first complete performance in Philadelphia on 4 April 1941 – two day's before Beecham's first WPA concert – by the soprano Barbara Troxell and the pianist Eugene Bossart.

hotel's front-desk. A few days later the composer received another call, telling him to return to the hotel, this time for a consultation. 'Beecham took me into his bedroom', Arnell remembered. 'The suitcase was under the bed and he pulled it out. I got the clear impression that he had hardly looked at its contents. He fished out my *Sinfonia quasi variazioni*, started to leaf through it and, before he had got very far, announced that he would perform it.'[33] Beecham was as good as his word and gave the work its first performance at Carnegie Hall with the WPA orchestra in March 1942.*

During his wartime years in the United States, Beecham was prudent enough to perform a number of contemporary American works, though only one of their composers, Virgil Thomson, was to leave any sort of mark on the nation's music.† Beecham conducted Thomson's Second Symphony on several occasions, as well as the suites drawn from his ballet *Filling Station*, and his film-score for Pare Lorentz's documentary *The River*. 'No one else has ever made my Second Symphony sound so glowing', wrote Thomson, 'though I do not think he was comfortable with the work.'[34] While it comes as no surprise that Beecham failed to include in his concert programmes any works by the three most important composers then living in America – Bartók, Schoenberg and Stravinsky – it is odd that he should have ignored the easily accessible music of leading American composers such as Aaron Copland and Samuel Barber.

As Beecham had hoped, the success of the WPA concerts gave a fillip to his faltering career. He signed a contract with the Metropolitan Opera for twelve performances during the following season, and accepted plenty of other offers of work. Suddenly the proposed visit to Britain vanished from his plans. His schedule for the forthcoming Montreal Festival was formidable, for it included three major choral works he had never conducted before – Bach's Mass in B minor, Fauré's Requiem and Elgar's *Dream of Gerontius*, as well as Mozart's motet *Ave verum corpus*. He spent all of May preparing for them, though he found time to give a lecture at New York's Town Hall on 'Mozart and the 18th Century'. He spoke without notes and played the musical illustrations himself on the piano, ending with *Ave verum corpus*, which, he told his audience, had all the leading qualities of its composer's work – high seriousness, beauty of melody, perfect craftsmanship and an intimate and exquisite tenderness.[35]

---

* Beecham continued to show an interest in the music of Richard Arnell (b. 1917) almost to the end of his life. He commissioned and conducted the first performances of *Ode to the West Wind* for soprano and orchestra (1955) and the orchestral piece *Landscapes and Figures* (1956). In 1949 he gave the first concert performance of Arnell's score for the ballet *Punch and the Child*, and recorded it a year later.

† The other composers, most of them now forgotten, included Courtlandt Palmer, Horace Johnson, Hermann Hans Wetzler, George McKay, Anis Fuleihan, Jerome Moross and Paul White.

Beecham's performance of *Ave verum corpus* in Montreal with the Disciples de Massenet choir made such an impression that it had to be repeated. After the festival, Beecham never conducted either the B minor Mass or *The Dream of Gerontius* again, which suggests that they were Montreal's choice, rather than his own. The city's French-language newspaper, *Le Devoir*, found the performance of the Bach 'excessivement brillante, théâtrale même', [36] while reviews of *Gerontius* suggest that Beecham injected a good deal of drama into that work, too. In an interview he gave about Elgar – 'the most sociable and genial of souls; well-read, too, with a wide circle of friends' – Beecham avoided giving an opinion on the work, but quoted an unnamed foreign colleague, who had once told him that it 'might have been written by Mendelssohn if he had come down from heaven and then gone to Bayreuth to hear a performance of *Parsifal*'. [37] At least he did not underline what may have been his true feelings about *Gerontius* by rounding off the evening with an unscheduled performance of the *Blue Danube*, as had happened at Hanley twenty-nine years earlier. In Montreal, *Gerontius* was followed by the *Enigma Variations*.

In July 1941 Beecham conducted eight outdoor concerts with the Chicago Symphony Orchestra at Ravinia Park, its summer home on the shore of Lake Michigan. Although it was his first opportunity to conduct one of America's 'big four' orchestras* during his current visit, he was not entirely happy with the venue. Writing to his daughter-in-law, Joyce, he complained that Ravinia would be agreeably idyllic if it were not for the close proximity of a railway line on which the trains ran with the most devastating racket every five minutes. Worse, his hotel did not sell alcoholic drinks. The critics commended Beecham for his unusual programmes, which included the first Chicago performance of Dvořák's Piano Concerto, with Rudolf Firkušný as soloist. At the end of the last concert he was awarded 'the most cheerful and extended fanfare we have ever heard the orchestra give'. [38] Beecham told Joyce that he had now become 'a success' in America, with enough work to keep him going through the next few years, which was mainly to the good, since the musical outlook in Europe was likely to be 'obscure and limited' for some time to come. [39]

Beecham was being disengenuous. What was keeping him in America was, not his work, but the presence in New York of the British pianist Betty Humby, whom he had last met in 1938, when he had conducted the concert for her Mozart series at the Cambridge Theatre in London. Like Beecham, Humby was managed by Andrew Schulhof, who reintroduced them and subsequently arranged for them to perform the Delius Piano Concerto together on 22 June 1941 at

---

* The other three were the Boston Symphony, the New York Philharmonic-Symphony and the Philadelphia Orchestra. The Cleveland Orchestra did not achieve similar status until after the Second World War, when George Szell became its conductor.

a studio-concert for the Columbia Broadcasting System. Humby had had the concerto in her repertoire for some years, but had never played it before with Beecham; indeed, she had never played anything with him, though she would often claim that she had. What little that was known about Humby in America came from an article that had appeared some months earlier in the *New York Herald Tribune*, which said that she had brought over her nine-year-old son, Jeremy Thomas, from war-torn Britain for reasons of safety and that she was now living in New York. Her husband, vicar of St Philip's church, Earl's Court, had remained behind in London. Meanwhile she was making a living in New York by teaching and giving recitals. She was also helping British–American war-relief agencies 'to provide vitamins, ambulances and other needed equipment for devastated areas of England'.[40] Humby came from a medical background. Five generations of her family, including her father, Morgan Humby, a dentist, had practised as doctors or dentists in Newgate Street, close by St Paul's Cathedral, until the premises were destroyed in the Blitz.

Some of Humby's claims in the *Tribune* – for example, that she had won a scholarship to the Royal Academy of Music in London at the age of ten and had earned her own living as a pianist since she was twelve – were on the fanciful side, but they were repeated unchecked by other publications for months to come.* In public-relations terms they paid dividends: a Seattle feature-writer hailed her in print as 'one of the world's most renowned pianists'.[41] In fact, she never reached the top rank of players, for she lacked the physical strength for the big romantic repertoire, though many American critics at the time appreciated her excellent technique, as well as her lightness of touch and refinement of phrasing. Some thought it over-refined.

By extraordinary coincidence, though it was not mentioned in the article, Humby had travelled to America in May 1940 on the same boat as Dora Labbette, who was on her way to meet Beecham before sailing to Australia with him. Humby had given her last concert in London on 27 April, when she had played Mozart's C minor concerto K491, with Boult and the LSO at the Royal Albert Hall. *The Times* found her playing 'neatly turned', but thought that the orchestra's contribution was 'on the whole so lax as to be sleepy'.[42] During the voyage Humby confided to Labbette that one reason for her going to America was to get a divorce from her husband, so that she could marry another man. He was not identified, but it can be said with confidence that it was not Beecham.[43]

---

* Humby, born in 1908, did not win one of the Academy's own scholarships at the age of ten, but was awarded an Associated Board scholarship when she was twelve, which provided her with free lessons at the RAM. She proved to be an excellent student, winning many prizes that enabled her to continue her studies at the Academy until 1925. Her teachers included Irene Scharrer and Tobias Matthay.

The CBS concert, which took place on a Sunday afternoon in the middle of an oppressive heat-wave, was not a major date in New York's musical calendar, but for Beecham and Humby it always held a particular significance, for it marked the start of what would turn out to be a close and lasting relationship. *Time* magazine marked the event with a photograph of the 'goateed, salt-&-peppery' conductor with the 'pretty, blonde' pianist (in fact she was brunette), but nobody else took much notice.[44] An off-the-air recording of the Delius concerto reveals a performance of engaging dash, greatly superior to the commercial recording of the work that Humby and Beecham made five years later, that surely reflects the excitement of their new-found relationship.

For many listeners, however, the most memorable feature of the event was, not the concerto, but the interruption of the final item, Dvořák's *Golden Spinning Wheel*, for Winston Churchill's broadcast from London about Germany's invasion that morning of Soviet Russia. Churchill promised Russia every possible help and ended with an oblique, but nonetheless powerful reminder to America's isolationists that they could not afford to ignore Germany's actions much longer: 'The Russian danger is therefore our danger, and the danger of the United States, just as the cause of any Russian fighting for his hearth and home is the cause of free men and free peoples in every quarter of the globe. Let us learn the lessons already taught by such cruel experience. Let us redouble our exertions and strike with united strength while life and power remain.'[45]

The talk was relayed coast-to-coast. 'Can any American ever again talk seriously of appeasing Hitler or trusting his promises?', asked the *New York Times* the following morning in a leading article that can have left little doubt in most readers' minds that America was now a step closer to war. Two days later Beecham gave an open-air concert at Newark, New Jersey, for the Essex County Symphony Society before an estimated 20,000 people. At the start of the evening he turned to face the audience while conducting 'The Star-Spangled Banner' and encouraged the audience to join in. During the interval a collection was taken for British War Relief.

Beecham's engagements in America were not confined to concerts and lectures. On 26 September 1941 he demonstrated his remarkable memory for literature in the first of three appearances he made on NBC radio's up-market quiz show *Information Please*, in which Clifton Fadiman of the *New Yorker* put literary, musical and historical questions submitted by listeners to a panel of regulars and guests. Fadiman asked Beecham's fellow-guest, Jan Struther, the begetter of *Mrs Miniver*, if she could identify the poem or piece of prose that included the words, 'the weariest river'. She produced the words that immediately followed – 'winds somewhere safe to sea' – but could not remember either the name of the poem or its author. Beecham got both, 'The Garden of Proserpine' by Swinburne, and went on to quote from memory the complete eight-line stanza from which the quotation came. 'Is there anything you don't know, Sir Thomas?', asked Fadiman at one point. Beecham remained uncharacteristically modest and quietly spoken throughout all three programmes, which, as always, were unrehearsed.[46]

Beecham's first season with the Seattle Symphony Orchestra began in mid-October 1941. On his way there he made a detour to British Columbia, where he gave a lecture on Mozart in Victoria and conducted a concert in Vancouver. Unbeknown to Emerald Cunard, Betty Humby went with him. As they crossed the border into Canada on 9 October, a United States immigration official noticed that Beecham's American visa had run out and told him that he would need a new one before he could get back into the country. Beecham, who was due to take his first rehearsal in Seattle only five days later, was warned that the process could take up to a month. Eventually, after urgent calls to the State Department in Washington, he was issued with a thirty-day waiver, which allowed him back into America. 'I've had fingerprints taken, and foot-prints, and blue prints', he announced on arrival in Seattle. 'I've discovered some of the most extraordinary things about myself that I've never even suspected. I have a strawberry mark on my left foot, and a brown spot on my left knee. I've been examined, diagnosed, signed, sealed, documented and delivered. There is not one chance in a million now that I'll ever be mistaken for anyone else.'[47]

In the 1940s many of Seattle's inhabitants could remember the days when it had been the main supply depot for both the Yukon and Alaskan gold rushes. Although it was now the largest city in America's Pacific Northwest, it still remained a cultural backwater. Its orchestra, whose previous conductors included Basil Cameron and the Russian-born Nikolai Sokoloff, had a poor reputation. Numbering up to sixty-five players, some of them students, it normally gave about eight subscription concerts a year, plus some school concerts and a couple of broadcasts; for the rest of the time it played for visiting dance and opera companies. The turnover of players was high. Beecham soon discovered that he had an uphill struggle ahead of him.

At the opening concert on 20 October there was an unfortunate incident involving a photographer from the *Seattle Post-Intelligencer*, who, to avoid the need for a flash-bulb, had armed himself with an infra-red camera. Sitting in the front row, he took a picture of Beecham conducting Delius's *Walk to the Paradise Garden*. Hearing the click, Beecham whirled round. 'Leave the hall', he shouted. 'This is an insult to the audience.' After the photographer had fled, Beecham, 'in the sweetest and calmest of tones', announced to applause that with the kind permission of the audience he would start the piece again.[48] Beecham had made his point, but the incident was not forgotten by the *Post-Intelligencer*'s music critic, who later would prove a thorn in his flesh.

By all accounts the orchestra played reasonably well at the concert, but three days later, during a broadcast for the Standard Hour, it got so lost in a movement from *The Gods Go a'Begging* that Beecham called a halt and started again. Using a mixture of cajolery and diplomacy, he began to gain the players' confidence. A recording from a second broadcast, given only a fortnight later, finds the orchestra playing the finale of Mozart's Symphony no. 29 with an immense rhythmic élan that is missing from the commercial recording he made with the LPO four years earlier. Seattle's critics recognised that something unusual was afoot, and responded with reviews that were enthusiastic, if not always musically informed. So great was the demand for tickets that the subscription series sold out for the first time in the orchestra's history and extra concerts were put on.

After the incident with the photographer, Beecham went to some length to smooth the press's ruffled feathers. On hearing that he was about to be served with a writ for non-payment of British income tax amounting to £1,298 (£37,300), he invited reporters to his apartment to witness – and photograph – the moment when it was handed to him by the Seattle attorney who was acting for the British Government. When everyone arrived, they found him clad in pyjamas, blue silk dressing-gown and bedroom-slippers. Close inspection of the writ revealed that it had been issued by one William Bernard Blatch, solicitor for the Inland Revenue, Grand Hotel, North Parade, Llandudno. 'It's footling', cried Sir Thomas, waiving the document above his head. 'This tuppenny-ha'penny, mutton-headed pip-squeak – this solicitor sitting safely somewhere safely in Wales, miles from the danger of bombing and firing off his harmless little squibs ... He is a mosquito of a lawyer, a gadfly. This is the most impracticable and most useless proceeding in law ever launched by a representative of His Majesty's Government.' He added that he would be sending a cable to his lawyer in London, telling him to settle the matter.

The reporters, thrilled by Beecham's shameless histrionics, filed hundreds of words for their newspapers. The *Seattle Times* even provided a glossary, so that its readers might miss none of the nuances, e.g. 'PIP-SQUEAK – A small, high velocity shell used by the Germans in the World War, made an odd sound; an insignificant or futile person.' As Beecham no doubt intended, the reporters went away believing that it was indeed ridiculous that a man they called a 'multi-millionaire' should have been hounded all the way to Seattle over such a 'trivial' matter.[49] In reality, Beecham was always short of funds during the war years in America, a situation exacerbated by the fact that he insisted on living in some style. The sum demanded by the British Revenue was a large one for him to find, for by twenty-first-century standards his US fees were not particularly high.*

That Betty Humby should have been staying in the same apartment as Beecham in Seattle caused some local curiosity, particularly as there was an age-gap between them of twenty-nine years, though no one quite knew what their relationship was, and at this stage it was never mentioned in the press. In November Humby gave three performances of the Mozart C minor concerto K491, with Beecham and the orchestra, and later charmed Seattle society with a recital at the Washington Athletic Club in aid of a fund to provide ambulances for London's Great Ormond Street Hospital for Sick Children, where her younger brother, Graham, was a surgeon.

As a curtain-raiser to the recital, Beecham made a speech in which he challenged Seattle to become more culturally aware. The city, he said, should not have to put up with being 'an aesthetic dust-bin', into which inferior promotions from the East were dumped. Instead it should create its own events and its own stars. The orchestra had made great strides, he said, but it was still at an 'embryonic' stage. He would do all he could to help, but only if Seattle was prepared to give him its co-operation.[50] The 'aesthetic dustbin' metaphor was widely misunderstood and greatly resented.

In mid-November 1941 Beecham took a three-month break from Seattle. He went first to Philadelphia, where he had been engaged for a series of six concerts with Eugene Ormandy's Philadelphia Orchestra, four of them in the city itself, plus one each in New York and Baltimore. The first concert in Philadelphia, a matinée that was being broadcast, got off to a farcical start. Beecham, who was staying just a block away at the Ritz-Carlton Hotel, arrived at the stage-door of the Academy of Music to find that the concert had begun without him. Saul Caston, the orchestra's first trumpet and associate conductor, had been called from his place in the brass section to direct *The Star-Spangled Banner*, and was now half-way through the first movement of Haydn's Symphony no. 93. 'What's this?', Beecham shouted at the orchestra's manager, Harl McDonald, who was waiting for him backstage. The hapless McDonald explained that when Beecham had still not arrived by 2.35 p.m., five minutes after the scheduled start of the concert, he had had no alternative but to tell the audience that Caston would conduct instead. 'The clocks in the hotel must have been late', snapped Sir Thomas. 'I left there at 2.25, in plenty of time.' Was he by any chance ill?

---

* In 1941 the Detroit Symphony Orchestra, for example, paid him $500 a concert (the equivalent in 2007 of £3,600), though during his forthcoming visit to the Metropolitan Opera he would be getting $750 a performance, which was considered generous. Only Bruno Walter was paid more by the Met – $1,000 a performance. The thirty-year-old Erich Leinsdorf's average fee was around $450.

asked a journalist who happened to witness the exchange. 'Yes, I was and am', came the lame reply. 'I have a sore throat.'

As the first movement of the Haydn ended, McDonald returned to the platform to announce that the missing conductor had turned up and would now take over from Caston. To a burst of applause, Beecham took the three steps leading up to the podium in one leap and launched into the rest of the symphony. 'With clenched fists and waving hands', wrote the *Inquirer*'s critic, 'he crouched threateningly over the musicians, searing the wits out of them, and searing out of them also one of the most responsive performances they have given this season.' The Haydn was followed by an intensely dramatic performance of Mozart's 'Jupiter' Symphony. Shortly after the start of its last movement Beecham thwacked his baton against the music stand so hard that it splintered in his hand. An incomplete recording of the broadcast testifies to the remarkable results that Beecham achieved with the Philadelphia Orchestra, with the two symphonies more urgent and less mannered than in the earlier commercial recordings he made of them with the LPO. When Beecham repeated the 'Jupiter' at the Philadelphians' New York concert, the critic of the *Musical Courier* hailed it as 'the biggest, breeziest, most exhilarating performance of the symphony that I, at least, have heard in years'. [51]

At the final concert in Philadelphia, on 6 December 1941, Beecham conducted the Delius Piano Concerto with Humby as soloist. The *Inquirer* noted that Humby 'was gallantly and literally led out on to the stage by Sir Thomas, who held her hand with courtly air'. [52] They had last given the work together at the CBS concert in New York that had been interrupted by Churchill's announcement of the Nazi invasion of Russia. On the day after the Philadelphia performance, America was shaken by news of an event that it found even more momentous – the bombing of Pearl Harbor by the Japanese. Suddenly, the United States found itself at war.

CHAPTER 16

Divorce in Boise

BY THE END OF 1941 Emerald Cunard had become alarmed about the
frequency of Betty Humby's appearances at Beecham's concerts. Always a
bad sleeper, she took to telephoning her friends in the middle of the night. Had
they heard anything about Sir Thomas? He was becoming harder to get hold
of when he was out of town. And who was this Miss Humby exactly? She had
heard from Willie Maugham that Sir Thomas was quite fond of her. Was there
anything in it? Frederic Prokosch, one of the recipients of the calls, detected a
note of anguish in her voice.[1]

Beecham told Virgil Thomson that he was greatly troubled about the
effect his new liaison might have on Lady Cunard.[2] As often happened when
Beecham was faced with awkward personal issues, evasion proved to be the better part of valour, and when Cunard finally gathered up courage to tackle him
about the rumours, he told her there was no truth in them. Humby, he said, was
'descended from a long line of dentists', as though that alone ruled her out as a
possible paramour.[3]

Despite Beecham's denials, Cunard was well aware that he had fallen under
the spell of a much younger and physically more attractive woman. 'He is deeply
sentimental, but also relentless', she told Thomson. 'When he wants a thing, no
one can stop him.'[4] One can only guess at Cunard's feelings when, on 15 January 1942, she entered her box at the Metropolitan Opera for Beecham's company debut in a double-bill of his own staged version of Bach's *Phoebus and Pan*
and Rimsky-Korsakov's *Golden Cockerel*, which, in defiance of the company's
custom, he insisted on giving complete.

When Edward Johnson, the Met's general manager, announced that both
Beecham and Bruno Walter would appear as guest conductors during the 1941–2
season, a feeling of excited anticipation ran through New York's critical fraternity, for the step heralded a distinct change of direction for the house. Walter
had appeared already during the previous season but, wrote Oscar Thompson,
veteran critic of the *New York Sun*, Beecham's arrival 'put the seal of approval on
conductors' opera, as distinguished from singers' opera'. This, said Thompson,
was something new in the history of the Met, for even the rivalry of Mahler
and Toscanini 'occasioned much less buzz in the corridors of the Metropolitan,
old timers will agree, than the rivalry of Caruso and Bonci, or that of Geraldine
Farrar and Mary Garden.'[5]

The Met's decision was dictated by events in Europe. The war was playing havoc with the company's artistic plans, and many favourite singers were missing from the season. Kirsten Flagstad had announced in Oslo that 'as long as there is a war I want to stay in my own country, together with my husband and my family';[6] Jussi Björling was stuck in Stockholm, unable to get a passage to New York; while Tito Schipa had been ordered home by Count Ciano, Italy's foreign minister and son-in-law of Mussolini. The Wagner repertory – banished from the Met when America entered the First World War, but not during the Second – was particularly threatened, not just by Flagstad's absence, but also because the company's second Brünnhilde, the Australian soprano Marjorie Lawrence, had had to withdraw from all her stage engagements after contracting polio. As a result the Met was forced into a greater reliance than usual on promising, but often inexperienced, home-grown talent, for example the St Louis-born soprano, Helen Traubel, who became the company's Brünnhilde and Isolde. Johnson recognised that strong leadership from the pit was essential if the company was to survive artistically. Olin Downes welcomed the change of direction: 'The Metropolitan is at last taking to heart the principle that in order for first-class opera to be given, conductors of the first rank are necessary.'[7]

It was generally agreed, however, that Beecham's double-bill was something of a disappointment. *Phoebus and Pan* was sung in English that was rarely intelligible, *The Golden Cockerel* in a French translation that was 'absurd when you could hear it' (Virgil Thomson). Apart from Ezio Pinza as Rimsky's King Dodon, 'who was in excellent voice and did capital fooling' (Olin Downes), the singers made little impression. The *New Yorker* thought that in *Phoebus* Beecham turned in an orchestral performance of 'animation and charm', but despite a lavish new production complete with ballet, the piece failed at the box-office and was dropped after only five performances, one of them on tour in Philadelphia.[8]

Beecham proposed that for his second appearance at the Metropolitan he should conduct a staged version of Handel's secular oratorio *Hercules*, a novel idea for the time, but it was turned down, no doubt on the grounds that *Phoebus and Pan* was quite enough by way of Baroque experiment for one season. Instead, he was given a revival of *Carmen*, which proved to be the ideal opera with which to make his mark on the house. 'I must bring electricity into this lazy body', he told Klemperer, who attended one of his orchestral rehearsals. Klemperer found him 'very energetic'.[9]

Beecham not only took the orchestra by the scruff of the neck, but, unusually for a conductor at the Met, attended most of the stage-rehearsals as well, though he could do little about the ancient stage-sets that, because of shortages of materials, were to bedevil most of the company's productions until the end of the war. By now he had been conducting Bizet's opera for forty years and had strong views on characterisation: 'Any singer who fails to make her portrayal of Carmen in accordance with the refinement of the music is doing something that is an aesthetic offence', he told the *New York Times*. 'To make a harridan of Carmen is at complete variance with fact, for the people of Spain have the best manners in the world. I have visited that country many times and never once have I seen anyone there, gypsy or native Spaniard, who was a vulgarian.' [10]

Beecham's Carmen was Lily Djanel, a thirty-two-year-old Belgian, who after singing the role at the Opéra-Comique in Paris on 9 June 1940, just five days before the Germans entered the city, had decided that rather than return home to Brussels she would head for Bordeaux, where she managed to take ship for Brazil. Eventually she reached New York, where the Met, in need of a Carmen, greeted her with relief. Frank St Leger, in charge of casting, wrote to Beecham: 'Here is an artist who is truly French and very chic. I am personally of the opinion that she will be a great asset to the Company. The material is so interesting; her vivacity and her enthusiasm are so infectious that in these days of more sombre personalities she may click. I believe we should gamble on her.' [11] Most of the critics, accustomed to the Met's usual, lackadaisical approach to the opera, were taken aback by the intensity that Beecham brought to Bizet's masterpiece, and not all of them liked it. For Olin Downes, the pace was 'sometimes so fast that it became jumbled and hurried. The fact that chorus and orchestra had occasional trouble in keeping up with Sir Thomas need not be a permanent evil. But singers must have time to breathe and articulate, and some leeway for dramatic action.' [12]

Downes's verdict reads oddly in the light of a recording taken from the broadcast of the opening matinée on 24 January 1942. Beecham is heard at the height of his powers as a theatre conductor, the opera fairly crackling with the electricity he sought in rehearsal. Even the small boys in the guard-mounting scene, their French diction admirably clear, manage to keep up with the headlong tempo he sets them. But Beecham also knows when to relax the pace and, far from failing to give his singers 'time to breathe and articulate', he accompanies them with care and sensitivity, notably in Licia Albanese's rendering of Micaela's Act 3 aria, where orchestra and singer are held in seamless unity.

Albanese's beautiful if rather uninvolved singing of the aria gets the biggest applause of the afternoon, but it is Djanel's performance that sticks most firmly in the memory for its commitment and identification with the character. With its sometimes intrusive flutter, the voice can hardly be described as beautiful, but Djanel marries the French text to the musical line to wonderfully expressive effect. She and Beecham, together with the American tenor Charles Kullman as a moving and finely sung José, drive the last act to a spine-chilling conclusion. For one reason or another, Djanel failed to match the older New York critics' idea of what a Carmen should be like, but Beecham held her in high regard as an exponent of French style. During the three seasons he worked with the Met company, he was to conduct no fewer than twenty-four performances of *Carmen*. Djanel sang in nineteen of them.*

Six days after the *Carmen*, Beecham conducted a revival of Gounod's *Faust* with Richard Crooks in the title-role, Albanese as Marguérite and Pinza as Méphistophélès. Although Albanese had enjoyed great success as Micaela in *Carmen*, some thought it strange that the Met should have decided to cast its Violetta and Butterfly in the quintessentially French role of Marguérite, but the management had a practical reason for doing so. Following the bombing of Pearl Harbor, *Madama Butterfly* had been dropped hurriedly from the company's repertory – an opera featuring a serving US naval officer and a geisha was thought highly inappropriate for the times – and as a result it had become necessary to find a substitute role for Albanese. She had never sung Marguérite in French before, and opinions of her performance were mixed. Pinza received the best reviews among the singers, but as far as both the *Times* and the *Tribune* were concerned, it was the conductor who was the real star of the evening. *Butterfly* would not return to the Met until January 1946, with Albanese once more in the title-role.

Although Beecham was close to some of the more established Met singers, among them Lauritz Melchior and the Australian John Brownlee, his Koanga at Covent Garden, many of the younger artists found him an unnerving figure, feared for his sarcasm. It was not unknown for singers to walk out of rehearsals after he had lambasted them for not following his wishes in matters of tempo or phrasing. The Hungarian-American soprano Astrid Varnay remembered a rehearsal when a well-known tenor was singing so flat that it got on everyone's nerves. The concertmaster suggested that it might help if he were to give the singer the correct pitch. 'No need to', said Beecham. 'Shortly he'll be an octave lower and we'll all be together again.' [13]

After a second performance of *Faust* on 7 February, Beecham took a month's break from the company to conduct an ambitious 'Pacific Northwest Mozart Festival' with the Seattle orchestra. Whether by accident or design is not known, but on 9 February, the day Beecham left New York for Seattle, Cholly Knicker-bocker, the bitchy social columnist of Randolph Hearst's *New York Journal-*

---

* Beecham's other Carmens at the Met were Irra Petina (three performances) and Gladys Swarthout and Jennie Tourel (one each).

American,* chose to blow the gaff on the affair with Humby in an article that was syndicated throughout the country. 'Excitement is i-n-t-e-n-s-e over the manner in which comely Betty Humby, a young and very talented English pianist, reportedly has injected herself, and a bit of crescendo, into the never-too-tantalizing Cunard–Beecham symphony. That Sir Thomas appreciates Betty – musically – is borne out by his statement in Seattle that she can "play Beethoven better than I can direct it." ... Naturally all this has sent "Dear Emerald's" blood pressure up like Vesuvius in an angry mood.'

Betty Humby was now in the remote but fashionable ski-resort of Sun Valley, Idaho, establishing the statutory period of residence that under state law would allow her to apply for a quick divorce from her husband. Her son Jeremy was with her. Beecham, who by now had left both the Ritz-Carlton and Emerald Cunard for good, joined them whenever his engagements allowed. Unlike Dora Labbette, Humby had no scruples about such divorces, though on being telephoned in Sun Valley by a newspaper for confirmation of Knickerbocker's story, she was uncharacteristically brusque: 'I know nothing about it. I'm sorry. Goodbye.' [14]

When Beecham's train from New York reached Tacoma on the West Coast, reporters armed with copies of Knickerbocker's article boarded it for the last thirty miles or so into Seattle. 'It was not the old outspoken and, at times, apoplectic Sir Thomas that newsmen found huddled in one corner of the parlor car', reported the *Seattle Post-Intelligencer*.

> He appeared weary to the point of exhaustion and much thinner than Seattle knew him last fall. ... [He] blinked, cupped a hand to his ear, spoke scarcely above a whisper. ... When Sir Thomas read the "romance" story, only a slight suggestion of annoyance crossed his face. Paragraph by paragraph he slowly perused it, pausing only twice to remark: "It's utterly imbecilic" and "It's all misquoted." "What's all misquoted?" he was asked. "I never said that anyone could play Beethoven better than I can direct it." [What he had actually said was that Humby had played a particular Mozart concerto better than he had conducted it.] "But what is your comment generally on the matter?" "My dear fellow", he replied, "there are two ladies' names mentioned here. It's a private matter; it's not the sort of thing the people of Seattle are interested in." [15]

Beecham, aware that he needed all the support he could get for the Mozart festival, was careful to keep the local press on his side, however. Within days he was telling the *Seattle Times* of his dismay over the fall of Singapore on 15 February 1942, which, he said, would not have happened if Britain had had the sense to mobilise and use the potential military power of India. He added with an imperialistic flourish that India had 'ninety millions of Mohammedans, a

* Pen-name of Igor Cassini, American gossip-writer of Russian descent and younger brother of the fashion designer Oleg Cassini. He is credited with coining the phrase 'jet set'.

stern fighting race which is one hundred per cent loyal to the Crown. As for the Hindu part of it – however much they want and clamour for absolute home rule, they do not desire to exchange the comparatively mild control of Great Britain for the heavier hand of the Axis'.[16]

The North-West Mozart festival commemorated the 150th anniversary of Mozart's death. In the space of sixteen days Beecham gave an opening lecture on the composer, and rehearsed and conducted nine concerts, four of them in Seattle itself, three in Oregon (at Pendelton, Eugene and Portland), and one each in Victoria, British Columbia, and Boise, Idaho. It would have been a tall order for an experienced orchestra, let alone one that had not played most of the works before. The programmes included seven of the late symphonies, Act 3 of *Figaro*, various operatic overtures, movements from two of the divertimenti, the *Sinfonia concertante*, K364, with Antonio Brosa and William Primrose as soloists, and motets sung by the University of Washington choir. Audrey Mild-may, Canadian wife of Glyndebourne's founder John Christie, sang arias from *Don Giovanni* and *Figaro*, while Betty Humby gave five performances of the G major piano concerto K453. To demonstrate his confidence in the Seattle players, Beecham asked their concert-master, Francis Aranyi, to play the Fourth Violin Concerto. It received a long ovation, which only stopped when soloist and conductor walked off the platform arm-in-arm, an unusually matey gesture on Beecham's part. The concerts marked the end of Beecham's first season in Seattle, where it was generally agreed that he had wrought a substantial improve-ment in the orchestra, though he told its management that he would not return for another season unless new players were hired. The demand was accepted.

With the Mozart festival over, Beecham returned to New York, where on 14 March 1942, the last day of the Met's season, he conducted a broadcast matinée of *Faust*. To the management's alarm, he turned up at the house only three min-utes before curtain-up. In a recording of extended excerpts from the perform-ance, Albanese still seems uncomfortable with the French text, but in the last act leads the trio to a thrilling conclusion, sending the audience into a frenzy of shouting and stamping that only stops when Charles Kullman, the ardent Faust, breaks in with the despairing cry of 'Marguérite!' Beecham turns the opera's final apotheosis into something grand and inspired. Virgil Thomson, a fervent francophile, went so far as to say that Beecham's *Faust* was the 'best single con-ducting job' he had heard at the Metropolitan Opera all season,[17] a season that had also included Bruno Walter conducting *Don Giovanni*, Gluck's *Orfeo* and an English-language *Magic Flute*.

No sooner had the Metropolitan's season ended in New York than the entire company entrained for its spring tour. The first stop was Baltimore, the second Boston, where the opening night on 20 March, a performance of *Lohengrin* under Erich Leinsdorf, made front-page news, second only in prominence to the announcement that General MacArthur had flown to secret headquarters in Australia to take command of all allied forces in the south-west Pacific. Beecham conducted *Carmen* in Boston and then *Faust*. For one critic, 'the orchestra was worth hearing for itself alone, a rare experience where *Faust* is concerned'. [18] Albanese was again the Marguérite. Ironically, Dora Labbette was singing the role in English that same week in far less glamorous circumstances – on tour in blacked-out Glasgow with the brave but hand-to-mouth Carl Rosa Opera, which was doing a three-week stint before full houses at the Theatre Royal. At least the company was getting rather better support than normal from the pit, for it had hired the Scottish Orchestra and its conductor, Warwick Braithwaite, for the visit. Labbette alternated Marguérite with Mimi in *La bohème*, for which the small chorus was boosted with amateur singers from the Glasgow Grand Opera Society. Unfortunately there was no time to rehearse them properly and the result was, in the discreet opinion of one Scottish reviewer, 'untidy'. [19]

Operatic life in Britain had changed beyond recognition since Beecham left Britain in 1940. Not only had Covent Garden become a dance-hall, but Sadler's Wells Theatre had been commandeered as a rest-centre for bombed-out families. The Sadler's Wells company, like the Carl Rosa, spent the war touring the length and breadth of the country, with sporadic forays to the capital. Because of military and civilian conscription, orchestras and choruses were much reduced in size and casts suffered from an acute shortage of young singers. Inevitably, the performances failed to reach pre-war standards, but new and appreciative audiences were being attracted to opera.

Despite problems posed by air-raids, the blackout, unreliable train schedules and a frequent lack of accommodation or even meals for the players, Britain's orchestras were also finding new audiences, in town halls, music halls, cinemas, schools, factories and miners' institutes. During March 1942, while Beecham was on tour with the Metropolitan Opera, the self-governing LPO gave no fewer than forty concerts in London and the provinces, sometimes two in one day. Its conductors that month included Wood, Sargent, Boult, Cameron and Leslie Heward, though the players also had to put up with the caprices of other, less competent, conductors brought in to fill the gaps. Inevitably, with so many of the LPO's original members now in the armed forces, the orchestra's standard of playing was not what it had been under Beecham, but at least it had survived.

When Lieutenant Harold C. Schonberg, later the music critic of the *New York Times*, arrived in London as a US Army code-breaker, he found the musical scene 'feverish. ... Never in history have so many people been clamoring to get into concerts.' But as he pointed out in an article he sent back to the *Musical Courier* in New York, there was an inevitable down-side to the situation. The new audiences demanded familiar repertoire, with the result that most pro-grammes had become disappointingly repetitive: 'Anyone who can play the Schumann, Tchaikovsky or "Emperor" concertos need not worry about the future for a long time to come.' Fortunately, wrote Schonberg, there were plenty of excellent pianists in Britain, Clifford Curzon, Myra Hess, Eileen Joyce, Louis Kentner, Moura Lympany, Benno Moiseiwitsch and Solomon among them, though when it came to violinists, singers and conductors, 'the census was woe-fully low'. Most European artists of international repute, including a number of Britons, were in America and there were 'not enough left to cope with the present state of affairs'. [20] The judgement might seem harsh, but to an American used to an exalted line-up of conductors that included Toscanini, Koussevitsky, Walter, Stokowski, Reiner, Szell, Ormandy, Mitropoulos and Monteux, not to mention Beecham, their British counterparts seemed rather unexciting.

Throughout his wartime years in America, Beecham invariably referred to the LPO as 'my orchestra', a claim that did not escape the notice of the orchestra's manager, Thomas Russell, who observed that the players themselves were now 'in possession of the key of the door, and meant to use it'. [21] Though Beecham may not have known it, there was an undercurrent of disappointment, even resentment, in Britain, shared by musicians and concert-goers alike, that he should have remained in America instead of returning home. Wood was now Britain's musical hero of the hour, just as Beecham had been during the First World War. Following the bombing of the Queen's Hall on the night of 10 May 1941 Wood had transferred the Proms to the Royal Albert Hall, where they have remained ever since. He was photographed posing defiantly in the ruins of the old hall, an image that was reproduced throughout the English-speaking world.*

By the spring of 1942 Emerald Cunard was beside herself with worry about the Humby situation. According to Frederic Prokosch, her eyes 'took on a wilder glitter. Her voice rose into an ever more despairing timbre. Her badi-nage at teatime grew faintly incoherent and the rouge on her cheeks took on a clownlike intensity.' [22] Cunard's problems were compounded by the fact that her funds were running low, with little hope of their being replenished with money from Britain. Beecham rubbed salt in the wound by bringing Humby to Car-negie Hall to play the Mozart G major concerto with the WPA orchestra. Per-haps anxious not to offend Cunard, neither Virgil Thomson nor Olin Downes

---

* The original photograph showed Wood standing between two BBC officials, but, before it was released, they were 'removed' to produce the more heroic effect of a man standing alone (Arthur Jacobs, *Henry J. Wood: Maker of the Proms* (London, 1994), p. 355).

reviewed the concert. Ross Parmenter, who took Downes's place, thought that the concerto was marred by Humby 'constantly letting her melodic lines fade out in her attempts to get ethereal pianissimos'.[23]

The 1941–2 season ended for Beecham with further tour performances of *Carmen* in Atlanta and in Cleveland, where, mindful that he had to catch a train to New York shortly after curtain-down, he took the ballet music in the last act so fast that the dancers could hardly stay on their feet.[24] He also conducted a single performance of Gounod's *Roméo et Juliette* on 28 April for the Montreal Festival, with Raoul Jobin and Stella Andreva as the lovers. At the end of the first act there was loud applause before the orchestra had finished playing, which provoked Beecham into shouting at the audience, 'My musicians are also artists and deserve to be heard to the very end.' To which a man high up in the auditorium shouted back, 'We have a right to applaud our artists when we want.'[25] When Beecham took his place at the start of the second act, he was greeted with booing from the upper reaches of the house, an occurrence probably unique in his career.

After the *Roméo* Beecham returned to Sun Valley, which became his base for the spring and summer months of 1942. He achieved a good rapport with Humby's son, Jeremy. They had first met two years earlier at Humby's tiny New York apartment on unfashionable East 33rd Street, within earshot of the old elevated railway running up Third Avenue. Lying in bed one evening, Jeremy had heard a man 'roaring' loudly in the next room and had gone to investigate. 'It's all right', said his mother, 'this is your Uncle Tom.' It turned out that the stranger had been reciting poetry. He took Jeremy on his knee and announced, 'I'm going to look after you now', which the boy accepted as natural enough. After that, in Jeremy's words, 'things moved fast'.[26]

Beecham gave Jeremy a good deal of his time in Sun Valley, teaching him to play chess and regaling him with poetry ranging from the Odes of Horace to Walter Scott's Ballads. Although the boy took lessons each morning from a White Russian governess, it was Beecham who stretched his mind more. 'How was that Old Cockleorum?', he might ask after a concert in expectation of a considered reply, or 'What do you think of this claret, old boy?' Beecham even took Jeremy along to Boise, the Idaho state capital, for a conference with his divorce lawyer. Later, in New York, Jeremy was taken to meet a genial tax-inspector with an office overlooking the Hudson River. Coffee was served, and the two men exchanged ribald stories. Jeremy found the encounter puzzling. Eventually, he recalled, 'Tom rose and, with elaborate courtesy, handed over a box of cigars. We left amid protestations of mutual esteem.' On the way home Jeremy asked Beecham if they were good cigars. 'No, not very', came the amused reply, 'but they cost a lot.' Beecham had filled the box with dollar bills. Jeremy could only imagine that he had been taken along to add an air of innocence and respectability to the proceedings.[27]

In Sun Valley, Jeremy was taught to ski by one of the few members of the resort's band of Austrian instructors who had not been interned by the FBI on the dubious grounds that they had been either receiving secret radio messages from the Fatherland or transmitting them back home from a mountain-top. Eventually almost all were released to serve with the American armed forces, many of them with distinction. When the snow finally melted, Beecham gave Jeremy a semi-automatic .22 Winchester rifle – 'a somewhat unsuitable weapon for an eleven-year-old', observed Jeremy years later[28] – and the boy roamed the mountains in search of mountain lions, though all he could find were jack-rabbits and ground-squirrels. He kept the squirrels' tails as trophies until they attracted a legion of red mites, which invaded the chalet apartment

Hollywood stars, among them Claudette Colbert and Gary Cooper, Ray Milland and Norma Shearer, were also in Sun Valley, for what would prove to be the resort's last season before the Navy took it over for a recuperation hospital. Already an American army ski battalion was in training there, while the Sun Valley Commandos – thirty local men equipped with horses and 300 rounds of ammunition each – were all set to conduct guerrilla warfare in the event of Japanese invaders attempting to cut the trans-continental railway. 'It is hard to believe now', wrote the resort's historian forty years later, 'but after the catastrophe of Pearl Harbor many people believed that the first line of defense would be the Rockies.'[29] Such was the unlikely setting for Beecham's own residency in Idaho that would eventually enable him to file for a divorce from Utica.

In June 1942 he paid a brief visit to New York, where he made a batch of recordings for American Columbia with the New York Philharmonic-Symphony Orchestra. This in no way signalled a rapprochement with Arthur Judson. Each year, from mid-June to mid-August, the orchestra was hired out to play for a season of open-air concerts at the now long-demolished Lewisohn Stadium, a fine amphitheatre on the upper West Side that belonged to City College. Since many of the Philharmonic's principals took their holidays at this time of year, the Lewisohn orchestra always included a good sprinkling of deputies. Although Beecham may not have realised it in advance, it was this version of the orchestra that played for his recording sessions. In Britain, he had enjoyed a leisurely approach to recording, with plenty of time available for retakes, but in New York he was faced with having to complete a number of works in just two days: Rimsky-Korsakov's *Golden Cockerel* suite, Mendelssohn's 'Italian' Symphony, Tchaikovsky's *Capriccio Italien* and Sibelius's Seventh Symphony, along with 'Melisande' from his *Pelleas and Melisande* incidental music.

Although Beecham had seemed pleased when he heard the playbacks during the sessions at Liederkranz Hall, he was less enthusiastic when Columbia sent him the first batch of test-pressings. He complained that the sound-quality of the *Capriccio Italien* and the *Golden Cockerel* excerpts was inferior to that of his London recordings, and that there were too many weak or dull players in the orchestra.[30] He sought an injunction to stop Columbia releasing the two symphonies and the Rimsky-Korsakov, and sued the company for $600,000 in damages for the 'libellous injury' that the records had inflicted on him. In its defence, Columbia pointed out that since Beecham had heard playbacks of the recordings as they were being made, and had been satisfied with them, there was no case to answer. Beecham withdrew his suit, and the company (though not its British associate) went ahead and issued all the recordings, except for the *Golden Cockerel* suite.*

Even if Columbia had agreed to let Beecham re-record the disputed sides, he would not have been able to do so, because just six weeks after the New York sessions, James Caesar Petrillo, president of the American Federation of Musicians, banned his members from taking part in any further recordings for either the gramophone companies or the broadcasting transcription services. The dispute arose because vagaries in the copyright laws gave American radio stations an excuse for not paying royalties on the records they broadcast. Beecham was not sympathetic to the ban, but argued in a letter to the *New York Times* that, since it was unlikely that the companies would ever agree to take on hundreds of extra musicians, it would make more sense for Petrillo to demand a short and simple act of legislation in Congress to change the copyright laws.[31] Beecham's suggestion received plenty of support, but in spite of interventions by the United States attorney-general and others, the ban was not lifted completely until November 1944.

Financially, the ban was a setback for Beecham, for he was unable to take advantage of a new contract he had signed with RCA to record with the Detroit Symphony and other orchestras. It came as a blow to the Detroit orchestra, which had already suffered a major loss of income following the Ford Motor Company's decision to drop the popular 'Ford Sunday Evening Hour' radio concerts in the aftermath of Pearl Harbor. Ironically the concerts had been started by members of the Ford family in the early thirties to provide work for the orchestra during the Depression. Now, at the beginning of the 1942–3 season, it found itself insolvent and was forced to suspend operations.

---

* *New York Times*, 6, 14 March, 4 April 1943. The recordings' true worth became apparent in 1997, when all of them, including the *Golden Cockerel* items, were transferred to CD, using the original lacquer masters (*Sir Thomas Beecham: American Columbia recordings, 1942–52*; Sony Classical MH2K 63366). Any blemishes in the playing seem a reasonable price to pay for the chance to hear readings of the Mendelssohn and Sibelius symphonies notable for their drive and feeling of spontaneity.

Beecham, who had a contract for six pairs of concerts with the orchestra, sued its board of directors for loss of earnings amounting to $7,500. The dispute rambled on for three years until one of the directors, against the advice of his own attorneys, decided to settle the matter for the sake of peace and quiet. He offered Beecham $1,000, which to the relief of all concerned was accepted.[32] In what at first sight seemed to be a magnanimous gesture, Beecham invited Karl Krueger, chief conductor of the now resurrected orchestra, to give some concerts in London with the LPO.[33] Krueger accepted the invitation happily, not realising that Beecham was in no position to make such an offer. The London concerts never took place.

Meanwhile Humby had been granted her divorce in Boise on 3 July 1942. For her husband, a priest of the Church of England, it had been a distressing experience, but he did not stand in his wife's way and declined to contest the suit. The judge awarded Humby custody of Jeremy, on the condition that his father was allowed to visit him at reasonable times. Under Idaho law Humby was not allowed to remarry in the state, except to her now divorced husband, for a period of six months.[34] Both Beecham and Humby declined to comment on their future.

During July and August Beecham auditioned new players in Seattle and successfully rebuilt bridges in Los Angeles, where he gave two concerts with the Los Angeles Philharmonic at the Hollywood Bowl. The press was much taken with the 'drama, enthusiasm and vigor' with which he conducted *The Star-Spangled Banner*, making 'the public sing and sing out loud, too'.[35] He was asked to sign a copy of the programme-book for a fan. 'You must excuse me', he said, 'my hand is shaking a bit. It always shakes before I conduct this orchestra.'[36]

On 26 August 1942, Beecham filed a petition for divorce from Utica in the near-derelict gold-mining town of Idaho City, which in its heyday in the 1860s had boasted a population of more than 30,000, but now had only 400 citizens. Beecham's lawyer chose this outpost in the hope that no one there would recognise his client's name. The strategem worked until, six weeks later, someone noticed that District Judge Charles F. Koelsch of Boise (the same judge who had granted Humby her divorce) had issued an order permitting Beecham's lawyer 'to take a deposition from Mrs Beecham in London'.[37] Beecham was evasive when faced by reporters, but then admitted that divorce was on the cards. The revelation came as something of a surprise in Seattle, where few people realised that he was married, let alone about to get a divorce.

In his petition, Beecham claimed that Utica had 'treated him in a cruel and inhuman manner, by inflicting upon him grievous mental suffering constituting extreme cruelty under the laws of the State of Idaho', that she had 'continuously and unreasonably found fault with [him] and his work', and that against his express wishes she had 'ceased cohabitation with [him] in 1909 and never has resumed such relationship'.[38] For Beecham it had now become a matter of urgency to secure Utica's agreement to an Idaho divorce, for he had been warned by Philip Emanuel, who still looked after his affairs in London, that if she were to withhold her consent, it could be considered invalid in the eyes of the British law. This would not matter as long as Beecham remained unmarried after the divorce had been granted, but if he were to marry Humby in America, and then return with her to the United Kingdom, there could be complications: Utica might accuse him of bigamy. If her case were proved, he might find himself under arrest.

Adrian and Joyce, who approved strongly of the liaison with Humby, were quick to offer Beecham their support. They engineered a meeting with Utica at Clopton House on 4 September, Adrian's thirty-ninth birthday, in the hope that they might be able to persuade her to agree to a divorce, but when after lunch Joyce broached the subject Utica went up like a sky-rocket and a furious slanging-match broke out between the two women. Utica refused to give an inch. Joyce soon realised that there was no point in continuing the argument. Writing to Humby about the incident, she said that it had been 'like two bull-dogs pulling at a bone'. On Beecham's instructions, Emanuel advised Adrian and Joyce that further disputes with Utica might only make matters worse, and called for a halt to the campaign of persuasion.[39]

By now Beecham and Humby had left Sun Valley for Canada and were living in a rented house in the small village of Caulfeild, on the North Shore of Vancouver Bay. The quickest way to reach the local shop, the wooden Hudson Bay store, was by boat, and each morning, no matter what the weather, Jeremy rowed there to collect the bread and milk. When Beecham needed a break from working on scores he played billiards with Jeremy on the full-size table in the basement of the house – he was remembered as a good player, though out of practice. Jeremy noted how exceptionally close Beecham and his mother had become. She started to look after his business affairs and to act as his touring manager, collecting up his sopping evening clothes at the end of each concert, dealing with fans, shooing away hangers-on and, most difficult of all, for he was a notorious procrastinator when it came to catching trains, making sure he reached railway stations on time. She even took on the task of answering Berta Geissmar's letters from Britain, some of them 4,000 words long, which Beecham had begun to find increasingly indecipherable.[40] Geissmar's devotion to him had remained unswerving, and in her letters she kept him informed, not only about the LPO, for which she continued to work throughout the war, but also about life with the younger Beechams in Warwickshire. She was a frequent and welcome visitor, both at Compton Scorpion and at the nearby home of Beecham's younger son Tommy, now an officer in the Royal Engineers.

In New York, Emerald Cunard continued to live in the hope that her erstwhile lover would return to her. To occupy her days she went to stay in the country with the society beauty Mona Harrison Williams, wife of a Wall Street financier. The English film-actress Leonora Corbett, who came to lunch, told her fellow guests that she had just had a letter from an old school-friend, Betty Humby, who said that she was going to marry Sir Thomas Beecham. Cunard almost fainted with shock, but said nothing until after the guests had gone, when she confided to her hostess that she only wanted to die. She returned to Manhattan, where in spite of the difficulties involved, she secured a passage to Lisbon on a neutral Portuguese liner, the *Serpa Pinto*, which during the subsequent voyage took on board survivors from another ship in the convoy that had been torpedoed.[41] After a three-week wait in Lisbon she flew to London, where her friends greeted her return with delight and relief. One of the first to dine with her was the Tory MP and man-about-town Sir Henry 'Chips' Channon, who noted in his diary: 'Her spritely gaiety is infectious. She kissed me affectionately goodnight and I admired her courage for I know her heart is broken over Thomas Beecham's desertion.'[42]

Cunard made one last bid to regain Beecham's affections. Hearing that the wife and daughters of the composer Arthur Bliss were stranded in California and unable to get passages home, she came up with an improbable solution to the problem. She told the mystified Bliss, who was now the BBC's Director of Music in London, that Beecham had become emotionally involved in America and that it was imperative that he should return to Britain as soon as possible. If, Cunard continued, the BBC's Director-General could be persuaded to invite Beecham to supersede Bliss as Director of Music, she, in turn, would use all her influence to enable the composer to get to America and bring his family home. Bliss was astounded: 'My first impulse was to laugh outright at the thought of Beecham behind my desk, administering a large department, punctiliously answering memos, attending conferences, interviewing would-be broadcasters, etc, etc, but this soon turned to anger at the unwarranted presumption behind this absurd deal.'[43] Bliss's family did return to Britain eventually, but without the help of Emerald Cunard.

After three months of living in Canada, Beecham returned with Humby to the United States in October 1942 for the opening of his second season with the Seattle orchestra. He stayed in the city for just over six weeks, giving six concerts in Seattle itself and one before 4,000 troops at Fort Lewis, the army's huge training camp in Washington State, where he stood to conduct beneath a basket-ball net in the sports arena. His efforts were greeted with thunderous applause. 'So soldiers don't like classical music', commented the *Seattle Times* ironically.[44] Members of the Seattle Symphony who had been drafted into the armed services were beginning to appear on the platform in uniform, while those of them who had been posted away were replaced temporarily by students from the University of Washington's orchestra.[45] Between concerts Beecham dictated the last pages of *A Mingled Chime* to a typist at the Olympic Hotel. He told a local gathering that the book was 'demi-semi-autobiographical. It's mingled because it concerns everything under the sun.'[46] By now Joyce Beecham had given birth to a second son, Robert, and Betty scoured the Seattle shops for woollen underwear for the two grandchildren, though she soon discovered that because of the war it was no longer being made in America. 'I tried to get you some silk stockings', she wrote to Joyce, 'but there are none to be had here in the West.'[47]

Half-way through the Seattle engagements, Beecham took the train to Boise for his divorce hearing on 4 November before Judge Koelsch. He repeated the claims he had made in his original petition and testified further that Utica had 'formed an aversion' to him and had 'belittled the success which he continually attained'.[48] In the absence of any counter-claims from Utica, the judge deferred his decision until he had received depositions in support of Sir Thomas's case from Philip Emanuel in London.

Immediately after the last Seattle concert on 16 November, Beecham left for New York and the start of the 1942–3 season at the Metropolitan Opera, where again he was to be responsible for the French repertoire. Reporters were at Seattle's Union Station when, with Humby on his arm, he arrived to board the Milwaukee Olympian. Was Miss Humby travelling with him? he was asked. 'I shan't answer such a question', he stormed, 'and you ought to know better than to ask it.' All concerned could have saved their breath, for the pair were clearly seen entering adjoining Pullman compartments. The rail company was under the impression that Humby was Beecham's secretary.[49]

To avoid the gaze of the New York press, they rented a house in the village of Spring Valley, some twenty-five miles to the north-west of Manhattan. Initially there had been doubts that the Met could mount a season at all, for the previous season, seriously affected by America's entry into the war, had shown an operating deficit of $214,374. Flagstad's absence in particular had caused a significant drop in box-office receipts. Rationing of car-tyres, petrol shortages and other transport restrictions had kept away many opera-goers who would otherwise have come in from Long Island, New Jersey, Westchester County and the Hudson valley.[50] Edward Johnson slashed the cost of the expensive seats by no less than 23 per cent, with corresponding bargains among the cheaper ones, a move that proved highly effective in filling what otherwise would have been empty seats. Beecham and Bruno Walter both agreed to accept a 10 per cent cut in their fees.*

When patrons, many of them in uniform, arrived for the opening of the season on 23 November 1942 – Donizetti's *Fille du régiment*, with the French-born Lily Pons in the title-role and Frank St Leger conducting – they found changes at the opera house. The vast iron grilles that once adorned the windows on the opera house's south-east corner had been ripped out for scrap-metal, while fire-buckets and stirrup-pumps were placed at strategic points in the auditorium in case of air-raids. *Time* magazine noted that, 'though a few Manhattan dowagers, of almost Egyptian preservation, clung valiantly to their tiaras and diamond necklaces', both Edward Johnson and the orchestra had 'descended to the informality of black ties'.[51] When Pons inserted the 'Marseillaise' into the Act 2 finale and unfurled, not the customary tricolour flag of France, but one bearing the Free French Cross of Lorraine, the audience rose spontaneously to its feet and cheered.

Three nights later Beecham conducted a revival of *Carmen*, which to many ears sounded under-rehearsed. There was a new Escamillo, the Hungarian baritone Alexander Sved. The critic Irving Kolodin thought he had 'the vigor of voice to make this music exciting, though the ferocity with which he roared it out made one wonder, at times, whether he was impersonating the toreador or the bull', a witticism that has been wrongly attributed to Beecham, though he often repeated it as his own.[52] Beecham followed *Carmen* with revivals of two operas that he had last conducted in London in 1919 – Massenet's *Manon*, with the Brazilian soprano Bidú Sayão, in the title-role, and Charpentier's *Louise*, with Grace Moore. Virgil Thomson thought the diminutive Sayão sang delightfully, but ruined her performance with 'mincing movements' more suited to musical comedy than opera.[53]

Writing about the *Louise* two years later, Grace Moore complained that although the dress rehearsal had been 'a real performance', the opening matinée on 15 January 1943 had been 'slow in tempo and fatigued'.[54] Perhaps she had still not forgiven Beecham for the brusque treatment she had received at Covent Garden in 1935, or she may have resented his claim that at the Met she had not been anxious to rehearse, but her verdict is not borne out by a recording of the performance, which shows Beecham bringing considerable panache to the proceedings. For Virgil Thomson, 'the sweeping musical conception and the great beauty of the symphonic passages, made it evident that a musico-dramatic

---

* Beecham was now paid $675 a performance (the equivalent today of almost £5,000), Walter $900 (later cut to $800). George Szell, a new addition to the conducting roster, was paid $400 a week, with the stipulation that he would not be asked to conduct more than four times a week.

occasion of some magnitude was in progress.'[55] Moore had studied the role of Louise with both the composer and one of its finest interpreters, Mary Garden, and her singing has Gallic grace and a sense of style. Though she sings the aria 'Depuis le jour' transposed down a semitone, it would not in those days have been considered a crime.

Beecham's divorce was finally granted in Boise on 14 January 1943, the day before *Louise* opened. The proviso that he could not legally remarry in Idaho within a period of six months presented no problem, since the State of New York allowed recently divorced people to remarry whenever it suited them, provided they lived within its boundaries. Just four days after the divorce came through, Beecham and Humby took out a marriage licence at their local township of Suffern. It allowed them to marry anywhere in the state, and on the following day, 19 January, they married in secret before a police justice in Manhattan. Shortly afterwards they moved into a splendid apartment close by Central Park, at 31 East 79th Street, described by *Time* magazine as 'a baronial Manhattan duplex with Tudor interiors'.[56] It was filled with suitably imposing furniture from Plaza Antiques, whose bill, despite repeated pleas for payment and threatened lawsuits, would remain unpaid for five years, when Beecham finally instructed his American manager to settle it for $5,000 (worth £33,000 in 2008).[57]

Whatever her private feelings, Utica reacted to the news of the divorce with dignity when approached by a reporter from a London newspaper. 'You cannot judge a man like Sir Thomas by ordinary rules and conventions', she said. 'For him music was all that mattered. And I am still proud that I had some part in giving this man and his music to the world.' Only once did a sharp note creep into her voice, when she referred to Beecham's claim that she had formed an aversion to him.[58]

One of the few people who knew about the marriage was young Jeremy, now a boarder at the Eaglebrook preparatory school at Deerfield, Massachusetts. Humby and Beecham went to visit him there on 21 February, the day of the thirty-two-strong Eaglebrook School Band's concert. Jeremy was one of the clarinet players. During the lunch that preceded the performance the headmaster's wife persuaded Beecham to conduct one of the items. He chose Schubert's *Marche militaire*, but when he gave the downbeat to begin, nobody came in. He tried again. Still nothing happened. Archibald Smith, the school's music master, rushed up to the podium. 'Sir Thomas, Sir Thomas', he explained, 'you have to say, "A one and a two and a ..."' Beecham, full of bonhomie, followed his advice, with a satisfactory result.[59]

When on 24 February the New York newspapers ran unconfirmed reports that Beecham and Humby were married, the couple admitted the story was true.

Newsmen turned up at the Town Hall, where Beecham was giving a lecture in aid of British War Relief on 'The Changing Patronage of Music'. Where and when, they asked, had the ceremony taken place? 'That's something we can't go into', said Beecham. 'There are various wagers on that subject.' [60] After the press had left, the War Relief committee gave a lunch for the newly-weds with, much to the couple's amusement, orchids for the bride and a wedding cake complete with candles. That night Betty wrote to Joyce Beecham to tell her about the marriage and to apologise for the secrecy surrounding it: 'We felt it would be easier for everyone this way, and necessary if we were to carry through our plans successfully. ... At present we don't know Clopton's attitude. ... But we hope for the best.' Such worries apart, the letter reflects the sense of relief she and Beecham felt now that the days of subterfuge were over. Beecham added a note saying that he would like to have a wedding cake all to himself for months to come.

Dora Labbette heard about the marriage, not from Beecham, but from his lawyer in London. The news came as a terrible blow, because Beecham had continued to write to her in the most affectionate terms, even though he was already deeply committed to Humby. In April 1943 Labbette embarked on rehearsals for a production of André Messager's operetta *Monsieur Beaucaire*,* set in Georgian Bath, which was to tour the provinces before coming into London's West End. Labbette, who continued to use the stage-name Lisa Perli, played the female lead, Lady Mary Carlisle. Despite wartime restrictions on stage materials, the sets and costumes looked opulent. The tour opened at the Grand Theatre, Blackpool, on 3 May and then continued, first to Leeds and then Edinburgh. Most reviewers liked the show, but box-office takings were not large enough to risk a London run. Georgian froth was out of step with the national *Zeitgeist*.

The final performance, at Glasgow's Theatre Royal on 22 May, marked the end of Labbette's singing career. The occasion had an added poignancy because it took place in the theatre where, seven years earlier, she had made her last operatic appearance with Beecham, as Mimi. Though aged only forty-five, and singing as well as ever, she felt betrayed by him and as a result had lost the will to continue performing. It was a melancholy end to a fine career. 'The stuffing went out of me', she told her son later, 'and I really felt that I didn't want to sing any more.' [61] With music no longer a part of her life, she moved to the village of Sidlesham, close to the West Sussex coast, where she grew tomatoes, kept

---

* *Monsieur Beaucaire*, written to an English book by Frederick Lonsdale, with lyrics by Adrian Ross, was first performed at the Prince of Wales Theatre, Birmingham, on 7 April 1919, prior to a London run at the Princes Theatre. Maggie Teyte played Lady Mary Carlisle. It was first given in Paris in 1925.

chickens and ducks, and bred spaniels. Some years later she made a heap in the garden of everything that reminded her of Beecham, including his letters to her, and put a match to it.

Beecham meanwhile was at the 1943 Montreal Festival, where on 27 May, five days after Labbette's last *Monsieur Beaucaire*, he conducted a performance of *Tristan und Isolde*, with Marjorie Lawrence as Isolde. Her legs were still paralysed as a result of the polio she had contracted, and she was unable to stand unassisted, let alone walk, though two months earlier she had managed to sing the relatively short role of Venus in *Tannhäuser* at the Met from a sitting position. Beecham had heard it and sent Lawrence a telegram, asking if she would sing Isolde for him in Montreal, with the British tenor Arthur Carron as Tristan. She assumed he was talking about a concert performance and was astonished to learn that it would be staged. Beecham brushed aside her objections, saying that he and the stage director, Herbert Graf of the Metropolitan Opera, had worked out a production that would make it possible for her to take part. The first two acts presented no problem, said Beecham; the action would simply revolve around her seated figure. Act 3 was more difficult, since Isolde did not make her entrance until two-thirds of the way through, but he and Graf had found a solution in Kurwenal's line, 'Sie trag ich herauf: trau meinen Armen' ('I will carry her up here: trust in my arms). After carrying Isolde on, Kurwenal would gently deposit her beside the dying Tristan. Sceptics feared the worst, but the scheme worked remarkably well. The critic Thomas Archer found Lawrence 'noble both visually and aurally'. [62]

Writing to his son Adrian in July 1943, Beecham said that in his marriage he had gained a happiness that he had 'never thought possible of achievement on this earth'. He hoped to visit Britain in the summer of 1944, but was worried that he might run disagreeable risks were he to do so. He asked for news of Adrian's brother Tommy who, on leave from the army, had opened the bill as a cornet-playing comic at a charity show, *Seventy Years of Song*, which Charles B. Cochran had mounted at the Royal Albert Hall. Beecham demanded more details of this 'unexpected manifestation of family genius'. [63] By now Beecham had become such a familiar figure in the United States that he appeared on the coveted front cover of *Time*, with a four-page profile inside. A reader from Lexington, Virginia, wrote to the magazine to say that the cover was like an oasis in the desert: 'After a great procession of military men and political leaders, it was a tremendous relief to see the Mephisophelean face of Orchestra Leader Beecham on that issue. The artists have been too neglected in this war time. Let the poet, the dramatist, the composer and the painter join the parade across the front of *Time* again.' Beecham, the profile declared, had 'become a treasured and crusty feature on the musical landscape of democratic

America'.[64]* The British Ministry of Information's New York office woke up to Beecham's potential as a propagandist, and he and Betty were often to be found at its exhibitions promoting Britain's war-effort and special showings of films such as Roy Boulting's documentary, *Desert Victory*.

The Beechams arranged dinner parties, at which influential Americans might meet visiting politicians, writers, diplomats and economists from Britain. There were military heroes, too. Jeremy remembered an RAF fighter-pilot who had been catapulted from the deck of merchant ships to attack German aircraft, and a kilted Scot with a hole in his knee who had survived the commando raid on Saint-Nazaire in March 1942. But it was not just the great and the good who enjoyed Beecham's hospitality. When he discovered that a performance of *Carmen* at the Met, to which he had invited a party of young Australian airmen, was sold out, he arranged for them to watch the performance from the wings, where – no doubt to the consternation of the stage-management – they joined in the better-known choruses.[65]

Beecham's third and final Seattle season opened on 26 September 1943 amid considerable controversy, most of it orchestrated by the *Seattle Post-Intelligencer*'s reviewer, Suzanne Martin, who a month earlier had written a series of articles criticising the orchestra's management. She argued that although Beecham's inspiration was 'self-evident and indisputable', what the Seattle Symphony actually needed was a conductor who was prepared to work with the orchestra, not for six weeks a season, but for nine or ten months a year. Only then would its playing standards really improve.[66]

Martin was not a good critic, nor was she much of a writer, but she had a point. Unfortunately, she overplayed her hand, claiming repeatedly that if Beecham were to rehearse the orchestra more often, it would play better. Beecham became increasingly irritated with Martin, who in the opinion of the players had misunderstood his attitude to rehearsing. 'Beecham often failed to use all his allotted rehearsal time', noted the cellist Gordon Epperson, later a distinguished string-teacher. 'He didn't really like to rehearse. He loved to conduct and he saved his electricity, which was abundant, for performances.' Epperson was one of many players who combined playing in the orchestra with war-work. He was in a car-pool with four or five other players from Tacoma: 'We'd drive to Seattle together, play the rehearsal or concert and then return to Tacoma to start work in the shipyards at midnight.'[67]

Beecham wrote to the orchestra's trustees complaining not only of 'the

---

* Beecham was also pictured at the time in full-page magazine advertisements endorsing the Magnavox radio-phonograph, for which he was presumably paid a suitably large fee: 'Like many another great artist he finds renewed inspiration and pleasant relaxation in listening to his Magnavox.'

unspeakable cultural thuggery' of Martin and one of her colleagues, but also of editors who tolerated articles on music that displayed the 'literary approach of a street Arab, the monumental vanity of the high school magazine editor, the range of knowledge of a stevedore and the vocabulary of a baboon.'[68] By the third concert, Beecham had became so exasperated by the carping that after conducting a pair of Sibelius pieces, *Valse triste* and the *Karelia* march, he addressed the audience. 'I have heard today from this orchestra two of the finest performances ever given in my life', he said, adding that if he were to read anything to the contrary in the next morning's papers, he would pursue the offending critics for as long as he lived. In her review of the concert Martin conceded that the *Karelia* march had been 'a stunner', but went on to draw the illogical and untenable conclusion that, because Beecham had failed to include in his praise the performances of the two preceding works, the *Meistersinger* prelude and Beethoven's Eighth Symphony, he could not have thought much of either of them.[69]

Beecham took his revenge four nights later, when he delivered the orchestra's annual Conductor's Lecture at the Moore Theater. 'Instead of music criticism', he told his listeners, 'the Seattle Symphony Orchestra has been receiving gossip criticism.' The city, he said, had a much finer orchestra than its detractors were prepared to admit, and, to prove his point, he would play recordings of items from recent Seattle concerts, which he had had made specially for the occasion. By way of comparison, he would also play commercial recordings of the same works, some of them conducted by himself. He would not reveal which recording was which, but would invite the audience to vote with a show of hands on the one it preferred in each case.

To Beecham's delight, and to the discomfort of his tormentors, most of whom were present, the audience chose the Seattle recordings in almost every instance. Beecham turned the knife further by reading out specific criticisms from the reviews and then refuting them by playing the relevant passages from the actual performances. It was a *tour de force*. 'If this action against me continues', he announced, 'I shall close up shop and leave.' The *Seattle Star*, which had stood up for Beecham consistently, observed that 'any music critic present must have found it hard to leave the Moore Theater without slinking'.[70]

In her next two reviews, Martin found it prudent to concentrate more on the soloists than on Beecham, though after praising Marjorie Lawrence for her singing in the *Götterdämmerung* Immolation Scene, she opined obscurely that the orchestral playing had been 'scuffled during its progress'. Her colleague from the *Seattle Times* accused the players of 'fumbling through Wagner'. For Beecham, these were jibes too far. He found an ally in Seattle's influential left-wing weekly, *New World*, which branded Martin's music criticism 'unintelligible caterwauling'. Beecham's ejection of her paper's photographer from a concert two years earlier might have been inadvisable, said the *New World*, but it was no justification for her 'malicious' and 'idiotic' feud.[71]

When Marjorie Lawrence repeated the Immolation Scene the next night, Beecham told the audience that the Seattle reviewers were 'ignorant, malicious, lying' and that their criticism would keep self-respecting artists away from the city. On the following day, 2 November 1943, he resigned. The orchestra's management announced that Beecham was ill and that he would be unable to conduct his last three scheduled concerts, though shortly afterwards it had to admit the truth of what had happened.[72] In a final ironic twist it turned out that the season had been one of the most financially successful in the orchestra's history. All its debts had been paid off and a sum of $30,000 placed in an endowment fund to secure its future stability.

Some years later Walter Legge wrote that Beecham's Seattle seasons 'must have been the very nadir of his artistic experiences', [73] but it is unlikely that Beecham saw them that way. His quarrel was with the critics, not the Seattle orchestra, with which he enjoyed an excellent rapport. The recordings Beecham played in the Moore Theater have survived and show the orchestra in a favourable light. The general standard of playing is far higher than might be expected from the reviews, no more so than in the blazing *Meistersinger* prelude and the incisive reading of Beethoven's Eighth Symphony that had been the target for Suzanne Martin's ill-advised sneers.

Back in New York, Beecham started rehearsals for the Metropolitan Opera's 1943–4 season, which, artistically speaking, would prove to be the high point of his sojourn in America. His first opera was *Tristan*, a work he had long wanted to conduct in New York. Originally the conductor was to have been Bruno Walter, but he had been told to rest after a bad attack of influenza. Three members of the cast had sung their roles with Beecham at Covent Garden before the war – Lauritz Melchior as Tristan, Herbert Janssen as Kurwenal and Kerstin Thorborg as Brangäne. The Isolde was Helen Traubel, who in the previous season had become the first American-born soprano to sing the role at the Met since Lilian Nordica thirty-three years earlier. At the start of his first orchestral rehearsal, Beecham affected shock on hearing that he was expected to accept the customary cuts imposed on the opera by Artur Bodanzky, who had been in charge of the Met's German repertoire until his sudden death in 1939. Beecham told the players that the cuts were 'vandalism' and that he would be restoring the missing passages. In fact he did no such thing. It seems he was merely indulging in his tactic of catching the players' attention with a demand that would excite their interest.

The first night, on 24 November, was fraught with problems. Traubel said

that she was feeling unwell and, to ensure that she got through the performance, Beecham was obliged to make further cuts in addition to Bodanzky's.
Traubel was one of the best Wagner singers of her generation, though, as she
admitted in her memoirs, she had a 'psychological block' about singing top Cs.
She transposed them down.[74] On this occasion it was not just the Cs that were
transposed. The Bs in Act 1 suffered the same treatment. Not surprisingly, the
act failed to ignite. Jerome D. Bohm of the *Tribune* felt that latecomers had
not helped matters by clattering down the aisles during the Prelude, so that 'Sir
Thomas found it difficult to immerse himself fully in the music'. It seems that by
the start of Act 2 Traubel had recovered her health and Beecham his composure,
because from then on, in the words of *Musical America's* critic, 'the true fascination and resplendence of Sir Thomas's reading – its luminous poetry, its breadth,
transparence and ravishing detail – came into perspective.' For Olin Downes
the performance 'was on the whole the most poetic and romantic interpretation
of this particular opera that we have heard for years in the Metropolitan Opera
House'.[75]

The critics returned for the sixth and last *Tristan* on 14 March 1944, when
Marjorie Lawrence repeated her Montreal success as Isolde, giving the audience
the chance to hear the role's high Cs, which, one reviewer pointed out, had not
been heard at the Met 'since Kirsten Flagstad began to ignore them in her last
years here'.[76] Before the performance started, Lawrence noticed that Beecham
was in an uncharacteristic mood of intense nervous excitement.[77] This time
Jerome Bohm thought his conducting 'was throughout of the utmost eloquence,
often overwhelming in its incandescent intensity'.[78]

In his history of the Metropolitan Opera, Irving Kolodin, who attended
the performance, says that although the house was crowded and the enthusiasm extraordinary, Edward Johnson told him that some patrons considered
Lawrence's participation 'unsightly'. A month later, on tour in Chicago, she
sang one more Isolde, again with Beecham, but she was never offered another
opportunity to sing at the Met, which Kolodin considered 'a sorry discrimina-
tion against a woman already severely tried'.[79] The heroic Lawrence, who was
never afraid to call a spade a spade, claimed in her memoirs that some of her
colleagues had complained that, 'regardless of how well they sang, if I sang the
same roles or if I were in a cast with them, mine would be the performance
that would attract all the notice and acclaim! This was downright nonsense, of
course, and the worst kind of jealousy.'[80] In spite of this, Marjorie Lawrence's
Isolde at the Met achieved legendary status, for in 1955 it provided the moving
climax to *Interrupted Melody*, the Hollywood bio-pic based on her life, with
Eleanor Parker playing the part of Lawrence, and the American soprano Eileen
Farrell singing the arias for her on the soundtrack.

Many singers at the Met noticed that Beecham had mellowed since the previous season, a change they ascribed to his marital happiness. Comments at rehearsal had become more good-humoured. 'You are addressing a charming young lady', he reminded a tenor, 'not the US Senate. This is no Friends, Romans, Countrymen affair.'[81] No one had more reason to be grateful for this new-found benevolence than the Met audition-winner, Patrice Munsel, who at the age of only eighteen sang Philine in Ambroise Thomas's *Mignon* under Beecham's direction and in doing so became the youngest singer ever to make his or her debut in a principal role at the house. Some critics wrote her off before she had even stepped on stage, but Beecham was supportive throughout the rehearsals.

On the first night, 4 December 1943, Munsel, perhaps over-confident, made a potentially disastrous blunder in the polonaise, 'Je suis Titania', when she sang the aria's second set of coloratura variations, rather than the first, thus making an inadvertent cut of some 40 bars. Beecham shouted out an instruction that got the orchestra to the right place, with the result that everyone ended up together. Munsel, who received an ovation for the aria lasting almost seven minutes, did not realise she had made a mistake until she was told about it during the interval by the stage-director, Désiré Defrère. She waited in trepidation for a tirade from Beecham but, though she sang in eight further performances of *Mignon* with him, it never came. She could only assume he knew that, if he were to bawl her out, she might lose her confidence for ever.[82] As it was, she sang with the company for fourteen seasons. A recording of the second performance of *Mignon*, a matinée on Christmas Day 1943, finds Munsel singing the polonaise with aplomb and without mishap, crowning it with a fizzing top F. That night the Beechams gave a Christmas dinner in their apartment for a few friends, including Virgil Thomson, Lauritz Melchior and his wife, Kleinchen, and Cecil Roberts. It marked the end of a year that had brought them great contentment.

At the fifth performance of *Mignon* on 5 February 1944, Beecham was disconcerted to find that Risë Stevens, in the title-role, was never where he expected her to be on stage. At the interval he went to her dressing-room and demanded an explanation. Nervously, she confessed to him that she was pregnant and that her doctor had told her to be careful. Beecham put his arms round her. 'My dear', he said, 'you must not do a single thing that is uncomfortable for you.' For the rest of the opera he followed her with his eyes like a hawk. When in Act 3 she affected to faint, she was surprised to find the Lothario, Nicola Moscona, supporting her, so that she did not have to slide to the floor. Beecham had tipped him off.[83]

Beecham sealed his reputation at the Met with revivals of Offenbach's *Contes d'Hoffmann* and Verdi's *Falstaff*. *Hoffmann*'s fine cast included Jobin in the title-role, Munsel as Olympia, Djanel as Giulietta, Jarmila Novotna as Antonia, Pinza as both Coppelius and Dr Miracle, and the French baritone, Martial Singher, as Dappertutto. Virgil Thomson wrote that Beecham conducted 'with a fire and a sweep as have not been heard at the Metropolitan since Toscanini left its pit some twenty-five years ago.' [84] A recording of the seventh performance on 26 February 1944 fully justifies Thomson's enthusiasm. Just before the end of the opera there is a typical example of the care Beecham lavished on the piece. He gives the spoken role of the Muse, not as is customary to the Nicklausse (in this case the American mezzo Lucielle Browning), but to the French-speaking Djanel, who delivers the lines over the orchestral accompaniment with a sinuous grandeur that evokes the style of a long-vanished epoch.

Falstaff was sung in an English translation that was largely Beecham's own work. The cast was all-American, apart from two Australians, John Brownlee as Ford and John Dudley as Dr Caius. The title-role was sung first by Lawrence Tibbett and then by Leonard Warren, who had been coached by Beecham himself and was by all accounts the better of the two. There were only twelve days of rehearsal, very little for this archetypal ensemble opera, bearing in mind that many of the singers were young and new to their roles. Nonetheless, Beecham, cigar in mouth, sitting on a chair with his head tilted back, remained calm and genial throughout as the producer, Herbert Graf, rehearsed the cast on the Met's 'roof-stage', high up above the house's main stage.

Beecham was full of suggestions. Above all he insisted on clear words. 'Don't think of notes', he urged Eleanor Steber, the Mistress Ford. 'Don't think of tone. Think only of words. The words cannot be too distinct.' [85] A recording of the third performance (with Warren) reveals English diction of unusual clarity. Oscar Thompson wrote of the first night that Beecham 'conducted expertly and with his accustomed spirit. The pace was fast, though perhaps not so fast as Toscanini's in the revival of 1908–09.' [86] The recording suggests that for the most part, if Beecham's pace had been any faster, it would have been beyond the capabilities of most singers and orchestral players alive or dead. The ensemble that closes the first act comes within a hair's breadth of coming apart as it is.

When the season closed at the end of March 1944, the company went out on tour and Ballet Theatre moved into the Metropolitan Opera House, where Beecham conducted nine performances of the one-act ballet *Romeo and Juliet*, choreographed by Antony Tudor to the music of Delius. Two years earlier he had helped Tudor to select the music for it – *Over the Hills and Far Away*, *The Walk to the Paradise Garden*, *Eventyr*, the *Irmelin* prelude and *Brigg Fair* – though it was Antal Dorati, the company's music director, who welded the pieces into a surprisingly successful score for dancing and subsequently conducted the ballet's premiere in April 1943.* Beecham knew Tudor's work because during the 1939 season at Covent Garden his dance company had taken part in *The Bartered Bride*, *La traviata* and (with the young Margot Fonteyn) *Aida*.

Edwin Denby of the *Tribune* wrote of the first night that with Beecham in the pit the two British principals, Alicia Markova and Hugh Laing, danced their roles less well than they had the year before, when the music had been played 'less as a show piece; more as a high-grade soundtrack'.[87] Markova took a different view of the conductor's contribution: 'Beecham knew that Delius's music must be allowed to "breathe" and he adopted the concert tempi for the score, rather than the sometimes faster speeds that had been taken for our [previous] performances. The music became so *sostenuto* that Hugh Laing used to mutter to me, "I'm going to die during these lifts", as he held me in his arms. One night Sir Thomas was particularly caught up in the music, but, despite the slowness of the tempi, the music did not disintegrate. ... I was in seventh heaven at such inspired accompaniment. The stage management, however, was not. We had run fourteen minutes over time on this one ballet – and extra fees loomed for the musicians.'[88]

Although Beecham was now enjoying great artistic success in America, it was also a time of acute frustration for him, for he was only too aware that if he were to play any significant role in the reconstruction of Britain's post-war musical life, he would have to make a move as soon as possible. Barbirolli had already left America for Manchester, where he would achieve notable success in restoring both his own fortunes and those of the Hallé Orchestra. No one could predict when exactly the war would end, though the allies were now confident that victory would eventually be theirs. Beecham had learned from Thomas Russell that the London Philharmonic would welcome him back as a conductor, though he would have to accept that he would not be given overall control. He was keen to accept the offer, but there still remained the problem of the Idaho divorce.

Beecham hit on a compromise. Rather than return to Britain, he would invite the London Philharmonic to tour America and Canada with him, an idea that appealed to the orchestra. He enlisted the help of Andrew Schulhof, who had managed his affairs at Boosey & Hawkes until he had lost his job in an office putsch, and was now working for a dairy company in California. When Schulhof put out feelers about the feasibilty of such a tour, the response from promoters all over North America was so enthusiastic that Beecham felt confident

---

* In her autobiography, *Distant Dances* (New York, 1980), Sono Osato, who danced the role of Rosaline at the premiere, makes the often repeated claim that no scores of the Delius works were available in America during the war, with the result that Dorati had to transcribe all of them, note by note, from Beecham's pre-war recordings. In fact, the only work Dorati transcribed was *Over the Hills and Far Away*, which was to remain unpublished until 1950.

enough to tell the press that it would take place in either September or October 1944, with concerts in at least twenty-six cities, stretching from Halifax in Nova Scotia to Kansas City.

Beecham brought Schulhof to New York to work on detailed planning. No sooner had he arrived than Beecham told him that he would also like him to become his manager, with responsibility for his business affairs in all countries except the United Kingdom; he could represent other artists as well, but for the time being Beecham was to be the sole conductor on the books. Schulhof immediately set about bringing order to Beecham's financial affairs. He negotiated higher fees for him, and used a portion of them to start paying off Sir Thomas's accumulated debts. He also insisted on Beecham's honouring all contracts he signed.

The British embassy in Washington reacted with alarm to news of the tour, for although it would not be too difficult to ship an orchestra from Britain to America, getting it home again would be next to impossible. With preparations for an invasion of France already well advanced, practically all allied shipping sailing from the United States to Britain was now crammed with service personnel and equipment. On 3 January 1944 the embassy cabled the Foreign Office in London, urging it not to approve the tour, because of 'the distress and ill-feeling which would be caused if we had to give 100 berths on eastbound ships to orchestra players at the expense of the unhappy people who have been waiting for so long to go home'.[89] The Ministry of Information warned the LPO about the official disquiet, only to be told by Thomas Russell that Beecham was already pressing the United States Government to issue an official invitation. The Foreign Office warned Washington that this 'might prove embarrassing'.

Beecham visited the Washington embassy on 25 January to discuss the situation. Disingenuously, he led officials to believe that it was not he, but American musical institutions that had invited the orchestra to the United States, and that the 'initiative and undertaking' were entirely theirs. He claimed that the embassy's worries about the return journey were immaterial, since the orchestra could get engagements in the United States and Canada for an indefinite period. The embassy was sceptical about the claims of 'this vigorous conductor', and a week later cabled the Foreign Office, saying that it had learned that the US State Department's Cultural Relations Department was 'not at all keen on [the] project though prepared to co-operate if it has your support'.

At the end of February the Foreign Office complained to the embassy that it was under 'high telegraphic pressure' from Beecham, who apparently had secured support for the tour from Britain's Minister of Production, Oliver Lyttelton. Beecham now planned to start it on 15 September 1944 with a three-week visit to Canada, followed by ten weeks in the United States. The Governor-General of Canada and the Canadian Government, he claimed, had both welcomed the project. It is doubtful if that was the case, for on 10 March the British High Commission in Ottawa cabled London, saying that, quite apart from the transport problem, it would be imprudent for the orchestra to be touring Canada at a time when the Canadian Army might be suffering heavy casualties in the invasion.

The *coup de grâce* was delivered a fortnight later by Richard Law, Britain's Under-Secretary of State for Foreign Affairs and, ironically, a friend of the Beechams. (Two of his sons were at Eaglebrook School with Jeremy.) In a cable marked 'secret', which was sent via the ambassador, Lord Halifax, Law informed Beecham that the tour could not be allowed to take place. It was a set-back, though Humby, in a letter to Halifax, said that her husband had taken the news 'grandly'. She asked if the tour might be postponed until April 1945, but Halifax turned down that idea, too. As a result Beecham decided there was nothing for it but to accept Russell's invitation to conduct the LPO in Britain, whatever the consequences, and a date was set for a tour of English towns beginning on 18 September 1944. Beecham would remain in Britain for three months and then return to the United States to fulfil a contract he had signed for a series of concerts with the Rochester Philharmonic Orchestra. The embassy promised to help secure passages for the Beechams.

It is a sign of Beecham's trust in his new wife that, instead of writing to Halifax himself, he left the job to her. By now she was writing quite a number of letters on his behalf. After hearing that Wilfred Pelletier would be conducting *Carmen* in Cleveland during the Met tour, Humby, jealously guarding what she believed to be her husband's exclusive territory, fired off an imperious complaint to Edward Johnson: 'Perhaps you would be good enough to let me know if there is any truth in the announcement as I am obliged to tell you that my husband cannot allow such a thing.'[90]

The invasion of Normandy started on 6 June, D-Day. A fortnight later Beecham began a week of outdoor concerts at the Lewisohn Stadium in New York. At the first, Mayor La Guardia told the 16,600-strong audience that the concerts were living proof that 'no dictator or group of dictators can interrupt the continuity of interpretative art in our country', while Fritz Kreisler played what one reviewer called his 'strangely altered and truncated' version of the Tchaikovsky Violin Concerto.[91] No sooner were the concerts over than Beecham was in Cincinnati, where in temperatures that soared to 35 degrees centigrade he conducted *Pagliacci*, *Carmen* and *Aida*, with casts drawn mainly from the Met. Jobin was the Canio and Don José, Djanel the Carmen, and Rose Bampton the Aida. The operas were given at the Pavilion, in the grounds of the city's zoo. The building was open-sided and from time to time the performances were punctuated – not inappropriately in *Aida* – by the cries of lions, elephants and seals.

An even more unusual operatic enterprise was planned for July, a two-week 'Festival Mozart' in Mexico City, arranged by a private, non-profit-making organisation called Opera de México and underwritten by the Mexican government. It was designed as an Anglo-American-Mexican gesture of solidarity.* Two performances each of *Don Giovanni*, *Die Zauberflöte* and *Le nozze de Figaro* were to be slotted into the Mexican Opera Nacional's regular season at the Palacio de Bellas Artes. Beecham was to be the sole conductor, with casts from the Met with Mexican reinforcements.

Beecham travelled to Mexico City early, in order to acclimatise himself to its high altitude. It was just as well he did. He was due to open with *Don Giovanni*, but discovered on arrival that the Opera Nacional had scheduled its own performance of the same work for the night before, with Jascha Horenstein conducting. Beecham promptly postponed his season by a week. On starting rehearsals with the Opera Nacional's orchestra, he found that not only was it bedevilled by the deputy system, but many of its players habitually arrived late. One morning when he gave the down-beat to begin, the orchestra failed to react. Beecham asked what was wrong. 'We don't have the music', said one of the players. 'The librarian hasn't turned up.' Trying to impart his own ideas about *Don Giovanni* to an orchestra that had Horenstein's reading in its head was not easy. 'You know what we do with a musician like him in England?', Beecham asked *Time*'s Mexican correspondent. 'We clap him in the Tower!' Stage-rehearsals also had their unnerving moments. One of the Mexicans in *Don Giovanni* carried a loaded pistol, because the father of a man he had shot dead some weeks earlier in an *affaire d'honneur* was threatening vengeance. Fortunately Andrew Schulhof was on hand to help Beecham sort out problems and calm nerves.

'I am willing to admit that there is an opera house here', Beecham told a local reporter, 'but nobody seems to be in charge of it.' The British ambassador thought that Beecham would be justified if he were to throw in the towel, but the conductor had no intention of doing so. Far from being downcast, he revelled in the situation. He was even more cheerful after the first night, for it was widely agreed that his performance of *Don Giovanni* had outclassed Horenstein's. Indeed, the 'festival' was such a success that it was extended by a week. After a final performance of *Figaro* on 16 August, the Mexican government gave a dinner in Beecham's honour, at which he was presented with a silver cigar-box inscribed with the message, 'Salud y Alegria' ('Health and Happiness'). After

---

* Mexico had declared war on the Axis powers in June 1942. Its main contribution to the war-effort was the supply of oil and raw materials to the United States, but it also provided air-support during the struggle for control of the Philippines in 1945.

the guests had gone, Beecham handed it to Andrew Schulhof's wife, Belle. 'Mrs Schulhof', he said, 'may I present you with this precious box. I think you and your husband deserve it for making this very peculiar Mozart festival possible.'[92]

The Mozart operas should have been Beecham's final engagement before returning to Britain for his concert tour. Rehearsals were due to begin in London on 13 September, but he had still not managed to secure a transatlantic passage. From Mexico he fired off cables to friends in London who, he hoped, might be able to put pressure on the authorities. The Tory MP Beverley Baxter recalled receiving one that read something like: 'Here in Mexico, the only country which has the faintest idea of how to govern itself, I ask you to stir up those senile but amiable folk masquerading as Ministers in Westminster. I wish to come home.'[93] But in Whitehall and Westminster Beecham's pleas must have seemed of low priority as the allied armies fought for the upper hand in France. Just before leaving Mexico City Beecham received an urgent message from the Hollywood Bowl, asking if he would conduct four concerts with the Los Angeles Philharmonic in place of Artur Rodzinski, who had suddenly withdrawn from the engagement for no clear reason. Beecham took the Mexicana night-flight to Los Angeles in a DC-3 fitted out with sleeping-berths and dubbed the 'Palacio Aereo'. It seems he had not flown before.

Artur Rubinstein was the soloist at the first concert on 22 August, Jascha Heifetz at the last one a week later. Star-soloists of this calibre tended to make Beecham nervous – probably because he knew they were even bigger crowd-pullers than he was – and his nervousness often manifested itself in truculence. When Heifetz, whom he had kept waiting to rehearse, went to the conductor's room before the first run-through of Vieuxtemps's Violin Concerto no. 4, he found Beecham looking through the score. 'What on earth are you doing playing garbage like this?', asked Beecham, who had not conducted the piece before. Heifetz was speechless.[94] Rubinstein was infuriated by having to sit at the piano doing nothing, while Beecham rehearsed the orchestral part of Tchaikovsky's B flat minor Piano Concerto in minute and, what seemed to Rubinstein, quite unnecessary detail. He got his own back at the end of the rehearsal, when Beecham asked him for a lift. Rubinstein, an experienced driver, pretended to be very nervous at the wheel. He warned his passenger that he had only received his driver's licence that very morning. When Beecham pointed out a red light to him, he affected not to have seen it. According to Rubinstein's own account, Beecham was 'sweating with anxiety', and at the end of the journey 'tottered out unsteadily, gave me a murderous look, and whispered, "Thank you".'[95]

Immediately after the second concert at the Bowl the Beechams returned to New York, where they were told that at last a passage to Britain had been found for them and that they should be ready to leave within a matter of days. On 7 September 1944 they underwent a second marriage ceremony, this time before a judge of the Supreme Court of the State of New York, rather than a lowly police-court justice. One of the witnesses was Herbert M. Karp, Beecham's New York lawyer, who issued a brief statement: 'Sir Thomas's attorneys believed that to assure compliance with technicalities of the English law it was advisable that a second marriage ceremony be performed at this time.'[96]

On the following day, in the port of Philadelphia, the Beechams boarded a Dutch freighter loaded with military vehicles that was bound eventually for Liverpool. The vessel took three days to reach New York, where on 11 September it joined fifty-nine other ships that were being assembled to form convoy HX 308, which set sail two days later. The crossing took fifteen days, a little longer than anticipated. On the day after leaving New York, the convoy was caught by a hurricane that had already caused devastation along North America's east coast from the Carolinas to Canada; five vessels had to return to port. Beecham reported that 'the boat stood up on end'. To add to the convoy's problems, there was the need to take evasive action against Germany's new long-distance submarines fitted with snorkels, which, though the main Battle of the Atlantic was over, posed a dangerous threat that could not be ignored. Lurking marauders were detected on three separate occasions and corvettes escorting the convoy dropped depth-charges to deter them.[97]

To while away the time in his cramped cabin, Beecham wrote a ballad of sixty-two stanzas, printed in the ship's journal, chronicling an occasion in the ship's history when a group of Australian passengers defied the captain's orders not to go ashore at Colombo:

> They tore off every stitch they had.
>   For no one they cared two hoots.
> They leapt through the portholes, coo-eed like mad.
>   And swam in their birthday suits.[98]

The convoy arrived intact in Liverpool on 28 September. One of the first things Beecham did on landing was to visit a barber, where an enterprising reporter from the London *Evening News* found him swathed in a white sheet. 'I always come to Liverpool', said Beecham, 'even if it's only for a shave.'[99]

CHAPTER 17

The Royal Years

THOMAS RUSSELL, the LPO's chairman and organiser, met the Beechams in Liverpool and travelled with them to London by train. Beecham seemed unsure as to how he should comport himself in wartime Britain, asking Russell if it was all right to be seen in public smoking a large cigar. Russell thought it would be. They were met at Euston by Betty Humby's parents and her son Jeremy, now thirteen, who had returned from America three months earlier with a group of evacuee schoolchildren. Because of the delays, Beecham had arrived two and a half weeks late for the LPO tour, and Basil Cameron had already conducted six of the concerts in his place. Beecham had no time to waste. His first concert was scheduled to take place in three days' time at Watford, to be followed immediately by dates in Leeds, Huddersfield, Sheffield and Peterborough, where blocks of seats had been bought up by the surrounding American camps for the use of servicemen.

At sixty-five, Beecham seemed in excellent physical shape, apart from his gout. On the morning after his arrival he was at Wembley Town Hall to start two full days of rehearsals.* On the second morning, making a particularly vigorous swish with his baton during Sibelius's Sixth Symphony, he drove it straight into his left hand. The tip broke off and had to be removed at the local hospital. Undeterred, Beecham returned for the afternoon rehearsal with his hand stitched and bandaged and his arm in a sling. His hand was still bandaged for the Watford concert.

The LPO, now led by Jean Pougnet, had changed considerably since 1940. Only eighteen of its seventy-five members had played at Beecham's last concert before leaving for Australia. Russell had given up playing, and was concerned solely with administration. He had joined the Communist party, but his new political affiliation in no way affected his admiration for the seigneurial Beecham. Russell had long hoped for his return, and in a preface to the printed programmes for the tour prophesied that he would 'bring back to British orchestral playing the high qualities of delicacy and brilliance which the pressure of

---

* Earlier in the year, in a remarkable gesture considering wartime stringency, the Committee for the Encouragement of Music and the Arts (CEMA) decided to provide Britain's orchestras with subsidies that would allow them to give slightly fewer concerts and hold more rehearsals, which in turn would help to raise performing standards. In 1945 CEMA became the Arts Council of Great Britain.

war-time routine work has done much to lose.' For the time being Beecham was content to accept that he was now reliant for work on one of his old employees. He was just pleased to be home again, if only for three months, and conducted his first batch of concerts without fee.

Beecham adapted easily to the privations and shortages of wartime Britain, though he was unnerved by the German V2 rockets, which caused havoc until March 1945. He was relieved that the validity of his American marriage was not being questioned. Dora Labbette, anticipating that on his arrival he would be arrested for bigamy, had decided that their son Paul would be known as Paul Strang, rather than Paul Beecham, so as to shield him from the publicity that would inevitably follow such a dramatic development. (After divorcing her husband, Labbette had continued to use her married surname, Strang.)

If audiences felt any residual resentment about Beecham's long absence in America, it was soon dissipated. Following the death of Henry Wood the previous August, he was once again the undisputed doyen of British conductors. The Royal Albert Hall was crowded for his first London concert on 7 October, which as well as the Sibelius Sixth included the *Carnaval romain* overture, *Brigg Fair* and Mozart's Symphony no. 34. The playing was not perfect but, wrote *The Times*, nothing like the Berlioz overture under Beecham's 'fiery direction' had been heard in London since he went away. When the programme was repeated in Birmingham ten days later, the *Post*'s reviewer Eric Blom found that in the LPO's playing there was 'none of that listlessness, born of various trying circumstances, one has had on occasion to deplore of late'.

The tour continued to Nottingham and Leicester, Oxford and Wembley, Coventry and Bristol. Beecham also started recording again after a gap of two years. The Petrillo ban had been lifted, and his contract with RCA Victor reactivated. The ensuing series of recordings, made for RCA by its British associate HMV, included several works that Beecham had not recorded before: Beethoven's Fourth Symphony, Schubert's Sixth (so little known in Britain that *The Gramophone*'s review of it filled almost a page) and, perhaps best of all, Mendelssohn's Fifth, the 'Reformation', not an easy work to pull off, but in Beecham's hands remarkable for its structural cohesion.[1] The recordings provided welcome extra income for the orchestra and brought Walter Legge back into Beecham's orbit. Legge, who had not been called up because of poor eyesight, had spent the war running the musical side of ENSA, the organisation that provided entertainment for the forces, while simultaneously working part-time for EMI.

Humby made her first appearance with the LPO on 29 November in Bristol, playing a four-movement piano concerto, based on music by Handel, that Beecham had written for her in America. Full of bravura and unashamed romanticism, it is the most outrageous of his Handel arrangements (Beecham called it a '*de*rangement'), but fun for those prepared to suspend temporarily their musicological preconceptions. After a further performance in London the Beechams recorded it.*

Christmas 1944 was spent at Studio Cottage, which Humby had built before the war at Selsey on the Sussex coast, though visits to it became sporadic when it was discovered that Dora Labbette was living only five miles away at Sidlesham. By the New Year Beecham should have been on his way to America, where the first concert of his visit was scheduled for 18 January 1945 at Rochester, but there was no chance of his arriving in time for it, because once again it was proving difficult to get a passage. He was left kicking his heels in London, unable to accept concert dates in case he had to leave suddenly. The delay gave him time to start a duel with the Hallé Concerts Society that was to provide a good deal of amusement and leave its chairman, the textile manufacturer Philip Godlee, with egg on his face.

The origins of the dispute went back to 1934, when Beecham, acting as the Hallé's chief guest conductor following Hamilton Harty's resignation, had been made the orchestra's honorary president in succession to Elgar and, before him, A. J. Balfour. He took the post more seriously than either of his predecessors, addressing at least two annual general meetings, handing out advice and conducting a large number of the concerts, which he continued to do until December 1939. When, four years later, Barbirolli returned from America to rejuvenate the orchestra – a task he carried out with considerable skill – it irked him that Beecham of all people should still be president. He made it clear to Godlee that he wanted Beecham removed from office.[2]

Hearing in July 1944 that Beecham was soon to return to Britain, Godlee wrote belatedly to tell him that in his absence his tenure of the presidency had been 'allowed to lapse', and that Manchester's Lord Mayor was to take his place. Beecham did not answer the letter (he may not even have received it), but as soon as he reached London in October he informed the press about the decision to unseat him – much to the embarrassment of Godlee, who had not got round to telling the Lord Mayor what was in store for him. His Worship declared himself 'amazed' at the news: it was, he said, the first he had heard of it.[3] Matters grew worse for Godlee when it became clear that a number of Hallé supporters wanted Beecham to remain as president. At the annual general meeting on 12 December 1944 Godlee side-stepped the issue, saying that further discussion would be postponed for two months, by which time, he hoped, a unanimous decision might be achieved 'in which Sir Thomas fully concurs'.

---

* Somm-Beecham CD 9. The concerto, first performed at New York's Town Hall on 15 March 1944, uses themes from clavichord and harpsichord pieces and music from *Il pastor fido*, *Ottone* and *Teseo*.

In an attempt to secure this concurrence, the orchestra's general manager Ernest Bean was dispatched to Liverpool, where Beecham was conducting two concerts with the Liverpool Philharmonic. In the course of a forty-minute discussion at the Adelphi Hotel (Bean described it as being more like 'a fantastic monologue') Beecham made it quite clear that he had no intention of giving in. The Hallé could not depose him – he was president for life. Each member of Godlee's 'ridiculous' committee would be served with a writ, and the matter would go to Chancery. He called Barbirolli 'an upstart'. The astonished but admiring Bean reported to Godlee that Beecham's harangue 'was as exhilarating as riding on the war-head of a V2, but of course it made mincemeat of my mission'. [4]

The committee was now convinced that Beecham was 'nursing a personal vendetta' against Barbirolli,[5] which at least evened things up, since Beecham thought it was Barbirolli who was conducting the feud. On being given an 'expurgated' version of the Liverpool interview by Bean, Barbirolli vowed to obtain evidence from New York of Beecham's 'sliminess'.[6] In a parting shot before finally leaving for America, Beecham wrote to the *Manchester Guardian* saying that henceforth he would take a close interest in the Hallé's affairs, since it was only too obvious that it required guidance from someone who 'was not wholly without qualifications for the task'.[7] In a ludicrous twist to the story, it was discovered that there was no mention in the constitution of a president, so technically the post did not exist

On 29 August 1945 Beecham visited Manchester for the first time in six years to give a concert with the BBC Northern Orchestra at the Albert Hall. (The Free Trade Hall had been destroyed in an air-raid.) Inevitably he was asked by a reporter if he was still the Hallé's president. 'Of course I am', he replied. He had nothing but 'kind thoughts and benevolent intentions' towards the society, and was certain he could be of service. Reviewing the BBC concert, the *Guardian*'s critic wrote that what Beecham had 'so generously and brilliantly done for the city's music has set him firmly and forever in our affection'. After the final item, Brahms's Second Symphony, he was greeted with 'mighty and prolonged torrents of applause'.*

There is little doubt that if someone other than Barbirolli had been the Hallé's conductor, Beecham would not have pursued the matter to such farcical lengths, because, whatever his faults, he was not normally a man who looked backwards

---

* The Hallé Society finally invited Beecham to give two concerts in Manchester under its auspices in 1955 – pointedly not with the Hallé Orchestra itself, but the RPO. When Beecham walked on to the platform for the first concert, the entire audience rose to its feet. 'He responded with a noise that matched the welcome,' wrote the *Guardian*'s critic, Colin Mason. 'The sound of the National Anthem would have quelled a rebellion' (3 November 1955).

or harboured grudges. That Barbirolli had effectively kept him away from the New York Philharmonic still rankled. Beecham's relations with other conductors were usually cordial and he enjoyed their foibles as much as he did his own. He had his blind spots. He was known to call Toscanini 'Toscaninny' (the Italian maestro branded him 'Pagliaccio') and habitually referred to the teetotal conductor of the BBC Symphony Orchestra as 'Dame Boult'. 'Adrian was there', he once said famously, 'reeking of Horlicks.' Boult disapproved of Beecham, whom he considered irresponsible. But it had never stopped Beecham being invited to conduct the BBC orchestra, or Boult appearing with the pre-war LPO.

It was not until the beginning of February 1945 that Beecham and Betty finally sailed for America. They sailed from Gourock on the Clyde estuary aboard the *Queen Mary*, camouflaged with grey paint and filled with wounded American troops returning to the United States. It is not known how the berths were secured, but clearly Beecham had contacts in high places. He arrived too late for his first two scheduled dates with the Rochester Philharmonic, but was able to give the third on 15 February and then took the orchestra on a tour of ten concerts starting at Utica, New York, which must have caused a wry smile.

Next came a series of Saturday afternoon concerts with the American Broadcasting Company's orchestra at the Ritz Theatre on West 48th Street. The second, on 14 April, became a memorial concert for President Roosevelt, whose funeral in Washington was taking place at the same time. The programme, chosen by Beecham himself, began with the Funeral March from *Götterdämmerung* and also included Schubert's 'Unfinished' Symphony, during which the transmission was interrupted for a report on the obsequies. For a vigorous, optimistic ending – the Allies had crossed the Rhine and the final phase of the war in Europe had begun – Beecham turned to Berlioz's Trojan March.

At the conclusion of the concert Beecham travelled eight blocks south to the Metropolitan Opera House, where that night he conducted the third of six performances of Antony Tudor's Delius ballet, *Romeo and Juliet*. He had been invited to take on the revival in compensation for Theatre Ballet's failure, for financial reasons, to mount the ballet *The Great Elopement*, set in the Bath of Beau Nash, for which Beecham had fulfilled a commission to provide both the scenario and a score based on the music of Handel.* The cancellation of *The Great Elopement* was a blow for Beecham, for he had expected to benefit handsomely from future royalties.[8]

---

* For *The Great Elopement* Beecham arranged and orchestrated music from various operas and the suites for harpsichord. He conducted fourteen of the nineteen numbers for the first time at Rochester in March 1945, and later that year recorded twelve of them with the LPO. In the 1950s he recorded the complete score, now called *Love in Bath,* with the Royal Philharmonic Orchestra.

VE Day on 7 May 1945, marking the German surrender and the end of the war in Europe, found Beecham in San Francisco. He and Betty had arrived that morning by train from the East for three concerts at the city's cavernous Civic Auditorium with a pick-up ensemble called the People's Symphony Orchestra. Many of its players were engaged in war-work at the local shipyards and factories. All tickets cost 50 cents (£3.53) plus 10 cents tax. What, the press asked Beecham, did he think about the end of the war in Europe? 'I'm so happy,' he said, 'I can hardly contain myself.' And 50-cent concerts? 'Just the idea of a millionaire seated next to the crossing-sweeper has always appealed to me.'[9] They were his last engagements of the visit.

The Beechams arrived back in London on 2 June by air, though there is no record of how they managed such a feat – America and Britain were still at war with Japan, and severe travel restrictions were still in place. They had bought for £8,000 (£180,600) a dilapidated but beautiful mid-nineteenth century house called Overnoons at Lodsworth, near Petworth, in Sussex. Beecham described it to his son Adrian, who it seems helped with its purchase, as being a manor of moderate proportions with two cottages, a tennis court and about eighty acres of garden, meadow and woodland.[10] Why the Beechams needed such a large place – for much of the year Jeremy was away at Eton – is not clear. The train service was poor, and after about two years they moved to London, to 39 Circus Road in St John's Wood, close to the Abbey Road studios and handy for the railway stations.

Virgil Thomson, on a trip to Europe for the *Herald-Tribune*, went to visit the Beechams at Overnoons, but first called on Lady Cunard. The Grosvenor Square house had been damaged by bombing, and she was now living in a seventh-floor suite at the Dorchester, cluttered with what was left of her furniture. Though her fortune had been greatly reduced, and her most valuable jewels long sold, she was still entertaining her friends as best she could in rationed Britain. She asked Thomson if he would be seeing Beecham, and extracted a promise that he would bring her news of him.[11] Thomson could not possibly have conveyed to her his true impressions, which he recorded in his memoirs: 'There is no question that at this time of Beecham's life, aged sixty-six, his still vast energies were better nurtured by a young wife-secretary-housekeeper-muse-companion and all-purpose Egeria than they would have been by a driving and driven ex-social leader of his age. For Betty was above all a musician ... and wholly occupied with Beecham and his life. No dinners with cabinet ministers and powerful ladies, no spending of money just for the fun. ... Betty's usefulness to Thomas was complete, and Emerald knew it.' Emerald died of throat cancer three years later, still mourning the loss of Beecham. Her ashes were scattered in Grosvenor Square.

VJ Day, 14 August 1945, when the war finally ended, after the dropping of atomic bombs on Hiroshima and Nagasaki, came between concerts at Swindon and Walthamstow. Beecham seemed to be everywhere, conducting as well as the LPO the Liverpool, Scottish and both the BBC Symphony and BBC Northern orchestras, On 18 November he even gave his first concert since 1932 with the London Symphony Orchestra, which had ended the war in rather worse condition than the LPO. It had still not forgiven Beecham for his 'treachery', but could not afford to lose the date, a Sunday afternoon promotion of Harold Holt's at the Royal Albert Hall.

In the same month Beecham and the LPO went to Paris, Antwerp and Brussels for concerts celebrating the end of the war. His programmes included the Four Sea Interludes and the Passacaglia from Benjamin Britten's opera *Peter Grimes*, which had had its triumphant premiere at the reopening of Sadler's Wells Theatre on 7 June, exactly a month after VE Day. Beecham had not been keen to conduct the *Grimes* excerpts, but eventually agreed to do so. During the Channel crossing he suggested to the orchestra's librarian that the parts might quietly be dropped into the sea. It is conceivable that he was jealous that one of the most significant events in British operatic history had occurred without his participation. Beecham would conduct only one other work of Britten's, the revised version of the Violin Concerto, whose first performance he gave in December 1951, with Bronsilav Gimpel as soloist. He took great pains over it, conducting it at concerts in Nottingham and Leicester before bringing it to London for a Royal Philharmonic Society concert on 12 December.

While the LPO was in France and Belgium, the Paris Conservatoire Orchestra came to Britain for a short tour with Charles Munch. On 11 November the orchestras swapped conductors: Munch conducted the LPO in Paris; Beecham the French orchestra in London. Munch's programme included Walton's (first) Symphony, Beecham's included Méhul and Berlioz. The initiative for the highly successful exchange came from Russell and the LPO's secretary, Felix Aprahamian,* with support from the French embassy in London, but with strong opposition from the British Council's music advisory committee, which 'categorically' refused to sponsor the tour because Beecham's 'irresponsible utterances are more potentially dangerous than his musicianship can possibly outweigh'. The Council thought that a gala concert with Constant Lambert and the Brussels orchestra would be a much better bet for Anglo-Belgian relations, 'particularly if we also sent Willie Walton to conduct his concerto with [Arthur] Grumiaux [a leading Belgian violinist] playing it.'[12] The pettifoggers on the advisory committee – Walton was one of its members – had no cause for concern. Beecham did not put a diplomatic foot wrong.

---

* Beecham found Aprahamian's wide knowledge of the French musical scene invaluable.

Though Russell did not know it, Beecham had for some time been planning to end his relationship with the LPO. Given the way in which the orchestra was managed, he could not see how its standard of playing, decent though it was, could be raised still further. To get what he wanted, he would have to form a new orchestra of his own. Beecham thought it might be possible to co-operate with Walter Legge, who was also thinking of starting an orchestra, albeit one of modest proportions. Legge was not uninterested. During the war he had set up the Philharmonia String Quartet for the purpose of making gramophone records. His new creation, to be called the Philharmonia Orchestra, would fulfil the same purpose, though it would also give concerts. Legge had been promised financial backing, not by EMI, but by Sir Victor Schuster of the merchant-banking family. Beecham, Legge reckoned, could provide artistic clout. But Beecham thought Legge was on the wrong track

In January 1945 he wrote to Legge deprecating the idea of a moderate-sized orchestra, and declaring that he found the name Philharmonia 'slightly preposterous'. Instead he envisaged a full-scale ensemble that would equal the pre-war LPO, bear the name 'Beecham Symphony Orchestra' and eliminate all competition in the space of twelve months. Beecham urged Legge to discuss the matter with him as soon as possible.[13] Legge stuck firmly to his original plan, but invited Beecham to conduct the Philharmonia's first concert, an all-Mozart programme at the Kingsway Hall on 27 October 1945. Legge forgot to negotiate a fee, and it was not until after the concert was over that he asked Beecham how much he wanted. Beecham said that he had got so much pleasure from conducting the 'magnificent consort of artists' that he would settle for a decent cigar.[14]

To muster an orchestra, even one of only thirty-five players, was no mean achievement in 1945, when so many of the country's musicians were still in the forces. But thanks to his ENSA experience Legge knew just how to get the ones he wanted. More then half the players at the concert were still members of military bands and orchestras based around London. The RAF Central Band at Uxbridge was a particularly rich source of talent. One of its members, the twenty-four-year-old Dennis Brain, acted as the Philharmonia's startlingly good principal horn. A number of Legge's other players – among them the principal clarinet Reginald Kell,* the first bassoon John Alexandra, the first trumpet Harry Mortimer and timpanist James Bradshaw – were well known to Beecham from the old LPO and Hallé days

Two days after the concert, Victor Schuster invited Legge and Beecham to lunch at Boodle's club in St James's Street. According to Legge's account,

---

* Kell played Mozart's Clarinet Concerto at Beecham's concert, which also included the Symphony no. 40, the *Don Giovanni* Overture, the Divertimento in D K131, and five German Dances.

Beecham announced that he wanted to take over the Philharmonia and build it up into an orchestra of 'full symphonic strength'. He claimed that he had access to money and said that he was in negotiation with the Royal Philharmonic Society for the use of the name 'Royal Philharmonic Orchestra'. Both he and Legge would benefit from the royalties on the recordings he would make with it. Legge, taken aback, told Beecham that under no circumstances would he hand over his orchestra, though a way might be found to share the musicians. Beecham, says Legge, 'left angrily'.[15]

Beecham also had a brief flirtation with John Christie of Glyndebourne, who in 1944 had attempted, without success, to buy the freehold of the Royal Opera House. On the face of it he and Christie seemed unlikely partners. Rebuffed by Beecham when Glyndebourne first opened, Christie had lost no opportunity to criticise the pre-war international seasons at Covent Garden, while Beecham talked of 'Christie's minstrels'. But Christie had come round to Beecham, largely because of the kindness he and Betty had shown to his wife Audrey in North America during the war. Beecham proposed that they should collaborate on a season at Glyndebourne in the summer of 1946, and it was eventually agreed that there should be three operas: *Carmen* in French with dialogue, *Figaro* in Italian, and *Die Zauberflöte* in English or German. Carl Ebert would return to Glyndebourne as producer.

By December 1945, however, the project had collapsed, not least because Beecham found Christie's approach to casting unacceptable. For Carmen, Christie had been pressed by an old Glyndebourne stalwart, Roy Henderson, into accepting one of his former pupils, Kathleen Ferrier, a young contralto with no stage experience. Beecham went to hear her, but came away convinced that she was not the right choice. His reason for rejecting Ferrier as Carmen was expressed succinctly in a letter sent by Betty to Audrey Christie, which had undoubtedly been dictated by Beecham, for its style is unmistakable. No contralto, said the Humby–Beecham epistle, had 'ever succeeded in doing anything with the role but make a complete ass of herself'. As for Christie's proposed tenor for the role of Don José (unidentified in the letter), 'after about one half hour of solid singing he would, in his present condition, peter out and dry up decisively'. Beecham was not prepared to act 'as a kind of nurse in a species of musical kindergarten'.[16]*

Beecham gave his last-ever concert with the LPO on 29 December 1945 at the Albert Hall. By chance it was an all-Sibelius programme, just as his final concert with the original LPO had been in April 1940. In an attempt to keep Beecham,

---

* Despite Beecham's withdrawal, Glyndebourne did reopen in July 1946 with fourteen performances of Benjamin Britten's new opera *The Rape of Lucretia*. Ferrier scored a notable success as Lucretia, a role far more suited to her talent than Carmen.

Russell had offered him a contract as artistic director, but Beecham found its clauses insulting: all offers he received for outside work were to be approved by the LPO; he could not broadcast, make records or conduct opera without the LPO's agreement; the management would have the right to appoint an assistant conductor for preliminary rehearsals.[17] He rejected the contract out of hand.

Once again Beecham went with Betty to America, where this time he remained for four months, conducting concerts from Detroit to San Antonio, Texas. He also went to Havana and Montreal. Such visits would remain an important source of income. After returning to England on the *Queen Mary* at the beginning of May 1946, he spent most of the next three months drawing up plans for his new orchestra. The Royal Philharmonic Society agreed that it could be called the Royal Philharmonic Orchestra.*

Recordings were to play a crucial part in its financing. Andrew Schulhof in New York was instructed to negotiate a new contract with RCA Victor for the RPO to take over from the LPO as Beecham's recording orchestra. Since RCA was not interested in Delius, it was agreed that there could be a second contract, this time with HMV, for the purpose of recording the composer's music with subsidies from the Delius Trust – which was controlled by Beecham. Another step forward came with the Philharmonic Society's agreement that the new orchestra should play for most of its concerts. To take care of the RPO's burgeoning business affairs, Philip Emanuel set up a new company, Anglo American Music Association Ltd, with Morgan Humby, Betty's father, as chairman.

For Beecham it was vital that the new orchestra should succeed, for it had been brought home to him forcefully that his future lay primarily in the concert hall. Throughout the war years in America he had believed that one day he would return to Covent Garden, preferably with his own company. What he had not bargained for was that it would reopen as a state-supported theatre, run on the lines of the major European houses. A resident opera company was to start performing in 1947, but the new Covent Garden Trust, chaired by the economist Lord Keynes (who was also chairman of the fledgling Arts Council), had not invited Beecham to play any part in it, a snub that hurt him deeply, though he never admitted it publicly.†

The post of musical director would go instead to Karl Rankl, a refugee from Austria (he had a Jewish wife) who had spent the war in Britain, where he

---

* The society granted its permission for this in the most casual manner, but later secured an agreement that the title would be used only during Beecham's lifetime. After his death the society tried – but failed – to stop the orchestra using the name.

† The Opera House had reopened as a theatre on 20 February 1946 with *The Sleeping Beauty*, given by the Sadler's Wells Ballet Company with Margot Fonteyn and Robert Helpmann in the leading roles. Under Ninette de Valois the ballet company, now resident at the Opera House, held the fort until it was joined a year later by the new opera company.

conducted many concerts for the LPO. His appointment was a perfectly reasonable one, for at the time he was the only conductor in the country with the
experience to create a large full-time company in a state-funded opera house.
After acting as chorus master at Vienna's Volksoper under Weingartner and
assisting Klemperer at the Kroll Oper in Berlin, Rankl had been musical director at Wiesbaden, Graz and the German opera house in Prague. His main difficulty would be finding a sufficient number of decent British singers to form
a company. Largely on the insistence of one of the trustees, Edward Dent, all
operas would be sung in English, which at the time was not such an odd idea.
Most German and Italian houses sang the entire repertory in the vernacular.

Keynes and his colleagues on the board have been much criticised over the
years for employing Rankl rather than Beecham, but with hindsight their decision was undoubtedly the right one. All too often, at the BBC, at the Opera
House under Toye, with the self-governing LPO, Beecham had proved himself incapable of subjecting himself to the dictates of others. Committees and
bureaucracy were anathema to him, and at heart he did not approve of state
funding for the arts, without which the new Covent Garden could not possibly
function. What was unforgivable on the part of the trustees was that they did
not ask Beecham to conduct even a single guest performance during the initial
seasons, which was unfair to both him and the public. Four years would pass
before a new generation of opera-goers had the chance to hear Britain's finest
opera conductor at Covent Garden.

It was not in Beecham's nature to mope, and he concentrated all his energies
on the Royal Philharmonic, which he aimed to have ready by October 1946.
He needed some special event to launch it and, as much for practical reasons as
anything else, hit on the idea of a second Delius festival. It would not have the
attraction of the composer's presence, and might seem down-beat to a nation
that needed to be cheered up, but it would have one thing its 1929 predecessor
lacked, adequate funding. Beecham persuaded the Royal Phiharmonic Society
to sponsor the opening concert, and the BBC to pay for the last one, a performance of *A Mass of Life*. The rest of the money would come from the Delius
Trust.

Victor Olof, violinist, conductor and Decca record producer, was appointed
the RPO's general manager. Finding players would prove far harder than it had
been for Fred Laurence in 1932. The war was over, but demobilisation of the
armed forces would take a long time, while young musicians who might otherwise have attended music colleges were being called up to help keep the peace.
In the search for good principals, Beecham telephoned old colleagues, among
them Gerald Jackson and Archie Camden, who both came to the rescue. He
did a deal with Walter Legge, who agreed that Dennis Brain, Reginald Kell

and others could work for Beecham provided they were not required for the Philharmonia, which initially had few public engagements. For leader Beecham picked a former LSO player, John Pennington, who happened to be in London on holiday from America, where during the war he had led the Paramount Studio's orchestra in Hollywood. Legge reported to a colleague at EMI that 'the bold bad baronet' was bound to get a strong team, because he was offering star players £1 (£28.55) more per concert than the Philharmonia.[18]

The biggest problem was finding good rank-and-file string players. In the first week of September Beecham auditioned possible recruits at the Midland Hotel, Manchester. One of them was a violin student from the Royal Manchester College of Music called Martin Milner. Coming as he did from a family of teetotallers, the eighteen-year-old Milner was unsure what to make of the collection of empty Guinness bottles in Beecham's suite (Beecham was avoiding wine because of his gout.) He was also surprised to find Beecham still in his dressing-gown, even though it was afternoon. From the four concerto scores that Milner had brought along Beecham picked out the Elgar – and threw it into a chair on the other side of the room. Then, choosing the Brahms, he sat down at an upright piano. Together he and Milner went through the first movement and half the second. Beecham got up and rolled his eyes. Did Milner want to play some unaccompanied Bach? Yes, said Milner, the Chaconne, which he was allowed to play right through. Beecham asked him to join the orchestra as one of the first violins, and offered him £10 a week. Milner said he earned more than that freelancing, so Beecham, amused by the boy's Lancastrian cheek, said he would ask the BBC what it paid its players. The next morning he telephoned Milner – or 'Mr Milnah', as he always called him – at home. The BBC, said Beecham, paid its principals £14, its rank-and-file players £12. He would give Milner £13 (£370). Shortly afterwards Milner left for London to join the RPO, but after about a year, despite Beecham's constant efforts to stave off the authorities, he was called up for National Service.[19] Later he would lead the Hallé for twenty-nine years.

Since it was all but impossible to gauge the orchestra's true quality, Beecham thought it would be prudent, before bringing it to central London, to knock it into shape at venues out of the limelight. To this end, Harold Holt fixed up a series of concerts, to be given at fortnightly intervals on Saturday afternoons, at the Davis Theatre in Croydon High Street, which doubled as a cinema, and at 4,000 seats was one of the largest in the country. Not only would the concerts allow the orchestra to play itself in, they would provide it with much-needed work. Plans were at last unveiled to the public at a press conference at the Savoy Hotel on 15 August. The news that the Royal Philharmonic was to make its debut nine and half miles to the south of Charing Cross caused some raised eyebrows. Why Croydon? Beecham was asked. Why not? he said. It was 'a salubrious spot'. He had been told that when it came to concerts the Croydon public was 'splendid'.[20] (Though he did not mention it, he had given several concerts at the Davis with the LPO before leaving for Australia.)

Beecham's first rehearsal with the RPO was held on 11 September 1946, only four days before the opening concert, which was packed. There was no list of players in the programme – indeed a year was to pass before one appeared – an indication that Beecham anticipated changes. For the *Times* critic the orchestra's playing was 'not exceptional', though there was 'evidently the making of a fine instrument here'.* On returning to the Davis a month later for the third Croydon concert, the same critic wrote that the RPO was 'settling down into a coherent organization, though the string-tone is still lacking in both suavity and fire'. By now the orchestra had fifty-five contracted players, with the rest on probation.[21] To provide further experience, Beecham took it to Eastbourne, Folkestone, Margate, Oxford and Cambridge.

Seven weeks after its debut the RPO was ready for the opening of the Delius Festival on 26 October. In all there were seven concerts, five of them at the Albert Hall, two at Central Hall, Westminster, spread over six weeks. Beecham shared the conducting with Richard Austin, late of the Bournemouth Municipal Orchestra and son of Beecham's fellow Delius Trust adviser, Frederic Austin. For Richard Capell, Beecham's 'feeling for the music seemed to be more passionate than ever, and its expression of surpassing fineness. The [RPO] gave in the course of this series the best performances by far of the autumn's multifarious music-making. ... There were large audiences, though perhaps not such responsive ones as seventeen years before. The lack of Queen's Hall was painfully felt.'[22] Eric Fenby, who might have been expected to attend the festival, stayed away. He disapproved of Beecham's strong grip on the Delius Trust.

On 3 November 1946, between the first and second Delius concerts, Beecham made another appearance with the London Symphony Orchestra, this time at an event celebrating the diamond jubilee of the socialist Fabian Society at the Royal Albert Hall. He had been invited to conduct because of his membership of the society more than forty years earlier, when, said the meeting's chairman, the economist Harold Laski, Beecham had been 'young and revolutionary'. There were speeches by the Prime Minister, Clement Attlee, and three of his ministers, Herbert Morrison, Ellen Wilkinson and John Strachey. To the audience's surprise there was a fifth, unscheduled, speaker. After bringing the evening to an end with the *Carmen* suite, Beecham swung round and delivered

---

* The programme consisted of the *William Tell* overture, Mozart's 'Linz' Symphony, Delius's *Over the Hills and Far Away*, Tchaikovsky's *Romeo and Juliet* and a suite from Bizet's *Carmen*.

an impassioned plea for a proper concert hall for London. If the Government obliged, he said to laughter and applause, he might even consider re-entering the Fabian ranks.

As predicted, there were many changes in the RPO's membership over the next two years. Some like Kell left because they had other work; others, less skilled, were dropped overboard. The orchestra's woodwind line-up became second to none, earning the sobriquet 'the Royal Family', with Gerald Jackson, first flute, Terence MacDonagh, who came from the BBC Symphony Orchestra, first oboe, Jack Brymer, a former schoolmaster who had never previously played in a professional orchestra, first clarinet, and, as first bassoon, Gwydion Brooke, who after almost six years in the army without touching his instrument had joined the Liverpool Philharmonic, where Beecham found him. For first trumpet, Beecham desperately wanted another of the original LPO players, Richard Walton, but he was still with the Irish Guards band in Palestine and the army would not release him. In late 1947 Beecham at last secured his release with an angry telephone call to Emanuel Shinwell, Attlee's Secretary of State for War.

John Pennington had to leave the RPO after the Musicians' Union belatedly woke up to the fact that he was not one of its members, and was replaced as leader by his number two, Oscar Lampe, who came from London's East End. The son of Russian immigrants, he had few social graces, but his playing was prodigious. Beecham loved him both as a character and musician. Lampe had an ancient BMW with a supercharged engine, from which he had removed all the seats, except the driver's. To the amazement of the rest of the orchestra, Beecham accepted a lift home in it after a rehearsal, sitting on the floor next to Lampe.

Richard Strauss, who in October 1947 came to London for a festival of his works, was so delighted with Lampe's playing of the tailors' dance from the *Bourgeois gentilhomme* music at the opening concert at Drury Lane that he burst into spontaneous applause. Beecham, who was conducting, shushed him with a withering glance. At the end of the evening, to cries from the audience of 'Strauss, Strauss', the eighty-three-year-old composer came on to the platform, arm in arm with Beecham. He clapped the RPO and boomed in French, 'Merci! Merci! Merveilleux!' At a second Drury Lane concert Beecham conducted, for the only time in his career, the closing scene from *Ariadne auf Naxos* in its revised version, with Maria Cebotari as Ariadne, and Karl Friedrich as Bacchus.

The festival, arranged by Beecham and Ernst Roth, Strauss's publisher at Boosey & Hawkes, was foremost an act of reconciliation, but it also provided an opportunity for the composer, living in straitened circumstances in Switzerland, to collect some of the blocked royalties that had accrued to him during the war years. He arrived by air – the first time he had flown – and stayed for almost a fortnight, conducting a concert of his own works with the Philharmonia at the Albert Hall and a performance of *Till Eulenspiegel* with the BBC Symphony Orchestra. The festival posed all sorts of problems for Denham Ford, the RPO's orchestral manager. In 1947 there were only two contrabassoons in London: if on the night one of them was already in use, and the owner of the other was on holiday, there was a problem. Bass oboes had disappeared in the war, and it proved impossible to find a decent harmonium. In the end Ford had to borrow a Mustel organ from the BBC's popular music series *Grand Hotel*. RPO players were interested to note that at rehearsal Beecham was unusually respectful in the composer's presence. The horn player Norman Del Mar, who acted as Beecham's assistant and conducted two of the works, the *Frau ohne Schatten* suite (its first British performance) and the tone poem *Macbeth*, was surprised to find how tall the composer was. He made Beecham look tiny.

In addition to the Drury Lane concerts, Beecham conducted two concert performances of *Elektra*, given with the RPO at the BBC's Maida Vale studios and broadcast on the year-old Third Programme. At the end of the first one Strauss, sitting in the gallery, let out a loud 'Bravo!' He embraced Beecham, overjoyed with a performance notable for both its power and, particularly in the Orest scene, its tenderness.[23] Strauss told the true-voiced Erna Schlüter from the Hamburg Opera, who sang the title-role, that he found in her the fulfilment (*Erfüllung*) of Elektra. There was strong support from Ljuba Welitsch (Chrysothemis), Elisabeth Höngen (Klytämnestra) and Paul Schöffler (Orest), all from the Vienna State Opera. With the Strauss festival the RPO came of age. For almost a decade, together with its rival, Legge's Philharmonia, it would dominate Britain's concert life, with Beecham more than holding his own against Legge's array of guest conductors, who included Furtwängler and Toscanini, Cantelli and von Karajan.

By now Beecham had conducted his first post-war concerts abroad with European orchestras. Along with Toscanini, Bruno Walter and Erich Kleiber, he had been asked to conduct at the first post-war Salzburg Festival in 1946, but like the others had turned down the invitation.[24] Ironically, their action opened the door for Karajan's return to respectability; in March of that year he was cleared by an Austrian denazification commission, which enabled him to conduct at Salzburg. In January 1947 Beecham made a successful visit to Switzerland, where he conducted the Zurich Tonhalle, the Suisse Romande and the Winterthur Musikkollegium orchestras. But a trip to the Netherlands two months later, for eleven concerts with the Amsterdam Concertgebouw Orchestra, was extremely *un*successful.

He had been to the Netherlands once before, for a concert at the Hague with the Concertgebouw Chamber Orchestra in 1932, when the Dutch critics had complained that his approach to eighteenth-century music was 'unstylish'. Undeterred, and unwisely, he offered them *The Great Elopement* at his two opening concerts in 1947, the first at the Hague on 1 March, the second in Amsterdam on the following day. The suite, wrote the *Algemeen Handelsblad*'s reviewer, was 'good for choreography', but 'without any value as a piece of music', adding for good measure that Beecham's reading of Haydn's Symphony no. 97 was 'cool and academic' and 'not correct'. The *Vrije Volk* found the symphony slow and heavy ('too much Beecham, not enough Haydn'), the Handel 'not in good taste'.

There was plenty of favourable comment about Beecham's musicianship, his ability to draw luminous playing from the Concertgebouw and, in contrast to Boult, who had conducted the orchestra in November 1945, his vitality. But for the press in general his programmes lacked a sense of seriousness. After the fourth concert – there were still seven to go – Beecham vented his irritation in a letter to the Dutch agent who had arranged the visit for him. He complained about the Danish pianist France Ellegaard, who had played the Grieg Concerto at the opening concerts and said that he had never heard of the violinist – the twenty-three-year-old Herman Krebbers, later the Concertgebouw Orchestra's leader – who was down to play the Brahms Violin Concerto at the final concert on 16 March. 'I shall not conduct this concert at all', wrote Beecham, 'and I wish to leave this town at the earliest opportunity, as I do not care to be associated one minute longer than I can help with what appears to be an unattractive company of young barbarians.'[25] He would also cancel the penultimate concert at the Hague. If the management refused to accept his decision, he would go to the press. He added a postscript: 'So far as the Orchestra itself is concerned I have had a completely satisfactory and pleasant experience.'

The programme for the sixth concert, on 10 March, included a cello concerto by the contemporary French composer Jean Hubeau, presumably chosen by the soloist, Paul Tortelier. *De Tijd* branded it 'an insignificant composition, easy-listening music, pleasant but nothing more'. Beecham had had enough. He withdrew, not just from the last two concerts, but from the last five. The orchestra's chief conductor Eduard van Beinum and his assistant Hein Jordans stepped into the breach, amending the programmes to reflect local taste with Bruckner's Seventh Symphony, Beethoven's Fourth and Seventh, César Franck's *Psyché* and several Dutch works. A note in the programmes explained, falsely, that Beecham had rheumatic problems in his right arm; he had 'consulted Prof. Dr. W. Noordenbos, who said he must rest for some weeks'. Beecham never conducted in the Netherlands again, though there was a happy footnote to the saga.

Beecham invited Tortelier to make his British debut at the Strauss festival with the cello part in *Don Quixote*. Two days after the performance they recorded it.

Beecham was under considerable strain at the time of the Concertgebouw concerts. In the previous December, at a morning rehearsal at the Davis Theatre, there had been an incident which, to the orchestra, seemed inexplicable. Humby, down to rehearse Mozart's C minor piano concerto K491 for that afternoon's concert, had turned up late. She seemed agitated. She started to rehearse, but seemed to be in difficulties, for which she blamed the piano. Half-way through the concerto she said, 'I'm sorry, I can't go on', and collapsed. After she had been helped out, Beecham asked his librarian George Brownfoot to go to Circus Road immediately and fetch the parts for Schubert's 'Unfinished' Symphony, which would be played instead. Beecham made light of the episode, telling the Croydon press that his wife had been recovering from a severe bout of 'flu, a situation not helped by the fact that she had had to play a piano that 'would disgrace a village hall in the Arabian desert'. [26]

A week later Humby had recovered her composure sufficiently to play the concerto with Beecham at the Royal Albert Hall, and again on the next afternoon for a BBC broadcast. But in May she withdrew unexpectedly from a concert at Drury Lane, at which she was to have played the same work. Beecham told the audience that she was suffering from acute rheumatic inflammation and that since she was the only pianist, with the possible exception of Bruno Walter, who could play the concerto properly with him, he was replacing it with purely orchestral pieces. Harold Fielding, the concert's promoter, was furious, calling Beecham's remarks 'tommyrot' and 'an insult to our foremost British pianists'; there were, he said, plenty of artists who could have stepped in. Betty's condition was more serious than inflammation. Cancer was suspected, and ten days later, on 28 May 1947, she underwent an abdominal operation. She survived it, but never fully recovered, though she remained undaunted. No one apart from her immediate family was aware of what had happened.

In January 1948 the Beechams sailed on the *Queen Elizabeth* to America, it seems to seek medical advice. Betty looked thin, her face drawn. Beecham explained to reporters that he had come for a three-week rest in New York after eighteen months of non-stop conducting: 'If I had conducted one more day, the musicians would have murdered me.' [27] In August they made a longer voyage, to South Africa for concerts with the country's radio orchestras. The trip did much to restore Betty's confidence, and she played the Delius concerto in Cape Town, Johannesburg and Durban. Beecham enjoyed the trip, though he was suffering from sciatica and had to walk with a stick. Asked at a press conference if he were part of the British government's export drive to build up its credits overseas, he said that he had 'nothing to do with the British Government, the British

Council of Arts or any other form of British humbug'. Someone suggested that the Arts Council was actually doing good work. 'I'd like to know what the devil it is', he replied.[28] This was Beecham humbug. Despite his oft-repeated boast that his orchestra was entirely unsubsidised and all the better for it, he was in reality more than happy to accept Arts Council contributions towards his multifarious enterprises.

No sooner had the Beechams returned to Britain than they moved again, this time to Ringmer, close to Glyndebourne, where they leased from John Christie the large Queen Anne-style Delves House, on the north side of the village green. 'Borrowed' might be a better word to describe the arrangement, for Christie never received much in the way of rent. The house was unfurnished, but was soon filled with Beecham's antique furniture and picture collection, which included two Crome landscapes and eighteenth-century portraits of Sir Richard Steele and David Garrick.

Beecham told a journalist that he was always changing his pictures. When he tired of them, he sold them, often to acquire funds for his orchestra.[29] Though he did not say it, Humby's jewellery was often lodged with an Oxford Street pawnbroker for the same purpose. When in 1948 he overspent the budget on a recording of Gounod's *Faust*, and it seemed that the sessions at Abbey Road would have to be suspended, he appealed to the members of the RPO to accept money from future royalties, rather than a fee. They agreed to the deal, and the recording was completed. Although Beecham's income from recordings was by now quite high, the Beechams' outgoings were considerable. There were school fees for both Jeremy and Paul (who was now at Harrow) and maintenance to be paid to Dora Labbette. There were also demands from the Inland Revenue. After leaving Harrow, Paul was articled to Underwood & Co., a firm of London solicitors in Welbeck Street, for which Beecham paid the fees; in due course he would became senior partner. Jeremy went to Oxford.

On 29 April 1949 Beecham celebrated his seventieth birthday with two concerts, the first on 27 April with the Liverpool Philharmonic, the second five days later at the Albert Hall in London, where he conducted a programme of works by composers with whom he was particularly associated: Mozart, Delius, Strauss, Sibelius and Berlioz. Bax also got a look in with *The Garden of Fand*, a piece Beecham had always liked. He told reporters that he would go on conducting to the end of his days, which was 'a hell of a long way off'.

The Beechams remained at Delves House for three years, though in all they cannot have spent more than six months there, since for most of the time they were in London, staying at Brown's Hotel or the Ritz. Beecham conducted a number of concerts in the theatre at Glyndebourne. No opera seasons were held there between 1948 and 1950, but the company mounted productions for the Edinburgh Festival, with which it was closely associated. The RPO played for the Edinburgh performances and would remain Glyndebourne's official orchestra until 1963.

Beecham was friendly with Rudolf Bing, Glyndebourne's general manager, who was also Edinburgh's artistic director. Bing would soon leave for New York to become general manager of the Metropolitan Opera, but not before he had planned with Beecham a magnificent extravaganza for the 1950 Edinburgh Festival, a production, under Glyndebourne's auspices, of the original version of Strauss's *Ariadne auf Naxos* with Hofmannsthal's version of *Le bourgeois gentilhomme* as prologue. It had not been given in this form in Britain since Beecham had given its London premiere at His Majesty's Theatre in 1913. Carl Ebert produced, with glittering sets and costumes designed by Oliver Messel. There was a new translation of the play by Miles Malleson, who also played the part of Monsieur Jourdain, and a strong cast for the opera headed by Hilde Zadek as Ariadne, Ilse Hollweg as Zerbinetta and Peter Anders as Bacchus. *The Times* noted admiringly that when it came to the five female singers there was not 'a wobble among them'.* Although Norman Del Mar assisted at rehearsals, Beecham conducted all nine performances.

On the last night of the festival, 9 September, he conducted Handel's *Music for the Royal Fireworks* on the Castle Esplanade, with the massed bands of the Royal Scots Grays, the 9th Queen's Royal Lancers, the Royal Scots and the Highland Light Infantry. They were joined by the RPO's eight double basses, though it is doubtful if anybody could have heard them. On the last chord there was a deafening salute from heavy cannon on the battlements, cued by Beecham who pushed a button on his rostrum, and the evening ended with a fifteen-minute firework display.

Ariadne was only one in a series of engagements in 1950 that might have brought a fitter and younger conductor to his knees. Before it, Beecham had spent five weeks at Shepperton film studios recording the soundtrack for Michael Powell and Emeric Pressburger's film of Offenbach's *Tales of Hoffmann*. Beecham did not just conduct, he arranged a short ballet for the opening sequence and made numerous suggestions about casting and production. Before filming began, he made a piano recording of the complete score for Powell and Pressburger, which was used as the blueprint for the scenario. Miraculously, it has been preserved. Beecham sings and shouts his way through the opera, at the

---

* Cuts were made in both the opera and the play's incidental music, while Hollweg sang a simplified version of the taxing 'Grossmächtige Prinzessin'. The score was not performed complete in Britain until Scottish Opera mounted a production of both play and opera for the 1997 Edinburgh Festival. A recording of one of Beecham's 1950 performances, includes part of the play (Melodram CD GM 6 0007).

same time calling out stage directions and changes of key. His piano playing is far from immaculate, but he provides a riveting commentary on the score.*

Hoffmann was not Beecham's first post-was venture into film-making. In 1947 he and the orchestra had pre-recorded Brian Easdale's music for the *Red Shoes* ballet sequence in Powell and Pressburger's celebrated film of the same name starring Moira Shearer; and in the following year performed Lennox Berkeley's score for the soundtrack of Alberto Cavalcanti's *The Perfect Gentleman*, an historical drama featuring Cecil Parker as the Prince Regent. Muir Mathieson, musical director at Denham Studios, conducted the RPO for a number of other films, a vital source of income for the orchestra.

The year ended with an epic tour of the United States with the RPO that began in Hartford, Connecticut, on 13 October, and ended – fifty concerts later – at Bethlehem, Pennsylvania, on 15 December. It had taken Andrew Schulhof three years to organise. The orchestra travelled as far north as Madison, Wisconsin, and as far south as New Orleans. David McCallum, who had led the pre-war LPO and was now leading the RPO, took on three of the concerts, but Beecham conducted the remaining forty-eight – which was one in the eye for the Hungarian conductor Ferenç Fricsay, who had been rehearsing *Figaro* for Edinburgh at the same time that Beecham was preparing *Ariadne*. On being told by Richard Walton about the tour to America, the acerbic Fricsay said that Beecham looked so decrepit he would probably be dead before he got there.[30] Humby played at five of the tour concerts and withdrew from three others. Her performance of the Delius concerto at Lafayette, Indiana, on 1 December 1950 marked the end of her playing career. By poignant coincidence it was the work with which she had started her association with Beecham nine years earlier.†

Back in London the Beechams moved yet again, to 31 Grove End Road in St John's Wood. Once more he was close to the Abbey Road studios, where at the end of January 1951 he resumed work with a recording of orchestral excerpts from *Hoffmann*. His contract with RCA had expired, and he had now transferred his allegiance to American Columbia. Betty was in poor health. To combat the pain of her condition she had been prescribed barbiturates at a time when little was understood about their side-effects. She became addicted to

---

* Excerpts from the piano recording, made at Shepperton on 17 and 24 February 1950, are included on Somm-Beecham CD 13-2, which also includes a cut version of the film's original soundtrack.

† Betty Humby had suffered a memory lapse when in September 1950 she played the concerto at a concert at Walthamstow in preparation for the tour. When George Brownfoot said at the interval that the piano should be pushed off the platform, the double-bass player Vincent Howard remarked quietly, 'Just leave it there, it will slink away by itself.' Several RPO veterans have testified that this is the origin of a joke that has been ascribed to Beecham at venues stretching from London to Montreal.

them, and as a result suffered from unpredictable mood-changes, which were widely misunderstood by those who did not know her. Beecham was patient, comforting and caring. She travelled with him practically everywhere.

The Beechams lived frugally at Grove End Road, though there were curious extravagances. Once a month Beecham hired a limousine with chauffeur to take him to the Midland Bank at 1 Poultry in the City where, in the hope of securing extra funds, he would confer with the manager who dealt with the Beecham Trust. The limousine would also be summoned for odd tasks such as changing library books. Occasionally, one of Beecham's friends would visit, the theatre impresario C. B. Cochran, the Arabist Sir Ronald Storrs, the odd orchestral player or, most frequently, Philip Emanuel,* but otherwise there was little entertaining.

1951 was the year of the Festival of Britain, the national jamboree designed to give the nation 'a lift', which at last brought London a proper concert hall to replace Queen's Hall. Far from welcoming the Royal Festival Hall – only five years earlier, in Fabian mode, he had called on the government to build just such a hall – Beecham derided it before he had set foot inside it. He found the outside 'repellent'. Tax-payers, he declared, should not have to provide money for musical enterprises.[31] Two years earlier he had mounted a savage and ill-advised attack on Covent Garden and its music director Karl Rankl.[32] The reason for such outbursts was transparently obvious – he had not been consulted about either the Opera House or the Festival Hall. Beyond the confines of the RPO he had no influence whatever over the nation's musical affairs.

In the case of the Festival Hall there was an additional reason for his ire. Although initially he and the RPO had been approached about taking part in the first week's events, it was Toscanini who had been invited to conduct the inaugural concert on 4 May 1951 – Beethoven's First and Ninth symphonies with the BBC Symphony Orchestra. 'I am not, nor ever have been, opposed to the appearance of eminent foreigners in this country', Beecham wrote to the *Daily Telegraph*, 'but I do hold the unshakable opinion that an event such as the opening week of this new hall should be dominated by native art and artists.' Which in the end is what happened. Toscanini withdrew after suffering a minor stroke, and Malcolm Sargent, Boult's successor as the BBC Orchestra's chief conductor, took his place. Beecham confined himself to some Festival of Britain concerts at the Albert Hall and took the RPO round the country with Stokowski as his co-conductor. By the following October, however, he had transferred his operations to the Festival Hall. He had to admit that its acoustics, though not perfect,

---

* Some months before his death in 1961 Beecham suddenly dropped Philip Emanuel as his solicitor and replaced him with a large City law firm. The action came as a kick in the teeth to Emanuel, who had been getting Beecham out of scrapes for the past thirty-five years.

were a huge improvement on those of the Albert Hall, and went on to conduct at the new hall on no fewer than ninety-three occasions.

On 29 June 1951 Beecham returned at last to Covent Garden after a gap of twelve years. The general administrator, David Webster, had asked him to conduct a new staging of *Die Meistersinger*, to be sung in German. (The English-language policy had begun to crack.) There were four performances, with Karl Kamann and Hans Hotter sharing the role of Hans Sachs, Elisabeth Grümmer as Eva, and Peter Anders, Beecham's Bacchus in Edinburgh, as Walther von Stolzing. The producer was Heinz Tietjen, who had been running the Berlin State Opera when Beecham had last seen him in 1938 and was now in charge of the Städtische Oper in the city's western sector.

Karl Rankl was deeply upset by Beecham's arrival, for he had been the target of some of his nastiest invective in his attack on the Opera House two years earlier. True there had been a lot of poor performances during the company's first four years, particularly in the Italian repertoire, but against the odds Rankl had built up a good orchestra, a fine chorus and a roster of British singers, some of whom were rather better than most people had dared hope for. A handful of recorded excerpts from *Götterdämmerung* and a *Tristan* with Flagstad show that his Wagner conducting at Covent Garden was far more impressive than legend would have it. But Webster believed, rightly, that the moment had come for the company to stretch its wings and, as well as Beecham, brought in Clemens Krauss and Erich Kleiber to conduct. Rankl felt humiliated and resigned.*

Several members of the Covent Garden orchestra had played there for Beecham before the war. One of them, the bass-clarinettist Richard Temple Savage, noted that when he entered the pit for the first orchestral rehearsal he was visibly moved. He looked up at the great crimson curtains, murmured 'very pretty' and plunged straight into the *Meistersinger* prelude.[33] There were disputes over individual players, the size of the chorus and the production; but the end result was magnificent. The critic of *The Times* wrote of the first night that 'as a distillation through the orchestra of Wagner's imaginative vision of what human sympathy is its heights and depths it could only be described as superlative. Brilliant, tender, incandescent by turns, it was never turgid in the Teutonic vein yet never less than majestic'. Klemperer attended the second performance on 2 July. His verdict was short and typically to the point: 'Beecham I found good. The direction of Tietjen of Berlin – this I found bad. But the orchestra was very good.'[34]

In August Beecham was back at Covent Garden. Webster had asked him

---

* The board awarded Rankl a special grant of £1,000 (£23,000). A year later he became chief conductor of the Scottish National Orchestra and was then appointed musical director of the opera company in Sydney. He died in 1968.

to conduct an appropriate opera to mark the Festival of Britain, which would first be performed in Liverpool. Beecham proposed *A Village Romeo and Juliet*, which was turned down on the grounds that it would not prove a box-office draw. Instead, surely tongue in cheek, he hit on Balfe's *The Bohemian Girl*, which had not been seen at the Opera House since 1893. Some thought Beecham had lost hold of his senses, not realising that forty-nine years earlier at the Shakespeare Theatre, Battersea, it had been the first opera he had ever conducted. He lavished as much care on the old piece as if it were *Die Meistersinger*. With the help of the producer, Dennis Arundell, a new edition was prepared, based on one that Balfe had made for the Paris Opéra. In all there were twenty-seven performances, eight in Liverpool, nineteen at Covent Garden. Nine were conducted by Beecham, the rest by Norman Del Mar. Work on the edition continued right to the last moment. Temple Savage, who was playing the basset-horn on this occasion, noticed that in his part for the tenor's third-act aria, 'When other lips and other hearts', the word 'cadenza' appeared, but there were no notes for it. He asked Beecham what he should do. 'Go and away and write yourself one', said Beecham, which he did.[35] Not even Beecham could persuade the world that Balfe's opera was really worth reviving, but it had its moments, including its most famous number, 'I dreamt that I dwelt in marble halls', sung, as a recording of it taken from the broadcast of the fifth Covent Garden performance testifies, quite ravishingly by the young American soprano Roberta Peters. Beecham, adopting a slow tempo, moulds the phrases lovingly and allows Peters to reprise the last verse.

At the end of the year Beecham returned yet again to the Opera House, for two further performances of *Die Meistersinger*, this time with Hans Hopf as Walther, but without Hans Hotter. The first of them, on 14 December, was said to be the 250th opera performance that Beecham had conducted there. When at the end of it David Webster presented him with a laurel wreath, Beecham wiped away a mock-tear with his handkerchief. Webster called him 'something of an institution', Beecham said that he would rather be thought of as an individual. The second performance came three days later. It would be some time before Beecham was asked to conduct at Covent Garden again. In 1956 he vented his frustration in a letter to *The Times*, in which he criticised the Opera House's new musical director, Rafael Kubelik, for over-optimism about the future of British singing. Kubelik was so upset that he offered to resign, but the board stood by him. Time has proved that Kubelik's optimism was justified.

Deep down Beecham cannot have minded about being called an institution, because as he got older he played up the image. Audiences began to expect regular speeches from him at concerts, and he indulged them happily. He also delighted in serving up as encores short pieces that he called 'lollipops', Delius's

Sleigh Ride, for instance, or the Bacchanale from *Samson et Dalila*. His comments were waggish rather than witty, and grew more laboured as the years passed. It is the spontaneous moments that have best stood the test of time, for example his solemn remark to an Edinburgh Festival audience that had started to applaud in the middle of a suite from Grétry's *Zémire et Azor*: 'Ladies and gentlemen, I deeply regret to say that we haven't come to the end of this piece.' [36] The walk to the rostrum, always deliberate and stately, became slower, but the music-making was as full of fire as ever.

In the summer of 1952 Beecham rented a villa on Round Island in Poole Harbour, Dorset. There he hoped to find peace to start writing the biography of Delius that he had promised Jelka eighteen years earlier. Essentially the book was to be a straightforward life of the composer, rather than a commentary on his music and its interpretation, invaluable though that would have been to future conductors. Inevitably Beecham's concert schedule interrupted progress, and after only two months he left the island. The book was shelved for at least four years. During the next five seasons Beecham and the RPO were inseparable, except when he made one of his almost annual trips to America. He conducted the orchestra at endless recording sessions and at concerts all over the country. He treated the players as his musical peers, though the social proprieties were always observed. He addressed them as Mr McCallum or Mr Brymer, and they in turn called him Sir Thomas, though among themselves he was always Tommy. Beecham's rehearsal methods invariably surprised newcomers. He never lectured the players. Before a rehearsal started, the dynamics and accents he wanted had already been copies into the parts in blue crayon by his librarian, George Brownfoot, or even by Beecham himself. He would get the orchestra to play through a piece without interruption and then discuss various points he thought might be improved. Then he would repeat it. Often the transformation astonished even the most hardened players. Only when a player, no matter how distinguished, stepped out of line was Beecham's displeasure invoked. When in December 1948 Dennis Brain told him that he could not play for a tour performance of *Ein Heldenleben* because of his Philharmonia commitments, Beecham gave him the choice of doing the concert or leaving the RPO. Brain chose to resign and did not resume his dual relationship with both orchestras until October 1950.

In May 1953 the RPO played for the premiere of Delius's first opera, *Irmelin*, which, more than sixty years after it was written, was given five performances at the New Theatre, Oxford. Beecham persuaded John Denison, the Arts Council's music director, to part with money for some basic scenery,[37] while further financial support came from the Delius Trust. The cast was no more than adequate, and there was a small professional chorus, bolstered by members of the Oxford University Opera Club. As producer, Dennis Arundell was faced with a virtually actionless story about a never-never-land princess who falls for a prince disguised as a swineherd.

Five days before the first night Beecham, alarmed by the lack of interest at the box-office, issued a-call-to-arms in the *Oxford Mail*, claiming loyally – but inaccurately – that Delius was 'the most popular of all composers here and in the United States', where, he said, an album of Delius records was 'selling better today than those of any other composer, dead or alive'. (A reader challenged him to substantiate the second part of the assertion, but failed to get a convincing answer.)

The reviews did nothing to help. They were strongly reminiscent of those for the 1935 *Koanga* at Covent Garden: Beecham's conducting was masterful and the orchestra's playing magical, but Delius's sense of theatre was all but non-existent. Arundell conducted the fourth performance after Beecham fell on the stairs at the Mitre Hotel and struck his knee on a fire-bucket. When a year later Beecham performed scenes from the second and third acts with the RPO for BBC television, he told viewers that the Oxford production had been unlucky – 'I say unlucky, of course, because from the practical and commercial point of view it was the most complete and fatal flop.'[38]

Beecham conducted just one more opera in Britain, Grétry's *Zémire et Azor* at the 1955 Bath Festival.* Produced by Anthony Besch with a more or less all-French cast and designs by Oliver Messel, it worked perfectly in the small Theatre Royal. The orchestra came from the ranks of the Bournemouth Symphony. Beecham handed over the fourth of the five performances to his chorus master, Denis Vaughan. Later in the year Beecham was rewarded for his devotion to the music of a composer who was still living. On 8 December, at a concert at the Festival Hall marking Sibelius's ninetieth birthday, the Finnish Ambassador presented him with the Order of the White Rose of Finland. A few days later, at the composer's request, Beecham and the RPO recorded his enigmatic tone poem, *The Oceanides*. Publicly, Beecham maintained that he did not know why Sibelius had asked him to do it, but the answer comes in a letter the composer had sent him a year earlier, saying that the only recording that existed at the time was 'not satisfactory', because 'the conductor [Boult] has taken the work too fast'.[39]

By now the Beechams had moved yet again, to Ramley House, on the edge of the New Forest at Pennington, near Lymington. The estate agents described it

---

* According to the programme, the edition used was by Beecham himself, but he fell behind with the work, which involved filling in the string parts, and asked his musical assistant, the composer Leonard Salzedo, who was one of the RPO's first violins, to complete it. Beecham repaid Salzedo by conducting the first performance of his Symphony no. 1 at a Festival Hall concert with the RPO in May 1956. (Interview with Salzedo, 1999.)

as 'Dignified Country Residence'. Betty's father Morgan Humby died there in February 1955 and at his funeral at the church at nearby Boldre, Beecham conducted an ensemble of fifteen string players from the RPO in Grieg's *The Last Spring* and one of his favourite lollipops, 'The Last Sleep of the Virgin' from Massenet's sacred drama *La Vierge*. John Kennedy, the RPO's first cello, played Massenet's *Élégie*.

Ramley did not remain in the Beechams' ownership for long. True to form, they put it back on the market in 1957, a year that started for them in North America. Toscanini had died on 16 January, and a week later Beecham conducted *The Last Spring* in his memory at a concert he gave with his old orchestra, the NBC Symphony, now renamed the Symphony of the Air. Beecham concluded his programme with a blazing performance of Brahms's Third Symphony, of which even 'Toscaninny' might have approved.[40]

When Beecham returned to Britain he gave concert-goers a shock. On 31 March, at the end of a Haydn–Mozart concert with the RPO at the Festival Hall, he informed the audience that it would be his last in London for eighteen months. He told the *Daily Mail*, 'I shall live from now on in the South of France or in some similar locality where the climate will enable me to exist. I have always had a weak throat, and now it is chronic.' But Beecham was masking his real reasons for going. First, he had arranged to become a tax exile, which meant that he could not stay in Britain for more than ninety days a year. Secondly, and more importantly, he was leaving, not for the sake of his own heath, but of Betty's. Her condition was deteriorating, and he was greatly concerned for her future. On 7 April, after recording Delius's *Songs of Sunset* and a few other bits and pieces at Abbey Road, the Beechams left for Cap Ferrat on the Côte d'Azur, where they had rented a villa. In June it was announced in the Birthday Honours list that Beecham had been made a Companion of Honour.*

Beecham did not lose complete contact with the RPO. In October 1957 EMI paid for the orchestra to go to Paris for nine days to record a batch of Haydn's 'London' symphonies with him at the Salle Wagram. After the sessions Beecham gave two concerts with the orchestra at the Salle Pleyel – at the end of the second one he shouted out hoarsely, 'Come on brass, give 'em hell', before launching into Berlioz's Trojan March[41] – and then set off with it on a tour of Switzerland, followed by two concerts at the Musikverein in Vienna, where he told the audience that it had always been his ambition to take his orchestra to

---

* The Order of the Companions of Honour, founded in 1917 by George V, is limited to sixty-five members, forty-five of them in the United Kingdom, the remainder in the Commonwealth. It is awarded for outstanding achievement in the arts, literature, science, religion, politics and industry.

the city. Karajan attended the first concert (the programme included Haydn's Symphony no. 93 and Schubert's Sixth) and afterwards went to see Beecham backstage. 'One can speak of the conductor only in terms of the highest respect', wrote *Die Presse*. For the *Neuer Kurier*, the RPO was 'a wonderfully homogeneous ensemble of the highest precision'.

In November the apparently indefatigable Beecham conducted concerts with Spanish and Portuguese orchestras in Madrid, Porto and Lisbon, and in December went to the Cine Città studios in Rome to record music with the Rome Radio Orchestra for the soundtrack of Michael Powell's latest film *Honeymoon* or *Luna de miel*, an Anglo-Spanish co-production that must be counted among his least inspired movies. The heavily cut version released in Britain amounts to little more than a poorly acted travelogue, but it is saved by its three dance sequences – Sarasate's *Zapateado* wittily performed by the great Spanish dancer Antonio in an orchestration by Leonard Salzedo; Falla's *El amor brujo* performed by Antonio's dance company with Leonide Massine in the role of the Ghost; and, the least interesting, a short ballet called *The Lovers of Teruel*, choreographed by Massine with a score by Mikis Theodorakis.

When Antonio questioned a certain tempo in *El amor brujo*, he received a magisterial rebuke from Beecham: 'Young man, I *knew* de Falla and this is how he intended it to go.' For the vocal numbers Beecham wanted a singer with a strong, almost raucous voice. The writer Monk Gibbon witnessed the auditions Beecham held in Madrid:

> An impresario had assembled half a dozen, delightfully nonchalant and easy-going vocalists, only one of whom had thought of bringing an accompanist with her. The first of them to sing, so far from being overawed at finding herself on trial, seemed rather more inclined to cross-examine Sir Thomas. Presently Clara Alcara, spontaneous, natural, full of verve and good humour, entered the room. She, also, had omitted to bring an accompanist, and [Beecham] chivalrously declared, 'I will accompany you, if I may.' 'Do you play the piano?' the lady demanded. Sir Thomas replied that he had, on various occasions, made the attempt. He was given the music of a little Spanish folk-song, which they successfully performed together. 'Now, do you think you could sing the ['Chanson bohème'] from *Carmen*?' he asked her. She could and would. Sir Thomas's hands banged down on the keys as though he must fill the Albert Hall with sound; the lady burst into vigorous song, and the general effect on all present was electric. After which Clara Alcara departed saying cheerfully, 'Well, I suppose I'll be hearing from you.' Which in due course she did.[42]

Beecham recorded the complete score of *El amor brujo*, though it was shortened by eight minutes for the purposes of the film – Beecham suggested possible cuts, but left the final choice to Powell.[43] Later the complete recordings of all three pieces were offered to EMI, which decided not to issue them on the grounds that it did not want to compete with its version of *El amor brujo* with Giulini,[44] which is sad, because Beecham's version is vitally idiomatic.

In the spring of 1958 he paid a nostalgic visit to Grez-sur-Loing with Salzedo and a French photographer, who took pictures of Delius's house and its garden for the biography of the composer that Beecham was at last close to completing. It would be published in the following year. In June, at the Salle Wagram, Beecham embarked on one of his best-known recordings, the *Carmen* with Victoria de los Angeles and Nicolai Gedda. Los Angeles had worked happily with Beecham during the sessions for his classic recording of *La bohème*, made in New York two years earlier, but this time things went far less smoothly. She not only complained about some of Beecham's tempi, but also his habit of recording numbers out of sequence, rather than consecutively. Eventually, in exasperation, she closed her score, announced that she had had enough, and the next day left for Spain. Beecham thought her intolerably conceited. At one point it seemed that the project might have to be abandoned, but good sense prevailed and the recording was completed the following year. Gedda suggested that perhaps he should re-record his bits, since his voice might have changed in the interval. 'For the better or the worse?', asked Beecham.[45]

After the 1958 sessions had petered out, Beecham set out with Betty for Buenos Aires. He had been invited to rehearse and conduct a series of five operas, spread over thirteen weeks, at the city's grand, marble-foyered opera house, the Teatro Colón, which was celebrating its fiftieth anniversary. The operas were *Otello*, *Carmen*, *Samson et Dalila*, *Die Zauberflöte* and *Fidelio*. Live recordings (of varying sound quality) exist of all five. That Beecham had to travel 7,000 miles to conduct a season that he could have been offered in London was the ultimate irony of his life. Covent Garden was celebrating its centenary, but Beecham had not received an invitation from that address.

Beecham's task would not be easy. The Colón had still not fully recovered from Juan Perón's second term of office as Argentina's president, when he had packed the theatre with his cronies. The orchestra was on the rough side, but the chorus was excellent, though it invariably sang in Italian, even when the principals were singing in German or French. Beecham made it clear who was in charge from the start. The first thing he did was to reseat the orchestra, which immediately resulted in a better blend of sound. He also ensured that all his markings were transferred into the orchestral parts. He found allies in the head of music staff, Roberto Kinsky, and in the chorus master, Tulio Boni, who persuaded his choristers to learn *Die Zauberflöte* in its original language (though they drew the line at *Fidelio* and *Carmen*).

Rehearsals for the opening opera, *Otello*, started badly. There were strong differences of opinion between Beecham and the Desdemona, Antonietta Stella, which led her to storm out with the cry, 'Vecchio maledetto!' ('Damned old man!'). Beecham, in the pit, threw his score to the ground and shouted, 'Bring me another soprano!' Stella returned, but Ramón Vinay, who seemed to be as fed up as Beecham, asked the theatre to release him from his contract 'for reasons of health'. The opening was postponed by three days. Four young female choristers took it upon themselves to go to the Plaza Hotel, where Vinay was staying. After they had pleaded with him not to leave, he handed out signed photographs of himself and agreed to talk to the Colón's management. Vinay, the press duly reported, had 'overcome the problems that had affected his health' and would stay in Buenos Aires after all. The women's intervention had not been in vain.[46]

The first night of *Otello* on 4 July was a major success. Vinay, Stella and the Iago, Giuseppe Taddei, all shone, but the greatest praise was reserved for Beecham. Several reviewers said they could barely believe they were listening to the Colón orchestra, such was the brilliance of its attack and its new feeling for colour. Under Beecham, said one critic, 'they changed from musicians into artists'. The *Otello* was no flash in the pan. Though the cast in *Carmen* was a relative disappointment, the Beecham magic was again evident in the pit. The German-language *Argentinisches Tageblatt* reported that not since the days of Fritz Busch and Erich Kleiber had such conducting been heard in Buenos Aires.

Beecham missed the last of the four performances of *Samson et Dalila* with Vinay and Blanche Thebom, as well as a charity performance of its third act in aid of flood victims. Betty was unwell, and he decided he should remain by her side at the Plaza Hotel. Up until then she had attended all his rehearsals and performances in Buenos Aires; he had called her his 'third ear'. A member of the music staff, Aldo Bonifanti, conducted in Beecham's place. There was a gap of four weeks before the opening of Beecham's next opera, *Die Zauberflöte*. He conducted a Mozart concert for the Amigos de la Música, and then, as soon as Betty felt strong enough, took her north to Salta in the foothills of the Andes for a rest. But while there she had a fall, which seemed to aggravate her condition.

Back in Buenos Aires Betty remained bed-ridden, while Beecham rehearsed *Die Zauberflöte*. On 2 September 1958 she died in her sleep of a heart attack. She was fifty years old. On the following day there was a funeral service at the British cemetery chapel, followed by cremation. There were wreaths from the British Embassy, the British Council, the Colón theatre and the Colón orchestra. Beecham asked for them to be laid on the graves of British ex-servicemen. The tenor Jon Vickers, who had been singing in Buenos Aires, was about to return to London; Beecham asked him to take Betty's ashes with him, so that they might be given to her son Jeremy, who was now in the diplomatic service.

Beecham was reported to be 'outwardly calm'. He told the *Buenos Aires Herald* that he was determined to carry on with the season, because there was 'too much at stake'. He stayed away from the dress-rehearsal of *Die Zauberflöte*, but conducted the first night on 5 September, with a cast that included Walter Berry as Papageno, Pilar Lorengar the Pamina and Anton Dermota the Tamino. Beecham adopted tempi often far quicker than those in his Berlin recording and secured needle-sharp playing.

The season ended with *Fidelio*. Gré Brouwenstijn was as an outstanding Leonore, Hans Hopf a wooden Florestan. At rehearsal there were complaints from some of the singers about Beecham's slow tempi. The recording of the first night shows the grave-digging to have been uncharacteristically ponderous, and the 'O namenlose Freude' equally lethargic, but Beecham bursts into life with an incandescent account of the third Leonora overture, which is greeted with thunderous applause. At the end of the last performance, on 30 September, flowers rained down from the upper reaches of the vast house as Beecham took his bow and he was besieged at the stage-door as left the theatre. The next morning he was interviewed in his dressing-gown at the Plaza by the *Buenos Aires Herald*. The Colón, he said, was ' positively and absolutely without the slightest semblance of management – a monument, in fact, to mismanagement'. But he had nothing but praise for the music staff. 'Tell your readers', he said, 'that they wouldn't have any opera if it wasn't for them.'

A fortnight later, on 19 October, Beecham gave his first concert in London for more than a year and a half. Just before it started, he said he would 'give £10,000 not to have to conduct tonight'.[47] He shuffled on to the platform in what appeared to be his bedroom slippers and wore a black tie with his tails as a mark of mourning for Betty. The audience rose to greet him. There was a chair for him on the rostrum, but he scarcely used it. There were no speeches and no jokes, but the music-making was full of energy – Mendelssohn's 'Italian' Symphony, Schubert's Third, graced by real *pianissimos* the likes of which, said *The Times*, had not been heard since the day Beecham went away, and Strauss's *Ein Heldenleben*. After the concert a woman acquaintance came up and asked Beecham how Betty was. 'She's on tour', he said, 'with Vaughan Williams.' The English composer had died a week before her.

Beecham stayed in London for a month, giving concerts and making recordings. Reviewing an all-Wagner programme at the Festival Hall on 17 December, Desmond Shawe-Taylor wrote that it was 'wonderful, rich, spellbinding Wagner, full of poetry and colour and magic; very different from the restrained and scrupulously balanced performances of the "The Ring" we have been hearing lately at Covent Garden' (under Rudolf Kempe).[48] On 28 December Beecham sailed on the *Queen Mary* for the United States, where he conducted nineteen concerts, nine with the Philadelphia Orchestra, five with the Chicago Symphony and four with the Houston Symphony. The tour went off without a hitch, and in the spring of 1959 he returned to London in buoyant spirits to celebrate his eightieth birthday on 29 April. On the actual day he gave a lunch at Brown's Hotel for friends, including Beverley Baxter, Lord Boothby, Neville Cardus and Shirley Hudson, the RPO's administrator. Two days later there was a more official lunch at the Dorchester, attended by many of his colleagues. Telegrams of congratulation from prominent musicians were read out. 'Nothing from Mozart?', asked Beecham.

On 22 August, not quite a year after Betty Humby's death, Beecham caused astonishment with an announcement he had placed in the *Daily Telegraph* that day. It read: 'The marriage took place quietly on Aug. 10 at Zurich, Switzerland, between Sir Thomas Beecham and Miss Shirley Hudson.' Not even Beecham's closest associates knew of the ceremony, at Zurich's Town Hall. Beecham's new wife was the RPO's administrator. Little was revealed about her, except that, at twenty-seven, she was fifty-three years younger than Beecham and that her parents lived in the north London suburb of Southgate. She had started work as the RPO's telephone-switchboard operator in 1947 and subsequently had become Beecham's secretary in 1955 and the orchestra's administrator in January 1959. On occasion she had helped to nurse Betty. 'I am a reformed character,' Beecham told the press when the news of the marriage came out. 'I no longer provoke, denounce or condemn. I coo like the proverbial dove.'

On 17 December 1959, four days after he had conducted a memorable performance of Berlioz's *Grande messe des morts* at the Albert Hall, Beecham and his new wife sailed to New York for what proved to be his last visit to the United States and Canada. His four-month tour was to start with concert performances for the American Opera Society of Berlioz's *Les troyens*, split over two nights. They were to be given in New York, Philadelphia, and finally Washington, with the Symphony of the Air and a cast led by Eleanor Steber as Cassandra, Regina Resnik as Dido, and Richard Cassilly as Aeneas. For the first time in America the work was to be given more or less complete and in French. The plan went awry. Beecham had a bad attack of gout, and withdrew from the New York performances, which were taken over by the society's associate conductor, Robert Lawrence. Meanwhile the Philadelphia dates were cancelled because of a poor response at the box office, which at least gave Beecham time to recover for *La prise de Troie* in Washington on 9 January 1960 and the second part, *Les troyens à Carthage* on the following day. To the cast he seemed to be on edge, but somehow he found the strength to pull off the performances. Beecham, wrote Paul Hume of the *Washington Post*, had 'wrought an overwhelming feeling of dramatic unity, winning for the incomparable Britisher a prolonged ovation from shouting, applauding admirers'. It was one thing to conduct *Les troyens* in the concert hall over two days, but Beecham must have wondered whether he would have strength to conduct the work in the theatre. In three months' time, on his eighty-first birthday, he was due to conduct the first of five performances of the huge work at Covent Garden.

Normally Andrew Schulhof travelled with Beecham to sort out problems as they cropped up, but not this time. He had fallen seriously ill. Before setting out for America, Beecham had written to him sympathetically: 'Do not worry at all about me because with Belle's sole assistance I can fend for myself.' [49] But Belle, Schulhof's wife and business associate, could help very little, for her husband was dying and she had to remain in New York to care for him. He died on 8 February. Many of the tasks that Schulhof would have dealt with now fell on Shirley Beecham's shoulders. There was a fortnight's respite before the next batch of concerts in Pittsburgh, San Francisco and Seattle, which Beecham had not visited since he left it in high dudgeon sixteen years earlier. Fourteen players from that time were on the platform to greet him when he arrived at Seattle's Union station. A television reporter asked Beecham if he was still composing. 'Good Lord, yes', came the reply, 'sometimes I think I'm decomposing.'

The new Lady Beecham was a source of particular fascination for the Seattle press: 'Sir Thomas' 27-year-old bride of six months', wrote June Anderson Almquist of the *Seattle Times*, 'is British (born in London) and looks it: Brown hair, which she wears short and curled; big, china-blue eyes (smartly accented with blue mascara) and smooth complexion. In fact, she resembles Queen Elizabeth, especially in profile.' Beecham should have conducted four concerts with the Seattle Symphony, three in Seattle itself and a fourth in Tacoma, but after the first one on 18 February he had to hand over the remaining dates to the orchestra's concert-master, Henry Siegl. He was suffering from heart-strain. The doctor attending him reported that he was responding to treatment, but he 'should attempt no activity until much further improvement is evidenced. His heart has been under severe strain for the last several weeks because of a demanding schedule, resulting in extreme shortness of breath. His breathing is much improved.' [50]

Only ten days later Beecham conducted the first of two concerts in Vancouver and then moved on to Chicago for seven dates with Fritz Reiner's superlative Chicago Symphony Orchestra, four of them at Orchestral Hall, two at the Sheraton Towers mounted specially for television, and one in Milwaukee. The telecasts, in colour, provide a fascinating glimpse of Beecham at eighty. He stands bolt upright throughout the fifty-minute programmes, sitting only for the slow movement of the 'Prague' Symphony at the first concert and part of *The Great Elopement* suite at the second one. He conducts with a baton, but without a score.[51] The gestures are less extravagant than they once were, but the players get as much from the expressive eyes as they do from the hands. The symphonies of Haydn (no. 102) and Mozart (the 'Prague') might seem old fashioned in the light of current practice, but few watching Beecham's handling of them could doubt his mastery as a conductor. After two television concerts in Toronto he flew back to Britain, arriving at Heathrow on 12 April.

His first act on returning was to tell Covent Garden's administrator, Sir David Webster, that it was impossible for him to conduct the performances of *Les troyens*, which were now only a fortnight away. He explained that the symptoms he had experienced in Seattle had returned in Toronto, and that he had been told that he must 'avoid for a period of not less than a month or six weeks any arduous musical work'. It was, he said, a great disappointment for him.[52] John Pritchard and John Matheson took over the performances. In spite of the setback, Beecham was determined to make his first appearance in opera at Glyndebourne with *Die Zauberflöte*, which was scheduled for 4 August. It was to be recorded by EMI.

Meanwhile, on 24 April, he conducted a concert with the RPO at the Festival Hall and another on 7 May, at Portsmouth. He gave a lunch for the players in the town's banqueting hall to mark his pleasure at being with them again. Afterwards everyone adjourned to the Guildhall for a brief rehearsal. 'And now, gentleman, to the important business of the day', said Beecham. A television set was pushed on to the platform and he and the football fans in the orchestra settled down to watch the Cup Final. To the Lancastrian Beecham's chagrin Wolverhampton Wanderers beat Blackburn Rovers 3–0. That night he sat to conduct a typical programme: the *Zauberflöte* Overture, Haydn's 'Military' Symphony, the *Love in Bath* suite, Schubert's Fifth Symphony, 'On the River' from Delius's *Florida* suite, and the Dance of the Priestesses from *Samson et Dalila*. There was an encore, Delius's *Sleigh Ride*. Though Beecham did not know it, it would turn out to be the last piece of music he ever conducted.

He was still determined to conduct *Die Zauberflöte* at Glyndebourne, and before rehearsals began went to Montreux to rest. There, on 21 June, he suffered a cerebral thrombosis and was forced to withdraw from the opera. In July he returned to England, where he spent time in a nursing home. In the autumn he expressed a wish to hear some music, and on 8 October was taken by Shirley to Abbey Road, where the RPO was recording Rachmaninov's Second Piano Concerto, with Moura Lympany as soloist and Sargent conducting. Victor Olof, in charge of the session, noted that Beecham was 'looking very ill, very thin, and in my opinion a dying man. ... However, he spoke through the microphone to the orchestra from the machine room and we recorded his speech, which was faltering, hazy and short. He stayed in the studio afterwards for "one take" and then left, his visit lasting about 25 minutes.'[53] A number of the players went outside to wave him off as he was pushed in a wheelchair to a waiting car.

By now Beecham had exceeded the ninety days he was allowed to remain in Britain. Help came from an unexpected quarter. Hearing of Beecham's plight, Sidney Bernstein, chairman of Granada Television, and one of its directors, Denis Forman, felt that it would be cruel for Beecham to have to leave Britain at this point. (They knew Beecham because he had acted briefly as the company's musical adviser.) Now they approached a senior civil servant, Sir Edward Play-fair, and laid before him Beecham's circumstances. 'To his credit (and one must add a plaudit for that universally disliked body, the Inland Revenue)', wrote Forman, 'it was agreed that Sir Thomas could stay on and die in England, with no tax penalties.' [54]

The Beechams were now living at Harley House, a large Edwardian block of flats in the Marylebone Road, where Shirley looked after his needs. Beecham began to feel better. He read books, occasionally ventured out for lunch and even began to talk of sharing concerts with Malcolm Sargent, one of his regular visitors. But he had another thrombosis and died on 8 March 1961. The London *Evening News* led that day's paper with an eight-column banner headline on page 1 announcing the death, with articles and pictures beneath, a remarkable, and probably unique, acknowledgment of a great musician's importance in Britain's cultural life. Two days later he was buried among the pine trees at Brookwood Cemetery in Surrey. As well as Shirley Beecham, those present included Beecham's three sons, Adrian, Tommy and Paul, two of his seven grandchildren, and his eldest sister, Emily, who more than sixty years earlier had been banished from Ewanville with him. There was a large contingent from the RPO, as well as Paul Beard, who had led the LPO at its first concert in 1932.

Beecham did not die a rich man. By the time his estate had been sorted out there was little left. The probate value was put at £3,498 15s 6d (£57,000). Utica, now seventy-nine and still living at Clopton House, where she showed visitors round at 2s 6d (£2) a head, demanded to see the will, but her name was not mentioned in it. Beecham had left everything to Shirley, his wife of nineteen months. Until she died sixteen years later Utica proclaimed to anyone who listened that she was still the only true wife of Sir Thomas Beecham. He was, she said, a great man. Nobody could dispute that.

In 1991 Shirley Beecham, worried that Beecham's grave might be disturbed by landscaping work at Brookwood, arranged for his body to be exhumed and reburied at Limpsfield churchyard, close to Delius's grave. This duly took place on what would have been Beecham's 112th birthday. Though few of those present realised it, the choice of Limpsfield was doubly appropriate. Betty's son Jeremy Thomas, later Britain's ambassador to Greece, had lived in the village for a time. On receiving his mother's ashes from Buenos Aires, he had them buried in his garden, not a stone's throw from the churchyard.

Source Notes

Abbreviations

CHAPTER I

The Birth of the Pill

1 *Tit-Bits*, 17 May 1890.
2 Anne Francis, *A Guinea a Box: A Biography* (London, 1968), pp. 47–8.
3 *Pharmaceutical Journal*, vol. 18 no. 3 (1858), p. 198.
4 *St Helens Reporter*, 9 April 1907.
5 *St Helens Intelligencer*, 6 August 1859.
6 British Medical Association, *Secret Remedies: What they Cost and What they Contain* (London, 1909).
7 *St Helens Intelligencer*, 7 February 1857.
8 Letter to Thomas Giles, 12 February 1872 (StH). Sales figures from T. A. B. Corley, *National to Multinational Enterprise: The Beecham Business, 1848–1945* (University of Reading, Department of Economics, 1983).
9 *St Helens Newspaper & Advertiser*, 24 August 1872.

CHAPTER 2

The Mecca of Globules

1 Thomas Beecham, *A Mingled Chime: Leaves from an Autobiography* (London, 1944), p. 11.
2 Interview with Unsworth, *St Helens Newspaper and Advertiser*, 25 February 1910.

3 *St Helens Reporter*, 1 August 1890.
4 *St Helens Reporter*, 1 August 1890.
5 Sale catalogue of Ewanville contents, 1919 (StH).
6 Anne Francis, *Letter to the Past* (London, 1994), p. 3.
7 Undated letter from the 1960s to her daughter, Anne Wintle.
8 C. L. Stocks, 'Some Memories of Sir Thomas Beecham, Bart', *The Rossallian*, December 1961.
9 Concert review, *Fleetwood Chronicle*, 3 August 1894.
10 *The Rossallian*, 18 February 1896, 10 February 1897.
11 *The Rossallian*, 23 July 1897.
12 *Fleetwood Chronicle*, 30 July 1897.
13 Charles Lancelot Stocks, *People and Places in Prose and Verse* (Aylesbury, 1970), p. 19.
14 *Wadham College Gazette*, Michaelmas term, 1897.
15 *St Helens Newspaper & Advertiser*, 16 December 1889.
16 *Musical Times*, 1 October 1910.
17 Ethel Smyth, *Beecham and Pharaoh* (London, 1935), p. 16.
18 From 'Some Memories of Sir Thomas Beecham Bart', *The Rossallian*, December 1961.
19 Affidavit of Charles Stuart Welles, 7 February 1902 (NA, J77/708).

20 Letter from Thomas Beecham, Ewanville, Huyton, to W. M. Lyon, St Helens, 14 May 1889 (StH).

21 Beecham, *A Mingled Chime*, pp. 35–7.

22 *St Helens Reporter*, 28 February 1969.

23 *St Helens Reporter*, 11 November 1899.

24 Charles Reid, *Thomas Beecham: An Independent Biography* (London, 1961), p. 30.

25 *St Helens Newspaper & Advertiser*, 9 December 1899.

26 *St Helens Newspaper & Advertiser*, 16 December 1899.

27 *St Helens Newspaper & Advertiser*, 16 December 1899.

28 *St Helens Newspaper & Advertiser*, 16 December 1899.

CHAPTER 3
Banishment

1 Law report, *Liverpool Daily Post*, 12 February 1901.

2 Affidavit of Dr Charles Stuart Wells, 7 February 1902 (NA, J77/708).

3 Josephine Beecham's petition, 14 December 1900 (NA, J77/708); affirmation of Helen McKey Taylor, 13 June 1917 (NA, Chancery papers, J4/8858).

4 Reid, *Thomas Beecham*, p. 35.

5 Law report, *The Times*, 15 December 1900.

6 *St Helens Newspaper and Advertiser*, 1 May 1903.

7 Law reports, *The Times*, 9 and 12 February 1901.

8 Order dated 15 February 1902 (NA, J77/708).

9 Beecham, *A Mingled Chime*, p. 47.

10 *Daily Telegraph*, 1 April 1902.

11 *The Era*, 5 April 1902.

12 *Musical Times*, 1 October 1910.

13 Letter from Pizzi, London, to Illica, Castell'Arquato, 29 October 1902 (IA, box 53). Practically all the information about the *Marlowe* saga comes from the extensive Illica archive (IA) housed at the Biblioteca Comunale Passerini-Landi, Piacenza.

14 Beecham, *A Mingled Chime*, p. 51.

15 Draft contract in Illica's handwriting (IA, box 3).

16 Letter from Beecham, 9 Roland Gardens, London SW, 20 December 1902 (IA, box 15/1902, fol. 7).

17 Undated letter, Pizzi to Illica (IA, box 34/ senza data, fol. 51).

18 *Daily Telegraph*, 16 July 1903.

19 Reid, *Thomas Beecham*, p. 41.

20 Indenture dated 22 July 1903 (NA, B9/1235; affidavit of Sir Thomas Beecham, 5 July 1934).

21 Summary of Appeal Court judgment, 28 April 1903 (NA, J77/708).

22 Stanley Jackson, *Monsieur Butterfly: The Story of Puccini* (London, 1974), p. 123.

23 Letter to Illica, 15 November 1904 (IA, box 34/, fol. 39).

24 Letter, Pizzi to Illica, 5 February 1906 (IA, box 53).

25 Letter to Pizzi from solicitors Frederick Walker & Co., 13 September 1913 (IA, box 53).

26 Scott, *My Years of Indiscretion* (London, 1924), p. 162.

27 Memorandum of the meeting between H. S. Oppenheim and Edgar Todd-Jones at the Hotel Victoria, St Helens, on 27 May 1905 (StH).

28 *Musical Standard*, 13 May 1905.

29 J. A. Fuller-Maitland, *A Door-Keeper of Music* (London, 1929), pp. 121–2. Reviews in *The Times*, 6 June 1905, and *Sunday Times*, 11 June 1905.

30 Beecham, *A Mingled Chime*, pp. 45–6; undated letter from Beecham to Morley, *c.* 1905 (author's collection).

31 Document drawn up by Loxdales of South Kensington and Oppenheim & Son of St Helens (StH).

CHAPTER 4
Orchestral Fireworks

1 *The Times*, 2 July 1906.

2 Cyril Ehrlich, *The Music Profession in Britain since the Eighteenth Century* (Oxford, 1985), p. 162.

3 Smyth, *Beecham and Pharaoh*, p. 18.

4 Letter from Henry Oppenheim to Joseph Beecham, 25 May 1906 (StH, BP/2/2/6a).

5 *The Tribune*, 13 December 1906.

6 *The Referee*, 31 March 1907.

7 *Musical Standard*, 20 April 1907.

8 Joseph Szigeti, *Szigeti on the Violin* (London, 1962), p. 6.

9 Denise Lassimone (ed.), *Myra Hess by her Friends* (London, 1966), p. 30.

10 Original letter in German dated 9 October 1907 (DT archive); English version in *Delius: A Life in Letters*, ed. Lionel Carley, 2 vols. (London, 1983, 1988), vol. 1, pp. 300–2).

11 Thomas Beecham, *Frederick Delius*, revised edition (London, 1975), p. 149.

12 *Delius*, ed. Carley, vol. 1, p. 333.

13 *Birmingham Daily Post*, 28 November 1907.

14 Havergal Brian, 'The Neglect of Holbrooke', *Musical Opinion*, November 1937.

15 *Morning Leader*, 21 January 1908.

16 *Birmingham Daily Post*, 21 January 1908.

17 Beecham, *A Mingled Chime*, p. 129.

18 Letter from Beecham, Borehamwood, to Delius, Grez-sur-Loing, 17 June 1908; *Delius*, ed. Carley, vol. 1, pp. 356–7.

19 Letter from Delius, Gendeboden, Norway, to Jelka Delius, Grez-sur-Loing, 18 August 1908; *Delius*, ed. Carley, vol. 1, pp. 357–9.

20 Letter quoted in *Delius*, ed. Carley, vol. 1, p. 368.

21 Letter to Delius, 21 September 1908 (DT archive).

22 'Musicus' [alias of the *Daily Telegraph*'s chief music critic, Robin Legge], 'Coming Music', *Daily Telegraph*, 21 November 1908.

23 *Staffordshire Sentinel*, 4 December 1908.

24 Letters from Delius to Jelka Delius, 8 October 1908 and 3 December 1908 (Grainger Museum, University of Melbourne).

25 Thomas Quinlan's statement of expenses, 6 December 1908.

26 James Agate, 'My Debt to Manchester', *Manchester Evening News*, 13 October 1944.

27 *Manchester Guardian*, 5 December 1908; *Musical Standard*, 12 December 1908; *Manchester Evening News*, 5 December 1905.

28 *Musical News*, 27 February 1909.

29 Eric Wetherell, *Albert Sammons, Violinist* (London, 1998), p. 20.

30 Letter to Delius, 28 January 1909 (DT archive).

31 *Staffordshire Sentinel*, 23 February 1909.

32 *The Star* [London], 15 January, 1941.

33 Letter to Delius, 1 March 1909; *Delius*, ed. Carley, vol. 2, pp. 7–8.

34 Letters to Delius, 1 March 1909 and 1 April 1909 (DT archive).

35 *The Music Bulletin*, December 1924.

36 Garry O'Connor, *The Pursuit of Perfection: A Life of Maggie Teyte* (London, 1979), p. 178.

37 Gerald Cumberland, *Set Down in Malice: A Book of Reminiscences* (London, 1919), p. 232.

38 Court report, *Daily Telegraph*, 26 October 1911.

39 *Daily Telegraph*, 24 March 1909; *The Times*, 24 March 1909.

40 Letter to Delius, 11 April 1909.

41 Letter read out as evidence in the High Court; *Daily Telegraph*, 25 October 1911.

42 Letter to Delius, 1 March 1909 (DT archive).

43 Letter read out in the High Court; *Daily Telegraph*, 26 October 1911.

44 Letter from Beecham to Delius, 23 June 1909 (DT archive).

45 Letter to Beecham, 3 May 1909 (DT archive).

46 *Birmingham Daily Post*, 9 June 1909; *Musical Standard*, 12 June 1909.

47 Smyth, *Beecham and Pharaoh*, p. 25.

48 Letter to Delius, 17 June 1908; *Delius*, ed. Carley, vol. 1, pp. 356–7.

49 Letter to Delius, 29 March 1909; *Delius*, ed. Carley, vol. 2, pp. 20–1.

50 Interview, *Daily Express*, May 1909, quoted in a Beecham Orchestra concert programme.

51 Smyth, *Beecham and Pharaoh*, p. 32.

52 Smyth, *Beecham and Pharaoh*, p. 33.

53 Eric Coates, *Suite in Four Movements: An Autobiography* (London, 1953), p. 152.

54 Smyth, *Beecham and Pharaoh*, p. 38.

55 Reid, *Thomas Beecham*, p. 32.

56 Smyth, *Beecham and Pharaoh*, p. 32; also letter from Smyth to Lady Cunard, 10/11 January 1915 (StH, BP/2/2/3/37).

57 Letter to Delius, 23 October 1909; *Delius*, ed. Carley, vol. 2, pp. 34–5.

58 Letter to Delius, 13 September 1909 (DT archive).

59 Annexe to George Foster's petition for divorce, 17 May 1910 (NA, J77/1001).

60 Letter to Delius, 2 August 1909; *Delius*, ed. Carley, vol. 2, pp. 27–9.

61 *Musical Standard*, 10 July 1909.

62 *Morning Post*, 7 July 1909.

63 Law report, *Daily Telegraph*, 26 October 1911.

64 Horace Fellowes, *Music in my Heart* (Edinburgh, 1958), pp. 68–9.

65 Lionel Tertis, *My Viola and I* (London, 1974), p. 32.

66 Coates, *Suite in Four Movements*, p. 122.

67 Reviews in *Malvern News*, 16 October 1909; *Malvern Gazette*, 15 October; *Manchester Guardian*, 28 October; *Staffordshire Sentinel*, 29 October; *Cambridge Daily News*, 31 October.

68 Michael Kennedy, *Portrait of Elgar*, rev. edn (London, 1982), p. 228.

69 *Torquay Times*, 15 October 1909; *Cheltenham Looker-On*, 16 October 1909.

70 Reginald Nettel, *The Orchestra in England* (London, 1946), p. 257.

71 Letter to Granville Bantock, 17 December 1908; *Delius*, ed. Carley, vol. 1, pp. 376–7.

72 Nettel, *Ordeal by Music: The Strange Experience of Havergal Brian* (London, 1945), p. 88.

73 Complaint filed at the Third Judicial District Court, Idaho City, 26 August 1942; *Seattle Times*, 6 October 1942.

CHAPTER 5

Elektra and the Baptist

1 Report by W. J. Henderson, *New York Sun*, 23 January 1907.

2 Resolution of the board of directors, 27 January 1908 (MO archives).

3 *New York Times* and *New-York Tribune*, 23 January 1907.

4 Letters written by Ethel Smyth (7 December), Viscount Althorp (9 December); G. A. Redford (10 December 1909) (BL, MS LCP CORR Salome 1910/815).

5 Reference to invitation in 'German influence on English music', *The Times*, 2 May 1933.

6 'Opera in England', *The English Review*, December 1911.

7 *The Observer*, 13 January 1910.

8 *Daily Sketch*, 18 February 1910; *Daily Mirror*, 19 February 1910.

9 *Musical America* interview reprinted in *Musical Standard*, 16 April 1910.

10 *The Observer*, 20 February 1908.

11 *The Observer*, 20 February 1910.

12 *Daily Sketch*, *Daily Mirror* and *Daily Graphic*, 21 February 1910.

13 *Birmingham Daily Post*, 21 February 1910; *The Nation*, 26 February – 6 August 1910.

14 *St Helens Reporter*, 11 March 1910.

15 *St Helens Newspaper and Advertiser*, 15 March 1910.

16 *St Helens Reporter*, 18 March 1910.

17 *Morning Leader*, 14 March 1910.

18 *Carmen* review, *Musical Standard*, 19 March 1910; Smyth quoted in Christopher St John, *Ethel Smyth: A Biography* (London, 1959), p. 144.

19 Philip Heseltine, *Frederick Delius* (London, 1952), p. 68.

20 Letters, Delius to Granville Bantock, 16 October 1910; Beecham to Delius, 27 August 1910 (DT archive).

21 *The Globe*, 21 March 1910.

22 Letter to Beecham, 13 March 1910 (DT archive).

23 *The Globe*, 21 March 1910.

24 Petition of George Sherwood Foster to the High Court of Justice, Probate, Divorce and Admiralty Division, 18 March 1910; answers of Maud Foster and Thomas Beecham, 12 July 1910 (NA, J77/1001).

25 *St Helens Reporter*, 29 April 1910.

26 Profile of Beecham, *Musical Times*, 1 October 1910.

27 *The Observer*, 15 May 1910.

28 *Daily Mail*, 23 May 1910.

29 *Sunday Times*, 19 and 26 June 1910.

30 'Opera in England', *The English Review*, December 1911.

31 Recorded for RCA with the Royal Philharmonic Orchestra, 11 April 1947. CD transfers: Biddulph WHL 056; Testament SBT 1147.

32 The 'Doll's Song' and the *Fledermaus* overture were transferred to LP in 1979 by EMI ('Sir Thomas Beecham, 1879–1961', World Records box SH 1001). A CD transfer of the overture is included in 'Sir Thomas Beecham Bart' (Symposium 1096-1097).

33 Osbert Sitwell, *Great Morning* (London, 1948), p. 198.

34 *St Helens Newspaper and Advertiser*, 25 November 1910.

35 *Sunday Times*, 23 October 1910.

36 Letter and subsequent correspondence in BL, MS LCP CORR Salome 1910/815.

37 *Daily News*, 9 April 1918.

38 *Daily Mirror*, 8 December 1910.

39 *The Nation*, 17 December 1910.

40 *The Times*, 9 December 1910; *Sunday Times*, 11 December 1910.

41 *Sunday Times*, 11 December 1910.

42 Archdeacon's and Dawson's letters both dated 23 December 1908 (BL, MS LCP CORR Salome 1910/815).

43 *The Times*, 2 January 1911; *The Observer*, 1 January 1911; letter to Delius, 15 January 1911; *Delius*, ed. Carley, vol. 2, pp. 66–7.

CHAPTER 6
Guilty – or Not Guilty?

1 Interview in *Musical America*, reprinted in *Musical Standard* [London], 19 November 1910.

2 *The Observer*, 1 January 1911.

3 *Musical Standard*, 4 February 1911; *The Stage*, 2 February 1911.

4 Brozel hearing, *The Times* and *Daily Telegraph*, 9, 14, 15 December 1911. Evans case, *The Times*, 1 November 1911.

5 *Sheffield Daily Telegraph*, 11–15 March 1911.

6 *Swansea and Glamorgan Herald*, 25 February 1911.

7 *Daily Express*, 23 May 1911.

8 Beecham, *A Mingled Chime*, p. 106.

9 Scott, *My Years of Indiscretion*, p. 160.

10 *The Diaries of Cynthia Gladwyn*, ed. Miles Jebb (London, 1995), p. 219.

11 Tony Gray, *A Peculiar Man: A Life of George Moore* (London, 1996), p. 10.

12 Dates from the Nevill Holt guest book (Harry Ransom Humanities Research Center, University of Texas, Austin, box 22, folder 1).

13 Anne Chisholm, *Nancy Cunard* (London, 1979), p. 23.

14 *Musical Standard*, 18 February 1911.

15 *St Helens Newspaper and Advertiser*, 25 November 1910.

16 *Daily News*, 22 June 1911.

17 *Musicians' Report and Journal*, September 1911, p. 14.

18 Letter from Beecham, Hotel Belmont, New York, to Delius, Grez-sur-Loing, 19 September 1911; *Delius*, ed. Carley, vol. 2, pp. 76–7.

19 *New York Times*, 23, 24 September 1911.

20 *Western Mail*, Cardiff, 22 August 1911.

21 Court reports, *Daily Telegraph*, *The Times*, *Daily Mirror*, *Daily Sketch*, *Daily Graphic* and *Western Mail*, 19 October – 1 November 1911; *News of the World* and *The Umpire* [Manchester], 22, 29 October, 5 November 1911.

22 Maud Foster's answer to her husband's petition for divorce, 12 July 1910 (NA, J77/1001).

23 Order for payment of costs, Divorce Division, High Court of Justice, 13 February 1912 (NA, J77/1001).

24 Reid, *Thomas Beecham*, p. 120.

25 'Open Letters and Post Cards', *Mrs Bull*, 25 November 1911.

26 *Manchester Evening Chronicle*, 10 June 1912; *Pall Mall Gazette*, 12 June 1912.

27 *Western Mail*, 11 November 1911.

28 Letter to Delius, 9 February 1912; *Delius*, ed. Carley, vol. 2, p. 83.

29 Francis, *Letter to the Past*, p. 166.

30 Smyth, *Beecham and Pharaoh*, p. 52.

31 *Staffordshire Sentinel*, 22 March 1912.

32 *Daily Express*, 10 June 1912.

33 Cyril W. Beaumont, *The Diaghilev Ballet in London: A Personal Record* (London, 1940), p. 9.

34 *Daily Telegraph*, 1 October 1912.

35 Letter, 10/23 December 1912, quoted in Stephen Walsh, *Stravinsky: A Creative Spring* (London, 1999), p. 189.

36 *The Observer*, 22 December 1912.

37 Letter written from the Devonshire Club, London, 26 December 1912; *Delius*, ed. Carley, vol. 2, pp. 95.

38 *Vossische Zeitung*, 19, 25 December 1912; *Signale*, 18 December; *Germania*, 22 December; *Allgemeine Musik-Zeitung*, 3 January 1913, etc.

CHAPTER 7

Towards the Abyss

1 *Musical Standard*, 1 October 1910.

2 *Musical Standard*, 19 November 1910.

3 *The Era*, 18 November 1911.

4 *The Standard*, etc, 10 June 1912.

5 Diaghilev–Beecham contract (New York Public Library for the Performing Arts, Astruc papers, GA 82-9).

6 Memorandum, 4 January 1913 (BL, MS LCP Der Rosenkavalier 1913/3).

7 Beecham, *A Mingled Chime*, p. 114.

8 *St Helens Newspaper and Advertiser*, 24 January 1913.

9 *The Lady*, 6 February 1913.

10 *The Journals of Arnold Bennett, 1911–1921*, ed. Flower Newman (London, 1932), p. 58.

11 Review by L. Leonhard, *Musik*, 1 March 1913.

12 *The Lady*, 13 February 1913.

13 *Daily Mail*, 5 February 1913.

14 Muriel Draper, *Music at Midnight* (New York, 1929), p. 205.

15 *Daily Mail*, 18 February 1913.

16 Interviews with Stravinsky and Diaghilev, *Daily Mail*, 6 February 1913.

17 *Daily Sketch*, 10 May 1913.

18 *Daily Chronicle*, 14 May 1913.

19 *Daily Telegraph*, 17 May 1913.

20 Letter sent from Schloss Ehrenburg, Coburg, Germany.

21 Berlin reviews in His Majesty's Theatre cuttings book, which dates them as 28 May 1913 (BTC, HBT/000044); *Pall Mall Gazette*, 28 May.

22 *Pall Mall Gazette*, 31 May 1913.

23 *Daily Mail*, 19 June 1913.

24 Beaumont, *The Diaghilev Ballet in London*, p. 74.

25 Beecham, *A Mingled Chime*, p. 128.

26 Alec Robertson, *More than Music* (London, 1961), pp. 28–9.

27 *Sunday News*, 25 January 1925.

28 *St Helens Newspaper and Advertiser*, 25 July; 1, 8 August 1913.

29 *St Helens Newspaper and Advertiser*, 12 September 1913.

30 *Evening Standard*, 13 September 1913.

31 Coates, *Suite in Four Movements*, p. 123; Beecham, *A Mingled Chime*, p. 115n.

32 *Comœdia Illustré*, 5 July 1913.

33 Letter to Heseltine, 28 June 1913: *Delius*, ed. Carley, vol. 2, pp. 107–8.

34 *Daily Mail*, Paris edition, 20 June 1913.

35 *Birmingham Daily Post* and *Birmingham Daily Mail*, 16–29 September 1913.

36 Letter from J. W. Preger, *Manchester Guardian*, 7 October 1913.

37 *Manchester Guardian*, 1–11 October 1913; *Manchester Evening News*, 4 October; *Daily Dispatch*, 6 October; *Evening Standard*, 8 October; *Musical Times*, 1 November.

38 *Sheffield Daily Post* and *Sheffield Daily Independent*, 14–21 October 1913.

39 *Yorkshire Evening News*, 22 October 1913.

40 *The Times*, 25 October 1913; *Yorkshire Post* and *Yorkshire Evening News*, 21–7 October 1913.

41 *Manchester Guardian*, 1–15 November 1913; *Daily Dispatch* and *Manchester Evening News*, 10 November 1913.

42 *The Scotsman*, 1 December 1913; *St Helens Newspaper and Advertiser*, 2 December 1913.

43 StH BP/2/2/3/3–5 and 54.

44 Letter from Beecham to Delius, 14 June 1914; letter from Delius to Jelka Delius, 23 June; *Delius*, ed. Carley, vol. 2, pp. 127–8, 129–30. Information about debts from StH, BP/2/2/3/34.

45 *Morning Post*, 9 June 1914.

46 'Opera in London', *The Times*, 13 May 1914.

47 'The Gramophone and the Singer', *The Gramophone*, August 1927.

48 Gabriel Astruc, *Le pavillon des fantômes: souvenirs* (Paris, 1987), p. 209.

49 Richard Buckle, *Diaghilev* (London, 1979), pp. 279–80.

50 Lynn Garafola, *Diaghilev's Ballets Russes* (New York, 1989), pp. 184–5, which quotes Diaghilev's contract with Joseph Beecham dated 13 March 1914 (Bibliothèque de l'Opéra, Paris, Fonds Kochno, Pièce 129).

51 Garafola, *Diaghilev's Ballets Russes*, p. 188.

52 Charles Ricketts, *Self-Portrait* (London, 1939), p. 236.

53 S. L. Grigoriev, *The Diaghilev Ballet, 1909–1929*, trans. Vera Bowen (London, 1953), p. 101.

54 Letter to Jelka Delius, 23 June 1914; *Delius*, ed. Carley, vol. 2, pp. 129–30.

55 Entry dated 15 November 1915, *The Duff Cooper Diaries, 1915–51*, ed. John Julius Norwich (London, 2005), p. 20.

56 Letters dated 28 November 1914, 23 December 1914 and 12 March 1915; H. H. Asquith, *Letters to Venetia Stanley*, ed. Michael and Eleanor Brock (Oxford, 1982), pp. 320, 337, 474.

57 *Morning Post*, 22 June 1914.

58 Chancery papers, 1917 (NA, J4/8854, fol. 248, and J4/8857, fol. 916); law report, *Estates Gazette*, 24 February 1917.

59 *The Times*, 4 June 1914.

60 Beecham, *A Mingled* Chime, p. 132; German visit reported in *Daily Telegraph*.

61 Lady Margherita Howard de Walden, *Pages from my Life* (London, 1965), p. 74.

62 *Evening News*, 6 July 1914.

63 *Daily Mail*, 4 July 1914; inquest reports, *Daily Telegraph* and *Islington Daily Gazette*, 9 July 1914.

64 Letter to Jelka Delius, 3 July 1914; *Delius*, ed. Carley, vol. 2, pp. 134–5.

65 Letter to Jelka Delius, 26 June 1914; *Delius*, ed. Carley, vol. 2, p. 130.

66 *Lloyd's Weekly News*, 5 July 1914.

67 Funeral report, *Islington Daily Gazette*, 13 July 1914.

68 Wynn Reeves, unpublished memoirs.

69 *Daily Telegraph*, 25 July 1914.

70 *The Referee*, 26 July 1914.

CHAPTER 8

Battle for Music

1 *Delius*, ed. Carley, vol. 2, p. 137.

2 *St Helens Reporter*, 20 October 1914.

3 Lewis Foreman, 'Watford sur Gade', *Delius Society Journal*, no. 131 (Autumn 2001).

4 Kenneth Young, *Music's Great Days in the Spas and Watering-places* (London, 1968), p. 61.

5 *Musical Times*, 1 September 1914.

6 RPS Cashbook (BL, RPS MS 308).

7 RPS Directors' Minute Book (BL, RPS MS 291, fols. 164–5, 194).

8 Letter from Welldon to the Hallé's hon. secretary, J. Aikman Forsyth, 11 March 1915 (Hallé archives).

9 Review of concert of 25 February 1915, *Musical Standard*, 6 March 1915.

10 Igor Stravinsky, *Themes and Conclusions* (London, 1972), p. 230.

11 *Delius*, ed. Carley, vol. 2, pp. 145, 150.

12 Arnold Bax, *Farewell, my Youth* (London, 1943), p. 91.

13 'The Musical Constitution of England', *New Statesman*, 26 February 1916.

14 Landon Ronald, *Myself and Others* (London., 1931), pp. 182–4.

15 *Manchester Guardian*, 5, 7, 11, 14 December 1914.

16 Archie Camden, *Blow by Blow: The Memories of a Musical Rogue and Vagabond* (London, 1982), p. 80.

17 'Report on the business carried on by the Executors of the will of Sir Joseph Beecham, Bart, deceased', November 1922 (StH, BP/2/2/10).

18 London Metropolitan Archives, E/BER/CG/E/12/006.

19 Affirmation of Helen McKey Taylor, 13 June 1917 (NA, J4/8858).

20 Anne Francis [the Ellises' daughter], *Letter to the Past*, pp. 4–5.

21 Letter to Joseph Beecham, 18 September 1915 (StH, BP/2/2/2/8).

22 Letter to Thomas Beecham (StH, BP/2/2/3/36).

23 *Daily Telegraph*, 4 October 1915.

24 Lady Elgar's diary, 21 November 1915, 18 March 1916 (University of Birmingham, special collections).

25 Accademia di Santa Cecilia, *I concerti dal 1895 al 1933* (Rome, 1933), pp. 128–30.

26 Quotations from reviews, 28 December 1915 and 4 January 1916.

27 Letter from Sir Henry Paget Cooke to Herbert Asquith, 31 December 1915 (Bodleian Library, Oxford, MSS Asquith 29, fol. 146.)

28 Letter dated 15 March 1915; Asquith, *Letters to Venetia Stanley*, p. 487.

29 *Giornale d'Italia*, 4 January 1916.

30 *Manchester Guardian*, 27 January 1916.

31 NA, FO372.

32 Beecham, *A Mingled Chime*, pp. 146–7.

33 *Giornale d'Italia*, 16 January 1916.

34 *La Tribuna*, 16 January 1916.

35 Letter to Beecham, 4 January 1916 (Accademia di Santa Cecilia archives, Rome).

36 Minutes of directors' meeting, 25 February 1916 (LSO archives).

37 RPS Directors' Minute Book, 23 June 1916 (BL, RPS MS 291, fol. 194).

38 Minutes of directors' meeting, 19, 30 August 1916 (LSO archives).

39 *Daily Express*, 28 February 1916; *The Queen*, 4 March 1916.

40 *The Times*, 17 June 1916.

41 *Daily Dispatch*, 12 June 1916.

42 *The Queen*, 17 June 1916.

43 *The Queen*, 12 August 1916.

44 Company press-release quoted in *The Queen*, 24 June 1916.

45 *The Era*, 16 August 1916.

46 Wynn Reeves, unpublished memoirs.

47 Minutes of directors' meetings, June–October 1916 (BL, RPS MS 291).

48 *Birmingham Daily Post*, 23 March 1916.

49 David Dilks, *Neville Chamberlain*, vol. 1: *Pioneering and Reform, 1869–1929* (Cambridge, 1984), pp. 184–5.

50 *Evening Chronicle* [Manchester], 20 October 1916.

51 *Musical Standard*, 5 February 1916.

52 *Delius*, ed. Carley, vol. 2, p. 169.

53 *St Helens Newspaper and Advertiser* and *Hampstead Record*, 27 October 1916.

CHAPTER 9

A Mountain of Debts

1 *St Helens Newspaper and Advertiser*, 27 October 1916.

2 Transcript of Beecham's examination in the Bankruptcy Court, 12 October 1921 (NA, B9/869).

3 Minutes of executors meeting, 15 April 1918 (StH, BP/1/3/16).

4 Beecham, letter to the executors, 21 June 1922 (StH, BP/3/16).

5 Tape of Elsie Olive Betts talking to Alan Jefferson, *c.* 1977.

6 Affidavit of Louis Nicholas, 25 July 1923 (NA, J4/9515 fol. 1436).

7 'Comments', *New Statesman*, 2 December 1916.

8 *Westminster Gazette*, 20 December 1917; *The Era*, 11 January 1918.

9 NA, WO339/117056.

10 Donald Brook, *Conductor's Gallery* (London, 1945), p. 63.

11 *Westminster Gazette*, 25 June 1917.

12 John Galsworthy, 'New Russia – Free Russia', *Russian Exhibition: Preliminary Notice*.

13 *The Nation*, 28 July 1917.

14 'Notes and Aspects of the Opera Season', *Musical Standard*, 4 August 1917.

15 *Evening Chronicle*, 17 September 1917; *Manchester Guardian*, 20 September; *The Observer* 23 September; *The Times*, 31 October.

16 Diary entry, September 1917 (Bodleian Library, Oxford, MS Eng.d.3216).

17 John Barfoot, *Over Here and Over There: Ilford Aerodromes and Airmen in the Great War* (Romford, 1998), p. 100.

18 *Daily Sketch*, 31 October 1917.

19 *The Queen*, 13 October 1917.

20 Diana Cooper, *The Rainbow Comes and Goes* (London, 1958), p. 156.

21 *Manchester Guardian*, 24 December 1917.

22 *Birmingham Daily Post*, 11 October, 1 November, 29 November 1917; 7 February 1918.

23 *Sporting Times*, 8 December 1917.

24 *Saturday Review*, 1 December 1917.

25 *The Globe*, 26 November 1917.

26 *The Queen*, 15 March 1918.

27 *The Era*, 20 June 1918.

28 *The Nation*, 22 June 1918.

29 *Daily Telegraph*, 17 June 1918.

30 *Daily Sketch*, 29 July 1918.

31 Directors' Minute Book, 27 September 1918 (BL, RPS MS 291).

32 *The Scotsman*, 12 November 1918.

33 *The Scotsman*, 18 November 1918.

34 Letter to Marie Clews, 20 December 1918; *Delius*, ed. Carley, vol. 2, pp. 200–2.

35 Bankruptcy Court transcript, 12 October 1921 (NA, B9/869).

36 Lists of shareholders, August 1919 (NA, BT31/24501/154006).

37 *Daily Telegraph*, 17 May 1919.

38 Mosco Carner, *Puccini: A Critical Biography*, 2nd edition (London, 1974), p. 217.

39 Letters from Puccini to Sybil Seligman dated 16 March and 6 April 1919; Vincent Seligman, *Puccini among Friends* (London, 1938), pp. 292–3.

40 Unidentified review, Harold Rosenthal, *Two Centuries of Opera at Covent Garden* (London, 1958), p. 400.

41 Beecham interviewed by Denis Forman, 27 November 1959 (Granada Television archives).

42 Robin H. Legge, *Daily Telegraph*, 13 May 1919.

43 Nellie Melba, *Melodies and Memories* (London, 1980), pp. 215–16.

44 Beecham, *A Mingled Chime*, pp. 170–1.

45 John Hetherington, *Melba: A Biography* (London, 1973), p. 198.

46 Wyn Reeves, unpublished memoirs.

47 Statement of Albert Hindle of L. Sherwood Ltd, New Bond Street, 5 June 1919 (NA, B9/869).

48 Letter to C. W. Orr, 16 May 1920; *Delius*, ed. Carley, vol. 2, p. 231.

49 'Stray Musings', *Musical Opinion*, May 1920.

50 *The London Mercury*, December 1919, p. 376.

51 *The Athenaeum*, 19 December 1919.

52 Hetherington, *Melba*, p. 213.

53 Beecham, *A Mingled Chime*, p. 180.

54 *The Times*, 13 May 1920.

55 *Hampstead and St John's Wood Advertiser*, 27 May 1920.

56 Interview with Irving Kolodin, *The Gramophone*, January 1957.

57 Letter quoted in Seligman, *Puccini among Friends*, p. 310.

58 Interview with Irving Kolodin, *The Gramophone*, January 1957.

59 Letter to Diaghilev from solicitor Charles Russell, 11 July 1922 (Theatre Museum dance collection); High Court papers, 9 October 1922 (NA, J13/9243).

60 NA, BT31/24501/154006.

61 NA, BT31/154006.

62 Affidavit of Henry Higgins, 13 September 1920 (NA, J13/8678).

63 *Glasgow Herald*, 18 September 1920.

64 Blamey v. Beecham; law reports, *The Times*, 14 November 1925, 9 June 1926, etc.

65 *Musical Herald*, 1 November 1920.

CHAPTER 10

The Bull of Bashan

1 Law report, *The Times*, 25 November 1920.

2 Letter to Bankruptcy Court from Dr Harry Overy, Lowndes Street, 7 January 1921; Beecham's statement to the court, 8 January (NA, B9/869).

3 Beecham's examination by W. P. Bowyer, transcript, 12, 20 October 1921 (NA, B9/869); law reports, *The Times*, 25 November 1920; 3 February, 17 March, 27 April, 30 June 1921.

4 Letter to Marie Clews, 31 July 1921; *Delius*, ed. Carley, vol. 2, pp. 244–7.

5 Law reports, *Times*, 29 March 1923.

6 *Hertfordshire Express*, 8, 22, 29 January; 25 June; 2, 23 July 1921.

7 Letter to executors, 24 August 1921 (StH, BPI/3/16).

8 Hallé executive committee meeting minutes, 14 June 1922 (Hallé archives).

9 Letter to executors, 10 August 1922 (StH, BPI/3/16).

10 Minutes of executors' meetings, 17 August, 1 September 1922; report by Louis Nicholas and solicitors Bremner, Sons & Corlett, 30 August 1922 (StH, BP/1/3/16); Nicholas, affidavit to Chancery Court, 27 February 1923 (NA, J4/9509, fol. 336).

11 Letter to Behrens, 18 February 1923 (Hallé archives).

12 *Evening Chronicle*, 16 March 1923.

13 Hallé executive committee minutes, 9 April, 25 June 1923 (Hallé archives).

14 Letter to Harty from Beecham's secretary, H. Trevor, 25 March 1923 (Hallé archives).

15 *Daily Telegraph*, 7 April 1923.

16 *Musical Mirror*, May 1923.

17 'Schaunard', *Musical Opinion*, May 1923.

18 *Musical News and Herald*, 14 April 1923.

19 *Musical News and Herald*, 15 December 1923.

20 Chancery papers (NA, J15/3620, fol. 1906).

21 Introduction to a Council petition, 1919.

22 Author's interview with Jane Brabyn.

23 Utica Beecham's affidavit, 6 July 1925 (NA, J4/9737, fol. 1320).

24 Thomas Beecham's affidavit, 6 July 1925 (NA, J4/9737, fol. 1346).

25 *Morning Post*, 30 May 1925; *Daily Express*, 1 June 1925, etc.

26 Law reports, *The Times*, 4, 8 July 1925, etc.

27 Affidavits of Adrian and Thomas Beecham, 24 June 1925, and Sir Thomas Beecham, 6 July 1925 (NA, J4/9737, fols. 1319, 1346).

28 *The Times*, 20 November 1922.

29 Glaskie v. Beecham, law report, *The Times*, 22 October 1925.

30 *Sunday Times*, 29 March 1925.

31 Directors' board minutes, 12 March 1924 (LSO archives).

32 Wyn Reeves, unpublished memoirs.

33 Camden, *Blow by Blow*, pp. 105–6.

34 William McBrien, *Cole Porter: A Biography* (New York, 1998), p. 107.

35 George Moore, *Letters to Lady Cunard, 1895–1933*, ed. Rupert Hart-Davis (London, 1957), pp. 149–50.

36 *Daily Telegraph*, 5 November 1926.

37 Stephen Sherwood, 'Sir Thomas Shakes the Dust', *The Sackbut*, December 1926.

38 LSO board minutes, 29 June 1922, etc. (LSO archives).

39 *Nottingham Guardian*, 19 November 1926.

40 *Manchester Guardian*, 16 December 1926; *New Statesman*, 24 December 1927.

41 Concert review, *West Australian*, 19 September 1940.

42 *The Gramophone*, January 1928.

43 *Central European Observer*, 28 January 1927.

44 Antal Dorati, *Notes of Seven Decades* (London, 1979), p. 76.

CHAPTER 11

The Twopenny Opera

1 *Newcastle Daily Journal*, 12 March 1927.

2 *Monthly Musical Record*, 1 June 1927.

3 *The Times*, 5 January 1927.

4 *Daily Mail*, 28, 29 October 1927.

5 *The Star*, 14 November 1927.

6 *The Times*, 28 November 1927.

7 *Birmingham Mail*, 24 November 1927.

8 Michael Kennedy, *Barbirolli: Conductor Laureate*, rev. edn (Uttoxeter, 2003), p. 62.

9 *Glasgow Herald*, 29 December 1927.

10 *New York Times*, 5 January 1928.

11 *Musical Courier*, 12 January.

12 Comments by Markham Lee, *New York Times*, 7 January 1928.

13 Editorial: 'A Blazing Indiscretion', *Scottish Musical Magazine*, 1 February 1928.

14 *New York Evening Post* and *New York Times*, 13 January 1928.

15 Letter, 21 January 1928; Library of Congress music divisioin, miscellaneous manuscripts collection.

16 *The Bulletin* [Philadelphia], 27 January 1928.

17 Letter to Judson from Clarence Mackay, chairman of the orchestra's board, 15 March 1928; contract between Beecham and the Philharmonic dated 15 June 1928 (NYPO archives).

18 *The Times*, 2 February 1928.

19 Robert Elkin, *Royal Philharmonic: The Annals of the Royal Philharmonic Society* (London, 1947), p. 114.

20 Letter from Balfour Gardiner to the society's treasurer, 7 June 1919 (BL, RPS MS 370, fols. 54–5).

21 *Monthly Musical Record*, 1 May 1928.

22 Beecham's memorandum to the Society (BL, RPS MS 370, fols. 134–6).

23 RPS minute book, 2 April, 1 May 1928 (BL, RPS MS 278). Correspondence between the society's secretary, Mewburn Levien, and Beecham, October 1928 (BL, RPS MS 370, fols. 154–5).

24 *New York Times*, 13, 22 January 1928.

25 Nicholas Kenyon, *The BBC Symphony Orchestra: The First Fifty Years, 1930–1980* (London, 1981), p. 16.

26 Harold Shipp, *The Sackbut*, August 1928.

27 Grigoriev, *The Diaghilev Ballet*, p. 248.

28 Buckle, *Diaghilev*, p. 505.

29 Letter quoted in Kenyon, *The BBC Symphony Orchestra*, p. 20.

30 Eric Fenby, *Delius as I knew Him* (London, 1966), p. 25.

31 Story confirmed to the author by her son, the seventh Earl of Harewood.

32 Note in the tour programme.

33 *Liverpool Echo*, 11 December 1929.

34 'Paris Notes', *Dancing Times*, February 1929.

35 *Hampshire Telegraph and Post*, 19 July 1929.

36 *Yorkshire Post*, 2 October 1928.

37 *Musical Opinion*, May 1929.

38 *Eastbourne Gazette*, 1 May 1929.

39 Letter from Delius to Beecham (dictated to Jelka Delius), 10 March 1929; *Delius*, ed. Carley, vol. 2, pp. 346–7.

40 The account of Beecham's visit draws on both Fenby's book *Delius as I Knew him*, and a talk he gave to the Beecham Society of London on 9 March 1974.

41 Robertson, *More than Music*, p. 131.

42 Lyndon Jenkins, *While Spring and Summer Sang: Thomas Beecham and the Music of Frederick Delius* (Aldershot, 2005), p. 49.

43 Fenby, talk to the Beecham Society, 9 March 1974.

44 LSO board minutes, 10 May 1929 (LSO archives).

45 Maurice Pearton, *The LSO at 70: A History of the Orchestra* (London, 1974), pp. 77–8.

46 *Evening Standard*, 21 March 1929.

47 *Manchester Guardian*, 28 November 1928.

48 *The Times*, 27 January 1930.

49 *Musical Standard*, 28 December 1929; *Monthly Musical Record*, February 1930.

50 Contract between Beecham and André, dated 28 February 1930.

51 General meeting of the Covent Garden Properties Company, *The Times*, 31 July 1930.

52 Figure given in ledger submitted to the Court of Chancery (NA, J90).

53 *The Times*, 17 December 1930.

54 Ledger submitted to the Court of Chancery (NA, J90).

55 Piers Brendon, *The Dark Valley: A Panorama of the 1930s* (London, 2001), p. 154.

56 *Monthly Musical Record*, December 1930.

57 *Morning Post*, 26 November 1930.

58 Law reports, *The Times*, 6, 10, 13, 17 December 1930.

59 *Birmingham Post*, 24 November 1930.

60 *Oxford Times*, 28 November 1930.

61 *Eastbourne Gazette*, 26 November 1930.

62 Berta Geissmar, *The Baton and the Jackboot: Recollections of Musical Life* (London, 1944), p. 175.

63 Arthur Bliss, *As I Remember* (London, 1970), p. 59.

64 *Monthly Musical Record*, 2 June 1930.

CHAPTER 12

'Just listen to this'

1 *Birmingham Gazette*, 8 January 1931.

2 Law report, *The Times*, 17 January 1931.

3 Transcript of Beecham's examination by H. Wheeler, senior assistant official receiver (NA, B9/109).

4 Law report, *The Times*, 19 May 1931.

5 *Monthly Musical Record*, 1 August 1930.

6 Board minutes, 20 June 1930 (LSO archives).

7 'The Russian Opera Example', *Musical Mirror*, July 1931.

8 *Daily Herald*, 26 June 1931.

9 Beecham, interview, *The Observer*, 17 May 1931.

10 'Chaliapin', unsigned article, *The Clarion*, July 1931.

11 Feodor Chaliapin, 'The Russian Opera', *Saturday Review*, 20 June 1931.

12 *Sunday Times*, 24 May 1931.

13 *Sunday Times*, 10 May 1931.

14 *Manchester Guardian*, 2 September 1931.

15 *Monthly Musical Record*, 1 October 1931.

16 *Salzburger Volksblatt*, 3 May 1931.

17 RPS committee minutes, 7 and 21 January 1931 (BL, RPS MS 239).

18 Memorandum, Gaisberg to Alfred Lack, HMV's manager, 1 October 1931 (EMI archives).

19 Michael Kennedy, *Portrait of Walton* (Oxford, 1989), p. 58.

20 This, the earliest and probably most accurate version of the story, comes from James Agate's journal, *Ego 4* (London, 1940), p. 81.

21 Memorandum, Gaisberg to Lack, 23 November 1931 (EMI archives).

22 Board minutes, 25 November 1931 (LSO archives).

23 Board minutes, 21 and 26 January 1932 (LSO archives).

24 Board minutes, 12–17 February 1932 (LSO archives).

25 Review by Olin Downes, *New York Times*, 24 March 1932.

26 Account details (NYPO archives).

27 Utica Beecham's affidavit, 4 Feb 1932 (NA, J4/10400).

28 Law report, *The Times*, 16 April 1932.

29 Chancery Court order, 15 June 1932 (Stratford Birthplace Trust Records Office, DR574/352/4).

30 *The Times* and *Daily Telegraph*, 14 July 1932.

31 Interview with Lyndon Jenkins, *Classical Music*, 18 December 1982.

32 Cables, Blois to Beecham, 15 and 17 March 1932 (ROH archives).

33 Letter quoted in Harold Rosenthal, *Opera at Covent Garden: A Short History* (London, 1967), p. 115.

34 Beverley Baxter, *Strange Street* (London, 1935), pp. 222–3.

35 RPS committee minutes, 29 October, 5 November 1931. Barbirolli represented Covent Garden in the discussions (BL, RPS MS 293).

36 Reid, *Malcolm Sargent*, p. 203.

37 Report by Geoffrey Toye, RPS committee minutes, 5 May 1932 (BL, RPS MS 293).

38 Letter from Jelka Delius to Fenby; ; *Delius*, ed. Carley, vol. 2, pp. 409.

39 *Delius*, ed. Carley, vol. 2, p. 409.

40 RPS committee minutes, 12 August 1932 (BL, RPS MS 293).

41 Reid, *Thomas Beecham*, p. 202.

42 Board minutes, 12 September 1932 (LSO archives).

43 Gwydion Brooke, interview with the author, 21 October 1999.

44 Richard Walton, interview with the author, 1999.

45 Leo Birnbaum, interview with the author, 23 August 1999.

46 *Sunday Times*, 9 October 1932.

47 *Monthly Musical Record*, November 1932.

48 Obituary of Horowitz, *New York Times*, 12 November 1989; review by William McNaught, *Musical Times*, 1 December 1932.

49 Keyworth, *Cabbages and Things: The Background and Story of the Covent Garden Property Companies to 1970* (n.p., 1990), p. 113.

50 *The Times*, 14 December 1932.

51 Rosenthal, *Opera at Covent Garden*, p. 118.

CHAPTER 13

The Shadows Lengthen

1 *Daily Telegraph*, 18 May 1933.

2 *Monthly Musical Record*, June 1933.

3 *Daily Telegraph*, 2 May – 17 June 1933.

4 Letter to Geoffrey Toye, 14 May 1934 (ROH archives).

5 Report by H. E. Wortham, *Daily Telegraph*, 22 May 1933.

6 *The Bystander*, 21 June 1933.

7 *Sunday Times*, 11 June 1933.

8 *The Times*, 10, 12 June 1933.

9 Alan Jefferson, *Sir Thomas Beecham: A Centenary Tribute* (London, 1979), p. 212.

10 *The Times*, 15 July 1933.

11 'The World of Music', *Daily Telegraph*, 30 March 1935.

12 Keyworth, *Cabbages and Things*, p. 167.

13 *The Music Lover*, 21 April 1934.

14 *The Times*, 22 April 1933.

15 Francis Toye, 'Facts about Opera', *Daily Telegraph*, 30 March 1935.

16 *Monthly Musical Record*, July–August 1934.

17 Wilfrid Blunt, *John Christie of Glyndebourne* (London, 1968), pp. 160–1.

18 *The Times*, 1 May 1934.

19 Otto Erhardt in *Diener der Musik*, ed. Martin Müller and Wolfgang Mertz (Tübingen, 1965), pp. 169–70.

20 Beecham, letter to Toye, 14 May 1934 (ROH archives); *The Times*, 1 May 1934.

21 Letter, Legge to Delius, 21 May 1934; *Delius*, ed. Carley, vol. 2, p. 450.

22 *The Gramophone*, September 1934, p. 139.

23 Information from Paul Strang, 2008.

24 Francis, *A Guinea a Box*, p. 167.

25 Ivor Newton, *At the Piano: The World of an Accompanist* (London, 1966), pp. 138–9.

26 Grace Moore, *You're Only Human Once* (London, 1947), p. 221–6.

27 *La Libre Belgique*, 2 July 1935; Paul Tinel, *Le Soir*, 1–3 July 1935.

28 *Daily Telegraph*, 23 August 1935.

29 *Liverpool Daily Post*, 28 December 1936 – 23 February 1937.

30 *The Times*, 30 September 1935.

31 *The Diaries of Sir Robert Bruce Lockhart*, ed. Kenneth Young (London, 1973), p. 331.

32 Letter to Beecham, 6 August 1935 (NYPO archives).

33 Letter to Judson, 27 September 1935 (NYPO archives).

34 *Musical Courier*, 11, 25 January 1936.

35 Letter from Judson to board member Charles Triller, 25 March 1936 (NYPO archives).

36 Cablegram from Beecham to Columbia Artists (NYPO archives).

37 Letter to Beecham, 9 April 1936 (NYPO archives).

38 Kennedy, *Barbirolli*, pp. 82, 127–8, 133.

39 Charles Reid, *John Barbirolli: A Biography* (London, 1971), p. 146.

40 *The Times*, 20 January 1936.

41 Sir Robert Mayer, interview with Alan Jefferson, 28 January 1977.

42 *The Times*, 3 February 1936.

43 Geissmar, *The Baton and the Jackboot*, pp. 177–8, etc.

44 Josephine O'Donnell, *Among the Covent Garden Stars* (London, 1936), pp. 239, 251.

45 Otto Erhardt in *Diener der Musik*, ed. Müller and Merz, p. 172.

46 Humphrey Procter-Gregg (ed.), *Beecham Remembered* (London, 1976), p. 111.

47 Brigitte Hamann, *Winifred Wagner: A Life at the Heart of Hitler's Bayreuth*, trans. Alan Bance (London, 2005), p. 255.

48 Leo Birnbaum, interview with the author.

49 Reid, *Thomas Beecham*, p. 212.

50 Friedelind Wagner, *The Royal Family of Bayreuth* (London, 1948), p. 133.

51 Confirmed by Leo Birnbaum, who, on the first desk of violas, was sitting almost at Beecham's feet.

52 Author's conversation with one of the diplomats, Reinhard Spitzy, February 1998.

53 Diary entry dated 14 November 1936; *Die Tagebücher von Josef Goebbels*, Teil I, Band 3/II (Munich, 2001), pp. 250–1.

54 Consul General D. St Clair Gainer's monthly report to Sir Eric Phipps, 27 November 1936 (NA, FO371/19924).

55 *Fifty Years of Tape Recording* (Chandos box DBTD 2007S).

56 *Daily Mail*, 23 November 1936.

57 Thomas Russell, *Philharmonic Decade* (London, 1945), p. 54.

58 Review by Henry Prunières, *La Revue Musicale*, April 1937.

59 Letter dated 6 May 1938; quoted by Geissmar, *The Baton and the Jackboot*, pp. 334–5.

60 Frederic Spotts, *Hitler and the Power of Aesthetics* (London 2002), p. 80.

61 Elisabeth Schwarzkopf, *On and Off the Record: A Memoir of Walter Legge* (London, 1982), p. 153.

62 Paul Strang, conversation with the author, 2008.

63 Ernest Irving, *Cue for Music: An Autobiography* (London, 1959), p. 84.

64 *The Bartered Bride*, Somm-Beecham CD 14-2. *Il trovatore*, Bel Canto Society CD BCS-5000. *Aida*, Eklipse CD3.

65 Letter to LPO committee, 13 October 1939 (LPO archives).

66 Geissmar, *The Baton and the Jackboot*, p. 365.

67 Letter from Arthur Mason, 18 October 1939 (ABC).

68 Dutton CDBP 9723.

69 Letter to Adrian Beecham, 26 April 1940.

70 *Philharmonic Post*, May 1940.

71 Letter from Arthur Mason to Charles Moses, 5 April 1940 (ABC).

CHAPTER 14
Adventures in Australia

1 Paul Strang, conversation with the author, 2003.
2 *Auckland Star*, 8 June 1940.
3 *Picture-News*, 8 June 1940.
4 *Sydney Morning Herald*, 13 June 1940.
5 *Daily Telegraph* [Sydney], 12 June 1940; *Melbourne Argus*, 18 June 1940.
6 Letter from Beecham, Hotel Australia, Sydney, 13 June 1940, to T. W. Bearup (ABC, SP1558/2/0, box 14).
7 *The Listener In*, 15 June 1940.
8 *Teleradio*, 20 July 1940.
9 *Melbourne Argus*, 29 June 1940; *The Herald* [Melbourne], 17 June 1940.
10 Dorati, *Notes of Seven Decades*, pp. 292–3.
11 *ABC Weekly*, 26 October 1940.
12 *Melbourne Argus*, 22 June 1940.
13 *The Herald* [Melbourne], 22 June 1940.
14 Charles Buttrose, *Playing for Australia: A Story about ABC Orchestras and Music in Australia* (Sydney, 1982), p. 73.
15 *Daily Telegraph* [Sydney], 29 June 1940.
16 Beecham, *Frederick Delius*, p. 92.
17 *Courier-Mail* [Brisbane], 18 July 1940.
18 *The Age* [Melbourne], 24 June 1940.
19 *The Listener In*, 12 July 1940.
20 *The Advertiser* [Adelaide], 28 August 1940.
21 *The Herald* [Melbourne], 8 July 1940.
22 Letter from Beecham, Hotel Australia, Melbourne, 11 July 1940, to Joyce Beecham.
23 Interview by Rupert Charlett, *Melbourne Argus*, 13 July 1940.
24 Rupert Charlett, *The Australasian* [Melbourne], 20 July 1940.
25 *Truth*, 6 July 1940.
26 *Sydney Morning Herald*, 17 September 1940.
27 Interview with Robert Renthwaite, *The Strand*, February 1945.
28 *ABC Weekly*, 26 October 1940.
29 *Courier-Mail* [Brisbane], 27 July 1940.
30 *Sunday Sun* [Sydney], 21 July 1940.
31 *The Telegraph* [Brisbane], 22 July 1940.
32 *The Telegraph* [Brisbane], 22 July 1940.
33 *Courier-Mail* [Brisbane], 25 July 1940.
34 *The Telegraph* [Brisbane]; *West Australian* [Perth], 26 July 1940.
35 *Courier-Mail* [Brisbane], 26 July 1940.
36 *The Telegraph* [Brisbane], 26 July 1940.
37 *Courier-Mail* [Brisbane], 25 July 1940.
38 ABC memo, Harry J. Stephens to General Manager, 31 July 1940 (ABC, SP1558/2/0, box 14).
39 *West Australian* [Perth], 2 August 1940.
40 *Sunday Telegraph* [Sydney], 5 August 1940.
41 Unidentified newspaper cutting.
42 *Daily Sun* [Sydney], 1 August 1940.
43 *Daily Telegraph* [Sydney], 31 August 1940.
44 *Toronto Daily Star*, 25 November 1940.
45 Interviews with Beecham, *West Australian*, 17 September 1940; *Toronto Daily Star*, 25 November 1940.
46 Letter from Beecham, Hotel Esplanade, Perth, 17 September 1940, to Adrian Beecham.
47 Memo from acting general manager T. W. Bearup to all ABC commissioners, 2 October 1940 (ABC, SP613/1/00).
48 *Sydney Morning Herald*, 4 October 1940.
49 *Auckland Star*, 7 October 1940.
50 *Sydney Sun*, 9 October 1940.
51 *Vancouver Sun* and *Daily Province* [Vancouver], 26 October 1940.
52 Isabelle Moresby, *Australia Makes Music* (Melbourne, 1948), p. 178.

CHAPTER 15
Enter Miss Humby

1 *Virgil Thomson by Virgil Thomson* (New York, 1966), p. 341.
2 Viscount Norwich, conversation with the author, 18 March 2003.
3 *The Telegram* [Toronto], 27 November 1940.
4 *The Gazette* [Montreal], 4 December 1940.
5 *Los Angeles Times*, 30 December 1940.
6 'Hedda Hopper's Hollywood', *Los Angeles Times*, 2 January 1941.
7 *San Francisco Chronicle* and *San Francisco Examiner*, 1 January 1941; *San Francisco Call-Bulletin*, 2 January 1941.
8 Letter from Evelyn Barbirolli, New York, to her mother-in-law, Mrs Louise Barbirolli, London, 17 February 1941 (NA, FO371/26215).
9 *San Francisco Chronicle*, 4 January 1941.

10 *Detroit News*, 14 February 1941.

11 Foreign Office minute (NA, FO371/26215).

12 Letter from Beecham, Palace Hotel, San Francisco, 7 January 1941, to Walter Legge; *Walter Legge: Words and Music*, ed. Alan Sanders (London, 1998), pp. 94–5.

13 Letter from Beecham, Hotel Utah, Salt Lake City, 11 January 1941, to Joyce Beecham, Compton Scorpion.

14 Letter from Beecham, Park Plaza Hotel, St Louis, 15(?) December 1940, to Eugene Goossens, Cincinnati (BL, MSS).

15 *Cincinnati Times-Star*, 23 January 1941.

16 Belle Schulhof, *Roundtrip, Budapest/New York* (New York, 1987), p. 88.

17 Diana Cooper, *Trumpets from the Steep* (London, 1960), p. 98.

18 *Los Angeles Times*, 23–6, 28 February, 2 March 1941.

19 *New York Times*, 27 February 1941.

20 Letter from Elizabeth Tibbles to Winston Churchill and subsequent correspondence (NA, FO371/26215 and FO371/26216).

21 James Chuter Ede, *Labour and the Wartime Coalition: The Diary of James Chuter Ede*, ed. Kevin Jefferys (London, 1987), pp. 40–1.

22 *Time*, 27 January 1941.

23 Richard Arnell, conversation with the author.

24 *New York Times*, 6 April 1941.

25 *New York Herald Tribune*, 7 April 1941.

26 *New York Times*, 7 April 1941.

27 *New York Times*, 13 April 1941.

28 *New York Herald Tribune*, 15 April 1941.

29 Howard Shanet, *Philharmonic: A History of New York's Orchestra* (New York, 1975), p. 289.

30 Letter from Toscanini, Riverdale on Hudson, New York, 28 October 1941, to Olin Downes; *The Letters of Arturo Toscanini*, ed. and trans. Harvey Sachs (London, 2002), pp. 382–3.

31 Cecil Roberts, *And so to America* (London, 1946), pp. 168–75.

32 Frederic Prokosch, *Voices: A Memoir* (New York, 1983), p. 136.

33 Richard Arnell, conversation with the author.

34 *Virgil Thomson by Virgil Thomson*, p. 343.

35 *New York Times*, 22 May 1941.

36 *Le Devoir* [Montreal], 19 June 1941.

37 *The Gazette* [Montreal], 17 June 1941.

38 *Chicago Daily News*, 13 July 1941.

39 Letter from Beecham, Moraine on the Lake Hotel, Highland Park, Illinois, 26 June 1941, to Joyce Beecham, Compton Scorpion.

40 *New York Herald Tribune*, 14 April 1941.

41 *Seattle Times*, 22 October 1941.

42 *The Times*, 29 April 1940.

43 Letter from Dora Labbette to Betty Humby Beecham, London, February 1948.

44 *Time*, 30 June 1941.

45 Transcript of broadcast, *New York Times*, 23 June 1941.

46 *Information Please* transcription discs, 26 September 1941, 20 March 1942, 31 May 1943 (Library of Congress Audio Collection, Washington, DC).

47 *Seattle Times*, 14 October 1941.

48 *Seattle Times*, 21 October 1941.

49 *Seattle Times*, 23 October 1941; *Seattle Post-Intelligencer*, 24 October 1941.

50 *Seattle Post-Intelligencer*, 15 November 1941.

51 Report and review by Liston Martin, *Philadelphia Inquirer*, 29 November 1941; *Musical Courier*, 15 December 1941.

52 *Philadelphia Inquirer*, 6 December 1941.

CHAPTER 16

Divorce in Boise

1 Prokosch, *Voices*, pp. 148–9.

2 *Virgil Thomson by Virgil Thomson*, p. 341.

3 Cecil Beaton, *The Strenuous Years: Diaries, 1948–55* (London, 1973), p. 15.

4 *Virgil Thomson by Virgil Thomson*, p. 342.

5 *New York Sun*, 30 August 1941.

6 *Musical Courier*, September 1941.

7 *New York Times*, 31 August 1941.

8 *New York Herald Tribune* and *New York Times*, 16 January 1942; *New Yorker*, 24 January 1942.

9 Tribute to Beecham by Otto Klemperer, *New Statesman*, 17 March 1961.

10 Interview with Noel Straus, *New York Times*, 18 January 1942.

11 Letter from Frank St. Leger, New York, to Beecham, Gainsborough Apartments, Seattle, 28 October 1941 (Metropolitan Opera archives).

12 *New York Times*, 25 January 1942.

13 Astrid Varnay, *Fifty-five Years in Five Acts: My Life in Opera* (Boston, 2000), p. 99.

14 *Seattle Post-Intelligencer*, 13 February 1942.

15 *Seattle Post-Intelligencer*, 13 February 1942.

16 *Seattle Times*, 16 February 1942.

17 *New York Herald Tribune*, 19 April 1942.

18 Review by Warren Storey Smith, *Boston Sunday Post*, 29 March 1942.

19 *The Bulletin* [Glasgow], 25 March 1942.

20 *Musical Courier*, 20 March 1944.

21 Russell, *Philharmonic Decade*, p. 76.

22 Prokosch, *Voices*, p. 149.

23 *New York Times*, 16 March 1942.

24 Typescript, *Recollections of Sir Thomas Beecham*, by the company's chief librarian, Harry G. Schumer (MO archives).

25 *Le Devoir* [Montreal], 30 April 1942.

26 Sir Jeremy Thomas, conversation with the author, 19 March 2002.

27 Sir Jeremy Thomas, unpublished memoir.

28 Sir Jeremy Thomas, conversation with the author, 22 August 2003.

29 Dorice Taylor, *Sun Valley* (Sun Valley, ID, 1980), p. 123.

30 Letter from Beecham, Olympic Hotel, Seattle, to Goddard Lieberson, Columbia Records, 19 August 1942.

31 *New York Times*, 25 July 1943.

32 Minutes of Detroit Symphony Society board meeting, 19 April 1945 (DSO archives).

33 *New York Times*, 14 March 1943; *New York Times*, 6, 14 March 1943 and 4 April 1943; notes by Michael Gray for the CD reissues, *Sir Thomas Beecham: American Columbia recordings, 1942–52* (Sony Classical MH2K 63366), 1945.

34 Ada County Judgement Book, no. 36, Idaho. Case no. 17685.

35 *Los Angeles Examiner*, 24 July 1942.

36 Lotte Klemperer, letter to the author, 8 April 2001.

37 *Seattle Times*, 6 October 1942.

38 Petition filed at the Third Judicial District Court, 26 August 1942; *Seattle Times*, 6 October 1942.

39 Joyce Beecham, draft of a letter to Betty Humby, November 1942.

40 Letter from Sir Thomas Beecham, New York, to Adrian Beecham, Compton Scorpion, 23 July 1943.

41 Daphne Fielding, *Emerald and Nancy: Lady Cunard and her Daughter* (London, 1968), p. 131.

42 *Chips: The Diaries of Sir Henry Channon*, ed. Robert Rhodes-James (London, 1967), entry for 16 November 1942, p. 342.

43 Bliss, *As I Remember*, p. 163.

44 *Seattle Times*, 6 November 1942.

45 *Musical America*, 10 January 1943.

46 *Seattle Times*, 4 October 1942.

47 Letter from Betty Humby, New York, to Joyce Beecham, Compton Scorpion, 20 October 1942.

48 *Idaho Daily Statesman*, 15 January 1943.

49 *Seattle Post-Intelligencer*, 17 November 1942.

50 *New York Times*, 15 March 1942.

51 *Time*, 7 December 1942.

52 *New York Sun*, 27 November 1942.

53 *New York Herald Tribune*, 13 December 1942.

54 Moore, *You're Only Human Once*, p. 222.

55 *New York Herald Tribune*, 16 January 1943.

56 *Time*, 5 April 1943.

57 Letter from Beecham, 39 Circus Road, London NW8, to Andrew Schulhof, New York, 24 April 1948.

58 *The Star*, 15 January 1943.

59 Sir Jeremy Thomas, conversation with the author, 19 March 2002.

60 *New York World-Telegram*, 24 February 1943.

61 Paul Strang, 'The Musical Side of the Family', BBC Radio 4, 13 June 2000.

62 *The Gazette* [Montreal], 28 May 1943.

63 Letter from Sir Thomas Beecham, New York, to Adrian Beecham, Compton Scorpion, 23 July 1943.

64 *Time*, 5 and 19 April 1943.

65 *Daily Telegraph*, 24 February 1943.

66 *Seattle Post-Intelligencer*, 22, 29 August; 5, 12 September 1943.

67 Gordon Epperson, 'At the hands of the mighty', *The Strad*, July 1997.

68 Jo Ann Patterson, 'Remembering Sir Thomas', included in the notes for a set of LPs issued by the American Beecham Society, WSA 517-20.

69 *Seattle Post-Intelligencer*, 11 October 1943.

70 *Seattle Star*, 15 October 1943.

71 *New World*, 28 October 1943.

72 *Seattle Post-Intelligencer*, 19 October, 1, 2, 3, 4 November 1943; *Seattle Times*, 1 November 1943.

73 Schwarzkopf, *On and Off the Record*, p. 160.

74 Helen Traubel, *St. Louis Woman* (New York, 1959), p. 267.

75 *New York Herald Tribune* and *New York Times*, 25 November 1943; *Musical America*, 10 December 1943.

76 Oscar Thompson, *New York Sun*, 15 March 1944.

77 Marjorie Lawrence, *Interrupted Melody: The Story of my Life* (London, 1952), p. 222.

78 *New York Herald Tribune*, 15 March 1944.

79 Irving Kolodin, *The Metropolitan Opera, 1883–1966* (New York, 1966), p. 443.

80 Lawrence, *Interrupted Melody*, p. 221.

81 Mary Ellis Peltz, *Spotlights on the Stars* (New York, 1945), p. 8.

82 Patrice Munsel, conversation with the author, New York, 30 October 2001.

83 'A Beecham Mosaic', *Musical America*, 18 May, where Stevens misremembers the Lothario as being Pinza.

84 *New York Herald Tribune*, 12 December 1943.

85 George Beiswanger, 'From Eleven to Two', undated cutting from *Theatre Arts*.

86 *New York Sun*, 15 January 1944.

87 *New York Herald Tribune*, 14 April 1944.

88 Alicia Markova, *Markova Remembers* (London, 1986), pp. 109–10.

89 Foreign Office and Dominions Office papers, including correspondence between Humby and Lord Halifax (NA, DO35/112).

90 Letter from Betty Humby, 31 East 79th Street, New York, to Edward Johnson, 14 March 1944 (MO archives).

91 Olin Downes, *New York Times*, 21 June 1944.

92 *Excelsior*, Mexico City, July/August 1944; Schulhof, *Roundtrip Budapest/New York*, pp. 94–5; *Time*, 31 July, 7 August 1944; *Lotos Leaf*, New York, April 1956.

93 *Evening Standard*, ? October 1944.

94 John S. Edwards, 'I Coddle the Maestros', *Saturday Evening Post*, 7 November 1959.

95 Artur Rubinstein, *My Many Years* (London, 1988), p. 501.

96 *New York Times*, 8 September 1944.

97 Convoy report (NA, ADM199/2102).

98 *Daily Telegraph*, 4 October 1944.

99 *Evening News*, 29 September 1944; *The Star*, 30 September 1944.

CHAPTER 17

The Royal Years

1 Biddulph CDs WHL041, 042, 043.

2 Kennedy, *Barbirolli*, p. 216.

3 *Manchester Evening News*, 4 November 1944.

4 Letter to Godlee, 15 December 1944 (Hallé archives).

5 Undated document headed 'The Question of Presidency' (Hallé archives).

6 Bean, letters to Godlee, 19 and 20 December 1944 (Hallé archives).

7 *Manchester Guardian*, 7, 20 February 1945.

8 Schulhof, *Roundtrip, Budapest/New York*, p. 87

9 *San Francisco Call-Bulletin*, 10 May 1945.

10 Letter dated 28 December 1944.

11 *Virgil Thomson by Virgil Thomson*, p. 360. Thomson mistakenly places Overnoons near Ringmer, where the Beechams were to live subsequently.

12 Minute written by Evelyn Donald of the British Council's music department, 17 October 1945 (NA, BW 14/2).

13 Letter dated 31 January 1945; *Walter Legge*, ed. Sanders, pp. 97–9.

14 Schwarzkopf, *On and Off the Record*, p. 93.

15 Schwarzkopf, *On and Off the Record*, p. 94.

16 Letter dated 3 November 1945 (Glyndebourne archives).

17 *News Review*, 26 September 1946.

18 Internal memo, Legge to B. Mittell, 22 August 1946 (EMI archives).

19 Martin Milner talk for the Beecham Society, London, 19 September 1987.

20 *Croydon Advetiser*, 16 August 1946; *Croydon Times*, 17 August 1946.

21 Internal memo, J. D. Bicknell to B. Mittell, 3 October 1946 (EMI archives).

22 *Musical Times*, December 1946.

23 Recording of second performance, Myto 2 MCD 946.117.

24 Robert C. Bachmann, *Karajan: Notes on a Career*, trans. Shaun Whiteside (London, 1990), p. 154

25 Letter to J. Beek, 7 March 1947 (Concertgebouw Orchestra archives, Gemeentearchief, Amsterdam).

26 *Croydon Times*, 14 December 1946.

27 *New York Herald-Tribune*, 24 January 1948.

28 *Natal Daily News*, 3 September 1948.

29 *Stage & Cinema* [South Africa], 6 August 1948.

30 Richard Walton, conversation with the author, 1999.

31 *The Times*, 22 August 1949.

32 *The Times*, 6 January 1949.

33 Richard Temple Savage, *A Voice from the Pit: Reminiscences of an Orchestral Musician* (Newton Abbot, 1998), p. 136.

34 Interview in English with Peter Heyworth, Canadian Broadcasting Corporation, 1969.

35 Savage, *A Voice from the Pit*, p. 137.

36 Usher Hall, 23 August 1956. Somm-Beecham CD 22. (Beecham's remark is slightly truncated.)

37 Denison, conversation with the author, 1998.

38 American Beecham Society LP, WSA 521-2

39 Facsimile of letter dated 3 December 1954 (Dominic Winter book auction catalogue, South Cerney, 7 November 2007).

40 American Beecham Society LP, WSA 508.

41 David Cairns, *Responses: Musical Essays and Reviews* (London, 1973), p. 154.

42 Essay prepared for publicity purposes (BFI archives).

43 Letter to Powell (dictated to Norman Miller), 23 December 1957 (BFI archives).

44 Correspondence between Powell and Victor Olof of HMV's artists' department, February 1949. (BFI archives).

45 Nicolai Gedda, *My Life and Art*, ed. Aino Sellermark, trans. Tom Geddes (Portland, OR, 1999), p. 142.

46 *La Prensa*, 2, 3 July 1958; *Buenos Aires Herald*, 2 October 1958. Interviews with the author, Buenos Aires, 1991.

47 Jefferson, *Sir Thomas Beecham*, p. 240.

48 *Sunday Times*, 21 December 1958.

49 Schulhof, *Roundtrip, Budapest/New York*, p. 115.

50 *Seattle Post-Intelligencer*, 17, 22 February 1960; *Seattle Times*, 17 February.

51 DVD, Chicago Symphony Orchestra.

52 *The Times*, 14 April 1960.

53 Letter to Belle Schulhof, 10 October 1960.

54 Denis Forman, *Persona Granada: Some Memories of Sidney Bernstein and the Early Years of Independent Television* (London, 1997), p. 128.

Bibliography

Accademia di Santa Cecilia, *I concerti dal 1895 al 1933* (Rome, 1933)

Agate, James, *Ego 4: Yet More of the Autobiography of James Agate* (London, 1940)

Asquith, Herbert Henry, *Letters to Venetia Stanley*, ed. Michael and Eleanor Brock (Oxford, 1982)

Astruc, Gabriel, *Le pavillon des fantômes: souvenirs* (Paris, 1987)

Bachmann, Robert C., *Karajan: Notes on a Career*, trans. Shaun Whiteside (London, 1990)

Baillie, Isobel, *Never Sing Louder than Lovely* (London, 1982)

Barfoot, John, *Over Here and Over There: Ilford Aerodromes and Airmen in the Great War* (Romford, 1998)

Barker, T. C. and J. R. Harris, *St Helens: A Merseyside Town in the Industrial Revolution, 1750–1900* (Liverpool, 1954)

Bax, Arnold, *Farewell, my Youth* (London, 1943)

Baxter, Beverley, *Strange Street* (London, 1935)

Beaton, Cecil, *The Strenuous Years: Diaries, 1948–55* (London, 1973)

Beaumont, Cyril W., *The Diaghilev Ballet in London: A Personal Record* (London, 1940)

Beecham, Michael, *That Reminds Me …* (Tavistock, 1983)

Beecham, Sir Thomas, *A Mingled Chime: Leaves from an Autobiography* (London, 1944)

—— *Frederick Delius*, revised edition (London, 1975)

Bennett, Arnold, *The Journals of Arnold Bennett, 1911–1921*, ed. Newman Flower (London, 1932)

Benson, Tony (ed.), *Sir Thomas Beecham, Bart, CH, 1879–1961: Supplement to Maurice Parker's Calendar of Sir Thomas's Concert and Theatrical Performances, Issue 2* ([Westcliff-on-Sea], 1998)

Bliss, Sir Arthur, *As I Remember* (London, 1970)

Blunt, Wilfrid, *John Christie of Glyndebourne* (London, 1968)

Brendon, Piers, *The Dark Valley: A Panorama of the 1930s* (London, 2001)

British Medical Association, *Secret Remedies: What they Cost and What they Contain* (London, 1909)

Brook, Donald, *Conductors' Gallery* (London, 1945)

Bruce Lockhart, Sir Robert, *The Diaries of Sir Robert Bruce Lockhart*, ed. Kenneth Young (London, 1973)

Buckle, Richard, *Diaghilev* (London, 1979)

—— *George Balanchine: Ballet Master* (London, 1988)

—— *Nijinsky* (London, 1971)

Buttrose, Charles, *Playing for Australia: A Story about ABC Orchestras and Music in Australia* (Sydney, 1982)

Cairns, David, *Responses: Musical Essays and Reviews* (London, 1973)

Camden, Archie, *Blow by Blow: The Memories of a Musical Rogue and Vagabond* (London, 1982)

Cardus, Neville, *Sir Thomas Beecham: A Memoir* (London, 1961)

Carley, Lionel (ed.), *Delius: A Life in Letters*, 2 vols. (London, 1983, 1988)

Carner, Mosco, *Puccini: A Critical Biography*, 2nd edition (London, 1974)

Chaliapin, Feodor, *Chaliapin: An Autobiography as Told to Maxim Gorky*, ed. Nina Froud and James Hanley (London, 1967)

Channon, Sir Henry, *Chips: The Diaries of Sir Henry Channon*, ed. Robert Rhodes-James (London, 1967)

Chase, C. Thurston, *Eaglebrook: The First Fifty Years* (Deerfield, MA, 1972)

Chisholm, Anne, *Nancy Cunard* (London, 1979)

Chuter Ede, James, *Labour and the Wartime Coalition: The Diary of James Chuter Ede*, ed. Kevin Jefferys (London, 1987)

Coates, Eric, *Suite in Four Movements: An Autobiography* (London, 1953)

Cooper, Diana, *Trumpets from the Steep* (London, 1960)

—— *The Rainbow Comes and Goes* (London, 1958)

Cooper, Duff, *The Duff Cooper Diaries, 1915–51*, ed. John Julius Norwich (London, 2005)

Corley, T. A. B., *From National to Multinational Enterprise:The Beecham Business, 1848–1945* University of Reading Discussion Papers in International Investment and Business Studies no. 76 (University of Reading, Department of Economics, 1983)

Cumberland, Gerald, *Set Down in Malice: A Book of Reminiscences* (London, 1919)

De Walden, Lady Margherita Howard, *Pages from my Life* (London, 1965)

Dean, Basil, *Mind's Eye: An Autobiography, 1927–1972* (London, 1973)

Dilks, David, *Neville Chamberlain*, vol. 1: *Pioneering and Reform, 1869–1929* (Cambridge, 1984)

Dorati, Antal, *Notes of Seven Decades* (London, 1979)

Draper, Muriel, *Music at Midnight* (New York, 1929)

Ehrlich, Cyril, *The Music Profession in Britain since the Eighteenth Century: A Social History* (Oxford, 1985)

—— *First Philharmonic: A History of the Royal Philharmonic Society* (Oxford, 1995)

Elkin, Robert, *Queen's Hall, 1893–1941* (London, 1944)

—— *Royal Philharmonic: The Annals of the Royal Philharmonic Society* (London, 1947)

Erskine, John, *The Philharmonic-Symphony Society of New York: Its First Hundred Years* (New York, 1943)

Fellowes, Horace, *Music in my Heart* (Edinburgh, 1958)

Fenby, Eric, *Delius as I Knew him* (London, 1966)

Fielding, Daphne, *Emerald and Nancy: Lady Cunard and her Daughter* (London, 1968)

Forman, Denis, *Persona Granada: Some Memories of Sidney Bernstein and the Early Years of Independent Television* (London, 1997)

Francis, Anne [Anne Wintle], *A Guinea a Box: A Biography* (London, 1968)

—— *Letter to the Past* (London, 1994)

Fuller-Maitland, J. A., *A Door-Keeper of Music* (London, 1929)

Garafola, Lynn, *Diaghilev's Ballets Russes* (New York, 1989)

Gedda, Nicholai, *My Life and Art*, ed. Aino Sellermark, trans. Tom Geddes (Portland, OR, 1999)

Geissmar, Berta, *The Baton and the Jackboot: Recollections of Musical Life* (London, 1944)

Gibbon, Monk, *The Red Shoes Ballet: A Critical Study* (London, 1948)

—— *The Tales of Hoffmann: A Study of the Film* (London, 1951)

Gilmour, J. D. (ed.), *Sir Thomas Beecham, The North American Tour, 1950: A Documentary Presentation of News Media Articles* (Ocean Shores, WA, 1979)

—— *Sir Thomas Beecham, The Seattle Years, 1941–1943: A Documentary Presentation of News Media Articles* (Aberdeen, WA, 1978)

Gladwyn, Cynthia, *The Diaries of Cynthia Gladwyn*, ed. Miles Jebb (London, 1995)

Goebbels, Josef, *Die Tagebücher von Josef Goebbels*, Teil I, Band 3/II (Munich, 2001)

Goossens, Eugene, *Overture and Beginners: A Musical Autobiography* (London, 1951)

Gray, Tony, *A Peculiar Man: A Life of George Moore* (London, 1996)

Grigoriev, S. L., *The Diaghilev Ballet, 1909–1929*, trans. and ed. Vera Bowen (London, 1953)

Hamann, Brigitte, *Winifred Wagner: A Life at the Heart of Hitler's Bayreuth*, trans. Alan Bance (London, 2005)

Heseltine, Philip, *Frederick Delius*, with additions by Hubert Foss (London, 1952)

Hetherington, John, *Melba: A Biography* (London, 1973)

Irving, Ernest, *Cue for Music: An Autobiography* (London, 1959)

Jackson, Paul, *Saturday Afternoons at the Old Met, 1931–1950* (Portland, OR, 1992)

Jackson, Stanley, *Monsieur Butterfly: The Story of Puccini* (London, 1974)

Jacobs, Arthur, *Henry J. Wood: Maker of the Proms* (London, 1994)

Jefferson, Alan, *Sir Thomas Beecham: A Centenary Tribute* (London, 1979)

Jenkins, Lyndon, *While Spring and Summer Sang: Thomas Beecham and the Music of Frederick Delius* (Aldershot, 2005)

Kennedy, Michael, *Barbirolli: Conductor Laureate*, revised edition (Uttoxeter, 2003)

—— *Portrait of Elgar*, revised edition (London, 1982)

—— *Portrait of Walton* (Oxford, 1989)

Kenyon, Nicholas, *The BBC Symphony Orchestra: The First Fifty Years, 1930–1980* (London, 1981)

Keyworth, J. Max, *Cabbages and Things: The Background and Story of the Covent Garden Property Companies to 1970* (n.p., 1990)

Kolodin, Irving, *The Metropolitan Opera, 1883–1966: A Candid History* (New York, 1966)

Lassimone, Denise (ed.), *Myra Hess by her Friends* (London, 1966)

Lawrence, Marjorie, *Interrupted Melody: The Story of my Life* (London, 1952)

Leiter, Robert D., *The Musicians and Petrillo* (New York, 1953)

McBrien, William, *Cole Porter: A Biography* (New York, 1998)

Markova, Dame Alicia, *Markova Remembers* (London, 1986)

Melba, Dame Nellie, *Melodies and Memories* (London, 1980)

Moore, George, *Letters to Lady Cunard, 1895–1933*, ed. Rupert Hart-Davis (London, 1957)

Moore, Grace, *You're Only Human Once* (London, 1947)

Moresby, Isabelle, *Australia Makes Music* (Melbourne, 1948)

Müller, Martin, and Wolfgang Mertz (eds.), *Diener der Musik: Unvergessene Solisten und Dirigenten unserer Zeit im Spiegel der Freunde* (Tübingen, 1965)

Nettel, Reginald, *The Orchestra in England: A Social History* (London, 1946)

—— *Ordeal by Music: The Strange Experience of Havergal Brian* (London, 1945)

Newton, Ivor, *At the Piano: The World of an Accompanist* (London, 1966)

O'Connor, Garry, *The Pursuit of Perfection: A Life of Maggie Teyte* (London, 1979)

O'Donnell, Josephine, *Among the Covent Garden Stars* (London, 1936)

Osato, Sono, *Distant Dances* (New York, 1980)

Parker, Maurice (ed.), *Sir Thomas Beecham, Bart, CH, 1879–1961: A Calendar of his Concert and Theatrical Performances* ([Westcliff-on-Sea], 1985)

Pearton, Maurice, *The LSO at 70: A History of the Orchestra* (London, 1974)

Peltz, Mary Ellis, *Spotlights on the Stars* (New York, 1945)

Pirouet, Edmund, *Heard Melodies are Sweet: A History of the London Philharmonic Orchestra* (Lewes, 1998)

Polunin, Vladimir, *The Continental Method of Scene Painting*, ed. Cyril W. Beaumont (London, 1980)

Powell, Michael, *Million-Dollar Movie: The Second Volume of his Life in Movies* (London, 1992)

Procter-Gregg, Humphrey (ed.), *Beecham Remembered* (London, 1976)

Prokosch, Frederic, *Voices: A Memoir* (New York, 1983)

Reid, Charles, *Thomas Beecham: An Independent Biography* (London, 1961)

—— *Malcolm Sargent: A Biography* (London, 1968)

—— *John Barbirolli: A Biography* (London, 1971)

Ricketts, Charles, *Self-Portrait*, compiled T. Sturge Moore, ed. Cecil Lewis (London, 1939)

Roberts, Cecil, *And so to America* (London, 1946)

Robertson, Alec, *More than Music* (London, 1961)

Ronald, Landon, *Myself and Others: Written, Lest I Forget* (London, 1931)

Rosenthal, Harold, *Opera at Covent Garden: A Short History* (London, 1967)

—— *Two Centuries of Opera at Covent Garden* (London, 1958)

Rossall School, *Centenary Celebrations at Rossall School, 1947* (Aldershot, 1947)

Rubinstein, Artur, *My Many Years* (London, 1988)

Russell, Thomas, *Philharmonic Decade* (London, 1945)

St John, Christopher, *Ethel Smyth: A Biography* (London, 1959)

Sanders, Alan (ed.), *Walter Legge: Words and Music* (London, 1998)

Savage, Richard Temple, *A Voice from the Pit: Reminiscences of an Orchestral Musician* (Newton Abbot, 1998)

Schulhof, Belle, with Allan Kozinn, *Roundtrip, Budapest/New York: The Experiences of an Impresario in the Music World* (New York, 1987)

Schwarzkopf, Elisabeth, *On and Off the Record: A Memoir of Walter Legge* (London, 1982)

Scott, Cyril, *My Years of Indiscretion* (London, 1924)

Seligman, Vincent, *Puccini among Friends* (London, 1938)

Shanet, Howard, *Philharmonic: A History of New York's Orchestra* (Garden City, NY, 1975)

Sheean, Vincent, *The Amazing Oscar Hammerstein: The Life and Exploits of an Impresario* (London, 1956)

Sitwell, Osbert, *Great Morning: Being the Third Volume of Left Hand, Right Hand* (London 1948)

Smyth, Ethel, *Beecham and Pharaoh* (London, 1935)

Spotts, Frederic, *Hitler and the Power of Aesthetics* (London 2002)

Stocks, Charles Lancelot, *People and Places in Prose and Verse* (Aylesbury, 1970)

Stravinsky, Igor, *Themes and Conclusions* (London, 1972)

Szigeti, Joseph, *Szigeti on the Violin* (London, 1962)

Taylor, Dorice, *Sun Valley* (Sun Valley, ID, 1980)

Tertis, Lionel, *My Viola and I* (London, 1974)

Thomson, Virgil, *Virgil Thomson by Virgil Thomson* (New York, 1966)

Toscanini, Arturo, *The Letters of Arturo Toscanini*, trans. and ed. Harvey Sachs (London 2002)

Traubel, Helen, *St. Louis Woman* (New York, 1959)

Varnay, Astrid, *Fifty-five Years in Five Acts: My Life in Opera* (Boston, 2000)

Wagner, Friedelind, *The Royal Family of Bayreuth* (London, 1948)

Walsh, Stephen, *Stravinsky: A Creative Spring: Russia and France, 1882–1934* (London, 1999)

Wetherell, Eric, *Albert Sammons, Violinist: The Life of 'Our Albert'* (London, 1998)

Williams, Gordon, *British Theatre in the Great War: A Revaluation* (London 2003)

Windsor, Wallis Warfield, Duchess of, *The Heart has its Reasons* (London, 1956)

Wood, Henry J., *My Life of Music* (London, 1938)

Young, Kenneth, *Music's Great Days in the Spas and Watering-places* (London, 1968)

Zanetti, Emilia, Annalisa Bini and Laura Ciancio (eds.), *Gli anni dell'Augusteo: cronologia dei concerti, 1908–1936* (Rome, 1990)

Ziegler, Philip, *Diana Cooper* (London, 1981)

Index

Beecham in Rehearsal

[1] **Haydn: Symphony no. 100 in G 'Military'**   5.24

[2] **Haydn: Symphony no. 104 in D 'London'**   12.45
Salle Wagram, Paris, May 1958

Mozart: Die Entführung aus dem Serail

[3] 'O! wie will ich triumphieren' (Osmin's Aria, Act 3)   7.39

[4] 'Verwünscht seist du samt deinem Liede' (Osmin & Belmonte's Duet, Act 1)
– 'Solche hergelauf'ne Laffen' (Osmin's Aria, Act 1)   7.00

[5] Accompaniment to Chorus of Janissaries (Act 1)
– Accompaniment to 'Ach ich liebte' (Constanze's Aria, Act 1)
– 'Welcher Wechsel herrscht in meiner Seele' (Constanze's Recit., Act 2)   4.44

[6] Vaudeville (Finale, Act 3)   2.26

Gottlob Frick, bass (Osmin) · **Léopold Simoneau**, tenor (Belmonte)
Lois Marshall, soprano (Constanze)
Beecham Choral Society (chorus master Denis Vaughan)
Kingsway Hall, London, May 1956

[7] **Handel arr. Beecham: The Gods Go A'Begging***   10.26

[8] **Liszt: A Faust Symphony** (Finale)*   7.31
Alexander Young (tenor) · **Beecham Choral Society**

[9] **Liszt: Orpheus** – Symphonic Poem*   4.30
Kingsway Hall, April 1958

[10] **Beethoven: Symphony No.5 in C minor** Op. 67*   6.47
III. Allegro – IV. Allegro – Presto
No.1 Studio, Abbey Road, London, 14 July 1951

    69.52

Royal Philharmonic Orchestra
Sir Thomas Beecham

Digitally remastered by Michael J. Dutton & John Holland

℗ 1958 & *1992 The copyright in these sound recordings is owned by EMI Records Ltd and licensed by courtesy of EMI Classics. This compilation and digital remastering ℗ 1992 by EMI Records Ltd. The author and publishers acknowledge the kind assistance of the John Ireland Trust for its contribution towards the cost of including the CD in this book.

All but the last of the excerpts on the compact disc that accompanies this book come from rehearsals with the Royal Philharmonic Orchestra for recording sessions in 1956 and 1958. By then Beecham was in his late seventies and approaching the end of his long career. His rehearsal methods were held to be more enjoyable than any other conductor's: 'You're never bored', the players used to say. Courtesy, raillery and humour were all employed, not only to get the best out of the orchestra, but also to create the atmosphere and mood in which the performance he sought would blossom. Yet if all seems to be easily achieved, a great deal of preparatory work went on beforehand, notably in the meticulous marking and editing of the orchestral material: no wonder Beecham complained occasionally that his capacity 'for sheer hard work' was never given sufficient recognition.

[1]   At his Paris recording venue, the Salle Wagram near the Arc de Triomphe, Beecham announces the first business of the day: Haydn's 'Symphony One Hundred' (the 'Military'). The brief passages and comments upon each of the movements that follow include a typical bit of fun when Beecham pretends not to know the number of percussion instruments required by Haydn's score (though his jocular threat to 'do something about it' was not subsequently carried out).

[2]   Haydn's 'London' Symphony is obviously at an earlier stage of preparation, and Beecham spends some time dealing with interpretative ideas. A suggestion from the orchestra's principal second violin, Guy Daines, for a technical improvement is accepted without hesitation. A new take ('numéro douze') is announced, but then the recording engineers find that the rain falling on the Salle Wagram roof is being picked up by the microphones. This is the cue for Beecham to set about entertaining his players with anecdotes. .

[3]–[6]   The complete recording of Mozart's opera *Die Entführung aus dem Serail* took place in London over eight days in May 1956. A few points are worth elucidating. In [3] the red light that gives the signal to begin recording has evidently been placed outside Beecham's sight-line; the female voice heard at the end of [4] is that of Betty Humby, his second wife; and in [5], though the transposition to A major is easily accomplished despite Beecham's exaggerated words of warning, the original key of A flat was reverted to for the recording.

[7]   We join the preparations to record *The Gods Go A'Begging* at a point where final checks of the orchestral material are being made. Beecham's own conducting score still seems to be in disarray, and a few notes remain to be corrected (though notice his laconic observation, 'Much worse things in Handel', when the cellos query having to play a C sharp against a D in his arrangement).

The 'sacred fire' allusion is another reference to the red recording light, while at the end of the session the significance of one of the players calling out 'See you in Paris' lies in the fact that the next time conductor and orchestra were due to meet was for an intensive series of recording sessions there.

[8]   Beecham is evidently satisfied with the way the recording of Liszt's *Faust Symphony* is progressing. Early on there's a further illustration of the way he relied on his principal players to help him secure the best results when clarinettist Jack Brymer suggests a longer take to cover an unnoticed deficiency in the playing. At the next pause comes an exchange with George Brownfoot, the RPO's librarian, about the tuning of the second harp. During the next take Beecham's preferred expression, 'We'll make a record', reminds us that he had been 'making records' since 1910 and evidently felt he had no need to bother himself with the nomenclature of modern processes; but it goes awry because the tenor, Alexander Young, and the chorus have mistaken the starting point. Only those nearest to Beecham would have heard his concluding remark, 'Not a bad little piece.' This was a characteristic understatement he reserved for large-scale works such as the *Faust Symphony*, Berlioz's *Requiem* or Strauss's *Ein Heldenleben*: the singer Dietrich Fischer-Dieskau's consternation when Beecham made the observation to him during rehearsals of Delius's *A Mass of Life* may easily be imagined.

[9]   'We'll make another record of this', announces Beecham at the beginning of this extract from Liszt's *Orpheus*. He sounds cheerful enough, but it takes his sudden discovery of an extra microphone placed nearby to put him in a really good mood. He well understands that it is there to catch his voice, hence his offer to 'recite a poem' into it. Wrong notes are obvious in the harps, but he merely pauses with a chuckle to ask for a different phrasing. Microphones fade out as the music gets under way, and pick up again during the final chord. After an ironic dig at the recording staff he seeks the opinion of what has just been taped from his players, who play up to him mightily.

[10]   This is something of a mystery. Beecham gave only three performances of Beethoven's Fifth Symphony with the RPO between its formation in 1946 and his death in 1961. None was near the date of this run-through of parts of the *scherzo* and *finale*. The original tape-box bears the marking 'Experiment'.

© 2008 Lyndon Jenkins